BRITISH GOVERNMENT PUBLICATIONS

An index to
chairmen of committees and commissions of inquiry

VOLUME I : 1800-1899

BRITISH GOVERNMENT PUBLICATIONS

An index to
chairmen of committees and commissions of inquiry

VOLUME I : 1800-1899

Compiled by
Stephen Richard
for the
Reference, Special and Information Section
of the
Library Association

LA

THE LIBRARY ASSOCIATION · LONDON

© Stephen Richard and The Library Association 1982. Published by
Library Association Publishing Limited, 7 Ridgmount Street, London
WC1E 7AE and printed and bound in Great Britain for the publishers
by Redwood Burn Limited, Trowbridge.

First published 1982

British Library Cataloguing in Publication Data

Richard, Stephen
    British government publications: an index to
    chairmen of Committees and Commissions of Inquiry.
    Vol. 1: 1800-1899
    1. Government investigations-Great Britain-
    Bibliography   2. Great Britain-Government
    publications-Bibliography
    I. Title   II. Library Association. *Reference,*
    Special and Information Section
    016.3209'041   Z2009

    ISBN 0 85365 743 2

Designed by Ron Jones
Typeset in 9 on 10pt Baskerville by Library Association Typesetting

Contents

Introduction

Just as many contemporary government reports are referred to by the chairman's name, so are many nineteenth century reports. The Chadwick report on the labouring classes is one of the most commonly known nineteenth century reports referred to in this way. There are also a number of reports made by individuals, which are not indexed by the authors' names in the published indexes to the parliamentary papers. As collections of nineteenth century parliamentary papers are rarely individually catalogued, there is no easy means of access to reports known by the author or chairman. Knowledge and experience of the requirement for an additional means of access to parliamentary papers has led me to the compilation of this index of chairmen.

This index covers committees of the House of Commons and the House of Lords, commissions of inquiry and selected reports by individuals to commissions and branches of government for the period, 1800-99. It also includes reports from the 18th century located in the reports from committees of the House of Commons not in the Journals[1] and from the microcard edition of the Abbot collection of the eighteenth century[2]. Reports for this period have been excluded where they are indexed by chairman's name in Grace Ford's list of reports printed in the House of Commons Journals[3]. Sheila Lambert's edition of the eighteenth century sessional papers[4] also includes chairmen's names and these two works should be consulted when searching for eighteenth century reports.

Certain kinds of material have been excluded. These are serials, reports on accidents (explosions, mining, railway and shipping), court-martials, equipment trials, preliminary reports on local acts, diplomatic and consular reports, and committees to search the Journal of either house of parliament. Poor law and public health reports are included only if they are not local or if they appear to have had wider than local significance.

This alphabetical index of authors and chairmen is arranged by surname with references from titles and variants of names. The chairmen of committees have been determined by reference to the appropriate Journal in cases of doubt. References have been made from other persons who also served as chairmen. Lists of holders of various official positions, for example, Lord Chancellor and the Archbishop of Canterbury, are included in the appropriate alphabetical location. No distinction has been made in this index between government servants and others.

The form of the entry is shown by the following examples:

> **MAULE-RAMSAY, Fox,** *11th E. Dalhousie*
> Select committee on the Supreme Court of Judicature
> in Scotland. Report, 28 May 1840. 1840 (332) xiv;
> (Legal Administration, 6).

> **PETTY-FITZMAURICE, Henry Charles Keith,** *5th M.*
> *Lansdowne*
> Committee on employment of officers of Royal Engineers in civil departments of the state. Report, 24 Sept
> 1870. 1871 C.276 xiv; (GO Civil Service, 8). War Office.

> **RICE, Thomas Spring,** *1st Bn. Monteagle*
> Select committee (HL) on consolidated annuities, Ireland. Report, 29 June 1852. HL 1852 (64) xx; HC repr.
> 1852 (585) vi.

The chairman's or author's surname is followed by christian names and any titles. The committee reports are filed alphabetically by title unless an alternative order is the more obvious choice, for example, numerical or chronological. The arrangement of each entry is: title, date of signature or printing and location details. Parliamentary papers are given the session, command number or House of Commons paper number in round brackets, and volume number in roman numerals. As House of Lords papers are also given numbers in round brackets, these papers are indicated by the prefix 'HL' before the session. If House of Lords papers were reprinted as House of Commons papers, the House of Commons reference follows the House of Lords. Papers included in the Abbot collection are noted by the convention 'Reps., 1731-1800' followed by the volume and number, all enclosed in round brackets. Papers in the House of Commons Journal are noted by the symbol 'CJ' followed by the volume and page; those in the collection of reports not printed in the House of Commons Journal are noted by use of the convention 'CJ Reports' with the volume and page number and enclosed in round brackets. A few reports have been located which were not issued in the numbered, bound sets of parliamentary papers; in these cases the publisher is given at the place where the sessional reference is found for other reports. The reference to the Irish University Press reprint of the House of Commons sessional papers is given in round brackets after the location details. The body of government responsible for the paper is given as the last element of the entry.

This work has been compiled from the volumes of parliamentary papers held in Edinburgh University Library, the National Library of Scotland, the House of Lords Record Office, the British Library Official Publications Library and the Bodleian Library, Oxford. I wish to thank the staff of all these institutions for their assistance in this project. Especial thanks are due to Edinburgh University which kindly gave me leave and clerical assistance for the major period of compilation and to Julian Roberts of the Bodleian Library who encouraged me to complete the index. The RSIS publication sub-committee has been a major factor in encouraging the compilation and publication of this and other indexes of chairmen of British government publications for the nineteenth and twentieth centuries.

Horton-cum-Studley
March 1978

1. Reports from committees of the House of Commons which have been printed by order of the House and are not inserted in the Journals, reprinted by order of the House. 16 vols. 1803-1806.

2. Papers printed by order of the House of Commons from the year 1731-1800, in the custody of the Clerk of the Journals, reprinted in microcard form by Readex Microprint with E.L. Erickson as editor. This series of volumes is also known as the "First Series" in the Hansard's Catalogue and Breviate of Parliamentary Papers, 1834, reprinted 1953, edited by P. and G. Ford.

3. Ford, Grace. Select list of reports and other papers in the House of Commons Journals, 1688-1800. Nendeln, KTC Press, 1976.

4. Lambert, Sheila. House of Commons sessional papers of the eighteenth century. 147 volumes. Wilmington, Delaware, 1976-1977.

Abbreviations

[ ]	Command papers (1 4222, 1833–1868-9)
( )	House of Commons papers
App.	Appendix
Archbp.	Archbishop
b	born
Bn.	Baron
C.	Command papers (1 9550, 1870-1899)
Capt.	Captain
CJ	House of Commons Journal
d	died
E.	Earl
Ev.	Evidence
GB	Great Britain
H.M.	His/Her Majesty('s)
HC	House of Commons
HL	House of Lords
HL [session] ( )	House of Lords papers
jr.	junior
LJ	House of Lords Journal
M.	Marquis
Memo.	Memorandum
Min. of ev.	Minutes of evidence
Oceana HL	Reprint of HL papers, 1660-1805. Oceana Press
(P.B.)	House of Commons papers on private bills printed at the objectors' expense
Proc.	Proceedings
Rep.	Report
Repr.	Reprint(ed)
(Reps., 1731-1800)	Parliamentary papers printed by order of the H.C. from 1731-1800. Reports, vol. 1-28. (also known as the First Series or the Abbot collection)
s	succeeded to title
Suppl.	Supplement
U.K.	United Kingdom
Vct.	Viscount

Index to chairmen

ABBOT, Charles, *1st Bn. Colchester*

Committee on expired and expiring laws. Report, 1796. CJ, vol.51, p.702.

Committee on expired and expiring laws: 3rd session, 17th Parliament. Report, 11 March 1799. CJ, vol.54, p.300; (Reps., 1731-1800, no.152, vol.22).

Committee on expired and expiring laws: 5th session, 18th Parliament. Report, 14 Nov 1800. (Reps., 1731-1800, no.173, vol.28).

Committee (HL) on the Office of the Clerk of Parliaments. Report, 5 April 1827. HL 1826/7 (82) ccxix.

Committee on offices under the Crown of Ireland, which shall disqualify persons from sitting in the HC of the united Parliament. Report, 8 May 1801. 1801 (63) iii.

Commission for making roads and building bridges in the highlands of Scotland. Report, 1 June 1804. (Oceana HL 1803/4 (44) vol.3, p.495).

Committee for promulgation of the statutes. Report, 5 Dec 1796. CJ Reports, vol.14, p.119; (reps., 1731-1800, no.137, vol.19).

Committee for promulgation of the statutes of the U.K. Report, 28 April 1801. 1801 (49) iii; CJ Reports, vol.14.

Committee (HL) on the state of laws concerning trial of peers for offences committed in Scotland. Report 14 April 1825. HL 1825 (43) cxcii.

Committee on temporary laws, expired or expiring. Report, 12 May 1796. CJ Reports, vol.14, p.34; (Reps., 1731-1800, no.127, vol.16).

Select committee (HL) on the appellate jurisdiction of the HL.
> Report, 17 June 1823. HL 1823 (65) cliii.
> 2nd report, 25 June 1823. HL 1823 (74) cliii; repr. HL 1824 (5) clxiii.
> Report, 3 June 1824. HL 1824 (99) clxiii.

Select committee on finance
> 1st report: Debt and taxes. 31 March 1797. CJ Reports, vol.12, p.1.
> 2nd report: Taxes. 21 April 1797. CJ Reports, vol.12, p.36.
> 3rd report: Unfunded debts and demands outstanding. 11 May 1797. CJ Reports, vol.12, p.41.
> 4th report: Collection of the public revenue — Customs. 19 July 1797. CJ Reports, vol.12, p.53.
> 5th report: Collection of the public revenue — Excise. 19 July 1797. CJ Reports, vol.12, p.107.
> 6th report: Collection of the public revenue — Stamp Office. 19 July 1797. CJ Reports, vol.12, p.154.
> 7th report: Collection of the public revenue — Post Office. 19 July 1797. CJ Reports, vol.12, p.178.
> 8th report: Collection of the public revenue — Tax Office. 19 July 1797. CJ Reports, vol.12, p.223.
> 9th report: Collection of the public revenue — Salt Office. 19 July 1797. CJ Reports, vol.12, p.242.
> 10th report: Collection of the public revenue — Hawkers and Pedlars. 19 July 1797. CJ Reports, vol.12, p.257.
> 11th report: Collection of the public revenue — Hackney Coach Office. 19 July 1797. CJ Reports, vol.12, p.261.
> 12th report: Collection of the public revenue — Duties on pensions, salaries, fees, *etc.* 19 July 1797. CJ Reports, vol.12, p.268.
> 13th report: Collection of the public revenue — First fruits and tenths. 19 July 1797. CJ Reports, vol.12, p.273.
> 14th report: Expenditure of the public revenue — Bank of England, and South Sea Co. 19 July 1797. CJ Reports, vol.12, p.276.
> 15th report: Expenditure of the public revenue — Treasury. 19 July 1797. CJ Reports, vol.12, p.286.
> 16th report: Expenditure of the public revenue — Secretaries of state. 19 July 1797. CJ Reports, vol.12, p.297.
> 17th report: Expenditure of the public revenue — Admiralty Board, *etc.* 19 July 1797. CJ Reports, vol.12, p.328.
> 18th report: Expenditure of the public revenue — Transport Office. 19 July 1797. CJ Reports, vol.12, p.344.
> 19th report: Expenditure of the public revenue — Secretary at War, *etc.* 19 July 1797. CJ Reports, vol.12, p.349.
> 20th report: Expenditure of the public revenue — Barrack Office. 19 July 1797. CJ Reports, vol.12, p.409.
> 21st report: Expenditure of the public revenue — Office of Ordnance. 19 July 1797. CJ Reports, vol.12, p.424.
> 22nd report: Auditing the accounts — Exchequer and concluding remarks. 20 July 1797. CJ Reports, vol.12, p.447.
> 23rd report: Public revenue for 1797. 26 June 1798. CJ Reports, vol.13, p.1.
> 24th report: Public debts and expenditure for 1797. 26 June 1798. CJ Reports, vol.13, p.149.
> 25th report: Privy Council Office. 26 June 1798. CJ Reports, vol.13, p.185.
> 26th report: Privy Seal Office. 26 June 1798. CJ Reports, vol.13, p.195.
> 27th report: Courts of Justice. 26 June 1798. CJ Reports, vol.13, p.199.
> 28th report: Police, including convict establishments. 26 June 1798. CJ Reports, vol.13, p.244; repr. 7 June 1810. 1810 (348) iv; (CP Transportation, 1).
> 29th report: Stationery Office. 26 June 1798. CJ Reports, vol.13, p.427.
> 30th report: Civil government of Scotland. 26 June 1798. CJ Reports, vol.13, p.439.
> 31st report: Admiralty, dock yards and transports. 26 June 1798. CJ Reports, vol.13, p.485.

ABBOT, Charles, *1st Bn. Colchester* (continued)

32nd report: Victualling Office. 26 June 1798. CJ Reports, vol.13, p.508.

33rd report: Office for Sick and Wounded Seamen. 26 June 1798. CJ Reports, vol.13, p.567.

34th report: Chatham Chest, Greenwich Hospital and Chelsea Hospital. 26 June 1798. CJ Reports, vol.13, p.593.

35th report: Army expenditure. 26 June 1798. CJ Reports, vol.13, p.621.

36th report: Offices of secretary at War; Judge Advocate General; Commissary General of Musters and the military government in G.B. 27 June 1798. CJ Reports, vol.13, p.681.

Select committee on the improvement of the port of London.

1st report. 1 June 1799. CJ Reports, vol.14, p.444.

2nd report. 11 July 1799. CJ Reports, vol.14, p.461.

Select committee (HL) on the law in regard to the trial of peers for offences committed in Scotland. Report, 14 April 1825. HL 1825 (43) cxcii.

Select committee on the state of the public records.

1st report. 4 July 1800. CJ Reports, vol.15, p.1.

2nd report. Analysis of the returns. 4 July 1800. CJ Reports, vol.15, p.509.

ABBOT, Charles, *2nd Bn. Colchester*

Select committee (HL) on the Metropolitan Railway (Improvements, *etc.*) Bill. Report, 15 March 1861. HL 1861 (47) xxiv.

Select committee (HL) on the North London Railway (Branch to the City) Bill. Report, 15 March 1861. HL 1861 (45) xxiv.

Select committee (HL) on the policy and operation of the navigation laws. SEE: Yorke, Charles Philip, *4th E. Hardwicke.*

ABBOTT, P.H.

Commission on public accounts. Report by the 3rd commissioner: Navy, Ordnance departments, *etc.* 12 June 1829. 1829 (325) vi. SEE ALSO: Brooksbank, T.C. and Beltz, Samuel.

ABERCROMBIE, James, *1st Bn. Dunfermline*

Commission on the state of Windsor Forest.

1st report, 12 April 1809. 1809 (132) iv.

2nd report, 12 April and 9 May 1809. 1809 (133) iv.

3rd report, 12 April and 9 May 1809. 1809 (134) iv.

Select committee on the Cold Bath Fields meeting, 1833. SEE: Hawes, Benjamin, *jr.*

Select committee on municipal corporations. Report, 4 June 1833. 1833 (344) xiii.

Select committee on the library of the HC. Reports, 30 March 1835. 1835 (104) xviii.

ABERDARE, Bn. SEE: Bruce, Henry Austin, *1st Bn. Aberdare* (1815-1895)

ABERDEEN, E. of SEE:

Gordon, George Hamilton, *4th E. Aberdeen* (s.1801-1860)

Gordon, George John James, *5th E. Aberdeen* (s.1860-1864)

Hamilton-Gordon, George, *6th E. Aberdeen* (s.1864-1870)

Hamilton-Gordon, John Campbell, *1st M. Aberdeen* (s.1870-1934)

ABERNETHY, James

Report on Birkenhead Dock Bills. 27 Feb 1847. 1847 (351) lxi. Admiralty.

ABNEY, William de Wiveleslie

Committee on the buildings and site of the Royal College of Science for Ireland. Dublin. Report. 1899 C.9159 xlv. Privy Council.

Report on the action of light on water colours. 30 June 1888. 1888 C.5453 lxxviii. Art Dept., Privy Council Committee on Education.

ACHESON, Archibald, *2nd E. Crosford*

Commission on grievances complained of in Lower Canada. 1st-5th general reports, 20 Feb 1837. 1837 (50) xxiv; (Canada, 4).

ACLAND, Arthur Herbert Dyke

Select committee on the Elementary Education (Blind and Deaf Children) Bill. Report, 10 July 1893. 1893/4 (317) xi.

ACLAND, Charles Thomas Dyke

Select committee on Stannaries Act (1869) Amendment Bill. Special report and report, 28 and 19 July 1887. 1887 (245) (252) xii.

ACLAND, Thomas Dyke, *Sir*

Select committee on the Pluralities Bill, 1885. SEE: Kennaway, John, *Sir.*

ADAIR, Hugh Edward

Select committee on the Lisburn election petition. Min. of proc. 18 April 1864. 1864 (182) x.

General committee on railway and canal bills, 1863. SEE: Smith-Stanley, Edward Henry, *15th E. Derby.*

Select committee on the Waterford County election petition. Min. of ev. 5 April 1867. 1867 (205) viii.

ADAM, William Patrick

Select committee on the kitchen and refreshment rooms (HC). Report, 10 August 1877. 1877 (411) xii.

Select committee on the kitchen and refreshment rooms (HC). Report, 12 August 1879. 1878/9 (372) x.

ADAMS, William

Committee on Mr. Koop's petition for establishing a company for remanufacturing paper. Report, 13 June 1800. CJ, vol.55, p.647.

ADAMS, William Henry

Select committee on the Poor Law Boards (Payment of Debts) Bill, 1859. SEE: Villiers, Charles Pelham.

ADDERLEY, Charles Bowyer, *Bn. Norton*

Committee on expiring laws, 3rd session, 17th Parliament. Report, 7 April 1859. 1859 sess.1 (199) iii.

Committee on expiring laws. 5th session, 17th Parliament. Report, 5 June 1863. 1863 (321) vii.

Royal sanitary commission

1st report: Evidence to 5 Aug 1869. 1868/9 [4218] xxxii.

2nd report:

Vol.1: Report, 1871. 1871 C.281 xxxv.

Vol.2: Arrangement of sanitary statutes, analysis of ev., paper on watershed boards and memo. on duties of medical officers of public health. 1871 C.281-I xxxv.

Vol.3, pt.1: Min. of ev. 1871 C.281-II xxxv.

Vol.3, pt.2: Tabular abstract of answers, letters, memoranda. 1874 C.1109 xxxi; (Health, 9-11)

Select committee on Chain Cables and Anchors Bill. Report, 30 June 1874. 1874 (252) vii.

Select committee on criminal and destitute children, 1852. SEE: Baines, Matthew Talbot.

Select committee on the Merchant Seamen Bill, 1878. SEE: Stanhope, Edward.

Select committee on Merchant Ships (Measurement of Tonnage) Bill. Report, 17 July 1874. 1874 (309) x.

Select committee on parliamentary and municipal election hours of polling, 1877. SEE: Forster, William Edward.

Select committee on the western coast of Africa. Report, 26 June 1865. 1865 (412) v; (Africa, 5).

ADDINGTON, Henry, *1st Vct. Sidmouth*
Committee (HL) to examine the physicians attending His Majesty (Geo. III) on the state of His health. Report, 15 Jan 1812. HL 1812 (4) liii.

Secret committee (HL) on the late disturbances; Nottingham, Midlands destruction of machinery, *etc.* Report, 9 July 1812. HL 1812 (158) liii.

ADDINGTON, John Hiley
Committee on cotton manufacture. Report, 28 March 1804. 1803/4 (41) v; (IR Textiles, 3).

ADEY, D.G.
Investigation into the conduct of the master of the Bath Union workhouse. Report, 27 Jan 1839. 1839 (489) xliv. Poor Law Com.

ADVOCATE FOR SCOTLAND, LORD
(years of appointment)

1789 Robert Dundas
1801 Charles Hope
1804 James Montgomery, *Sir*
1806 Henry Erskine
1807 Archibald Campbell (afterwards Colquhon)
1816 Alexander Maconochie
1819 William Rae, *Sir*
1830 Francis Jeffrey
1834 John Archibald Murray
1839 Andrew Rutherford
1841 William Rae, *Sir*
1842 Duncan McNeill
1846 Andrew Rutherford
1851 James Moncreiff
1852 Adam Anderson
1852 John Inglis
1853 James Moncreiff
1858 John Inglis of Glencorse
1858 Charles Baillie
1859 David Mure
1859 James Moncreiff
1866 George Patton
1867 Edward Strathearn Gordon
1868 James Moncreiff
1869 George Young
1874 Edward Strathearn Gordon
1876 William Watson
1880 John McLaren
1881 John Blair Balfour
1885 John Hay Athole Macdonald
1886 John Blair Balfour
1886 John Hay Athole Macdonald
1888 James Patrick Bannerman Robertson
1891 Charles John Pearson, *Sir*
1892 John Blair Balfour
1895 Charles John Pearson, *Sir*
1896 Andrew Graham Murray

ADYE, John Miller
Report on the Crimean cemetaries. Dec 1872. 1873 C.719 xl. War Office.

AGLIONBY, Henry Aglionby
Select committee on Capt. Wynne's letters. Report, 22 July 1847. 1847 (732) xiv.

Select committee on Enfranchisement of Copyholds Bill. Report, 17 July 1851. 1851 (550) xiii.

Select committee on the Plymouth election petitions. Report, 10 May 1853. 1852/3 (470) xviii. Min. of ev. 13 May 1853. 1852/3 (497) xviii.

Select committee on public bills. Report, 20 Aug 1836. 1836 (606) xxi.

AGNEW, Andrew, *Sir*
Select committee on the observance of the Sabbath day. Report, 6 Aug 1832. 1831/2 (697) vii.

AIKIN, James
Report on the Liverpool Marine Bd. in the case of Capt. Noble of the 'Tayleur' 1854 (167) lx. Bd. of Trade.

AIREY, James Talbot, *Lord*
Committee on Army re-organisation. Report, 8 March 1880. 1881 C.2791 xxi. War Office.

AIREY, Richard, *Sir*
Barrack and hospital improvement commission. Report on ventilation of cavalry stables, 31 Oct 1863. 1864 [3290] xvi. War Office.

Report on the organisation of the Royal Artillery. May 1872. 1872 C.561 xiv. War Office.

AIRLIE, *E. of* SEE: Olgilvy, David Graham Drummond, *7th E. Airlie (b.1826, s.1846, d.1881).*

AIRTH, *Lord* [Claim of peerage]. 1839. SEE: Cooper, C.A.; 1870. SEE: Freeman-Mitford, J.T.

AIRY, George Biddell
Commission for the restoration of the standards of weight and measure.
    Report, 21 Dec 1841. 1842 [356] xxv.
    Abstract of the report, repr., 1854/5 (177) xv. Treasury.
    SEE ALSO: Bethune, J.E. Drinkwater.

Commission on the construction of new Parliamentary standards of length and weight. Report, 28 March 1854. 1854 [1786] xix. Treasury.

Standards Commission.
    1st report, 24 July 1868. 1867/8 [4077] xxvii.
    2nd report: Metric system. 3 April 1869. 1868/9 [4186] xxiii.
    3rd report: Abolition of the troy weight. 1 Feb 1870. 1870 C.30 xxvii.
    4th report: Inspection of weights and measures. 21 May 1870. 1870 C.147 xxvii.
    5th report: Business of the Standards Dept, and the condition of the official standards and apparatus. 3 Aug 1870. 1871 C.271 xxiv.
    General index. 1873 C.716 xxxviii.

Report on the equipment for preventing fraud in the sale of gas to the public. 11 Feb 1860. 1860 (100) lix. Treasury; (FP Gas, 6).

AITCHISON, Charles Umpherston, *Sir*
Consumption of opium in British Burma. 30 April 1880. 1881 (266) lxviii. India Office.

Public service commission, India. Report, 23 Dec 1887. 1888 C.5327 xlviii. India Office.

AITCHISON, John, *Sir*
Indian officers' commission. Report, 14 Sept 1865. 1865 [3598] xxvii.

AKERS-DOUGLAS, Aretas
Select committee on the Customs Offices (Southampton) Bill and the Customs and Other Offices (Barry Dock) Bill. Report, 5 May 1898. 1898 (193) (194) ix.

Select committee on the Edinburgh General Register House Bill. Report, 12 May 1896. 1896 (177) ix.

Select committee on government offices; appropriation of sites
    Report, 23 July 1896. 1896 (310) x.
    Report, 22 July 1897. 1897 (335) x.

Select committee on the Post Office Extension Bill. Report, 7 May 1897. 1897 (204) xiii.

Select committee on the Public Offices (Site) Bill. Report, 11 May 1896. 1896 (172) xiii.

Select committee on the Public Offices (Whitehall) Bill. Report, 7 May 1897. 1897 (203) xiii.

ALBEMARLE, E. of SEE:
Keppel, George Thomas, *6th E. Albemarle* (b.1799, s.1861, d.1891).
Keppel, William Coutts, *7th E. Albemarle* (b.1832, s.1891, d.1894).

ALBERT, *Prince* SEE:
Saxe-Coburg, Francis Albert Augustus Charles Emanuel, *Prince of Saxe-Coburg-Gothe, etc.*

ALBERT EDWARD, *Prince of Wales* SEE:
Saxe-Coburg, Albert Edward, *Prince of Wales* (b.1841, c.1841).

ALCOCK, Rutherford
Commission on the claims of the British Auxiliary Legion against the Spanish government. Reports, 26 Oct 1839 and 20 March 1840. HL 1840 [unnumbered command paper] xxxvi.

ALCOCK, William Congreve
Committee of privileges. Report on his lunacy. SEE: Williams-Wynne, C.W.

ALEXANDER, Henry
Committee on the civil list accounts. Report, 13 March 1802. 1801/2 (27) ii.

Committee on expired and expiring laws
    2nd session, 1st Parliament. Report, 31 March 1802. CJ Reports, vol.14, p.73; 1801/2 (39) ii.
    1st session, 2nd Parliament. Report, 30 Nov 1802. 1802/3 (4) v.
    3rd session, 2nd Parliament. Report, 22 Jan 1805. 1805 (3) iii.
    4th session, 2nd Parliament. Report, 24 Jan 1806. 1806 (3) ii.

Select committee on the 10th Naval report. Report, 27 May 1805. 1805 (140) ii.

ALEXANDER, William
Commission on duties, salaries and emoluments in courts in England and Wales.
    Court of Exchequer and Exchequer Chambers. Report, 27 March 1822. 1822 (125) xi.
    Consistory Court of the Bishop of London. Commissary court for London and Deaneries of Middlesex and Barking. Report, 20 Feb 1824. 1824 (43) ix.
    High Court of Admiralty, High Court of Delegates and High Court of Appeals for Prizes. Report, 15 April 1824. 1824 (240) ix.
    SEE ALSO: Campbell, J.

ALFRED ERNEST ALBERT, *D. of Edinburgh.* SEE: Saxe-Coburg, Alfred Ernest Albert, *D. of Edinburgh* (b.1844, c.1866).

ALLPORT, James Joseph
Royal Commission on Irish public works.
    1st report, 9 April 1887. 1887 C.5038 xxv.
    2nd report, 4 Jan 1888. 1888 C.5264 xlviii.

ALSAGER, Richard
Select committee on the Thames tunnel. Report, 10 July 1837. 1837 (499) xx.

ALTHORPE, *Vct.* SEE:
Spencer, J.C. *3rd E. Spencer* (1782-1845).

ALVERSTONE, *Vct.* SEE:
Webster, Richard Everard, *Vct. Alverstone.*

AMIENS, *Vct.* [Peerage claim]. SEE:
Freeman-Mitford, J.T.

AMOS, Andrew
Indian law commission
    Report, 15 Jan 1841. 1841 (262) xxviii.
    Special reports, 30 May 1843. 1843 (300) xxxvi.
    Special reports, 9 Aug 1844. 1844 (632) xxxvii.
    Special reports, 6 April 1847. 1847 (585) xxx. India Office.
    SEE ALSO: Macaulay, T.B.

AMPHLETT, R. Paul
Committee of the Courts of Justice commission to examine the plans submitted to the commission. Report, 1868/9 (274) xlvii. Treasury.

ANDERSON, Henry Percy, *Sir*
Committee on railway communication with Uganda. Report, 27 April 1895. 1895 C.7833 lxxi. Colonial Office; (Africa 67).

ANDERSON, John William, *Sir*
Committee on London bakers' petition. Report, 27 April 1804. 1803/4 (76) v.

Committee on the petition of Messrs. Chalmers and Cowie on Swedish herrings. Report, 29 March 1805. 1805 (65) iii; (Fisheries, 1).

ANDERSON, W.G.
Commission on the accounts of the Commission of Public Works in Ireland. Report, 14 Dec 1847. 1847/8 [926] xxxvii. Treasury.

ANDERSON-PELHAM, Charles Anderson Worsley, *1st E. Yarborough*
Select committee on commons inclosure. Report, 5 Aug 1844. 1844 (583) v; (Agriculture, 7).

Select committee on Epworth (corn laws) petition, 1843. SEE: Christopher, Robert Adam.

Select committee on the General Terminus and Glasgow Harbour Railway Bill, the Glasgow Harbour Grand Junction Railway Terminus Bill, and the Glasgow Harbour and Mineral Railway Bill. Min. of ev. 17 April 1846. 1846 (212) xii.

Select committee on the Glasgow Harbour Mineral Railway Bill, and the Glasgow Harbour Grand Junction Railway Terminus Bill. Min. of ev. 5 May 1846. 1846 (267) xii.

Select committee (HL) on the Langton's Discovery Bill. Min. of ev. 28 May 1829. HL 1829 (82) cclxii.

ANDREWES, Frederick William
Report on the condition of the Aldershot camp sewage farm and of the dairy maintained upon it. 1899 C.9339 lxxvii. War Office.

ANGLESEY, *Lord* [Peerage claim]. SEE:
Cooper, C.A.

ANNANDALE, *Lord* [Peerage claim, 1825-44]. SEE: Cooper, C.A.; 1876-81. SEE: Freeman-Mitford, J.T.

ANNESLEY, *E.* [Peerage claim]. SEE:
Freeman-Mitford, J.T.

ANNESLEY, Arthur, *11th Vct. Valentia*
Select committee on kitchen and refreshment rooms (HC). Report, 1 Aug 1899. 1899 (316) x.

ANNESLEY, Francis
Committee on Isaac Du Bois's petition. Report, 28 June 1803. 1802/3 (131) v.

Committee on the petition for rebuilding Greenwich church, *etc.* Report, 6 April 1711. CJ, vol.16, p.580.

ANSON, George, *Sir*
Select committee on army colonels. Report, 26 July 1870. 1870 (385) v.

Select committee on Royal gun factories. Report, 24 July 1868. 1867/8 (459) vi.

ANSTEY, Thomas Chisholm
Papers on consolidation of the statutes relating to finance. 1854 (302-I) xxiv. Lord Chancellor's Office.

Select committee on fisheries in Ireland. Report, 20 July 1849. 1849 (536) xiii; (Fisheries, 3).

Select committee on import duties on wines. Report, 18 June 1852. 1852 (495) xvii.

ANSTRUTHER, John, *Sir*
Committee of the whole House on the expedition to the Scheldt. Min. of ev. 5 Feb 1810. 1810 (12) viii.

Select committee on the affairs of the East India Co. Report, 11 May 1810. 1810 (255) v; (East India, 1). 2nd report, 1810. SEE: Wallace, Thomas, *1st Bn. Wallace.*

ANSTRUTHER, Robert, *Sir*
Select committee on Lord Cochrane's petition. Report, 16 July 1877. 1877 (338) x.

ANTRIM, *E.* [Peerage claim]. SEE:
Freeman-Mitford, J.T.

ARBUTHNOT, Charles
Commission on the Dept. of Stamps. Report, 5 March, 1821. 1821 (156) x.

ARBUTHNOT, G.
Reports on Japanese currency. 24 Dec 1862 to 2 Dec 1863. 1866 (513) l. Treasury.

ARCHER, Forster
Commission appointed to investigate abuses in the Convict Dept. at Cork. Report, 9 June 1817. 1817 (343) viii.

ARDROSSAN, *Lord* SEE:
Montgomerie, Archibald William, *13th E. Eglinton* (s.1819, d.1861).
Montgomerie, Archibald William, *14th E. Eglinton* (1841-1892).

ARESKINE, Charles
Copy of report and certificate from the Lords of Council and Session, respecting the abolition of heritable jurisdictions, Scotland. 18 March 1748. (Reports, 1731-1800, no.2, vol.1).

ARGYLL, *D.* SEE:
Campbell, George Douglas, *8th D. Argyll* (b.1823, s.1847, d.1900).

ARMAGH, *Bp.* SEE:
Beresford, John George, *Bp. of Armagh,* 1822-62.
Beresford, Marcus Gervais, *Bp. of Armagh,* 1862-86.

ARMSTRONG, J.W.
Committee on the Army short service system. Report, 19 Nov 1878. 1881 C.2817 xx. War Office.

ARNOLD, Matthew
Report on the systems of education in use in France, Holland and the French cantons of Switzerland. June 1860. *In:* 1861 [2794-IV] xxi, pt.4; (Education, 4).

ARNOTT, Neil
Committee for scientific inquiries in relation to the cholera epidemic of 1854. Report, 14 July 1854. 1854/5 [1980], [1996] xxi. General Board of Health; (HE Infectious Diseases, 3).

Inquiry on the prevalence of disease at Croydon and on the plan of sewerage. Medical report, 21 April 1853. 1852/3 [1648] xcvi. Home Dept. (UA Sanitation, 3). SEE ALSO: Page, Thomas.

ARROW, F.
Committee on regulations for preventing collisions at sea. Report. 1876 (58) xlix. Admiralty.

ASHBOURNE, *Bn.* SEE:
Gibson, Edward, *1st Bn. Ashbourne*

ASHBURTON, *Lord* SEE:
Baring, Francis, *3rd Bn. Ashburton* (1800-1868).
Baring, Alexander Hugh, *4th Bn. Ashburton* (1835-89).

ASHER, Alexander
Select committee on the Presumption of Life (Scotland) Bill. Report, 17 June 1881. 1881 (287) xii.

Select committee on the Sale of Goods Bill. Report, 15 Aug 1893. 1893/4 (374) xv.

ASHLEY, *Lord* SEE:
Cooper, Anthony Ashley, *7th E. Shaftesbury* (b.1801, s.1851).

ASHLEY, Anthony Evelyn Melbourne
Select committee on fishing vessels; regulations as to lights. Report, 14 July 1880. 1880 (285) viii.

Select committee on railway charges. Report, 4 Aug 1881. 1881 (374) xiii, xiv; (Transport, 16, 17).

Select committee on railways' rates and fares. Report, 27 July 1882. 1882 (317) xiii; (Transport, 18).

ASHLEY, Evelyn SEE:
Ashley, Anthony Evelyn Melbourne.

ASHMEAD-BARTLETT, Ellis
Select committee on Greenwich Hospital; age pensions. Report, 7 April 1892. 1892 (138) xii.

ASHTOWN, *Bn.* [Peerage claim]. SEE:
Freeman-Mitford, J.T.

ASHURST, William Henry
Select committee on allowances to bakers where assize of bread is set. Report, 8 April 1824. 1824 (212) vi.

ASPINALL, John Bridge
Royal commission on corrupt practices in the city of Gloucester. Report, 22 March 1881. 1881 C.2841 xli.

ASQUITH, Herbert Henry
Select committee on HC: admission of strangers. Report, 21 March 1893. 1893/4 (126) xii.

Select committee on HC: vacating of seats. Report, 9 Aug 1894. 1894 (278) xii.

Select committee on HC: vacating of seats. Report, 20 May 1895. 1895 (272) x.

Select committee on Leicester writs. Report, 3 May 1895. 1895 (247) xi.

ASTELL, William
Select committee on the Helleston election petition. Report, 25 March 1813. 1812/3 (108) iii.

ATHENRY, *Lord* [Peerage claim]. SEE: Cooper, C.A.

ATHERTON, Henrietta Maria
Committee on petition on Lancaster canal. SEE: Stanley, Thomas.

ATHLUMNEY, *Lord* [Peerage claim]. SEE: Freeman-Mitford, J.T.

ATKINS, John
Committee on petition respecting property sequestrated in Sweden. Report, 30 March 1813. 1812/3 (121) iii.

Select committee on laws relating to auctions. Report, 26 May 1818. 1818 (360) iii.

Select committee on Weymouth and Melcombe Regis election. Report, special report, and further report, 1 March 1813. 1812/3 (65) iii.

ATKINSON, John
Remarks on alterations in the poor laws to lessen the many inconveniences and unnecessary expenses and to show what are the effects produced upon those who receive parochial aid. 2 March 1830. *In:* 1834 (44) xxvii.

ATKINSON, John, *1st Bn. Atkinson*
Select committee on the Galway Infirmary Bill. Report, 15 June 1892. 1892 (272) xii.

ATTORNEYS-GENERAL
(years of appointment)

1799 J. Mitford, *Bn. Redesdale*
1801 E. Law, *Bn. Ellenborough*
1802 S. Perceval
1806 A. Pigot, *Sir*
1807 V. Gibbs, *Sir*
1812 T. Plumer, *Sir*
1813 W. Garrow, *Sir*
1817 S. Shepherd, *Sir*
1819 R. Gifford, *Bn. Gifford*
1824 S. Copley, *Bn. Lyndhurst*
1826 C. Wetherell, *Sir*
1827 J. Scarlett, *Lord Abinger*
1828 C. Wetherell, *Sir*
1829 J. Scarlett, *Lord Abinger*
1830 T. Denman, *Lord Denman*
1832 W. Horne, *Sir*
1834 J. Campbell, *Bn. Campbell*
1834 F. Pollock, *Sir*
1835 J. Campbell, *Bn. Campbell*
1841 F. Pollock, *Sir*
1844 W. Follett, *Sir*
1845 F. Thesinger, *Bn. Chelmsford*
1846 J. Jervis, *Sir*
1850 J. Romilly, *Bn. Romilly*
1851 A.J.E. Cockburn, *Sir*
1852 F. Thesinger, *Sir*
1853 A.J.E. Cockburn, *Sir*
1856 R. Bethell, *Sir*
1858 F. Kelly, *Sir*
1859 R. Bethell, *Sir*
1861 W. Atherton, *Sir*
1863 R. Palmer, *Sir*
1866 H. Cairns, *E. Cairns*
1866 J. Rolt, *Sir*
1867 J.B. Karslake, *Sir*
1868 R.P. Collier, *Sir*
1871 J.D. Coleridge, *Sir*
1873 H. James, *Sir*
1874 J.B. Karslake, *Sir*
1874 R. Baggallay, *Sir*
1875 J. Holker, *Sir*
1880 H. James, *Sir*
1885 R.E. Webster, *Sir*
1886 C. Russell, *Sir*
1886 R.E. Webster, *Sir*
1892 C. Russell, *Sir*
1894 J. Rigby, *Sir*
1894 R.T. Reid, *Sir*
1895 R.E. Webster, *Sir*

ATTORNEYS-GENERAL FOR IRELAND
(years of appointment)

1798 John Toler
1800 Patrick Stewart
1803 Standish O'Grady
1805 William C. Plunkett
1807 William Saurin
1822 William C. Plunkett
1827 H. Joy
1831 F. Blackburne
1835 Louis Perrin
1835 M. O'Loughlen
1836 John Richards
1837 Stephen Wolfe
1838 Nicholas Ball
1839 Maziere Brady
1840 David R. Pigot
1841 Francis Blackburne
1842 Thomas B.C. Smith
1846 Richard W. Green
1846 Richard Moore
1847 J.H. Monahan
1850 John Hatchell
1852 J. Napier
1853 Abraham Brewster
1855 William Keogh
1856 John D. Fitzgerald
1858 James Whiteside
1859 John D. Fitzgerald
1860 Richard Deasy
1861 Thomas O'Hagan
1865 James A. Lawson
1866 J.E. Walsh
1866 Michael Morris, *Lord Morris*
1867 H.E. Chatterton
1867 Richard Warren
1868 J.T. Ball

1868 E. Sullivan
1869 Charles Robert Barry
1871 R. Dowse
1872 C. Palles
1874 J.T. Ball
1875 H. Ormsby
1875 George A.C. May
1877 Edward Gibson, *Lord Ashbourne*
1880 Hugh Law
1881 W.M. Johnson
1883 A.M. Porter
1884 John Naish
1885 Samuel Walker
1885 Hugh Holmes
1887 John G. Gibson
1888 Peter O'Brien
1889 D.H. Madden
1892 John Atkinson, *Bn. Atkinson*
1892 H.H. Macdermot (session 2)
1895 John Atkinson, *Bn. Atkinson*

AUBERON-HERBERT, E.W.M. SEE:
Herbert, Edward William Molyneux Auberon.

AUCKLAND, *Lord* **SEE:**
Eden, William, *1st Bn. Auckland* (1774-1814).
Eden, George, *1st E. Auckland* (1784-1849).

AUSTIN, Alfred
Committee on the increased cost of the telegraph service since the acquisition of the telegraphs by the state. Report, 17 July 1875. 1875 C.1309 xx. Treasury.

Committee on the rating of houses held by government officials. Report, 1 April 1863. 1865 (325) xxx. Treasury.

Report on certain post mortem examinations of paupers who died in workhouses of the Dudley Union. 28 March 1844. 1844 (385) xl. Poor Law Commission.

Report on the conduct of the relieving officer at Dudley. 14 March 1844. 1844 (117) xl. Poor Law Commission.

Report on the employment of women and children in agriculture: Wiltshire, Dorset, Devon and Somerset. 25 March 1843. 1843 [510] xii. Poor Law Commission; (Agriculture, 6).

Report on the workhouses of Keighley Union. 25 May 1846. 1846 (413) xxxvi. Poor Law Commission.

AUSTIN, Anthony
Report on hand-loom weavers of the south western parts of England. 9 Jan 1839. 1840 (43-I) xxiii; (IR Textiles, 9).

AUSTIN, Henry
Report on the Croydon drainage. 19 Aug 1853. 1852/3 [1009] xcvi. Board of Health; (UA Sanitation, 3).

Report of an examination of Croydon and of the new [sewage] works, in relation to the outbreak of fever. 17 Feb 1853. *In:* 1852/3 [1683] xcvi. Board of Health; (HE Infectious Diseases, 2).

Report on the means of deodorizing and utilizing the sewage of towns. March 1857. 1857, session 2 [2262] xx. General Board of Health; (UA Sanitation, 4).

Report on St. Giles Cemetary, St. Pancras. 13 June 1850. 1850 [1228] xxi. General Board of Health.

Statement of the various schemes proposed for the improvement of the supply of water to the Metropolis. *In:* 1850 [1282] xxii. General Board of Health.

AUSTIN, Horatio T.
Committee of inquiry into the capabilities of the mercantile steam navy for purposes of war. Reports, 15 Nov 1852, 12 March 1853. 1852/3 (687) lxi. Board of Ordnance.

AUSTIN, John
Commission on the affairs of the Island of Malta.
Report and correspondence, pts I and II. 1837/8 (141) xxix.
Report and correspondence, pt.III. 27 March 1839. 1839 (140) xvii.
Further correspondence. 22 April 1839. 1839 (211) xvii.
Copies or extracts of reports and correspondence. 16 Feb 1838. 1837/8 (141) xxix.

AUSTRALIA, W.G.
Committee of the legislative council of New South Wales on Immigration. Report, 12 Nov 1839. 1840 (612) xxxiii; (Australia, 6). Colonial Office.

Committee of the legislative council of New South Wales on Emigration. Report, 2 Sept 1840. 1841 (241) xvii; (Australia, 6). Colonial Office.

AVEBURY, *Lord* **SEE:**
Lubbock, John, *Bn. Avebury.*

AWDRY, John Wither, *Sir*
Commission on the civil, municipal and ecclesiastical laws of the Island of Jersey.
Report. 1860. 1860 [2725] xxxi.
Report. 1861. 1861 [2761] xxiv.

AYLESFORD, *Lord* [Peerage claim]. **SEE:**
Freeman-Mitford, J.T.

AYMER, *Lord* [Peerage claim]. **SEE:**
Freeman-Mitford, J.T.

AYNSLEY, Charles Murray
Committee on boilers.
(1st and 2nd reports not located)
3rd report, 9 Aug 1877. 1877 C.1874 xix.
Ev., addenda, appendices. 1877 C.1723 xx.

AYRTON, Acton Smee
Select committee on the Cheltenham election petition, Min. of ev. 7 June 1866. 1866 (333) x.

Select committee on coal. Report, 18 July 1873. 1873 (313) x; (FP Coal Trade, 5).

Select committee on East India finance. Report, 23 July 1871. 1871 (363) viii; (East India, 19).

Select committee on East India finance. Report, 23 July 1872. 1872 (327) viii; (East India, 20).

Select committee on East India finance
1st report, 2 May 1873. 1873 (179) xii.
2nd report, 9 May 1873. 1873 (194) xii.
3rd report, 28 July 1873. 1873 (354) xii; (East India, 21).

Select committee on East London water bills, *etc.* Report, 27 June 1867. 1867 (399) ix.

Select committee on Factories and Workshops Bill. Report, 21 July 1870. 1870 (378) viii; (IR Factories, 2).

Select committee on Houses of Parliament new refreshment rooms. Report, 25 May 1870. 1870 (257) vi.

Select committee on the Lee River Conservancy Bill. Special report, 28 May 1868. 1867/8 (306) xi. Min. of ev. 29 May 1868. 1867/8 (307) xi.

AYRTON, Acton Smee (continued)
Select committee on Metropolis local taxation.
  1st report, 2 May 1861. 1861 (211) viii.
  2nd report, 24 June 1861. 1861 (372) viii.
  3rd report, 26 July 1861. 1861 (476) viii.

Select committee on Metropolitan local government, *etc.*
  1st report, 16 April 1866. 1866 (186) xiii.
  2nd report, 30 July 1866. 1866 (452) xiii.

Select committee on Metropolitan local government and local taxation.
  Report, 15 March 1867. 1867 (135) xii.
  2nd report, 6 May 1867. 1867 (267) xii.
  3rd report, 20 May 1867. 1867 (301) xii.

Select committee on mines. Report, 22 June 1865. 1865 (398) xii; (FP Mining Accidents, 9).

Select committee on mines, 1866. SEE: Neate, Charles.

Select committee on the Municipal Corporations (Borough, *etc.*, Funds) Bill. Report, 12 July 1871. 1871 (349) xi.

Select committee on pawnbrokers. Report, 4 Aug 1871. 1871 (419) xi.

Select committee on pawnbrokers, 1870, 1872. SEE: Whitwell, John.

Select committee on poor rates assessment, *etc.* Report, 22 June 1868. 1867/8 (342) xiii; repr. 1868/9 (0.47) xi; repr. 1873 (0.89) xvi.

Select committee on the Royal Parks and Gardens Bill. Min. of proc. 19 July 1871. 1871 (366) xi.

Select committee on the Thames Navigation Bill. Special report, 30 May 1870. 1870 (261) ix.

Select committee on thanksgiving in the Metropolitan Cathedral. Report, 19 Feb 1872. 1872 (49) xii.

Select committee on tribunals of commerce, *etc.* Report, 12 July 1858. 1857/8 (413) xvi; repr. 1873 (0.36) ix.

Select committee on tribunals of commerce. Report, 3 Aug 1871. 1871 (409) xii.

BABINGTON, Thomas
Committee of the Whole House on petitions against orders in council. Min. of ev. 29 April to 13 June 1812. 1812 (210) iii.

BADEN-POWELL, George Smyth
Behring Sea commission. Report, 21 June 1892. 1893/4 C.6919 cx. Foreign Office.

Royal Commission on the West Indies. Report.
  Pt.1: Jamaica. Sept 1883. 1884 C.3840 xlvi.
  Pt.2: Grenada, St. Vincent, Tobago and St. Lucia. Feb 1884. 1884 C.3840-I xlvi.
  Pt.3: Leeward Islands. Feb 1884. 1884 C.3840-II xlvi.
  Pt.4: Supplementary remarks. March 1884. 1884 C.3840-III xlvi; (West Indies, 6).

BAGWELL, John
Committee on tolls on the grand canal of Ireland. Report, 14 June 1805. 1805 (169) iv.

Select committee on destitution in Gweedore and Cloughancely district, County of Donegal. Report, 12 July 1858. 1857/8 (412) xiii.

BAILEY, Joseph Russell, *1st Bn. Glanusk*
Select committee on the London County Council (General Powers) Bill. Report, 27 May 1892. 1892 (232) xii.

Select committee on workmen at Woolwich Arsenal. Report, 18 June 1889. 1889 (197) xvi.

BAILLIE, Henry James
Select committee on Ceylon.
  1st report, 19 Feb 1850. 1850 (66) xii.
  2nd report, 4 March 1850. 1850 (106) xii.
  3rd report, 6 July 1850. 1850 (605) xii; repr. 1851 (36) viii, 2 pts.

Select committee on Ceylon and British Guiana.
  1st report, 18 May 1849. 1849 (297) xi.
  2nd report, 27 July 1849. 1849 (573) xi.
  3rd report, 31 July 1849. 1849 (591) xi; (Colonies, 1).

Select committee on emigration, Scotland.
  1st report, 26 March 1841. 1841 (182) vi.
  2nd report, 24 May 1841. 1841 (333) vi; (Emigration, 3).

Select committee on the London (City) Traffic Regulation Bill. Report, 14 July 1863. 1863 (440) x.

BAILLIE, Matthew
Committee on petition respecting purchase of the Hunterian collection. SEE: Evelyn, G.A.W.S.

BAILLIE, Thomas, *9th E. Haddington*
Select committee (HL) on the Chimney Sweepers Bill. Min. of ev. 13 July 1840. HL 1840 (206) xxii.

BAILLIE-COCHRANE, Alexander Dundas Wishart Ross
Select committee on public offices and buildings in the Metropolis. Report, 6 July 1877. 1877 (312) xv.

BAINES, Edward
Select committee on the London Corporation Regulation Bill. Min. of proc. 14 May 1858. 1857/8 (273) xi; repr. 1872 (137) xi.

Select committee on the Queen's printers' patent. Report, 4 Aug 1859. 1859, session 2, (144) v.

Select committee on the Queen's printers' patent. Report, 22 March 1860. 1860 (162) xxii.

Select committee on the suppression of the *Calcutta Journal.* Report, 4 Aug 1834. 1834 (601) viii.

BAINES, Matthew Talbot
Select committee on criminal and destitute juveniles. Report, 24 June 1852. 1852 (515) vii; (CP Juvenile Offenders, 2).

Select committee on criminal and destitute children. Report, 28 June 1853. 1852/3 (674) xxiii; (CP Juvenile Offenders, 3).

Select committee on the Dulwich College Bill Min. of ev. 31 July 1857. 1857, session 2, (222) ix.

Select committee on the London Corporation Regulation Bill. Min. of proc. 14 May 1858. 1857/8 (273) xi.

Select committee on the Statute Law Commission. Report, 10 March 1857. 1857, session 1, (99) ii.

Select committee on transportation
  1st report, 27 May 1856. 1856 (244) xvii.
  2nd report, 20 June 1856. 1856 (296) xvii.
  3rd report, 11 July 1856. 1856 (355) xvii; (CP Transportation, 4).

Select committee on poor removal. Report, 21 July 1854. 1854 (396) xvii; (Poor Law, 22).

BAIRD, George H.
Committee of the General Assembly [of the Church

of Scotland] on the management of the poor in Scotland. Supplementary report, 23 June 1820. 1820 (195) vii.

BAKER, Edward
Inquiry on allegations about Milbank Prison. SEE: Crawford, William.

BAKER, William Henry
Select committee on petition. SEE: Hotham, Beaumont.

BALD, William
Report on Holyhead and Portdynllaen as a harbour of refuge for the Channel trade. 13 June 1846. 1846 (640) xlv. Admiralty.

Report on Sutton Pool Harbour Improvement Bill. 27 April 1847. 1847 (736) lxi. Admiralty.

BALDWIN, Arthur
Select committee on Local Government Provisional Order (No.15) Bill. Report, 13 July 1899. 1899 (277) x.

BALDWIN, Thomas
Royal commission on agriculture. Preliminary report of the assistant commissioner for Ireland. 1 Jan 1880. 1881 C.2951 xvi; (Agriculture, 16).

BALFOUR OF BURLEIGH, *Bn*. SEE:
Bruce, Alexander Hugh, *6th Bn. Balfour of Burleigh.*

BALFOUR, Arthur James
Royal commission on recent changes in the relative values of the precious metals, 1887-8. SEE: Herschell, Farrer, *Bn. Herschell.*

BALFOUR, John Blair, *Bn. Kinross*
Select committee on the Burgh Police and Health (Scotland) Bill. Report, 18 July 1884. 1884 (286) viii.

Select committee on the Civil Imprisonment (Scotland) Bill. Report, 19 July 1882. 1882 (288) viii.

Select committee on feus and leases in Scotland. Report, 31 July 1893. 1893/4 (354) xii. 2nd report, 9 Jan 1894. 1893/4 (477) xii.

Select committee on laws, feus and buildings leases in Scotland. Report, 26 July 1894. 1894 (238) xi.

Select committee on Limited Owners (Scotland) Bill. Special report, 27 July 1887. 1887 (242) x.

Select committee on the Married Women's Property (Scotland) Bill. Report, 29 March 1881. 1881 (152) ix; (Marriage and Divorce, 2).

Select committee on the Poor Relief and Audit of Accounts (Scotland) Bill. Report, 3 Aug 1881. 1881 (373) xii.

Select committee on rating and valuation in Scotland. Report, 12 July 1888. 1888 (274) xvii.

Select committee on rating and valuation in Scotland. Report, 30 July 1890. 1890 (335) xvii.

BALFOUR OF BURLEY [Peerage claim]. SEE: Freeman-Mitford, J.T.

BALL, Alexander Francis
Commission on charges against the magistracy of Dungannon. SEE: Coffey, J.C.

BALL, John Thomas
Commission on corrupt practices in elections of members to service in Parliament in the County of the Town of Galway. Report, 1857/8 [2291] xxvi.

BALY, William
Report on quarantine at Gibraltar. 6 May 1854. 1854/5 (161) xxxvi. Colonial Office.

Report on the sanitary state of Gibraltar. 20 July 1854. 1854/5 (274) xxxvi. Colonial Office.

BANDON, *E*. [Peerage claim]. SEE:
Freeman-Mitford, J.T.

BANGOR, *Vct*. [Peerage claim]. SEE:
Palmer, R.

BANKES, George
Select committee on the land tax as affecting Roman Catholics. Report, 18 July 1828. 1828 (550) iv.

Select committee on the ophthalmic hospital. Report, 3 July 1821. 1821 (732) iv.

BANKES, Henry
Committee on abuses in the disposal of the patronage of the East India Company. Report, 23 March 1809. 1809 (91) ii.

Committee of Dr. Jenner's petition, respecting his discovery of vaccine inoculation. Report, 6 May 1802. CJ Reports, vol.14, p.189; 1801/2 (114) ii.

Committee on Dr. Smyth's petition, respecting his discovery of nitrous fumigation. Report, 10 June 1802. CJ Reports, vol.14, p.189; 1801/2 (114) ii.

Committee on the high price of provisions, 1801. SEE: Yorke, C.

Committee on petitions relating to the General Post Office. Report, 26 July 1814. 1813/4 (338) iii.

Committee on the petition of the Trustees of the British Museum relating to the collection of the late Dr. Burney. Report, 17 April 1818. 1818 (205) iii.

Committee of public expenditure
1st report: Pay Office. 1807 (61) ii; (Monetary Policy, 1).
2nd report: Bank of England. 1807 (108) ii.
3rd report: Pensions, sinecures, reversions, *etc.* 1807 (109) ii; repr. 1808 (331) iii. Supplement, 31 May 1809. 1809 (200) iii.
4th report: Dutch prizes. 1809 (99) iii.
5th report: Office of Paymaster of Marines. 18 April and 20 June 1810. 1810 (216), (372) ii.
6th report: Collection of taxes in Scotland. 20 June 1810. 1810 (369) ii.
7th report: Buildings, civil and military. 20 June 1810. 1810 (370) ii.
8th report: Linen Board, Ireland. 20 June 1810. 1810 (371) ii.
9th report: Printing and stationery. 20 June 1810. 1810 (373) ii.
10th report: Audit of accounts. 26 June 1811. 1810/1 (253) iii.
11th report: Continuation of 5th-7th reports. 1 July 1811. 1810/1 (257) iii.
12th report: Balances and defaulters. 10 July 1812. 1812 (339) ii.
13th report: Proc. relating to regimental accounts; commissioners sent to the West Indies. 10 July 1812. 1812 (340) ii.

Select committee on committee rooms and printed papers. Report, 26 May 1826. 1826 (403) iii.

Select committee on the Earl of Elgin's collection of sculptured marbles, *etc.* Report, 25 March 1816. 1816 (161) iii.

BANKES, Henry (continued)

Select committee on the general index to the Journals of the' HC. Report, 10 July 1823. 1823 (541) iv.

Select committee on the general index to the Journals of the HC. Report, 24 June 1825. 1825 (477) v.

Select committee on the improvements in Westminster. Report, 20 June 1809. 1809 (272) iii.

Select committee on the intended improvements in the Post Office. Report, 15 April 1815. 1814/5 (235) iii.

Select committee on the Office of Works and Public Buildings. Report, 19 June 1828. 1828 (446) iv.

Select committee on public buildings at Westminster. Report, 14 May 1824. 1824 (307) vi.

Select committee on sinecure offices.
1st report, 20 June 1810. 1810 (362) ii.
2nd report, 18 June 1811. 1810/1 (246) iii.
3rd report, 23 April 1812. 1812 (181) ii.

Select committee on the standing order relating to bills respecting trade. Report, 23 May 1823. 1823 (376) iv.

BANKES, Joseph

Commission on preventing the forgery of bank notes.
Report, 22 Jan 1819. 1819 (2) xi.
Final report, 18 Feb 1820. 1819/20 (64) ii.

Committee of the Royal Society on the state of the reservoir of gas belonging to the Gas-Light Co. Report, 26 March 1823. 1823 (193) v; (FP Gas, 6).

BANNATYNE, Andrew

Commission on the state of the registers of land rights in the counties and burghs of Scotland. Report, July 1862 and Feb 1863. 1863 [3110] xv.

BANNERMAN, Alexander

Select committee on the petition on Liverpool Borough. Report, 1 April 1833. 1833 (139) x.

Select committee on Liverpool Borough elections. Report, 29 July 1833. 1833 (583) x.

BANTRY, E. [Peerage claim]. SEE:
Freeman-Mitford, J.T.

BARBOUR, David Miller

Report on the finances of Jamaica. July 1899. 1899 C.9412 xli. Colonial Office.

BARCLAY, Charles

Select committee on Blackfriars Bridge. Report, 1 July 1836. 1836 (418) xx.

Select committee on petition of inhabitants of Athlone, 1827. SEE: Dawson, Alexander.

BARHAM, Lord SEE:
Noel, C.N., 2nd Bn. Barham.

BARHAM, Joseph Forster

Committee on West India Dock Co's accounts. Report, 22 March 1810. 1810 (130) iv.

BARING, Alexander

Select committee on members accepting offices abroad. Report, 2 June 1829. 1829 (307) iii.

Select committee on reduction of salaries. Report, 30 March 1831. 1830/1 (322) iii.

BARING, Francis, 3rd Bn. Ashburton

Committee on expired and expiring laws: 2nd session,

12th Parliament. Report, 15 Feb 1836. 1836 (27) xxi.

Select committee on malt drawback on spirits. Report, 4 Oct 1831. 1831 (295) vii.

Select committee (HL) on the operation of the Poor Removal Act. Report, 11 March 1847. HL 1847 (47) xxv; HC repr. 1847 (369) viii.

Select committee on public documents, 1833. SEE: Russell, John.

BARING, Francis Thornhill, Sir

Committee on the Carlow County election petition. Min. of ev. 11 May 1837. 1837 (307) x.

Committee on expired and expiring laws: 1st session, 13th Parliament. Report, Feb 1838. 1837/8 (134) xxiii.

Committee of public accounts, 1862.
1st report, 8 May 1862. 1862 (200) xi.
2nd report, 16 July 1862. 1862 (414) xi.
3rd report, 29 July 1862. 1862 (467) xi.

Committee of public accounts, 1863.
1st report, 19 May 1863. 1863 (286) vii.
2nd report, 2 June 1863. 1863 (309) vii.

Committee of public accounts, 1864. SEE: Bouverie, Edward Pleydell.

General committee of elections on the Cashel election petition. Report, 25 March 1858. 1857/8 (157) xii.

Secret committee on commercial distress.
1st report, 8 June 1848. 1847/8 (395) viii, pt.1.
2nd report, 2 Aug 1848. 1847/8 (584) viii, pt.1.
Appendix. 1847/8 (395), (584) viii, pt.2; (MP Commercial Distress, 1, 2).

Select committee on Clerk of the Crown in Chancery. Report, 31 July 1835. 1835 (457) xviii.

Select committee on public accounts.
1st report, 11 June 1861. 1861 (329) xi.
2nd report, 21 June 1861. 1861 (367) xi.
3rd report, 9 July 1861. 1861 (418) xi.
4th report, 19 July 1861. 1861 (448) xi.
5th report, index, 25 July 1861. 1861 (468) xi; (National Finance, 4).

Select committee on public monies. Report, 21 July 1856. 1856 (375) xv.

Select committee on public monies. Report, 13 March 1857. 1857, session 1 (107) ii.

Select committee on public monies. Report, 18 Aug 1857. 1857, session 2 (279) ix.

Select committee on Sandhurst Royal Military College. Report, 18 June 1855. 1854/5 (317) xii.

Select committee on sinecure offices. Report, 12 Aug 1835. 1835 (507) xviii.

BARING, Henry

Select committee on Worcester election petitions. Report, 23 March 1819. 1819 (149) iv.

BARING, Henry Bingham

Select committee on the Salmon Fishery Act (1861) Amendment Bill. Min. of proc. 13 June 1865. 1865 (358) xii.

BARING, Thomas, Sir

Committee on the Limerick election. Min. of ev. 2 March 1819. 1819 (77) iv.

Report of the visiting magistrates of the gaol and

bridewell at Winchester, 13 April 1832. 1831/2 (383) xxxiii. Home Office.

Select committee on Indian territories, 1851. SEE: Wood, Charles.

Select committee on Indian territories. Report, 29 June 1852. 1852 (533) x; (East India, 12).

Select committee on the militia estimates, 1861-62. Report, 23 July 1861. 1861 (461) xiii.

Select committee on Mr. McAdam's petition relating to his improved system for constructing roads. Report, 20 June 1823. 1823 (467) v.

BARING, Thomas George, *1st E.Northbrook*
Royal commission on mining royalties.
1st report, 31 July 1890. 1890 C.6195 xxxvi.
2nd report, 31 March 1891. 1890/1 C.6331 xli.
3rd report, 22 July 1891. 1890/1 C.6529 xli.
4th report, 8 March 1893. 1893/4 C.6979 xli.
Final report, 24 March 1893. 1893/4 C.6980 xli; (FP Mining Royalties, 1-3).

BARING, Thomas George, *2nd Bn. Northbrook*
Committee on Capt. Moncrieff's letter of 5 Dec 1868 with reference to his invention for mounting guns. Report, 3 Feb 1869. 1868/9 [4092] xii. War Office.

Committee on arrangements for conduct of the Army Depts. 1st to 3rd reports. 11 March 1869 to 12 Feb 1870. 1870 C.54 xii; (Military and Naval, 4). War Office.

Committee of the Ordnance Council of the proposed 35-ton gun competition. Report, June 1870. 1870 (308) xliii. War Office.

Joint committee of the HL and the HC on canal rates, tolls and charges provisional order bills. Report, 20 July 1893. 1893/4 (395) x; HL report, 1 Sept 1893. HL 1893/4 (270) x.

Select committee on Cattle Diseases Prevention, and Cattle, *etc.* Importation bills. Report, 27 June 1864. 1864 (431) vii.

Select committee on the Chemists and Druggists Bill and the Chemists and Druggists (No.2) Bill. Special report, 19 June 1865. 1865 (381) xii; (HE Food and Drugs, 3).

BARING, William Bingham
Select committee on atmospheric railways. Report, 24 April 1845. 1845 (252) x.

Select committee on Metropolitan sewage manure. Report, 13 July 1846. 1846 (474) x; (UA Sanitation, 1).

BARLOW, Peter
Committee on railway communications between London and Dublin. Report, 16 April 1840. 1840 (250) xlv. Treasury.

Committee on railway communication between London, Dublin, Edinburgh and Glasgow.
Report, 16 May 1840. 1840 (312) xlv.
(2nd report not identified)
3rd report, 14 Nov 1840. 1841 (8) xxv.
4th report, 15 March 1841. 1841 (132) xxv. Treasury.

Report on the atmospheric railway. 15 Feb 1842. 1842 [368] xli. Board of Trade.

BARLOW, William Henry
Report of the court of inquiry upon the fall of a portion of the Tay Bridge, 28 Dec 1879. 30 June 1880. 1880 C.2616 xxxix. Board of Trade.

BARNEBY, John
Select committee on Gilbert Unions. Report, 25 June 1845. 1845 (409) xiii.

Select committee on Hereford lunatic asylum. Report, 27 June 1839. 1839 (356) ix; (HE Mental, 2).

Select committee on the Highways Act. Report, 11 June 1838. 1837/8 (436) xxiii.

Select committee on poor relief, Gilbert Unions. Report, 25 July 1844. 1844 (534) x.

BARNEY, George
Commission appointed to inquire into the execution of the contracts for certain union workhouses in Ireland. Report, 12 Feb 1845. 1845 (170) xxvi. Treasury.

BARRINGTON, *Vct.* [Peerage claim]. SEE: Giffard, H.S.

BARRON, Henry Page Turner
Report on the cattle plague in Belgium. 22 Jan 1866. 1866 [3628] lix. Foreign Office.

BARRON, Winston
Select committee on perogative and ecclesiastical courts in Ireland. Report, 22 June 1837. 1837 (412) vi.

BARRY, *Lord* [Peerage claim]. SEE: Cooper, C.A.

BARRY, Charles
Commission to visit quarries and inquire into the qualities of the stone to be used in building the new House of Parliament. Report, 16 March 1839. 1839 (574) xxx. Commissioners of H.M. Woods, Forests, *etc.*

BARRY, Charles R.
Commission of inquiry, 1864, into the magisterial and police jurisdiction arrangements and establishment of the Borough of Belfast. Report, 8 March 1865. 1865 [3466] xxviii; (CP Civil Disorder, 7).

BARRY, Frederick William
Enteric fever in the Tees Valley. Report, Nov 1892. 1893/4 C.7054 xlii. Local Government Board.

Report on an epidemic of small-pox at Sheffield during 1887-88. Dec 1888. 1889 C.5645 lxv. Local Government Board.

BARRY, John Maxwell
Committee on Holyhead harbour. Report, 12 June 1816. 1816 (462) viii.

Committee on Holyhead roads. Report, 30 May 1811. 1810/1 (197) iii.

Committee on the petition of John McClintock. Report, 24 March 1808. 1808 (131) iii.

Committee respecting the draining of bogs in Ireland. Report, 22 March 1810. 1810 (148) iv.

BARSTOW, Thomas Irwin
Commission on corrupt practices at the last election for the Borough of Lancaster. Report, 1867. 1867 [3777] xxvii.

BARTTELOT, Walter Barttelot, *Sir*
Committee of public accounts, 1884-85. SEE: Salt, Thomas.

Select committee on commons. Report, 5 May 1885. 1884/5 (179) viii.

BARTTELOT, Walter Barttelot, Sir (continued)
Select committee on commons. Report, 31 March 1886. 1886, session 1 (98) vii.

Select committee on commons. Report, 12 June 1888. 1888 (216) ix.

Select committee on commons. Report, 9 April 1889. 1889 (103) x.

Select committee on commons. Report, 17 April 1890. 1890 (132) xiii.

Select committee on commons, 1891. SEE: Bryce, James.

Select committee on malt tax. Report, 25 July 1867. 1867 (470) xi.

Select committee on malt tax. Report, 13 July 1868. 1867/8 (420) ix.

Standing committee on law. Police Bill. Report, 22 July 1890. 1890 (317) xvii.

BASING, Bn. SEE:
Sclater-Booth, George, 1st Bn. Basing.

BATEMAN, John Frederick
Report on the inundations of the River Shannon. 7 June 1867. 1867 (383) lix. Treasury.

Report on the means of preventing injury by flooding of lands adjoining the River Shannon. 7 May 1863. 1863 (292) l. Treasury.

BATHURST, E. SEE:
Bathurst, Henry, 3rd E. Bathurst (s.1794, d.1834).
Bathurst, Henry George, 4th E. Bathurst (1790-1866).
Bathurst, William Lennox, 5th E. Bathurst (1791-1878).
Bathurst, Allen Alexander, 6th E. Bathurst (1832-1892).
Bathurst, Seymour Henry, 7th E. Bathurst (1864-   ).

BATHURST, Allen Alexander, 6th E. Bathurst
General committee on railway and canal bills, 1870. SEE: Goldsmid, Francis Henry, Sir.

BATHURST, Charles
Committee on Calcutta bankers petition. Report, 29 July 1822. 1822 (603) v.

Committee of precedents on expulsion of members. Report, 16 Feb 1807. 1806/7 (79) iii.

Committee of secrecy. Report on papers presented (sealed up) to the HC on 5 June 1817, by command of HRH the Prince Regent. 20 June 1817. 1817 (387) iv.

Committee of secrecy. Report on papers presented (sealed up) to the HC by command of HRH the Prince Regent. 27 Feb 1818. 1818 (69) iii.

Select committee on the printed *Votes and Proceedings* of the HC. Report, 27 March 1817. 1817 (156) iii.

Select committee on the regularity of proceedings upon private bills. Report, 28 May 1810. 1810 (301) ii.

Select committee on the state of gaols. Report, 12 July 1819. 1819 (579) vii; (CP Prisons, 1).

BATHURST, Henry, 3rd E. Bathurst
Select committee (HL) on the affairs of the East India Co. Report. HL 1830 (11) cclxxiv; HC repr. 1830 (646) vi.

Select committee (HL) on the state of the British wool trade. Report, 27 June 1828. HL 1828 (90) ccxxxvi; HC repr. 1828 (515) viii.

Select committee (HL) on the state of the coal trade. Report, 15 June 1829. HL 1829 (37) ccxlvii; HC repr. 8 Feb 1830. 1830 (9) viii; (Coal Trade, 1).

BATHURST, Henry George, 4th E. Bathurst
Berbice and Demerara Manumission Order in Council. Min. of ev. 18 April 1828. 1828 (261) xxx. Privy Council.

Select committee on the general index to the journals of the HC. Report, 3 June 1818. 1818 (396) iii.

Select committee (HL) on the Irish Great Western Railway Bill. Report, 25 July 1845. HL 1845 (325) xviii.

BAXTER, William Edward
Select committee on the Bridgewater election petition. Min. of ev. 8 May 1866. 1866 (247) x.

Select committee on East India Railway communication. Report, 18 July 1884. 1884 (284) xi.

Select committee on standing order 167. Report, 19 May 1882. 1882 (196) xiii.

BAYFIELD, Henry W.
Report on the necessity of erecting a lighthouse on Cape Pine, Newfoundland. 26 Aug 1847. 1849 (225) li. Admiralty.

BAYLEY, E.C.
Report on certain claims against the late native government of Oude. 11 July 1862. 1862 (428) xl. India Office.

BAYLEY, S.C.
Committee of the legislative council of India on the Bengal Tennancy Bill. Report, 14 March 1884. 1884 (228) lx. India Office.

BAZALGETTE, J.W.
Reports on tubular-pipe drains or sewers. 24 June 1853. 1852/3 (669) xcvi. Metropolitan Com. of Sewers.

BEACH, Michael Hicks. SEE:
Hicks-Beach, Michael

BEARDMORE, Nathaniel
Report on the Aldborough Harbour of Refuge and Improvement Bill. 9 March 1852. 1852 (269) xlix. Admiralty.

Report of the failure and bursting of a reservoir embankment belonging to the Sheffield Waterworks Co., 11 March 1864. 20 May 1864. 1864 (290-I) l. Home Department.

BEARDSLEY, B.C.
Select committee of the House of Assembly, Upper Canada on the conduct of Capt. Phillpotts. Report, 18 July 1833. *In:* 1833 (543) xxvi.

BEAUCHAMP, Lord SEE:
Lygon, William, 1st E. Beauchamp (cr.1815, d.1816).
Lygon, William Beauchamp, 2nd E. Beauchamp (s.1816, d.1823).
Lygon, John Beauchamp, 3rd E. Beauchamp (s.1823, d.1853).
Lygon, Henry Beauchamp, 4th E. Beauchamp (s.1853, d.1863).
Lygon, Henry, 5th E. Beauchamp (1829-1866).
Lygon, Frederick, 6th E. Beauchamp (1830-1891).
Lygon, William, 7th E. Beauchamp (1872-1938).

BEAUCHAMP, *Vct.* SEE:
Seymour-Conway, Francis, *2nd E. Hertford* (1743-1822).

BEAUFORT, F.
Report on the plans of Mr. Cubitt for constructing a harbour of refuge at Dover. 9 Dec 1841. 1842 (444) xxxix. Admiralty.

BEAUMONT, *Lord* [Peerage claim]. SEE:
Cooper, C.A., SEE ALSO: Stapleton, Miles Thomas, *1st Bn. Beaumont* (1805-54).

BEAUMONT, Wentworth Blackett
Select committee on the Forest of Dean Turnpike Trust. Report, 7 June 1888. 1888 (209) xii.

Select committee on the Shrewsbury and Holyhead turnpike road. Report, 13 June 1890. 1890 (224) xvii.

Select committee on the Turnpike Acts Continuance Act, 1880. Report, 10 May 1881. 1881 (210) xii.

Select committee on Turnpike Acts continuance. Report, 3 May 1882. 1882 (178) xiii.

Select committee on Turnpike Acts continuance. Report, 4 May 1883. 1883 (153) xiv.

Select committee on the Turnpike Acts continuance. Report, 13 May 1884. 1884 (173) xv.

Select committee on Turnpike Acts continuance. Report, 12 May 1885. 1884/5 (187) xii.

BEAUMONT, William A.
Report on the prevention of accidents from machinery in the manufacture of cotton. Aug 1899. 1899 C.9456 xii. Home Office.

BECKETT, Gilbert A.
Report on the operation of the laws of settlement and removal of the poor in the counties of Suffolk, Norfolk, Essex and the Reading Union, Berkshire. 24 Oct 1848. 1850 [1152] xxvii. Poor Law Bd., (Poor Law, 21).

BECKETT, William
Select committee on the Devon and Dorset Railway Bill. Min. of ev. 4 July 1853. 1852/3 (705) xxiv.

Select committee on the Metropolis water bills. Min. of ev. 24 May and 25 June 1852. 1852 (395), (527) xii; (UA Water supply, 3).

BEDFORD, George Augustus
Report on the harbours of Holyhead. 29 July 1869. 1868/9 [4201] liv. Board of Trade.

BEECHEY, Frederick W.
Committee on a code of signals to be used at sea. Report, 24 Sept 1856. 1857, session 1 [2194] ix. Board of Trade.

Committee on the suitableness and capabilities of the ports of Galway and the Shannon for a transatlantic packet station in connexion with a harbour of refuge. Report, 31 July 1852. 1852/3 (22) xcv. Admiralty.

Inquiry into the loss of the steamship 'Amazon'. Report, 17 Feb 1852. 1852 [1425] xlix. Board of Trade.

Inquiry into the present system of pilotage in the Bristol Channel. Min. of ev. 2 June 1854. 1854 (286) lx. Board of Trade.

Report on the best means of communication between

London and Dublin. 14 Jan 1840. 1840 (250) xlv. Admiralty.

Report of an investigation into the loss of the 'Annie Jane'. 30 Dec 1853. 1854 [1724] lx. Board of Trade.

Report of an investigation into the loss of the steamship 'Forerunner' on the coast of Madeira, 25 Oct 1854. 25 Nov 1854. 1854/5 [1858] xlvi. Board of Trade.

Report on the loss of the 'Victoria' of Hull off the Wenga lighthouse, 8 Nov 1852. 16 April 1853. 1852/3 (450) xcviii. Board of Trade.

Report of a survey of the Selby Rocks in the Straits of Menai. 30 Sept 1846. 1850 (314) xxxv.

BELHAVEN, *Lord* [Peerage claim]. SEE:
Freeman-Mitford, J.T.

BELL, Andrew Beatson
Committee on accommodation of prisoners awaiting trial in Scotland. Report, 14 March 1889. 1889 C.5683 xli. Scottish Office; (CP Prisons, 18).

BELL, George Joseph
Law commission, Scotland.
    1st report, 12 May 1834. 1834 (295) xxvi.
    2nd report, 30 June 1835. 1835 [63] xxxv.
    3rd report: Conveyancing. 13 Jan 1838. 1837/8 [114] xxix.
    4th report, 25 Nov 1839. 1840 [241] xx.

BELL, Jacob
Select committee on the Pharmacy Bill. Report, 21 May 1852. 1852 (387) xiii; (HE Food and Drugs, 1).

BELL, Robert
Commissioners of religious instruction, Scotland
    Report, 7 Feb 1837. 1837 (31) xxi.
    2nd report, 1837/8 [109] xxxii.
    3rd report. 1837/8 [113] xxxiii.
    4th report. 1837/8 [122] xxxiii.
    5th report. 1839 [152] xxiii.
    6th report. 1839 [153] xxiv.
    7th report. 1839 [154] xxv.
    8th report. 1839 [162] xxvi.
    9th report. 1839 [164] xxvi.

BELLENDEN KER, H. SEE:
Ker, H.B.

BELLEW, *Bn.* [Peerage claim]. SEE:
Freeman-Mitford, J.T.

BELMORE, *E.* [Peerage claim]. SEE:
Freeman-Mitford, J.T. SEE ALSO: Lowry-Corry, Somerset Richard, *4th E. Belmore* (*b.*1835, *s.*1845).

BELPER, *Lord* SEE:
Strutt, Edward, *1st Bn. Belper* (1801-1880).
Strutt, Henry, *2nd Bn. Belper* (*s.*1880).

BELTZ, Samuel
Papers on the mode of keeping public accounts. 25 June 1831. 1831 (50) xiv.

BENNET, Henry Gray
Committee on employment of boys in sweeping chimneys. Report, 23 June 1817. 1817 (400) vi, (IR Children's Employment, 1).

Committee on King's Bench, Fleet and Marshalsea prisons. Report, 1 May 1815. 1814/5 (152) iv; (CP Prisons, 7).

Committee on the police of the Metropolis. Report,

BENNET, Henry Gray (continued)
1 July 1816. 1816 (510) v; (CP Police, 1).

Committee on the state of the police of the Metropolis.
>1st report: Licensing. 2 May 1817. 1817 (233)
>vii; repr. 1852/3 (292) xxxviii.
>2nd report: Rewards and Prions. 8 July 1817.
>1817 (484) vii.
>3rd report, 5 June 1818. 1818 (423) viii; (CP
>Police, 2-3).

Select committee on the contagious fever in London. Report, 20 May 1818. 1818 (332) vii.

Select committee on the penitentiary at Milbank. Report, 8 July 1823. 1823 (533) v.

Select committee on the penitentiary at Milbank. Report, 11 June 1824. 1824 (408) iv; (CP Prisons, 10).

Select committee on returns made by members of the HC to the several orders of the HC on 8 June 1821 [on offices and emoluments]. Report, 9 July 1822. 1822 (542) iv.

BENNETT, James Risdon
Commission on the death of John Nolan in Clerkenwell Prison. Report, 8 Feb 1879. 1878/9 (79) lix; (CP Prisons, 18). Home Office.

BENNETT, John
Select committee on Liverpool election petition. Min. of ev. 28 March 1831. 1830/1 (307) iii.

BENSON, Edward White, *Archbp. of Canterbury*, 1883-69
Royal commission on the constitution and working of the ecclesiastical courts. Report. 1883 C.3760 xxiv. 2 vols.

Select committee (HL) on the Church Patronage Bill. Report, 4 June 1886. HL 1886 (145) vii.

BENSON, Ralph
Select committee on petitions relating to the duty on leather. Report, 5 April 1813. 1812/3 (128) iv.

BENTINCK, Cavendish. SEE:
Cavendish-Bentinck, George Augustus Frederick, *Lord*

BENTINCK, George William Pierrepont
Select committee on accidents on railways. Report, 25 June 1858. 1857/8 (362) xiv.

Select committee on Sheep, *etc.* Contagious Diseases Prevention Bill. Report, 26 June 1857. 1857, session 2 (129) ix.

BENTINCK, H.
Commission on purchase and sale of commissions in the Army. Note of dissent. 3 Aug 1857. 1857/8 [2293] xix; (Military and Naval, 3). SEE ALSO: St. Maur, Edward Adolphus, *12th D. Somerset.*

BERE, Montague
Commission on corrupt practices at elections for the Borough of Totnes. Report, 29 Jan 1867. 1867 [3776] xxix.

Report and ev. on the wreck of the 'North' on the Goodwin Sands, 30 Aug 1866 and the alleged plunder on that occasion. 21 June 1867. 1867 (389) lxiii. Board of Trade.

Report on the inquiry into the accident to the ship 'Olivia' off Deal on 21 April 1867. 1867 (539) lxiv. Board of Trade.

BERESFORD, Charles William de la Poer, *Lord*
Select committee on saving life at sea. Report, 29 July 1887. 1887 (249) xii.

BERESFORD, Henry de la Poer, *6th M. Waterford*
Select committee (HL) on land law in Ireland, 1882. SEE: Cairns, Hugh MacCalmont, *1st E. Cairns.*

Select committee (HL) on the Poor Law Guardians (Ireland) Bill, 1885. SEE: Leeson, Edward Nugent, *6th E. Milltown.*

BERESFORD, John George, *Archbp. of Armagh*, 1822-62
Commission of ecclesiastical inquiry, Ireland. Report, 13 July 1831. 1831 (93) ix.

Commission on ecclesiastical revenue and patronage, Ireland
>Report, 28 Aug 1833. 1833 (762) xxi.
>2nd report, 8 Aug 1834. 1834 (589) xxiii.
>3rd report, 9 May 1836. 1836 (246) xxv.
>4th report, 10 July 1837. 1837 (500) xxi.

BERESFORD-HOPE, Alexander James Bresford
Select committee on Foreign Office reconstruction. Report, 13 July 1858. 1857/8 (417) xi.
Select committee on the Woodhouse collection. SEE: Cardwell, Edward.

BERKELEY, *Lord* [Peerage claim], 1829. SEE:
Cooper, C.A. [Peerage claim], 1858. SEE:
Freeman-Mitford, J.T.

BERKELEY, Craven
Select committee on corn laws (Cheltenham petition). Report, 23 March 1846. 1846 (139) viii.

BERKELEY, Francis Henry Fitzhardinge
Select committee on the Sale of Beer, *etc.* Act
>1st report, 20 July 1855. 1854/5 (407) x.
>2nd report, 26 July 1855. 1854/5 (427) x; (SP
>Sunday Observance, 2).

BERKELEY, George Charles Grantley Fitzhardinge
Select committee on admission of ladies to the strangers gallery. Report, 28 July 1835. 1835 (437) xviii.

BERNAL, Ralph
Committee on expired and expiring laws. 2nd session, 10th Parliament. Report, 26 Jan 1832. 1831/2 (86) v.

Select committee on expired and expiring laws. 1st session, 11th Parliament. Report, 20 Feb 1833. 1833 (24) xvi.

Select committee on expired and expiring laws. 2nd session, 11th Parliament. Report, 26 Feb 1834. 1834 (69) xviii.

Select committee on expired and expiring laws: 3rd session, 12th Parliament. Report, 22 March 1837. 1837 (130) xx.

Committee on expired and expiring laws: 2nd session, 13th Parliament. Report, 22 March 1839. 1839 (121) xiii.

Select committee on Hertford Borough. Report, 27 June 1833. 1833 (449) ix.

Select committee on Hertford election petition. Report, 3 April 1833. 1833 (152) ix.

BERNARD, Scrope
Committee on laws relating to lotteries.
>Report, 13 April 1808. 1808 (182) ii.
>2nd report, 24 June 1808. 1808 (323) iii; (SP
>Gambling, 2).

BERNERS, Lord SEE:
Wilson, Henry William, *2nd Bn. Berners.*
[Peerage claim]. SEE: Cooper, C.A.

BERTHON, E.L.
Report on collapsing life boat. SEE: Cradock, H.

BERTOLACCI, Francis Robert
Select committee on the Duchy of Lancaster. SEE: Southeron-Estcourt, T.H.S.

BESSBOROUGH, Lord SEE:
Ponsonby, John William, *4th E. Bessborough* (1781-1847).
Ponsonby, John George Brabazon, *5th E. Bessborough* (1809-1880).
Ponsonby, Frederick George Brabazon, *6th E. Bessborough* (1815-95).
Ponsonby, Walter William Brabazon, *7th E. Bessborough* (1821-1906).

BEST, William Draper, *1st Bn. Wynford*
Select committee (HL) on agriculture in England and Wales. Report, 7 July 1836. HL 1836 (9) xi; HC repr. 1837 (464) v; (Agriculture, 5).

BETHELL, Richard, *1st Bn. Westbury*
Committee on Kingston-upon-Hull Docks Bill (1840) Min. of ev. 26 Feb 1841. 1841 (83) ix.

Digest of law commission.
1st report. SEE: Rolfe, Robert Monsey, *Bn. Cranworth.*
2nd report, 11 May 1870. 1870 C.121 xviii.

Select committee on the Augmentation of Benefices Bill. Report, 5 May 1863. HL 1863 (91) xxxiii.

Select committee (HL) on the Bankruptcy and Insolvency Bill. Report, 30 May 1861. HL 1861 (110) xxiv.

Select committee on the Copyright (Works of Art) Bill. Report, 10 July 1862. HL 1862 (172) xxix.

Select committee (HL) on the Declaration of Title Bill, the Security of Purchasers Bill, the Transfer of Land Bill, the Title to Landed Estates Bill, the Registry of Landed Estates Bill, and the Real Property (Title of Purchasers) Bill. Report, 3 April 1862. HL 1862 (50) xxix; HC repr. 1862 (320) xvi.

Select committee (HL) on the divorce court and dissolution of marriage in Scotland. Report, 22 July 1861. HL 1861 (63) xxiv.

Select committee on the Fine Arts Copyright Consolidation and Amendment (No.2) Bill. Report, 9 July 1869. HL 1868/9 (181) xxvii.

Select committee on harbours of refuge. Report, 16 June 1836. 1836 (334) xx.

Select committee (HL) on the Insane Prisoners Act Amendment Bill. Report, 3 June 1864. HL 1864 (110) xxvii.

Select committee on the Judgements, *etc.* Law Amendment Bill. Report, 25 July 1864. HL 1864 (250) xxvii.

BETHUNE, Charles Ramsay Drinkwater
Commission on local charges upon shipping.
Report: England. July 1854. 1854 [1836] xxxvii.
Report: Ireland. 20 March 1855. 1854/5 [1911] xxvii.
Report: Scotland and the Channel Islands. July 1855. 1854/5 [1967] xxvii.

Report on the state of the River Clyde and Port of Glasgow. 25 May 1846. 1846 (242) lxi. Admiralty.

BETHUNE, J.E. Drinkwater
Letter of dissent from the report of the commission for the restoration of the standards of weight and measure. 21 Dec 1841. 1842 [357] xxv. SEE ALSO: Airy, G.B.

BEWLEY, Edmund T.
Commission on disturbances in Londonderry on 1st Nov 1883. Report, 11 Feb 1884. 1884 C.3954 xxxviii; (CP Civil Disorder, 8). Irish Secretary's Office.

BEXLEY, Lord SEE:
Vansittart, Nicholas, *1st Bn. Bexley.*

BEYTAGH, Edward
Lurgan riots inquiry commission. Report, 31 Oct 1879. 1880 (130) lx. Irish Secretary's Office.

BICKERSTETH, Henry, *1st Bn. Langdale*
Registration and conveyancing commission.
1st report, 1 July 1850. 1850 [1261] xxxii.
(No others identified)

BIDDER, G.P.
Report to Metropolitan Board of Works upon main drainage of the Metropolis. 6 April 1858. 1857/8 (419) xlviii; (UA Sanitation, 4). Office of Works.

BIDDULPH, Michael Anthony Shrapnel, *Sir*
Ordnance committee. Report on the accident to the 12-inch B.L. gun, mark II, on board the 'Collingwood' and construction of B.L. guns. 18 Aug 1886. 1886 C.4871 xiii. War Office.

BIDDULPH, Robert
Education of officers. Report by the Director-General of military education.
1st report, 31 March 1873. 1873 C.875 xviii.
Report, 1 Jan 1876. 1876 C.1491 xv.
3rd report, 23 Aug 1883. 1883 C.3818 xv.
4th report. 1889 C.5793 xvii. War Office.

BIGGE, John Thomas
Commission of inquiry at the Cape of Good Hope.
Report on memorial and petition of Mr. Cooke on the disposal of prize slaves by Mr. Blair. 13 Dec 1826. 1826/7 (42) xxi; (Slave Trade, 71).
Reports on the administration and finance. 1 May 1827. 1826/7 (282) xxi.
Documents. 30 May 1827. 1826/7 (406) xxi.
Further papers on administration. 21 May 1827. 1826/7 (371) xxi; (Africa, 19, 20).

Commission of inquiry on the Hottentot population of the Cape of Good Hope and of the missionary institutions. Report, 1 July 1830. 1830 (584) xxi; (Africa, 20).

Commission of inquiry on the judicial establishments of New South Wales and Van Diemen's Land. Report, 21 Feb 1823. 1823 (33) x; (Australia, 3).

Commission of inquiry on the state of agriculture and trade in the colony of New South Wales. Report, 31 March 1823. 1823 (136) x; (Australia, 3).

Commission of inquiry on the trade, navigation and harbours of the Cape of Good Hope. Report, 2 June 1829. 1829 (300) v; (Africa, 20).

BINNING, Lord. SEE:
Hamilton, Thomas, *9th E. Haddington.*

BIRCHAM, Francis Thomas
Supplement to 2nd report of commission on friendly

BIRCHAM, Francis Thomas (continued)
and benefit building societies. 27 Jan 1873. 1873 C.678 xxii; (Insurance, 4). SEE ALSO: Northcote, Stafford, Henry, *Sir*.

BLANCHFORD, Bn. SEE:
Rogers, Frederick, *1st Bn. Blanchford*.

BLACK, Adam
Select committee on the Copyright (No.2) Bill. Report, 29 June 1864. 1864 (441) ix.

BLACK, George
Report on Holyhead and Port Dynllaen harbours. 9 June 1843. 1844 (43) xlv. Admiralty.

BLACK, William Henry
Report on the state of the rolls and records now lying in Chester Castle. 31 Dec 1852. 1852/3 (214) lxxviii. Master of Rolls.

BLACKBURN, Bn. SEE:
Blackburn, Colin, *Bn. Blackburn*.

BLACKBURN, Colin, Bn. Blackburn
Royal commission on a criminal code bill. Report, 12 June 1879. 1878/9 C.2345 xx; (LA Criminal Law, 6).

Trial of the Bewdley election petition. Min. of ev. 25 Jan 1869. 1868/9 (9) xlviii.

Trial of the Bridgwater election petition, 1868. Min. of ev. 26 Feb 1869. 1868/9 (65) xlix.

BLACKBURNE, Francis
Commission to inquire and report concerning the ancient laws and institutes of Ireland. Report, 19 Feb 1852. 1852 (356) xviii. Irish Secretary's Office.

Commission for publication of the ancient laws and institutes of Ireland (Brehon law commission).
Preliminary report, 19 Feb 1852. 1859, session 2 (190) xiii, pt.2.
1st report, Jan 1857. 1859, session 2 (190) xiii, pt.2
3rd and 4th reports, 16 Jan 1861 and 1 March 1863. 1864 (192) xlviii. Irish Secretary's Office.
SEE ALSO: Gibson, Edward, *1st Bn. Ashbourne*.

Commission on the superior courts of common law and courts of chancery of England and Ireland.
1st report, 27 July 1863. 1863 [3238] xv.
2nd report, 23 May 1866. 1866 [3674] xvii; (Legal Administration, 10).

Report and evidence on the Royal Dublin Society, the Museum of Irish Industry and the system of scientific instruction in Ireland. 18 Oct 1862. 1863 [3180] xvii.

BLACKBURNE, John
Commission on municipal corporations in England and Wales.
1st report, 30 March 1835. 1835 (116) xxiii, xxiv, xxv, xxvi.
2nd report: London and Southwark; London Companies. 25 April 1837. 1837 (239) xxv.
Analytical index. 15 July 1839. 1839 (420) xviii; (GO Municipal Corporations, 2-7).

Committee on Louis Borell's petition for a reward for the discovery of his method for the dyeing of the colour of turkey red upon cotton hanks and in the piece. Report, 3 April 1786. CJ, vol.41, p.467.

Committee on Mr. Crompton's petition [regarding a spinning invention]. Report, 24 March 1812. 1812 (126) ii.

Committee on the petition of journeymen callico printers.
Min. of ev. 4 July 1804. 1803/4 (150) iv; repr. 1806/7 (129) ii.
Report, 17 July 1805. 1806 (319) iii; repr. 1806/7 (130) ii.

BLACKBURNE, John
Committee on the petitions of journeymen cotton weavers, cotton manufacturers, and operative cotton weavers. Report, 29 March 1809. 1809 (111) iii; (IR Textiles, 3).

BLACKSTONE, William Seymour
Select committee on the Shaftesbury election petition. Min. of ev. 9 April 1838. 1837/8 (290) xii.

BLACKWELL, J. Kenyon
Report on the ventilation of mines. 25 March 1850. 1850 [1214] xxiii; (FP Mining Accidents, 6). Home Office.

BLACKWELL, Thomas E.
Report on the drainage and water supply of Sandgate, in connection with the outbreak of cholera in that town. 21 Feb 1855. 1854/5 (82) xlv. General Board of Health.

BLACKWOOD, Frederick Temple, 5th Bn. Dufferin and Claneboye
Royal commission on military education.
1st report, 9 Aug 1869. 1868/9 [4221] xxii.
2nd report, 14 July 1870. 1870 C.214 xxiv.

BLACKWOOD, Frederick Temple H.T. SEE:
Hamilton-Temple-Blackwood, Frederick Temple, *1st M. Dufferin and Ava*.

BLAIR, Charles
Commission of inquiry at the Cape of Good Hope. SEE: Bigge, John Thomas.

BLAIR, W.
Commission of inquiry on the slave trade at Mauritius, 1829. SEE: Colebrooke, W.M.G.

BLAKE, A.R.
Commission appointed to revise the grand jury laws, Ireland. Report, 2 April 1842. 1842 [386] xxiv.

BLAKE, John Aloysius
Commission on methods of oyster culture in the U.K. and France and their introduction into Ireland. Report, 22 June 1870. 1870 C.224 xiv. Irish Secretary's Office.

Select committee on the Sea Coast Fisheries (Ireland) Bill. Report, 19 July 1867. 1867 (443) xiv.

BLAKISTON, Reyton
Report on the administration and effects of the poor laws, especially in the county of Hants. 22 Feb 1834. 1834 (44) xxxvii.

BLANDFORD, M. SEE:
Spencer-Churchill, John Winston, *6th D. Marlborough*.

BLENNERHASSETT, Rowland, Sir
Dublin hospitals commission. Report of committee of inquiry. 4 April 1887. 1887 C.5042 xxxv. Irish Secretary's Office.

BLIGH, Edward, 5th E. Darnley
Committee (HL) on the Gravesend Pier Bill. Min. of ev. 9 May 1832. HL 1831/2 (125) cccxii.

BLOMEFIELD, Thomas Wilmot Peregrine, *Sir*
Committee on railway passenger communication. Report, June 1898. 1898 C.8918 lxxxii. Board of Trade.

BLOMFIELD, Charles James, *Bp. of London,* 1828-56
Select committee (HL) on the Religious Worship Bill. SEE: Stanley, Edward Geoffrey, *14th E. Derby.*

BLYTH, Lindsay
Report on the chemical quality of the supply of water to the Metropolis. 1856. 1856 [2137] lii. General Board of Health.

BOASE, W.D.
Report on vagrancy. 1848. 1847/8 [987] liii. Poor Law Board.

BOLD, Peter Patten
Select committee on duties payable on printed cotton goods. Report, 8 May 1818. 1818 (279) iii; (IR Textiles, 3).

BOLDERO, Henry George
Select committee on contracts for public departments. Report, 13 Aug 1857. 1857, session 2 (269) xiii.

Select committee on contracts for public departments.
1st report, 4 June 1858. 1857/8 (319) vi.
2nd report, 10 June 1858. 1857/8 (328) vi.
3rd report, 2 July 1858. 1857/8 (398) vi.
4th report, 13 July 1858. 1857/8 (418) vi.
5th report, 16 July 1858. 1857/8 (438) vi.

BOLITHO, Thomas S.
Report of the inquiry on the loss of the steamer 'Garonne'. 18 June 1868. 1867/8 (408) lxiii. Board of Trade.

BLOOMFIELD, *Bn.* [Peerage claim]. SEE: Cooper, C.A.

BOLTON, Thomas Henry
Select committee on the Patent Agents Bill. Special report, 25 July 1894. 1894 (235) xiv.

BONHAM-CARTER, John
Committee of selection on the grouping of private bills, 1852/3. SEE: Sotheron, T.H.S.

Committee of selection on the grouping of private bills, 1864. SEE: Wilson-Patten, John.

Committee of selection relative to the grouping of private bills, 1870. SEE: Wilson-Patten, John.

Committee of selection relative to the grouping of private bills, 1871. SEE: Wilson-Patten, John.

Select committee on Chancery officers. Report, 17 Aug 1833. 1833 (685) xiv.

Select committee on the police of the Metropolis. Report, 13 Aug 1834. 1834 (600) xvi; (CP Police, 6).

BOOTH, George Sclater. SEE: Sclater-Booth, George.

BORELL, Louis
Committee on petition for a reward for his method for dyeing of the colour of turkey red upon cotton hanks and in the piece. SEE: Blackburne, John.

BORTHWICK, *Lord* [Peerage claim, 1814]. SEE: Cooper, C.A. [Peerage claim, 1869-71]. SEE: Freeman-Mitford, J.T.

BOSANQUET, John Bernard, *Sir*
Commission on courts of common law. SEE: Pollock, Jonathan Frederick.

BOTREAUX, *Lord* [Peerage claim]. SEE: Freeman-Mitford, J.T.

BOUDIER, John
Report of the visiting magistrates of Warwick Gaol on the allegations in the petition of Messrs. Lovett and Collins. 23 July 1839. 1839 (462) xxxviii; (CP Prisons, 11). Home Office.

BOURKE, Richard
Report and minutes of ev. taken at the investigation held at Ballinrobe workhouse with reference to the conduct of Rev. Mr. Anderson. 5 July 1851 and 3 May 1852. 1852 (294) xlvi. Poor Law Commission in Ireland.

Report on the condition of the Kilrush Union. 8 April 1850. 1850 (259) l. Poor Law Board.

BOURKE, Richard Southwell, *6th E. Mayo*
Committee on the cattle plague in Ireland.
1st report, 6 Dec 1865. 1866 (67) lix.
Sequel to the report. Report of experts. 1866 [3639] lix.
Prof. Hugh Ferguson's report. 10 Feb 1866. 1866 [3647] lix. Irish Secretary's Office.

Select committee on the Curragh of Kildare Bill. Report, 25 June 1868. 1867/8 (404) x.

Select committee on Dublin hospitals. Report, 29 June 1854. 1854 (338) xii.

Select committee on the Huddersfield election petition. Min. of ev. 7 May 1866. 1866 (243) x.

Select committee on Tramways (Ireland) Acts Amendment Bill. SEE: Monsell, William.

BOURNE, William Sturges
Select committee on poor laws.
Report, 4 July 1817. 1817 (462) vi.
Report, 10 March 1818. 1818 (107) v.
2nd report: Mines. 28 April 1818. 1818 (237) v.
3rd report, 26 May 1818. 1818 (358) v.

Committee on the poor laws. Report, 30 June 1819. 1819 (529) ii.

BOUVERIE, Edward Pleydell
Committee of public accounts. Report, 15 July 1864. 1864 (494) viii.

Committee of public accounts. Report, 26 June 1865. 1865 (413) x.

Committee of public accounts. Special report on the Exchequer and Audit Departments Bill. 15 March 1866. 1866 (113) vii.

Committee of selection on the grouping of private bills. SEE: Wilson-Patten, John.

General committee on railway and canal bills.
1st report, 3 March 1854. 1854 (82) vii.
2nd report, 8 March 1854. 1854 (96) vii.
3rd report, 15 March 1854. 1854 (106) vii.
4th report, 7 April 1854. 1854 (164) vii.
5th report, 5 May 1854. 1854 (216) vii.
6th report, 8 May 1854. 1854 (222) vii.
7th report, 18 May 1854. 1854 (256) vii.
8th report, 14 June 1854. 1854 (308) vii.
9th report, 19 June 1854. 1854 (317) vii.

Select committee on the Bridgnorth election petition. Min. of ev. 7 March 1853. 1852/3 (203) viii.

BOUVERIE, Edward Pleydell (continued)

Select committee on the Corrupt Practices Prevention Act, 1854, *etc.* Report, 22 May 1860. 1860 (329) x; (GO Elections, 3).

Select committee on diplomatic and consular services. Report, 25 July 1870. 1870 (382) vii; (GO Diplomatic Service, 3).

Select committee on diplomatic and consular services, 1871. SEE: Sclater-Booth, George.

Select committee on the Edinburgh Annuity Tax Act. SEE: Ingham, Robert.

Select committee on expiring laws: 2nd session, 17th Parliament. Report, 17 March 1854. 1854 (111) vii.

Select committee on extradition. Report, 6 July 1868. 1867/8 (393) vii.

Select committee on fees in courts of law and equity. Report, 25 July 1849. 1849 (559) viii; (Legal Administration, 7).

Select committee on fees in courts of law and equity, *etc.*
    1st report, 17 May 1850. 1850 (386) xiii.
    2nd report, 14 Aug 1850. 1850 (711) xiii; (Legal Administration, 7).

Select committee on the Kidderminster election petition. Min. of ev. 30 April 1850. 1850 (286) xiii.

Select committee on the Kinsale election petition. Min. of ev. 2 March 1848. 1847/8 (138) xiii.

Select committee on the militia estimates, 1851/2. Report, 7 July 1851. 1851 (496) x.

Select committee on parliamentary proceedings. Report, 2 July 1862. 1862 (373) xvi.

Select committee on Queen Anne's Bounty Board. Report, 17 July 1868. 1867/8 (439) vii.

Select committee on railway labourers. Report, 28 July 1846. 1846 (530) xiii; (Industrial Relations, 4).

Select committee on sites for churches in Scotland.
    1st report, 29 March 1847. 1847 (237) xiii.
    2nd report, 26 April 1847. 1847 (311) xiii.
    3rd report, 5 July 1847. 1847 (613) xiii.

Select committee on the Tithe Commutation Acts Amendment Bill. Report, 16 June 1873. 1873 (250) xvii.

Select committee on the Totnes election petition. Min. of ev. 23 March 1866. 1866 (139) xi.

BOUVERIE, Jacob Pleydell, *Vct. Folkstone.* SEE: Pleydell-Bouverie, Jacob, *Vct. Folkstone.*

BOWEN, Charles Synge Christopher, *Lord Justice Bowen*
Commission on the truck system. SEE: Guthrie, W.

Featherstone inquiry committee. Report, 6 Dec 1893. 1893/4 C.7234 xvii; (CP Civil Disorder, 4). Home Department.

BOWEN, James William
Royal commission on corrupt practices in the Borough of Boston. Report, 28 Jan 1881. 1881 C.2784 xxxviii.

BOWLES, T.H.
Reports on captured Negroes at St. Christopher's Nevis and Tortola. 12 June 1827. 1826/7 (463) xxii; (Slave Trade, 72).

BOWLES, William
Commission of inquiry into the present state of the River Tyne. Report, 19 May 1855. 1854/5 [1948] xxviii.

Committee respecting the expeditions in search of Sir John Franklin. Report, 20 Nov 1851. 1852 [1435] l. Admiralty.

Tidal harbours commission.
    1st report, 8 July 1845. 1845 [665] xvi.
    2nd report, 20 March 1846. 1846 [692], [756] xviii, pts 1 and 2.
        App. C with supplement and index 1847. 1847 [874] xxxii.
        App. C with supplement II. 1847/8 [943] xxvi.

BOWLY, James D.
Report on the home and cottage system of training and educating the children of the poor. 4 Feb 1878. 1878 (285) lx; (ED Poorer Classes, 7). Local Government Board.

BOWRING, John
Commerce and manufacturers of Switzerland. Report, 1836. 1836 (60) xlv.

Commercial relations between France and Great Britain.
    1st report, 1834. 1834 [64] xix.
    2nd report: Silks and wine. 1835. 1835 [65] xxxvi.

Public accounts of France.
    Report, 5 July 1831. 1831 (78) xiv.
    2nd report, 29 Sept 1831. 1831 (289) xiv.
    3rd report: Military expenditure. 9 July 1832. 1831/2 (586) xxviii.

Public accounts of the Netherlands. Report, 5 March 1832. 1831/2 (236) xxviii.

Report on the commercial statistics of Syria. 17 July 1839. 1840 [278] xxi.

Report on Egypt and Canada. 27 March 1839. 1840 [277] xxi.

Report on the Prussian commercial union. 23 Dec 1839. 1840 [225] xxi.

Report on the statistics of Tuscany, Lucca, the Pontifical and the Lombardo-Venetian States, with special reference to their commercial relations. 28 April 1837. 1839 [165] xvi. Foreign Office.

Select committee on accounts of colonial receipt and expenditure. Report, 13 July 1837. 1837 (516) vii; (Colonies, 2).

Select committee on colonial accounts. Report, 17 July 1845. 1845 (520) viii.

BOYCE, Samuel
Report of inquiry on charges against him. SEE: Cox, Joseph *and* Ffrench, M.J.

BOYD, *General*
Committee on his petition. SEE: Wilberforce, William

BOYLE, Courtenay, *Sir*
Departmental committee on the dissemination of commercial information.
    Report, July 1898. 1898 C.8962 xxxiii.
    Min. of ev. 1898 C.8963 xxxiii. Board of Trade.

Electrical standards committee. Supplementary and final reports, 29 Nov 1892 and 2 Aug 1894. 1894 C.7552 xxxiii. Board of Trade.

BOYLE, Richard Edmund St. Lawrence, *9th E. Cork and Orrey*
Royal commission on horsebreeding. SEE: Cavendish-Bentinck, William John Arthur Charles James, *6th D. Portland.*

BOYNE, *Vct.* [Peerage claim]. SEE:
Freeman-Mitford, J.T.

BRABAZON, John Cambre, *10th E. Meath*
Commission on the corporation for paving, cleansing and lighting the streets of Dublin. Report, 18 Feb 1806. 1806 (17) viii.

BRABAZON, William, *11th E. Meath*
Commission on the revenues and condition of the established church in Ireland. Report, 27 July 1868. 1867/8 [4082] xxiv.

BRADBURY, John Leigh
Committee on petition relative to machinery for engraving and etching. SEE: Moore, Peter.

BRADY, Francis M. *Sir*
Report of the Board of Superintendence of Dublin Hospitals on evidence of neglect on the part of the hospital officials. 19 Dec 1878. 1880 (103) xxiii. Irish Secretary's Office.

BRADY, John
Committee on sewage of towns.
　1st report, 10 April 1862. 1862 (160) xiv.
　2nd report, 29 July 1862. 1862 (469) xiv; (UA Sanitation, 1).

BRADY, Maziere
Incumbered estates inquiry commission, Ireland. Report, 21 May 1855. 1854/5 [1938] xix.

BRADY, Thomas F. *Sir*
Mackerel fishing off the coast of Ireland during the Spring of 1890. Report. 1890 C.6177 xxi.

Report and min. of ev. on the changing of the fishing season on the River Shannon. 30 Dec 1861. 1862 (452) liii. Commission of Fisheries in Ireland.

BRAGGE, Charles
Committee on accounts relating to HM civil list. Reports and accounts. 15 March 1802. CJ Reports, vol.11, p.193.

Committee on HM message respecting the Mogador ships. Report, 8 May 1800. (Rep., 1731-1800, vol.28).

Committee on linen and hempen manufacture and importation of flax seed to Ireland. Report, 10 May 1802. 1801/2 (79) ii; CJ Reports, vol.10, p.531.

Committee on orders respecting Ireland.
　Report, 6 Feb 1801. 1801 iii (number not on paper).
　2nd report, 23 Feb 1801. 1801 (10) iii.
　3rd report, 25 June 1801. 1801 (136) iii.

Committee respecting the interference of peers, *etc.* in elections. Report, 10 Nov 1801. 1801/2 (1) ii.

Committee on the restriction of payments in cash by the Bank of England. Report, 17 Nov 1797. CJ Reports, vol.11, p.192; repr. 1826 (26) iii.

Second committee on standing orders relating to bills of inclosure.
　Report, 22 June 1801. 1801 (132) iii.
　2nd report, 24 June 1801. 1801 (134) iii.

Select committee on the charge upon HM civil list revenue. Report, 8 July 1803. 1803 (147) v; repr. 6 July 1830. 1830 (614) ix.

Select committee on the eligibility of persons in Holy Orders to sit in the House [of Commons]. Report, 2 April 1801. 1801 (36) iii.
　2nd report, 14 April 1801. 1801 (40) iii; CJ Reports, vol.14, p.150, 162.

BRAMAH, Joseph
Committee on petition for patent on his locks. SEE: Steward, Tuckers.

BRAMSTON, John
Departmental committee on investment of trust funds in colonial stocks. Report, 19 March 1890. 1890/1 C.6278 lvi. Treasury.

BRAMSTON, Thomas William
Select committee on the Athlone election petition. Report, 12 April 1853. 1852/3 (321) viii.
Min. of ev. 22 April 1853. 1852/3 (383) viii.

Select committee on the Chatham election petition. Report, 9 June 1853. 1852/3 (588) xii.
Min. of ev. 1 June 1853. 1852/3 (596) xii.

Select committee on Durham election petition. Report, 9 June 1853. 1852/3 (588) xii.
Min. of ev. 10 June 1853. 1852/3 (596) xii.

Select committee on the Horsham election petition. Min. of ev. 5 Sept 1848. 1847/8 (737) xii.

BRAMWELL, Frederick
Interdepartmental committee on the national science collections. Report, 27 July 1885. 1886, session 1 (246) li. Treasury.

BRAMWELL, George William Wilshire, *Bn. Bramwell*
Bristol election petition trial. Report, 14 June 1870. 1870 (309) lvi.

New Windsor Borough election petition trial.
　Ev. 5 Aug 1874. 1874 (373) liii.
　Judgement. 7 May 1874. 1874 (152) liii.

Royal commission on Metropolitan sewage discharge.
　1st report, 31 Jan 1884. 1884 C.3842 xli.
　2nd and final report, 27 Nov 1884. 1884/5 C.4253 xxxi; (UA Sanitation, 7).

Select committee (HL) on the Bills of Exchange Bill. Report, 10 Aug 1882. HL 1882 (233) vii.

BRAND, David
Royal commission on the highlands and islands. Report, 19 March 1895. 1895 C.7681 xxxviii.
Min. of ev. 2 vols. 1895 C.7668 xxxviii, xxxix, pt.1
App. 1895 C.7668-II xxxix, pt.2

BRAND, Henry Bouverie William
Select committee on the Metropolis Water (No.2) Bill. Special Report, 25 July 1871. 1871 (381) xi.

BRAND, Thomas, *20th Bn. Dacre*
Committee (HL) on the Equitable Loan Bank Companies Bill. Min. of ev. 20 June 1825. HL 1825 (159) cxcvii. SEE ALSO: Yorke, P., *3rd E. Hardwicke*

Committee of the whole HC on Grampound bribery indictments, 1891. SEE: Moore, P.

BRANDON, *E.* [Peerage claim]. SEE:
Freeman-Mitford, J.T.

BRANDRETH, H.R.
Committee on metals. Iron and its uses in the naval service of this country. 26 Feb 1846. 1867 (394) xliv. Admiralty.

BRASSEY, Thomas, *Bn. Brassey*
Committee on the entry, training and promotion of the professional officers of the dockyards. Report, 10 March 1883. 1883 (277) xvii. Admiralty.

BRASSEY, Thomas, *Bn. Brassey* (continued)
Royal commission on opium.
   1st report, 30 Dec 1893. 1894 C.7313 lx.
   Min. of ev. 18 Nov to 29 Dec 1893. 1894 C.7397 lxi.
   Min. of ev. 3-27 Jan 1894. 1894 C.7419 lxi.
   Min. of ev. 29 Jan to 22 Feb 1894. 1894 C.7471 lxii.
   Proc., app., correspondence. 1894 C.7473 lxii.
   Final report, 16 April 1895. 1895 C.7723 xlii.
   Historical app. 1895 C.7723-I xlii.
   Supp. to report, Note by the Maharaja Bahadur of Durbhanga. 1895 C.7751 xlii.

Select committee on the Employers' Liability Act (1880) Amendment Bill. Report, 11 June 1866. 1866 (192) viii; (Industrial Relations, 19).

BRAYE, *Lord* [Peerage claim]. SEE:
Cooper, C.A.

BREADALBANE, *Lord* [Peerage claim]. SEE:
Freeman-Mitford, J.T.

BREADALBANE, *M. of* SEE:
Campbell, John, *2nd M. of Breadalbane.*

Brehon law commission. SEE:
Blackburne, Francis.

BRETT, Peircy, *Sir*
Report and estimate relating to Ramsgate Harbour. 24 Dec 1755. (Reps., 1731-1800, no.3, vol.1).

BRETT, William Baliol, *Vct. Esher*
Committee on the duties and salary of Clerk of Assize. Report, 10 Aug 1868. 1868/9 (313) li. Treasury.

Committee on the existence of corrupt practices in the Borough of Kingston-upon-Hull. Report, 30 Aug 1853. 1854 [1729] xxii, pts.1 and 2.

Committee on rules as to the distribution of business and clerical staff in the Chancery Court. Report, 7 Aug 1885. 1886, session 1 (92) liii; (Legal Administration, 16).

BRETTON, Monk, *Bn.* SEE:
Dodson, John George, *1st Bn. Monk Bretton.*
Dodson, John William, *2nd Bn. Monk Bretton.*

BREWER, J.S.
Report on the publication of the calendar of the Patent and Close rolls of Ireland. 4 Oct 1864. 1865 (35) xlv. Master of the Rolls *and* the Treasury.

BRICKDALE, M.I.
Papers on consolidation of statutes relating to wills and apportionment. 1854 (302-I) xxiv. Lord Chancellor's Office.

BRIDGE, John
Interdepartmental committee on riots. Report, 12 Nov 1894. 1895 C.7650 xxxv; (CP Civil Disorder, 4). Home Dept.

Report on inquiry into the tithe rent charge disturbances in Wales. 19 Aug 1887. 1887 C.5195 xxxviii. Home Office.

BRIDGES, John Henry
Report on the effects of heavy sizing in cotton weaving upon the health of the operatives employed. 1 Oct 1883. 1884 C.3861 lxxii; (IR Factories, 28). Home Dept.

Report on the proposed changes in hours and ages of employment in textile factories. 7 April 1873.

1873 C.754 lv; (IR Factories, 28). Local Government Board.

Report on smallpox in the hospitals of the Metropolitan Asylums Board, 1876 to 1878. 3 May 1879. 1880 (75) lxii. Local Government Board.

BRIGHT, John
Select committee on the growth of cotton in India. Report, 17 July 1848. 1847/8 (511) ix.

BRISCOE, Henry
Committee on dietaries of the prisons in England and Wales subject to the Prison Acts 1865 and 1877. Report, 27 Feb 1878. 1878 (95) xlii; (CP Prisons, 18). Prison Commission.

BROCKLEBANK, Thomas
Liverpool compass committee.
   1st report, 5 Feb 1856. 1857/8 [2293] lii.
   2nd report, Feb 1857. 1857/8 [2293] lii.
   3rd report, 1861. 1862 [2921] liv. Board of Trade.

BRODERICK, William St. John Freemantle, *1st E. Middleton*
Committee on the decentralization of War Office Business. Report, 16 March 1898. 1898 C.8934 xiii; (Military and Naval, 6). War Office.

Select committee on Aldershot Roads Bill. Report, 14 July 1890. 1890 (299) x.

Select committee on the Dublin Barracks Improvement Bill. Report, 9 May 1892. 1892 (179) xi.

Select committee on rifle ranges. Report, 4 May 1891. 1890/1 (223) xvi.

BRODLAUGH, Charles
Select committee on parliamentary oath. SEE:
Walpole, S.H.

BROGDEN, James
Committee on expired and expiring laws. 3rd session, 5th Parliament. Report, 10 Nov 1814. 1814/15 (4) iii.

Committee on expired and expiring laws. 4th session, 5th Parliament. Report, 5 Feb 1816. 1816 (2) iii.

Committee on expired and expiring laws. 5th session, 5th Parliament. Report, 1 Feb 1817. 1817 (4) iii.

Committee on expired and expiring laws. 6th session, 5th Parliament. Report, 29 Jan 1818. 1818 (3) iii.

Committee on expired and expiring laws. 1st session, 6th Parliament. Report, 25 Jan 1819. 1819 (3) ii.

Committee on expired and expiring laws. 2nd session, 6th Parliament. Report, 27 Nov 1819. 1819/20 (4) ii.

Committee on expired and expiring laws. 1st session, 7th Parliament. Report, 1 May 1820. 1820 (4) ii.

Committee on expired and expiring laws. 2nd session, 7th Parliament. Report, 25 Jan 1821. 1821 (5) iv.

Committee on expired and expiring laws. 3rd session, 7th Parliament. Report, 8 Feb 1822. 1822 (5) iv.

Committee on expired and expiring laws. 4th session, 7th Parliament. Report, 10 Feb 1823. 1823 (7) iv.

Committee on expired and expiring laws. 5th session, 7th Parliament. Report, 6 Feb 1824. 1824 (2) iv.

Committee on expired and expiring laws. 6th session, 7th Parliament. Report, 7 Feb 1825. 1825 (13) iv.

Committee on expired and expiring laws. 7th session, 7th Parliament. Report, 6 Feb 1826. 1826 (3) iii.

Committee on the manner of the HC going to St.

Paul's Church on Thursday, 7 July 1814. Report, 4 July 1814. 1813/4 (280) iii.

Committee on the Royal Naval Asylum estimate. Report, 9 June 1817. 1817 (340) iii.

Committee of the whole HC on the Penryn Bribery Bill
  Min. of ev. 12-19 May 1819. 1819 (303) iv.
  Report, 8 May 1827. 1826/7 (370) iv.

Committee of the whole HC on the private business of the HC. Report, 22 June 1824. 1824 (453) vi.

Committee of the whole HC on Grampound bribery indictments. SEE: Moore, P.

Select committee on accommodation for the court of Chancery. Report, 15 May 1816. 1816 (357) iv.

Select committee on tolls and customs in Ireland. Report, 17 March 1826. 1826 (170) v.

BROMLEY, R. Maddox
Committee to investigate certain acts of fraud and abuse in connection with the funds of the Committee for improvement of the navigation of the River Shannon. Report, 30 Nov 1847. 1847/8 (251) lvii. Treasury.

Report on the Poor Law Commission, Ireland. 4 March 1854. 1854/5 (0.28) xlvi. Treasury.

BROMLEY, Richard M., *Sir*
Report on the organisation and working of Greenwich Hospital. 7 Jan 1864. 1864 (202) xxxvii. Admiralty.

BROOKE, James, *Sir*
Commission of inquiry into matters connected with his position in Borneo. SEE: Prinsep, C.R.

BROOKFIELD, Arthur Montague
Select committee on retired soldiers' and sailors' employment. Report, 27 June 1895. 1895 (338) xii. SEE ALSO: Chesney, George Tomkyns, *Sir*

Select committee on the Uniforms Bill. Report, 10 July 1894. 1894 (212) xv.

BROOKS, William Alexander
Report on the Harwick Railway lines. 23 Feb 1847. 1847 (433) lxiii. Admiralty.

BROOKSBANK, Thomas C.
Committee on public accounts. Report: Navy, Army and Ordnance grants and summary. 1 June 1829. 1829 (290) vi. SEE ALSO: Abbott, P.H.

Papers on the mode of keeping public accounts. 25 June 1831. 1831 (50) xiv.

BROS, Thomas
Commission on the state of criminal law in the Channel Islands.
  1st report: Jersey. 1847 [865] xv.
  2nd report: Guernsey. 1847/8 [945] xxvii.

BROUGHAM, Henry, *Bn. Brougham and Vaux*
Commission of public instruction, Ireland.
  1st report. 1835 [45], [46] xxxiii.
  2nd report. 1835 [47] xxxiv.

Committee for privileges (HL).
  Crawfurd and Lindsay claim of peerage. Ev. 2 March to 30 July 1845. HL 1846 (47) xxi.

Select committee (HL) on the administration of oaths, 1842. SEE: Cooper, Cropley Ashley, *6th E. Shaftesbury.*

Select committee (HL) on the Bankrupt Law Consolidation Bill. Report, 27 July 1841. HL 1847/8 (263) xxiii.

Select committee (HL) on bankruptcy and insolvency.
  1st report, 9 March 1849. HL 1849 (23) xxx; HC repr. 1849 (372) viii.
  2nd report, 18 May 1849. HL 1849 (23-II) xxx; HC repr. 1849 (372) viii.

Select committee (HL) on criminal law.
  1st report, 26 April 1847. HL 1847 (49) xxiv; HC repr. 1847 (447) vii.
  2nd report, 14 June 1847. HL 1847 (49) xxiv; HC repr. 1847 (534) vii; (CP Juvenile Offenders, 1).

Select committee (HL) on the Criminal Law Consolidation (No.2) Bill. Report, 10 July 1848. HL 1847/8 (217) xxiv.

Select committee on education of the lower orders in the Metropolis.
  Min. of ev. 7 to 20 June 1816. 1816 (427), (469), (495), (497) iv.
  Report, 20 June 1816. 1816 (498) iv; (ED Poorer Classes, 1).

Select committee on education of the lower orders in the Metropolis. Report, 7 July 1817. 1817 (479) iii; (ED Poorer Classes, 2).

Select committee on the education of lower orders.
  Report, 17 March 1818. 1818 (136) iv.
  2nd report, 25 May and 15 June 1818. 1818 (356) iv.
  3rd report, 3 and 8 June 1818. 1818 (426) iv.
  4th report: app. A. 5 June 1818. 1818 (427) iv.
  5th report: app. B. 8 June 1818. 1818 (428) iv.
  Digest of parochial returns. 3 vols. 1 April 1819. 1819 (224) ix, 3 parts; (ED Poorer Classes, 2-5).

Select committee (HL) on the execution of the criminal law, especially with reference to juvenile offenders and transportation.
  1st report, 12 March 1847. HL 1847 (49) xxiv.
  2nd report, 14 June 1847. HL 1847 (49-II) xxiv.

Select committee (HL) on the Masters' Jurisdiction in Equity Bill.
  1st report, 21 July 1851. HL 1851 (202) xix; HC repr. 1852 (564) xiii.
  (no further reports identified).

Select committee (HL) on the operation of the criminal law, 1847. SEE: Petty-Fitzmaurice, Henry, *3rd M. Lansdowne.*

Select committee (HL) on the petitions on the law of debtor and creditor. Report, 8 May 1845. HL 1845 (153) xix.

Select committee (HL) on the Privy Council Appellate Jurisdiction Act Amendment Bill. SEE: Copley, John Singleton, *1st Bn. Lyndhurst.*

BROUGHAM, William
Select committee on Bankrupts' Estates Bill. Report, 10 June 1834. 1834 (362) xviii.

Select committee on a general register of real property. Report, 18 July 1832. 1831/2 (609) xviii.

BROUGHAM AND VAUX, Bn. SEE:
Brougham, Henry, *Bn. Brougham and Vaux.*

BROUGHTON, *Lord* SEE:
Hobhouse, John Cam., *Bn. Broughton.*

BROUGHTON, W.E. Delves
Supplementary reports on the boundary between the British possessions in North America and the United States of America. 28 Nov 1840 and 11 Feb

BROUGHTON, W.E. Delves (continued)
1842. 1842 [413] xxviii. Foreign Office. SEE ALSO: Featherstonhaugh, J.D.

BROWN, Alexander
Select committee on the Public Health Act (1875) Amendment Bill. Report, 5 April 1878. 1878 (134) xviii. (Health, 11).

BROWN, G.T.
Departmental committee on swine fever.
　　Report, 11 Dec 1895. 1896 C.8023 xxiv.
　　2nd report, 25 Feb 1897. 1897 C.8372 xxiii.
　　Board of Agriculture.

Report on the eruptive diseases of the teates and udders of cows in relation to scarlet fever in man. July 1888. 1888 C.5481 xxxii. Privy Council Office; (AG Animal Health, 3).

Report on swine-fever in G.B., 1886. 1886 C.4843 xix; (AG Animal Health, 3). Privy Council Office, Agriculture Department.

Report on Texas fever. 31 Aug 1880. 1880 C.2693 lvi. Privy Council Office, Veterinary Department.

BROWN, William
Select committee on decimal coinage. Report, 1 Aug 1853. 1852/3 (851) xxii; (MP Decimal Coinage, 1).

BROWNE, A.
Remarks on West Indian fever. 3 Jan 1851. *In:* 1852 [1473] xx. General Board of Health.

BROWNE, Anthony
Committee on petitions of persons interested in estates on the Island of St. Vincent. Report, 7 May 1813. 1812/3 (182) iii.

BROWNE, Dominick
Select committee on Connaught lakes. Report, 3 July 1835. 1835 (354) xx.

Select committee on Irish election laws. Report, 19 May 1817. 1817 (281) viii.

BROWNE, Isaac Hawkins, *the younger*
Committee on the high price of provisions. SEE: Yorke, C.

Committee on Dr. Cartwright's petition respecting his weaving machine. Report, 13 April 1808. 1808 (179) ii.

Committee on the survey of the coasts, *etc.* of Scotland.
　　Report: Emigration. 13 May 1803. 1802/3 (80) iv.
　　2nd report: Roads and Bridges. 3 June 1803. 1802/3 (94) iv.
　　3rd report: Caledonian Canal. 14 June 1803. 1802/3 (110) iv.
　　4th report: Naval stations and fisheries. 20 June 1803. 1802/3 (118) iv.

Select committee on the petition on the election and return of the town and county of Nottingham. Report, 10 March 1803. 1802/3 (35) iii.

BROWNLOW, *Lord* SEE:
Cust, Adelbert Wellington Brownlow, *3rd E. Brownlow.*

BRUCE, Alexander Hugh, *6th Bn. Balfour of Burleigh*
Royal commission on colonisation of Canada of crofters and cottars from the western Highlands and Islands of Scotland.
　　1st report. 1890 C.6067 xxvii.

2nd report. 1890/1 C.6287 xxvi.
3rd report. 1892 C.6693 xxvii.
4th report. 1893/4 C.7226 lxxi.
5th report. 1894 C.7445 lxix.
6th report. 1895 C.7738 lxxix.
7th report. 1896 C.8220 lxviii.
8th report. 1897 C.8576 lxxii.
9th report. 1899 C.9140 lxxviii.
10th report. 1900 Cd.14 lxviii.
11th report. 1901 Cd.456 lx.
12th report. 1902 Cd.812 lxxxiii.
13th report. 1903 Cd.1395 lv.
14th report. 1904 Cd.1967 lxxviii.
15th report. 1906 Cd.3145 xcvii; (Canada, 32-33)

Royal commission on local taxation.
　　1st report: Local rates in England and Wales, valuation and collection. 1898 C.9142 xxv.
　　2nd report: Tithe rent charge valuation and rating. 1899 C.9142 xxxv.
　　Report on valuation in Ireland. 14 Feb 1902. 1902 Cd.973 xxxix.
　　Final report
　　　　England and Wales 28 May 1901. 1901 Cd.638 xxiv.
　　　　　　Appendix. 1902 Cd.1221 xxxix.
　　　　Ireland. 11 April 1902. 1902 Cd.1068 xxxix.
　　　　Scotland. 10 April 1902. 1902 Cd.1067 xxxix.
　　Evidence and appendices
　　　　Vol.1: 1st to 29th days. 1898 C.9863 xli.
　　　　　　Appendices (2 parts). 1898 C.8764, C.8765 xlii.
　　　　Vol.2: 30th to 36th, 43rd to 49th days. 1899 C.9150 xxxvi.
　　　　Vol.3: Scotland, 37th to 42nd days. 1899 C.9319 xxxvi.
　　　　Vol.4: 50th to 56th, 64th days. 1900 Cd.201 xxxvi.
　　　　Vol.5: Ireland, 57th to 63rd days. 1900 Cd.383 xxxvi.
　　Classification and incidence of imperial and local taxes, *etc.* 1899 C.9528 xxxvi.
　　Index. 1903 Cd.1480 xxiii.

Royal commission on the operation of the Sunday Closing (Wales) Act, 1881. Report. 1890 C.5994 xl; (Sunday Observance, 3).

Royal commission on the water supply of the Metropolis. Report, 8 Sept 1893. 1893/4 C.7172 xl, pts. 1 and 2; (UA Water Supply, 7-8).

Select committee (HL) on the Provisional Order (Scotland) Bill. Report, 19 July 1897. HL 1897 (166) ix.

BRUCE, Gainsford, *Sir*
Interdepartmental committee on target practice seawards. Report, 30 Jan 1893. 1893/4 C.6931 lv. Board of Trade.

BRUCE, Henry Austin, *1st Bn. Aberdare*
Committee on intermediate and higher education in Wales. Report, 18 Aug 1881. 1881 C.3047 xxxiii. Education Department, Privy Council Office.

Royal commission on the aged poor.
　　Vol.1 Report, 26 Feb 1895. 1895 C.7684 xiv.
　　Vol.2 Ev., 1895 C.7684-I xiv.
　　Vol.3 Ev., app., index. 1895 C.7684-II xv; (Poor Law, 28-29).

Royal commission on noxious vapours. Report, 13 Aug 1878. 1878 C.2159 xliv.

Royal commission on reformatories and industrial schools. Report, 8 Sept 1883. 1884 C.3876 xlv.

Select committee on Burials Bill. Report, 10 May 1870. 1870 (220) vi.

Select committee on Cattle Diseases Prevention and Cattle, *etc.* Importation Bills. SEE: Baring, Thomas George.

Select committee (HL) on intemperance. SEE: Grosvenor, Hugh Lupus, *1st D. Westminster.*

BRUCE, Herbert
Report on the income and expenditure of British Burma. 15 Dec 1860. 1865 (405) xxxix. India Office.

BRUCE, Thomas, *7th E. Elgin and 11th E. Kincardine*
Select committee on his collection of sculptured marbles, *etc.* SEE: Bankes, Henry.

BRUCE, Victor Alexander, *9th E. Elgin and 13th E. Kincardine*
Committee on the means of distributing the grant in aid of secondary education in Scotland.
    Report, 10 Aug 1892. 1892 C.6826 lxii.
    Min. of ev. 1892 C.6840 lxii. Privy Council Committee on Education in Scotland.

BRUCE, William R.
Commission on corrupt practices at the last election for Sligo. Report, 3 March 1870. 1870 C.48 xxxii.

BRYCE, James
Committee on distribution of a grant for university colleges in G.B. Report, 18 May 1894. 1894 (204) lxvi. Treasury.

Royal commission on secondary education.
    Vol.1: Report, 13 Aug 1895. 1895 C.7862 xlii.
    Vol.2-4: Min. of ev. 1895 C.7862 I-III xliv, xlv, xlvi.
    Vol.2 supplement. 1896 C.8077 xlv.
    Vol.5: Memoranda and answers to questions. 1895 C.7862-IV xlvii.
    Vol.6: Reports of assistant commissioners on the counties of Bedford, Devon, Lancaster, Norfolk. 1895 C.7862-V xlviii.
    Vol.7: Reports of assistant commissioners on the counties of Surrey, Warwick and Yorkshire, and on certain features of secondary education in the U.S.A. 1895 C.7862-VI xlviii.
    Vol.8: Summary and index. 1895 C.7862-VII xlix.
    Vol.9: Statistical tables. 1895 C.7862-VIII xlix; (Education, 40-46).

Select committee on commons. Report, 14 April 1891. 1890/1 (179) xii.

Select committee on the India Office (Store Depot) Bill. Report, 13 July 1898. 1898 (298) x.

BUCCLEUCH, D. SEE:
Montagu-Douglas-Scott, Walter Francis, *5th D. Buccleuch and 7th D. Queensbury.*

BUCHANAN, George
Report on certain sizing processes used in the cotton manufacture at Todmorden, and their influence upon health. April 1872. 1872 (203) liv; (IR Factories, 28). Local Government Board.

Royal commission on tuberculosis.
    Part 1. Report, 3 April 1895. 1895 C.7703 xxxv.
    Parts 2 and 3: Witnesses, min. of ev., index and appendix; special inquiries. 1896 C.7992 xlvi.

BUCKHURST, *Lord* [Peerage claim]. SEE:
Freeman-Mitford, J.T.

BUCKINGHAM, D. SEE:
Temple-Nugent-Chandos-Grenville, Richard Plantagenet *2nd D. Buckingham and Chandos* (1797-1861).
Temple-Nugent-Chandos-Grenville, Richard Plantagenet Campbell, *3rd D. Buckingham and Chandos* (1823-1889).

BUCKINGHAM, James Silk
Select committee on the causes of shipwrecks. Report, 15 Aug 1836. 1836 (567) xvii; (Shipping, 2).

Select committee on drunkenness. Report, 5 Aug 1834. 1834 (559) viii.

BUCKINGHAMSHIRE, E. SEE:
Hobart, John, *2nd E. Buckinghamshire* (s.1756, d.1793).
Hobart, George, *3rd E. Buckinghamshire* (s.1793, d.1804).
Hobart, Robert, *4th E. Buckinghamshire* (s.1804, d.1816).
Hobart, George Robert, *5th E. Buckinghamshire* (s.1816, d.1849).
Hobart, Augustus Edward, *6th E. Buckinghamshire* (s.1849, d.1885).

BUCKLAND, Francis Trevelyan
Commission on the outbreak of disease among salmon in certain rivers of England and Scotland. Report, 2 Aug 1880. 1880 C.2660 xiv. Home Office.

Inquiry on the fisheries of Norfolk, especially crabs, lobsters, herrings and the Broads. Report, 9 Aug 1875. 1875 (428) xvii. Home Office.

Inquiry respecting an application for an order restricting the taking of crabs and lobsters on the coast of Norfolk. Report, 1 Dec 1879. 1880 (70) xiv. Board of Trade.

Inquiry on the use of dynamite for killing fish. Report, 17 July 1877. 1877 C.1819 xxiv. Home Office.

Special commission on salmon fisheries in Scotland. Report, July 1871. 1871 C.419 xxv. Home Department.

BUCKLAND, Frank SEE:
Buckland, Francis Trevelyan.

BUCKNER, J., *Bp. of Chichester,* 1797-1824
Select committee (HL) on the Southwark Parish Rector Bill. Min. of proc. 8 Aug 1807. HL 1806/7 (35) xiv.

BUCKNILL, Thomas Townsend
Departmental committee on Metropolitan police court district. Report, 22 Feb 1893. 1893/4 C.6962 lxxiv, pt.2. Home Department.

BUDDLE, John
Dean Forest mining commission.
    1st report, 17 June 1839. 1839 (328) xxix.
    2nd report, 7 Aug 1840. 1840 (630) xxviii.
    3rd report, 12 March 1841. 1841 (247) xii; (FP Mining Districts, 1).

BULLER, Alexander
Navy boiler committee. Conclusions and recommendations. 9 Dec 1892. 1892/3 C.6991 liv. Admiralty.

Select committee on controverted elections.
    Report, 27 July 1836. 1836 (496) xxi; repr. 1837/8 (44) x; (GO Elections, 2).

Select committee on the National Land Company.
    1st report, 9 June 1848. 1847/8 (398) xix.

BULLER, Alexander (continued)
2nd report, 21 June 1848. 1847/8 (420) xix.
3rd report, 30 June 1848. 1847/8 (451) xix.
4th report, 14 July 1848. 1847/8 (503) xix.
5th report, 28 July 1848. 1847/8 (557) xix.
6th report, 1 Aug 1848. 1847/8 (577) xix; (Agriculture, 13).

BULLER, Charles
Select committee on the Record Commission.
Report, 11 July 1836. 1836 (429) xvi.
Report, 15 Aug 1836. 1836 (565) xvi.

Select committee on settlement and poor removal.
1st report, 19 Feb 1847. 1847 (82) xi.
2nd and 3rd reports, 2 and 4 March 1847. 1847 (135) xi.
4th report, 23 March 1847. 1847 (218) xi.
5th report, 23 March 1847. 1847 (226) xi.
6th report, 20 May 1847. 1847 (409) xi.
7th and 8th reports, 17 June and 6 July 1847. 1847 (518) xi; (Poor Law, 20).

BULLER, Edward Manningham, *Sir*
Select committee on the Public Offices Concentration Bill. Report, 6 July 1869. 1868/9 (296) x.

BULLER, John Yarde. SEE:
Yarde-Buller, John, *3rd Bn. Churston*.

BULWER, Edward Lytton
Select committee on dramatic literature. Report, 2 Aug 1832. 1831/2 (679) vii.

BUNBURY, Charles, *Sir*
Committee on felons return. Report, 1 April 1779. CJ, vol.37, p.306; (Rep., 1731-1800, no.56a, vol.6).

Committee on the laws relating to transportation, imprisonment and other punishment of certain offenders. Report, 22 March 1784. CJ, vol.39, p.1040; (Rep., 1731-1800, no.61a, vol.6).

Committee on punishment of convicts by hard labour. Report, 15 April 1778. CJ, vol.36, p.926.

BURDETT, C.W.
Report on captured Negroes at Demerara. 12 June 1827. 1826/7 (464) xxii; (Slave Trade, 72).

BURDETT, Francis, *Sir*
Committee on the petition respecting the New Street Act, 53 Geo III (Charing Cross). Report, 27 Feb 1817. 1817 (79) iii.

Select committee on proceedings. SEE: Giddy, D.

Select committee on Regent Street paving. Report, 14 Aug 1835. 1835 (520) xx.

Select committee on the supply of water to the Metropolis. Report, 19 July 1828. 1828 (567) viii; (UA Water Supply, 1).

BURDON, Rowland
Committee on the General Highway Acts, *etc.* Report, 21 March 1800. CJ Reports, vol.10, p.759; (Reps., 1731-1800, no.165, vol.27). SEE ALSO: Lushington, W.

Committee on London coal admeasurement petition. Report, 19 March 1806. 1806 (40) ii.

Committee on Mr. Greathead's petition respecting his new invention of a life-boat. Report, 31 March 1802. 1801/2 (37) ii; CJ Reports, vol.10, p.729.

Committee on standing orders respecting bills of inclosure.

Report, 2 April 1801. 1801 (38) iii.
2nd report, 28 April 1801. 1801 (50) iii.

Select committee on regulations for the use of short-hand writers at the trials of controverted elections. Report, 31 March 1803. 1802/3 (40) iii.

BURDON-SANDERSON, John
Report of the results of an inquiry into the epidemics of cerebro-spinal meningitis prevailing about the Lower Vistula in the beginning of 1865. 26 May 1865. *In:* 1865 (435) xlvii. Privy Council.

BURELL, Charles, *Sir*
Select committee on Parrett navigation petition. Report, 1 May 1839. 1839 (238) xiii.

BURGOYNE, J.F.
Commission for improvement of the navigation of the River Shannon.
Report, 18 March 1836. 1836 (143) xlvii.
2nd report, 5 Dec 1837. 1837/8 [130] xxxiv.
3rd report, 24 May 1838. 1837/8 [142] xxxiv.
4th report. 1839 [172], [208] xxvii, xxviii.
5th report, 28 Feb 1839. 1839 [173] xxviii.

Relief commission, Ireland.
1st report, 10 April 1847. 1847 [799] xvii.
2nd report, 15 May 1847. 1847 [819] xvii.
3rd report, 17 June 1847. 1847 [836] xvii.
4th report, 19 July 1847. 1847 [859] xvii.
5th report, 17 Aug 1847. 1847/8 [876] xxix.
6th report, 11 Sept 1847. 1847/8 [876] xxix.
7th report, 12 Oct 1847. 1847/8 [876] xxix.
Supplementary appendix. 1847/8 [956] xxix; (Famine, 8). Treasury.

BURLINGTON, *E.* SEE:
Cavendish, William, *7th E. Devonshire*.

BURN, Robert
Committee of inquiry into the capabilities of the mercantile steam navy for purposes of war. Reports, 6 Nov and 23 Dec 1852. 1852/3 (687) lxi.

Committee on the machinery of the U.S.A. Report, 23 Aug 1854. 1854/5 (0.11) l. Board of Ordnance.

BURNLEY, William H.
Committee on the Council of Trinidad on the Negro character. Extracts from the min. of ev. 14 June 1827. 1826/7 (479) xxiii.

BURRELL, Charles, *Sir*
Select committee on St. Margaret's Church, Westminster. Report, 10 July 1844. 1844 (474) vi.

BURRELL, Peter, *1st Bn. Gwidir*
Committee on the Houses of Parliament and the offices thereto belonging. Report, 22 July 1789. CJ, vol.44, p.548; (Reps., 1731-1800, no.93, vol.9)

Committee (HL) on the Worcester Roads Bill. Min. of proc. 27 May 1803. HL 1802/3 vol.[7]; Oceana 1802/3, vol.4, p.389.

BURRELL, W.H.
Report on quarantine. 2nd report: Yellow fever, appendix V. Report on the plague of Malta in 1813. 8 July 1852. 1853/4 [1869] xlv. General Board of Health. SEE ALSO: Cooper, Anthony Ashley, *7th E. Shaftesbury*.

Report on the subject of yellow fever. 29 May 1850. In 1852 [1473] xx. General Board of Health.

BURSTAL, Edward
Report on the state of the River Thames from Putney to Rotherhithe. 27 Jan 1857. 1857, session 1 (17) xiii. Commission of Works.

BURT, Thomas
Committee on railway accidents returns. Report, 11 Dec 1894. 1895 C.7603 lxxxvi. Board of Trade.

Committee on the transmission of seamen's wages. Report, June 1893. 1893/4 C.7179 lxxx. Board of Trade.

Select committee on the Clubs Registration Bill. Report, 7 July 1893. 1893/4 (314) x.

BURTON, John
Report on the state of the Walsall Union workhouse. 30 Nov 1867. 1867/8 (40) lx. Poor Law Board.

BURTON, John Hill
Report on arrestment of wages, the effect of abolishing imprisonment for small debts, and the practice of truck in Scotland. 11 Jan 1854. 1854 (0.3) lxix. Lord Advocate's Office.

BURY, *Vct.* SEE:
Keppel, William Coutts, *7th E. Albemarle.*

BUTT, George Medd
Select committee on the Barnstaple election petition. Min. of ev. 6 March 1855. 1854/5 (100) vii.

Select committee on the Sligo Borough election petition. Min. of ev. 22 May 1856. 1856 (234) vii.

BUTTEVANT, *Lord* [Peerage claim]. SEE:
Cooper, C.A.

BUTTS, R.G.
Commission of inquiry on emigration from Sierra Leone to the West Indies. Reports, 23 July 1844 to 13 March 1845. 1847/8 (732) xliii. Colonial Office.

BUXTON, Charles
Select committee on paper (export duties on rags). Report, 25 July 1861. 1861 (467) xi.

BUXTON, J.F.
Select committee on criminal laws. SEE: MacKintosh, J.

BUXTON, Thomas Fowell, *Sir*
Select committee on aborigines (British settlements). Report, 5 Aug 1836. 1836 (538) vii; (Anthropology, 1)

Select committee on aborigines (British settlements). Report, 26 June 1837. 1837 (425) viii; (Anthropology, 2)

Select committee on Mauritius slave trade
Report, 31 May 1826. 1826 (430) iii.
Min. of ev., 13 to 23 May 1826. 1826/7 (90) vi; (Slave Trade, 1).

BYNG, George, *7th Vct. Torrington*
Committee on the agreement between Mr. Palmer and the Post Office for its reform and improvement. Min. of ev. 3 June 1813. 1812/3 (260) iv.

Committee (HL) on the bill giving relief to bankers of Madras (Messrs. Chase and Co.). Min. of ev. 16 June 1819. HL 1819 (111) cxi.

Select committee (HL) on the Edgware, Highgate and London Railway Bill. Report, 15 March 1861. HL 1861 (50) xxiv.

Committee on notices for poor bills. Report, 13 March 1810. 1810 (116) ii.

BYNG, George Henry Charles, *3rd E. Stafford*
Select committee on gas for the Metropolis. Report, 6 July 1858. 1857/8 (393) xi; (FP Gas, 1).

Select committee on gas for the Metropolis. Report, 15 April 1859. 1859, session 1 (224) iii; (FP Gas, 1).

Select committee on the Juries Bill. Report, 27 June 1870. 1870 (306) vi.

Select committee on special and common juries. Report, 8 July 1867. 1867 (425) ix.

Select committee on special and common juries. Report, 7 July 1868. 1867/8 (401) xii.

BYNG, John, *Sir*
Select committee on Carrickfergus Borough. Report, 15 July 1833. 1833 (527) viii.

Select committee on colonial military expenditure. SEE: Gordon, Robert.

Select committee on Newry Borough election petition. Report, 14 March 1833. 1833 (76) x.

BYRNE, John Alexander
Commission on corrupt practices at the last election for Sligo. Report, 3 March 1870. 1870 C.48 xxxii.

BYRNE, William Patrick
Departmental committee on inebriate reformatories. Report, 12 Dec 1898. 1898 C.9112 xi. Home Office.

CADOGAN, *E.* SEE:
Cadogan, George Henry, *5th E. Cadogan.*

CADOGAN, George Henry, *5th E. Cadogan*
Joint select committee of the HL and the HC on the publication of debates and proceedings in Parliament. Report, 17 July 1888. HL 1888 (217) xv; 1888 (284) x.

Select committee (HL) on high sheriffs, 1888. SEE: Gathorne-Hardy, Gathorne, *1st E. Cranbrook.*

Select committee (HL) on the standing orders of the HL. Report, 31 July 1888. HL 1888 (242) x.

Select committee (HL) on standing orders relating to standing committees. Report, 3 Feb 1891. HL 1890/1 (26) xi.

CAIRD, James
Commission on the sea fisheries of the U.K.
Report. 1866 [3596] xvii.
Min. of ev. 1866 [3596-I] xvii; (Fisheries, 4-5).

CAIRNS, *E.* SEE:
Cairns, Hugh MacCalmont, *1st E. Cairns (s.1867, d.1885)*
Cairns, Arthur William, *2nd E. Cairns (s.1885, d.1890)*
Cairns, Herbert John, *3rd E. Cairns (s.1890, d.1905)*

CAIRNS, Hugh MacCalmont, *1st E. Cairns*
Judicature commission
1st report, 25 March 1869. 1868/9 [4130] xxv.
2nd report, 3 July 1872. 2 vols. 1872 C.631 xx.
3rd report: Tribunals of commerce. 21 Jan 1874. 1874 C.957 xxiv.
4th report: Chamber practice. 25 March 1874. 1874 C.984 xxiv.
5th and final report, 10 July 1874. 1874 C.1090 xxiv; (Legal Administration, 13)

Royal commission on the Royal Hospital of St. Katherine. SEE: Wood, William Page, *Bn. Hatherley.*

CAIRNS, Hugh MacCalmont, *1st E. Cairns* (continued)
Royal commission on the supersession of colonels of the British Army. Report, 13 March 1871. 1871 (276) xxxix.

Select committee (HL) on the County Courts Bill. Report, 24 April 1879. HL 1878/9 (61) vii.

Select committee (HL) on the HL construction and accommodation, 1883. SEE: Freeman-Mitford, John Thomas, *1st E. Redesdale.*

Select committee (HL) on the land law in Ireland
  1st report, 28 April 1882. HL 1882 (37) ix; HC repr. 1882 (249) xi.
  2nd report, 1 Aug 1882. HL 1882 (37-I) ix; HC repr. 1882 (379) xi.
  3rd report, 10 May 1883. HL 1883 (37) ix; HC repr. 1883 (204) xiii.
  4th report, 9 July 1883. HL 1883 (139) ix; HC repr. 1883 (279) xiii.
  Index to 3rd and 4th reports. HL 1883 (139-IND) ix.

Select committee (HL) on the law relating to the protection of young girls.
  Report, 26 July 1881. HL 1881 (145) viii; repr. HL 1883 (109) ix; HC repr. 1881 (448) ix.
  Report, 10 July 1882. HL 1882 (188) vii; repr. HL 1883 (109) ix; HC repr. 1882 (344) xiii.
  Index to reports, 1881-2. HL 1882 (188-IND) vii; (CP Juvenile Offenders, 5).

Select committee (HL) on the Married Women's Property Bill. Report, 11 July 1870. HL 1870 (196) viii.

Select committee (HL) on poor law in Ireland.
  1st report, 28 April 1882. HL 1882 (37) vii.
  2nd report, 1 Aug 1882. HL 1882 (37-I) vii.
  Indexes. HL 1882 (37-IND, 37-I, IND) vii.

Select committee on rivers pollution; River Lee. Report, 18 June 1886. 1886, session 1 (207) xi.

CALCRAFT, John, *the younger* (1765-1831)
Committee on the petition of William Lee and petty constables relating to further renumeration for attendance on Parliament. Report, 24 Feb 1818. 1818 (62) iii.

Select committee on laws relating to salt duties. Report, 1 June 1818. 1818 (393) v.

CALCRAFT, John
Select committee on the improvements of Windsor Castle. Report, 9 July 1830. 1830 (656) ix.

Select committee on the sale of beer. Report, 6 April 1830. 1830 (253) x; repr. 1852/3 (292) xxxviii.

CALDER, John
Report of the conditions of work in the fish-curing trade of the U.K. 1 Feb 1898. 1898 C.8753 xiv; (IR Factories, 31). Home Office.

CALVER, Edward Killwick
Reports on encroachments on the foreshore of the River Tyne. 23 Nov and 17 Dec 1853. 1854 (312) xlii. Admiralty.

Report on the Victoria (Redcar) Harbour and Docks Bill. 25 April 1851. 1851 (390) xxix. Admiralty.

CALVERT, John M.
On dispensary associations. 22 Feb 1833. *In* 1834 (44) xxxvii.

CALVERT, Nicholson
Select committee on forfeitures of recognizances. Report, 13 June 1821. 1821 (636) iv.

Select committee on recognizances. Report, 29 March 1822. 1822 (135) iv.

CAMBRIDGE, D. SEE:
Guelph, George William Frederick Charles, *2nd D. of Cambridge.*

CAMDEN, E. SEE:
Pratt, Charles, *1st E. Camden* (cr.1756, d.1794).
Pratt, John Jeffreys, *1st M. Camden* (cr.1794 d.1840).

CAMERON, Charles, *Sir*
Departmental committee on habitual offenders, vagrants, beggars, inebriates and juvenile delinquents, Scotland. Report, 25 April 1895. 1895 C.7753 xxxvii. Scottish Office.

Departmental committee on the transit by water of animals carried coast-wise. Report, 7 Aug 1894. 1894 C.7511 lxix; (AG Animal Health, 4). Board of Agriculture.

Select committee on the Fraudulent Debtors (Scotland) Bill. Report, 28 July 1880. 1880 (313) ix.

CAMERON, Charles A.
Report on the prevalence of enteric fever at the Royal Barracks, Dublin. 13 Aug 1887. 1888 C.5292 xxv. War Office.

CAMERON, Charles Duncan
Report respecting imprisonment in Abyssinia. 28 Sept 1868. 1868/9 [4089] lxiii. Foreign Office.

CAMERON, Charles Hay
Commission of inquiry on Ceylon. SEE: Colebrook, William M.G.

Commission on the state and operation of the law of marriage. SEE: Wortley, James Stuart.

Indian Law Commission. Special Report: Civil judicature in the Presidency towns. 2 May 1845. 1845 (272) xxiv.

Indian penal code.
  Report, 23 July 1846. 1846/7 (19) xxviii.
  2nd report, 24 June 1847. 1846/7 (330) xviii.
  India Office.

CAMERON, D.A.
Council of military education. General report. SEE: Napier, William C.E.

CAMOYS, *Lord* SEE:
Stonor, Thomas, *5th Bn. Camoys.*

[Peerage claim]. SEE: Cooper, C.A.

CAMPBELL, Alexander
Committee on papers relating to the Crinan Canal. Report, 13 June 1816. 1816 (467) iv.

Report on certain atrocities of slave traders. 9 Aug 1838. 1839 (157) 1; (Slave Trade, 87). Colonial Office.

CAMPBELL, Archibald SEE:
Colquhon-Campbell, Archibald.

CAMPBELL, *Lord* SEE:
Campbell, John, *1st Bn. Campbell* (1779-1861)

CAMPBELL, George Douglas, *8th D. Argyll*
Chancery funds commission. Report, 17 Feb 1864. 1864 [3280] xxix.

Commission on coal in the U.K.

Vol.1: General report and sub-reports, 27 July 1871. 1871 C.435 xviii.

Vol.2: General min. and proc. of committees A to D. 1871 C.435-I xviii.

Vol.3: Report of committee E. Statistics of production, consumption and export of coal. 1871 C.435-II xviii; (FP Coal Trade, 4).

Education commission, Scotland
1st report: Ev. 18 March 1865. 1865 [3483] xvii. Appendix. 1867 [3858] xxv.
2nd report
Elementary schools. 1867 [3845] xxv.
Statistical report on the state of education in the lowland country districts of Scotland. 1867 [3845-I] xxv.
Report on the state of education in Glasgow. 20 March 1866. 1867 [3845-II] xxv.
Report on the state of education in the country districts of Scotland. 1 March 1866. 1867 [3845-III] xxv.
Report on the state of education in the Hebrides. May 1866. 1867 [3845-IV] xxv.
Statistics relative to schools in Scotland collected by Registrars of Birth, *etc*. 1865. 1867 [3845-V] xxvi.
3rd report: Burgh and middle-class schools
Vol.1: Report. 1867/8 [4011] xxix.
Vol.2: Special reports. 1867/8 [4011-II] xxix; (Education, 13-16).

Select committee (HL) on the Entail Amendment (Scotland) Bill. Report, 28 March 1878. HL 1878 (51) vii.

Select committee (HL) on the government of Indian territories, 1852/3. SEE: Cavendish, Spencer Compton, 8th D. Devonshire.

Select committee (HL) on the government of Indian territories, 1853. SEE: Leveson-Gower, Granville George, 2nd E. Granville.

Select committee on the Hypothec Amendment (Scotland) Bill. Report, 18 March 1867. HL 1867 (49) xxvii.

Select committee (HL) on the management of the Crown Estate of Kinconcouse. Report, 28 July 1854. HL 1854 (192) xxi.

Select committee (HL) on the printing of papers for the HL. SEE: Leveson-Gower, Granville George, 2nd E. Granville.

CAMPBELL, Ilay, *Sir*
Commission on duties, salaries, fees and emoluments in courts in Scotland. SEE: Montgomery, James.

CAMPBELL, J.
Commission on duties, salaries, and emoluments in courts of justice in England and Wales
Court of Chancery. Report, 6 June 1816. 1816 (428) viii.
2nd report, 6 April 1818. 1818 (156) vii. 1819/20 (3) ii.
Court of Kings Bench. Report, 14 May 1818. 1818 (292) vii.

CAMPBELL, John, *1st Bn. Campbell*
Commission on the law of divorce. Report. 1852/3 [1604] xl; (Marriage and Divorce, 1).

Commission on the law of real property
1st report, 20 May 1829. 1829 (263) x.
2nd report, 29 June 1830. 1830 (575) xi.
3rd report, 24 May 1832. 1831/2 (484) xxiii.
Report, 25 April 1833. 1833 (226) xxii.

Commission on the mode of taking evidence in Chancery and its effects. Report. 1860 [2698] xxxi; (Legal Administration, 9).

Common law (judicial business) commission. Report, 31 July 1857. 1857, session 2 [2268] xxi; (Legal Administration, 9).

Select committee on copyhold enfranchisement. Report, 13 Aug 1838. 1837/8 (707) xxiii.

Select committee (HL) on the Bankruptcy and Insolvency Bill. Report, 30 May 1861. HL 1861 (110) xxiv; HC repr. 1861 (320) xiv.

Select committee (HL) on the Criminal Law Administration Amendment Bill. Report, 15 May 1848. HL 1847/8 (134) xxiv; HC repr. 1847/8 (523) xvi; (LA Criminal Law, 6).

Select committee (HL) on the law of defamation and libel. Report, 1 June 1843. HL 1843 (18) xx; HC repr. 1843 (513) v.

CAMPBELL, John, *2nd M. Breadalbane*
Select committee (HL) on the Oxford and Great Western Union Railway Bill. Min. of ev. 26 June 1838. HL 1837/8 (227) xx.

CAMPBELL, John Frederick
Select committee on administration of justice in Wales. Report, 13 July 1820. 1820 (273) ii.

Select committee on administration of justice in Wales. Report, 14 June 1821. 1821 (662) iv.

CAMPBELL, William Frederick, *2nd Bn. Stratheden and Campbell*
Select committee (HL) on the Smoke Nuisance Abatement (Metropolis) Bill. Report, 15 July 1887. HL 1887 (174) ix; HC repr. 1887 (321) xii.

CAMPBELL, William G.
Report on the death of Rees Price in the Carmarthen Asylum. 7 Feb 1870. 1870 (148) lvii; (HE Mental, 8). Poor Law Board.

Report on the death of Santi Nistri in the Hanwell Asylum. 8 Nov 1869. 1870 (148) lvii; (HE Mental, 8). Poor Law Board.

CAMPBELL-BANNERMAN, Henry, *Sir*
Select committee on the Birmingham Corporation Water Bill. Report, 19 May 1892. 1892 (197) xi.

Select committee on the Caledonian Railway (Conversion of Stock) Bill, the Great Northern Railway (Capital) Bill, the London and Southwestern Railway (Conversion of Stock) Bill, and the Isle of Wight Railway Bill. Reports and special report, 13 June 1890. 1890 (225) xi.

Select committee on distress from want of employment
1st report, 11 March 1895. 1895 (111) viii.
2nd report, 7 May 1895. 1895 (253) viii.
3rd report, 2 July 1895. 1895 (365) ix; (Industrial Relations, 23-24).

Select committee on Navy estimates
1st report, 2 May 1888. 1888 (142) xii.
2nd report, 8 June 1888. 1888 (213) xiii.
3rd report, 27 July 1888. 1888 (304) xiii.
4th report, 6 Aug 1888. 1888 (328) xiii.

Standing committee on law. Clergy Discipline (Immorality) Bill. Report, 24 May 1892. 1892 (223) xi.

CAMPBELL-BANNERMAN, Henry, *Sir* (continued)
Standing committee on law. Court of session and

Bill Chamber (Scotland) Clerks Bill and the Judicial
Factors (Scotland) Bill. Report, 27 June 1889. 1889
(216), (217) x.

Standing committee on law. Lunacy Acts Amendment
Bill. Report, 15 July 1889. 1889 (252) xi.

Standing committee on law. Stamp Duties Bill and
the Stamp Duties Management Bill. Report, 26 June
1891. 1890/1 (297), (298) xvii.

Standing committee on law. Universities and College
Estates Bill. Report, 14 June 1898. 1898 (238) xiii.

Standing committee on law. Vaccination Bill. Report,
5 July 1898. 1898 (275) xii.

CAMPERDOWN, *E.*   SEE:
Duncan-Haldane, Robert Dundas, *1st E. Camperdown*
(1785-1859)
Duncan-Haldane, Adam, *2nd E. Camperdown* (d.1867)
Duncan-Haldane, Robert Adam Philips, *3rd E. Camper-*
down (d.1913)

CANDLISH, John
Select committee on the Abyssinian expedition.
Report, 29 July 1870. 1870 (401) v; (Africa, 7).

Select committee on the Abyssinian war. Report,
30 July 1869. 1868/9 (380) vi; (Africa, 6).

CANE, Richard Basil
Report of an inquiry into the treatment of the sick
in the Strand Union Workhouse. 11 June 1866. 1866
(362) lxii. Poor Law Board.

Report on the pauperism of the County of Lancaster
and parts of the counties of Chester, Derby and York
(West Riding). 20 Jan 1870. 1870 (69) lviii. Poor
Law Board.

CANNING, Charles John, *1st E. Canning*
Commission to investigate the projects for establishing
railway termini within or in the immediate vicinity
of the Metropolis. Report, 27 June 1846. 1846 [719],
[750] xvii.

Committee on contract packets. Report, 8 July 1853.
1852/3 [1660] xcv. Treasury.

CANTERBURY, *Archbp.* SEE:
Moore, John, *Archbp. Canterbury,* 1783-1805
Manners-Sutton, Charles, *Archbp. Canterbury,* 1805-28
Howley, William, *Archbp. Canterbury,* 1828-48
Sumner, John Bird, *Archbp. Canterbury,* 1848-62
Longley, Charles Thomas, *Archbp. Canterbury,* 1862-68
Tait, Charles Campbell, *Archbp. Canterbury,* 1868-83
Benson, Edward White, *Archbp. Canterbury,* 1883-96
Temple, Frederick, *Archbp. Canterbury,* 1896-1903

CAPEL, Arthur Algernon, *6th E. Essex*
Commission on the best mode of distributing the
sewage of towns and applying it to beneficial and
profitable uses.
Preliminary report, 26 March 1858. 1857/8 [2372]
xxxii.
2nd report, Aug 1861. 1861 [2882] xxxiii.
3rd report, March 1865. 1865 [3472] xxvii; (UA
Sanitation, 4-5). Treasury.

CAPERN, H.
Select committee of the Bahamas Assembly on petition. SEE: Meadows, J.G.

CAPPER, John Henry
Report on the treatment of convicts in the hulks at

Woolwich. 10 Feb 1847. 1847 (149) xlviii; (CP Prisons,
12). Home Department.

CARDWELL, Edward, *Vct. Cardwell*
Commission appointed to inquire into the costs of
prosecutions. Report, 1859, session 2 [2575] xiii, pt.1.

Committee on expiring laws: 6th session, 14th Parliament. Report, 13 March 1846. 1846 (128) xv.

Royal commission on vivisection.
Report, 8 Jan 1876. 1876 C.1397 xli.
Index. 1877 C.1864 xxvii.

Select committee on Bank Acts, 1857. SEE: Lewis,
George Cornewall, *Sir*

Select committee on Bank Acts. Report, 1 July 1858.
1857/8 (381) v; (MP Commercial Distress, 4).

Select committee on the Births, Deaths and Marriages
(Ireland) Bill, and the Registration of Births, *etc.*
(Ireland) Bill. Report, 11 July 1861. 1861 (425) xiv.

Select committee on Callan schools. Report, 18 June
1873. 1873 (255) ix.

Select committee on the Church Building and New
Parishes Acts Amendment Bill. Report, 22 July 1862.
1863 (482) vi.

Select committee on the Markets and Fairs (Ireland)
Bill. Special report, Markets (Ireland) Bill. 11 July
1861. 1861 (424) xiv; (LA Criminal Law, 6).

Select committee on the Metropolis Gas Bill. Special
report, 8 Aug 1867. 1867 (520) xii; (FP Gas, 3).

Select committee on the Nawals of Surat Treaty Bill.
Min. of ev. 9 June 1856. 1856 (256) x.
Min. of ev., documents, 2 pts. 1856 (265-I, 265-II)
x.

Select committee on poor relief in Ireland. Report,
5 July 1861. 1861 (408) x.

Select committee on railway and canal bills.
1st report, 16 Dec 1852. 1852/3 (79) xxxviii.
2nd report, 28 Feb 1853. 1852/3 (170) xxxviii.
3rd report, 18 March 1853. 1852/3 (246) xxxviii.
4th report, 8 April 1853. 1852/3 (310) xxxviii.
5th report, 8 July 1853. 1852/3 (736) xxxviii;
(Transport, 9).

Select committee on Smithfield Market Removal Bill.
Report, 6 June 1851. 1851 (376) x.

Select committee on sugar duties. Report, 8 July
1862. 1862 (390) xiii.

Select committee on the Woodhouse collection.
Report, 9 Aug 1867. 1867 (521) ix.

CARLISLE, *Lord* SEE:
Howard, George William Frederick, *7th E. Carlisle*
(1802-64)
Howard, William George, *8th E. Carlisle* (1808-89)
Howard, George James, *9th E. Carlisle* (1843-1911)

CARNARVON, *E.* SEE:
Herbert, Henry George, *2nd E. Carnarvon* (1772-1833)
Herbert, Henry John George, *3rd E. Carnarvon* (1800-
1849)
Herbert, Henry Howard Molyneux, *4th E. Carnarvon*
(1831-1890)

CARRINGTON, *Lord* SEE:
Wynn-Carrington, Charles Robert, *1st E. Carrington.*

CARTER, John Bonham SEE:
Bonham-Carter, John.

CARTON, Richard P.
Commission on the Queen's colleges in Ireland. Report, 1885. 1884/5 C.4313 xxv. Irish Secretary's Office.

CARTWRIGHT, Emund
Committee on weaving machine, 1808. SEE: Browne, I.H.

CARTWRIGHT, William Cornwallis
Select committee on wine duties. Report, 9 July 1879. 1878/9 (278) xiv.

CASTLETOWN, *Bn.* SEE:
Fitzpatrick, Bernard Edward Barnaby, *2nd Bn. Castletown.*

CASTLEREAGH, *Lord* SEE:
Stewart, R., *Vct. Castlereagh.*

CATHCART, William Schaw, *1st E. Cathcart*
Committee of privileges. Chandos peerage claim, 1802. SEE: De Grey, Thomas.

CAUSTON, Richard Knight
Select committee on parliamentary papers distribution. 1st report, 20 June 1894. 1894 (181) xiv. (No other reports identified).

CAVE, Lewis William
Royal commission on corrupt practices in the city of Oxford. Report, 5 April 1881. 1881 C.2856 xliv.

CAVE, Stephen
Royal commission on municipal boundaries. Report, 2 parts. 1880 C.2490 xxxi.

Select committee on commons
1st report, 4 April 1878. 1878 (130) xi.
2nd report, 27 May 1878. 1878 (197) xi; (Agriculture, 14).

Select committee on East India finance. Report, 28 July 1874. 1874 (329) viii; (East India, 22).

Select committee on lunacy law. Report, 28 March 1878. 1878 (113) xvi; (HE Mental, 5).

Select committee on lunacy law, 1877. SEE: Dillwyn, Lewis Llewellyn.

CAVENDISH, Frederick Charles, *Lord*
Committee of public accounts. Report, 16 May 1877. 1877 (217) vii.

Committee of public accounts
1st report, 13 March 1878. 1878 (83) x.
2nd report, 10 July 1878. 1878 (277) x.

Committee of public accounts
1st report, 12 March 1879. 1878/9 (96) viii.
2nd report, 14 May 1879. 1878/9 (186) viii.

CAVENDISH, George Henry, *Lord*
Select committee on Turnpike Acts continuance
Report, 14 June 1869. 1868/9 (262) xi.
Report, 22 May 1871. 1871 (244) xii.
Report, 7 May 1872. 1872 (184) xii.
Report, 19 May 1873. 1873 (215) xvii.
Report, 5 June 1874. 1874 (205) xi.
Report, 13 May 1875. 1875 (208) xiv.
Report, 25 May 1876. 1876 (241) xiv.
Report, 15 May 1877. 1877 (207) xvii.
Report, 14 May 1878. 1878 (169) xviii.
Report, 24 June 1879. 1878/9 (243) xiv.
Report, 16 March 1880. 1880 (133) xii.

Select committee on Turnpike Acts continuance

(Bruton Trust). Report, 16 July 1872. 1872 (313) xii.

CAVENDISH, Spencer Compton, *8th D. Devonshire*
Committee on the claims of Capt. Grant to remuneration for the introduction of his system of cookery. Report, 27 Jan 1864. 1864 [3279] xxxv. War Office.

Committee on the organisation of the War Office 1st to 4th reports, 6 Sept 1864 to 28 March 1865. 1865 (184) xxxi; (Military and Naval, 4). War Office

Royal commission on the administration of the Naval and Military departments. Preliminary and further reports, 10 July 1889 and 11 Feb 1890. 1890 C.5979 xix; (Military and Naval, 6).

Royal commission on labour
1st report, 16 March 1892. 1892 C.6708 xxxiv.
2nd report, 20 June 1892. 1892 C.6795 xxxvi.
3rd report, 2 Feb 1893. 1893/4 C.6894 xxxii.
4th report, 1 June 1893. 1893/4 C.7063 xxxix, pt.1
5th report
  Report, 24 May 1894. 1894 C.7421 xxxv.
  Secretary's report, summaries of ev., appendix. 1894 C.7421-I xxxv.
  Papers showing action taken by the Board of Trade. 1894 C.7540 xxxv.
Min. of ev. (sitting as a whole). 1893/4 C.7063-I xxxix, p.1.
Digest of ev. (sitting as a whole). 1893/4 C.7063-II xxxix, pt.1.
Appendix to ev. 1893/4 C.7063-III.A xxxix, pt.1.
Ev. before group A
  Min. of ev.
    Vol.1: Mining. 1892 C.6708-IV xxxiv.
    Vol.2: Mining, iron, engineering and hardware. 1892 C.6795-IV xxxvi, pt.1.
    Vol.3: Mining and quarrying, iron and steel, chain making, nail making, engineering and shipping trades. 1893/4 C.6894-VII xxxii.
  Digest of ev.
    Vol.1: Mining. 1892 C.6708-I xxxiv.
    Vol.2: Mining, iron, engineering and hardware. 1892 C.6795-I xxxvi, pt.3.
    Vol.3, including indexes to precis, vols.1-3. 1893/4 C.6894-X xxxii.
Ev. before group B
  Min. of ev.
    Vol.1: Docks, wharves and shipping. 1892 C.6708-V xxxv.
    Vol.2: Transport by water. 1892 C.6795-V xxxvi, pt.2.
    Vol.3: Transport by water and land. 1893/4 C.6894-VIII xxxiii.
  Digest of ev.
    Vol.1: Docks, wharves and shipping. 1892 C.6708-II xxxiv.
    Vol.2: Transport by water. 1892 C.6795-II xxxvi, pt.3.
    Vol.3: Including indexes to precis, vols.1-3. 1893/4. C.6894-XI xxxiii.
Ev. before group C
  Min. of ev.
    Vol.1: Textiles. 1892 C.6708-VI xxxv.
    Vol.2: Textile, clothing, chemical, building and miscellaneous trades. 1892 C.6795-VI xxxvi, pt.2.
    Vol.3: Textile, clothing, chemical, building, and miscellaneous trades. 1893/4 C.6894-IX xxxiv.
  Digest of ev.
    Vol.1: Textiles. 1892 C.6708-III xxxiv.
    Vol.2: Textile, clothing, chemical, building

CAVENDISH, Spencer Compton, *8th D. Devonshire* (continued)

and miscellaneous trades. 1892 C.6795-III xxxvi, pt.3.

Vol.3: including indexes to precis, vols.1-3. 1893/4 C.6894-XII xxxiv.

Index to ev.

Vol.1: Subject groups A-C. 1893/4 C.7063-IV xxxviii.

Vol.2: Trades groups A-C. 1893/4 C.7063-V, -V.A, -V.B. xxxviii.

Vol.3: Glossary of technical terms. 1893/4 C.7603-V.C xxxviii.

Vol.4: Ev. before the commission as a whole, witnesses, subjects and trades. 1893/4 C.7063-III xxxix, pt.1.

Assistant commissioners' reports on agricultural labour

Vol.1: England. pts.1-6. 1893/4 C.6894-I–IV xxxv.

Pt.7: Index. 1893/4 C.6894-XIII xxxvi.

Vol.2 and 3: Scotland. 1893/4 C.6894-XV–XVII xxxvi.

Vol.4: Ireland. Pts.1-4. 1893/4 C.6894-XVIII-XXI xxxviii, pt.1.

Vol.5: General report. 1893/4 C.6894-XXV, XXVI xxxvii, pt.2.

Foreign reports

Vol.1: United States. 1892 C.6795-X xxxvi, pt.5.

Vol.2: Colonies and Indian Empire, with an appendix on the migration of labour. 1892 C.6795-XI xxxvi, pt.5.

Vol.3: Holland. 1893/4 C.7063-VI xxxix, pt.2.

Vol.4: Belgium. 1893/4 C.7063-VIII xxxix, pt.2.

Vol.5: Germany. 1893/4 C.7063-VII xxxix, pt.2.

Vol.6: France. 1893/4 C.7063-IX xxxix, pt.2.

Vol.7: Switzerland. 1893/4 C.7063-X xxxix, pt.2.

Vol.8: Italy. 1893/4 C.7063-XII xxxix, pt.2.

Vol.9: Denmark, Sweden and Norway, and Spain and Portugal.1893/4 C.7063-XIII xxxix, pt.2.

Vol.10: Russia. 1893/4 C.7063-XIV xxxix, pt.2.

Vol.11: Austria, Hungary and the Balkan States. 1893/4 C.7063-XI xxxix, pt.2.

Reports on the employment of women. 1893/4 C.6894-XXIII xxxvii, pt.1.

Rules of associations of employers and of employed. 1892 C.6795-XII xxxvi, pt.5.

Answers to the schedules of questions.

Group A. 1892 C.6795-VII xxxvi, pt.3.

Group B. 1892 C.6795-VIII xxxvi, pt.3.

Group C. 1892 C.6795-IX xxxvi, pt.4; (Industrial Relations, 25-44).

Royal commission on railways

Ev. and papers relating to railways in Ireland, extracted from the proc. of the commission. 1866 [3607] lxiii.

Report, 7 May 1867. 1867 [3844] xxxviii, pt.1.

Min. of ev. 1867 [3844-I] xxxviii, pt.1.

Appendix, 2 vols. 1867 [3844-II] [3844-III] xxxviii, pt.2; (Transport, 10-11).

Royal commission on scientific instruction and the advancement of science

1st report, 9 March 1871. 1871 C.318 xxiv.

Supplement with min. of ev. 14 June 1870 to 11 July 1871. 28 Feb 1872. 1872 C.536 xxv.

2nd report, 22 March 1872. 1872 C.536 xxv.

3rd report, 1 Aug 1873. 1873 C.868 xxviii.

4th report, 16 Jan 1874. 1874 C.884 xxii.

5th report, 4 Aug 1874. 1874 C.1087 xxii.

Min. of ev. vol.2: 12 Feb 1872 to 21 March 1873. 1874 C.958 xxii.

6th report, 18 June 1875. 1875 C.1279 xxviii.

7th report, 18 June 1875. 1875 C.1279 xxviii.

8th report, 18 June 1875. 1875 C.1298 xxviii.

Min. of ev. vol.3: 1875. 1875 C.1363 xxviii; (ED Scientific and Technical, 3-4).

Select committee on estimates procedure for grants of supply. Report, 13 July 1888. 1888 (281) xii.

Select committee of juries in Ireland. 1st, 2nd and special reports, 7 July 1873. 1873 (283) xv.

Select committee on the law of rating in Ireland. Report, 4 Aug 1871. 1871 (423) x.

Select committee on law of rating in Ireland. Report, 7 May 1872. 1872 (187) xi.

Select committee on London Corporation, charges of malversation. Report, 20 May 1887. 1887 (161) x.

Select committee on parliamentary and municipal elections. Report, 23 July 1869. 1868/9 (352) viii; (GO Elections, 4).

Select committee on parliamentary and municipal elections. Report, 15 March 1870. 1870 (115) vi; (GO Elections, 4).

Select committee on the Telegraph Acts Extension Bill. Report, 5 July 1870. 1870 (336) x; (Posts and Telegraphs, 5).

Select committee on the Telegraph Bill. Report, 22 July 1869. 1868/9 (348) vi; (Posts and Telegraphs, 3).

Select committee on Westmeath, *etc.* unlawful combinations. Report, 31 March 1871. 1871 (147) xiii.

CAVENDISH, William, *7th D. Devonshire*

Select committee (HL) on the government of Indian territories.

1st report, 12 May 1853. HL 1852/3 (20) xxviii.

2nd report, 4 Aug 1853. HL 1852/3 (20-II) xxix.

3rd report, 18 Aug 1853. HL 1852/3 (20-III) xxx.

Committee (HL) on the Parrett Navigation Bill. Report 13 June 1866. HL 1866 (135) xxxiii.

Committee (HL) on the Sheffield and Rotherham Railway Bill. Report, 21 June 1836. HL 1836 (158) xii.

Select committee (HL) on the Sheffield Gas Bill. SEE: Cooper, Cropley Ashley, *6th E. Shaftesbury.*

CAVENDISH-BENTINCK, George Augustus Frederick, *Lord*

Select committee on the Registration of Trade Marks Bill. Report, 28 July 1875. 1875 (365) xiv.

CAVENDISH-BENTINCK, William George Frederick, *Lord*

Select committee on steam communication with India. Report, 15 July 1837. 1837 (539) vi.

Select committee on sugar and coffee planting.

1st report, 24 Feb and 15 June 1848. 1847/8 (123), (409) xxiii, pt.1.

2nd report, 2 March 1848. 1847/8 (137) xxiii, pt.1.

3rd report, 14 March 1848. 1847/8 (167) xxiii, pt.1.

4th report, 17 March 1848. 1847/8 (184) xxiii, pt.2.

5th report, 27 March 1848. 1847/8 (206) xxiii, pt.2.

6th report, 3 April 1848. 1847/8 (230) xxiii, pt.2.

7th report, 6 April 1848. 1847/8 (245) xxiii, pt.3.

8th report, 29 May 1848. 1847/8 (361-II) xxiii, pt.3.

Supplement to 8th report, 29 May 1848. 1847/8 (361-II) xxiii, pt.4.

Statements given in evidence to the committee showing the transit loss on Scotch and Irish spirits imported into London. 18 July 1848. 1847/8 (518) xxiii, pt.4.

Index. 29 May 1848. 1847/8 (361) xxiii, pt.4.

CAVENDISH-BENTINCK, William John Arthur Charles James, *6th D. Portland*
Royal commission on horse breeding.
Report, 20 Dec 1887. 1888 C.5419 xlviii.
2nd report, 5 Dec 1888. 1888 C.5595 xlviii.
3rd report, 5 May 1890. 1890 C.6034 xxvii.
4th report, 9 Feb 1894. 1893/4 C.6897 xxxi.
5th report, 3 July 1895. 1895 C.7811 xxxv.
6th report, 26 July 1897. 1897 C.8593 xxxiv.
7th report, 7 Aug 1899. 1899 C.9487 xxxiii.
8th report, 23 July 1901. 1901 Cd.712 xxiv.
9th report, 3 July 1903. 1903 Cd.1678 xxiii.
10th report, 28 July 1905. 1905 Cd.2646 xxx.
11th report. 1907 Cd.3712 xxxvii.
12th report. 1908 Cd.4039 xlvii.
13th report, 27 July 1910. 1910 Cd.5307 xxvi.
Final report, 11 Oct 1911. 1911 Cd.5936 xxix, pt.1.

CAWLEY, Charles Edward
Select committee on locomotives on roads. Report, 18 July 1873. 1873 (312) xvi.

CAYLEY, Edward Stillingfleet
Select committee on coal mines. Report, 22 June 1852. 1852 (509) v; (FP Mining Accidents, 3).

Select committee on hand-loom weavers' petitions. SEE: Maxwell, John.

Select committee on Mr. Gurney's case on steam carriages. Report, 10 July 1835. 1835 (373) xiii; (Transport, 1).

Select committee on ventilation of the HC.
1st report, 31 March 1854. 1854 (149) ix.
2nd report, 26 May 1854. 1854 (270) ix.
3rd report, 24 July 1854. 1854 (403) ix.

CECIL, Eustace, *Lord* SEE:
Gascoyne-Cecil, Eustace Brownlow Henry, *Lord*.

CECIL, James Brownlow Gascoyne SEE:
Gascoyne-Cecil, J.B.W., *2nd M. Salisbury*.

CHADS, Henry Ducie, *Sir*
Committee on lights for steam and sailing vessels. Report, 29 March 1856. 1857, session 2 (196) xxxix. Admiralty.

CHADWICK, Edwin
Commission on employment of children in factories (Factories Inquiry Commission). SEE: Tooke, Thomas

Inquiry into the sanitary condition of the labouring population of G.B.
Report, May 1842. HL 1842 (unnumbered command paper) xxvi.
Local reports: England. HL 1842 (unnumbered command paper) xxvii.
Local reports: Scotland. HL 1842 (unnumbered command paper) xxviii.
Poor Law Commission.

Inquiry into the sanitary condition of the labouring population of G.B. Supplementary report on the practice of internment in towns. 1843 [509] xii. Poor Law Commission. SEE ALSO: Mackinnon, William Alexander.

Letter to Mr. N.W. Senior explanatory of communications and evidence on half school-time teaching; on military drill and physical training; and on the administration of funds applicable to popular education. 1862 (120-I) xliii; (ED General, 8). Education Commission.

On the half-time school system. 1862 (120) xliii; (ED General, 8). Education Commission.

On the teaching of the Naval and military drill in popular schools. 1862 (120) xliii; (ED General, 8). Education Commission.

On the time and cost of education on a large and on a small scale. 1862 (120) xliii; (ED General, 8). Education Commission.

Report on Metropolitan drainage. 4 Aug 1854. 1854 (180) lxi; (UA Sanitation, 4). General Board of Health.

CHALMERS, Charles
Committee on petition on Swedish herrings. SEE: Anderson, J.W., *Sir*.

CHALMERS, David Patrick
Report and correspondence on the insurrection in the Sierra Leone Protectorate.
Pt.1. Report and correspondence. 21 Jan 1899. 1899 C.9388 lx.
Pt.2. Ev. and documents. 1899 C.9391 lx. Colonial Office.

Report on the effect of steps taken by the colonial government to abolish slavery within the Gold Coast Protectorate. 27 June 1878. 1878 C.2148 lv; (Slave Trade, 98). Colonial Office.

CHAMBERLAIN, Joseph Austin
Royal commission on explosions from coal dust in mines
1st report, 30 July 1891. 1890/1 C.6543 xxii.
2nd report, 13 June 1894. 1894 C.7401 xxiv.
Min. of ev. 1894 C.7401-I xxiv; (FP Mining Accidents, 12).

Select committee on merchant shipping. Report, 23 July 1880. 1880 (305) xi.

Select committee on small holdings. Report, 10 Aug 1888. 1888 (358) xviii; (Agriculture, 20).

Select committee on small holdings. Report, 9 Aug 1889. 1889 (313) xii; (Agriculture, 20).

Select committee on small holdings. Report, 13 June 1890. 1890 (223) xvii; (Agriculture, 20).

CHAMBERS, Thomas
Select committee on members holding contracts (*Sir* Sidney Waterlow). Report, 15 March 1869. 1868/9 (78) vii.

Select committee on Metropolitan Commons Act, 1866, Amendment Bill. SEE: Cowper, William Francis

Select committee on Portuguese claims. Report, 24 July 1854. 1854 (404) xvi.

CHAMBERS, William
Report on the cases of pleuro-pneumonia among cattle recently imported from Ireland into Norfolk. 25 Jan 1875. 1875 (193) lx; (AG Animal Health, 2). Privy Council, Veterinary Department.

CHANCELLOR, *Lord*
(years of appointment)
1793 Lord Loughborough
1801 Lord Eldon

CHANCELLOR, *Lord* (continued)

(years of appointment)

1806 Lord Erskine
1807 Lord Eldon
1827 Lord Lyndhurst
1830 Lord Brougham
1834 Lord Lyndhurst
1836 Lord Cottenham
1841 Lord Lyndhurst
1846 Lord Cottenham
1850 Lord Truro
1852 Lord St. Leonards
1852 Lord Cranworth
1858 Lord Chelmsford
1859 Lord Campbell
1861 Lord Westbury
1865 Lord Cranworth
1866 Lord Chelmsford
1868 Lord Cairns
1868 Lord Hatherley
1872 Lord Selborne
1874 Earl Cairns
1880 Earl Selborne
1885 Lord Halsbury
1886 Lord Herschell
1886 Lord Halsbury
1892 Lord Herschell
1895 Lord Halsbury

CHANCELLOR OF THE EXCHEQUER

(years of appointment)

1783 William Pitt
1801 H. Addington
1804 William Pitt
1806 H. Petty, *Lord*
1807 S. Perceval
1812 N. Vansittart
1823 F.J. Robinson
1827 G. Canning
1827 J.C. Herries
1828 H. Goulburn
1830 *Vct.* Althorpe
1834 R. Peel, *Sir*
1835 T. Spring-Rice
1839 F.T. Baring
1841 H. Goulburn
1846 C. Wood
1852 B. Disraeli
1852 W.E. Gladstone
1855 G.C. Lewis, *Sir*
1858 B. Disraeli
1859 W.E. Gladstone
1866 B. Disraeli
1868 G.W. Hunt
1868 R. Lowe
1873 W.E. Gladstone
1874 S. Northcote, *Sir*
1880 W.E. Gladstone
1882 H.C.E. Childers
1885 M.E. Hicks-Beach, *Sir*
1886 W. Harcourt, *Sir*
1886 R. Churchill, *Lord*
1887 G.J. Goschen
1892 W. Harcourt, *Sir*
1895 M.E. Hicks-Beach, *Sir*

CHANDOS, *M.* SEE:
Temple-Nugent-Brydges-Chandos-Grenville, Richard Plantagenet, *2nd D. Buckingham* (*b.*1797, *s.*1839, *d.*1861)
Temple-Nugent-Brydges-Chandos-Grenville, Richard Plantagenet Campbell, *3rd D. Buckingham* (*b.*1823, *s.*1861, *d.*1869)

[Peerage claim]. SEE: De Grey, Thomas, *2nd Bn. Walsingham.*

CHAPLIN, Henry
Departmental committee on the transatlantic cattle trade. Report. 1890/1 C.6350 lxxviii. Board of Trade *and* Board of Agriculture.

Select committee on aged deserving poor. Report, 27 July 1899. 1899 (296) viii.

Select committee on the Metropolitan Water Companies (Government) Bill. Report, 27 March 1899. 1899 (132) x.

CHAPMAN, Henry S.
Report on hand-loom weavers in Yorkshire (West Riding). 25 Nov 1838. 1840 (43-II) xxiii; (IR Textiles, 9).

Report on immigration to the Canadas. 22 Feb 1834. *In* 1834 (44) xxxvii.

CHARLES, Arthur
Royal commission on corrupt practices in the City of Canterbury. Report, 24 Dec 1880. 1881 C.2775 xxxix.

CHARLEVILLE, *E.* [Peerage claim]. SEE:
Freeman-Mitford, J.T.

CHARLTON, Edmund Lechmere
Committee of privileges. Report concerning his contempt of court. SEE: Williams-Wynne, C.W.

CHARTERIS, Francis SEE:
Wemyss-Charteris-Douglas, Francis, *8th E. Wemyss.*

CHATTERTON, Hedges Eyre
Royal commission on registration of deeds and assurances in Ireland. SEE: May, G.A.C.

CHELMSFORD, *Bn.* SEE:
Thesiger, Frederick, *1st Bn. Chelmsford* (1794-1878).
Thesiger, Frederick Augustus, *2nd Bn. Chelmsford* (1827-1905).

CHESNEY, George Tomkyns, *Sir*
Select committee on retired soldiers' and sailors' employment. Report, 3 Aug 1894. 1894 (258) xv.

Select committee on retired soldiers' and sailors' employment, 1895. SEE: Brookfield, A.M.

CHESTER, *Bp.* SEE:
Graham, John, *Bp. Chester*

CHESTER, J.
Cambridge University commission. Report, 22 Jan 1861. 1861 [2852] xx.

CHESTERFIELD, *Lord* [Peerage claim]. SEE:
Freeman-Mitford, J.T.

CHETWYND, George
Select committee on laws relating to vagrants. Report, 23 May 1821. 1821 (543) iii.

CHETWYND-TALBOT, Henry John Chetwynd, *3rd E. Talbot*
Select committee on Post Office communication with Ireland. Report, 11 June 1841. 1841 (399) ix.

Select committee on Post Office communication with Ireland. Report, 27 June 1842. 1842 (373) ix.

CHEYNE, John
Boundary commission for Scotland. Report, 31 Dec 1892. 1893/4 C.6940 xliv.

CHICHESTER, *E.* SEE:
Pelham, Henry Thomas, *3rd E. Chichester* (1804-86).

CHICHESTER, *Bp.* SEE:
Buckner, J. 1797-1824
Carr, Robert James, 1824-31
Maltby, Edward, 1831-36
Otter, William, 1836-40
Shuttleworth, Philip Nicholas, 1840-42
Gilbert, Ashhurst Turner, 1842-70
Durnford, Richard, 1870-95
Wilberforce, Ernest, 1895-1908

CHIEF JUSTICE OF IRELAND, *Lord,* 1879. SEE:
May, George Augustus Chichester.

CHILDERS, Hugh Culling Eardley
Committee on the administration and organisation of the Metropolitan police force. Report, 19 July 1886. 1886 C.4894 xxxiv. Home Department. (CP Police, 10).

Committee on the origin and character of the disturbances in the Metropolis, Monday 8 Feb 1886, and the conduct of the police. Report, 22 Feb 1886. 1886 C.4665. Home Department.

Committee of public accounts
1st report, 29 May 1867. 1867 (333) x.
2nd report, 7 Aug 1867. 1867 (519) x.

Committee of public accounts. Report, 21 July 1868. 1867/8 (452) xiii.

Official statistics committee
1st report, Customs. 6 Aug 1878. 1878/9 (107) xxi.
2nd report, 6 Aug 1878. 1881 (39) xxx.
3rd report, 23 Dec 1879. 1881 (39) xxx. Treasury.

Royal commission on the financial relations between G.B. and Ireland. SEE: O'Connor, Charles Owen, *the O'Connor Don.*

Royal commission on the spontaneous combustion of coal in ships. Report, 18 July 1876. 1876 C.1586 xli.

Select committee on the Army system of retirement. Report, 26 July 1867. 1867 (482) vii.

Select committee on civil service expenditure
1st report, 31 March 1873. 1873 (131) vii.
2nd report, 12 June 1873. 1873 (248) vii.
3rd report, 25 July 1873. 1873 (352) vii; (National Finance, 5).

Select committee on Contagious Diseases Act, 1866. SEE: Vivian, J.C.W.

Select committee on East India public works, 1878. SEE: Hamilton, G.F.

Select committee on education, science and art; administration of votes. Report, 21 Aug 1883. 1883 (341) xiii.

Select committee on education, science and art; administration of votes. Report, 31 July 1884. 1884 (312) xiii.

Select committee on the Hanover Chapel Bill. Report, 21 July 1891. 1890/1 (356) xii.

Select committee on the Pontefract election. SEE: Walpole, S.H.

Select committee on soldiers', sailors' and marines' civil employment. Report, 13 July 1876. 1876 (356) xiv.

Select committee on soldiers' and marines' civil employment. Report, 31 July 1877. 1877 (383) xv.

Select committee on the Thames Watermen and Lightermen Bill. Special report, 24 June 1890. 1890 (244) xvii.

Select committee on transportation. Report, 28 May 1861. 1861 (286) xiii; (CP Transportation, 3).

CHILDERS, John Walbanke
Select committee on the Derby election petition. Min. of ev. 28 March 1848. 1847/8 (212) xi.

Select committee on Kingstown and Holyhead mails. Report, 4 July 1850. 1850 (501) xiv.

CHISHOLM, H.W.
Report on the formation and proc. of the International Metric Commission, Paris, 1869-72. 8 Jan 1873. 1873 C.714 xxxviii. Board of Trade.

Report on the trial of the Pyx and the coinage subjected to this public trial. 10 Feb 1866. 1866 (293) xl; (MP Currency, 3).

CHRISTIE, W.D.
Select committee on the Bridport election petition. Report, 13 July 1846. 1846 (478) viii.

CHRISTOPHER, Robert Adam
Select committee on Epworth (corn laws) petitions.
1st report, 19 July 1843. 1843 (447) xi.
2nd report, 31 July 1843. 1843 (511) xi.

CHURCHILL, Henry Adrian
Committee on East African slave trade. 24 Jan 1870. 1870 C.209 lxi; (Slave Trade, 91). Foreign Office.

CHURCHILL, Randolph, *Lord* SEE:
Spencer-Churchill, Randolph Henry, *Lord.*

CHURSTON, *Lord* SEE:
Yarde-Buller, John, *3rd Bn. Churston.*

CLANCARTY, *E.* SEE:
De Burgh, Ulick John, *14th E. and 1st M. Clanricarde* (*b.*1802, *s.*1808, *d.*1874).
De Burgh, Hubert George, *15th E. and 2nd M. Clanricarde* (*b.*1832, *d.*1916).

CLARENCE AND AVONDALE, *D.*
Precedence. SEE: Parker, A.E.

CLARENDON, *Lord* SEE:
Villiers, John Charles, *3rd E. Clarendon* (*s.*1786, *d.*1838).
Villiers, George William Frederick, *4th E. Clarendon* (*d.*1870).
Villiers, Edward Hyde, *5th E. Clarendon* (*d.*1914).

CLARK, W. Tierney
Report on the Metropolitan Sewage Manure Company. 8 May 1846. 1846 (338) xliii. Commission of H.M. Woods, Forests, *etc.*

CLARKE, Andrew
Report on Alderney harbour. 27 June 1870. 1870 (354) lix. Board of Trade.

CLARKE, Edward George, *Sir*
Select committee on the Statute Law Revision Bill, the Lunacy Consolidation Bill, and the Inland Revenue Regulation Bill. Special report and reports, 25 March and 5 and 6 May 1890. 1890 (110) xvii.

Select committee on the Statute Law Revision (No.2) Bill. Report, 7 Aug 1890. 1890 (359) xvii.

Select committee on the Statute Law Revision Bill. Report, 28 July 1891. 1890/1 (376) xvii.

Select committee on the Yorkshire Provident Insurance Company. Report, 18 July 1889. 1889 (262) xvi; (Insurance, 10).

CLAUSSEN, P.
Report on processes proposed for the preparation and uses of flax fibre. SEE: Kane, Robert.

CLAY, John, *Jr.*
Royal commission on agriculture. Report on American agriculture. 20 Jan 1882. 1882 C.3375-VI xv; (Agriculture, 19). SEE ALSO: Gordon-Lennox, Charles Henry, *6th D. Richmond.*

CLAY, William, *Sir*
Select committee on the Cheltenham election petition. Min. of ev. 4 Sept 1848. 1847/8 (727) xi.

Select committee on Hertford Borough. SEE: Bernal, Ralph.

CLEATON, J.D.
Report on the death of Rees Price in the Carmarthen Asylum. 7 Feb 1870. 1870 (148) lvii; (HE Mental, 8). Poor Law Board.

CLEMENTS, Charles S.
Report on the Carlton, Great Ouseburn, Barwick-in-Elment and Great Preston incorporations under Gilbert's Act. 28 Feb 1842. 1842 (172) xlv. Poor Law Commission.

Report on inmates of the Skipton workhouse sent to a factory. 6 March 1843. 1843 (143) xlv. Poor Law Commission.

CLEMENTS, Edward
Commission of inquiry into the turnpike trusts of Ireland. Report, 4 June 1856. 1856 [2110] xix.

Select committee on pawnbroking in Ireland. Report, 3 Aug 1838. 1837/8 (677) xvii.

CLERK, George, *Sir*
Commission on the licensing system in Scotland.
Report, 1860. 1860 [2684], [2684-I] xxxii, xxxiii.
Report, 1861. 1861 (403) xxxi.

Commission on weights and measures
1st report, 7 July 1819. 1819 (565) xi.
2nd report, 8 Sept 1820. 1820 (314) vii.
3rd report, 5 April 1821. 1821 (383) iv.

Committee on Edinburgh and Leith Docks Bill. Min. of ev. 12 May 1825. 1825 (PB.1) v.

Committee on expired and expiring laws: 1st session. 12th Parliament. Report, 30 March 1835. 1835 (105) xviii.

Committee on expired and expiring laws: 3rd session, 14th Parliament. Report, 13 June 1843. 1843 (338) xi.

Committee on expiring laws: 4th session, 14th Parliament. Report, 1 April 1844. 1844 (168) xiv.

Committee on petition of Royal Burghs of Scotland respecting jails. Report, 22 May 1818. 1818 (346) vi; (CP Prisons, 8).

Committee of the whole HC on Lord Ellenborough's Divorce Bill. Min. of ev. 1 April 1830. 1830 (214) x; (Marriage and Divorce, 3).

Report on the administration of Scinde. 24 April 1848. 1854 (483) xlix. East India Office.

Select committee appointed to prepare the militia estimates. Report, 8 July 1842. 1842 (424) xiv.

Select committee on the Caledonian canal. Report, 2 May 1842. 1842 (218) xiv.

Select committee on controverted elections. Report, 19 March 1840. 1840 (138) ix; (GO Elections, 2).

Select committee on postage. Report, 14 Aug 1843. 1843 (564) viii; (Posts and Telegraphs, 4).

Select committee on Rochester Bridge. SEE: Gilbert, D.

Select committee on weights and measures. Report, 1 July 1814. 1813/4 (290) iii.

CLERMONT, *Bn.* [Peerage claim]. SEE:
Freeman-Mitford, J.T.

CLEVELAND, *D.* SEE:
Powlett, Harry George, *4th D. Cleveland.*

CLIFTON, *Lord* SEE:
Bligh, John, *4th E. Darnley* (1767-1831).

Bligh, Edward, *5th E. Darnley* (1795-1835).
Bligh, John Stuart, *6th E. Darnley* (1827-1896).

CLINTON, Henry Pelham Fiennes Pelham. SEE:
Fiennes-Pelham-Clinton, Henry Pelham, *5th D. Newcastle.*

CLIVE, *Vct.* SEE:
Herbert, Edward, *2nd E. Powis.*
Herbert, Edward James, *3rd E. Powis.*

CLIVE, *Lord* [Peerage claim]. SEE:
Freeman-Mitford, J.T.

CLIVE, Edward Bolton
Select committee on Evesham election petition. Min. of ev. 14 Dec 1830. 1830/1 (73) iii.

CLIVE, George
Committee on group 13 of railway bills. Min. of proc. relative to the Carlisle, Langholm and Hawick Railway Bill, the Border Counties Railway Bill, and the North British Railway (Hawick and Carlisle Junction Railway) Bill. Report, 17 May 1858. 1857/8 (0.75) xv.

Select committee on the Galway Town election petition. Min. of ev. 17 July 1857. 1857, session 2 (187) vi.

Select committee on turnpike trusts. Report, 14 June 1864. 1864 (383) ix.

CLIVE, Henry
Select committee on Wexford election petition. Min. of ev. 23 March 1830. 1830 (175) iv.

Select committee on Canterbury election. Proc., min. of ev. 5 April 1841. 1841 (219) ix.

CLONCURRY, *Bn.* [Peerage claim]. SEE:
Freeman-Mitford, J.T.

COBBETT, John Morgan
Select committee on the Beverley election petition. Min. of ev. 11 Aug 1859. 1859, session 2 (187) iii.

Select committee on bleaching and dyeing works. Report, 11 May 1858. 1857/8 (270) xi; (IR Children's Employment, 12).

Select committee on the Carlisle election petition. Min. of ev. 2 March 1860. 1860 (126) xi.

Select committee on law as regards contracts of service between master and servant. Report, 15 June 1865. 1865 (370) viii; (Industrial Relations, 18).

COBDEN, *Vct.* SEE:
Lyttelton, Charles George, *1st Vct. Cobham.*

COBDEN, Richard
Select committee on packet and telegraphic contracts, 1860. SEE: Dunlop, Alexander Murray.

Select committee on packet and telegraphic contracts. Report, 10 Aug 1859. 1859, session 2 (188) vi.

COCHRANE, *Lord*
Report on arrest in HC. SEE: Rose, George.

COCHRANE, Alexander D.W.R. Baillie. SEE:
Baillie-Cochrane, Alexander Dundas Wishart Ross.

COCHRANE, Thomas
Committee to inquire into the system of keeping the victualling accounts of HM ships. Report, July 1851. 1852 (342) xxx. Admiralty.

COCKBURN, Alexander James Edward, *Sir*
Committee on the present practice at the chambers of the Queen's Bench, Common Pleas and Exchequer divisions. Report, 1878. 1878 C.2064 xxv; (Legal Administration, 16).

Royal commission on extradition. Report, 30 May 1878. 1878 C.2039 xxiv.

Royal commission on labour laws
    1st report, 31 July 1874. 1874 C.1094 xxiv.
    2nd and final report, 17 Feb 1875. 1875 C.1157 xxx; (Industrial Relations, 18).

Letter containing comments and suggestions in relation to the Criminal Code (Indictable Offences) Bill. 12 June 1879. 1878/9 (232) lix. Lord Chancellor's Office.

COCKBURN, George, *Sir*
Select committee on Morton's patent slip. Report, 13 April 1832. 1831/2 (380) v.

COCKBURN, James Edmund, *Sir*
Royal commission on the superior courts of common law
    1st report, 30 June 1851. 1851 [1389] xxii.
    2nd report, 30 April 1853. 1852/3 [1626] xl.
    3rd report. 1860 [2614] xxxi; (Legal Administration, 9).

COCKELL, William
Report on a new system of shoeing horses introduced by Monsieur Charlier of Paris. July 1868. 1867/8 (503) xlii. War Office.

COCKS, John Somers, *2nd E. Somers*
Select committee on limits of the Borough of Arundel. Report, 19 June 1832. 1831/2 (537) v.

CODDINGTON, J.
Report on a central railway terminus in or near the City of Perth. 4 Aug 1845. 1846 (149) xxxviii. Board of Trade, Railway Dept.

Report on the state of the North British Railway. March 1847. 1847 (248) lxiii. Board of Trade, Railway Commission.

CODRINGTON, William, *Sir*
Select committee on the billiting system. Report, 25 June 1858. 1857/8 (363) x.

Committee on the Enfield and Whitworth rifles. SEE: Hutchinson, W.N.

COFFEY, James Charles
Commission on the charges made by A.F. Ball against the magistracy of Dungannon. Report, 13 Nov 1871. 1872 C.482 xx. Irish Secretary's Office.

Report on the qualification and fitness of Francis M'Keon to be on the roll of the magistracy for the Court of Leitrim. 29 June 1870. 1870 C.178 lvii. Irish Secretary's Office.

COFFIN, Edward Pine
Commission to investigate certain acts of fraud and abuse in connection with the funds of the Commission for Improvement of the Navigation of the River Shannon. Report, 30 Nov 1847. 1847/8 (251) lvii. Treasury.

COHEN, Benjamin Louis
Select committee on gas companies' Metropolitan charges. Report, 4 Aug 1898. 1898 (359) x; (FP Gas, 6).

COKE, Daniel Parker
Committee on law between masters and servants. Report, 8 May 1801. 1801 (62) iii.

Select committee on framework-knitters' petitions. Report, 27 May 1812. 1812 (247) ii.
    2nd report, 16 July 1812. 1812 (349) ii.

COLBORNE, *Bn.* SEE:
Ridley-Colborne, Nicholas William, *1st Bn. Colborne.*

COLCHESTER, *Bn.* SEE:
Abbot, Charles, *1st Bn. Colchester* (1757-1829).
Abbot, Charles, *2nd Bn. Colchester* (1798-1867).

COLE, Henry, *Sir*
Reports on the Paris Universal Exhibition, 1867.
    Vol.1: Report of the executive commission. 15 July 1868. 1867/8 [3968] xxx, pt.1.
    Vol.2-5: Reports on products and apparatus. 1867/8 [3968-I-IV] xxx, pt.1-3.
    Vol.6: Returns relative to the new order of award. 1867/8 [3969] xxx, pt.3.
    Index to reports. 1868/9 [4195] xxiii. Privy Council.

Special report on the annual international exhibitions of the years 1871, 1872, 1873 and 1874. 6 May 1875. 1878/9 C.2379 xxi. Commission for the Exhibition of 1851.

COLEBROOKE, Thomas Edward, *Sir*
Royal commission on endowed schools and hospitals in Scotland
    1st report, 1873 C.755 xxvii.
    2nd report, Ev. 1 May 1874. 1874 C.976 xvii.
    3rd report, 15 Feb 1875. 1875 C.1123 xxix.

COLEBROOKE, William M.G.
Commission of inquiry at the Cape of Good Hope. Report on Memorial and petition of Mr. Cooke on the disposal of prize slaves by Mr. Blair. 13 Dec 1826. 1826/7 (42) xxi; (Slave Trade, 71).

Commission of inquiry on Ceylon
    Reports on the administration and revenues of the government. 13 March 1832. 1831/2 (274) xxxii.
    Report of the judicial establishment and procedure. 13 March 1832. 1831/2 (274) xxxii.
    Report on revenues of Ceylon. 13 March 1832. 1831/2 (274) xxxii. Colonial Department.

Commission of inquiry on the slave trade at Mauritius. Report, 1 June 1829. 1829 (292) xxv; (Slave Trade, 76).

COLEMAN, John
Royal commission on agriculture. Reports on Northumberland, Lancashire and Cheshire. 1 Sept 1881. 1882 C.3375-V xv; (Agriculture, 19). SEE ALSO: Gordon-Lennox, Charles Henry, *6th D. Richmond.*

COLERIDGE, John Duke, *1st Bn. Coleridge*
Committee on the central office of the Supreme Court of Judicature. Report, 22 March 1887, 1887 (181) lxvii; (Legal Administration, 18). Lord Chancellor's Office.

Report from the committee of judges on assizes and sessions. 1 May 1878. 1878 (311) lxiii; (Legal Administration, 16). Lord Chancellor's Office.

Select committee (HL) on the Bills of Sale Act (1878) Amendment Bill. Report, 21 July 1882. HL 1882 (189) vii.

COLERIDGE, John Taylor, *Sir*
Commission on the expediency of bringing together all the superior courts of law and equity, *etc.* Report, 3 July 1860. 1860 [2710] xxxi.

COLLET, C.E.
Report on the money wages of indoor domestic servants. April 1899. 1899 C.9346 xcii. Board of Trade, Labour Department.

COLLIER, Robert, *2nd Bn. Monkswell*
Select committee (HL) on the Copyright Bill. Report, 9 Aug 1899. HL 1899 (362) viii.

Select committee (HL) on the Copyright Bill and the Copyright (Artistic) Bill. Report, 24 July 1899. HL 1899 (178) x.

Select committee (HL) on the Copyright (Amendment) Bill. Report, 16 July 1897. HL 1897 (163) ix; HC repr. 1897 (385) x.

COLLINGS, Jesse
Departmental committee on friendly societies (shop clubs). Report, 8 March 1899. 1899 C.9203 xxxiii.

Select committee on fire brigades. Report, 25 July 1899. 1899 (303) ix.

Select committee on petroleum, 1897. SEE: Mundella, A.J.

Select committee on petroleum. Report, 13 July 1898. 1898 (299) xi.

COLLINGWOOD, Edward
Committee on the petitions concerning the harbours of Rye and Dover. Report, 13 Dec 1756. (Reps. 1731-1800, nos.4 and 5, vol.1).

COLLINS, Arthur Hammond
Royal commission on corrupt practices in the City of Chester. Report, 14 March 1881. 1881 C.2824 xl.

COLLINSON, R.
Committee on lights of fishing vessels
Report, 19 Feb 1880. 1880 C.2508 lxv.
Report, 1881 (78) lxxxii.
Further report, April 1881. 1881 (187) lxxxii.
Board of Trade *and* Admiralty. SEE ALSO: Murray, D.

COLONSAY, Bn. SEE:
McNeill, Duncan, *Bn. Colonsay.*

COLQUHOUN, J.N.
Committee of inquiry into the capabilities of the mercantile steam navy for purposes of war. Reports, 15 Nov 1852, 12 March 1853. 1852/3 (687) lxi. Board of Ordnance.

COLQUHOUN-CAMPBELL, Archibald
Committee respecting the stock fund of the Court of Session. Report, 4 May 1808. 1808 (199) ii.

COLVILLE, Charles Robert William, *1st Vct. Colville of Culross*
Select committee (HL) on the jubilee service in Westminster Abbey. 1st and 2nd reports, 9 and 20 June 1887. HL 1887 (114), (130) ix.

COLVILLE, Bn. [Peerage claim]. SEE:
Cooper, C.A.

COLVILLE, James William
Commission of inquiry into the defalcations of Sir T.E.M. Turton, late Registrar of the Supreme Court of Calcutta. Report, 25 Jan 1849. 1849 (417) xxxix. East India Office. SEE ALSO: Roebuck, John A.

COMPTON, Spencer Joshua Alwyne, *2nd M. Northampton*
Committee on papers relating to African forts. Report, 13 June 1816. 1816 (470) iv; (Africa, 1).

Select committee on papers relating to African forts. Report, 26 June 1816. 1816 (506) vii; (Africa, 1).

CONEYS, Thomas
Commission of legal inquiry on the case of the Indians at Honduras. Report, 10 July 1828. 1828 (522) xxvi; (Slave Trade, 75).

CONGREVE, William, *Sir*
State of the gas works in the Metropolis. Report, Jan 1822 and further report and tables, 26 March 1823. 1823 (239) v.

CONNELLAN, J. Corry
Report on the escape of James Stephens from Richmond Bridewell. 7 Dec 1865. 1866 (147) lviii; (CP Prisons, 21). Irish Secretary's Office.

CONNOLLY, W.P.J.
Committee on the proceedings of charitable loan societies in Ireland. Report, 5 Dec 1896. 1897 C.8381 xvii. Loan Fund Board for Ireland.

CONWAY, Francis Seymour, *1st M. Hertford*
Committee on transportation of felons and other offenders. Report 28 July 1785. CJ, vol.40, p.954; (Reps., 1731-1800, no.71, vol.7).

Committee on the usage of Parliament to interpose touching on discretionary powers vested in servants of the Crown or any body of men for public purposes. Report, 12 Feb 1784. (Reps., 1731-1800, no.57, vol.6)

CONYNGHAM, Francis Nathaniel, *2nd M. Conyngham*
Commission of Post Office Inquiry
Report: Postal arrangements between France and G.B. 20 July 1835. 1835 (416) xlviii.
2nd report: Contract for mail coaches. 22 June 1835. 1835 (313) xlviii.

Commission on the public offices on the civil list establishment. Report. 1873 [72] xxiv, pt.1; (GO Civil Service, 1).

COODE, George
Papers on the consolidation of the statutes. 1853. 1854 (438) xxiv. Lord Chancellor's Office.

Report on fire insurance duties in England and Wales. 29 Nov 1856. 1857, session 1 [2168] iii; (Insurance, 3). Treasury.

Revised report on fire insurance duties. 4 March 1863. 1863 [3118] xxvi; (Insurance, 3). Exchequer.

Report on the state of popular education in the specimen manufacturing districts of Dudley, Wolstanton, Newcastle-under-Lyne and Stoke-upon-Trent. 26 Aug 1859. *In* 1861 [2794-II] xxi, pt.2; (Education, 4).

COODE, John
Report on Wexford harbour improvements. 27 Dec 1859. 1860 (148) lxii. Admiralty.

COOKE, Anthony Charles
Routes in Abyssinia. 1868. 1867/8 [3964] xliv. War Office.

COOKE, D.P. SEE:
Coke, D.P.

COOKE, George
Committee on laws respecting bankrupts. Report, 12 March 1773. CJ, vol.28, p.602.

COOKE, Launcelot
Commission of inquiry at the Cape of Good Hope. SEE: Bigge, John Thomas.

COOPE, Octavius Edward
Select committee on Thames flood prevention. Report, 27 July 1877. 1877 (367) xvii.

COOPER, Anthony Ashley, *7th E. Shaftesbury*
Commission on lunacy
Report. HL 1844 xxvi (unnumbered command paper); London, Bradbury and Evans, 1844. 274p.
Statistical appendix. 8 Aug 1844. 1844 (621) xviii.
Supplemental report, relative to the general condition of the insane in Wales. 25 Aug 1844. HL 1844 xxvi (unnumbered command paper); London, Bradbury and Evans, 1844. 61p.
Further report. 24 June 1847. HL 1847 xxxvi (unnumbered command paper); HC repr. 1847/8 [858] xxxii. Lord Chancellor's Office.

Report of the commission in lunacy on the state and management of Bethlehem Hospital. 7 Feb 1852. 1852/3 (75) xlix; (HE Mental, 6).

Select committee on the Durham City election petitions. Min. of proc., ev. 14 July 1843. 1843 (433) vi.

Report on the epidemic cholera of 1841 and 1849. 14 Aug 1850. 1850 [1273], [1274], [1275] xxi;

(HE Infectious Diseases, 1). General Board of Health.

Report on a general scheme of extramural sepulture for country towns. 2 April 1851. 1851 [1348] xxiii; General Board of Health.

Report on the Haydock Lodge Lunatic Asylum. 20 Jan 1847. 1847 (147) xlix; (HE Mental, 6). Commission in Lunacy, Home Department.

Report on the present conditions of Broadmoor criminal lunatic asylum and its inmates. 31 March 1864. 1864 (216) xlix. Commission in Lunacy.

Report on quarantine
    Report, 1849. 1849 [1070] xxiv.
    2nd report: Yellow fever, 7 April 1852. 1852 [1473] xx.
    Appendix V: Report on the plague of Malta in 1813. 8 July 1852. 1853/4 [1869] xlv. General Board of Health.

Select committee on the Longford election petition. Proc. 26 April 1842. 1842 (208) vi.

Select committee on the Lyme Regis election petition. Min. of ev. 9 March 1848. 1847/8 (162) xiv.

Select committee on medical poor relief
    1st report, 22 May 1844. 1844 (312) ix.
    2nd report, 17 June 1844. 1844 (387) ix.
    3rd report, 29 July 1844. 1844 (531) ix; (Health, 1)

Select committee on mills and factories
    1st report, 3 April 1840. 1840 (203) x.
    2nd report, 13 April 1840. 1840 (227) x.
    3rd report, 20 May 1840. 1840 (314) x.
    4th report, 29 May 1840. 1840 (334) x.
    5th report, 26 June 1840. 1840 (419) x.
    6th report, 17 July 1840. 1840 (504) x; (IR Factories, 1).

Select committee on mills and factories. Report, 18 Feb 1841. 1841 (56) ix; (IR Factories, 1).

Select committee on the Newcastle-under-Lyme election petition (No.2). Min. of ev. 9 Aug 1842. 1842 (549) viii.

Select committee on payment of wages. Report, 20 July 1842. 1842 (471) ix.

COOPER, Cropley Ashley, *6th E. Shaftesbury*

Committee (HL) on Chimney Sweepers Regulation Bill. Report, 15 May 1818. HL 1818 (61) xci.

Committee (HL) on Deptford Pier Junction Railway Bill. Report, 16 June 1836. HL 1836 (143) xii.

Committee (HL) on the Eastern Counties Railway Bill. Report, 23 June 1836. HL 1836 (169) xii.

Committee (HL) on gas street lighting in the Metropolis. Min. of ev. 1 May 1817. HL 1817 (32) lxxxvii.

Committee (HL) on the Hayle Railway Bill. Report, 20 June 1836. HL 1836 (156) xii.

Committee (HL) on the London and Croydon Railway Bill. Report, 30 June 1836. HL 1836 (188) xii.

Committee (HL) on the London and Dover (South Eastern) Railway Bill. Report, 14 June 1836. HL 1836 (136) xii.

Committee (HL) on the Merthyr Tydfil and Cardiff Railway Bill. Report, 16 June 1836. HL 1836 (146) xii.

Committee (HL) on the Newcastle-upon-Tyne and North Shields Railway Bill. Report, 16 June 1836. HL 1836 (144) xii.

Committee (HL) on the North of England Railway Bill. Report, 17 June 1836. HL 1836 (150) xii.

Committee (HL) on the offices of Clerk of the Parliament, and Black Rod.
    Report, 4 June 1824. HL 1824 (101) clxviii.
    2nd report, 21 June 1824. HL 1824 (132) clxviii.
    1st and 2nd reports repr. HL 1825 (206) cxcii.

Committee on precedents for divorce bills expired in one session and renewed in another. Report, 21 May 1829. HL 1829 (66) ccxliv.

Committee (HL) on precedents of lists of witnesses for bills of attainer, impeachment, *etc.* Report, 14 July 1820. HL 1820 (96) cxvii.

Committee (HL) on precedents for the reversal of attainders
    Report, 31 May 1824. HL 1824 (86) clxviii.
    Addenda. HL 1824 (102) clxviii.

Committee (HL) on the Preston and Longridge Railway Bill. Report, 28 June 1836. HL 1836 (180) xii.

Committee for privileges (HL). Airth claim of peerage. Min. of ev. 9 July 1839. HL 1839 (162) xvii.

Committee of privileges (HL). Anglesey claim of peerage. Report, 11 May 1819. HL 1819 (65) ci.

Committee of privileges (HL). Annandale claim of peerage.
    Ev. 28 April, 19 May 1825. HL 1825 (128) cxcvi; repr. HL 1844 (100) xvi.
    Ev. 6 March to 25 May 1826. HL 1826 (34) ccix.
    Ev. 7 May 1830 to 30 June 1834. HL 1834 (56) xxiii, pt.1.
    Ev. 14 May to 11 June 1844. HL 1844 (101) xvi.

Committee of privileges (HL). Athenry claim of peerage. Ev. 10 March 1836. HL 1836 (17) xxix.

Committee of privileges (HL). Barry claim of peerage. Ev. 16 to 20 June 1825. HL 1825 (215) cxcvi.

Committee of privileges (HL). Beaumont claim of peerage. Min. of ev. 19 March 1840. HL 1840 (64) xxi. SEE ALSO: De Grey, Thomas, *2nd Bn. Walsingham.*

Committee of privileges (HL). Berkeley claim of peerage. Ev. and report, 19 June 1829. HL 1829 (115) cclxi.

Committee of privileges (HL). Berners claim of peerage. Ev. 9 March 1832. HL 1831/2 (73) cccxi.

Committee of privileges (HL). Bloomfield claim to vote at the election of Irish peers. Ev. 8 May 1849. HL 1849 (109) xxvi.

Committee of privileges (HL). Borthwick claim of peerage. Ev. 14, 26 July 1814. HL 1814/5 (49) lxxvi.

Committee of privileges (HL). Braye claim of peerage.
    Ev. 25 March 1836. HL 1836 (40) xxix.
    Min. of ev. 7 to 27 March 1837. HL 1837/8 (91) xix.
    Min. of ev., proc. 3 May 1838 to 28 June 1839. HL 1839 (171) xvii.

Committee of privileges (HL). Buttevant claim of peerage. Ev. 16 June 1825. HL 1825 (215) cxcvi.

Committee of privileges (HL). Camoys claim of peerage.
    Min. of ev. 6 April 1838. HL 1837/8 (118) xix.
    Min. of ev., proc. 14 Aug 1838 to 28 June 1839. HL 1839 (167) xvii.

Committee of privileges (HL). Crawfurd and Lindsay claim of peerage
    Ev. 12 June 1845. HL 1845 (206) xvii.
    Ev. 22 June, 5 July 1847. HL 1847 (231) xxii.
    Ev. 16 May to 11 Aug 1848. HL 1847/8 (135) xxii.

Committee of privileges (HL). Colville claim to vote at the elections of Scotch peers. Ev. 22 Feb 1850. HL 1850 (36) xxi.

COOPER, Cropley Ashley, *6th E. Shaftesbury* (continued)
Committee of privileges (HL). Darnley claim to vote at the election of Irish peers. Ev. 31 July 1849. HL 1849 (239) xxvi.

Committee of privileges (HL). De L'Isle claim of peerage.
    Ev. 17 June 1824. HL 1824 (140) clxxiii.
    Ev. 6 to 28 June 1825. HL 1825 (177) cxcvi.
    Ev. 13 April to 25 May 1826. HL 1826 (59) ccix.

Committee of privileges (HL). Dufferin and Claneboye claim to vote at the election of Irish peers. Ev. 18 July 1848. HL 1847/8 (245) xxii.

Committee of privileges (HL). Dunsandle and Clanconal claim to vote at the election of Irish peers. Ev. 12 July 1849. HL 1849 (211) xxvi.

Committee of privileges (HL). Dunsany claim of peerage. Min. of ev. 4 June 1823. HL 1823 (49) clvi.

Committee of privileges (HL). Fitzwalter claim to peerage.
    Min. of ev. 28 June 1842. HL 1842 (159) xvi.
    Ev. 9 May 1843. HL 1843 (104) xix.
    Ev. 18 March 1844. HL 1844 (51) xvi.

Committee of privileges (HL). Gardner claim of peerage
    Ev. 15 June 1825. HL 1825 (175) cxcvi.
    Ev. 2 March, 6 April 1826. HL 1826 (32) ccix.

Committee of privileges (HL). Grandison claim of peerage. Ev. 16 June 1829. HL 1829 (102) cclxi.

Committee of privileges (HL). Hastings claim of peerage.
    Min. of ev. 16 July 1840. HL 1840 (211) xxi.
    Ev. 25 March to 4 May 1841. HL 1841 (55) xx.

Committee of privileges (HL). Herries claim of peerage. Ev. 8 May to 19 July 1849. HL 1849 (108) xxvi.

Committee of privileges (HL). Huntley claim of peerage. Min. of ev. 8 June 1838. HL 1837/8 (197) xix.

Committee of privileges (HL). Kellie claim of peerage.
    Ev. 17 May 1832. HL 1831/2 (133) cccxi.
    Ev. 25 July 1834. HL 1834 (212) xxiii, pt.1.
    Ev. 28 Aug, 2 Sept 1835. HL 1835 (206) xlv.

Committee of privileges (HL). Lanesborough claim to vote at the election of Irish peers. Ev. 11 April 1841. HL 1847/8 (96) xxii.

Committee of privileges (HL). Leigh claim of peerage.
    Min. of ev. 3 June 1828. HL 1828 (117) ccxxxix.
    Ev. 18 May to 11 June 1829. HL 1829 (59) cclxi.

Committee of privileges (HL). Lovat claim of peerage.
    Min. of ev. 21 June 1827. HL 1826/7 (178) ccxxii.
    Report of ev. before judges in Scotland. 5 May 1826. HL 1826/7 (93) ccxxii.
    Min. of ev. 29 June 1831 to 24 April 1855. HL 1854/5 (G) xxi.

Committee of privileges (HL). Marchmont claim of peerage.
    Min. of ev. 23 May 1822. HL 1822 (40) cxli; repr. HL 1824 (40) clvi.
    Min. of ev. 20 March 1838. HL 1837/8 (113) xix.
    Min. of ev. 18 June 1839. HL 1839 (141) xvii.
    Min. of ev. 19 March and 16 June 1840. HL 1840 (67) xxi.
    Ev. 18 Feb 1842. HL 1842 (33) xvi.
    Ev. 8 May 1843. HL 1843 (103) xix.

Committee of privileges (HL). Marmyon claim of peerage.

Min. of ev. 22 April 1818. HL 1818 (47) xcv.
Min. of ev. 21 May 1818 to 11 May 1819. HL 1819 (48) cxi.

Committee of privileges (HL). Mayo claim to vote at the election of Irish peers. Ev. 31 July 1849. HL 1849 (294) xxvi.

Committee of privileges (HL). Molesworth claim to vote at election of Irish representative peers. Min. of ev. 17 May 1821. HL 1821 (76) cxxvii.

Committee of privileges (HL). Monck claim to vote at the election of Irish peers. 18 May 1849. HL 1849 (121) xxvi.

Committee of privileges (HL). Netterville claim of peerage. SEE: Freeman-Mitford, John Thomas, *2nd Bn. Redesdale.*

Committee of privileges (HL). North claim of peerage. Min. of ev. 9 May 1837. HL 1837 (72) xvi.

Committee of privileges (HL). Nugent of Riverston claim to peerage. Min. of ev. 30 July 1839. HL 1839 (208) xvii.

Committee of privileges (HL). Ormonde claim to vote at the election of Irish representative peers. Min. of ev. 14 June 1821. HL 1821 (104) cxxvii.

Committee of privileges (HL). Perth claim of peerage.
    Ev. 23, 30 July 1846. HL 1846 (233) xxi.
    Ev. 20 April to 17 June 1847. HL 1847 (107) xxii.
    Ev. 11 Aug 1848. HL 1847/8 (326) xxii.

Committee of privileges (HL). Polwarth claim of peerage.
    Min. of ev. 14 May 1818. HL 1818 (101) xcvi.
    Ev. 8 Aug 1831. HL 1831 (45) ccxciv.

Committee of privileges (HL). Precedents on arrest of peers not having seats in the HL (arrest of *Vct.* Hawarden). Report, 11 Feb 1828. HL 1828 (6) ccxxxvii.

Committee of privileges (HL). Precedents of peers advanced to higher dignity entering their proxies according to their former titles. 13 May 1817. HL 1817 (42) lxxxiv.

Committee of privileges (HL). Rokeby claim of peerage. Ev. 28 May 1830. HL 1830 (153) cclxxix.

Committee of privileges (HL). Roscommon claim of peerage.
    Min. of ev. 17 July 1823. HL 1823 (122) clvi.
    Ev. 5 April to 24 May 1824. HL 1824 (62) clxxiii.
    Ev. 24 March to 2 June 1825. HL 1825 (46) cxcvi.
    Ev. 27 April 1826. HL 1826 (116) ccix.
    Ev. 2 March to 7 June 1827. HL 1826/7 (40) ccxxii.
    Ev. Session 1828. HL 1828 (138) ccxxxix.
    Min. of ev. 21 May 1828. HL 1828 (138) ccxxxix.

Committee of privileges (HL). Saye and Sele claim of peerage.
    Ev. 21 July 1847. HL 1847 (316) xxii.
    Ev. 11 April to 16 May 1848. HL 1847/8 (101) xxii.

Committee of privileges (HL). Slane claim of peerage.
    Ev. 19 May 1830. HL 1830 (157) cclxxix.
    Ev. 20 July to 31 Aug 1831. HL 1831 (41) ccxciv.
    Ev. 27 Feb to April 1832. HL 1831/2 (75) cccxi.

Committee of privileges (HL). Southesk claim of peerage. Ev. 7 Aug 1848. HL 1847/8 (283) xxii.

Committee of privileges (HL). Stafford claim of peerage. Ev. 17 June 1825. HL 1825 (129) cxcvi.

Committee of privileges (HL). Strathmore claim

of peerage. Ev. 5 April to 22 May 1821. HL 1821 (39) cxxvii.

Committee of privileges (HL). Sussex claim of peerage. Ev. 14 June 1844. HL 1844 (142) xvi.

Committee of privileges (HL). Tracy claim of peerage.
Ev. 7 May, 18 June 1839. HL 1841 (46) xx.
Ev. 21 March 1843. HL 1843 (59) xix.
Ev. 23 March to 15 June 1847. HL 1847 (62) xxii.
Ev. 22 June to 3 Aug 1848. HL 1847/8 (156) xxii.
Ev. 8 May 1849. HL 1849 (107) xxvi.

Committee of privileges (HL). Vaux claim of peerage. Ev. 25 March 1836. HL 1836 (41) xxix.

Committee of privileges (HL). Wharton claim of peerage.
Ev. 16 April 1844. HL 1844 (66) xvii.
Ev. 10 June 1845. HL 1845 (202) xvii.

Committee (HL) on the Thames Haven Railway and Dock Bill. Report, 20 June 1836. HL 1836 (157) xii.

Committee on the York and North Midland Railway Bill. Report, 16 June 1836. HL 1836 (145) xii.

Select committee (HL) on the administration of oaths.
Report, 9 Aug 1842. HL 1842 (267) xvi.
Min. of ev. 9 Aug 1842. HL 1842 (267) xvi; repr. HL 1849 (141) xxvii.

Select committee (HL) on the accommodation of the HL.
1st report, 24 May 1849. HL 1849 (127) xxvii.
2nd report, 27 July 1849. HL 1849 (127-II) xxvii.

Select committee (HL) on the business of the HL. Report, 29 June 1837. HL 1837 (155) xx.

Select committee (HL) on the dignity of a peer. SEE: Freeman-Mitford, John Thomas, *1st E. Redesdale.*

Select committee (HL) on dwellings for labouring classes. Report, 25 April 1853. HL 1852/3 (157) xxxi.

Select committee (HL) on the expenses of witnesses and others on the Sudbury Disfranchisement Bill. Report, 11 April 1843. HL 1843 (83) xx.

Select committee (HL) on fees and charges on private bills. Report, 12 June 1827. HL 1826/7 (114) ccxix.

Select committee (HL) on the Needlewomen Limitations of Hours of Labour Bill.
Min. of ev. 22 June 1855. HL 1854/5 (167) xxii.
Proc. 10 July 1855. HL 1854/5 (215) xxii.

Secret committee (HL) on papers (sealed up) presented by command of the Prince Regent. Report, 6 March 1818. HL 1818 (95) iii.

Secret committee (HL) on the Office of the Clerk of the Crown in Chancery. Report, 30 March 1844. HL 1844 (58) xix.

Select committee (HL) on the Parliament Office and Office of the Black Rod.
1st report, 4 June 1824. HL 1824 (101) clxvii.
2nd report, 21 June 1824. HL 1824 (132) clxviii; both repr. HL 1825 (1) cxcii.

Select committee (HL) on the Parliament Office. Report, 17 and 16 May 1826. HL 1826/7 (57) ccxix.

Select committee (HL) on the permanent accommodation of the Houses of Parliament. Report, 12 June 1835. HL 1835 (73) xxviii.

Select committee (HL) on the Office of the Clerk of the Parliaments. Report, 25 July 1828. HL 1828 (181) ccxxxvii.

Select committee (HL) on the Office of the Clerk of the Parliaments. Report, 19 June 1829. HL 1829 (105) ccxliv.

Select committee (HL) on the Parliament Office. Printing of papers.
Report, 11 March 1834. HL 1834 (21) xxi.
2nd report, 18 April 1834. HL 1834 (55) xxi.
3rd report, 12 Aug 1834. HL 1834 (222) xxi.

Select committee (HL) on the Parliament Office. Report, 21 July 1847. HL 1847 (320) xxv.

Select committee (HL) on the petition of the Oxford, Worcester and Wolverhampton Railway Co. Report, 23 July 1850. HL 1850 (276) xxiii.

Select committee (HL) on the plan for the ventilation and warming the Houses of Parliament. Report, 4 Aug 1842. HL 1842 (251) xvi.

Select committee (HL) on the Prisoners Defence Bill.
Min. of ev. 17 July 1835. HL 1835 (130) xlvi.
Min. of ev. Session 1836. HL 1836 (119) xxxii.

Select committee (HL) on the progress of the building of the Houses of Parliament.
1st report. HL 1844 (46) xix; HC repr. 1844 (269) vi.
2nd report. HL 1844 (46) xix; HC repr. 1844 (629) vi.

Select committee (HL) on the promulgation of the statutes. Min. of ev. 24 March 1836. HL 1836 (35) ix; HC repr. 1836 (313) xxi.

Select committee (HL) on the Stafford Bribery Bill. Report, 8 May 1833. HL 1833 (43) cccxviii.

Select committee (HL) on the Sheffield Gas Bill. Min. of ev. 10 July 1835. HL 1835 (108) xliv.

Select committee (HL) on the state and progress of railway bills in Parliament. Report, 26 June 1845. HL 1845 (225) xix; HC repr. 1845 (427) x.

Select committee (HL) on the Parliament Office and Office of the Gentleman Usher of the Black Rod.
1st report, 23 April 1850. HL 1850 (120) xxiii.
2nd report, 19 July 1850. HL 1850 (267) xxiii.

Select committee on the Warwick Borough Bill. Ev. 5 May to 5 Aug 1834. HL 1834 (69) xxiv.

COOPER, Edward
Select committee on grand jury presentments of Ireland. Report, 12 June 1815. 1814/5 (283) vi.

COOPER, Synge
Select committee on Irish Grand Jury presentments
Report, 21 May 1816. 1816 (374) ix.
2nd report, 10 June 1816. 1816 (435) ix.

COOPER-KEY, Astley SEE:
Key, Astley Cooper.

COPE, C.W.
Committee of artists employed in the decoration of Westminster Palace. Report, 6 July 1871. 1872 (19) xlvi. Office of Works.

COPINGER, Christopher
Commission of inquiry into the state of the municipal affairs of the Borough of Belfast.
Report, 1859, session 1 [2470] xii; repr. 1859, session 2 [2470] x.
Min. of ev. and plans. 1859, session 2 [2526] x.

COPLEY, John Singleton, *1st Bn. Lyndhurst*
Select committee (HL) on the allegations of the Baron De Bode's petition. Report, 28 June 1852. HL 1852 (194) xix; HC repr. 1860 (482) xxii.

Select committee (HL) on appointment of sheriffs in Ireland. Report, 3 Aug 1838. HL 1837/8 (330) xxi.

Select committee (HL) on the Charitable Trusts Bill. Min. of ev. 12 June 1845. HL 1845 (204) xviii.

Select committee (HL) on the Divorce and Matrimonial Causes Bill and on the law and practice of divorce. Report, 24 June 1856. HL 1856 (181) xxiv.

Select committee on the petitions on the law of debtor and creditor. SEE: Brougham, Henry, *Bn. Brougham and Vaux.*

Select committee (HL) on the Privy Council Appellate Jurisdiction Act Amendment Bill. Report, 25 June 1844. HL 1844 (84) xix.

CORBALLIS, John R.
Report on the embezzlement of several sums of money by E.W. Mathews, late accountant to the Board of Charitable Donations and Bequests for Ireland. 10 April 1849. 1850 (454) xxv.

CORBETT, Uvedale
Local government and taxation of towns inquiry commission, Ireland.
　Part I. General. 15 Feb 1877. 1877 C.1696 xxxix.
　Part II. Report: Belfast, Antrim and Wicklow. 14 May 1877. 1877 C.1755 xl.
　Part III. Report and supplement, 28 June 1877. 1877 C.1787 xl. Irish Secretary's Office.

Report on the Metropolitan workhouses. 18 Jan 1867. 1867 (18) lx. Poor Law Board.

CORDER, James
Report on the progress of crime, particularly in reference to infanticide. 17 May 1838. *In* 1837/8 [147] xxviii.

CORK AND ORRERY, *E.* SEE:
Boyle, Richard Edmund St. Lawrence, *9th E. Cork.*

CORNEWALL, George, *Sir*
Select committee on petitions complaining of an undue election and return for the Borough of Aylesbury. Report, 29 Feb and 4 March 1804. 1803/4 (25) ii.

CORRIGAN, D.J.
Report on the condition and treatment of infant children in the workhouse of the North Dublin Union. SEE: Hall, Richard.

CORRY, Somerset Richard Lowry SEE:
Lowry-Corry, Somerset Richard, *4th E. Belmore.*

CORT, Coningsby
Committee on petition. SEE: Giddy, D.

COTES, John
Committee on the separate incorporation of surgeons Report, 27 Feb 1774. CJ vol.24, p.729, 738, 778

COTTENHAM, *E.* SEE:
Pepys, Charles Christopher, *1st E. Cottenham.*

COTTON, Arthur T.
Report on the irrigation of the Delta of the Godavery River. 17 April 1845. 1850 (127) xli. India Office.

Report on the irrigation, *etc.* of the Rajahmundry district of India. Report, 12 Aug 1844. 1850 (127) xli. India Office.

Report on sugar cultivation in India. 27 Aug 1845. 1850 (127) xli. India Office.

COTTON, Charles P.
Committee on municipal boundaries in Ireland.
　Report, part 1. Ev. 1880. 1880 C.2725 xxx.
　Report, part 2. 1881. 1881 C.2827 l.
　Report, part 3. 21 June 1881. 1881 C.3089 l.
　Report, part 4: Cork and Belfast. 27 June 1881. 1881 C.3089-II l. Irish Secretary's Office.

COUGH, Richard, *Sir*
Committee on the charges laid against the Gaekwar of Baroda. Proc., and appendix. 1875 C.1272 lvi. India Office.

COURTENAY, *Vct.* SEE:
Courtenay, William, *11th E. Devon* (1777-1859)
Courtenay, William Reginald, *12th E. Devon* (1807-1888).

COURTENAY, Thomas Peregrine
Committee on Lascars and other Asiatic seamen. Report, 11 July 1815. 1814/5 (471) iii.

Committee on Mr. Lee's patent petition. Report, 1 March 1813. 1812/3 (67) iii.

Committee on petitions of creditors of the Nabob of the Carnatic. Report, 5 June 1818. 1818 (407) vi.

Select committee on laws relating to prisons. Report, 7 May 1822. 1822 (300) iv; (CP Prisons, 8).

Select committee on laws respecting friendly societies. Report, 5 July 1825. 1825 (522) iv.

Select committee on laws respecting friendly societies. Report, 29 June 1827. 1826/7 (558) iii; (Insurance, 1).

Select committee on poor rate returns. Report, 15 July 1822. 1822 (556) v.

Select committee on poor rate returns. Report, 16 July 1823. 1823 (570) v.

Select committee on poor rate returns. Report, 15 June 1824. 1824 (420) vi.

Select committee on poor rate returns. Report, 20 May 1825. 1825 (334) iv.

Select committee on the poor rate returns of 1825. Report, 1 May 1826. 1826 (330) iii.

Select committee on the state of the West Indies. Report, 13 April 1832. 1831/2 (381) xx; (West Indies, 2).

COURTENAY, William, *11th E. Devon*
Commission on accommodation of public departments. SEE: Manners, John.

Commission appointed to inquire into the Exchequer bills forgery. Report, 2 Aug 1842. 1842 [409] xviii; (National Finance, 2).

Commission appointed to inquire into the occupation of land in Ireland.
　Report, 14 Feb 1845. 1845 [606], [616], [657], [672], [673] xix, xx, xxi, xxii.
　Digest of ev. pt.1. 1845 [605] xix.
　Digest of ev. 1847. HL 1847 xxxv.

Select committee on Bankruptcy Court. Report, 27 May 1819. 1819 (370) ii.

Select committee (HL) on carriage of passengers

on the River Thames. Report, 15 July 1837. HL 1837 (245) xx; HC repr. 1837/8 (563) xxiii.

Select committee (HL) on the 3rd report of the commission on criminal law, larceny. Report, 22 June 1838. HL 1837/8 (224) xxi.

Select committee (HL) on Grant's patent for ventilation. Report, 4 Aug 1846. HL 1846 (261) xxvi; repr. HL 1852/3 (17) xxxi. SEE ALSO: Stapleton, Miles Thomas, *1st Bn. Beaumont*.

Select committee (HL) on the state of the islands of New Zealand. Report, 3 April 1838. HL 1837/8 (123) xxi; HC repr. 1837/8 (680) xxi; (New Zealand, 1).

COURTENAY, William Reginald, *12th E. Devon*

Commission on the treatment of treason-felony convicts in English prisons. Report, 20 Sept 1870. 2 pts. 1871 C.319 xxxii; (CP Prisons, 21). Home Department.

Committee of enquiry on the Poor Law Board. Report, 20 July 1853. 1854 [1715] xxvii. Treasury.

Report on the petition on improper admission of an aged pauper into the workhouse of the Weymouth Union. 30 May 1849. 1849 (388), (578) xlvii. Poor Law Board.

Select committee on Andover Union. Report, 20 Aug 1846. 1846 (663) v, parts 1 and 2.

Select committee on the Chester County (Northern Division) election petition. Min. of ev. 1 Aug 1848. 1847/8 (567) xi.

Select committee on classification of railway bills, 1847. SEE: Wilson-Patten, John.

Select committee on the Horsham election petition. Min. of ev. 24 March 1848. 1847/8 (200) xii.

Select committee (HL) on the Poor Relief Bill. Report, 22 May 1868. HL 1867/8 (110) xxx.

Select committee on railway classification, 1846. SEE: Wilson-Patten, John.

COURTNEY, Leonard Henry

Commission on criminal lunacy. Report, May 1882. 1882 C.3418 xxxii; (HE Mental, 8).

Committee on the census. Report, 23 May 1890. 1890 C.6071 lviii. Treasury.

Committee of inquiry on the Mercantile Marine Fund. Report, 22 July 1896. 1896 C.8167 xli. Min. of ev. 1896 C.8168 xli. Board of Trade.

Royal commission on the amalgamation of the City and the County of London. Report, 7 Aug 1894. 1894 C.7493 xvii. Min. of ev., *etc.* 1894 C.7493-I xvii. Appendix, index. 1893 C.7493-III xviii.

Select committee on Stationery Office printing contracts, 1895. SEE: Hibbert, John Tomlinson, *Sir*.

Select committee on stationery contracts. Report, 12 June 1896. 1896 (230) xiii; (Industrial Relations, 22).

COURTNEY, Reginald

Report on the transit of animals from Ireland to ports in G.B. Feb 1878. 1878 C.2097 xxv. Veterinary Department of the Privy Council.

COURTNEY, W.

Commission for Post Office inquiry, India. Report, 1 May 1851. 1852/3 (87) lxxvi. East India Office.

COWIE, Robert

Committee on petition on Swedish herrings. SEE: Anderson, J.W., *Sir*.

COWPER, Francis Thomas De Grey, *7th E. Cowper*

Royal commission on the draft charter for the proposed Gresham University in London. Report, 24 Jan 1894. 1893/4 C.7529 xxxi. Min. of ev. 1894 C.7425 xxxiv.

Royal commission on the land acts, Ireland. Report, 21 Feb 1887. 1887 C.4969 xxvi. Separate report by Thomas Knipe. 17 March 1887. 1887 C.5051 xxvi.

COWPER, William Francis

Committee on inquiry into the appropriation of the site of Smithfield and the establishment of a new Metropolitan meat market. Report, 3 July 1856. 1856 [2115] xxxvii. Treasury.

Select committee on the Courts of Justice Building Act (Money) Bill. Min. of ev. 17 July 1861. 1861 (441) xiv.

Select committee on the Courts of Justice Concentration (Site) Bill. Min. of ev. 14 March 1865. 1865 (124) xii.

Select committee on the Inclosure Act. Report, 7 July 1869. 1868/9 (304) x; (Agriculture, 14).

Select committee on labouring poor, allotments of land. Report, 4 July 1843. 1843 (402) vii.

Select committee on Metropolitan Commons Act, 1866, Amendment Bill. Special report. 19 July 1869. 1868/9 (333) x.

Select committee on postal communication between London and Paris, etc. Report, 28 May 1850. 1850 (381) xiv.

Select committee on the Serpentine. Report, 30 March 1860. 1860 (192) xx.

Select committee on the Thames Embankment Bill. Report, 23 June 1862. 1862 (344) xv.

Select committee on the Thames Embankment (North Side) Bill. Report, 28 April 1863. 1863 (219) xii.

Select committee on the Thames Embankment (South Side) Bill. Report, 19 June 1863. 1863 (367) xii.

COWPER-TEMPLE, William Francis

Select committee on the Ecclesiastical Officers and Fees Bill. Report, 16 April 1877. 1877 (159) x.

Select committee on the Wildfowl Protection Bill. Report, 12 July 1872. 1872 (295) xii.

COX, Joseph

Report of inquiry on charges against sub-inspector Boyce of the police station at Dundrum, County Tipperary. 22 Feb 1864. 1864 (236) xlix. Irish Secretary's Office.

COX, Ponsonby

Report on Thames Valley sewerage. 11 Jan 1876. 1876 (184) lxiii; (UA Sanitation, 5). Local Government Board.

COX, Samuel C.

Commission of military inquiry. SEE: Drinkwater, J.

CRADOCK, H.

Report on Berthon's collapsing life boat. 19 May 1854. 1854 (336) xlii. Admiralty.

CRAIG, William Gibson
Committee of inquiry on the Colonial Office. Report, 15 Dec 1854. 1854 [1715] xxvii. Treasury.

Committee of inquiry on the Treasury. Reports, 2 March and 21 May 1849. 1854 [1715] xxvii. Treasury.

Select committee on railway bills classification, 1846. SEE: Wilson-Patten, John.

CRAIK, Henry
Report on Highland schools. 31 Oct 1884. 1884/5 C.4261 xxvi. Scotch Education Department.

CRAMP, William Dawkins
Chemical works committee of inquiry.
    Report on conditions of labour, *etc.* Oct 1893. 1893/4 C.7235 xvii.
    Report on lucifer match works. Oct 1893. 1893/4 C.7236 xvii; (IR Factories, 29-30). Home Department.

Department committee on the conditions of labour in the brass trades. Report. 1896 C.8091 xix; (IR Factories, 31). Home Department.

CRAMPTON, Philip
Commission of health on the epidemics of 1846-1850. Report. 1852/3 [1562] xli; (Famine, 8). Irish Secretary's Office.

CRANBOURNE, *Vct.* SEE:
Gascoyne-Cecil, James Brownlow William, *2nd M. of Salisbury.*

CRANBROOK, *Vct.* SEE:
Gathorne-Hardy, Gathorne, *1st E. Cranbrook.*

CRANWORTH, *Lord* SEE:
Rolfe, Robert Monsey, *Bn. Cranworth.*

CRAUFURD, Edward Henry John
Select committee on the Poor Law in Scotland. Report, 6 July 1869. 1868/9 (301) xi.

Select committee on the Poor Law in Scotland. Report, 18 July 1870. 1870 (357) xi.

Select committee on the Poor Law in Scotland. Report, 3 July 1871. 1871 (329) xi.

CRAUFURD, J.R.
Committee on the means of instruction and employment of soldiers and their children. Report, 31 March 1862. 1863 [3133] xxxii. War Office.

CRAWFORD, E. SEE:
Lindsay, James Ludovic, *26th E. Crawford and 9th Balcarres.*
[Peerage claim]. SEE: Cooper, C.A.

CRAWFORD, Charles S.
Report on an investigation held on the validity of certain claims to vote by proxy at the election for guardians of the North Dublin Union. 6 March 1855. 1854/5 (257) xlvi. Poor Law Commission, Ireland.

CRAWFORD, Robert Wygram
Select committee on East India communications. Report, 20 July 1866. 1866 (428) ix.

Select committee on the Weighing of Grain (Port of London) Bill. Report, 12 July 1864. 1864 (479) viii; repr. 1872 (0.49) xii.

CRAWFORD, William
Committee on the Middlesex County Court Bill. Report, 1838. 1843 (10) xi.

Inquiry by the inspectors of Milbank Prison into the allegations contained in a petition of Edward Baker complaining of certain proceedings on the part of the governor of the prison.
    Min. of proc. 24 July 1846. 1846 (521) xx.
    Supplementary report, 5 Aug 1846. 1846 (575) xx.
    Home Department.

Proceedings connected with the recent dismissal of Rev. C.S. Stanford from his office as Protestant Chaplain of the North Dublin Union. 27 Feb 1852. 1852 (120) xlvi. Poor Law Commission, Ireland.

Report on the system of prison discipline. Jan 1843. 1843 [457] xxv, xxvi; (CP Prisons, 11). Home Department.

Report on the penitentiaries of the United States. 11 Aug 1834. 1834 (593) xlvi; (CP Prisons, 2).

CRICHTON, John Henry, *4th E. Erne*
Committee on the Board of Works, Ireland. Report, 10 June 1878. 1878 C.2060 xxiii. Treasury. SEE ALSO: McKerlie, J.G.

CROGGON, Thomas
Select committee on his imprisonment. SEE: Wortley, J.A.S.

CROKER, John Wilson
Committee on the petition relating to Ardglass harbour. Report, 29 March 1809. 1809 (113) iii.

Report on the port of Dublin. 11 July 1804. 1803/4 (170) v.

CROMPTON, Samuel
Committee on his petition. SEE: Blackburne, John.

CROSS, *Vct.* SEE:
Cross, Richard Assheton, *1st Vct. Cross*

CROSS, John Kynaston
General committee on railway and canal bills, 1868/9, 1870, 1871. SEE: Goldsmid, F.

CROSS, Richard Assheton, *1st Vct. Cross*
Joint committee on electric powers; protective clauses. Report, 13 July 1893. 1893/4 (331) xi; HL 1893/4 (196) x.

Joint committee on electrical energy; generating stations and supply. Report, 23 May 1898. 1898 (213) ix; HL 1898 (75) ix.

Royal commission on the Elementary Education Acts.
    1st report, June 1886. 1886 C.4863 xxv.
    2nd report: Evidence. 1887 C.5056 xxix.
    3rd report: Evidence. 1887 C.5158 xxx.
    Final report, 27 June 1888. 1888 C.5485 xxxv.
    Foreign returns. 1888 C.5485-I xxxv.
    Statistical report. 1888 C.5485-II xxxvi.
    Training colleges. 1888 C.5485-III xxxvi.
    Digest and index of evidence. 1888 C.5329 xxxviii; (Education, 34-39).

Royal commission on prisons in Ireland.
    Preliminary report, 3 Feb 1883. 1883 C.3496 xxxii.
    Reports, 3 Feb 1883 and 1 Aug 1884. 1884/5 C.4233 xxxviii.
    2nd report, 1 Aug 1884. 1884 C.4145 xlii.

Select committee on artizans' and labourers' dwellings improvement. Report, 2 Aug 1881. 1881 (358) vii; (UA Housing, 1).

Select committee on artizans' and labourers' dwellings. Report, 19 June 1882. 1882 (235) vii; (UA Housing, 1)

Select committee on the Church Patronage Bill. SEE: Forster, William Edward.

Select committee on Clare County writ. Report, 8 Aug 1878. 1878 (343) xiii.

Select committee on Clare County writ. Report, 3 April 1879. 1878/9 (130) viii.

Select committee on the Conveyancing and the Settled Land Bills. Reports, 3 and 20 July 1882. 1882 (262) viii.

Select committee (HL) on the Debtors Act. Report, 20 June 1893. HL 1893/4 (156) ix.

Select committee (HL) on the East India Company's charter. Report, 29 June 1852. HL 1852 (88) xix.

Select committee (HL) on the Lord's Day Act.
    Report, 27 June 1895. HL 1895 (178) vi.
    2nd report, 14 July 1896. HL 1896 (196) ix.

Select committee on the Summary Jurisdiction Bill. Report, 29 April 1879. 1878/9 (154) xiii.

CROSSMAN, William
Report on the legation and consular buildings in China and Japan. March 1867. 1867/8 (315) xlviii. Treasury.

Royal commission on the West Indies. Report.
    Part 1: Jamaica. Sept 1883. 1884 C.3840 xlvi.
    Part 2: Grenada, St. Vincent, Tobago and St. Lucia. Feb 1884. 1884 C.3840-I xlvi.
    Part 3: Leeward Islands. Feb 1884. 1884 C.3840-II xlvi.
    Part 4: Supplementary remarks. March 1884. 1884 C.3840-III xlvi; (West Indies, 6).

CUBITT, Thomas
Commission on the fall of the cotton mill at Oldham and part of the prison at Northleach. Report, 28 Feb 1845. 1845 [628] xvi.

CUBITT, William, *Sir*
Report on Dover harbour. 23 Aug 1845. 1847/8 (476) lx. Admiralty. SEE ALSO: Thomson, Robert.

Report on Ramsgate harbour. 21 June 1853. 1852/3 (806) xcviii. Admiralty.

Report on Ramsgate harbour. 7 Jan 1856. 1856 (203) li. Board of Trade.

Thames embankment commission.
    Report, 22 July 1861. 1861 [2872] xxxi.
    Report, 29 July 1862. 1862 [3043] xxviii.
    Report, 7 Feb 1863. 1863 [3093] xxvi.

CUFFE, John Otway, *2nd E. Desart*
Committee on inland navigation in Ireland.
    1st report, 11 May 1813. 1812/3 (198) vi.
    2nd report, 3 June 1813. 1812/3 (266) vi.
    3rd report, 15 June 1813. 1812/3 (284) vi.

CULLY, George
Report on friendly societies in Scotland and northern counties of England. 1874 C.998 xxiii, pt.2; (Insurance, 8). SEE ALSO: Northcote, Stafford Henry, *Sir*.

CUMIN, Patrick
Report on educational charities. July 1860. In: 1861 [2794-IV] xxi, pt.4; (Education, 6).

Report on the state of popular education in the mari-

time districts of Bristol and Plymouth. June 1859. *In:* 1861 [2794-III] xxi, pt.3; (Education, 5).

CUMMING, Alexander
Report on the state of the hospitals of the British army in the Crimea and Scutari. 23 Feb 1855. 1854/5 [1920] xxxiii. War Office.

CUNNINGHAM, George
Report on the use of phosphorus in the manufacture of lucifer matches. Jan 1899. 1899 C.9188 xii. Home Office.

CUNYNGHAME, Henry Hardinge Samuel
Departmental committee on the testing of explosives for use in coal mines. Report, 6 Oct 1898. 1898 C.8698 xiii; (FP Mining Accidents, 12). Home Office.

CURRAN, William Henry
Report of an inquiry into the conduct of police employed in the collection of tithes in the county of Monaghan. 10 March 1834. 1834 (239) xliii.

CURTIS, Cockburn
Report in regard to the proposed Severn Navigation Improvement Commission Bill. 5 April 1848. 1847/8 (636) xxxi.

CURTIS, William, *Sir*
Committee on petitions from the City of London and the Grand Junction Canal Company. Report, 10 June 1802. 1801/2 (111) ii.

Committee on the petition from Dominica respecting the losses by the fire at Roseau. Report, 27 July 1807. 1807 (73) iii; CJ, vol.62, p.947.

Select committee on the petition from Dominica respecting the fire at Roseau. Report, 11 May 1808. 1808 (268) ii.

Select committee on the intended new post-office, London. Report, 17 July 1820. 1820 (290) ii.

CURWEN, John Christian
Committee on Capt. Manby's petition. Report, 26 March 1810. 1810 (163) iv.

Committee on the Isle of Man port petition. Report, 5 May 1804. 1803/4 (87) v.

Committee on petitions relating to machinery for manufacturing of flax. Report, 23 May 1817. 1817 (311) iii.

Committee on Wrexham Enclosure Bill. Copy of ev. 10 June 1819. 1819 (429) viii.

Select committee on Capt. Manby's apparatus for saving the lives of shipwrecked seamen. Report, 16 May 1823. 1823 (351) iv.

Select committee on poor laws. Report, 18 June 1816. 1816 (485) iv.

Select committee on the poor laws. Report, 18 June 1817. 1819 (532) ii.

CUSACK-SMITH, Thomas Berry SEE:
Smith, Thomas Berry Cusack.

CUST, Adelbert Wellington Brownlow, *3rd E. Brownlow*
Committee on the condition of the Yeomanry. Report, 17 March 1892. 1892 C.6675 xx. War Office.

Committee on Navy cutlasses and sword bayonets responsibility of General *Sir* John Ayde. Report, 9 Sept 1887. 1887 C.5241 xvi. War Office.

CUST, Adelbert Wellington Brownlow, *3rd E. Brownlow* (continued)

Local government boundaries commission. Report, 5 July 1888. 1888 (360) li (2 vols). Local Government Board.

Select committee (HL) on the Waterworks Clauses Act (1847) Amendment Bill. Report, 16 July 1885. HL 1884/5 (179) vii.

DACRE, *Lord* SEE:
Brand, Thomas, *20th Bn. Dacre.*

DAGLISH, Robert
Commission on control and management of H.M. naval yards. SEE: Willoughby, Henry Polard, *Sir.*

DALHOUSIE, *E.* SEE:
Maule-Ramsay, Fox, *11th E. Dalhousie* (1801-1874).
Maule-Ramsay, George, *12th E. Dalhousie* (1806-1880).
Maule-Ramsay, John William, *13th E. Dalhousie* (1847-1887).
Maule-Ramsay, Arthur George, *14th E. Dalhousie* (1878-1928).

[Peerage claim]. SEE: Freeman-Mitford, J.T.

DALRYMPLE, Charles, *Sir*
Select committee on public petitions. Special report, 30 Aug 1893. 1893/4 (393) xiii.

Select committee on public petitions. Mins. of ev. 11 April 1894. 1894 (102) xv.

DALRYMPLE, Donald
Select committee on habitual drunkards. Report, 13 June 1872. 1872 (242) ix; (SP Drunkenness, 2).

DALY, St. George
Commission on the state prisons and other gaols in Ireland. Report, 25 May 1809. 1809 (265) vii.

DANIELL, E. Lynch
Report on friendly societies in Ireland and Wales. 1874 C.995 xxiii, pt.2; (Insurance, 8). SEE ALSO: Northcote, Stafford Henry, *Sir.*

DARLING, Charles John, *Sir*
Select committee on the Royal National Lifeboat Institution. Report, 15 July 1897. 1897 (317) xiv.

DARLING, Henry Charles
Select committee on conduct while governor of New South Wales. SEE: Tooke, William.

DARNLEY, *E.* [Peerage claim]. SEE:
Cooper, C.A.

DARTMOUTH, *E.* SEE:
Legge, George, *3rd E. Dartmouth* (1775-1810).
Legge, William, *4th E. Dartmouth* (1784-1853).
Legge, William Walter, *5th E. Dartmouth* (1823-1891).
Legge, William Heneage, *6th E. Dartmouth* (1851-1936).

DARTREY, *E.* SEE:
Dawson, Richard, *3rd E. Dartrey.*

DAVENPORT, Davies
Committee on petition for Manchester and Salter's Brook Roads Bill. Proc. 2 March 1818. 1818 (77) iii.

DAVEY, Horace, *Bn. Davey*
Departmental committee on amendments relating to joint stock companies incorporated with limited liability under the Companies Acts, 1862 to 1890.

Report, 27 June 1895. 1895 C.7779 lxxxviii. Board of Trade.

Select committee on the Partnership Bill. Report, 17 July 1889. 1889 (260) xi.

DAVEY, Robert R.F.
Report on the probable cost of abolishing purchase in the Army. Feb 1871. 1871 (47) xxxix. War Office.

DAVIES, H.R.
Report on the trade of central Asia. 1 July 1862. 1864 (65) xlii. Colonial Office.

DAVIES, Lloyd
Select committee on civil service estimates, class 7. Report, 23 June 1856. 1856 (304) vii; (GO Civil Service, 4).

DAVIES, Thomas Henry Hastings
Committee on the adulteration of clover and trefoil seeds. Report, 31 May 1821. 1821 (595) iv.

Select committee on business of the H.C.
1st report, 12 May 1834. 1834 (284) xi.
2nd report, 4 June 1834. 1834 (350) xi.

Select committee on secondary punishments. Report, 27 Sept 1831. 1831 (276) vii.

Select committee on secondary punishments. Report, 22 June 1832. 1831/2 (547) vii.

DAVIS, H.
Committee of the Board of Excise on the observations and recommendations of the Commission of Excise inquiry. Report, Jan 1837. 1837 [96] xxx. SEE ALSO: Parnell, H.

DAVISON, Henry
Commission on the existence of corrupt practices in the Borough of Tynemouth. Report, Feb 1854. 1854 [1729] xxi.

DAVY, J.S.
Inquiry on the epidemic of typhoid fever in the Borough of Maidstone, 1897. Report, 1898 C.9000 xl. Local Government Board.

DAWSON, Alexander
Select committee on petition of inhabitants of Athlone. Report, 25 May 1827. 1826/7 (389) iv.

DAWSON, George Robert
Committee on Grand Jury presentments in Ireland. Report, 2 June 1819. 1819 (378) viii.

Select committee on conveyance and porterage of parcels. Report, 28 June 1825. 1825 (498) v.

DAWSON, Richard, *3rd E. Dartrey*
Select committee (HL) on the West Hartlepool Harbour and Railway Bill.
Min. of ev. 9 June 1863. HL 1863 (127) xxxiv.
Special report, 1 June 1863. HL 1863 (113) xxxiv.

DAY, William
Report on the operation and administration of the Poor Laws. *In:* 1834 (44) xxxvii.

DEAN, R.B.
Commission of Customs. Report on Customs frauds. 16 Nov 1842. 1843 [481] xxix. Treasury.

Report of H.M. Commission of Excise respecting the corn trade in the Isle of Man, Guernsey and Jersey. 23 March 1835. 1835 (74) xlviii.

General report on the report of the Commission of Revenue inquiry report on Custom-House frauds. 22 July 1843. 1843 [502] xxix. Treasury.

DEANE, Thomas
Commission appointed to ascertain the equitable amount to be repaid by the counties in Ireland transferred to other lunatic asylum districts. Report, 2 Feb 1857. 1857, session 2, (277) xvii. Lunatic Asylum Commission.

DEASY, Richard, *3rd E. Dartrey*
Select committee on the Cambridge Borough election petition. Min. of ev. 28 July 1857. 1857, session 2, (217) v.

Valuations for poor rates and registered elective franchise in Ireland. SEE: Haig, Charles.

DE BLAQUIERE, Lord [Peerage claim]. SEE: Freeman-Mitford, J.T.

DE BODE, Clement Joseph Philip Pen, *Bn. Bode*
Select committee on allegations in his petition. SEE: Copley, J.S., *1st Bn. Lyndhurst,* and Denman, George.

DE BROGLIE, D.
Min. of ev. on the right of search [of ships in suppression of the slave trade]. 31 March to 4 April 1845. 1847 [851] lxvii; (Slave Trade, 89).

DE BURGH, Ulick Canning, *Lord Dunkellin*
Select committee on the Galway Harbour (Composition of Debt) Bill. Special report, 18 June 1867. 1867 (378) x.

Select committee (HL) on the ventilation and lighting of the HL. Report, 7 July 1854. HL 1854 (60) xxi; HC repr. 1854 (384) ix.

DE BURGH, Ulick John, *14th E. Clanrickarde*
Select committee (HL) on the allegations of the several petitions in reference to the London and York Railway Bill. Report, 9 Aug 1845. HL 1845 (372) xix.

Select committee (HL) on breakwaters and harbours. Report, 2 Aug 1860. HL 1860 (207) xxiv; HC repr. 1860 (544) xv.

Select committee (HL) on the lighting of the HL and of the Lord's robing rooms. Report, 14 Dec 1852. HL 1852/3 (16) xxxi.

Select committee (HL) on the progress of the building of the Houses of Parliament.
Report, 2 April 1846. HL 1846 (38) xxvi.
2nd report, 11 May 1846. HL 1846 (136) xxvi.
3rd report, 23 June 1846. HL 1846 (203) xxvi.
4th report, 17 Aug 1846. HL 1846 (288) xxvi; HC repr. 1846 (719) xv.

Select committee (HL) on the progress of the building of the Houses of Parliament.
Min. of ev. 21 July 1847. HL 1847 (318) xxv.
Report, 20 July 1847. HL 1847 (314) xxv.

Select committee (HL) on the River Shannon navigation and drainage. Report, 29 May 1865. HL 1865 (130) xxi; HC repr. 1865 (464) xi.

Commission on the question of Sunday labour in the Post Office. Report, 10 Aug 1850. 1850 [1262] xx. Treasury.

Select committee (HL) on the Tenure (Ireland) Bill. Report, 2 Aug 1867. HL 1867 (196) xxvii; HC repr. 1867 (518) xiv.

Select committee (HL) on the Tenure (Ireland) Bill. Report, 28 May 1868. HL 1867/8 (129) xxx.

Select committee (HL) on the ventilation and lighting of the HL. Report, 7 July 1854. HL 1854 (60) xxi.

DEEDES, John
Commission on the existence of corrupt practices in the Borough of Kingston-upon-Hull. Report, 30 Aug 1853. 1854 [1729] xxii, pts. 1 and 2.

DEEDES, William
Committee of selection relative to the grouping of private bills. 1857/8, 1861, 1862. SEE: Wilson-Patten, John.

Committee on the Blackburn election petition. Min. of ev. 9 March 1853. 1852/3 (217) viii.

Select committee on the Harwich election petition.
Proc. 15 July 1851. 1851 (543) xii.
Min. of ev. 8 Aug 1851. 1851 (694) xii.

DE GREY, E. SEE:
Robinson, George Frederick Samuel, *1st M. Ripon.*

DE GREY, Thomas, *1st Bn. Walsingham*
Committee (HL) on the descent of peerages of Ireland. Report, 18 March 1802. (Oceana HL 1801/2, vol.2, p.231).

Committee (HL) on the Glenkenns Canal Bill. Min. of proc. 17 June 1802. HL 1801/2 vol. [3]; (Oceana HL 1801/2, vol.2, p.349).

Committee (HL) on the manner of receiving and proceeding upon peerage claims from Ireland. Report, 18 May 1802. HL 1801/2 vol. [3]; (Oceana HL 1801/2 vol.2, p.317).

Committee (HL) on the precedents for enabling persons to give testimony before this House by indemnifying them against criminal prosecutions and civil suits (Witnesses Indemnity Bill). Report, 1 March 1806. HL 1806 (4) v.

Committee of privileges (HL).
Airlie claim of peerage.
Min. of ev. 6 May 1813. HL 1812/3 (67) lxvii.
Ev. 28 April to 7 June 1814. HL 1813/4 (60) lxxii.

Committee for privileges (HL).
Banbury claim of peerage.
Report of proc. heretofore. 13 April 1808. HL 1808 (48) xxii.
Ev. HL 1808 (87) xxii.
Ev. 21 Feb to 8 June 1809. HL 1809 (20) xxxi.
Ev. 27 March to 16 June 1810. HL 1810 (64) xxxi.
Min. of ev. 2 April 1811. HL 1810/1 (11), (33) xlvi B.

Committee for privileges (HL).
Barnewall claim of peerage.
Ev. 10 April 1810, 10 March 1812. HL 1812 (44) lvii.
Ev. 6 April 1813. HL 1812/3 (27) lxvii.
Ev. 7 June 1814. HL 1813/4 (61) lxxii.

Committee of privileges (HL).
Beaumont claim to peerage. Min. of ev. 1794 and 1795; repr. HL 1840 (64) xxi. SEE ALSO: Cooper, Cropley Ashley, *6th E. Shaftesbury.*

Committee for privileges (HL).
Berkeley claim of peerage.
Min. of ev., 1799; repr. HL 1810/1 (14) xlvi A.
Min. of ev., 8 March 1811. HL 1810/1 (16) xlvi A.

DE GREY, Thomas, *1st Bn. Walsingham* (continued)
> Min. of ev., 8 March 1811. HL 1810/1 (16) xlvi B.

> Committee for privileges (HL).
>> Borthwick claim of peerage.
>>> Ev. 1 May 1809 to 14 April 1812. HL 1812 (83) lvii.
>>> Ev. 9 May 1812, 16 and 25 March 1813. HL 1812/3 (26) lxvii.
>>> Ev. 23 June, 5 July 1814. HL 1813/4 (77) lxxii.

> Committee of privileges (HL).
>> Chandos (*Bn.*) peerage claim. Min. of ev. 4 March 1802. (Oceana. HL 1801/2 vol.2, p.1.)

> Committee of privileges (HL).
>> Clarence claim to vote at elections of peers for Ireland. Min. of ev. 4 July 1805. HL 1805, vol.[15].

> Committee for privileges (HL).
>> Howard de Walden claim of peerage.
>>> Min. of ev. 15 Jan 1807. HL 1806/7 (3) xiv.
>>> Report of Attorney General. 16 Jan 1807. HL 1806/7 (3) xiv.
>>> Proc. 1804. HL 1806/7 (9) xiv.

> Committee for privileges (HL).
>> Killmorey claim to vote at elections for Irish peers.
>>> Ev. 25 July 1812. HL 1812 (187) lvii.
>>> Ev. 13 May 1813. HL 1812/3 (84) lxvii.

> Committee for privileges (HL).
>> Queensberry claim of peerage. Ev. 29 June 1812. HL 1812 (142) lvii.

> Committee of privileges (HL).
>> Roos peerage claim. Min. of ev. 16 March 1804. (Oceana, HL 1803/4 (15) vol.5, p.1).

> Committee of privileges (HL).
>> Roxburghe claim of peerage.
>>> Ev. 2 July 1808. HL 1808 (124) xxii.
>>> Ev. 16 to 21 Feb 1809. HL 1809 (15) xxxi.
>>> Ev. 5 April to 18 June 1809. HL 1809 (66) xxxi.
>>> Ev. 13 to 17 March 1812. HL 1812 (39) lvii.

> Committee for privileges (HL).
>> Stafford claim of peerage.
>>> Ev. 16 June 1809. HL 1809 (107) xxxi.
>>> Ev. 28 Jan to 18 Feb 1812. HL 1812 (18) lvii.

Committee (HL) on proc. on impeachments for high crimes and misdemeanors; Henry, *Vct. Melville.* Report, 12 March 1806. HL 1806 (10) v.

Committee (HL) to search the HL journals in relation to their lordships proceedings on impeachments; and to whom the further article of impeachments exhibited against Henry, *Vct. Melville.* Report, 12 March 1806. HL 1806 (10) v.

Committee (HL) on standing orders respecting private bills. Report, 2 July 1801. (Oceana, HL 1801, vol.1, p.641).

Committee of whole HL on complaints against Mr. Justice Fox. Min. of ev. 5-22 June 1805. HL 1805 (48) [15] ; (Oceana HL 1805 (48) [3]).

Committee of the whole HL on the impeachment against Warren Hastings. Proc. and report, 1 April 1795. LJ, vol.40, p.364; repr. HL 1806 (48) v.

Committee of the whole HL on the petition on orders in Council. Min. of ev. 29 March 1808. HL 1808 (33) xix.

Select committee (HL) on allegations against Mr. Justice Fox. Min. of ev. 10 June 1805. HL 1805 (47) vol. [15] .

Select committee (HL) on HL appeals. Report, 20 May 1811. HL 1810/1 (70) xliv.

Select committee (HL) on precedent of the manner of proceeding to judgement upon impeachments for high crimes and misdemeanors. Report, 17 Feb 1795. Repr. HL 1806 (42) v.

DE GREY, Thomas, *6th Bn. Walsingham*
Private ensilage commission.
> Report, 5 Aug 1885. 1884/5 (308) xx.
> Final report, March 1886. 1886, session 1 (119) xix.
> Agriculture Department, Privy Council Office.

DE LA BECHE, Henry Thomas, *Sir*
Coals suited to the steam navy
> 1st report, 5 Jan 1848. 1847/8 [915] xxviii.
> 2nd report, 24 May 1849. 1849 [1086] xxxii.
> 3rd report, 2 April 1851. 1851 [1345] xxxiii.
> Museum of Practical Geology *and* Admiralty.

Commission of the fall of the cotton mill at Oldham and part of the prison at Northleach. Report, 28 Feb 1845. 1845 [628] xvi.

Report on the gasses and explosions in collieries. 1 June 1846. 1846 (529) xliii; (FP Mining Accidents, 6). Home Department.

Report on the gasses and explosions in collieries. 1 June 1846. 1847 [815] xiv; (FP Mining Accidents, 5). Home Department.

Report on the Metropolitan Sewage Manure Company Bill. 14 May 1846. 1846 (308) xliii; (UA Sanitation, 3). Commission of HM Woods, Forests, etc.

Report on smoke prohibition. 30 March 1846. 1846 (194) xliii. Home Department.

DE LISLE, *Lord* [Peerage claim] . SEE:
Cooper, C.A.

DE SCALES, *Lord* [Peerage claim] . SEE:
Freeman-Mitford, J.T.

DE VESCI, *Vct.* [Peerage claim] . SEE:
Freeman-Mitford, J.T.

DE WORMS, Henry, *Bn. Pirbright*
Committee on the Merchant Shipping (Transfer of Registry, *etc.*) Bill. Report, 18 July 1887. 1887 (261) lxxiii. Board of Trade.

Select committee on Merchandise Marks Act (1862) Amendment Bill. Report, 30 June 1887. 1887 (203) x.

Select committee on Merchandise Marks Act, 1887. Report, 30 July 1890. 1890 (334) xv.

Select committee on the Western Australia Constitution Bill. Report, 6 May 1890. 1890 (160) xviii; (Australia, 32).

DENBIGH, *E.* SEE:
Feilding, Rudolph Robert Basil Aloysius Augustine, *9th E.Denbigh.*

DENHAM, H.M.
Report on passenger accommodation in steamers between Ireland and Liverpool. 21 May 1849. 1849 (339) li. Board of Trade.

Report on the restoration of Ardglass harbour. 1 Dec 1851. 1852/3 (1007-I) xciv. Admiralty.

DENISON, Edmund B.
Select committee on prison discipline. Report, 29 July 1850. 1850 (632) xvii; (CP Prisons, 5).

DENISON, John Evelyn
Select committee on the Ecclesiastical Commission. Report, 14 Aug 1848. 1847/8 (645) vii.

Select committee on the Larne, Belfast and Ballymena Railway Bill petition. Report, 17 July 1846. 1846 (495) xii.

Select committee on local acts (preliminary inquiries), 1850. SEE: Wilson-Patten, John.

Select committee on the New Forest Deer Removal, *etc*. Bill. Reports, 26 June and 17 July 1851. 1875 (192) xiii.

Select committee on public business. Report, 14 Aug 1848. 1847/8 (644) xvi.

Select committee on the Registration of Assurances Bill. Report, 5 Aug 1853. 1852/3 (889) xxxvi.

DENISON, Stephen Charles
Report on the employment of women and children in agriculture. Suffolk, Norfolk and Lincoln. 2 Feb 1843. 1843 [510] xii; (Agriculture, 6). Poor Law Commission.

DENISON, W.
Report on Dover harbour. 2 July 1845. 1847/8 (476) lx. Admiralty.

Report on the state of the River Clyde and Port of Glasgow. 25 May 1846. 1847 (242) lxi. Admiralty.

DENISON, William Thomas
Commission on preventing the pollution of rivers, 1868. SEE: Frankland, Edward.

DENMAN, George
Bewdley election petition trial. Ev. and judgement. 29 June 1880. 1880 (322) lvii.

Canterbury petition trial. Ev. and judgement. 16 June 1880. 1880 (263) lvii.

Macclesfield election petition trial. Ev. and judgement. 22 June 1880. 1880 (262) lviii.

Select committee on the *Bn.* De Bode's petition. Report, 1 Aug 1861. 1861 (502) xi.

DENT, John Dent
Select committee on main contracts. Report, 23 March 1869. 1868/9 (106) vi.

DERBY, E. SEE:
Stanley, Edward Geoffrey, *14th E. Derby* (1799-1869)
Stanley, Edward Henry, *15th E. Derby* (1826-1893)
Stanley, Frederick Arthur, *16th E. Derby* (1841-1908)
Stanley, Edward George Villiers, *17th E. Derby* (1865-1948)

DERWENTWATER, E. SEE:
Gage, H.H.

DESART, E. SEE:
Cuffe, J.O., *2nd E. Desart.*

DESMARETZ, J.P.
Report and estimate relating to Ramsgate harbour. 24 Dec 1755. (Reps., 1731-1800, no.3, vol.1).

DEVEREUX, H.B.
Commission of inquiry into certain matters connected with the position of Sir James Brooke, consul-general in Borneo. Reports, 6 and 11 Jan 1855. 1854/5 [1976] xxix. East India Office.

DEVON, E. SEE:
Courtenay, William, *11th E. Devon* (1777-1859)

Courtenay, William Reginald, *12th E. Devon* (1807-1888).
Courtenay, Edward Baldwin, *13th E. Devon* (1811-1891).
Courtenay, Henry Hugh, *14th E. Devon* (1891-1904).

DEVONSHIRE, Lord SEE:
Cavendish, William, *7th D. Devonshire* (1808-1891).
Cavendish, Spencer Compton, *8th D. Devonshire* (1833-1908).

DICK, John
Commission on the fees, gratuities, etc. of public offices.
  1st report: Secretaries of State, 11 April 1786, repr. 1806 (309) vii.
  2nd report: Treasury, 20 June 1786, repr. 1806 (309) vii.
  3rd report: Admiralty, 27 Dec 1787, repr. 1806 (309) vii.
  4th report: Treasurer of the Navy, 10 Jan 1788, repr. 1806 (309) vii.
  5th report: Commissioners of the Navy, 14 Feb 1788, repr. 1806 (309) vii.
  6th report: Dock yards, 10 March 1788, repr. 1806 (309) vii.
  7th report: Sick and Hurt Office, 20 March 1788, repr. 1806 (309) vii.
  8th report: Victualling Office, 17 April 1788, repr. 1806 (309) vii.
  9th report: Naval and victualling departments at foreign and distant ports, 1 May 1788, repr. 1806 (309) vii.
  10th report: Post Office, 30 June 1788, repr. 1806 (309) vii.

DICKENS, T.
Committee on exportation of hill coolies. Report, 14 Oct 1840. 1841 (45) xvi. India Office.

DICKINSON, Joseph
Report on the rock-salt mines and brine pits relative to landslips. 31 March 1873. 1873 (185) liii. Home Office.

DICKINSON, William (ca. 1745-1806)
Committee on Mr. Edward Sealy's petition respecting his patent for tanning of leather with elm bark. Report, 7 May 1798. CJ. vol.53, p.543; (Reps., 1731-1800, no.145, vol.22).

DICKINSON, William, Jr. (1771-1837)
Committee on the petition of the Dean and Chapter of the Collegiate Church of St. Peter, Westminster. Report, 23 March 1810. 1810 (155) ii.
  Min. of ev. 28 March 1810. 1810 (170) ii.

Committee on petitions for the repair of King Henry VII's Chapel. Report, 29 March 1811. 1810/1 (209) ii.

Committee respecting persons to be appointed commissioners, surveyors, *etc*, in inclosure and drainage bills. Report, 19 May 1801. 1801 (77) iii.

Committee respecting persons to be appointed commissioners, surveyors, *etc*, in inclosure and drainage bills. Re-committed report, 5 June 1801. 1801 (106) iii.

Select committee on expenditure of county rates. Report, 21 June 1825. 1825 (461) vi.

DICKSON, Collingwood, Sir
Ordnance committee. Recommendations on the construction of ordnance. 28 July 1885. 1884/5 C.4508 xiv. War Office.

DICKSON, Samuel Auchmuty
Select committee on the Drainage (Ireland) Bill. Min. of ev. 2 June 1862. 1862 (297) xvi.

DILKE, Charles Wentworth, *Sir*
Report on the organisation of the New York Industrial Exhibition, 1854. 1854 [1801] xxxvi. Foreign Office.

Royal commission on the housing of the working classes
    1st report. 1884/5 C.4402 xxx.
    2nd report: Scotland. 1884/5 C.4409 xxxi.
    3rd report: Ireland. 1884/5 C.4547 xxxi. (UA Housing, 3).

Select committee on Parliamentary and municipal elections. Report, 7 April 1876. 1876 (162) xii; (GO Elections, 5).

DILLWYN, Lewis Llewellyn
Select committee on lunacy law. Report, 30 July 1877. 1877 (373) xiii; (HE Mental, 5).

Select committee on the Patent Office Library and Museum. Report, 19 July 1864. 1864 (504) xii.

Select committee on the Salmon Fisheries (No.2) Bill. Min. of proc. 31 May 1872. 1872 (214) xii.

DINGWALL, *Lord* [Peerage claim]. SEE: Freeman-Mitford, J.T.

DIONNE, Joseph
Commission appointed to inquire into the losses occasioned by the troubles in Canada during the years 1837 and 1838, and into the damages arising therefrom.
    1st report, 18 April 1846. In: 1849 (253) xxxv.
    Appendix to 1st report, 6 June 1849. 1849 (353) xxxv; (Canada, 18). Colonial Office.

DISRAELI, Benjamin
Select committee on corrupt practices. Report, 23 June 1870. 1870 (302) vi; (GO Elections, 5).

DIVETT, Edward
Select committee on Athlone Borough election. Proc., 10 June 1842. 1842 (548) v.

Select committee on the Carlisle election petition. Min. of ev. 8 March 1848. 1847/8 (156) x.

Select committee on the Lancaster Borough election petition. Min. of ev. 22 Feb 1853. 1852/3 (152) xiv.

Select committee on the Leicester election petition.
    Report, 15 April 1853. 1852/3 (336) xiv.
    Min. of ev. 21 April 1853. 1852/3 (375) xiv.

Select committee on Lichfield Borough election. Proc. 27 June 1842. 1842 (548) v.

Select committee on the Sligo Borough election petition
    Report, 6 June 1853. 1852/3 (572) xviii.
    Min. of ev. 10 June 1853. 1852/3 (600) xviii.

DOBSON, Thomas
Report on the use of barley, malt, sugar and molasses in breweries and distilleries. 14 Nov 1846. 1847 (26) lix. Board of Excise.

DODD, Cyril
Commission on the Sudbury, Suffolk, Trustee Savings Bank. Interim report, 22 Jan 1894. 1893/4 C.6884 lxxxiii, pt.1; (MP Savings Bank, 4).

DODDS, Joseph
Select committee on salmon fisheries. Report, 27 July 1869. 1868/9 (361) vii.

Select committee on salmon fisheries. Report, 20 July 1870. 1870 (368) vi.

DODSON, John George, *1st Bn. Monk Bretton*
Committee of public accounts. Report, 16 June 1874. 1874 (242) vi.

Committee of public accounts.
    1st report, 19 March 1875. 1875 (107) viii.
    2nd report, 14 July 1875. 1875 (336) viii.
    3rd report, 30 July 1875. 1875 (373) viii.

Committee of public accounts.
    1st report, 24 March 1876. 1876 (133) viii.
    2nd report, 3 May 1876. 1876 (207) viii.
    3rd report, 29 June 1876. 1876 (324) viii; (National Finance, 5).

Joint select committee on private bill legislation. Report, 12 July 1888. 1888 (276) xvi.

Select committee on Cape of Good Hope and Zanzibar mail contracts. Report, 23 July 1873. 1873 (334) ix.

Select committee on hop duties. Report, 7 Aug 1857. 1857, session 2, (252) xiv.

Select committee on railways. Report, 17 May 1867. 1867 (302) viii.

Select committee on registration of county voters. Report, 14 April 1864. 1864 (203) x.

Select committee on the Rivers Conservancy and Flood Prevention Bill. Report, 29 June 1881. 1881 (303) xii.

Select committee on the University Elections Bill. Report, 31 May 1861. 1861 (297) xiv.

DOMBRAIN, J.
Committee of the Ballast Office, Dublin. Report on the better marking of the coast of Ireland from the Tuskar to the Kish, 16 April 1863. 1863 (256) lxiii. Board of Trade.

DONALDSON, Stuart A.
Select committee of the Legislative Council of New South Wales on the steam communication with Europe. 3 Sept 1850. 1851 (430) xxxv. Colonial Office.

DONCASTER, *E.* SEE:
Montagu-Douglas-Scott, Walter Francis, *5th D.Buccleuch and 7th D. Queensferry.*

DONEGAL, *M.* [Peerage claim]. SEE:
Palmer, R.

DONERAILE, *Vct.* [Peerage claim]. SEE:
Freeman-Mitford, J.T.

DONNELLY, John Fletchville Dykes
Report on the expediency of granting a charter of incorporation to the Borough of Reigate. May 1863. 1864 (77) 1. Privy Council.

Reports on the petition of the inhabitant householders of Aberavon, praying for a municipal charter. 1 Feb 1860 and 1 Jan 1861. 1861 (458) lvii. Privy Council.

DONOUGHMORE, *E.* SEE:
Hely-Hutchinson, Richard John, *4th E. Donoughmore.*
Hely-Hutchinson, John Luke George, *5th E. Donoughmore.*

[Peerage claim]. SEE: Freeman-Mitford, J.T.

DORINGTON, John Edward, *Sir*
Departmental committee on the Ordnance Survey. Report, 31 Dec 1892. 1893/4 C.6895 lxxii. Board of Agriculture.

Select committee on gas companies' Metropolitan charges. SEE: Cohen, Benjamin Louis.

DOUGAN, John
Remarks on his report on the state of captured Negroes at Tortola. SEE: Moody, Thomas.

Report on the state of captured Negroes at Tortola. Report, 12 June 1827. 1826/7 (462) xxii.
Further report, 12 July 1828. 1828 (535) xxvi; (Slave Trade, 72, 75).

DOUGLAS, Akers SEE:
Akers-Douglas, Aretas.

DOUGLAS, Dunbar James, *6th E. Selkirk*
Select committee (HL) on the York, Newcastle and Berwick Railway (Construction of Docks, *etc.*) Bill. Min. of ev. 17 July 1854. HL 1854 (229) xxi.

DOUGLAS, Francis Wemyss Charteris SEE:
Wemyss-Charteris-Douglas, Francis, *8th E. Wemyss.*

DOUGLAS, Sylvester, *Lord Glenbervie*
Committee on the corn trade between G.B. and Ireland. Report, 26 March 1802. 1801/2 (36); CJ Reports vol.9, p.161.

Committee on Mr. McDowall's petition on the loan of Exchequer bills to merchants of Grenada and St. Vincent. Report, 28 April 1800. CJ, vol.55, p.425; (Reps., 1731-1800, no.171, vol.28).

Committee on Scotch distillery duties. Report, 11 June 1798. CJ Reports, vol.11, p.319; (Reps., 1731-1800, no.144, vol.21).

Select committee on the 11th naval report. Report, 24 June 1805. 1805 (184) ii.

Committee of secrecy on the 11th naval report. Report, 27 June 1805. 1805 (198) ii.

DOUGLAS-COMPTON, Spencer Joshua Alwyne, *2nd M. Northampton*
Select committee (HL) on the Edinburgh and Glasgow Railway Bill. Min. of ev. 31 May 1838. HL 1837/8 (185) xx.

DOUGLAS-HAMILTON, William Alexander Louis Stephen, *12th D. Hamilton*
Select committee (HL) on the Glebe Lands (Scotland) Bill. Report, 13 July 1866. HL 1866 (191) xxviii.

DOUGLAS-SCOTT, Walter Francis Montagu SEE:
Montagu-Douglas-Scott, Walter Francis, *5th D.Buccleuch and 7th D. Queensferry.*

DOWDESWELL, George Morley
Commission on corrupt practices at the last election for the City of Norwich.
Report, 15 Feb 1870. 1870 C.13 xxxi.
Min. of ev. 1870 C.14 xxxi.

DOWDESWELL, William
Committee on the better supply of timber for H.M. Navy. Report, 6 May 1771. CJ Reports, vol.3, p.13; (Reps., 1731-1800, no.9, vol.1).

DOWELL, William Montagu, *Sir*
Committee on the naval manoeuvres, 1888. Extract from the report. 21 Nov 1888. 1889 C.5632 l. Admiralty.

DOWLING, E.
Commission appointed by the Governor-General of Canada to inquire into the state of the Canadian Post Office. Report, 31 Dec 1841. 1846 (721) xxvii; (Canada, 16). Colonial Office.

DOWNE, *Vct.* [Peerage claim]. SEE:
Freeman-Mitford, J.T.

DOWSE, Richard, *Lord*
Commission of inquiry, 1864, into the magisterial and police jurisdiction arrangements and establishment of the Borough of Belfast. Report, 8 March 1865. 1865 [3466] xxviii; (CP Civil Disorder, 7).

Select committee on the Juries Bill. Report, 5 July 1872. 1872 (286) x.

Louth County election petition trial. Ev. and judgement. 19 June 1880. 1880 (300) lviii.

DOYLE, Andrew
Emigration of pauper children to Canada. Reply to Miss Maria S. Rye's report, 14 May 1877. 1877 (263) lxxi. Local Government Board.

Report on the condition of the Anglesey and Holyhead unions. 13 Feb 1867. 1867 (84) lx. Poor Law Board.

Report on the education and training of children in Wales and West Midlands. 31 Dec 1850. 1851 (646) xlix. Poor Law Board.

Report on the education of pauper children. 12 April 1862. 1862 (510) xlix; (ED Poorer Classes, 7). Poor Law Board.

Report on the emigration of pauper children to Canada. 1 Dec 1874. 1875 (9) lxiii; (Canada, 28). Local Government Board.

Report on the state of the Walsall Union workhouse. 30 Nov 1867. 1867/8 (40) lx. Poor Law Board.

Royal commission on agriculture. Reports on Wales, *etc.* 7 Sept 1881. 1882 C.3375-III xv; (Agriculture, 19). SEE ALSO: Gordon-Lennox, Charles Henry, *6th D. Richmond.*

DOYLE, Francis Hastings, *Sir*
Report on the employment of women and children in agriculture: Yorkshire and Northumberland. 1 March 1843. 1843 [510] xii; (Agriculture, 6). Poor Law Commission.

DRINKWATER, J.
Commission of military inquiry
1st report: Office of the Barrack Master General, arrears of barrack office accounts. 21 March 1806. 1806 (46) vi.
2nd report: Establishment of the Barrack Office. 18 July 1806. 1806 (317) vi.
3rd report: Office of the Barrack Master General; stores and supplies. 22 Dec 1806. 1806/7 (4) ii.
4th report: Office of the Barrack Master General; buildings, with a supplement to the 1st and 3rd reports. 3 March 1807. 1806/7 (99) ii.
5th report: Army; Medical Department. 26 Jan 1808. 1808 (6) v.
6th report: Office of the Secretary at War, with a supplement to the 5th report. 25 June 1808. 1808 (327) v.
7th report: Office of the Secretary at War. 20 Jan 1809. 1809 (3) v.
8th report: Office of the Secretary at War. 20 Jan 1809. 1809 (4) v.
9th report: Commission on examination of public

DRINKWATER, J. (continued)

expenditure for H.M. forces in the West Indies. 14 April 1809. 1809 (141) v.

10th report: Royal Military College. 26 Feb 1810. 1810 (78) ix.

11th report: Departments of the Adjutant General and Quarter-Master General, and supplement to 8th report. 26 Feb 1810. 1810 (79) ix.

12th report: Office of Ordnance; Treasurer. 27 Feb 1810. 1810 (81) ix.

13th report: Master General and Board of Ordnance. 27 Feb 1811. 1810/1 (32) iv.

14th report: Ordnance estimates. 29 April 1811. 1810/1 (135) iv.

15th report: Ordnance fortifications and buildings, barracks, small gun department, shipping. 23 July 1811. 1810/1 (261) iv.

16th report: Ordnance. 9 Jan 1812. 1812 (4) iv.

17th report: Ordnance. 9 Jan 1812. 1812 (5) iv.

18th report: Office of the Commissariat. 20 March 1812. 1812 (119) iv.

19th report: Royal Hospital Chelsea; Commissary General Musters; Royal Military Asylum. 26 May 1812. 1812 (251) iv.

General index to reports, 1806-12. 23 Feb 1816. 1816 (51) x.

DRUCE, S.B.L.

Royal commission on agriculture. Report on Bedfordshire, Buckinghamshire, Cambridgeshire, Derbyshire, Essex, Hertfordshire, Huntingdonshire, Leicestershire, Middlesex, Norfolk, Northamptonshire, Nottinghamshire, Rutland, Suffolk. Dec 1881. 1882 C.3375-II xv; (Agriculture, 19). SEE ALSO: Gordon-Lennox, Charles Henry, *6th D. Richmond.*

DRUMMOND, Henry

Select committee on Crown forests. Report, 17 July 1854. 1854 (377) x.

DRUMMOND, Henry Home

Select committee on Wakefield Borough election. Proc. 21 April 1842. 1842 (584) v.

DRUMMOND, Thomas

Commission on railways for Ireland

1st report, 11 March 1837. 1837 [75] xxxiii.

2nd report, 13 July 1838. 1837/8 (145) xxxv.

Report on the distress experienced on the western coast of Ireland in the Summer of 1835 and of the measures adopted by the government for its relief. 1835. 1836 [734] xxxvii. Irish Secretary's Office.

DUBLIN, *Archbishop* SEE:

Whatley, Richard, *Archbp. of Dublin,* 1831-64.

Trench, Richard Chenevix, *Archbp. of Dublin,* 1864-85.

DU BOIS, Isaac

Committee on petition. SEE: Annesley, Francis; SEE ALSO: Vansittart, G.

DU CANE, Charles

Committee on Greenwich hospital and schools. Report, 19 March 1868. 1867/8 [4034] xvi. Admiralty.

DU CANE, Edmund F., *Sir*

Committee on employment of convicts. Report, 1882. 1882 C.3427 xxxiv; (CP Prisons, 18).

DUDLEY, E. SEE:

Ward, William Humble, *2nd E. Dudley.*

DUFF, Robert William

Select committee on herring brand, Scotland. Report, 21 June 1881. 1881 (293) ix.

DUFF, Mountstuart E. Grant SEE:

Grant-Duff, Mountstuart Elphinstone.

DUFFERIN AND CLANDEBOYE, *Bn.* SEE:

Hamilton-Temple-Blackwood, Frederick Temple, *1st M. Dufferin and Ava.*

[Peerage claim]. SEE: Cooper, C.A.

DUGDALE, Dugdale Stratford

Committee on the Birmingham and London Junction Canal petitions.

Min. 7 April 1830. 1830 (260) x.

Report, 5 April 1830. 1830 (251) x.

DUGDALE, W.S.

Select committee on the London and Birmingham Railway Bill. Min. of ev. 2 May 1839. 1839 (242) xiii.

DUIGENAN, Patrick

Committee on the petition of six clerks of Chancery in Ireland. Report, 26 May 1813. 1812/3 (238) vi.

DUNALLEY, *Lord* [Peerage claim]. SEE:

Freeman-Mitford, J.T.

DUNBAR, William

Second committee on the account branch of the War Office.

(1st report not identified)

2nd report, 19 March 1861. 1861 (169) xxxvi.

3rd report, 18 May 1861. 1861 (501) xxxvi. Treasury.

DUNBOYNE, *Lord* [Peerage claim]. SEE:

Freeman-Mitford, J.T.

DUNCAN, *Vct.* SEE:

Duncan-Haldane, Robert Dundas, *1st E. Camperdown* (1785-1859)

Duncan-Haldane, Adam, *2nd E. Camperdown* (1812-1867)

Duncan-Haldane, Robert Adam Philips, *3rd E. Camperdown* (1841-1918).

DUNCAN-HALDANE, Adam, *2nd E. Camperdown*

Select committee on expiring laws: 3rd session, 16th Parliament. Report, 29 March 1855. 1854/5 (149) vii.

Select committee on the Ordnance Survey of Scotland. Report, 6 May 1856. 1856 (198) xiv.

DUNCAN-HALDANE, Robert Adam Philips, *3rd E. Camperdown*

Commission on certain civil departments in Scotland. Report, 11 March 1870. 1870 C.64 xviii. Treasury.

Committee on medical officers of the Army and Navy. Report, 31 July 1889. 1889 C.5810 xvii. War Office

Report on the arrangements of H.M. victualling yards. Feb 1870. 1870 (56) xlvi. Admiralty.

Royal commission on the Medical Acts. Report, June 1882. 1882 C.3259 xxix; (HE Medical Profession, 5).

Select committee (HL) on the Electric Lighting Act (1882) Amendment Bills, nos. 1-3. Report, 4 June 1886. HL 1886 (147) vii; HC repr. 1886, session 1 (252) vii.

Select committee (HL) on high sheriffs. Report, 23 Feb 1894. HL 1893/4 (304) ix.

Select committee (HL) on high sheriffs. Report, 5 June 1894. HL 1894 (84) viii.

Select committee (HL) on the Trawlers' Certificates Suspension Bill. Report, 9 June 1899. HL 1899 (109) x.

Select committee (HL) on the Water Companies (Regulation of Powers) Bill. Report, 27 April 1885. HL 1884/5 (86) vii; HC repr. 1884/5 (197) xii.

DUNCAN-HALDANE, Robert Dundas, *1st E. Camperdown*
Select committee on the woods, forests and land revenues of the Crown. Report, plans, index, 25 July 1848. 1847/8 (538) xxiv, pts. 1 and 2.

Select committee on the woods, forests and land revenues of the Crown.
1st report, 17 July 1849. 1849 (513) xx.
2nd report, 27 July 1849. 1849 (574) xx.

DUNCANNON, *Lord* SEE:
Ponsonby, John William, *4th E. Bessborough* (1781-1847)
Ponsonby, John George Brabazon, *5th E. Bessborough* (1809-1880).

DUNCOMBE, Arthur
Select committee on the Hereford City election petitions. Min. of ev. 9 May 1866. 1866 (255) x.

DUNCOMBE, Charles, *1st Bn. Feversham*
Committee (HL) on the Clarence Railway Company's Bill. Min. of ev. 7 May 1829. HL 1829 (42) cclxii.

Committee (HL) on the Stockton and Darlington Railway Bill. Min. of ev. 1-2 May 1828. HL 1828 (73) ccxl.

DUNCOMBE, Thomas
Select committee on the land transport corps. Reports, 10 July 1857. 1857, session 2 (172) ix.

Select committee on Regent Street paving. Report, 16 June 1836. 1836 (335) xx.

DUNCOMBE, Thomas Slingsby
Select committee on Norwich election petitions withdrawal. Report, 17 March 1853. 1852/3 (243) xvii.

DUNDAS, *Lord* SEE:
Dundas, Lawrence, *1st E. Zetland.*

DUNDAS, Charles
Committee on Shetland Islands petition. Report, 29 March 1804. 1803/4 (42) v.

Committee on standing orders relative to navigation bills, *etc.* Report, 22 June 1814. 1813/4 (245) iv.

DUNDAS, David, *Sir*
Inquiry on the armistice and convention, *etc.* made in Portugal in August 1809. HL 1809 (6) xxviii. War Office.

Select committee on the case of Mr. Bewicke. Report, 17 June 1864. 1864 (395) v.

DUNDAS, Henry, *3rd Vct. Melville*
Commission on General Register House, Edinburgh
1st report, 8 May 1826. 1826 (347) xi.
2nd report, 25 May 1827. 1826/7 (384) vii.
(3rd report not identified)
4th report, 13 March 1845. 1845 (123) xxvi.

Commission of inquiry on the poor laws in Scotland
Report, 2 May 1844. 1844 [557] xx.
Appendix I-III: Min. of ev. 1844 [563], [564], [565] xxxi, xxii, xxiii
Appendix IV-VII. 1844 [597], [598], [543], [544] xxiv, xxv, xxvi
Analytical index. 1844 [544] xxvi.

Commission on fees, gratuities, perquisites, emoluments, which are or have been lately received in several public offices.
1st report: Secretaries of State. 17 June 1793.
2nd report: Treasury. 17 June 1793.
3rd report: Admiralty. 17 June 1793.
4th report: Treasurer of the Navy. 17 June 1793.
5th report: Commissioners of the Navy. 17 June 1793.
6th report: Dockyards. 17 June 1793.
7th report: Sick and Hurt Office. 17 June 1793.
8th report: Victualling Office. 17 June 1793.
9th report: Naval and victualling departments at foreign or distant ports. 17 June 1793.
10th report: Post Office. 17 June 1793. (Reps., 1793-1800, no.103, vol.10).

Committee on the agreement made with Mr. Palmer for reform and improvement of the Post Office. Report, 13 July 1797. (Reps., 1731-1800, no.136, vol.19); repr. 1807 (1) ii; 1812/3 (222) iv.

Committee of secrecy on seditious societies. Report on the Society of United Irishmen. 15 March 1799. CJ Reports, vol.10, p.787; (Reps., 1731-1800, no.157, vol.25).

Committee on the state of Cold Bath Fields Prison, Clerkenwell. Report, 19 April 1799. CJ, vol.54, 441; (Reps., 1731-1800, no.148, vol.22).

Committee to draw up articles of impeachment. SEE: Whitbread, S.

St. Andrews' University Commission, Scotland. Report, 18 Aug 1845. 1846 [717] xxiii.

Select committee on the charge on H.M. Civil List revenue. Report, 29 March 1804. 1803/4 (42) v.

University commission, Scotland. Commission to visit the University of Glasgow. Report, 16 March 1839. 1839 [175] xxix.

DUNDAS, Lawrence, *1st E. Zetland*
Committee (HL) on the Glenkenns Canal Bill. SEE: De Grey, Thomas, *4th Bn. Walsingham.*

Committee (HL) on the Sunderland Dock Bill. Min. of ev. 3 July 1832. HL 1831/2 (193) cccxi.

DUNDAS, Robert
Committee on an alteration made in the Sugar Distillery Bill
Min. of ev. 6 Feb 1809. 1809 (24) iii.
Report, 15 May 1809. 1809 (268) iii.

Committee appointed to examine the physicians who have attended His Majesty during his illness. Report, 17 Dec 1810. 1810/1 (2) ii.

Committee on Crinan Canal Company's petition. Report, 25 June 1804. 1803/4 (138) v.

DUNDAS, William
Committee on Edinburgh University buildings petition. Report, 25 May 1815. 1814/5 (324) iii.

Committee on estimate for the Caledonian Canal. Report, 13 June 1816. 1816 (463) iv.

Committee on estimate for highland roads and bridges. Report, 13 June 1816. 1816 (468) iv.

DUNDAS, William (continued)

Committee on petitions relating to East India shipping. Report, 22 May 1817. 1817 (301) iii.

Secret committee on the detention of Colville in the house of correction, Cold Bath Fields. Report, 1 March 1811. 1810/1 (37) ii.

DUNDONALD, *Lord* [Peerage claim]. SEE: Freeman-Mitford, J.T.

DUNKELLIN, *Lord* SEE: De Burgh, Ulick Canning, *Lord Dunkellin.*

DUNLOP, Alexander Murray

Report on the management of the poor in Scotland, by a committee of the General Assembly [of the Church of Scotland]. 25 March 1839. 1839 [177] xx.

Select committee on packet and telegraphic contracts, 1859. SEE: Cobden, Richard.

Select committee on packet and telegraphic contracts.
1st report, 22 May 1860. 1860 (328) xiv.
2nd report, 26 June 1860. 1860 (407) xiv.
3rd report, 5 July 1860. 1860 (431) xiv.

Select committee on the valuation of lands and heritages in Scotland. Report, 22 May 1865. 1865 (300) vii.

DUNLOP, James Crawford

Report on prison dietaries, Scotland. July 1889. 1899 C.9514 xliii. Prison Commission for Scotland.

DUNMORE, *E.* SEE: Murray, Charles Adolphus, *7th E. Dunmore.*

DUNNE, Francis Plunket

Select committee on contracts for public departments. Report, 9 March 1857. 1857, session 1 (93) ii.

Select committee on Holyhead harbour. Report, 14 July 1863. 1863 (445) vii.

Select committee on taxation of Ireland. Report, 22 July 1864. 1864 (513) xv.

Select committee on the taxation of Ireland, 1865. SEE: Northcote, Stafford Henry, *Sir.*

DUNRAVEN, *E.* SEE: Wyndham-Quinn, Windham Thomas, *2nd E. Dunraven and Mount-Earl.*

[Peerage claim]. SEE: Freeman-Mitford, J.T.

DUNSANDLE, *Bn.* [Peerage claim]. SEE: Cooper, C.A.

DUNSANY, *Bn.* [Peerage claim]. 1823. SEE: Cooper, C.A.; 1854. SEE: Freeman-Mitford, J.T.

DURHAM, *Bp.* SEE:
Maltby, Edward, 1836-56.
Longley, Charles Thomas, 1856-60.
Villers, Henry M., 1860-61.
Baring, Charles, 1861-78.
Lightfoot, Joseph Barber, 1879-89.
Westcott, Brook Foss, 1890-1901.

DWARRIS, Fortunatus

Commission of inquiry on civil and criminal justice in the West Indies
1st report: Barbados, Tobago, Grenada. 5 July 1825. 1825 (157) xv.
2nd report: St. Vincent, Dominica. 18 April 1826. 1826 (276) xxvi.

3rd report: Antigua, Montserrat, Nevis, St. Christopher, Virgin Islands and general conclusions. 11 Dec 1826. 1826/7 (36) xxiv; (West Indies, 3). SEE ALSO: Henry, Jabez.

Commission of legal inquiry on the colony of Trinidad. Report, 29 June 1827. 1826/7 (551) xxiii; (West Indies, 3).

Commission on titles to lands in Trinidad. Report, 14 June 1827. 1826/7 (478) xxiii.

DYCE, William

Observations on fresco painting. 31 Aug 1846. *In:* 1846 [749] xxiv; (ED Fine Arts, 2).

Report on state schools of design in Prussia, Bavaria and France. 27 April 1838. 1840 (98) xxix; (IR Design, 3). Board of Trade.

DYKE, William Hart, *Sir*

Committee on the inland transit of cattle. SEE: Smith, James Parker.

Select committee on kitchen and refreshment rooms (HC)
Report, 19 May 1881. 1881 (234) ix.
Report, 15 Aug 1881. 1881 (400) ix.

Select committee on kitchen and refreshment rooms (HC)
1st report, 1 March 1882. 1882 (81) x.
2nd report, 14 Aug 1882. 1882 (359) x.

Select committee on the kitchen and refreshment rooms (HC)
1st report, 21 Feb 1883. 1883 (13) xiii.
2nd report, 16 Aug 1883. 1883 (310) xiii.

Select committee on kitchen and refreshment rooms (HC)
1st report, 3 July 1884. 1884 (250) xiii.
2nd report, 28 July 1884. 1884 (304) xiii.

Select committee on kitchen and refreshment rooms (HC)
Report, 24 June 1886. 1886, session 1 (243) x.
Report, 15 Sept 1886. 1886, session 2 (35) x.
2nd report, 22 Sept 1886. 1886, session 2 (50) x.

Select committee on the Local Government Provisional Order (Poor Law) Bill. Report, 15 June 1893. 1893/4 (256) xii.

Select committee on the London County Council (General Powers) Bill. SEE: Stuart-Wortley, Charles Beilby, *1st Bn. Stuart.*

Select committee on the Lower Thames Valley Main Sewerage Bill. Report, 9 June 1885. 1884/5 (217) x; (UA Sanitation, 7).

Select committee on the Teachers' Registration and Organisation Bill. Special report, 14 July 1891. 1890/1 (335) xvii.

DYSART, *Lord* [Peerage claim]. SEE: Freeman-Mitford, J.T.

EARDLEY-WILMOT, F. Marrow

Special committee on Moncrieff [gun] carriages. Reports, 22 March 1870 18 July 1874. 1875 (427) xv. War Office.

EARDLEY-WILMOT, John Eardley, *Sir*

Select committee on the County Courts Jurisdiction (No.2) Bill. Report, 5 July 1878. 1878 (267) xi; (Legal Administration, 16).

Select committee on industries in Ireland. Report, 24 July 1885. 1884/5 (288) ix.

EARNSHAW, Thomas
Committee on his petition. SEE: Giddy, D.

EASTLAKE, C.L.
Royal Academy of Arts. Members' observations on the report of the commission on the Royal Academy in relation to fine arts. 15 March 1864. 1864 [3332] xix pt.1; (ED Fine Arts, 5).

Styles and methods of painting suited to the decoration of public buildings. 1845. *In:* 1846 [685] xxiv; (ED Fine Arts, 2).

EASTNOR, *Vct.* SEE:
Cocks, John Somers, John Somers, *2nd E. Somers.*

ERRINGTON, *Vct.* SEE:
Fortescue, Hugh, *2nd E. Fortescue.*

EBOR, T.
Commission on the subdivision of parishes.
    1st report, 27 July 1849. 1849 (582) xxii.
    Min. of ev. 1849. 1854 (0.4) lxix.
    2nd report, 3 May 1850. 1850 [1224] xx.
    3rd report, 14 March 1855. 1854/5 [1922] xv.

EBURY, *Bn.* SEE:
Grosvenor, Robert, *1st Bn. Ebury.*

EDEN, George, *1st E. Auckland*
Commission for sale and redemption of land tax on church and corporation estates. Report, 30 May 1810. 1810 (325) ix.

Commission for sale and redemption of land tax on church and corporation estates. Report, 3 March 1813. 1812/3 (71) v.

Committee (HL) on Chimney Sweepers Regulation Bill. Min. of ev. 18 March 1818. HL 1818 (25) xcv.

Committee on Mr. Palmer's account [of Post Office revenues due to him]. Report, 9 June 1808. 1808 (294) iii.

Committee on the state of gaols in the City of London. Report, 9 May 1814. 1813/4 (157) iv; (CP Prisons, 7).

Select committee (HL) on the County Courts Bill. Report, 16 June 1825. HL 1825 (157) cxcii.

Select committee (HL) on the Croydon and Epsom Railway Bill. Report, 18 July 1844. HL 1844 (197) xix.

Select committee (HL) on the law relating to insolvent debtors in England. Report, 20 June 1820. HL 1820 (117) cxvii.

Select committee (HL) on the Limerick Taxation Bill. Min. of ev. 9 July 1823. HL 1823 (106) clvii.

Select committee on transportation. Report, 10 July 1812. 1812 (341) ii; (CP Transportation, 1).

EDGCUMBE, William Henry, *4th E. Mount Edgcumbe*
Royal commission on electrical communication with lighthouses, *etc.*
    1st report, 8 Dec 1893. 1893/4 C.6844 xxxi.
    2nd report, March 1894. 1894 C.7338 xxxiii.
    3rd report, 26 April 1895. 1895 C.7736 xxxv.
    4th report, 12 May 1896. 1896 C.8092 xxxiii.
    5th and final report, Sept. 1897. 1898 C.8675 xxxiii.

EDGAR, J.W.
Report on tea cultivation in Bengal and production of tobacco in India. 1874 C.982 xlviii. India Office.

EDINBURGH, *D.* SEE:
Saxe-Coburg, Alfred Ernest Albert, *D. Edinburgh.*

EDWARDES, William, *4th Bn. Kensington*
Select committee on the kitchen and refreshment rooms (HC)
    1st report, 21 Feb 1883. 1883 (13) xiii.
    2nd report, 16 Aug 1883. 1883 (310) xiii.

Select committee on kitchen and refreshment rooms (HC), 1884. SEE: Dyke, William Hart.

Select committee on kitchen and refreshment rooms (HC). Report, 16 July 1885. 1884/5 (268) x.

EDWARDS, Clement Alexander
Committee on the age of recruits sent to India. Report, 19 April 1872. 1872 (230) xxxvii. War Office.

EGERTON OF TATTON, *Bn.* SEE:
Egerton, Wilbraham, *1st E. Egerton of Tatton.*

EGERTON, Caledon R.
Committee on the supersession of British Colonels by Colonels of H.M. Indian Army. Report, 5 Jan 1869. 1868/9 (283) xxxvi. War Office.

EGERTON, Edward Christopher
Select committee on the Great Grimsby election petition. Min. of ev. 11 April 1862. 1862 (169) xvi.

Select committee on the Oxford City election petition. Min. of ev. 9 July 1857. 1857, session 2 (170) viii.

Select committee on the Weymouth and Melcombe Regis election petition. Min. of ev. 1 March 1860. 1860 (121) xi.

EGERTON, Francis Leveson, *1st E. Ellesmere*
Commission of inquiry into the constitution and management of the British Museum. Report. 1850 [1170] xxiv; (ED British Museum, 3).

Commission of inquiry into the state of fairs and markets in Ireland. SEE: Robinson, Hercules George R.

Commission on the New York Industrial Exhibition. General report. 1854 [1716] xxxvi. Foreign Office.

Select committee on Great Yarmouth election petition. Report, 14 Aug 1835. 1835 (521) x.

Select committee on the Irish miscellaneous estimates. Report, 19 June 1829. 1829 (342) iv.

Select committee on New Zealand. SEE: Grey, Henry George, *3rd E. Grey.*

Select committee on tolls and customs in Ireland. Report, 13 Aug 1834. 1834 (603) xvii.

EGERTON, Philip Grey, *Sir*
Select committee on the Coventry election petition. Min. of ev. 24 March 1868. 1867/8 (165) viii.

Select committee on the Tipperary election petition. Min. of ev. 8 April 1867. 1867 (211) viii.

EGERTON, Wilbraham, *1st E. Egerton of Tatton*
Royal commission on the blind, the deaf and dumb, *etc.* Report, 10 July 1889. 1889 C.5781 xix, xx.

Select committee (HL) on the Church of England Fire Insurance Bill. Report, 16 July 1872. HL 1872 (215) ix.

EGERTON, William Tatton
Select committee on the York, Newcastle and Berwick Railway (Construction of Docks, *etc.*) Bill. Min. of ev. 19 July 1854. 1854 (386) vii.

EGLINTON, *E.* SEE:
Montgomerie, Archibald William, *13th E. Eglinton*
(s.1819, d.1861).
Montgomerie, Archibald William, *14th E. Eglinton*
(1841-1892).

EGREMONT, *E.* SEE:
Wyndham, George O'Brien, *3rd E. Egremont* (1751-
1837).
Wyndham, George Francis, *4th E. Egremont* (1785-
1835).

ELCHO, *Bn.* SEE:
Wemyss-Charteris-Douglas, Francis, *8th E. Wemyss*
(1796-1883)
Wemyss-Charteris-Douglas, Francis, *9th E. Wemyss*
(1818-   )

ELDON, *Lord* SEE:
Scott, John, *1st E. Eldon.*

ELFORD, William, *Sir*
Committee on Matthias Koops' petition on making
paper from refuse materials. Report, 4 May 1801.
1801 (55) iii.

ELGIN, *Lord* SEE:
Bruce, Thomas, *7th E. Elgin and 11th E. Kincardine*
(1766-1841).
Bruce, James, *8th E. Elgin and 12th E. Kincardine*
(1811-1863).
Bruce, Victor Alexander, *9th E. Elgin and 13th E.
Kincardine* (1849-1917).

ELIOT, *Lord* SEE:
Eliot, John, *1st E. St. Germans* (1767-1823).
Eliot, William, *2nd E. St. Germans* (1767-1845)
(Lord Eliot, 1815-23).
Eliot, Edward Granville, *3rd E. St. Germans* (1798-
1877) (Lord Eliot, 1823-45).

ELIOT, Edward Granville, *3rd E. St. Germans*
Indian penal code. Reports. SEE: Cameron, C.H.

Select committee (HL) on the Bankruptcy and Insolvency (Ireland) Act Amendment Bill. Report, 23
March 1865. HL 1865 (43) xxi.

Select committee on the Drainage (Ireland) Bill.
Min. of proc. 13 May 1842. 1842 (246) xiv.

Select committee (HL) on the Drainage and Improvement of Lands (Ireland) Bill. Report, 7 July 1863.
HL 1863 (197) xxxiii.

Select committee on the Fisheries (Ireland) Bill.
Min. of proc. 6 July 1842. 1842 (403) xiv; repr,
1863 (70) vii; (Fisheries, 2).

Select committee (HL) on the Furness Railway Bill,
the Chester and Holyhead Railway (Power to Purchase, *etc*) Bill, the London, Brighton, and South
Coast Railway (London Bridge and New Cross Stations) Bill, and the London and South-Western Railway Company's Acts Amendment, Extension, Devia-
tion and New Works Bill. Report, 27 July 1848. HL
1847/8 (265) xxvi.

Select committee (HL) on the Irish Poor Law. SEE:
Petty-Fitzmaurice, Henry, *3rd M. Landsdowne.*

Select committee on New Zealand. Report, 3 Aug
1840. 1840 (582) vii; (New Zealand, 1).

Select committee (HL) on salmon fisheries in Scotland. Report, 5 July 1860. HL 1860 (135) xxvi;
HC repr. 1860 (465) xix.

Select committee on Walsall election. Proc., min.
of ev. 5 April 1841. 1841 (219) ix.

ELIOT, John, *1st E. St. Germans*
Committee (HL) on Mr. Palmer's agreement (for
reform and improvement of the Post Office). Report, 17 June 1808. HL 1808 (111) xviii; repr. HL
1812 (137) liii.

ELLENBOROUGH, *E.* SEE:
Law, Edward, *1st E. Ellenborough.*

ELLESMERE, *E.* SEE:
Egerton, Francis, *1st E. Ellesmere* (1800-1857).
Egerton, George Granville Francis, *2nd E. Ellesmere*
(1823-1862).

ELLICE, C.H.
Committee on the formation of territorial regiments.
Report, 25 Feb 1881. 1881 C.2793 xx. War Office.

ELLICE, Edward
Commission on purchase and sale of commissions
in the Army. Note of dissent. 3 Aug 1857. 1857/8
[2293] xix; (Military and Naval, 3). SEE ALSO:
St. Maur, Edward Adolphus, *12th D. Somerset.*

Select committee appointed to prepare the militia
estimates. Report, 10 July 1833. 1833 (506) vii.

Select committee appointed to prepare the militia
estimates. Report, 27 June 1834. 1834 (425) xviii.

Select committee on Army and Ordnance expenditure. SEE: Maule-Ramsay, Fox.

Select committee on St. Alban's election petition
Min. of ev. 9 April 1851. 1851 (193) xii.
Min. of ev. 10 April 1851. 1851 (202) xii.
Min. of ev. 15 April 1851. 1851 (220) xii.

ELLIOT, Charles Gilbert John Brydone
Committee on the position of masters of the Royal
Navy. Report, 25 March 1862. 1866 (109) xlvii.

ELLIOT, E.F.
Commission for the investigation of alleged cases
of torture in the Madras Presidency. Report, 16 April
1855. 1854/5 (420) xl. East India Office.

ELLIOT, George
Committee on the designs upon which ships of war
have recently been constructed. Dissenting report.
14 Oct 1871. 1872 C.489 xiv. Admiralty. SEE ALSO:
Hamilton-Temple-Blackwood, Frederick Temple, *1st
M. Dufferin and Ava.*

Committee on Navy boilers. SEE: Aynsley, Charles
Murray.

Memorandum report on the design of ships of war:
'Devastation' and 'Thunderer' class. 11 March 1871.
In: 1871 C.333 xiv. Admiralty.

Select committee on lighthouses. SEE: Hume, Joseph.

ELLIOT, Thomas Frederick
Colonial land and emigration commission. Report on
colonization of the Falkland Islands and comments
on a British Port. 22 Aug 1840. 1841, session 2 (3) iii.

Colonial land and emigration commission. Report on
the course which should be pursued in the settlement
of the Falkland Islands. 30 March 1841. 1841, session
2 (3) iii.

Colonial land and emigration commission. Report on
the Passengers' Act. 22 July 1842. 1842 [355] xxv;
(Emigration, 10). Colonial Office.

Report on the applicability of emigration to relief
of distress in the Highlands. 29 July 1837. 1837 (60)
xxvii; (Emigration, 20). Colonial Office.

ELLIOT-MURRAY-KYNYMOUND, Gilbert, *2nd E. Minto*
Commission of religious instruction in Scotland. SEE:
Bell, Robert.

Committee on the Signet and Privy Seal offices.
Report, 30 Jan 1849. 1849 [1099] xxii.

Select committee (HL) on accommodation in the HL
to ambassadors and foreign ministers during debates.
Report, 25 June 1850. HL 1850 (226) xxii.
Report, 27 June 1850. HL 1850 (230) xxii.

Select committee (HL) on the county and burgh
police systems of Scotland. Report, 17 July 1868.
HL 1867/8 (112) xxx; HC repr. 1867/8 (486) ix;
(CP Police, 9).

Select committee (HL) on the East India Company's
charter. Report, 29 June 1852. HL 1852 (88) xix;
HC repr. 1852/3 (41) xxx; (East India, 15).

ELLIOT, T.H.
Report on the relation of wages in certain industries
to the cost of production. 4 Aug 1891. 1890/1 C.6535
lxxviii; (Industrial Relations, 21). Board of Trade.

ELLIS, Charles Rose
Committee on the commercial state of the West
India Colonies. Report, 24 July 1807. 1807 (65)
iii; (West Indies, 2).

Select committee on local taxation of Dublin. Report,
5 June 1822. 1822 (394) vii.

ELLIS, Francis W.
Report on the Harwich railway lines. 23 Feb 1847.
1847 (433) lxiii. Admiralty.

ELLIS, George Agar
Select committee on the present state of the library
of the HC. Report, 7 June 1820. 1820 (496) iv.

ELLIS, John Edward
Select committee on the Charity Commission. Report,
16 July 1894. 1894 (221) xi.

Standing committee on trade. Light Railways Bill.
Report, 30 April 1896. 1896 (159) x.

Standing committee on trade. Locomotives on Highways Bill. Report, 9 June 1898. 1898 (233) x.

Standing committee on trade. Market Gardners'
Compensation (Scotland) Bill. Report, 17 May 1897.
1897 (215) xi.

Standing committee on trade. Merchant Shipping
(Liability of Shipowners) Bill. Report, 2 May 1898.
1898 (189) x.

Standing committee on trade. Merchant Shipping
(Mercantile Marine Fund) Bill. Report, 31 March
1898. 1898 (140) x.

Standing committee on trade. Merchant Shipping
(Under Manning) Bill. Report, 13 May 1897. 1897
(209) xi.

Standing committee on trade. Plumbers' Registration
Bill. Report, 13 May 1897. 1897 (208) xiii.

Standing committee on trade. Sale of Food and Drugs
Bill. Report, 12 May 1899. 1899 (195) x.

Standing committee on trade. Shops (Early Closing)
Bill. Report, 26 March 1896. 1896 (126) xiii.

Standing committee on trade. Telegraphs (Telephonic
Communication, *etc*.) Bill. Report, 6 July 1899.
1899 (266) x.

Standing committee on trade. Truck Bill. Report,
21 May 1896. 1896 (196) xiv.

ELLIS, John Whitakker, *Sir*
Select committee on the Salmon Fisheries (Ireland)
Acts Amendment Bill. Report, 31 May 1892. 1892
(236) xvii.

ELLIS, Thomas Flower
Commission on the state of criminal law in the Channel
Islands.
1st report: Jersey. 1847 [865] xv.
2nd report: Guernsey. 1847/8 [945] xxvii.

ELLIS, Welbore
Committee appointed to examine precedents respecting cases of the personal exercise of the Royal authority being prevented or interrupted. Report, 12 Dec
1788. CJ, vol.44, p.11; (Reps., 1731-1800, no.90,
vol.8).

ELPHINSTONE, James Dalrymple Horn, *Sir*
Select committee on anchors, etc for the merchant
service. Report, 27 March 1860. 1860 (182) viii.

Select committee on East India communication.
Report, 22 May 1862. 1862 (266) vii.

ELTON, Charles Isaac
Select committee on the Temporary Dwellings Bill.
Report, 11 Aug 1887. 1887 (279) xiii.

ELWYN, Thomas
Special committee on Moncrieff [gun] carriages.
SEE: Eardley-Wilmot, F.M.

EMMERSON-TENNENT, James, *Sir*
Committee on the Executive council on the fixed
establishments of Ceylon. 13 Dec 1849. 1852 (568)
xxxvi. Colonial Office.

Report on the finance and commerce of the island
of Ceylon. 22 Oct 1846. 1847/8 [933] xlii. Colonial
Office.

Select committee on copyright of designs. Report,
6 July 1840. 1840 (442) vi; (IR Design, 2).

ENFIELD, *Vct.* SEE:
Byng, George Henry Charles, *3rd E. Strafford.*

ENGLEHEART, John Leonhard Dillman, *Sir*
Departmental committee on encouraging the increase
of allotments upon the lands belonging to the Duchy
of Lancaster. Report, 1 May 1894. 1894 (122) lxviii;
(Agriculture, 20).

ENNISKILLEN, *E.* [Peerage claim]. SEE:
Giffard, H.S.

ERLE, William
Commission of inquiry into the state and practice of
county courts. SEE: Romilly, John.

Trades unions commission
1st report. 1867 [3873] xxxii.
2nd report. 1867 [3897] xxxii.
3rd report. 1867 [3910] xxxii.
4th report. 1867 [3952] xxxii.
5th report. 1867/8 [3980-I] xxxix.
6th report. 1867/8 [3980-II] xxxix.
7th report. 1867/8 [3980-III] xxxix.
8th report. 1867/8 [3980-IV] xxxix.
9th report. 1867/8 [3980-V] xxxix.
10th report. 1867/8 [3980-VI] xxxix.
11th and final report (2 vols) 9 March 1869. 1868/9
[4123] xxxix; (Industrial relations, 8-9).

ERNE, *E.* SEE:
Crichton, John Henry, *4th E. Erne.*

ERROLL, E. SEE:
Hay, William George, *16th E. Eroll* (1810-1846)
Hay, William Henry, *17th E. Eroll* (1823-).

ERSKINE, Charles SEE:
ARESKINE, Charles.

ERSKINE, Thomas
Commission on bankruptcy and insolvency. Report, 30 July 1840. 1840 [274] xvi.

ESHER, *Vct.* SEE:
Brett, William Baliol, *Vct. Esher.*

ESLINGTON, *Bn.* SEE:
Liddell, Henry George, *2nd E. Ravensworth.*

ESSEX, E. SEE:
Capel, Arthur Algernon, *6th E. Essex.*

ESTCOURT, Thomas Grimston Bucknall
Commission on the state of Ilchester gaol. Report, 8 and 22 Feb 1822. 1822 (7), (54) xi; (CP Prisons, 9).

Select committee on the British Museum. Report, 6 Aug 1835. 1835 (479) vii; (ED British Museum, 1).

Select committee on the British Museum. Report, 14 July 1836. 1836 (440) x; (ED British Museum, 2).

Select committee on the Metropolitan police. Report, 16 Aug 1833. 1833 (675) xii.

Select committee on the police of the Metropolis. Report, 11 July 1828. 1828 (533) vi; (CP Police, 4).

Select committee on the police of the Metropolis, 1834. SEE: Bonham-Carter, John.

Select committee on standing orders revision, 1840. Report, 5 Aug 1840. 1840 (594) xv.

Select committee on standing orders revision, 1840 as agreed to and made standing orders of the HC. Report, 10 Aug 1840. 1840 (618) xv.

Select committee on standing orders revision, 1846. Report, 20 Aug 1846. 1846 (662) xii.

ESTCOURT, Thomas Sutton Sotheron. SEE:
Sotheron-Estcourt, Thomas Sutton.

EUSTON, *Lord* SEE:
Fitzroy, C., E. Euston.

EVANS, De Lacy, *Sir*
Select committee on East India, transport of troops. Report, 1 July 1858. 1857/8 (382) x.

EVANS, Frederick John
Sub-committee on the most suitable place for a harbour of refuge on the East coast of Scotland to be constructed by convicts. Report, 28 March 1884. 1884 C.4035 xliii. Treasury. SEE ALSO: Du Cane, E.F.

EVANS, J. Emrys
Report on the trade, commerce and gold mining industry of the South African Republic, 1897. 12 May 1898. 1899 C.9093 lxiv. Colonial Office.

EVANS, John
Committee on the science collections at South Kensington. Report, 23 July 1889. 1889 C.5831 xxxiv.

EVANS, Richard
Select committee on victualling house licenses, Hol-

born division. Report, 29 July and 14 Aug 1833. 1833 (585), (664) xv; repr. 1852/3 (292) xxxviii.

EVANS, Thomas William
Select committee on the Beverley election petition. Min. of ev. 18 April 1860. 1860 (224) xi.

Select committee on the Lisburn election petition. Min. of ev. 11 June 1863. 1863 (343) vii.

Select committee on the Maidstone and Ashford Railway Bill. Special report, 22 June 1880. 1880 (238) ix.

Select committee on the Norwich election petition. Min. of ev. 3 Aug 1859. 1859, session 2 (140) iv.

Select committee on the Rye election petition. Min. of ev. 26 April 1866. 1866 (211) xi.

EVELYN, George Augustus William Shuckburgh, *Sir*
Committee on the petition of Matthew Baillie and Everard Home, trustees in the will of John Hunter, respecting the purchase of the Hunterian Collection. Report, 16 March 1796. CJ, vol.51, p.512; (Reps., 1731-1800, no.126, vol.16).

EVERSLEY, *Vct.* SEE:
Shaw-Lefevre, Charles, *1st Vct. Eversley.*

EWART, James Cossar
Committee on the regulation of trawling and other modes of fishing in territorial waters. Report, 10 April 1888. 1888 C.5486 xxviii. Fishery Board for Scotland.

EWART, William
Select committee on arts and manufacturers. Report, 4 Sept 1835. 1835 (598) v; (IR Design, 1).

Select committee on arts and manufacturers. Report, 16 Aug 1836. 1836 (568) ix; (IR Design, 1).

Select committee on colonization and settlement in India
    1st report, 6 May 1858. 1857/8 (261) vii, pt.1.
    2nd report, 10 June 1858. 1857/8 (326) vii, pt.1.
    3rd report, 12 July 1858. 1857/8 (415) vii, pt.1.
    4th report, 23 July 1858. 1857/8 (461) vii pt.2;
    (East India, 17).

Select committee on the colonization and settlement of India. Report, 7 April 1859. 1859, session 1 (198) iv; (East India, 18).

Select committee on colonization and settlement in India. Report, 9 Aug 1859. 1859, session 2 (171) v; (East India, 18).

Select committee on the Oxford and Cambridge Universities Education Bill. Special report, 31 July 1867. 1867 (497) xiii.

Select committee on public libraries. Report, 23 July 1849. 1849 (548) xviii; (ED Public Libraries, 1).

Select committee on public libraries. Report, 1 Aug 1850. 1850 (655) xviii; (ED Public Libraries, 2).

Select committee on public libraries. Report, 2 Aug 1851. 1851 (630) x; (ED Public Libraries, 2).

Select committee on public libraries. Report, 25 June 1852. 1852 (532) v; (ED Public Libraries, 2).

Select committee on weights and measures. Report, 15 July 1862. 1862 (411) vii.

EXETER, *Bp.* SEE:
Courtenay, Henry Reginald, 1797-1803
Fisher, John, 1803-07
Pelham, George, 1807-20

Carey, William, 1820-30
Bethell, Christopher, 1830
Phillpotts, Henry, 1831-69
Temple, Frederick, 1869-85
Bickersteth, Edward Henry, 1885-1900

EXHAM, William Allan
Commission on municipal boundaries in Ireland. SEE: Cotton, Charles P.

Commission on the charges made by Alexander Francis Ball against the magistracy of Dungannon. Report, 13 Nov 1871. 1872 C.482 xx. Irish Secretary's Office.

Commission of inquiry into the riots and disturbances in the City of Londonderry, 1869. Report, 30 Nov 1869. 1870 C.58 xxxii; (CP Civil Disorder, 7). Irish Secretary's Office.

EYRE, Henry
Committee on infantry equipment
    1st report, 28 July 1865
    2nd report, 16 March 1867
    3rd report, 20 Feb 1868
    4th report, 11 Nov 1868. *All in:* 1871(72) xxxix. War Office.

Committee on libraries, reading rooms and day rooms for the troops. Report, 24 Aug 1861. 1862 [2920] xxxii. War Office.

Committee on regimental quartermasters. Report, 28 Dec 1864. 1865 (123) xxxii. War Office.

FAIR, Robert
Report on Holyhead and Port Dynllaen harbours. 9 June 1843. 1844 (43) xlv. Admiralty.

FAIRBAIRN, William
Commission of inquiry on the warming and ventilating the apartments of dwelling-houses and barracks. Report, 25 Aug 1857. 1857, session 2 (320) xli. General Board of Health.

Report on experiments for ascertaining the strength of iron structures. 19 Jan 1864. 1864 [3289] liii. Board of Trade.

FAIRFAX, Lord
Committee on petitions on his will. SEE: Vansittart, G.

FANE, John
Committee on Lyme Regis harbour petitions.
    Report, 12 June 1817. 1817 (356) iii.
    Report on re-committed report, 5 July 1817. 1817 (463) iii.

FANE, Henry
Committee on standing orders. SEE: Graham, J.

FARADAY, Michael
Report on electric light to the Commission on lights, buoys and beacons. 11 Oct 1862. 1862 (489) liv. Board of Trade.

Report on the explosion at the Haswell Collieries and on the means of preventing similar accidents. 21 Oct 1844. 1845 (232) xvi. Home Department.

Commission appointed to consider the lighting of picture galleries by gas. Report, 20 July 1859. 1859, session 2 (106) xv. Privy Council Committee for Education. (ED Fine Arts, 3).

FARNALL, Harry Burrard
Reports on the distress in the cotton manufacturing

district. 21 May to 20 June 1862. 1862 (413) xlix. Poor Law Board.

Report on distress in the cotton manufacturing districts. 4 Jan and 11 Feb 1864. 1864 (60) lii. Poor Law Board.

Report on distress in the cotton manufacturing district. 28 June 1864. 1864 (471) lii. Poor Law Board.

Report on the education and training of children in the north of England. 14 Jan 1851. 1851 (646) xlix. Poor Law Board.

Report on the infirmary wards of the several Metropolitan workhouses and their existing arrangements. 12 June 1866. 1866 (387) lxi. Poor Law Board.

Report of the inquiry into complaints against the management of the Rotherhithe Workhouse Infirmary. 5 July 1866. 1866 (518) lxi. Poor Law Board.

FARNBOROUGH, Bn. SEE:
Long, Charles, *1st Bn. Farnborough.*

FARR, William
Abstracts of causes of death, England and Wales, June to Dec 1837. 6 May 1839. *In:* 1839 [187] xvi.

Report on the epidemic cholera in England, 1866. 25 July 1866. *In* 1867/8 [4072] xxxvii; (HE Infectious Diseases, 3). Registrar-General's Office.

Report on the Northampton table of mortality, 1845. *In:* 1847/8 [967] xxv.

FARRE, Arthur
Report on 38 Metropolitan workhouses. 26 March 1849. 1850 (133) xxi; (HE Infectious Diseases, 1). General Board of Health.

FARREN, R.T.
Report on the condition of Castlebar Union Workhouse. 17 May 1850. 1850 (461) l. Poor Law Board.

FARRER, Thomas Henry
Committee on bankruptcy administration orders. Report, June 1887. 1887 C.5139 lxxv. Lord Chancellor's Office *and* Board of Trade.

Committee on the navigation of the River Thames
    Preliminary report, 5 Dec 1878. 1878/9 C.2198 xli.
    Report, 16 June 1879. 1878/9 C.2338 xli. Board of Trade.

Memorandum on the Merchant Shipping Law Consolidation Bill. 1854 (0.1) lxix. Board of Trade.

FAWCETT, Henry
Select committee on Post Office annuities and life assurance policies. Report, 28 March 1882. 1882 (138) xii.

FAZAKERLEY, John Nicholas
Select committee on the accounts and papers relating to the Rideau Canal. Report, 22 April 1831. 1830/1 (395) iii; (Canada, 6).

Select committee on canal communications in Canada. Report, 29 June 1832. 1831/2 (570) v; (Canada, 6).

Select committee on Leith harbour. Report, 4 July 1836. 1836 (403) xx.

Select committee on lower Canada. Report, 3 July 1834. 1834 (449) xviii; (Canada, 1).

Select committee on the affairs of lower Canada. SEE: Rice, Thomas Spring.

Select committee on the Poor Law Amendment Act
    Report, 5 July 1837. 1837 (481) xvii, pt.1.

FAZAKERLEY, John Nicholas (continued)

    1st report, 20 March 1837. 1837 (131) xvii, pt.1.
    2nd report, 22 March 1837. 1837 (138) xvii, pt.1.
    3rd report, 24 April 1837. 1837 (225) xvii, pt.1.
    4th report, 28 April 1837. 1837 (250) xvii, pt.1.
    5th report, 1 May 1837. 1837 (257) xvii, pt.1.
    6th report, 3 May 1837. 1837 (260) xvii, pt.1.
    7th report, 5 May 1837. 1837 (276) xvii, pt.1.
    8th report, 8 May 1837. 1837 (278) xvii, pt.1.
    9th report, 10 May 1837. 1837 (296) xvii, pt.1.
    10th report, 22 May 1837. 1837 (329) xvii, pt.2.
    11th report, 26 May 1837. 1837 (339) xvii, pt.2.
    12th report, 1 June 1837. 1837 (350) xvii, pt.2.
    13th report, 2 June 1837. 1837 (368) xvii, pt.2.
    14th report, 5 June 1837. 1837 (369) xvii, pt.2.
    15th report, 7 June 1837. 1837 (385) xvii, pt.2.
    16th report, 9 June 1837. 1837 (386) xvii, pt.2.
    17th report, 12 June 1837. 1837 (395) xvii, pt.2.
    18th report, 14 June 1837. 1837 (399) xvii, pt.2.
    19th report, 16 June 1837. 1837 (404) xvii, pt.2.
    20th report, 23 June 1837. 1837 (415) xvii, pt.2.
    21st report, 26 June 1837. 1837 (426) xvii, pt.2.
    22nd report, 28 June 1837. 1837 (446) xvii, pt.2.
    Index. 5 July 1837. 1837 (481-II) xvii, pt.2; (Poor
      Law Board, 1-2).

Select committee on the Poor Law Amendment Act
    Report, 7 Aug 1838. 1837/8 (681-I) xviii, pt.1.
    1st report, 9 Feb 1838. 1837/8 (136) xviii, pt.1.
    2nd report, 13 Feb 1838. 1837/8 (138) xviii, pt.1.
    3rd report, 14 Feb 1838. 1837/8 (140) xviii, pt.1.
    4th report, 16 Feb 1838. 1837/8 (144) xviii, pt.1.
    5th report, 19 Feb 1838. 1837/8 (145) xviii, pt.1.
    6th and 7th reports, 23 Feb 1838. 1837/8 (161)
      xviii, pt.1.
    8th report, 27 Feb 1838. 1837/8 (167) xviii, pt.1.
    9th report, 28 Feb 1838. 1837/8 (174) xviii, pt.1.
    10th report, 2 March 1838. 1837/8 (183) xviii, pt.1.
    11th report, 6 March 1838. 1837/8 (191) xviii, pt.1.
    12th report, 7 March 1838. 1837/8 (192) xviii, pt.1.
    13th report, 9 March 1838. 1837/8 (194) xviii, pt.1.
    14th report, 14 March 1838. 1837/8 (202) xviii,
      pt.1.
    15th report, 14 March 1838. 1837/8 (210) xviii,
      pt.1.
    16th report, 16 March 1838. 1837/8 (220) xviii,
      pt.1.
    17th report, 20 March 1838. 1837/8 (222) xviii,
      pt.2.
    18th report, 21 March 1838. 1837/8 (225) xviii,
      pt.2.
    19th report, 23 March 1838. 1837/8 (233) xviii,
      pt.2.
    20th report, 27 March 1838. 1837/8 (246) xviii,
      pt.2.
    21st report, 28 March 1838. 1837/8 (258) xviii,
      pt.2.
    22nd report, 30 March 1838. 1837/8 (262) xviii,
      pt.2.
    23rd report, 3 April 1838. 1837/8 (273) xviii,
      pt.2.
    24th report, 4 April 1838. 1837/8 (279) xviii,
      pt.2.
    25th report, 6 April 1838. 1837/8 (283) xviii,
      pt.2.
    26th and 27th reports, 4 May 1838. 1837/8 (359)
      xviii, pt.2.
    28th report, 8 May 1838. 1837/8 (374) xviii,
      pt.2.
    29th report, 9 May 1838. 1837/8 (378) xviii,
      pt.2.
    30th report, 10 May 1838. 1837/8 (380) xviii,
      pt.2.

    31st report, 15 May 1838. 1837/8 (390) xviii,
      pt.2.
    32nd report, 16 May 1838. 1837/8 (400) xviii,
      pt.2.
    33rd report, 18 May 1838. 1837/8 (405) xviii,
      pt.2.
    34th report, 22 May 1838. 1837/8 (414) xviii,
      pt.2.
    35th report, 24 May 1838. 1837/8 (428) xviii,
      pt.3.
    36th report, 25 May 1838. 1837/8 (429) xviii,
      pt.3.
    37th, 38th, 39th reports, 1 June 1838. 1837/8
      (439) xviii, pt.3.
    40th report, 7 June 1838. 1837/8 (452) xviii,
      pt.3.
    41st report, 12 June 1838. 1837/8 (469) xviii,
      pt.3.
    42nd report, 13 June 1838. 1837/8 (479) xviii,
      pt.3.
    43rd report, 15 June 1838. 1837/8 (501) xviii,
      pt.3.
    44th, 45th, 46th reports: Medical inquiry. 20 and
      22 June 1838. 1837/8 (518) xviii, pt.3.
    47th report, 22 June 1838. 1837/8 (526) xviii, pt.3.
    48th report, 11 July 1838. 1837/8 (579) xviii, pt.3.
    49th report, 11 July 1838. 1837/8 (625) xviii, pt.3.
    Index. 7 Aug 1838. 1837/8 (681-II) xviii, pt.3;
      (Poor Law, 3-5).

FEATHERSTONHAUGH, J.D.
    British commission on the north-eastern boundary
    of the United States. Report, 16 April 1840. 1840
    [257] xxxii. Foreign Office.

    Supplementary reports on the boundary between
    the British possessions in North America and the
    United States of America. 28 Nov 1840 and 11 Feb
    1842. 1842 [413] xxviii. Foreign Office.

FEILDING, Rudolph Robert Basil Aloysius Augustine,
9th E. Denbigh
    Select committee (HL) on the Infant Life Protection
    Bill and the Safety of Nurse Children Bill. Report,
    7 July 1896. HL 1896 (186) ix; HC repr. 1896 (343) x.

FELL-PEASE, H. SEE:
Pease, H.F.

FERGUSON, Hugh
    Report on the cases of pleuro-pneumonia among
    cattle recently imported from Ireland into Norfolk.
    25 Jan 1875. 1875 (193) lx; (AG Animal Health, 2).
    Privy Council, Veterinary Department.

    Report on the cattle plague in Ireland. 10 Feb 1866.
    1866 [3647] lix. Irish Secretary's Office. SEE ALSO:
    Bourke, R.S., *6th E. Mayo.*

    Report on the trade in and the movement of animals
    intended for exportation from Ireland to G.B. 19 July
    1878. 1878 C.2104 xxv. Veterinary Department.
    Irish Privy Council.

FERGUSON, Robert, *Sir*
    Committee of selection on the grouping of private
    bills. SEE: Sotheron, T.H.S. and SEE: Wilson-Patten,
    John.

    Select committee on classification of railway bills,
    1847. SEE: Wilson-Patten, John.

    Select committee on county cess, Ireland. Report,
    4 Aug 1836. 1836 (527) xii.

FERGUSON, Ronald Craufurd, *Sir*
    Select committee on Warwick Borough. Report,
    22 July 1833. 1833 (556) xi.

Select committee on the Warwick Borough election petition. Report, 17 May 1833. 1833 (295) xi.

FERGUSSON, James, *Sir*

Commission on the Factory and Workshop Acts. Report, 10 Feb 1876. 1876 C.1443 xxix, xxx; (IR Factories, 4-5).

Royal commission on grocers' licences in Scotland. Report, 1878. 1878 C.1941 xxvi.

Select committee on colonisation, 1889. SEE: Ritchie, Charles Thomson.

Select committee on colonisation. Report, 31 July 1890. 1890 (354) xii; (Emigration, 9).

Select committee on colonisation Report, 17 March 1891. 1890/1 (152) xi; (Emigration, 9).

Select committee on the London Improvements Bill. Report, 13 June 1893. 1893/4 (251) xii.

Select committee on merchanise marks. Report, 27 July 1897. 1897 (346) xi.

Select committee on the Sale of Liquors on Sunday Bill. Special report, 7 July 1868. 1867/8 (402) xiv.

Standing committee on law. Benefices Bill. Report, 28 April 1896. 1896 (155) ix.

Standing committee on law. Benefices Bill and the Benefices (No.2) Bill. Report, 1 April 1898. 1898 (147) viii.

Standing committee on law. Berriew School Bill. Report, 30 April 1897. 1897 (189) viii.

Standing committee on law. Board of Education (Lords) Bill. Report, 7 July 1899. 1899 (270) viii.

Standing committee on law. Habitual Inebriates Bill. Report, 8 July 1898. 1898 (286) x.

Standing committee on law. Improvement of Land Bill. Report, 14 July 1899. 1899 (279) x.

Standing committee on law. Infant Life Protection Bill. Report, 16 July 1897. 1897 (323) x.

Standing committee on law. Judicial Trustees Bill. Report, 15 May 1896. 1896 (187) x.

Standing committee on law. Labourers (Ireland) Bill. Report, 30 June 1896. 1896 (268) x.

Standing committee on law. Land Transfer Bill. Report, 16 July 1897. 1897 (324) x.

Standing committee on law. Locomotives on Highways Bill. Report, 10 July 1896. 1896 (293) x.

Standing committee on law. London University Commission Bill. Report, 19 July 1898. 1898 (306) x.

Standing committee on law. Poor Law Officers' Superannuation Bill. Report, 1 May 1896. 1896 (164) xiii.

Standing committee on law. Preferential Payments in Bankruptcy Act (1888) Amendment Bill. Report, 9 March 1897. 1897 (118) xiii.

Standing committee on law. Metropolitan and Other Police Courts Bill. Report, 29 June 1897. 1897 (270) xi.

Standing committee on law. Military Manoeuvres Bill. Report, 27 July 1897. 1897 (345) xi.

Standing committee on law. Public Health (Ireland) Bill. Report, 8 May 1896. 1896 (170) xiii.

Standing committee on law. Public Health (Scotland) Bill. Report, 3 June 1897. 1897 (243) xiii.

Standing committee on law. Vexatious Actions (Scotland) Bill. Report, 12 July 1898. 1898 (295) xii.

FERMOY, *Bn.* [Peerage claim]. SEE:
Freeman-Mitford, J.T.

FEVERSHAM, *Lord* SEE:
Duncombe, Charles, *1st Bn. Feversham of Duncombe Park* (1746-1841)
Duncombe, William, *2nd Bn. Feversham* (1798-1867)

FFRENCH, Martin Joseph

Report of inquiry on charges against sub-inspector Boyce of the police station at Dundrum, County Tipperary. 22 Feb 1864. 1864 (236) xlix. Irish Secretary's Office.

FIENNES-PELHAM-CLINTON, Henry Pelham, *5th D. Newcastle*

Commission for the improvement of the Metropolis. SEE: Howard, G.W.F., *7th E. Carlisle.*

Select committee on the Houses of Parliament. Report, 4 July 1844. 1844 (448) vi.

FILDER, William

Committee of inquiry into the Naval, Ordnance and Commissariat establishments and expenditure in the colonies. General report, 12 April 1852. 1852 [1515] xxx. Treasury.

FILMER, Edmund, *Sir*

Select committee on Thames marshes. Report, 17 July 1854. 1854 (378) xviii.

FINLAISON, Alexander Glen

Report on the Merchant Seamen's Fund. 18 March 1850. 1850 (178) liii. Board of Trade.

Report and tables on sickness and mortality among members of friendly societies. 1 Aug 1853. 1852/3 (955) c. National Debt Office.

Report on tontines and life annuities and on the duration of life among the nominees of government life annuitants. 1 Aug 1860. 1860 (585) xl; (Insurance, 3). National Debt Office.

FINLAISON, John

Report on the evidence and elementary facts on which the tables of life annuities are founded. 31 March 1829. 1829 (122) iii; (Insurance, 3).

FINLAY, Alexander Struthers

Select committee on the Game Laws (Scotland) Bill. Min. of proc., 8 July 1867. 1867 (426) x.

FINLAY, Robert Bannatyne

Joint select committee on statute law revision bills, *etc.*, 1897, 1899. SEE: Giffard, H.S., *1st E. Halsbury.*

Select committee on the Court of Criminal Appeal Bill. Report, 1 July 1895. 1895 (351) vii.

Select committee on election petitions. Report, 2 Aug 1898. 1898 (340) ix; (GO Elections, 5).

Select committee on parliamentary election petitions. Report, 27 July 1897. 1897 (347) xiii; (GO Elections, 5).

FISHER, William Hayes

Departmental committee on the sale of Ordnance Survey maps
    Report, 9 July 1896. 1896 C.8147 lxviii.
    Appendix, index. 1896 C.8148 lxviii.

FITZGERALD, *Lord* SEE:
Fitzgerald, John David, *Bn. Fitzgerald.*

FITZGERALD, Charles William, *5th D. Leinster*
Commission on endowed schools, Ireland. Report, 1 Feb 1858. 1857/8 [2336 I-IV] xxii, pts. I-IV. SEE ALSO: Stephens, Archibald John.

Commission of inquiry on the Queen's colleges at Belfast, Cork and Galway. Report, 30 June 1858. 1857/8 [2413] xxi.

Commission on the Science and Art Department, Ireland. Report, 2 Oct 1868. 1868/9 [4103] xxiv. Privy Council.

FITZGERALD, F.A.
Trial of the Cashel election petitions. Min. of ev. April 1869. 1868/9 (121) xlix.

FITZGERALD, Gerald, *Sir*
Committee on administration and management of dock yards. Sub-committee on dockyard accounts and audit. Report, 14 April 1886. 1887 C.4979 xvi. Admiralty.

FITZGERALD, William Seymour V.
Report on Mr. Murray's plan for the revision of consular fees. 26 May 1859. 1859, session 2 [2554] xv. Foreign Office.

FITZGERALD, John David, *Bn. Fitzgerald*
Commission on the High Court of Admiralty in Ireland. Report, 21 May 1864. 1864 [3343] xxix.

Down County election petition trial. Judgement and ev. 29 June 1880. 1880 (260) lvii.

Report on the trial of the Longford election petition. 9 April 1870. 1870 (178) lvi.

Select committee on Court of Chancery (Ireland) Bills. SEE: Keogh, William.

Select committee (HL) on the Infants Bill. Report, 17 March 1885. HL 1884/5 (45) vii.

Select committee on the Sligo Borough election (Mr. Somers' petitions). Report, 23 July 1857. 1857, session 2 (206) viii.

FITZGERALD, Robert Uniacke Penrose, *Sir*
Select committee on the Fisheries Act (Norfolk and Suffolk) Amendment Bill. Report, 19 May 1896. 1896 (190) ix.

Select committee on Great Southern and Western, Waterford, Limerick and Western Railway Companies Amalgamation Bill. Report, 21 July 1899. 1899 (290) ix.

FITZGERALD, Vesey
Committee on the establishment of the Royal household at Windsor. Report, 17 Feb 1819. 1819 (56) ii.

Committee on the lunatic poor in Ireland. Report, 25 June 1817. 1817 (430) viii.

Committee on the Royal Canal of Ireland. Report, 7 July 1817. 1817 (470) viii.

FITZGERALD, William
Committee on the petition of the Royal Canal Company, Ireland. Report, 14 June 1811. 1810/11 (235) iv.

FITZGERALD, William Robert Seymour, *Sir*
Select committee on the Dover Pier and Harbour Bill. Report, 1 June 1875. 1875 (236) x.

Select committee on the Metropolitan Buildings and Management Bill. Special report, 14 July 1874. 1874 (285) x.

FITZGERALD, William Vesey
Committee on petition for promoting the education of the poor of Ireland. 14 June 1815. 1814/5 (399) vi.

FITZGIBBON, Gerald
Education endowments (Ireland) commission. Final report, 18 Dec 1894. 1894 C.7517 xxx, pt.1. Irish Secretary's Office.

FITZMAURICE, Edmund George, *Lord*
Departmental committee on swine fever. Report, 27 March 1893. 1893/4 C.6999 xxiii; (AG Animal Health, 3). Board of Agriculture.

Standing committee on trade. Agriculture and Technical Instruction (Ireland) Bill. Report, 20 July 1899. 1899 (284) viii.

FITZMAURICE, George
Report of the inquiry into the conduct of the constabulary during the disturbances at Belfast in July and September 1857. 11 Feb 1858. 1857/8 (333) xlvii; (CP Civil Disorder, 7). Irish Secretary's Office.

FITZMAURICE, W.T.P. SEE:
Petty-Fitzmaurice, W.T.

FITZPATRICK, Bernard Edward Barnaby, *2nd Bn. Castletown*
Commission on the drainage of the district of the River Barrow and its tributaries. Report, 12 Feb 1886. 1886 C.4666 xix. Irish Secretary's Office.

FITZROY, Charles, *E. Euston*
Select committee on election for Dunfermline. Extracts of min. of ev. 31 March 1803. 1802/3 (39) iii.

FITZROY, Henry
Committee on expiring laws. 4th session, 16th Parliament. Report, 4 April 1856. 1856 (115) vii.

Select committee on coroners. Report, 24 July 1851. 1851 (584) x.

FITZWALTER, *Lord* [Peerage claim]. SEE:
Cooper, C.A.

FITZWILLIAM, *Lord* SEE:
Wentworth-Fitzwilliam, Charles William, *5th E. Fitzwilliam (s.1833, d.1857)*
Wentworth-Fitzwilliam, William Thomas Spencer, *6th E. Fitzwilliam (1815-1902)*

FLANAGAN, S. Woulfe
Commission for the sale of encumbered estates in Ireland. Report, 5 Aug 1850. 1850 [1268] xxv.

FLEETWOOD, Peter Hesketh, *Sir*
Select committee on consular establishment. Report, 10 Aug 1835. 1835 (499) vi; (GO Diplomatic Service, 1).

FLETCHER, Henry Charles
Special committee on breech-loading rifles.
Report on selection of a breech-loading rifle for the service. 11 Feb 1869. 1868/9 [4119] xii.
Report on repeating arms. 11 Feb 1869. 1868/9 [4119] xii.
Report on compressed powder. 11 Feb 1869. 1868/9 [4119] xii. War Office.

Special committee on the experimental Martini-Henry arms issued for trial in 1869. Abstract of reports. 12 July 1870. 1870 C.198 xii. War Office.

Special committee on Martini-Henry breech-loading rifles. Reports. 1871 C.299 xiv. War Office.

Special sub-committee of the Ordnance select committee on breech-loading arms. Reports, 11 June 1867 to 12 Feb 1868. 1867/8 [4020] xvi. War Office.

FLETCHER, Joseph
Report on hand-loom weavers in the Midland districts of England. 21 Oct 1839. 1840 [217] xxiv; (IR Textiles, 9).

FODEN, Thomas
Committee on petition on discovery of his crystalline size. SEE: Peel, R.

FOLKSTONE, *Vct.* SEE:
Pleydell-Bouverie, Jacob, *Vct. Folkstone.*

FORBES, Bernard Arthur William Patrick Hastings, *8th E. Granard*
Royal commission on horsebreeding. SEE: Cavendish-Bentinck, W.J.A.C.J., *6th D. Portland.*

FORBES, George John, *Vct. Forbes*
Select committee on the Galway election. Report, 12 April 1827. 1826/7 (264) iv.

FORSTER, Charles, *Sir*
Select committee on Azeem Jah (signatures to petitions). Report, 28 April 1865. 1865 (231) vii.

Select committee on Azeem Jah (signatures to petitions), (re-committed report). Report, 26 May 1865. 1865 (317) vii.

Select committee on Felony Bill. Report, 25 April 1870. 1870 (183) vi; (LA Criminal Law, 6).

Select committee on Payment of Wages Bill and Payment of Wages (Hosiery) Bill. Report, 22 July 1854. 1854 (382) xvi; (Industrial Relations, 5).

Select committee on public petitions
Special report, 21 March 1878. 1878 (97) xviii.
Special report, 11 April 1878. 1878 (145) xviii.
Special report, 20 May 1878. 1878 (188) xviii.

Select committee on public petitions. Special report, 20 April 1883. 1883 (134) xiv.

Select committee on public petitions. Special report, 14 June 1887. 1887 (175) xi.

FORSTER, Frank
Report on Mr. Joseph Smith's report on the state and condition of the Victoria Street Sewer. 2 May 1851. 1851 (338) xlviii; (UA Sanitation, 3). Metropolitan Commission of Sewers.

FORSTER, William Edward
Select committee on the Canal Boats Act (1877) Amendment Bill. Report, 11 July 1884. 1884 (263) viii.

Select committee on the Church Patronage Bill. Special report, 24 July 1884. 1884 (297) ix.

Select committee on contagious diseases in animals. Report, 25 July 1873. 1873 (353) xi.

Select committee on Endowed Schools Acts, 1869. Report, 17 June 1873. 1873 (254) viii.

Select committee on Endowed Schools Bill. Report, 11 May 1869. 1868/9 (208) viii.

Select committee on Endowed Schools (No.2) Bill. Report and special report, 8 June 1869. 1868/9 (256) viii.

Select committee on the Medical Act (1858) Amend-

ment (No.3) Bill. Special report, 29 July 1879. 1878/9 (320) xii; (HE Medical Profession, 4).

Select committee on the Medical Act (1858) Amendment (No.3) Bill. Special report, 12 March 1880. 1880 (121) ix; (HE Medical Profession, 4).

Select committee on the Metropolis Gas Companies Bill. 28 June 1875. 1875 (281) xii; (FP Gas, 4).

Select committee on the Metropolis Gas (Surrey Side) Bill. Report, 28 July 1876. 1876 (384) xi; (FP Gas, 6).

Select committee on parliamentary and municipal electors hours of polling. Report, 10 July 1877. 1877 (320) xv.

Select committee on school board elections; voting. SEE: Mundella, A.J.

Select committee on the Thames River (Prevention of Floods) Bill. Report, 13 May 1879. 1878/9 (178) xiii.

Select committee on trade with foreign nations. Report, 15 July 1864. 1864 (493) vii.

Select committee on the Vaccination Act, 1867. Report, 23 May 1871. 1871 (246) xiii.

FORSYTH, William
Report on a petition of the inhabitant householders of Brighton praying for a municipal charter. Report, 11 Nov 1852. 1852 (280) lxxviii.

FORTESCUE, Chichester Parkinson
Joint select committee on railway companies amalgamation. Report, 2 Aug 1872. HL 1872 (32) xii; HC repr. 1872 (364) xiii. 2 vols; (transport, 12-13).

FORTESCUE, Hugh, *2nd E. Fortescue*
Select committee on army and navy appointments. Report, 12 Aug 1833. 1833 (650) vii; (Military and Naval, 2).

Select committee on colonial military expenditure. Report, 7 Aug 1834. 1834 (570) vi.

Select committee on the HC. Admission of strangers. Report, 30 April 1888. 1888 (132) xii.

Select committee (HL) on the Irish Poor Law. SEE: Petty-Fitzmaurice, Henry, *3rd M. Lansdowne.*

Select committee (HL) on the operation of the Irish Poor Law
1st report, 9 March 1849. HL 1849 (19-I) xxxi.
2nd report, 22 March 1849. HL 1849 (19-II) xxxi.
3rd report, 29 March 1849. HL 1849 (19-III) xxxii.
4th report, 10 May 1849. HL 1849 (19-IV) xxxii.
5th report, 25 May 1849. HL 1849 (19-V) xxxii.
6th report, 2 July 1849. HL 1849 (19-VI) xxxii.
Appendix. HL 1849 (19-APP) xxxii.

Select committee on Weights and Measures Bill. Min. of ev. 7 July 1834. 1834 (464) xviii.

Select committee on the Weights and Measures Act. Report, 17 June 1835. 1835 (292) xviii.

FORWOOD, Arthur Bower
Committee on the system of purchase and contract in the Navy. Report, 5 Feb 1887. 1887 C.4987 xvi.

FOSTER, Alexander Frederick
Report on the state of popular education in specimen mining districts in Durham and Cumberland. 26 July 1859. *In* 1861 [2794-II] xxi, pt.2; (Education, 4).

FOSTER, Balthazar Walter, *Sir*
Select committee on death certification
1st report, 15 Aug 1893. 1893/4 (373) xi.
2nd report, 1 Sept 1893. 1893/4 (402) xi; (Health, 15).

Select committee on food products adulteration. Report, 1 Aug 1894. 1894 (253) xii; (HE Food and Drugs, 4).

Select committee on food products adulteration. Report, 2 July 1895. 1895 (363) x; (HE Food and Drugs, 5).

Select committee on the Locomotive Threshing Engines Bill. Report, 20 June 1894. 1894 (180) xiv.

Select committee on the public libraries (Ireland) Acts Amendment Bill. Report, 17 July 1894. 1894 (223) xv.

Select committee on the Suffolk County Council Committee (Borrowing Powers) Bill. Report, 21 March 1893. 1893/4 (125) xv.

FOSTER, Clement Le Neve
Departmental committee on Merionethshire slate mines. Report, 10 Dec 1894. 1895 C.7692 xxxv. Home Department.

Departmental committee on mining and mineral statistics. Report, Sept 1894. 1895 C.7609 xlii. Home Department.

FOSTER, John
Committee on Irish exchange
Report, 13 June 1804. 1803/4 (86) iv.
Min. of ev. 4 May 1804. 1803/4 (25) iv.

Select committee on state of commercial credit. Report, 7 March 1811. 1810/1 (52) ii; (Monetary Policy, 1).

FOSTER, John Leslie
Commission on bogs in Ireland
1st report, 20 June 1810. 1810 (363) x.
2nd report, 1 April 1811. 1810/1 (96) vi.
3rd report, 28 April 1814. 1813/4 (130) vi, pt.1.
4th report, 28 April 1814. 1813/4 (131) vi, pt.2.

Committee on the circulating paper, the specie, the current coin and exchange of Ireland. Report, 13 June 1804; repr. 1810 (86) iii, and 1826 (407) v.

Committee on Howth harbour. Report, 13 April 1810. 1810 (203) iv.

FOSTER, M.H.
Report on the financial condition of Turkey. 7 Dec 1861. 1862 [2972] lxiv. Foreign Office.

FOSTER, Thomas Henry
Committee on Holyhead roads and harbour
Report, 21 March 1810. 1810 (166) iv.
2nd report, 9 June 1810. 1810 (352) iv.

FOSTER, Walter, *Sir*   SEE:
Foster, Balthazar Walter, *Sir*.

FOURDRINIER, Henry (and Sealy)
Select committee on patent. SEE: Mackinnon, W.A. and SEE: Mosley, Oswald, *Sir*.

FOWLER, Henry Hartley, *1st Vct. Wolverhampton*
Committee on the expenditure and practice of different government departments in regard to stationery and printing. Report, 30 Dec 1884. 1884/5 C.4367 xxii. Treasury.

Committee on Indian currency
Report, 7 July 1899. 1899 C.9390 xxxi.
Min. of ev. 1899 C.9222 xxxi.
Index and appendix. 1899 C.9376 xxxi.
Despatch of the Secretary of State for India to the Governor General of India, 25 July 1899. 1899 C.9421 xxxi. India Office.

Report on local taxation, with especial reference to the proportion of local burdens borne by urban and rural ratepayers, and different classes of property in England and Wales. 10 April 1893. 1893/4 (168) lxxvii. Local Government Board.

Select committee on the Hyde Park Corner (New Streets) Bill. Report, 31 March 1887. 1887 (91) ix.

Select committee on the London Streets (Strand Improvement) Bill. Special report, 20 June 1890. 1890 (239) xv; (UA Planning, 10).

Select committee on woods and forests and land revenues of the Crown. Report, 26 July 1889. 1889 (284) xvi.

Select committee on woods and forests and land revenues of the Crown. Report, 30 July 1890. 1890 (333) xviii.

FOWNES, George
Reports on the production of spirit from sugar and molasses. 16 Feb, 6 May and 7 June 1847. 1847 (426), (529) lix. Board of Excise.

FRANCE, R.S.
Select committee (HL) on his pamphlet. SEE: Spencer-Churchill, J.W., *6th D. Marlborough*.

FRANKLAND, Edward
Commission on means of preventing the pollution of rivers, 1868.
1st report: Mersey and Ribble Basins
Vol.1: Report, 16 Feb 1870. 1870 C.37 xl.
Vol.2: Ev. 1870 C.109 xl.
2nd report: The A.B.C. process of treating sewage. 4 July 1870. 1870 C.181 xl.
3rd report: Pollution arising from the woollen manufacture and processes connected therewith. 1873 C.347 xxv.
Ev. 1873 C.347-I xxxvi.
4th report: Pollution of rivers of Scotland. 29 June 1872. 2 pts. 1872 C.603 xxxiv.
5th report: Pollution arising from mining operations and metal manufactures. 18 Oct 1873. 1874 C.951 xxxiii.
6th report: Domestic water supply of G.B. 30 June 1874. 1874 C.112 xxxiii. SEE ALSO: Rawlinson, Robert.

FRANKLIN, John, *Sir*
Committee respecting the expeditions in search of him. SEE: Bowles, W.

Report on the search for his expedition to the Arctic. SEE: Richardson, J.

FRANKLAND, William
Committee on Ramsgate harbour. Report, 14 March 1755. CJ, vol.27, p.213, 463.

FRANKS, John
Committee of the whole HC on the Charge against W. Kenrick. SEE: Gordon, R.

FRASER, Alexander
Report on the condition of the cottar population of Lews. 21 Jan 1888. 1888 C.5265 lxxx; (Agriculture, 25). Scottish Office.

FRASER, James

Report on the common school system of the United States and Canada. 1 March 1866. 1867 [3857] xxvi; (Education, 15). Schools Inquiry Commission. SEE ALSO: Labouchere, Henry, *Bn. Taunton.*

Report on the state of popular education in specimen agricultural districts in the counties of Dorset, Devon, Somerset, Hereford and Worcester. 17 May 1859. *In* 1861 [2794-II] xxi, pt.2; (Education, 4).

FRAZER, George Alexander

Report on the navigation and weirs of the Blackwater River. 25 Jan 1851. 1851 (194) l. Admiralty.

FREEMAN, William Deane

Commission on the Paving Board of Dublin. Report, 9 May 1827. 1826/7 (329) xi.

FREEMAN-MITFORD, John, *1st Bn. Redesdale*

Select committee (HL) on the Patent for the Fourdrinier Paper Making Machine Bill. Min. of proc. 10 Aug 1807. HL 1806/7 (36) xiv.

FREEMAN-MITFORD, John Thomas, *1st E. Redesdale*

Chairman's committee on the Norfolk Railway Bill. Report, 30 June 1856. HL 1856 (195) xxiv.

Chairman's committee on the Oxford, Worcester and Wolverhampton Railway (Additional Capital, *etc.*) Bill. Report, 30 June 1856. HL 1856 (196) xxiv.

Committee (HL) on the Coleorton Railway Bill. Min. of ev. 10 May 1833. HL 1833 (68) cccxxv.

Committee (HL) on the dignity of the peerage
1st report, 12 July 1819. HL 1820 (172) cxvi; repr. HL 1824 (46) clxvi; repr. HL 1829 (117) cclii.
2nd report, 26 July 1820. HL 1820 (101) cxvi; repr. HL 1829 (118) ccliii.
3rd report, 29 July 1822. HL 1822 (88) cxxxv; repr. HL 1829 (118) ccliii.
4th report, 2 July 1825. HL 1825 (176) cxcii; repr. HL 1829 (118), (119) ccliii, ccliv, cclv, cclvi.
Appendix. HL 1825 (172) clxvii.
5th report, 19 June 1829. HL 1829 (122) cclvi; HL repr. 1826 (391), (392), (393), (394) vi, vii, viii, ix.

Committee (HL) on Lees Invention for Hemp and Flax Bill. Min. of ev. 24 June 1816. HL 1816 (110) lxxxi.

Committee for privileges (HL)
Airth claim of peerage
Min. of ev. HL 1870 (G) x.
Ev., 26 July 1871. HL 1871 (E) x.
Proc., 4 Aug 1874. HL 1874 (F) xii.

Committee for privileges (HL)
Amiens (*Vct.*) and E. Aldborough claim to vote at elections of representatives for Ireland. Min. of ev. 9 June 1854. HL 1854 (155) xx.

Committee for privileges (HL)
Annandale peerage claim
Ev. 30 May 1876. HL 1876 (C) ix.
Ev. 12 June to 26 July 1877. HL 1877 (B) xi.
Ev. 4 April 1878. HL 1878 (A) x.
Ev. 29, 30 May 1879. HL 1878/9 (A) ix.
Ev. 22 to 30 June 1880. HL 1880 (A) viii.
Ev. 30 May to 20 July 1881. HL 1881 (A), (B) xi.

Committee for privileges (HL)
Annesley claim to vote at elections of representa-

tive peers for Ireland. Min. of ev. 12 July 1855. HL 1854/5 (K) xxi.

Committee for privileges (HL)
Antrim claim to vote for representative peers for Ireland. Ev. 16 July 1858. HL 1857/8 (G) xix.

Committee for privileges (HL)
Ashtown claim to vote for representative peers for Ireland. Ev. 12 July 1855. HL 1854/5 (M) xxi.

Committee for privileges (HL)
Athlumney claim to vote for representative peers for Ireland. Ev. 17 March 1864. HL 1864 (C) xxvi.

Committee for privileges (HL)
Aylesford claim of peerage. Ev. 6 July 1885. HL 1885 (159) xi.

Committee for privileges (HL)
Aymer claim to vote for representative peers for Ireland. Ev. 10 July 1860. HL 1860 (222) xxiii.

Committee of privileges (HL)
Balfour of Burley and Kilwinning claim of peerage
Ev. 25 July 1861. HL 1861 (273) xxiii.
Ev. 19 June 1862. HL 1862 (G) xxviii.
Ev. 27 July 1863. HL 1863 (G) xxxii.
Ev. 17 March 1864. HL 1864 (A) xxvi.
Proc. 18 to 22 July 1864. HL 1864 (A) xxvi.
Proc. 21 July 1868. HL 1867/8 (C) xxix.
Ev. 21 June 1869. HL 1868/9 (F) xxvi.

Committee for privileges (HL)
Bandon claim to vote for representative peers for Ireland. Ev. 21 March 1857. HL 1857 (B) ix.

Committee for privileges (HL)
Bantry and Bearhaven claim to vote at elections of representative peers for Ireland. Ev. HL 1851 (216) xvii.

Committee for privileges (HL)
Belhaven and Stenton claims of peerage
Ev. 7 July 1874. HL 1874 (C) xii.
Ev. 10 May to 20 Aug 1875. HL 1875 (B) xii.

Committee for privileges (HL)
Bellew claim to vote for representative peers for Ireland. Ev. 7 July 1856. HL 1856 (J) xxiii.

Committee for privileges (HL)
Belmore claim to vote for representative peers for Ireland. Ev. 7 July 1856. HL 1856 (G) xxiii.

Committee for privileges (HL)
Berkeley claim of peerage
Ev. 23 July 1858. HL 1857/8 (H) xix.
Ev. 7 April 1859. HL 1859, session 1 (D) xi.
Ev. 11 Aug 1859. HL 1859, session 2 (C) xvi.
Ev. 13 June to 10 Aug 1860. HL 1860 (A) xxiii.
Ev. 26 Feb 1861. HL 1861 (A) xxiii.
Judgement. 26 Feb 1861. HL 1861 (B) xxiii.

Committee for privileges (HL)
Borthwick claim of peerage
Ev. 13 July 1869. HL 1868/9 (C) xxvi.
Min. of ev. HL 1870 (B) x.
Ev. 21 July 1871. HL 1871 (H) x.

Committee for privileges (HL)
Botreaux, Hungerford, *etc.* claim of peerage
Min. of ev. HL 1870 (D) x.
Ev. 7, 21 July 1871. HL 1871 (D) x.

Committee for privileges (HL)
Boyne claim to vote for representative peers for Ireland. Ev. 12 July 1855. HL 1854/5 (O) xxi.

Committee for privileges (HL)

FREEMAN-MITFORD, John Thomas, *1st E. Redesdale*
(continued)
>Brandon claim to vote for representative peers for Ireland. Ev. 21 March 1857. HL 1857, session 1 (B) ix.

Committee for privileges (HL)
>Breadalbane claim of peerage
>>Ev. 5 Dec 1867. HL 1867/8 (A) xxix.
>>Ev. 21 June 1872. HL 1872 (B) xiii.
>>Ev. 14 Aug 1877. HL 1877 (F) xi.

Committee for privileges (HL)
>Buckhurst peerage claim. Ev. 17 July 1876. HL 1876 (E) ix.

Committee for privileges (HL)
>Charleville claim to vote at the elections of representative peers for Ireland. Min. of ev. 12 May 1853. HL 1852/3 (198) xxvi.

Committee for privileges (HL)
>Chesterfield claim of peerage. Ev. 8 July 1873. HL 1873 (E) xii.

Committee for privileges (HL)
>Clermont claim to vote at the elections of representative peers for Ireland. Min. of ev. 22 July 1853. HL 1852/3 (330) xxvi.

Committee for privileges (HL)
>Clive claim to vote for representative peers for Ireland. Ev. 25 July 1861. HL 1861 (238) xxiii.

Committee for privileges (HL)
>Cloncurry claim to vote at elections of representative peers for Ireland. Min. of ev. 9 June 1854. HL 1854 (160) xx.

Committee for privileges (HL)
>Dalhousie and Panmure claim to vote for representative peers for Scotland. Ev. 8 July 1862. HL 1862 (I) xxviii.

Committee for privileges (HL)
>De Blaquiere claim to vote for representative peers for Ireland. Ev. 17 March 1864. HL 1864 (B) xxvi.

Committee for privileges (HL)
>De Scales claim of peerage
>>Min. of ev. 6 Feb 1857. HL 1857, session 1 (A) ix.
>>Ev. 15 July 1858. HL 1857/8 (E) xix.
>>Ev. 13 June 1860. HL 1860 (B) xxiii.
>>Ev. 21 May 1863. HL 1863 (C) xxxii.
>>Ev. 22 July 1864. HL 1864 (H) xxvi.
>>Ev. 7 April 1865. HL 1865 (C) xxi.

Committee for privileges (HL)
>De Vesci claim to vote for representative peers for Ireland. Ev. 8 April 1856. HL 1856 (B) xxiii.

Committee for privileges (HL)
>Dingwall and Butler of Moore Park claim of peerage
>>Min. of ev. HL 1870 (C) x.
>>Ev. 6 June and 15 Aug 1871. HL 1871 (C) x.

Committee for privileges (HL)
>Doneraile claim to vote for representative peers for Ireland. Min. of ev. 9 June 1854. HL 1854 (163) xx.

Committee for privileges (HL)
>Donoughmore and Hutchinson claim to vote at elections of representative peers for Ireland. Min. of ev. 12 May 1853. HL 1852/3 (195) xxvi.

Committee for privileges (HL)
>Downe claim to vote for representative peers for Ireland. Ev. 8 June 1871. HL 1871 (B) x.

Committee for privileges (HL)
>Dunalley claim to vote for representative peers for Ireland. Ev. 12 July 1855. HL 1854/5 (N) xxi.

Committee for privileges (HL)
>Dunboyne claim of peerage
>>Ev. 5 April 1859. HL 1859, session 1 (C) xi.
>>Ev. 2 Aug 1859. HL 1859, session 2 (A) xvi.
>>Ev. 10 July to 9 Aug 1860. HL 1860 (C) xxiii.
>>Ev. 16 April to 15 June 1863. HL 1863 (A) xxxii.

Committee for privileges (HL)
>Dundonald claim of peerage
>>Min. of ev. 18 July 1861. HL 1861 (203) xxiii.
>>Ev. 2 Aug 1861 to 27 June 1862. HL 1862 (A), (H) xxviii.

Committee for privileges (HL)
>Dunraven claim to vote at the elections of representative peers for Ireland. Min. of ev. HL 1851 (107) xvii.

Committee for privileges (HL)
>Dunsany claim to vote at elections of representative peers for Ireland. Min. of ev. 9 June 1854. HL 1854 (158) xx.

Committee for privileges (HL)
>Dysart claim of peerage
>>Ev. 30 July to 3 Aug 1880. HL 1880 (B) viii.
>>Ev. 21 Jan to 21 Feb 1881. HL 1881 (A), (B) xi.

Committee for privileges (HL)
>Fermoy claim to vote for representative peers for Ireland. Ev., proc. 8 April 1856. HL 1856 (C) xxiii.

Committee for privileges (HL)
>Garvagh claim to vote at elections of representative peers for Ireland. Min. of ev. 12 May 1853. HL 1852/3 (192) xxvi.

Committee for privileges (HL)
>Gordon claim of peerage. Ev. 22 March 1872. HL 1872 (A) xiii.

Committee for privileges (HL)
>Grandison claim of peerage
>>Min. of ev. 7 April 1854. HL 1854 (82) xx.
>>Min. of ev., proc. 7 Aug 1855. HL 1854/5 (B) xxi.
>>Ev. 7 July 1856. HL 1856 (M) xxiii.
>>Ev. 23 and 26 June 1858. HL 1857/8 (C) xix.

Committee for privileges (HL)
>Grey de Ruthyn peerage claim. Ev. 30 May 1876. HL 1876 (B) ix.

Committee for privileges (HL)
>Grimston claim to vote for representative peers for Ireland. Ev. 20 July 1860. HL 1860 (274) xxiii.

Committee for privileges (HL)
>Guillamore claim to vote for representative peers for Ireland. Ev. 7 July 1856. HL 1856 (I) xxiii.

Committee for privileges (HL)
>Hawarden claim to vote for representative peers for Ireland. Ev. 21 March 1857. HL 1857, session 1, (C) ix.

Committee for privileges (HL)
>Herries claim of peerage
>>Min. of ev. HL 1851 (130) xvii.
>>Min. of ev. 8 April 1853. HL 1852/3 (154) xxvi.
>>Min. of ev. 30 May to 16 June 1854. HL 1854 (172) xx.
>>Min. of ev. 12 July 1855. HL 1854/5 (L) xxi.

Ev., proc. 23 June and 15 July 1858. HL 1857/8 (D) xix.

Committee for privileges (HL)
Inchiquin claim to vote for representative peers for Ireland. 30 July 1861 HL 1861 (275) xxviii.

Committee for privileges (HL)
Kensington claim to vote at elections of representative peers for Ireland. Min. of ev. 1 March 1853. HL 1852/3 (74) xxvi.

Committee for privileges (HL)
Kerry and Shelburne claim to vote at elections for representative peers for Ireland. Min. of ev. 7 April and 27 June 1865. HL 1865 (A) xxi.

Committee for privileges (HL)
Kinloss claim of peerage (HL). Ev. 18 June to 21 July 1868. HL 1867/8 (B) xxix.

Committee for privileges (HL)
Lauderdale claim of peerage. Min. of ev. 18 June 1885. HL 1885 (139) xi.

Committee for privileges (HL)
Lifford claim to vote for representative peers for Ireland. Ev. 12 July 1855. HL 1854/5 (P) xxi.

Committee for privileges (HL)
Lindsay peerage claim
Ev. 19 June 1877. HL 1877 (D) xi.
Ev. 26 Feb and 5 April 1878. HL 1878 (D) x.

Committee for privileges (HL)
Listowel claim to vote for representative peers for Ireland. Ev. 7 July 1856. HL 1856 (F) xxiii.

Committee for privileges (HL)
Londonderry claim to vote at elections of representative peers for Ireland. Min. of ev. 7 Aug 1854. HL 1854 (316) xx.

Committee for privileges (HL)
Loudoun claim to vote at elections of Scotch peers. Min. of ev. 31 July 1877. HL 1877 (E) xi.

Committee for privileges (HL)
Lovat claim of peerage
Ev. 7 July 1856. HL 1856 (L) xxiii.
Ev. 18 June 1885. HL 1885 (140) xi.

Committee for privileges (HL)
Mar claim of peerage
Ev. 16, 17 July 1868. HL 1867/8 (D) xxix.
Proc. 20 July 1869. HL 1868/9 (D) xxvi.
Min. of ev. HL 1870 (F) x.
Ev. 6 June and 21 July 1871. HL 1871 (A) x.
Ev. 25 July 1872. HL 1872 (D) xiii.
Ev. 15 to 25 July 1873. HL 1873 (C) xii.
Ev. 5 to 16 June 1874. HL 1874 (B) xii.
Proc. 25 Feb 1875. HL 1875 (A) xii.
Judgement. 25 Feb 1875. HL 1875 (A*) xii.

Committee for privileges (HL)
Massy claim to vote for representative peers for Ireland. Ev. 7 July 1856. HL 1856 (H) xxiii.

Committee for privileges (HL)
Midleton claim to vote at elections of representative peers for Ireland. Min. of ev. 9 June 1854. HL 1854 (161) xx.

Committee for privileges (HL)
Monacute claim of peerage
Min. of ev. 6 Aug 1861. HL 1861 (297) xxiii.
Ev. 19 June 1862. HL 1862 (D) xxviii.
Ev. 21 May 1863. HL 1863 (D) xxxii.
Ev. and proc. 17 March to 19 July 1864. HL 1864 (E) xxvi.
Ev. 7 July 1874. HL 1874 (E) xii.
Min. of ev. 6 Aug 1861. HL 1861 (298) xxiii.

Ev. 21 May 1863. HL 1863 (E) xxxii.
Proc. and ev. 17 March to 21 July 1864. HL 1864 (F) xxvi.

Committee for privileges (HL)
Dukedom of Montrose. Min. of ev. 28 July 1853. HL 1852/3 (347) xxvi.

Committee for privileges (HL)
Mountgarrett's claim to vote for representative peers for Ireland
Min. of ev. 9 June 1854. HL 1854 (159) xx.
Proc. 12 and 24 July 1855. HL 1854/5 (Q) xxi.

Committee for privileges (HL)
Mowbray claim of peerage
Ev. 30 May 1876. HL 1876 (D) ix.
Ev. 23 March to 26 July 1877. HL 1877 (A) xi.

Committee for privileges (HL)
Nairne claim of peerage
Ev. 8 July 1873. HL 1873 (A) xii.
Ev. 6 July and 4 Aug 1874. HL 1874 (D) xii.

Committee for privileges (HL)
Netterville claim of peerage
Ev. 7 July 1830. HL 1830 (206) cclxxix.
Ev. 27 July 1831 to 25 May 1833. HL 1833 (35) cccxxiii.
Ev. 30 June 1834. HL 1834 (141) xxiii, pt.1.
Min. of ev. 30 July 1861. HL 1861 (273) xxiii.
Ev. 28 July 1862. HL 1862 (E) xxviii.
Ev. 27 July 1863. HL 1863 (F) xxxii.

Committee for privileges (HL)
Newburgh claim of peerage
Ev. 15 to 30 July 1858. HL 1857/8 (F) xix.

Committee for privileges (HL)
Perth claim of peerage
Min. of ev. 19 July 1853. HL 1852/3 (432) xxvi.

Committee for privileges (HL)
Rathdonnell claim to vote for representative peers for Ireland. Ev. 7 May 1869. HL 1868/9 (B) xxvi.

Committee for privileges (HL)
Saltoun claim to vote for representative peers for Scotland. Ev. 7 July 1856. HL 1856 (E) xxiii.

Committee for privileges (HL)
Segrave claim of peerage
Ev. 19 May to 26 July 1877. HL 1877 (C) xi.

Committee for privileges (HL)
Shrewsbury claim to vote at elections for representative peers for Ireland. Min. of ev. 9 June 1854. HL 1854 (162) xx.

Committee for privileges (HL)
Shrewsbury claim of peerage.
Ev., proc. 20 April to 1 June 1858. HL 1857/8 (A) xix.

Committee for privileges (HL)
Southesk claim of peerage
Min. of ev. 2 June to 7 Aug 1854. HL 1854 (164) xx.
Min. of ev. 24 July 1855. HL 1854/5 (A) xxi.

Committee for privileges (HL)
Stuart de Decies peerage claim.
Ev. 7 April 1876. HL 1876 (A) ix.

Committee for privileges (HL)
Taaffe claim of peerage
Ev. 26 April 1858. HL 1857/8 (B) xix.
Ev. 2 Aug 1859. HL 1859, session 2 (B) xvi.
Ev. 9 and 17 Aug 1860. HL 1860 (D) xxiii.

Committee for privileges (HL)
Talbot of Malahide claim to vote at elections of representative peers for Ireland. Min. of ev. HL 1851 (106) xvii.

FREEMAN-MITFORD, John Thomas, *1st E. Redesdale*
(continued)

> Committee for privileges (HL)
>> Tracey claim of peerage
>>> Min. of ev. 7 Aug 1854. HL 1854/5 (R) xxi.

> Committee for privileges (HL)
>> Wensleydale's letters patent
>>> Letters patent creating Sir James Parke, *Bn. Wensleydale.* HL 1856 (5) xxiii.
>>> Ev. 21 Feb 1856. HL 1856 (18) xxii.

> Committee for privileges (HL)
>> Wentworth claim of peerage
>>> Ev. 27 July 1863. HL 1863 (H) xxxii.
>>> Ev. 15 March 1864. HL 1864 (G) xxvi.

> Committee for privileges (HL)
>> Westmeath claim to vote for representative peers for Ireland. Ev. 7 July 1871. HL 1871 (F) x.

> Committee for privileges (HL)
>> Wicklow claim to vote for representative peers for Ireland
>>> Ev. 22 June 1869. HL 1868/9 (E) xxvi.
>>> Speeches of counsel. 5 Aug 1869. HL 1868/9 (274) xxvi.
>>> Speeches of counsel and judgements. 31 March 1870. HL 1870 (E) x.

> Committee for privileges (HL)
>> Willoughby de Eresby claim of peerage. Ev. 21 July 1871. HL 1871 (G) x.

> Committee for privileges (HL)
>> Wiltes claim of peerage
>>> Ev. 22 July 1862. HL 1862 (K) xxviii.
>>> Ev. 21 May 1863. HL 1863 (B) xxxii.
>>> Ev. 7 April 1865. HL 1865 (B) xxi.
>>> Proc. 4 May 1869. HL 1869 (A) xxvi.
>>> Report, 7 May 1869. HL 1868/9 (100) xxvi.
>>> Opinions of judges. 4 May 1869. HL 1868/9 (101) xxvi.

> Committee for privileges (HL)
>> Winterton claim to vote for representative peers for Ireland. Ev. 24 June 1872. HL 1872 (C) xiii.

Joint select committee on parliamentary agency. Report, 17 July 1876. HL 1876 (360) xii.

Select committee (HL) on altering standing order number 185 regarding railway bills. Report, 30 June 1852. HL 1852 (249) xxi.

Select committee (HL) on the business of the HL. Report, 30 July 1867. HL 1867 (259) xxviii.

Select committee (HL) on companies subscribing, *etc.* powers. Report, 19 July 1861. HL 1861 (218) xxiv.

Select committee (HL) on HL construction and accommodation. Report, 17 July 1883. HL 1883 (147) ix.

Select committee (HL) on the destruction and sale of Exchequer documents. Min. of ev. 2 July 1840. HL 1840 (80) xxii.

Select committee (HL) on the dignity of the peerage
> Report, 13 June 1816. HL 1816 (115) lxxviii; HC repr. 1821 (709) xi.
> Report, 8 July 1817. HL 1817 (104) lxxxiv; HC repr. 1821 (709) xi.
> Report, 2 June 1818. HL 1818 (118) xci; HC repr. 1821 (709) xi.
> Report, 25 May 1820. HL 1820 (101), (172) cxvi; HC repr. 1821 (709) xi.
> Report, 29 June 1821. HL 1821 (130) cxxiii.

Select committee (HL) on the Duke of Wellington's funeral
> 1st report, 16 Nov 1852. HL 1852/3 (6) xxxi.
> 2nd report, 17 Nov 1852. HL 1852/3 (13) xxxi.

Select committee (HL) on the Gardens in Towns Protection Bill. Report, 26 June 1862. HL 1862 (127) xxix.

Select committee (HL) on the Improvement of Land Act, 1864 Bill, and the Mortgage Debentures Bill. Report, 14 June 1864. HL 1864 (130) xxvii.

Select committee (HL) on the library of the HL. Report, 14 April 1856. HL 1856 (71) xxiv.

Select committee (HL) on the Office of Messenger to the Great Seal Abolition Bill. Report, 27 May 1852. HL 1852 (154) xxi; HC repr. 1852 (185) xiii.

Select committee (HL) on the Metropolitan Railway (Extension to Finsbury Circus) Bill. Report, 21 March 1861. HL 1861 (56) xxiv.

Select committee (HL) on the Office of the Clerk of the Parliaments and the Office of the Gentleman Usher of the Black Rod.
> 1st report; Messenger of the Great Seal. HL 1851 (113) xix.
> 2nd report; Messenger of the Great Seal. HL 1852 (154) xxiv.

Select committee (HL) on the Office of the Clerk of the Parliaments and the Office of the Gentleman Usher of the Black Rod. Report, 24 July 1856. HL 1856 (291) xxiv.

Select committee (HL) on the Parliament Office and the Black Rod Office.
> (1st report not identified)
> 2nd report, 23 May 1865. HL 1865 (120) xxi.
> 3rd report, 4 July 1865. HL 1865 (253) xxi.

Select committee (HL) on the Parliament Office and the Black Rod Office
> 1st report, 3 July 1866. HL 1866 (183) xxviii.
> 2nd report, 6 Aug 1866. HL 1866 (283) xxviii.

Select committee (HL) on the Parliament Office and the Black Rod Office
> 1st report, 31 May 1867. HL 1867 (125) xxvii.
> 2nd report, 26 July 1867. HL 1867 (261) xxvii.

Select committee (HL) on the Parliament Office and the Office of the Black Rod. Report, 24 July 1868. HL 1867/8 (289) xxx.

Select committee (HL) on the Parliament Office and the Office of the Black Rod. Ev. of John Percy, 27 July 1869. Report, HL 1886 (26) x.

Select committee (HL) on the Parliament Office and the Office of the Black Rod. Report, 5 Aug 1869. HL 1868/9 (278) xxvii.

Select committee (HL) on the Parliament Office and the Office of the Black Rod
> 1st report, 16 May 1870. HL 1870 (99) viii.
> 2nd report, 23 June 1870. HL 1870 (156) viii; HC repr. 1870 (318) vi.
> 3rd report, 4 July 1870. HL 1870 (177) viii; HC repr. 1870 (342) vi.

Select committee (HL) on the Parliament Office and the Black Rod Office. Report, 1 April 1873. HL 1873 (58) ix.

Select committee (HL) on the Parliament Office and the Black Rod Office. Report, 15 June 1874. HL 1874 (111) viii.

Select committee (HL) on the Parliament Office and the Black Rod Office.
> 1st report, 16 March 1875. HL 1875 (42) x.
> 2nd report, 28 June 1875. HL 1875 (176) x.

Select committee (HL) on the Parliament Office and the Black Rod Office

Report, 27 April 1876. HL 1876 (56) vii.

2nd report, 10 July 1876. HL 1876 (166) vii.

Select committee (HL) on the Parliament Office and the Black Rod Office
1st report, 11 April 1878. HL 1878 (73) vii.
2nd report, 12 Aug 1878. HL 1878 (201) vii.

Select committee (HL) on the Parliament Office and the Black Rod Office
1st report (session 1) 12 March 1880. HL 1880 (41) vii.
1st report (session 2) 13 Aug 1880. HL 1880 (194) vii.

Select committee (HL) on the Parliament Office and the Black Rod Office
1st report, 7 July 1881. HL 1881 (150) viii.
2nd report, 22 Aug 1881. HL 1881 (220) viii.

Select committee (HL) on the Parliament Office and the Black Rod Office
1st report, 7 July 1881. HL 1881 (150) viii.
2nd report, 22 Aug 1881. HL 1881 (220) viii.

Select committee (HL) on the Parliament Office and the Black Rod Office
1st report, 14 June 1883. HL 1883 (93) ix.
2nd report, 20 Aug 1883. HL 1883 (206) ix.

Select committee (HL) on the Parliament Office and the Black Rod Office. Report, 11 July 1884. HL 1884 (187) vii.

Select committee (HL) on the Parliament Office and the Black Rod Office
1st report, 24 Feb 1885. HL 1884/5 (22) vii.
2nd report, 2 March 1885. HL 1884/5 (25) vii.
3rd report, 19 March 1885. HL 1884/5 (49) vii.
4th report, 4 May 1885. HL 1884/5 (97) vii.
5th report, 27 July 1885. HL 1884/5 (210) vii.

Select committee (HL) on the Parliament Office and the Black Rod Office. 1st report, 22 March 1886. HL 1886 (41) vii. (no other reports identified).

Select committee (HL) on the peers robing room. Report, 25 July 1861. HL 1861 (236) xxiv.

Select committee (HL) on the Railways (Guards and Passengers Communication) Bill. Report, 1 Aug 1867. HL 1867 (255) xxvii.

Select committee (HL) on standing order no. 184, section 2. Report, 10 July 1866. HL 1866 (168) xxviii.

Select committee (HL) on the Waterford, Wexford, Wicklow and Dublin Railway Bill. Report, 10 July 1851. HL 1851 (206) xix.

FREEMANTLE, Thomas, *Sir*
Select committee appointed to prepare the militia estimates. Report, 15 July 1844. 1844 (492) xiv.

Select committee on Stafford Borough. Report, 17 July 1833. 1833 (537) xi.

FREEMANTLE, William Henry
Select committee on supply of water to the Metropolis
Report, 18 May 1821. 1821 (537) v.
Min. of ev. 29 June 1821. 1821 (706) v; (UA Water Supply, 1).

FREMANTLE, C.W.
Reports on the administration of the Mint. 6 and 17 Nov 1869. 1870 (7) xli; (MP Currency, 3). Treasury.

Report on European mints. 10 Aug 1870. 1870 (466) xli; (MP Currency, 3). Treasury.

FRENCH, Fitzstephen
Select committee on general valuation, *etc.* Ireland. Report, 27 July 1869. 1868/9 (362) ix.

Select committee on the kitchen and refreshment rooms (HC)
Report, 24 April 1863. 1863 (215) vii.
2nd report, 17 June 1863. 1863 (366) vii.
3rd report, 23 June 1863. 1863 (384) vii.
4th report, 15 July 1863. 1863 (448) vii.

Select committee on the kitchen and refreshment rooms (HC)
Report, 5 April 1864. 1864 (175) x.
2nd report, 12 July 1864. 1864 (480) x.

Select committee on the kitchen and refreshment rooms of the HC. Report, 29 June 1865. 1865 (428) vii.

Select committee on the kitchen and refreshment rooms (HC). Report, 2 May 1866. 1866 (228) xi.

Select committee on kitchen and refreshment rooms (HC). Report, 5 June 1867. 1867 (351) viii.

Select committee on the kitchen and refreshment rooms (HC). Report, 8 July 1868. 1867/8 (409) viii.

Select committee on kitchen and refreshment rooms (HC)
1st report, 12 May 1969. 1868/9 (209) vii.
2nd report, 5 Aug 1869. 1868/9 (398) vii.

Select committee on kitchen and refreshment rooms (HC). Report, 29 July 1870. 1870 (395) vi.

Select committee on kitchen and refreshment rooms (HC). Report, 19 July 1871. 1871 (367) ix.

Select committee on kitchen and refreshment rooms (HC). Report, 11 April 1872. 1872 (148) x.

Select committee on medical charities. SEE: Hamilton, George Alexander.

Select committee on the Shannon River. Report, 23 June 1865. 1865 (400) xi.

Select committee on the Shannon River. Report, 25 April 1866. 1866 (213) xi.

Select committee on the Shannon River. Report, 18 May 1868. 1867/8 (277) x.

FRERE, William Edward
Commission on the treatment of immigrants in British Guiana. Report, 23 Feb 1871. 3 pts. 1871 C.393 xx; (Emigration, 24). Colonial Office.

Royal commission on the treatment of immigrants in Mauritius. Report, 5 Nov 1874. 1874 C.1115 xxxiv, xxxv.

FRESHFIELD, James William
Select committee on West India mails
1st report, 15 June 1841. 1841 (409) viii.
2nd report, 21 June 1841. 1841 (424) viii.

FRY, Edward, *Sir*
Royal commission on the Irish Land Acts and the Land Purchase Acts
Vol.1: Report, 4 Feb 1898. 1898 C.8734 xxxv.
Vol.2: Min. of ev. 1898 C.8859 xxxv.
Vo..3: Appendix. 1899 C.9107 xxxvi.

FRY, Lewis
Select committee on town holdings. Report, 31 July 1888. 1888 (313) xxii; (UA Planning, 6).

Select committee on town holdings. Report, 12 July 1889. 1889 (251) xv; (UA Planning, 7).

FRY, Lewis (continued)

Select committee on town holdings. Report, 1 Aug 1890. 1890 (341) xviii; (UA Planning, 8).

Select committee on town holdings. Report, 9 July 1891. 1890/1 (325) xviii; (UA Planning, 9).

Select committee on town holdings. Report, 23 May 1892. 1892 (214) xviii; (UA Planning, 9).

FULTON, Hamilton

Select committee on Holyhead roads. Report on mail roads in North Wales to the select committee. 1813. 1814/5 (363) iii.

FYNES, Henry

Committee on Westminster Abbey petition. Report, 10 July 1807. 1807 (23) ii.

GALE, Samuel

Commission on non-parochial registers of births, deaths, marriages, *etc.* in England and Wales. Report, 31 Dec 1857. 1857/8 [2331] xxiii.

GALE, William

Remarks on siting of reservoirs. 22 April 1850. *In* 1850 [1282] xxii. General Board of Health.

GALLY-KNIGHT, Henry

Select committee on first fruits and tenths, and administration of Queen Anne's Bounty. Report, 7 June 1837. 1837 (384) vi.

Select committee on the Kinsall election petition. Min. of ev. 30 April 1838. 1837/8 (332) xii.

Select committee on Trafalgar Square. Report, 27 July 1840. 1840 (548) xii.

GALTON, Douglas

Cam experiments. *In* 1849 [1123] xxix.

Consideration of plans for the main drainage of the Metropolis submitted by the Metropolitan Board of Works. Report, 31 July 1857. 1857, session 2 (233) xxxvi. Commission of Works.

Experiments made in Portsmouth Dockyard for determining the effects produced by passing weights over bars at different velocities. *In* 1849 [1123] xxix.

Experiments with slowly moving weights. *In* 1849 [1123] xxix.

Joint committee on the construction of submarine telegraph cables. Report, April 1860. 1860 [2744] lxii. Board of Trade.

Report on the Herbert Hospital, Woolwich. Report, 19 June 1865. 1865 [3579] xxvi. War Office.

Report on the railways of the United States of America. 1857, session 1 [2181] xvi. Board of Trade.

Sanitary condition and improvement of the Mediterranean stations. SEE: Sutherland, John.

GALTON, Francis

Committee on the Meteorological Department of the Board of Trade. Report. 1866 [3646] lxv. Board of Trade.

GALWAY, *Vct.* [Peerage claim]. SEE:
Palmer, R.

GANNON, J.P.

Reports on captured Negroes at St. Christopher's, Nevis and Tortola. 12 June 1827. 1826/7 (436) xxii; (Slave Trade, 72).

State and condition of apprenticed Africans at Antigua. Report, 17 May, 29 June 1827. 1826/7 (355), (553) xxii; (Slave Trade, 72).

GARDNER, *Lord* [Peerage claim]. SEE:
Cooper, C.A.

GARNETT, William James

Select committee on the Locomotive Bill. Min. of ev. 25 July 1859. 1859, session 2 (116) v.

GARSTIN, William Edmund, *Sir*

Report on the Soudan. 3 May 1899. (Egypt, no.5, 1899). 1899 C.9332 cxii. Foreign Office.

GARVAGH, *Bn.* [Peerage claim]. SEE:
Freeman-Mitford, J.T.

GASCOYNE-CECIL, Eustace Brownlow Henry, *Lord*

Select committee on Indian native troops' transport and employment abroad. Report, 29 July 1878. 1878 (321) x.

GASCOYNE-CECIL, James Brownlow William, *2nd M. Salisbury*

Commission appointed to inquire into the establishment, organisation, *etc.* of the militia of the United Kingdom. Report, 17 Jan 1859. 1859, session 2 [2553] ix.

Committee (HL) on the London and Blackwall Commercial Railway Bill. Report, 12 July 1836. HL 1836 (205) xii.

Committee (HL) on the North Midland Railway Bill
Min. of ev. HL 1836 (114) xxxii.
Report, 20 June 1836. HL 1836 (155) xii.

Select committee on the Army in India and the colonies. Report, 26 July 1867. 1867 (478) vii.

Select committee on the Army in India and the colonies. Report, 3 April 1868. 1867/8 (197) vi.

Select committee (HL) on the Canonries Bill. Report, 20 June 1873. HL 1873 (168) viii.

Select committee (HL) on the East India Company's Charter. Report, 29 June 1852. HL 1852/3 (8) xxvii.

Select committee (HL) on the Islington Market Bill. Min. of ev. 25 June 1835. HL 1835 (85) xlii.

Select committee (HL) on the means of divine worship in populous districts. Report, 18 June 1858. HL 1857/8 (79) xx; HC repr. 1857/8 (387) ix.

Select committee (HL) on poor laws
1st report, 15 Feb 1831. HL 1830/1 (30) cclxxxvii.
2nd report (not printed)
3rd report, 22 April 1831. HL 1830/1 (84) cclxxxvii.
Ev. 7 Dec 1830 to March 1831. HL 1830/1 (19) cclxxxvii.

Select committee (HL) on powers invested in companies for the improvement of land. Report, 25 May 1855. HL 1854/5 (119) xxii; HC repr. 1854/5 (403) vii.

Select committee on laws relating to game. Report, 18 April 1823. 1823 (260) iv.

Select committee (HL) on the Tolls on Steam Carriages Bill. Report, 19 July 1836. HL 1836 (230) xii.

GASCOYNE-CECIL, Robert Arthur Talbot, *3rd M. Salisbury*

Select committee (HL) on the improvement of land. Report, 8 July 1873. HL 1873 (81) ix; HC repr. 1873 (326) xvi.

Select committee (HL) on university tests. Report, 4 Aug 1870. HL 1870 (238) viii.

Select committee (HL) on university tests
    1st report, 23 March 1871. HL 1871 (17) viii; HC repr. 1871 (179-I) ix.
    2nd report, 27 April 1871. HL 1871 (78) viii; HC repr. 1871 (237) ix
    Report. HL 1871 (238) viii; HC repr. 1871 (179) ix.

GASKELL, James Milnes
Select committee on the Belfast Improvement (No.2) Bill. Min. of ev. 31 May 1864. 1864 (348) vi.

Select committee on the Clitheroe election petition. Min. of ev. 11 March 1853. 1852/3 (224) x.

Select committee on the Dover election petition. Min. of ev. 30 March 1860. 1860 (191) xi.

Select committee on the Limerick City election petition. Min. of ev. 5 Aug 1859. 1859, session 2 (147) iv.

Select committee on the New Windsor election petition. Min. of ev. 5 April 1853. 1852/3 (289) xix.

Select committee on the Peterborough election petition. Report, 15 Aug 1853. 1852/3 (934) xvii.

Select committee on Wareham election petitions. Min. of ev. 7 July 1857. 1857, session 2 (163) viii.

GATHORNE-HARDY, Gathorne, *1st E. Cranbrook*
Royal commission on the condition of cathedral churches in England and Wales. SEE: Howard, George James, *9th E. Carlisle.*

Select committee on the Benefices Resignation Bill, the Ecclesiastical Dilapidations Bill, the Sequestration Bill and the Sequestration of Benefices Bill. Reports, 2 and 20 June 1871. 1871 (266) vii.

Select committee on the Bury St. Edmund's Borough election petition. Min. of ev. 7 Aug 1857. 1857, session 2 (242) v.

Select committee on the Gloucester City election petition. Min. of ev. 1 Aug 1859. 1859, session 2 (127) iii.

Select committee on the Harwich election petition. Min. of ev. 3 May 1866. 1866 (233) x.

Select committee on high sheriffs. Report, 14 May 1888. HL 1888 (109) x; HC repr. 1888 (257) xii.

Select committee on the Master and Servant (Wages) Bill. Min. of proc. 6 May 1872. 1872 (183) xi.

Select committee on the Public Prosecutors Bill. Min. of proc. 30 May 1870. 1870 (260) viii.

Select committee (HL) on rabies in dogs. Report, 4 Aug 1887. HL 1887 (208) ix; HC repr. 1887 (322) xi; (HE Infectious Diseases, 8).

GATHORNE-HARDY, John Stewart, *2nd E. Cranbrook*
Departmental committee on the adulteration of artificial manures and fertilizers and feeding stuffs used in agriculture. Report, 27 Oct 1892. 1892 C.6742 xxvi. Board of Agriculture.

Select committee on the Boulogne sur Mer petition. Report, 16 May 1876. 1876 (232) viii.

GATHORNE-HARDY, John
Select committee on the Brine Pumping (Compensation for Subsidence) Bill. Report, 28 April 1891. 1890/1 (206) xi.

GEALE, Edward
Committee on the collection of fees under the County

Courts and Officers Act, 1877 in Ireland. Report, 31 Aug 1878. 1878/9 (310) lix.

GENNADIUS, P.
Report on agriculture in Cyprus. May 1899. 1899 C.9289 lix. Colonial Office.

GEOGHEGAN, J.
Report on coolie emigration from India. 1874 (314) xlvii. India Office.

GEORGE, John
Select committee on the Births, Deaths and Marriages (Ireland) Bill, and the Registration of Births, *etc.* (Ireland) Bill. SEE: Cardwell, Edward.

Select committee on the Peterborough City election petition. Min. of ev. 21 March 1860. 1860 (160) xi.

GIBBONS, Barry D.
Report on the improvement of Lough Erne, with a view to navigation and drainage. 21 May 1853. 1852/3 (694) xciv. Board of Works in Ireland.

GIBBON, Phillipps
Committee on distillation from corn. Report, 27 March 1745. CJ, vol.24, p.833.

Committee on petitions on Rye and Dover harbours. Report, 1756. CJ, vol.27, p.449.

GIBBS, John
Compulsory vaccination, briefly considered in its scientific, religious and political aspects. 30 June 1855. 1856 (109) lii. General Board of Health.

GIBBS, Vicary, *Sir*
Report on the Stafford peerage claim. 27 May 1808. HL 1808 (80) xxii.

GIBSON, Edward, *1st Bn. Ashbourne*
Commission for the publication of the ancient laws and institutes of Ireland (Brehon Law Commission).
    Report, 22 Dec 1886. 1887 C.5074 xliv.
    Report, 1888. 1888 C.5277 lx.
    Report, 29 Jan 1889. 1889 C.5634 xliii.
    Report, 8 Aug 1892. 1893/4 C.6847 xlviii.
    Report, 14 Feb 1893. 1893/4 C.6930 xlviii.
    Report, Jan 1894. 1893/4 C.7265 xlviii.
    Report, Jan 1895. 1895 C.7665 lvii.
    Report, Jan 1896. 1896 C.8040 xlviii.
    Report, Jan 1898. 1898 C.8845 li. Irish Secretary's Office. SEE ALSO: Blackburne, Francis.

Select committee on the County Officers and Courts (Ireland) Bill. Report, 17 July 1877. 1877 (341) x.

GIBSON, Thomas Milner
Select committee on the County Rates and Expenditure Bill. Report, 20 June 1850. 1850 (468) xiii.

Select committee on education in Manchester and Salford, *etc.* Report, 6 June 1853. 1852/3 (571) xxiv.

Select committee on election petition recognizances. Report, 15 July 1853. 1852/3 (775) xxxiv; (GO Elections, 3).

Select committee on Manchester and Salford education. Report, 21 June 1852. 1852 (499) xi.

Select committee on merchant shipping. Report, 7 Aug 1860. 1860 (530) xiii.

Select committee on navigation laws
    1st report, 26 March 1847. 1847 (232) x.
    2nd report, 30 March 1847. 1847 (246) x.

GIBSON, Thomas Milner (continued)
3rd report, 12 May 1847. 1847 (392) x.
4th report, 23 June 1847. 1847 (556) x.
5th report, index, 17 July 1847. 1847 (678) x;
repr. 1st-4th reports. 1847/8 (7) xx, pt.1; (TI
Navigation Laws, 1).

Select committee on newspaper stamps. Report,
18 July 1851. 1851 (558) xvii; (Newspapers, 1).

Select committee on private bill legislation. Report,
24 June 1863. 1863 (385) viii.

Select committee on the Railways Committee, 1846.
SEE: Wilson-Patten, John.

Select committee on the School of Design. Report,
27 July 1849. 1849 (576) xviii; (IR Design, 3).

Select committee on the Thames Navigation Bill.
Min. of ev. 5 July 1866. 1866 (391) xii.

Select committee on the Thames River. Report,
22 June 1865. 1865 (399) xii.

GIBSON-CRAIG, William, *Sir*
Commission on the law relating to the landlord's
right of hypothec in Scotland. Report. 1865 [3546]
xvii.

GIDDY, Davies
Committee on the Cambridge and London Junction
Canal Bill, in reference to non-compliance with the
standing orders of the House. Report, 13 May 1814.
1813/4 (172) iv.

Committee on copyright of printed books
Report, 17 June 1813. 1812/3 (292) iv.
Min. of ev. 20 July 1813. 1812/3 (341) iv.

Committee on Mr. Cort's petition (regarding iron
manufacture inventions). Report, 20 March 1812.
1812 (118) ii.

Committee on Mr. Earnshaw's petition (on chrono-
meters). Report, 31 May 1809. 1809 (245) iii.

Select committee on the civil list. Report, 7 July
1812. 1812 (330) ii; repr. 1830 (617) ix.

Select committee on proceedings relative to Sir Francis
Burdett
Report, 11 and 23 May 1810. 1810 (256), (295) ii.
Recommitted report, 11 May and 15 June 1810.
1810 (354) ii.

Select committee on public income and expenditure
of Ireland. Report, 19 June 1815. 1814/5 (214) vi.

Select committee on laws relating to bleaching powder. Report, 3 March 1815. 1814/5 (129) iii.

GIFFARD, Hardinge Stanley, *1st E. Halsbury*
Committee for privileges (HL)
Barrington peerage claim. Report, 15 Jan 1887.
HL 1887 (21) ix.

Committee for privileges (HL)
Enniskillen peerage claim. Report, 18 April 1887.
HL 1887 (62) ix.

Committee for privileges (HL)
Leinster peerage claim. Report, 26 July 1887.
HL 1887 (191) ix.

Committee for privileges (HL)
Meath peerage claim. Report, 6 Sept 1887. HL
1887 (253) ix.

Joint select committee on statute law revision bills
Report on the Friendly Societies Bill. 16 July
1896. HL 1896 (200) ix; HC 1896 (301) xiv.
Report on the Collecting Societies Bill. 16 July
1896. HL 1896 (201) ix.

Report on the Post Office Consolidation Bill.
11 June 1896. HL 1896 (125) ix.

Joint select committee on Statute Law Revision
Bill, *etc.* Report, 24 March 1897. 1897 (139) xiv
(HL version not identified).

Joint select committee on Statute Law Revision
Bill, *etc.* Report, 30 March 1898. 1898 (137) xi
(HL version not identified).

Select committee on British South Africa, 1897.
SEE: Jackson, William Lawies.

Select committee (HL) on the Companies Bill. Report,
17 July 1897. HL 1896 (207) ix; HC repr. 1896
(342) ix.

Select committee (HL) on the Companies Bill. Report,
8 Aug 1898. HL 1898 (207) ix; HC repr. 1898 (392)
ix.

Select committee (HL) on the Companies Bill. Report,
18 May 1899. HL 1899 (98) x; HC repr. 1899 (361)
viii.

Select committee (HL) on the Copyright Bill, and
the Copyright (Amendment) Bill. Report, 29 July
1898. HL 1898 (189) ix; HC repr. 1898 (393) ix.

Select committee (HL) on elections; interventions
of peers and prelates in parliamentary elections.
Report, 6 July 1888. HL 1888 (204) x.

Select committee (HL) on the Land Transfer Bill,
and the Land Charges Registration and Searches
Bill. Reports, 14 Dec 1888. HL 1888 (294) x.

Select committee (HL) on town improvements; better-
ment. Report, 10 July 1894. HL 1894 (159) viii;
HC repr. 1894 (292) xv; (UA Planning, 10).

GILBERT, Davies
Committee on the measurement of the tonnage of
ships. Report, 27 Feb 1834. HL 1834 (12) xv. Admiralty.

Committee on the measuring of the tonnage of ships.
Report, 21 Feb 1834. 1834 (43) xlix. Admiralty.

Committee on returns relative to the state of the
poor and charitable donations. Report, 23 May 1787;
repr. 1816 (22) iv.

Select committee on Acts regarding turnpike roads
and highways in England and Wales. Report, 10 July
1821. 1821 (747) iii.

Select committee on finance
1st report, 27 March 1817. 1817 (159) iv.
2nd report, 29 March 1817. 1817 (162) iv.
3rd report: Ordnance. 16 May 1817. 1817 (275) iv.
4th report: Public income and expenditure. 5 June
1817. 1817 (318) iv.
5th report: Irish civil estimates. 14 June 1817.
1817 (366) iv; repr. 1826/7 (209) iii.
6th report: Navy. 1817 (410) iv.
7th report, 23 Feb 1818. 1818 (57) iii.
8th report, 6 March 1818. 1818 (97) iii.
9th report: Ordnance. 18 March 1818. 1818 (183)
iii.
10th report: Civil contingencies. 7 May 1818.
1818 (269) iii.
11th report, 25 May 1818. 1818 (355) iii.

Select committee on finance (1819)
1st report: Income and expenditure. 6 April 1819.
1819 (205) ii.
2nd report: Army. 6 April 1819. 1819 (206) ii.
3rd report: Navy. 30 April 1819. 1819 (257) ii.
4th report: Ordnance. 10 May 1819. 1819 (289) ii.
5th report: Audit Office. 2 July 1819. 1819 (539)
ii.

Min. of ev. 19 March 1821. 1821 (184) viii.

Select committee on petitions complaining of the malt duties in Scotland. Report, 31 May 1821. 1821 (598) viii.

Select committee on the Population Bill
    Min. of ev. 11 May 1830. 1830 (385) iv; repr. 1840 (396) xv.
    Min. of ev. on re-committed Bill. 26 May 1830. 1830 (460) iv; repr. 1840 (396) xv.

Select committee on Rochester Bridge. Report, 11 July 1820. 1820 (267) iii.

Select committee on the table of fees. Report, 31 May 1821. 1821 (597) iv.

Select committee on turnpike roads and highways in England and Wales. Report, 18 July 1820. 1820 (301) ii.

Select committee on weights and measures. Report, 28 May 1821. 1821 (571) iii.

GILBERT, Edward
Gilbert and Sinclair's Patent Bill. SEE: Temple-Nugent-Chandos-Grenville, R.P.C., *3rd D. Buckingham.*

GILBERT, Francis Yarde
Report on the proposed extension of the boundaries of the Borough of Belfast. 11 Feb 1853. 1852/3 (958) xciv. Irish Secretary's Office.

GILBERT, Thomas
Committee on charitable donations. Report, 10 June 1788. CJ Reports, vol.9, p.733; repr. 1810 (48) ii.

GILES, Alfred
Select committee on Local Government Provisional Orders (No.3) Bill. Special report, 15 July 1884. 1884 (272) xiii; (UA Sanitation, 7).

GILES, Daniel
Committee to inspect the HL Journals in relation to their proceedings upon the impeachment of Henry, Viscount Melville. Report, 24 June 1806. 1806 (241) ii.

Committee on the petition respecting the fever institution. Report, 5 July 1804. 1803/4 (154) v.

GILLKREST, J.
Report on yellow fever. 28 Oct 1850. *In* 1852 [1473] xx. General Board of Health.

GILLON, William Downe
Select committee on internal communication taxation. Report, 30 June 1837. 1837 (456) xx.

GILPIN, Charles
Select committee on slave trade on the east coast of Africa. SEE: Gurney, Russell.

GIPPS, George, Sir
Report of the progressive discovery and occupation of New South Wales during Sir G. Gipps' administration of government. 28 Sept 1840. 1841 (120) xvii; (Australia, 6). Colonial Office.

GLADSTONE, Herbert John
Departmental committee on prisons. Report, 10 April 1895. 1895 C.7702 lvi; (CP Prisons, 19). Home Department.

Select committee on the Building Societies (No.2) Bill. Special report and report, 29 June 1893. 1893/4 (297) ix; (Insurance, 10).

Select committee on HC accommodation. Report, 7 Aug 1894. 1894 (268) xii.

Select committee on the Union Officers' Superannuation (Ireland) Bill. Report, 11 Aug 1882. 1882 (353) xiii.

GLADSTONE, William Ewart
Select committee on the Coalwhippers Bill. Min. of proc. 4 Aug 1843. 1843 (532) xi.

Select committee on the Farmers' Estate Society (Ireland) Bill. Report, 25 July 1848. 1847/8 (535) xvii.

Select committee on his funeral. SEE: Hicks-Beach, M.E.

Select committee on joint stock companies. Report, 2 Aug 1843. 1843 (523) xi.

Select committee on joint stock companies. Report, 15 March 1844. 1844 (119) vii.

Select committee on Merchant Seamen's Fund. Report, 1 July 1844. 1844 (431) viii.

Select committee on railways
    1st report, 16 Feb 1844. 1844 (37) xi.
    2nd report, 1 March 1844. 1844 (79) xi.
    3rd report, 1 April 1844. 1844 (166) xi.
    4th report, 15 May 1844. 1844 (283) xi.
    5th report, 24 May 1844. 1844 (318) xi.
    6th report, 22 July 1844. 1844 (524) xi; (Transport, 6).

GLANUSK, Lord SEE:
Bailey, Joseph Russell, *1st Bn. Glanusk.*

GLENBERVIE, Lord SEE:
Douglas, S., *Lord.*

GLOVER, George
Report on the common and model lodging houses of the Metropolis, with reference to epidemic cholera in 1854. 20 Jan 1855. 1854/5 [1892] xlv. General Board of Health.

GLOVER, John H.
Report on the conduct of the deputy commissioners, officers and men composing the expedition under his command on the Gold Coast (Ashantee invasion). 6 April 1874. 1874 C.962 xlvi; (Africa, 60). Foreign Office.

GODDARD, Norris M.
Report on the harbour of Holyhead as a harbour of refuge. 4 July 1844. 1846 (630-II) xlv. Admiralty.

GODERICH, Vct. SEE:
Robinson, Frederick John, *1st E. Ripon.*

GOLDNEY, Gabriel
Select committee on Ecclesiastical Dilapidations Acts. Report, 1 June 1876. 1876 (258) ix.

Select committee on the Metropolitan Board of Works (Shoreditch Improvement) Bill. Report, 30 March 1871. 1871 (142) xi.

GOLDSMID, Francis Henry, Sir
General committee on railway and canal bills. 1st to 6th reports, 16 March to 25 June 1869. 1868/9 (81), (81 I-V) vii.

General committee on railway and canal bills. 1st to 7th reports. 1 March to 23 June 1870. 1870 (87) (87 I-VI) vi.

GOLDSMID, Francis Henry, *Sir* (continued)
General committee on railway and canal bills. 1st to 6th reports, 3 March to 26 June 1871. 1871 (65) (65 I-V) ix.

Select committee on Wisley Common. Report, 26 April 1869. 1868/9 (169) x.

GOLDSMID, Julian, *Sir*
Standing committee on trade. Market Gardeners' Compensation Bill, and the Market Gardeners' Compensation (No.2) Bill. Special report and reports. 25 March 1895 (185) xii.

Standing committee on trade. Rating of Machinery Bill. Report, 14 March 1895. 1895 (116) xii.

GOOCH, Thomas Sherlock
Select committee on petitions complaining of the distressed state of the agriculture of the U.K., 1822. SEE: Wodehouse, E.

Select committee on petitions complaining of the depressed state of agriculture in the U.K. Report, 18 June 1821. 1821 (668) ix.

GOODENOUGH, James Graham
Report on the offer of the cession of the Fiji Islands to the British crown. 13 April 1874. 1874 C.1011 xlv. Colonial Office.

GOOLD, George J.
Report of the inquiry into the conduct of the constabulary during the disturbances at Belfast in July and September 1857. 11 Feb 1858. 1857/8 (333) xlvii; (CP Civil Disorder, 7). Irish Secretary's Office.

GORDON, *Lord* [Peerage claim]. SEE: Freeman-Mitford, J.T.

GORDON, Alexander Hamilton, *Sir*
Select committee on ecclesiastical and mortuary fees. Report, 25 July 1882. 1882 (309) x.

Commission to hold a local inquiry with a view to legislation on the Curragh of Kildare. Report, 28 Sept 1866. 1867/8 (329) lv. Treasury.

GORDON, Arthur
Commission on the working of the Western Pacific Orders in Council. Report. 1884 C.3905 lv. Colonial Office.

GORDON, Edward Strathearn
Select committee on Writs Registration (Scotland) Bill. Report, 2 July 1866. 1866 (395) viii.

GORDON, George Hamilton, *4th E. Aberdeen*
Select committee (HL) on the use of corn in distillation
Report, 13 June 1810. HL 1810 (67) xxxvi.
Appendix: William Rushton's account of corn arrived at the port of London. HL 1810 (67) xxxvi.

GORDON, James A., *Sir*
Commission appointed to survey the harbours of the south-eastern coast (of England). Report, 30 May 1840. 1840 (368) xxviii. Admiralty.

Committee on the port for departure and arrival of the West Indian mails. Report, 6 Aug 1840. 1840 (625) xliv. Admiralty.

Committee on the port for steam vessels to be employed in the conveyance of mails between England and Alexandria direct. Report, 11 Aug 1840. 1840 (626) xliv. Admiralty.

Committee on ports for Channel Islands mail. Report, 25 March 1841. 1841 (216) xxvi. Treasury.

Committee on ports for West India mails (1st and 2nd reports not identified)
3rd report, Oct 1840. 1841 (67) xxvi.

Report on the best means of communication between London and Dublin. 14 Jan 1840. 1840 (250) xlv. Admiralty.

GORDON, Osborne
Committee on the Royal Naval College, Greenwich. Report, 24 March 1877. 1877 C.1733 xxi. Admiralty.

Committee on fees and emoluments of public offices
1st report, 23 March 1837. 1837 (192) xliv.
2nd and final report, 5 May 1837. 1837 (277) xliv; (GO Civil Service, 1). Treasury.

GORDON, Robert
Committee of the whole HC on the charge against William Kenrick in relation to the case of John Franks. Min. of ev. 17 Feb 1826. 1826 (44) iii.

Committee on the whole HC on the East Retford Disenfranchisement Bill. Min. of ev. 3 to 7 March 1828. 1828 (80) iv.

Dean Forest Commission
1st and 2nd reports, 11 June 1835. 1835 (283) xxxvi.
3rd report, 13 Aug 1835. 1835 (515) xxxvi.
4th and 5th reports, 9 Sept 1835. 1835 (610) xxxvi.

Select committee on Bath and Weymouth Railway subscription list. Report, 26 April 1837. 1837 (243) xviii, pt.2.

Select committee on city of Dublin election petition. Report, 8 Aug 1831. 1831 (145) iv.

Select committee on colonial military expenditure. Report, 4 Aug 1835. 1835 (473) vi.

Select committee on pauper lunatics and asylums. Report, 29 June 1827. 1826/7 (557) vi; (HE Mental, 2).

Select committee on public offices (Downing Street). Report, 29 July 1839. 1839 (466) xii.

Select committee on rating of tenements.
1st report, 14 March 1838. 1837/8 (209) xxi.
2nd report, 1 June 1838. 1837/8 (440) xxi.

Select committee on Smithfield Market
1st report, 8 July 1828. 1828 (516) viii.
2nd report, 19 July 1828. 1828 (551) viii.

Select committee on Windsor Castle and Buckingham Palace
1st report, 27 Sept 1831. 1831 (272) iv.
2nd report, 14 Oct 1831. 1831 (329) iv.

GORDON, Samuel Enderby
Special committee on ordnance. Report on experiments with a 12-inch R.M.L. Gun returned from 'Thunderer'. 30 April 1880. 1880 C.2722 xiii. War Office.

GORDON, William
Select committee on salmon fisheries. SEE: Kennedy, T.F.

GORDON-LENNOX, Charles, *5th D. Richmond*
Commission for emigration. Report, 15 Aug 1832. 1831/2 (724) xxxii.

Commission on the establishment, organisation, *etc.* of the militia of the U.K. SEE: Gascoyne-Cecil, James Brownlow William, *2nd M. Salisbury.*

Commission for inquiring into the state of roads in England and Wales. Report, 17 July 1840. 1840 [256], [280] xxvii.

Committee (HL) on the Sale of Bread Bill. Min. of ev. 5-12 May 1836. HL 1836 (95) xxxix.

Committee (HL) on the Trinity (North Leith) Harbour and Dock Bill. Min. of ev. 24 June 1836. HL 1836 (173) xxxiii.

Select committee (HL) on the administration of oaths, 1842. SEE: Cooper, C.A., 6th E. Shaftesbury.

Committee (HL) on the Brighton Railway Bill. Min. of ev. 7 July 1836. HL 1836 (195) xxxiii.

Select committee (HL) on the charges of the county rates in England and Wales
    1st report, 24 June 1834. HL 1834 (24) xxi; HC repr. 1835 (206) xiv.
    2nd report, 24 June 1834. HL 1834 (24) xxi; HC repr. 1835 (206) xiv.

Select committee (HL) on the charging of entailed estates for drainage. Report, 18 April 1845. HL 1845 (119) xviii; repr. HL 1849 (11) xxx.

Select committee (HL) on the charging of entailed estates for drainage
    1st report, 30 April 1849. HL 1849 (4) xxx; HC repr. 1849 (350) xii.
    2nd report, 2 July 1849. HL 1849 (4-II) xxx.

Select committee (HL) on the Contagious Diseases (Animals) Bill. Report, 12 April 1878. HL 1878 (42) vii.

Select committee (HL) on county rates in England and Wales. 1st and 2nd reports, 24 June 1834. HL 1834 (24) xxi.

Select committee (HL) on gaols and houses of correction
    1st report, 12 May 1835. HL 1835 (42) xxvii.
    2nd report, 12 May 1835. HL 1835 (42) xxvii.
    3rd report, 8 July 1835. HL 1835 (42) xxvii.
    4th report, 9 July 1835. HL 1835 (42) xxvii.
    5th report, 2 Sept 1835. HL 1835 (42) xxvii.

Select committee (HL) on the High Constables Bill. Report, 24 April 1846. HL 1846 (89) xxvi.

Select committee on intercourse between the U.K. and the colonies of North America. SEE: Petty-Fitzmaurice, Henry, 3rd M. Lansdowne.

Select committee (HL) on the laws respecting gaming. 1st to 3rd reports, 26 April, 22 July and 5 Aug 1844. HL 1844 (80) xix; HC repr. 1844 (468), (544), (604) vi; (SP Gambling, 1).

Select committee (HL) on locomotive engines used in narrow streets
    1st report, 28 June 1836. HL 1836 (178) xii.
    2nd report, 7 July 1836. HL 1836 (168) xii.

Select committee (HL) on the operation of the act for the prevention of infectious diseases in cattle, etc. Report, 21 June 1850. HL 1850 (159) xxiii.

Select committee (HL) on prisons in England and Wales
    1st report, 12 May 1835. HL 1835 (42) xxvii; HC repr. 1885 (438) xi.
    2nd report, 12 May 1835. HL 1835 (42) xxvii; HC repr. 1835 (439) xi.
    3rd report, 8 July 1835. HL 1835 (42) xxviii; HC repr. 1835 (440) xii.
    4th and 5th reports, 9 July and 2 Sept 1835. HL 1835 (42) xxviii; HC repr. 1835 (441) xii; (CP Prisons, 3-4).

Select committee (HL) on the Sheffield Gas Bill.

SEE: Cooper, Cropley Ashley, 6th E. Shaftesbury.

Select committee (HL) on substituting declarations in lieu of oaths. Report, 3 July 1834. HL 1834 (64) xxi; HC repr. 1835 (186) xiv.

Select committee (HL) on substitution of declarations in lieu of oaths
    Report, 1835. HL 1837 (95) xx; HC repr. 1837 (411) xx.
    Min. of ev. 1835. HL 1835 (95) xx.

Select committee (HL) on substitution of declarations in lieu of oaths. Report, 22 May and 27 June 1837. HL 1837 (88), (144) xx; HC repr. 1837 (547) xx.

Committee (HL) on the Taff Vale Railway Bill. Min. of ev. 28 April 1837. HL 1837 (62) xix.

Select committee (HL) on turnpike road trusts
    1st report, 18 July 1833. HL 1833 (24) cccxxiii; HC repr. 1833 (422) xv.
    2nd report, 30 July 1833. HL 1833 (81) cccxxiii; HC repr. 1833 (703) xv.

Select committee (HL) on the West India colonies
    Report, 9 Aug 1832. HL 1831/2 (239) cccvi.
    Report, ev., appendix, index. 9 Aug 1832. HL 1831/2 (127) cccvi, cccvii.

GORDON-LENNOX, Charles Henry, 6th D. Richmond
Capital punishment commission. Report, 8 Jan 1866. 1866 [3590] xxi.

Joint select committee on canal rates, tolls and charges provisional order bills. Report, 27 July 1894. HL 1894 (97) ix; HC 1894 (232) x.

Joint select committee on canal rates, tolls and charges provisional order bills. Report, 18 May 1896. HL 1896 (103) ix; HC 1896 (188) ix.

Joint select committee on parliamentary deposits
    1st report, 11 July 1867. HL 1867 (213) xxvii; HC repr. 1867 (432) viii.
    2nd report, 6 Aug 1867. HL 1867 (308) xxvii; HC repr. 1867 (511) viii.

Joint committee on the railway acts and charges provisional order bills. Report, 27 July 1891. HL 1890/1 (268) xii, xiii; HC 1890/1 (394) xiv, xv; (Transport, 19-20).

Joint select committee on the railway rates and charges provisional order bills. Report, 10 May 1892. HL 1892 (99) x; HC 1892 (182) xv; (Transport, 21).

Oaths commission. Report. 1867 [3885] xxxi; (GO Civil Service, 8).

Reports on the Philadelphia International Exhibition. 30 April 1877. 1877 C.1774, C.1848, C.1890 xxxiv, xxxv, xxxvi. Privy Council Education Committee.

Royal commission on agriculture
    Preliminary report, ev. 14 Jan 1881. 1881 C.2778, C.3096 xv, xvi, xvii.
    Preliminary report of the assistant commissioner for Ireland. 1 Jan 1880. 1881 C.2952 xvi.
    Final report. 1882 C.3309 xiv.
    Min. of ev. 1882 C.3309-I xiv.
    Digest of min. of ev. 1882 C.3309-II xiv.
    Reports of assistant commissioners. 6 parts. 1882 C.3375 xv.
    Reports of assistant commissioners. July 1880. 1880 C.2678 xviii; (Agriculture, 15-19).

Royal commission on water supply. Report, 9 June 1869. 1868/9 [4169] xxxiii; (UA Water Supply, 5).

Select committee (HL) on the Compulsory Church Rates Abolition Bill. Report, 12 June 1868. HL 1867/8 (143) xxx.

GORDON-LENNOX, Charles Henry, *6th D. Richmond* (continued)

Select committee (HL) on conservancy boards, etc. Report, 24 July 1877. HL 1877 (159) vii; HC repr. 1877 (371) x.

Select committee (HL) on the Contagious Diseases (Animals) Bill. Report, 12 April 1878. HL 1878 (42) vii; HC repr. 1878 (154) xi.

Select committee (HL) on the East Gloucestershire Railway Bill. Min. of ev. 19 June 1862. HL 1862 (108) xxxix.

Select committee (HL) on the Promissory Oaths Bill. Report, 23 March 1868. HL 1867/8 (51) xxx.

Select committee (HL) on the Railway Companies Bill and the Railway Companies (Scotland) Bill. Report, 22 July 1867. HL 1867 (251) xxxvii.

Select committee (HL) on the Sea Fisheries Regulation (Scotland) Bill. Report, 28 March 1895. HL 1895 (51) vi.

Select committee on the Great Yarmouth Borough election petition. Min. of ev. 3 Aug 1857. 1857, session 2 (235) viii.

Select committee to join with a committee on the HL on parliamentary deposits
    1st report, 11 July 1867. (HL version not identified); HC 1867 (432) viii.
    2nd report, 6 Aug 1867. (HL version not identified); HC 1867 (511) viii.

Select committee (HL) on the Parliament Office and the Office of the Black Rod
    1st report, 26 May 1851. HL 1851 (113) xix.
    2nd report, 27 May 1852. HL 1852 (154) xxi.

Select committee (HL) on the Public Health (Scotland) (Nos. 1 and 2) Bills. Report, 30 April 1896. HL 1896 (72) ix.

Select committee (HL) on the Truro Cathedral Fabric and Services Bill. Report, 16 March 1888. HL 1888 (45) x.

GORDON-LENNOX, Charles Henry, *7th D. Richmond and March*

Wye River byelaws commission. Report, 8 June 1876. 1876 C.1537 xvi. Home Office.

GORE, Charles

Report on arrangements for the trying for and raising gold in England and Wales. 3 Feb 1854. 1854 (358) xxxix. Treasury.

Report on the claims of the Crown and of the Consolidated Fund under the Thames Embankment Act, 1862. 3 May 1871. 1871 (212) lvii. Treasury.

GORE, William Ormsby SEE:
Ormsby-Gore, William.

GORST, John Eldon, *Sir*

Committee on the distribution of science and art grants
    Report. 1897 C.8417 xxxiii.
    Appendix. 1898 C.8708 xxxii.
        Science and Art Department

Committee of public accounts
    1st report, 17 March 1886. 1886, session 1 (83) vii.
    2nd report, 28 May 1886. 1886, session 1 (169) vii.

Select committee on the Companies Act (1862) Amendment Bill. Special report, 3 July 1891. 1890/1 (314) xii.

Select committee on East India civil servants. Report, 29 July 1890. 1890 (327) xiii.

Select committee on museums of the Science and Art Department. SEE: Powell, Francis Sharp, *Sir.*

Select committee on Parliamentary debates. Report, 10 June 1892. 1892 (253) xiv.

Select committee on the Superannuation Acts Amendment (No.2) Bill. Report, 14 June 1892. 1892 (271) xvii; (GO Civil Service, 12).

Standing committee on trade. Fertilizers and Feeding Stuffs Bill. Report, 9 Aug 1893. 1893/4 (369) xi.

GOSCHEN, George Joachim

Report of the commission appointed to represent HM Government at the monetary conference held in Paris in August 1878. 27 Nov 1878. 1878/9 C.2196 xxi; (MP Currency, 4). Treasury.

Report on increase of local taxation, with especial reference to the proportion of the burden borne by the different classes of real property. March 1871. 1870 (470) lv; repr. 1893/4 (201) lxxvii. Poor Law Board.

Select committee on Admiralty expenditure and liabilities. Report, 3 Aug 1885. 1884/5 (311) vii.

Select committee on business of the HC; abridged procedure on partly considered bills. Report, 14 July 1890. 1890 (298) xi.

Select committee on depreciation of silver. Report, 5 July 1876. 1876 (338) viii; (MP Currency, 6).

Select committee on financial relations between England, Scotland and Ireland. Report, 18 Aug 1890. 1890 (412) xiii; (National Finance, 6).

Select committee on law of distress. Report, 17 July 1882. 1882 (284) viii.

Select committee on local taxation. Report, 15 July 1870. 1870 (353) viii.

Select committee on theatrical licenses and regulations. Report, 28 June 1866. 1866 (373) xvi; (Stage and Theatre, 2).

Select committee on town holdings. SEE: Sclater-Booth, George.

Standing committee on trade. Bankruptcy Bill. Report, 25 June 1883. 1883 (224) xi.

GOSFORD, *Lord* SEE:
Acheson, Archibald, *2nd E. Gosford.*

GOULBURN, Henry

Committee appointed to prepare militia estimates. Report, 26 March 1824. 1824 (171) vi.

Select committee on Clerk of the Crown in Chancery. Report, 5 July 1844. 1844 (455) xiv.

Select committee on the Derby election; petition of inhabitant householders. Report, 16 Dec 1852. 1852/3 (78) xii.

Select committee on HC offices. Report, 4 May 1849. 1849 (258) xii.

Select committee on oaths of members. Report, 10 April 1848. 1847/8 (256) xvi.

Select committee on ventilation of the new Houses of Parliament. Report, 5 Aug 1842. 1842 (536) xiv.

GOULD, Charles

Report on the subject of gold in the colony of Van Diemen's Land, Tasmania. 1862. 1864 (331) xli. Colonial Office.

GOULD, Edward

Departmental committee on factory statistics. Report,

30 Aug 1894. 1895 C.7608 xix; (IR Factories, 31).
Home Department.

Departmental committee on the various lead industries.
Report, 1893/4 C.7239 xvii; (IR Factories, 29). Home
Department.

GOWER, Francis Leveson   SEE:
Egerton, Francis, *1st E. Ellesmere.*

GOWER, Granville George Leveson   SEE:
Leveson-Gower, Granville George, *2nd E. Granville.*

GOWER, Granville Leveson, *Vct. Granville-Leveson*
Committee on county bridges. Report, 30 May 1800.
(Reps., 1731-1800, no.160, vol.25).

Committee on county bridges. Report, 19 May 1801.
1801 (78) iii.

Committee on county bridges. Report, 29 April 1803.
1802/3 (61) v.

GRAHAM, James, *3rd D. Montrose*
Secret committee (HL) on papers from H.R.H. the
Prince Regent. Report, 23 Feb 1818. HL 1818 (8) xci.

GRAHAM, James, *M. Graham*
Select committee (HL) on the Cork and Youghal
Railway Bill. Report, 23 March 1866. HL 1866 (63)
xxviii; HC repr. 1866 (209) xi.

GRAHAM, James, *Sir*
Committee on communication between England and
Ireland by the North-west of Scotland. Report, 15
June 1809. 1809 (269) iii.

Committee on Darlington and Stockton Railway
petition. Report, 25 March 1819. 1819 (163) viii.

Committee on expired and expiring laws. 4th session.
4th Parliament. Report, 26 Jan 1810. 1810 (3) ii.

Committee on the petition of the London clergy
incumbents. Report, 15 March 1819. 1819 (105)
viii.

Committee on roads between Carlisle and Port Patrick. Report, 13 May 1811. 1810/1 (119) iii.

Committee on standing orders
  Report, 9 April 1810. 1810 (190) ii.
  2nd report, 26 May 1810. 1810/1 (303) ii.
  3rd report, 18 June 1810. 1810 (321) ii.

GRAHAM, James Robert George, *Sir*
Select committee on agriculture. Report, 2 Aug 1833.
1833 (612) vi; (Agriculture, 2).

Select committee on Ameer Ali Moorad's claim (Coffey's petition). Report, 12 March 1858. 1857/8 (115)
xii.

Select committee on the business of the HC. Report,
19 April 1861. 1861 (173) xi.

Select committee on the Metropolis Water Bill. Min.
of ev. 5 Aug 1851. 1851 (643) xv; (UA Water Supply,
2).

Select committee on military organisation. Report,
9 July 1860. 1860 (441) vii; (Military and Naval, 5).

Select committee on slavery. Report, 11 Aug 1832.
1831/2 (721) xx; (Slave Trade, 2).

GRAHAM, John, *Bp. Chester,* 1848-1865
Commission on Cambridge University
  Report, 30 Aug 1852. 1852/3 [1559] xliv.
  Index. 20 Aug 1853. 1852/3 (1017) xliv.

GRAHAM, Thomas
Commission on the chemical quality of the supply
of water to the Metropolis. Report, 17 June 1851.
1851 (421) xxiii; (UA Water Supply, 5). Home Department.

Report on the International Monetary Conference,
Paris, June 1867. 2 Dec 1867. *In* 1867/8 [4021]
xxvii; (MP Currency, 3).

Reports on the supply of spirit of wine, free from
duty, for use in arts and manufactures. 24 July, 2 Nov
1854 and 8 Jan 1855. 1854/5 (201) l. Inland Revenue.

GRAHAM, William, *Sir*
Committee on administration and management of
dockyards. Sub-committee on dockyards returns,
etc. Report, 31 May 1886. 1887 C.4979 xvi. Admiralty.

Committee on dockyard expenditure. 1st and 2nd
reports, 8 Sept and 24 Oct 1885. 1886 C.4615 xiii.
Admiralty.

Committee on dockyard management
  1st report, 12 Jan 1886. 1886 C.4615 xiii. Admiralty.
  (no further reports identified)

GRAINGER, Richard Dugard
Committee of the Epidemiological Society on small-
pox and vaccination. Report, 26 March 1853. 1852/3
(434) ci. Home Department.

Medical report on the epidemic attack of fever at
Croydon. 18 Feb 1853. *In* 1852/3 [1683] xcvi;
(HE Infectious Diseases, 2).

Report on 38 Metropolitan workhouses. 26 March
1849. 1850 (133) xxi; (HE Infectious Diseases, 1).
General Board of Health.

Report on the sanitary condition of Agar Town,
St. Pancras. 31 May 1851. 1851 (388) xxiii; (Health,
7). Board of Health.

GRANDISON, *Lord*   [Peerage claim, 1829].   SEE:
Cooper, C.A.; 1854-58, SEE: Freeman-Mitford, J.T.

GRANT, Alexander, *Sir*
Committee on expired and expiring laws. 2nd session,
8th Parliament. Report, 1 Feb 1828. 1828 (4) iv.

Committee on expired and expiring laws. 3rd session,
8th Parliament. Report, 9 Feb 1829. 1829 (3) iii.

Committee on expired and expiring laws. 1st session,
9th Parliament. Report, 8 Nov 1830. 1830/1 (6) iii.

Report on the note of Mr. A. Monteath on the state
of education in India. 9 Dec 1867. 1867/8 (244) l.
India Office.

GRANT, Charles
Committee on the repair of the Cobb at Lyme Regis.
Report, 10 June 1818. 1818 (432) iii.

Select committee on the butter trade of Ireland.
Report, 26 May 1826. 1826 (406) v.

Select committee on steam navigation to India. Report,
14 July 1834. 1834 (478) xiv.

GRANT, Donald
Select committee on patent for ventilation.   SEE:
Courtenay, William, *11th E. Devon.*

GRANT, Henry Duncan
Committee on administration and management of
dockyards. Sub-committee on supplies of stores

GRANT, Henry Duncan (continued)
and materials at dockyards. Report, 20 May 1886. 1887 C.4979 xvi.

Report and evidence on the wreck of the 'San Francisco'. 23 April 1867. 1867 (265) lxvi. Board of Trade.

GRANT, James Hope, *Sir*
Army sanitary committee. Report on the epidemic of scarlet fever among children in Aldershot camp. 20 April 1866. 1866 [3708] xvii. War Office.

GRANT, John
Committee on claims for remuneration for introduction of his system of cookery. SEE: Cavendish, Spencer Compton, *8th D. Devonshire.*

GRANT, Robert
Committee on the Zemindar of Nozeed Bill. Min. of ev. 4 Oct 1831. 1831 (P.B. 2) iv.

Select committee on the affairs of Lower Canada. SEE: Rice, Thomas Spring.

Select committee on the Arigna Mining Company. Report, 3 April 1827. 1826/7 (243) iii.

GRANT-DUFF, Mountstuart Elphinstone
Select committee on the Thames River (Prevention of Floods) Bill. Report, 21 June 1877. 1877 (280) xvii.

GRANVILLE, E. SEE:
Leveson-Gower, Granville George, *2nd E. Granville.*

GRANVILLE-LEVESON, *Lord* SEE:
Gower, G.L., *Vct. Granville-Leveson.*

GRAVES, Charles
Commission for the publication of the ancient laws and institutes of Ireland (Brehon Law Commission). SEE: Blackburne, Francis.

GRAY, Edmond Dwyer
Select committee on privileges. Report on his commitment. SEE: James, Henry, *Sir.*

GRAY, Thomas
Committee on lights for fishing vessels. SEE: Collinson, R.

Committee on tests of cast steel anchors. Report, 21 July 1887. 1887 C.5229 lxvi. Board of Trade.

International code of signals committee. SEE: Murray, D.

Report on the Bristol Channel pilotage. 14 Jan 1870. 1870 (70) lx. Board of Trade.

Report on the supply of British merchant seamen. 21 Dec 1872. 1873 C.752 lix. Board of Trade.

GREATHEAD, Henry
Committee on petition respecting his new invention of a life-boat. SEE: Burdon, R., SEE ALSO: Ward, R.

GREAVES, Charles Sprengal
Report on criminal procedure. 30 June 1855. 1856 (456) l. Lord Chancellor's Office.

GREEN, Joseph Henry
Commission of inquiry on Northleach house of correction. Report, 27 Jan 1843. 1843 [463] xliii.

GREEN, Thomas
General committee on railway and canal bills. SEE: Bouverie, Edward Pleydell.

GREENE, Richard Wilson
Commission on the offices of the common law courts in Ireland. Report, 7 April 1842. 1842 [378] xxiii. Secretary for Ireland Office.

Committee on expired and expiring laws. 4th session, 13th Parliament. Report, 3 May 1841. 1841 (286) ix.

Select committee on classification of railway bills, 1847. SEE: Wilson-Patten, John.

GREENE, Thomas
Committee of selection, 1849. SEE: Wilson-Patten, John.

Committee of selection to the grouping of private bills. 1st to 12th reports. 23 Feb to 5 June 1855. 1854/5 (256) vii.

Committee of selection relative to the grouping of private bills, 1857. SEE: Wilson-Patten, John.

Select committee on Aylesbury election petitions. Report, 4 June 1851. 1851 (365) xii.

Select committee on the new House of Commons 1st report, 1 Aug 1850. 1850 (650) xv.
Proc., 1 Aug 1850. 1850 (650-II) xv.

Select committee on petitions relating to the Manchester and Birmingham Extension (Stone and Rugby) Railway Bill. Report, 12 June 1839. 1839 (306) xiii.

Select committee on standing orders revision, 1855. SEE: Heathcote, William, *Sir.*

Select committee of standing orders revision (1856). Report, 17 July 1856. 1856 (363) vii.

Select committee on strangers (in the HC). Report, 12 July 1849. 1849 (498) xii.

Select committee on witnesses expenses before select committees. Report, 29 July 1840. 1840 (555) xv.

GREENHOW, Edward Headlam
On the different prevalence of certain diseases in different districts in England and Wales. May 1858. 1857/8 [2415] xxiii; (Health, 8). General Board of Health.

GREENSHIELDS, John B.
Commission on municipal corporations in Scotland General report. 1835 [30] xxix.
Appendix. 1836 [34] xxiii.
Local reports, pt.1: Aberborthwick to Fortrose. 1835 [31] xxix.
Local reports, pt.2: Glasgow to Wigtown. 1836 [32] xxiii.
Local reports, pt.3: Burghs of Regality and Barony and Unincorporated towns, and appendix. 1836 [33] xxiii; (GO Municipal Corporations, 8-9).

GREENWOOD, John
Committee for inquiry into the misappropriation of monies entrusted to Mr. H. Swavey, late Registrar of the High Court of Admiralty. Report, 31 May 1854. 1854 (351) xlii. Treasury.

Report of inquiry into the Patent Office accounts. 12 July 1864, 31 Jan 1865, 28 Feb 1865. 1865 (173) xliii; (GO Civil Service, 7). Commission of Patents. SEE ALSO: Leveson-Gower, G.G., *2nd E. Granville.*

Report on the Office of Registrar of Deeds in Middlesex. 1 Aug 1867. 1867 (573) lvii. Home Department.

GREGORY, John
Report on the seizure of packages landed by the ships 'Hope' and 'Lelia' and directed to Rev. Mr. Capern. 20 May 1853. 1854 (362) xliii. Colonial Office.

GREGORY, John S.
Committee on the Incorporated Law Society on equity practice. Report, 2 Dec 1851. 1852 (216) xlii; (Legal Administration, 8).

GREGORY, William Henry
Select committee on the British Museum. Report, 10 Aug 1860. 1860 (540) xvi; (ED British Museum, 4).

Select committee on the Royal Atlantic Steam Navigation Company. Report, 23 July 1861. 1861 (463) xii.

Select committee on scientific institutions (Dublin). Report, 15 July 1864. 1864 (495) iii.

GREGSON, Samuel
Select committee on public institutions. SEE: Trelawny, John, *Sir*.

GREIG, James
Report on the state of education in Glasgow. 20 March 1866. 1867 [3845-II] xxv; (Education, 14). Education Commission, Scotland. SEE ALSO: Campbell, G.D., *8th D. Argyll*.

GRENVILLE, William Wyndham, *1st Bn. Grenville of Wooton-under-Bernwood*
Select committee (HL) on precedents relative to the impeachment against Warren Hastings. Report, 19 April 1791. Repr. HL 1806 (9) v.

Select committee (HL) on public income and expenditure. Report, 21 March 1786. CJ Reports, vol.11, p.39; [Reps. 1731-1800, no.78, vol.7].

GREVILLE, C.C.
Committee of inquiry on the Privy Council Office. Report, 6 Aug 1853. 1854 [1715] xxvii. Treasury.

GREY, *E*. SEE:
Grey, Henry George, *3rd E. Grey*.

GREY, Frederick William
Committee on the construction, condition and cost of fortifications. Report, 28 April 1869. 1868/9 [4135] xii. War Office.

GREY, George, *Sir*
Commission on over-regulation payments on promotion in the Army. Report. 1870 C.201 xii.

Committee on the Glasgow and Belfast Union Railway Bill petitions. Report, 3 July 1846. 1846 (459) xii.

Select committee on bribery at elections. SEE: Ord, W.H.

Select committee on the Cold Fields Bath meeting. SEE: Hawes, B., *jun*.

Select committee on County Courts Bill. Report, 8 July 1839. 1839 (387-II) xiii.

Select committee on Ecclesiastical Corporations Bill and the Ecclesiastical Commission, *etc*. Bill. SEE: Russell, John, *1st E. Russell*.

Select committee on the Highways Bill. Min. of proc. 12 May 1862. 1862 (226) xvi.

Select committee on private business, 1839. SEE: Poullett-Thomson, C.E.

Select committee on private business
    1st report, 7 Feb 1840. 1840 (56) xv.
    2nd report, 9 July 1840. 1840 (463) xv.
    3rd report, 17 July 1840. 1840 (503) xv.

Select committee on private business. Report: Severn navigation. 15 March 1841. 1841 (131) ix.

Select committee on railway bills, Ireland. Report, 23 May 1845. 1845 (315) x.

Select committee on South Australia
    1st report, 9 March 1841. 1841 (119) iv.
    2nd report, 10 June 1841. 1841 (394) iv; (Australia, 2).

Select committee on the Taunton election petition. Report, 18 April 1853. 1852/3 (355) xix.

GREY, Henry George, *3rd E. Grey*
Commission on consolidation of the different departments connected with the civil administration of the Army. Report, 21 Feb 1837. 1837 [78] xxxiv, pt.1: (Military and Naval, 4).

Commission on the operation of the acts relating to transportation and penal servitude
    Vol.1: Report, 20 June 1863. 1863 [3190] xxi.
    Vol.2: Min. of ev. 1863 [3190-I] xxi; (CP Transportation, 5).

Select committee appointed to prepare the militia estimates. Report, 27 Aug 1835. 1835 (570) vi.

Select committee appointed to prepare the militia estimates. Report, 2 Aug 1836. 1836 (515) xxi.

Select committee appointed to prepare the militia estimates. Report, 28 June 1837. 1837 (444) xx.

Select committee appointed to prepare militia estimates. Report, 23 July 1838. 1837/8 (616) xxiii.

Select committee appointed to prepare the militia estimates. Report, 25 July 1839. 1839 (457) xiii.

Select committee (HL) on the Charing Cross Railway (City Terminus) Bill. Report, 14 March 1861. HL 1861 (43) xxiv.

Select committee (HL) on the elective franchise in counties and boroughs. Report, 28 June 1860. HL 1860 (87) xxv; HC repr. 1860 (455) xii; (GO Elections, 3).

Select committee (HL) on the Hammersmith, Paddington and City Junction Railway Bill. Report, 15 March 1861. HL 1861 (49) xxiv.

Select committee (HL) on poor rates and highway rates and the Municipal Franchise Acts. Report, 14 April 1859. HL 1859, session 1 (46) xxii; HC repr. 1859, session 2 (56) vii.

Select committee on publication of the printed papers by order of the HC. 1st report, 18 March 1840. 1840 (130) xv. (no others identified).

Select committee (HL) on the Stamford and Spalding Railway Bill. Report, 16 June 1846. HL 1846 (192) xxvi.

Select committee on New Zealand. Report, 29 July 1844. 1844 (556) xiii; (New Zealand, 2).

Select committee on printed papers (Stockdale v Hansard)
    1st report, 10 June 1839. 1839 (297) xiii.
    2nd report, 15 June 1839. 1839 (321) xiii.
    3rd report, 20 Aug 1839. 1839 (546) xiii.

Select committee on publication of the printed papers. Report, 8 May 1837. 1837 (286) xiii.

Select committee (HL) on the West London Extension Railway Bill. Report, 15 March 1861. HL 1861 (48) xxiv.

GREY, John
Committee on petition of John Harrison respecting

GREY, John (continued)
the construction of a time-keeper
Report, 12 March 1763. CJ, vol.29, p.546.
Report, 16 March 1763. CJ, vol.29, p.566.

GREY DE RUTHYN, *Lord*   [Peerage claim]. SEE:
Freeman-Mitford, J.T.

GRIFFITH, Charles Marshall
Royal commission on corrupt practices in the Borough of Knaresborough. Report, 11 Jan 1881. 1881 C.2777 xlii.

GRIFFITH, Richard
Commission of inquiry on arterial drainage in Ireland. Report, 11 June 1853. 1852/3 [1641] xli. Treasury.

Progress of roads and land improvements on the Crown estates of King William's Town, County of Cork
Report, 3 June 1836. 1836 (315) xlvii.
Further report, 8 Aug 1839. 1839 (515) xlvii.
Further report, 31 Aug 1841. 1841, session 2 (8) ii.
Report, 24 July 1844. 1844 (612) xliii.
Report, 5 June 1851. 1851 (637) l. Commission of HM Woods, *etc.*

Report on the Bann Navigation Improvement Bill. 13 May 1851. 1851 (342) xxiv. Board of Works in Ireland.

Report on the experimental improvements on the Crown estate of King William's Town, County Cork. 5 June 1851. 1851 (637) l. Commission of HM Woods, *etc.*

Report on Kilkenny Canal. 23 Aug 1833. 1833 (723) xxxv.

Report on roads made at the public expense in the southern district of Ireland. 27 July 1831. 1831 (119) xii.

GRIFFITHS, A.M.
Commission of inquiry on the plan of Mr. Harris, relating to the protection of ships from the effects of lightning. Report, 11 Feb 1840. 1840 (63) xlv. Admiralty.

GRIMSHAW, Thomas W.
Report on the prevalence of enteric fever at the Royal barracks, Dublin. 13 Aug 1887. 1888 C.5292 xxv. War Office.

GRIMSTON, *Vct.* [Peerage claim]. SEE:
Freeman-Mitford, J.T.

GROSVENOR, *E.* SEE:
Grosvenor, Robert, *2nd M. Westminster.*

GROSVENOR, Hugh Lupus, *1st D. Westminster*
Select committee (HL) on intemperance
1st report, 23 March 1877. HL 1877 (12) viii; HC repr. 1877 (171) xi.
2nd report, 17 May 1877. HL 1877 (12-I) viii; HC repr. 1877 (271) xi.
3rd report, 13 July 1877. HL 1877 (12-II) viii; HC repr. 1877 (418) xi.
Index. HL 1877 (12-III) viii; (SP Drunkenness, 3).
4th report, 26 July 1878. HL 1878 (25) vii; HC repr. 1878 (338) xiv; (SP Drunkenness, 4).

Select committee (HL) on intemperance. Report, 10 March 1879. HL 1878/9 (28) vii; HC repr. 1878/9 (113) x; (SP Drunkenness, 4).

GROSVENOR, Robert, *2nd M. Westminster*
Select committee on the silk trade. SEE: Stuart, D.C.

Select committee (HL) on the supply of water to the Metropolis. Report, 27 Feb 1840. HL 1840 (29) xxii; HC repr. 1840 (354) xii; (UA Water Supply, 1).

Committee (HL) on the Chester and Birkenhead Railway Bill. Min. of ev. 6 June 1837. HL 1837 (107) xvii.

GROSVENOR, Robert, *1st Bn. Ebury*
Metropolitan sanitary commission
1st report, 19 Nov 1847. 1847/8 [888] xxxii.
Min. of ev. 1847/8 [895] xxxii.
2nd report, 19 Feb 1848. 1847/8 [911] xxxii.
Min. of ev. 1847/8 [921] xxxii.
3rd report, 13 July 1848. 1847/8 [979] xxxii; (Health, 7).

Select committee on the Bolton election petition. Report, 2 May 1853. 1852/3 (429) viii.

Select committee on the Malden election petition. Min. of ev. 5 April 1853. 1852/3 (290) xvi.

Select committee on Metropolis turnpike roads. Report, 4 July 1856. 1856 (333) xiv.

Select committee on the Tavistock election petition. Min. of ev. 11 March 1853. 1852/3 (227) xix.

Select committee on ventilation and lighting of the HC
1st report, 6 April 1852. 1852 (243) xvi.
2nd report, 24 May 1852. 1852 (402) xvi.

GROTE, George
Committee of privileges. Report, 14 Feb 1834. 1834 (51) xi.

Select committee on the Carlow Borough election petitions. Min. of ev. 17 July 1839. 1839 (414) vi, vii.

Select committee on sinecure offices. Report, 25 July 1834. 1834 (519) vi.

GROVE, William Robert, *Sir*
Trial of the Boston election petition. Ev. and judgement. 5 Aug 1874. 1874 (375) liii.

Taunton election petition. Judgement. 26 Jan 1874. 1874 (74) lii.

Wigan election petition. Ev. and judgement. 1 April 1881. 1881 (207) lxxiv.

GUELPH, George William Frederick Charles, *2nd D. Cambridge*
Royal commission for the Adelaide Jubilee International Exhibition of 1887. Report. 1888 C.5440 xxiv; (Australia, 30).

GUEST, Josiah John
Select committee on the establishment of the HC. Report, 12 Aug 1833. 1833 (648) xii.

Select committee on official houses
1st report, 17 July 1834. 1834 (480) xi.
2nd report, 5 Aug 1834. 1834 (558) xi.

GUILLAMORE, *Vct.* [Peerage claim]. SEE:
Freeman-Mitford, J.T.

GULLY, William Court
Inquiry into the causes of death of the patient Thomas Weir at St. Ann's Heath, Virginia Water. Report, 20 April 1895. 1895 (394) lxxx. Home Department.

GULSON, Edward
Removal of Irish paupers to Ireland, and the case of

William Kelly. 12 April 1856. 1856 (202) xlix. Poor Law Board.

Report on the distress in Nottingham. 23 April 1837. 1837 (376) li. Poor Law Commission.

GUPPY, Robert
Commission of inquiry on emigration from Sierra Leone to the West Indies. Report, 18 October 1844. 1847/8 (732) xliii. Colonial Office.

GURDON, W.B.
Departmental committee on the Register House Departments, Edinburgh, relating to the system of registration and searching in the Register of the Sasines. 3 Feb 1881. 1882 C.3377 xxi. Treasury.

GURNEY, Goldsworthy
Report on experiments for withdrawing and decomposing the noxious effluvia from the sewers in the neighbourhood of the Houses of Parliament. 8 Jan 1855. 1854/5 (105) liii; (UA Sanitation, 4). Office of Works.

Report on the lighting of the HC. 30 June 1853. 1852/3 (911) lxxxiii.

Select committee on his case. SEE: Molesworth, W.

Select committee on steam carriages. SEE: Cayley, E.S.

Ventilation, lighting and warming of the new HC
1st report, 5 April 1852. 1852 (237) xlii.
2nd report, 13 April 1852. 1852 (252) xlii.
3rd report, 19 May 1852. 1852 (371) xlii.

GURNEY, Russell
Commission of inquiry on the existence of bribery in the Borough of Sudbury. Report, 12 March 1844. 1844 [538] xviii.

Select committee on Married Women's Property Bill. 13 May 1869. 1868/9 (210) viii; (Marriage and Divorce, 2).

Select committee on slave trade on the east coast of Africa. Report, 4 Aug 1871. 1871 (420) xii; (Slave Trade, 7).

GUTHRIE, W.
Commission on the truck system
Vol.1: Report, 20 April 1871. 1871 C.326 xxxvi.
Vol.2: Min. of ev. 1871 C.327 xxxvi.
2nd report: Shetland. 15 June 1872. 1872 C.555 xxxv; (Industrial Relations, 11-12). Home Department.

GUY, William A.
Committee on the dietary of convicts in separate confinement. Report, 19 Dec 1863. 1864 (467) xlix; (CP Prisons, 17). Home Department.

GWILT, Joseph
Report on the Metropolitan Buildings Act. 14 Dec 1850. 1851 (114) xlviii. Commission of H.M. Woods, etc.

GWYDIR, Lord SEE:
Burrell, Peter, *1st Bn. Gwidir.*

GYBBON, P. SEE:
Gibbon, Phillipps.

HADDINGTON, E. SEE:
Baillie, Thomas, *9th E. Haddington* (1780-1858)
Baillie-Hamilton, George, *10th E. Haddington* (1802-70)

Baillie-Hamilton-Arden, George, *11th E. Haddington* (1827-1917).

HADFIELD, George
Select committee on the Judgements, *etc.* Law Amendment Bill. Report, 17 June 1864. 1864 (396) v.

HAIG, Charles
Valuations for poor rates and registered elective franchise in Ireland
General report. 1841 [292] xxii.
2nd general report. 9 March 1841. 1841 [306] xxii.
3rd general report. 1841 [329] xxiii.
Index. 1842 [401] xxxviii. Poor Law Commission.

HALCOMB, John
Select committee on British Channel fisheries. Report, 16 Aug 1833. 1833 (676) xiv.

HALDANE, George, Jr.
Committee on ministers, *etc* in Scotland. Report, 24 May 1751. CJ Reports, vol.2, p.317.

HALDANE, Robert Dundas Duncan SEE:
Duncan-Haldane, Robert Dundas, *1st E. Camperdown.*

HALIFAX, Vct. SEE:
Wood, Charles, *1st Vct. Halifax.*

HALL, Benjamin, Sir
Select committee on the Chelsea New Bridge Bill. Report, 7 Aug 1857. 1857, session 2 (250) ix.

Select committee on the Public Health Bill, and the Nuisances Removal Amendment Bill. Report, 18 May 1855. 1854/5 (244) xiii; (Health, 8).

Select committee on public offices. Report, 18 July 1856. 1856 (368) xiv.

Select committee on St. James Park. Report, 7 March 1856. 1856 (85) vii.

Select committee on the Tynmouth election petition
Report, 15 April 1853. 1852/3 (425) xix.
Min. of ev. 1852/3 (345) xix.

Select committee on Westminster Bridge. Report, 6 Aug 1857. 1857, session 2 (246) ix.

HALL, Charles, Sir
Committee on alterations in the regulations for preventing collisions at sea, recommended at the Washington International Maritime Conference
Report. 1890/1 C.6293 lxxvi. Board of Trade
Further reports, 12 Dec 1891 to 13 July 1892. 1892 C.6833 lxxi. Board of Trade.

Committee on rule of the road at sea. Reports on lights and signals of fishing and pilot vessels and right-of-way of steam fishing vessels
Reports, 4 Feb and 13 May 1898. 1898 C.8888 lxxxiii.
Min. of ev. 1898 C.8889 lxxxiii. Board of Trade.

HALL, Henry
Report on coal dust experiments. 20 Aug 1893. 1893/4 C.7185 xx; (FP Mining Accidents, 12). Home Department. SEE ALSO: Chamberlain, Joseph.

HALL, James
Committee on Gas-Light and Coke Companies Bill. Min. of ev. 19 May 1809. 1809 (220) iii; (FP Gas, 6).

HALL, James Trail
Commission on the Paving Board of Dublin. Report, 9 May 1827. 1826/7 (329) xi.

HALL, John, *Sir*
Report on the Board of medical officers on plans of a proposed hospital for Aldershot. 20 Nov 1856. 1857/8 (361) xxxvii. War Office.

HALL, Richard
Report on inquiry into the treatment, condition and mortality of infant children in the workhouse of the North Dublin Union. 20 Jan 1842. 1842 [370] xxxvi. Poor Law Commission.

Report on the relief of casual poor. 6 Feb 1844. *In:* 1844 [589] xix. Poor Law Commission.

Reports on the formation of the Metropolis into districts for the relief of the casual poor. 17 Jan 1845 and 13 May 1845. *In:* 1846 [745] xix.

Reports on the Strand Union School at Edmonton. 24 Nov 1851 and 24 Jan 1852. 1852 (177) xlv. Poor Law Commission.

HALSBURY, *Lord* SEE:
Giffard, Hardinge Stanley, *1st E. Halsbury.*

HAMILTON, D. SEE:
Douglas-Hamilton, William Alexander Anthony Archibald, *11th D. Hamilton* (1811-1863)
Douglas-Hamilton, William Alexander Louis Stephen, *12th D. Hamilton* (1845-1895)
Douglas-Hamilton, Alfred Douglas, *13th D. Hamilton* (1862-1940).

HAMILTON, Archibald, *Lord*
Committee on the petition of duties on corn. Report, 31 May 1805. 1805 (154) iii.

Select committee on Carlisle and Glasgow Road. Report, 28 June 1815. 1814/5 (463) iii.

Select committee on petitions from the Royal Burghs of Scotland. Report, 12 July 1819. 1819 (571) vi.

Select committee on petitions of the Royal Burghs of Scotland. Report, 14 July 1820. 1820 (277) iii.

Select committee on petitions from the Royal Burghs of Scotland. Report, 14 and 15 June 1821. 1821 (666) viii.

HAMILTON, Claude John, *Lord*
Select committee on pilotage. Report, 3 Aug 1888. 1888 (324) xiv.

HAMILTON, Frederick William
Council of military education. Report on Army school libraries and rooms. SEE: Napier, William C.E.

HAMILTON, *Lord* **George** SEE:
Hamilton, George Francis, *Lord.*

HAMILTON, George Alexander
Commission appointed to inspect charitable institutions, Dublin. Report, 2 May 1842. 1842 (337) xxxviii. Irish Secretary's Office.

Committee on the expense of military defences in the colonies. Report, 24 Jan 1860. 1860 (282) xli. War Office.

Committee to inquire into the Navy estimates from 1852 to 1858 and into the comparative state of the navies of England and France. Report, 6 Jan 1859. 1859, session 1 (182) xiv. Treasury.

Committee on expiring laws, 5th session, 15th Parliament. Report, 19 March 1852. 1852 (165) v.

Select committee on the Aylesbury election petition. Min. of ev. 28 April 1851. 1851 (231) xii.

Select committee on the Clitheroe election petition Report, 1 Aug 1853. 1852/3 (848) x.
Min. of ev. 1852/3 (868) x.

Select committee on the Cokermouth election petition Report, 19 April 1853. 1852/3 (357) x.
Min. of ev. 1852/3 (384) x.

Select committee on county and district surveyors, Ireland. Report, 13 Aug 1857. 1857, session 2 (270) ix.

Select committee on the Frome election petition. Report, 6 April 1853. 1852/3 (347) xiii.

Select committee on the Maidstone election petition. Min. of ev. 17 July 1857. 1857, session 2 (186) vii.

Select committee on medical charities, Ireland. Report, 7 July 1843. 1843 (412) x.

HAMILTON, George Francis, *Lord*
Select committee on East India (Compensation of Officers). Report, 23 March 1875. 1875 (116) x.

Select committee on East India Public Works. Report, 1 Aug 1878. 1878 (333) xii.

Select committee on East India public works, 1879. SEE: Stanhope, Edward.

Select committee on the East India Railway Bill. Special report, 13 June 1879. 1878/9 (226) ix.

HAMILTON, James, *3rd E. Clanbrassil*
Committee on linens, threads and tapes. Report, 11 March 1744. CJ Reports, vol.2, p.65.

HAMILTON, James Hans
Committee on expiring laws, 2nd session, 17th Parliament. Report, 29 June 1858. 1857/8 (373) xii.

HAMILTON, Robert George Crookshank, *Sir*
Departmental committee on the Department of the Charity Commission. Report, Nov.1893. 1895 (261) lxxiv. Treasury.

Report on the supply of British merchant seamen. 21 Dec 1872. 1873 C.752 lix. Board of Trade.

Royal commission on the island of Dominica. Report, 10 March 1894. 1894 C.7477 lvii.

HAMILTON, Thomas, *9th E. Haddington*
Commission for the issue of exchequer bills. Report, 15 Dec 1813. 1813/4 (53) iii.

Committee on the distillation of sugar and molasses Report, 13 April 1808. 1808 (178) iv.
2nd report, 31 May 1808. 1808 (278) iv.
3rd report, 10 June 1808. 1808 (300) iv.
4th report, 22 June 1808. 1808 (318) iv.

Committee on the drawbacks and countervailing duties on spirits
Report, 9 and 30 May 1809. 1809 (199), (215) iii.
Appendix of accounts. 1809 (199) iii.

Committee on petitions of creditors of the Nabob of the Carnatic. SEE: Courtenay, T.P.

Select committee on the civil list. Report and appendix, 16 June 1815. 1814/5 (401) iii; repr. 1830 (619) ix.

Select committee on finance. SEE: Gilbert, Davies.

Select committee on Morpeth and Edinburgh road. Report, 2 July 1822. 1822 (506) viii.

Select committee on printing and stationery. Report, 30 July 1822. 1822 (607) iv.

HAMILTON, William Alexander Baillie
Commission on lights, buoys and beacons. Report, 5 March 1861. 1861 [2793] xxv; (Shipping, 5).

HAMILTON-GORDON, John Campbell, 7th E. Aberdeen
Royal commission on loss of life at sea. SEE: Shaw-Lefevre, George John.

Royal commission on railway accidents. Report, 2 Feb 1877. 1877 C.1637 xlviii; (Transport, 14-15).

HAMILTON-TEMPLE-BLACKWOOD, Frederick Temple, 1st M. Dufferin and Ava
Committee on designs of ships of war
    Report, 26 July 1871. 1872 C.477 xiv.
    Dissenting report, 14 Oct 1871. 1872 C.489 xiv.
    Report on the 'Cyclops' and 'Devastation' classes. 11 March 1871. 1871 C.333 xiv. Admiralty.

Royal commission on military education
    Min. of ev. 1870 C.25 xxiv.
    2nd report, 14 July 1870. 1870 C.214 xxiv.
    Accounts of the systems of military education in France, Prussia, Austria, Bavaria and the United States. 1870 C.47 xxv. War Office.

HAMMOND, Anthony
Present state of the law of forgery. Report, draft bill and plan of consolidation, 2 April 1824. 1824 (205) iv; (LA Criminal Law, 2).

HAMPTON, Lord SEE:
Pakington, John Slaney, 2nd Bn. Hampton.

HANBURY, Robert William
Select committee on the Boyne Navigation Transfer Bill. Report, 4 June 1896. 1896 (212) ix.

Select committee on the Post Office (Sites) Bill. Report, 22 July 1897. 1897 (333) xiii.

Select committee on telephones. Report, 9 Aug 1898. 1898 (383) xii; (Posts and Telegraphs, 8).

HANBURY, W.
Medical and surgical history of the British Army which served in Turkey and the Crimea in the war against Russia, 1854-56
    Vol.1: Military medical history of individual corps.
    Vol.2: History of disease; history of wounds and injuries. 1857/8 [2434] xxxviii. pts.1 and 2. War Office.

HANBURY-TRACY, Charles Douglas Richmond, 4th Bn. Sudeley
Select committee (HL) on reporting. SEE: Lygon, Frederick, 6th E. Beauchamp.

HANCOCK, Henry
Commission of inquiry into the organisation of the Indian Army. Note of dissent, 5 March 1859. 1859, session 1 [2516] v; repr. 1859, session 2 [2516] viii. SEE ALSO: Peel, Jonathan.

HANCOCK, William Neilson
Commission on the laws of pawnbroking in Ireland. Report, 28 Feb 1868. 1867/8 [3985] xxxii. Irish Secretary's Office.

History of the landlord and tenant question in Ireland
    1st report, 11 Oct 1859
    2nd report, 11 April 1866. Both 1868/9 [4204] xxvi. Irish Secretary's Office.

HANKEY, Thomas
Select committee on fires in the Metropolis. Report, 8 May 1862. 1862 (221) ix.

HANMER, John, Sir
Select committee on the Manchester, Sheffield and Lincolnshire, and Great Northern Railway Companies Bill. Min. of ev. 17 May 1858. 1857/8 (0.77) xv.

HANNEN, James
Royal special commission [on charges and allegations made against certain members of Parliament in the action O'Donnell vs. Walter and another]. Report, 13 Feb 1890. 1890 C.5891 xxvii.

HANNING, William
Inquiry into charges against the Keeper of Ilchester gaol. Report, 21 Feb 1822. 1822 (30) xi.

HANSARD, Luke Graves
Petition in case of Stockdale vs. Hansard. SEE: Shaw-Lefevre, C.

HARBOURD, Edward
Select committee on regulations relative to the making and sale of bread. Report, 17 April 1821. 1821 (426) v.

HARCOURT, George Granville
Select committee on the D. of Marlborough's pension. Report, 2 June 1837. 1837 (365) xx.

HARCOURT, William George Granville Venables Vernon, Sir
Select committee on London water supply. Report, 3 Aug 1880. 1880 (329) x; (UA Water Supply, 6).

Select committee on registration of voters. Report, 2 July 1869. 1868/9 (294) vii.

Select committee on Mutiny and Marine Mutiny Acts. Report, 26 July 1878. 1878 (316) x.

Select committee on the Telegraphs Bill. Special report and report, 16 June 1892. 1892 (278) xvii.

Committee on the office of public prosecutor. 9 May 1884. 1884 C.4016 xxiii.

HARDING, J.D.
Report on hand-loom weavers, East of Scotland. 27 March 1839. 1839 (159) xlii; (IR Textiles, 9). Home Department.

HARDINGE, Lord SEE:
Hardinge, Henry, 1st Vct. Hardinge (1785-1856)
Hardinge, Charles Stewart, 2nd Vct. Hardinge (1822-94).

HARDINGE, Charles Stewart, 2nd Vct. Hardinge
Committee on the condition of the frescoes by D. Maclise in the Royal Gallery at the Houses of Parliament. Report, 3 Feb 1875. 1875 (71) lx. Board of Works.

Report of the judges to consider the designs for a new national gallery. 28 Feb 1867. 1867 (91) lv. Commission of Works and Public Buildings.

HARDINGE, Henry, 1st Vct. Hardinge
Select committee appointed to prepare the militia estimates. Report, 25 July 1843. 1843 (485) xi.

HARDWICKE, Lord SEE:
Yorke, P., 3rd E. Hardwicke (1757-1834)
Yorke, Charles Philip, 4th E. Hardwicke (1800-73)

HARDWICKE, Lord SEE : (continued)
Yorke, Charles Philip, *5th E. Hardwicke* (1836-97)
Yorke, Albert Edward, *6th E. Hardwicke* (1867-1904).

HARDY, Gathorne Gathorne SEE:
Gathorne-Hardy, Gathorne, *1st E. Cranbrook.*

HARDY, John Stewart Gathorne SEE:
Gathorne-Hardy, John Stewart.

HARDY, T. Duffas
Report on the publication of the calendar of the Patent and Close rolls of Ireland. 4 Oct 1864. 1865 (35) xlv. Master of the Rolls *and* Treasury.

HARE, John Middleton
Report on the state of popular education in the maritime districts of Hull, Yarmouth and Ipswich. 22 June 1859. *In:* 1861 [2794-III] xxi, pt.3; (Education, 5).

HAREWOOD, E. SEE:
Lascelles, Henry, *2nd E. Harewood* (1767-1841)
Lascelles, Henry, *3rd E. Harewood* (1797-1857)
Lascelles, Henry Thynne, *4th E. Harewood* (1824-1892)
Lascelles, Henry Ulick, *5th E. Harewood* (1846-1929).

HARGRAVE, Francis
Committee on petition relating to his books and manuscripts. SEE: Whitbread, Samuel.

HARLAND, Edward James, *Sir*
Committee on the spacing and construction of watertight bulkheads in merchant ships. (Bulkheads Committee). Report. 1890/1 C.6405 lxxvi. Board of Trade.

HARLEY, Thomas
Committee on hat manufacture. Report on foreign trade. 5 May 1764. CJ, vol.29, p.905.

Committee on hat manufacture. Report on internal management of the trade. 18 Feb 1777. CJ, vol.36, p.192.

Committee of secrecy on the East India Company
1st report, 7 Dec 1772. CJ Reports, vol.4, p.1; (Reps., 1731-1800, no.20, vol.3).
2nd report, 17 Dec 1772. CJ Reports, vol.4, p.15; (Reps., 1731-1800, no.21, vol.3).
3rd report, 9 Feb 1773. CJ Reports, vol.4, p.37; (Reps., 1731-1800, no.22, vol.3).
4th report, 24 March 1773. CJ Reports, vol.4, p.93; (Reps., 1731-1800, no.23, vol.3).
5th report, 30 March 1773. CJ Reports, vol.4, p.255; (Reps., 1731-1800, no.24, vol.3).
6th report, 26 April 1773. CJ Reports, vol.4, p.297; (Reps., 1731-1800, no.25, vol.3).
7th report, 6 May 1773. CJ Reports, vol.4, p.321; (Reps., 1731-1800, no.26, vol.3).
8th report, 11 June 1773. CJ Reports, vol.4, p.353; (Reps., 1731-1800, no.27, vol.3).
9th report, 30 June 1773. CJ Reports, vol.4, p.457; (Reps., 1731-1800, no.28, vol.3).

HARMAN, Edward Robert King SEE:
King-Harman, Edward Robert.

HARNESS, Henry Drury
Board of visitors to inspect the Royal Military Academy, Woolwich
Report, 26 July 1873. 1873 C.845 xviii.
Report, 13 June 1874. 1874 C.1093 xii. War Office.

Commission of inquiry into Dublin turnpikes. Report, 1854/5 (0.1) xix.

HARRIS, George Robert Canning, *Bn. Harris*
Committee on the Militia. Report, 6 Dec 1889. 1890 C.5922 xix. War Office.

Committee on the organisation of the Royal Artillery. Report, 27 April 1888. 1888 C.5491 xxv. War Office.

Select committee (HL) on the Oysters Bill. Report, 20 July 1899. HL 1899 (172) x.

Volunteer capitation committee. Report, 11 Jan 1887. 1887 C.4951 xvi. War Office.

HARRIS, James Edward, *2nd E. Malmesbury*
Select committee (HL) on the London to Southampton Railway Bill. SEE: Pleydell-Bouverie, William, *3rd E. Radnor.*

HARRIS, William C.
Report on the control of common lodging houses and on the condition of single rooms occupied by families in the Metropolis. 7 March 1859. 1859, session 1 (215) xxii. Home Department.

HARRISON, John
Committee on the corn trade. Report, 14 May 1804. 1803/4 (96) v.

Committee on petition respecting the construction of a time-keeper. SEE: Grey, John. SEE ALSO: Stephens, Philip.

HARROWBY, E. SEE:
Ryder, Dudley, *1st E. Harrowby* (1762-1847)
Ryder, Dudley, *2nd E. Harrowby* (1798-1882)
Ryder, Dudley, *3rd E. Harrowby* (1823-1900).

HART, Robert
Foreign customs establishment in China. Report, Nov 1864. 1865 [3509] xxxviii. Foreign Office.

HART-DYKE, William SEE:
Dyke, William Hart.

HARTINGTON, M. SEE:
Cavendish, Spencer Compton, *8th D. Devonshire.*

HARVEY, Charles
Select committee on steam boats. Report, 24 June 1817. 1817 (422) vi; (Transport, 2).

HARVEY, Daniel Whittle
Select committee to consider the reports of the Charities Commission. Report, 30 July 1835. 1835 (449) vii.

HARVEY, Eliab, *Sir*
Select committee on gas-light establishments. Report, 7 July 1823. 1823 (529) v; (FP Gas, 6).

HARVEY, Thomas
Report on the state of education in the Burgh and middle-class schools in Scotland. 1867/8 [4011-I] xxix; (Education, 16). SEE ALSO: Campbell, George Douglas, *8th D. Argyll.*

Report on the state of education in Glasgow. 20 March 1866. 1867 [3845-II] xxv; (Education, 14). Education Commission, Scotland. SEE ALSO: Campbell, George Douglas, *8th D. Argyll.*

HASSALL, Arthur Hill
Report on the microscopical examination of the Metropolitan water supply. 31 Jan 1857. 1857, session 1 [2203] xiii. General Board of Health.

HASSARD, Michael Dobbyn
General committee on railway and canal bills. SEE: Smith-Stanley, Edward Henry, *15th E. Derby.*

HASTINGS, *Lord* SEE:
Rawdon-Hastings, Francis, *1st M. Hastings.*

[Peerage claim]. SEE: Cooper, C.A.

HASTINGS, George Woodyatt
Select committee on police and sanitary regulations. Special report, 29 July 1887. 1887 (250) xi.

Select committee on police and sanitary regulations. Special report, 26 July 1888. 1888 (300) xv.

Select committee on police and sanitary regulations bills. Special report, 13 Aug 1889. 1889 (321) xi.

Select committee on police and sanitary regulations bills. Special report, 23 July 1890. 1890 (320) xvii.

Select committee on police and sanitary regulations bills. Report, 9 July 1891. 1890/1 (324) xiii.

HASTINGS, Warren
Committee on impeachment. SEE: Burke, Edmund.

Committee of whole HL on impeachment. SEE: De Grey, Thomas, *2nd Bn. Walsingham.*

HATCHELL, John
Committee on the National Board of Education in Ireland to inquire into the conduct of J.W. Kavanagh, Inspector of National Schools. Report, 26 Nov 1857. 1857/8 (386) xlvi.

Select committee on the law of mortmain. SEE: Headlam, T.E.

Select committee on outrages in Ireland. Report, 4 June 1852. 1852 (438) xiv.

HATHERLEY, *Bn.* SEE:
Wood, William Page, *Bn. Hatherley.*

HATHERTON, *Bn.* SEE:
Littleton, Edward John, *1st Bn. Hatherton* (1791-1863)
Littleton, Edward Richard, *2nd Bn. Hatherton* (1815-1888).

HAVERSHAM, *Bn.* SEE:
Hayter, Arthur Divett, *Bn. Haversham.*

HAWARDEN, *Vct.*
Committee for privileges. Precedents on arrest of peers. SEE: Cooper, C.A.

[Peerage claim]. SEE: Freeman-Mitford, J.T.

HAWES, Benjamin
Committee appointed for the review and consideration of the colonial reports on the finance and commerce of the Island of Ceylon. Report, 13 April 1847. 1847/8 [933] xlii. Colonial Office.

Report upon the evidence given by Sir Charles Trevelyan before the commission on the purchase and sale of commissions in the Army. 3 June 1858. 1857/8 (498) xxxvii; (Military and Naval, 3). War Office.

Select committee on the Athlone election petition. Min. of proc., and ev., 9 June 1843. 1843 (317) vi.

Select committee on Blackfriars Bridge. SEE: Barclay, Charles.

Select committee on the Cold Bath Fields meeting. Report, 23 Aug 1833. 1833 (718) xii.

Select committee on fine arts. Report, 18 June 1841. 1841 (423) vi; (ED Fine Arts, 2).

Select committee on the Kafir tribes. SEE: Labouchere, Henry.

Select committee on London and York Railway subscription list. Report, 9 Aug 1845. 1845 (657) x.

Select committee on Lyme Regis Borough election petition. Min. of proc. and ev., 3 June 1842. 1842 (285) vi.

Select committee on Metropolis police officers. Report, 29 June 1837. 1837 (451) xii; (CP Police, 7).

Select committee on Metropolis police officers. Report, 11 July 1838. 1837/8 (578) xv; (CP Police, 7).

Select committee on the South Eastern Railway petition. Report, 10 July 1845. 1845 (480) x.

Select committee on the ventilation of the Houses of Parliament. Report, 2 Sept 1835. 1835 (583) xviii.

Select committee on Wigan Borough election. Proc., 11 April 1842. 1842 (548) v.

HAWKESBURY, *Lord* SEE:
Jenkinson, R.B., *Lord Hawkesbury.*

HAWKINS, Henry, *Sir*
Evesham election petition trial. Judgement and ev., 8 June 1880. 1880 (228) lviii.

HAWKINSHAW, John, *Sir*
Commission on the purification of the River Clyde. Report, 21 March 1876. 1876 C.1464 xxxviii.

Committee on the practicability of assigning a safe co-efficient for use of steel in railway structures. Report, 19 March 1877. 1877 (136) lxxiii. Board of Trade.

Committee on wind pressure on railway structures. Report, 20 May 1881. 1881 C.3000 lxxxi. Board of Trade.

Final report on completion of the public works at Holyhead harbour. 30 June 1873. 1873 (296) lviii. Board of Trade.

Report on Alderney harbour. 27 June 1870. 1870 (354) lix. Board of Trade.

HAWLEY, W.H.T.
Report on a table [giving statistics of parishes] in the County of Northumberland. 29 Jan 1849. 1850 [1152] xxvii; (Poor Law, 21). Poor Law Board.

Report on the agricultural statistics of Hampshire. 31 Jan 1854. 1854 [1761] lxv. Poor Law Board.

Report on the parish of Alverstoke with Gosport. 20 Oct 1851. 1852 (270) xlv. Poor Law Board.

Report on vagrancy. 29 Feb 1848. 1847/8 [987] liii. Poor Law Board.

Report on the education of pauper children. 18 Dec 1861, 25 Feb 1862. 1862 (510) xlix; (ED Poorer Classes, 7). Poor Law Board.

HAY, Andrew Leith, *Sir*
Committee on the Trinity (North Leith) Harbour and Docks (No.2) Bill. Min. of ev. 28 July 1836. 1836 (503) xx.

Select committee on private bill fees. Report, 30 July 1834. 1834 (540) xi.

Select committee on statute labour, Scotland. Report, 11 July 1836. 1836 (430) xviii.

HAY, Charles Crawfurd
Report on application of gun cotton to mining and quarrying operations. 1868/9 (179) xlvii; (FP Mining Accidents, 10). War Office.

HAY, John
Committee on the defects of the method of measuring ships for tonnage. 15 Feb 1850. 1850 (49) liii. Admiralty.

HAY, John Charles Dalrymple, *Sir*
Select committee on explosive substances. Report, 26 June 1874. 1874 (243) ix; (TI Explosives, 1).

Special committee on iron shields supplied for Gibraltar and Malta. Report, 11 Feb 1868. 1867/8 [4003] xvi. War Office.

HAY, William
Common lodging-houses in the Metropolitan police district
    Report, Dec 1852. 1852/3 (237) lxxviii.
    Supplementary report, 15 April 1853. 1852/3 (435) lxxviii.
    2nd report, April 1854. 1854 [1780] xxxv. Home Department.

HAY, William George, *16th E. Erroll*
University Commission, Scotland, for visiting King's College and Marischal College, Aberdeen
    1st report, 1837/8 [123] xxxiii.
    2nd report, 1 Feb 1839. 1839 [176] xxix.

HAYES, Edmund Samuel, *Sir*
Select committee on Blackburn Borough election. Proc., 27 April 1842. 1842 (548) v; (GO Elections, 2).

Select committee on Flint County election. Proc., 14 May 1842. 1842 (548) v.

HAYES, John
Committee appointed to investigate Mr. Kyan's patent for the prevention of dry rot. Report, 9 July 1835. 1835 (367) xlviii.

HAYES, Joseph
Report on the principal oyster fisheries of France. 1878 C.1984 xxi. Irish Secretary's Office.

HAYLLAR, Thomas Child
Commission on the working of the Hong Kong Contagious Diseases Ordnance, 1867. Report, Dec 1878. 1880 (118) xlix. Colonial Office.

HAYTER, Arthur Divett, *Bn. Haversham*
Select committee on the Artillery Ranges Bill. Report, 25 May 1882. 1882 (206) vii.

Select committee on commons. Report, 7 May 1894. 1894 (106) xi.

Select committee on commons
    1st report, 2 May 1895. 1895 (243) vii.
    2nd report, 7 May 1895. 1895 (252) vii.
    3rd report, 17 May 1895. 1895 (270) vii.
    4th report, 17 May 1895. 1895 (271) vii.

Select committee on the Strensall Common Bill. Report, 27 June 1884. 1884 (245) xv.

HAYTER, William Goodenough, *Sir*
Committee on Broadmoor Criminal lunatic asylum. Report, 15 Jan 1877. 1877 C.1674 xli. Home Department.

Select committee on Belfast Borough election. Proc., 2 June 1842. 1842 (548) v.

Select committee on Cardigan Borough election. Proc., 16 April 1842. 1842 (548) v.

Select committee on the Cork County election. Min. of proc. and ev., 27 May 1842. 1842 (271) vi.

Select committee on expiring laws. 3rd session, 15th Parliament. Report, 26 March 1850. 1850 (194) xiii.

Select committee on the National Land Company. SEE: Buller, Charles.

HAYWARD, Abraham
Commission of inquiry into Dublin turnpikes. Report, 1854. 1854/5 (0.1) xix.

HEAD, Edmund, *Sir*
Report on the law of bastardy; with a supplementary report on a cheap civil remedy for seduction. March 1840. *In* 1840 [253] xvii.

HEADLAM, Thomas Emerson
Select committee on the Dublin City election petition. Min. of ev. 20 Aug 1857. 1857, session 2 (293) vi.

Select committee on the Harwich election petition
    Report, 6 May 1853. 1852/3 (449) xiii.
    Min. of ev. 1852/3 (467) xiii.

Select committee on HC arrangements. Report, 19 July 1867. 1867 (451) viii; repr. 1886, session 1 (0.61) x.

Select committee on HC arrangements. Report, 12 May 1868. 1867/8 (265) viii; repr. 1868/9 (0.29) vii; repr. 1886, session 1 (0.61) x.

Select committee on the law of mortmain. Report, 17 July 1851. 1851 (483) xvi.

Select committee on the law of mortmain. Report, 18 June 1852. 1852 (493) xiii.

Select committee on the Metropolis Sewage and Essex Reclamation Bill. Special report, 30 March 1865. 1865 (171) viii; (UA Sanitation, 5).

Select committee on the New Ross election petition
    Report, 18 April 1853. 1852/3 (356) xvi.
    Min. of ev. 1852/3 (463) xvi.

Select committee on noxious businesses. Report, 8 July 1873. 1873 (284) x.

Select committee on the Pontefract Borough election petition. Min. of ev. 9 July 1857. 1857, session 2 (169) viii.

Select committee on railway companies. Report, 7 July 1870. 1870 (341) x.

HEARTLEY, David
Committee on experiments respecting fire prevention. SEE: Townsend, Thomas.

HEATHCOTE, Gilbert, *Sir*
Committee on the late riotous proceedings in the Mint
    Report, 23 Feb 1705. CJ, vol.15, p.169.
    Report, 1772. CJ, vol.20, p.155.

HEATHCOTE, William, *Sir*
Committee of selection
    1st report, 17 March 1848. 1847/8 (181) xvi.
    2nd report, 24 March 1848. 1847/8 (199) xvi.
    3rd report, 14 April 1848. 1847/8 (266) xvi.
    4th report, 16 May 1848. 1847/8 (328) xvi.
    5th report, 22 May 1848. 1847/8 (346) xvi.
    6th report, 29 May 1848. 1847/8 (363) xvi.
    7th report, 30 May 1848. 1847/8 (367) xvi.
    8th report, 2 June 1848. 1847/8 (397) xvi.

Select committee on the Cambridge Borough election petition. Min. of proc. and ev., 9 June 1843. 1843 (316) vi.

Select committee on standing orders revision, 1847. Report, 7 July 1847. 1847 (631) xii.

Select committee on standing orders revision, 1848. Report, 25 July 1848. 1847/8 (537) xvi.

Select committee on standing orders. Report on petitions against the Edinburgh and Perth Railway Bill. 26 March 1847. 1847 (227) xii.

Select committee on standing orders revision, 1855. Report, 4 July 1855. 1854/5 (362) vii.

Select committee on the Wigan election petition. Min. of ev. 27 April 1846. 1846 (236) viii.

HEDLEY, Robert
Commission of inquiry into allegations concerning the treatment of children in the St. John's Industrial School for Roman Catholic Boys at Walthamstow. Report, 31 Oct 1894. 1895 (107) lxxx. Home Department.

HEDLEY, Thomas
Report on the state of popular education in specimen agricultural districts in counties of Lincoln, York, Nottingham, Suffolk, Norfolk and Cambridge. 9 May 1859. *In* 1861 [2794-II] xxi, pt.2; (Education, 4).

HELPS, Arthur
Committee on the transit of animals by sea and land. Report, 11 Feb 1870. 1870 C.116 lxi; (AG Animal Health, 2).

HELY-HUTCHINSON, John Luke George, *5th E. Donoughmore*
Report and ev. taken at a visitation of Clonmel Endowed School. 9 July 1850. 1851 (117) l. Commission of Education.

Select committee (HL) on the expenses incurred by Scotch and Irish peers proving their right to vote for representative peers. Report, 17 July 1856. HL 1856 (257) xxiv.

HELY-HUTCHINSON, Richard John, *4th E. Donoughmore*
Select committee on the Mortgage Debentures Bill, Land Debentures (Ireland) Bill and the Land Debentures Bill. Report, 19 June 1865. HL 1865 (173) xxi.

Select committee (HL) on railway companies 'borrowing' powers. Report, 21 July 1863. HL 1863 (175) xxxiv.

Select committee (HL) on railway companies borrowing powers. Report, 15 July 1864. HL 1864 (127) xxvii; HC repr. 1864 (518) xi.

Select committee (HL) on the West Hartlepool Harbour and Railway Bill. SEE: Dawson, Richard, *3rd E. Dartrey.*

HELY-HUTCHINSON, Richard Walter John, *6th E. Donoughmore*
Select committee (HL) on the land law in Ireland. SEE: Cairns, Hugh MacCalmont, *1st E. Cairns.*

HENDERSON, James
Departmental committee on the various lead industries. SEE: Gould, Edward.

HENLEY, Joseph John
Report on the boarding out of pauper children in Scotland. 15 Feb 1870. 1870 (176) lviii. Poor Law Board.

HENLEY, Joseph Warner
Select committee on the Board of Admiralty. Report, 16 July 1861. 1861 (438) v.

Select committee on contract packet service. Report, 27 July 1849. 1849 (571) xii.

Select committee on income and property tax. Report, 21 July 1851. 1851 (563) x; (NF Income Tax, 1).

Select committee on the new Westminster bridge. Report, 23 July 1856. 1856 (389) xiv.

Select committee of privileges. Report on complaint of a paragraph in the 'Times' as containing calumnious reflections on Irish members. 19 June 1854. 1854 (314) viii.

Select committee on railway and canal bills. SEE: Cardwell, Edward.

Select committee on Registrar's Office, Bankruptcy. Report, 18 March 1850. 1850 (153) xviii.

Select committee on the Rochdale election (Newall's petition). Report, 24 June 1857. 1857, session 2 (128) viii.

Select committee on Stade tolls. Report, 14 July 1858. 1857/8 (429) xvii.

HENRY, Jabez
Commission of enquiry on civil and criminal justice in the West Indies
    1st report: Jamaica. 29 June 1827. 1826/7 (559) xxiv.
    2nd report: United colony of Demerara and Essequebo, and the colony of Berbice. 25 July 1828. 1828 (577) xxiii.
    3rd report: Honduras and the Bahama Islands. 24 Feb 1829. 1829 (334) xxiv; (West Indies, 3). SEE ALSO: Dwarris, F.

Commission of legal enquiry on the case of the Indians at Honduras. Report, 10 July 1828. 1828 (522) xxvi; (Slave Trade, 75).

Commission of legal inquiry on the colony of Trinidad. Report, 29 June 1827. 1826/7 (551) xxiii; (West Indies, 3).

HERBERT, Arthur James
Committee on regulations for the employment of soldiers at trades. Report, 1871. 1871 (62) xxxix. War Office.

HERBERT, Edward, *2nd E. Powis*
Select committee on finance, 1819. SEE: Gilbert D.

Committee on the Longford County election petitions. Min. of ev. 17 May 1837. 1837 (319) x.

Committee on the re-committed Birmingham and Liverpool Canal Bill. Min. of ev., 26 April 1826. 1826 (309) iv.

Select committee on the Barnstaple election. Report, 9 March 1819. 1819 (86) iv.

Select committee on the Tregony election petition. Report, 9 March 1813. 1812/3 (76) iii.

HERBERT, Edward James, *3rd E. Powis*
Commission on primary education in Ireland
    Vol.1, pt.1: Report, 21 May 1870. 1870 C.6 xxviii, pt.1.
    Vol.1, pt.2: Appendix, special reports on model schools, the Central Training Institution, Dublin, and on agricultural schools. 1870 C.6A xxviii, pt.2.
    Vol.2: Reports of assistant commissioners. 1870 C.6-I xxviii, pt.2.

HERBERT, Edward James, *3rd E. Powis* (continued)
Vol.3-5: Min. of ev., analysis and index. 1870
C.6 II-IV xxviii, pts.3-4.
Vol.6: Educational census. 1870 C.6-V xxviii, pt.5.
Vol.7: Returns finished by the National Board of
Education, Ireland. 1870 C.6-VI xxviii, pt.5.
Vol.8: Miscellaneous papers and returns. 1870
C.6-VII xxviii, pt.5.

Select committee (HL) on the Presbyterian Church
(Ireland) Bill, and the Primitive Wesleyan Methodist
Society of Ireland Regulation Bill. Report, 4 May
1871. HL 1871 (89) viii.

HERBERT, Edward William Molyneux Auberon
Select committee on wild birds protection. Report,
23 July 1873. 1873 (338) xiii.

HERBERT, Henry Arthur
General committee of elections. Report on the withdrawal of the Lisburn election petition. 8 May 1863.
1863 (246) vii.

Select committee on communications between London
and Dublin. Report, 13 July 1853. 1852/3 (747) xxiv.

Select committee on the Huddersfield election petition. Min. of ev. 9 Aug 1859. 1859, session 2 (170)
iii.

Select committee on the Southampton election petition. Report, 6 April 1853. 1852/3 (354) xviii.

HERBERT, Henry George, *2nd E. Carnarvon*
Select committee on sinecure offices. SEE: Bankes,
Henry.

HERBERT, Henry Howard Molyneux, *4th E. Carnarvon*
Select committee (HL) on the construction of the
H.L. Report, 10 July 1868. HL 1867/8 (136) xxx.

Select committee (HL) on the construction of the
H.L. relative to hearing. Report, 6 Aug 1867. HL
1867 (203) xxvii.

Select committee (HL) on the London Bridge Bill.
Report, 14 July 1870. HL 1878/9 (139) vii.

Select committee (HL) on discipline in gaols and
houses of correction. Report, 6 July 1863. HL 1863
(37) xxxiii; HC repr. 1863 (499) ix; (CP Prisons, 6).

Select committee (HL) on public petitions. 1st to
8th and supplementary reports, 23 April to 6 July
1868. 9 parts. HL 1867/8 (91) xxx.

HERBERT, Percy Egerton, *Sir*
Barrack works committee. Report, 23 June 1862.
1862 [3041] xxxiii. War Office.

Select committee on the Thames Embankment (Land)
Bill. Min. of ev. 5 July 1872. 1872 (287) xii.

HERBERT, Sidney, *14th E. Pembroke*
Commission of inquiry into the question of promo-
tion and retirement in the higher ranks of the Army.
Report, 10 July 1858. 1857/8 [2417] xix.

Commission of inquiry into the regulations affecting
the sanitary conditions of the Army, the organisation
of military hospitals and the treatment of the sick
and wounded
Report, 1858. 1857/8 [2318] xviii.
Appendix. 1857/8 [2379] xix.

Commission on promotion in the army. Report, 17
June 1854. 1854 [1802] xix.

Commission on the sanitary state of the Army in
India. SEE: Stanley, Edward Henry, *15th E. Derby.*

Committee on the preparation of Army medical
statistics. Report, June 1858. 1861 (366) xxxvii.
War Office.

Departmental committee on beer materials. Report,
Jan 1899. 1899 C.9171, C.9172 xxx. Treasury.

Select committee on kitchen and refreshment rooms,
H.C. Report, 8 Sept 1887. 1887 (320) ix.

Select committee on kitchen and refreshment rooms
(HC)
Report, 9 Aug 1888. 1888 (343) xii.
2nd report, 20 Dec 1888. 1888 (434) xii.

Select committee on the kitchen and refreshment
rooms, HC. Report, 28 Aug 1889. 1889 (352) xi.

Select committee on kitchen and refreshment rooms,
HC. Report, 14 Aug 1890. 1890 (390) xv.

Select committee on the kitchen and refreshment
rooms, HC. Report, 4 Aug 1891. 1890/1 (408) xii.

Select committee on the kitchen and refreshment
rooms, HC. Report, 23 June 1892. 1892 (314) xii.

Select committee on the kitchen and refreshment
rooms, HC
1st report, 31 May 1894. 1894 (136) xii.
2nd report, 15 Aug 1894. 1894 (297) xii.

Select committee on kitchen and refreshment rooms,
HC, 1895. SEE: Leveson-Gower, George Granville.

Select committee on military organisation. SEE:
Graham, James, *Sir.*

Select committee on the militia estimates. Report,
15 July 1853. 1852/3 (777) xxxix.

Select committee on the militia estimates, 1859/60.
Report, 27 July 1859. 1859, session 2 (121) v.

Select committee on the militia estimates, 1860/1.
Report, 16 Aug 1860. 1860 (551) viii.

Select committee on Passengers' Act. Report, 2 Aug
1851. 1851 (632) xix; (Emigration, 6).

HERON, Denis Caulfield
Commission on corrupt practices at the last election
for Sligo. SEE: Byrne, John Alexander.

HERON, Robert, *Sir*
Committee of the whole H.C. on the conduct of the
Sheriff of Dublin. Min. of ev. 2-27 May 1823. 1823
(308) vi.

HERRIES, Lord   [Peerage claim, 1849]. SEE:
Cooper, C.A.; 1851-58, SEE: Freeman-Mitford,
J.T.

HERRIES, C.J.
Brewers' license inquiry committee. Report, 1880.
1880 C.2582 xviii. Treasury.

HERRIES, John Charles
Committee on expired and expiring laws. 1st session,
8th Parliament. Report, 27 Nov 1826. 1826/7 (3) iii.

Committee on the petition of the British Museum
relating to Mr. Rich's collection. Report, 25 March
1825. 1825 (152) v.

HERRIES, W.L.
Commission of audit. Report on the expenditure
occasioned by the Kaffir War. 17 Feb 1849. 1849
(186) xxx; (Africa, 22).

HERSCHELL, Farrer, *Bn. Herschell*
Committee on the Indian currency
Report, correspondence, min. of ev. 31 May

1893. 1893/4 C.7060, C.7060 I-II lxv.

Index. 1893/4 C.7086 lxv.

Further papers. 1893/4 C.7098 lxv; (MP Currency, 7). India Office.

Committee of inquiry into the Patent Office. Report. 1887 C.4968 lxvi. Board of Trade.

Joint select committee on private bills; alteration of memorandum of association. Report, 12 Aug 1889. HL 1889 (224) x; HC 1889 (317) xi.

Joint select committee on the Merchant Shipping Bill. Report, 18 Dec 1893. HL 1893/4 (290) x; HC 1893/4 (466) xiii.

Joint select committee on statute law revision. Report, 13 June 1892. HL 1892 (148) x; HC 1892 (258) xvii.

Joint select committee on statute law revision bills. Report, 18 July 1893. HL 1893/4 (204) x; HC 1893/4 (348) xv.

Joint select committee on statute law revision bills. Report, 3 Aug 1894. HL 1894 (170) ix; HC 1894 (259) xv.

Patent Office inquiry committee. Report, 16 March 1888. 1888 C.5350 lxxxi. Board of Trade.

Royal commission on the metropolitan Board of Works
Interim report. 1888 C.5560 lvi.
Final report, 8 April 1889. 1889 C.5705 xxix.

Royal commission on recent changes in the relative values of the precious metals
1st report, 10 June 1887. 1887 C.5099 xxii.
2nd report, 1888 C.5248 xlv.
Final report, Oct 1888. 1888 C.5512 lxv; (MP Currency, 4-5).

Royal commission on vaccination
1st report, 12 Aug 1889. 1889 C.5845 xxxix.
2nd report, 29 May 1890. 1890 C.6066 xxxix.
3rd report, 7 Aug 1890. 1890 C.6192 xxxix.
4th report. 1890/1 C.6527 xliv.
5th report, 21 April 1892. 1892 C.6666 xlvii.
6th report, 14 Feb 1896. 1896 C.7993 xlvii.
Final report, Aug 1896. 1896 C.8270 xlvii.
 Appendix 3: Report on the outbreak of small-pox in the Dewsbury Union, 1891-2. 1897 C.8609 xlv.
 Appendix 4: Reports on outbreaks of small-pox in London, 1892-3. 1897 C.8610 xlv.
 Appendix 5: Report on the outbreak of small-pox in the Borough of Warrington, 1892-3. 1897 C.8611 xlv.
 Appendix 6: Report on the outbreak of small-pox in the Borough of Leicester, 1892-3. Session 1897 C.8612 xiv.
 Appendix 7: Report on the outbreak of small-pox in the City of Gloucester. 1897 C.8613 xlvi.
 Appendix 8: Report on the prevalence of small-pox in Glasgow, Liverpool, Salford, Manchester, Oldham, Chadderton, Leeds, Sheffield, Halifax and Bradford, 1892-3. 1897 C.8614 xlvi.
 Appendix 9: Papers on cases in which death or injury was alleged to have been connected with vaccination. 1897 C.8615 xlvii; (HE Infectious Diseases, 8-13).

Select committee on the Bills of Exchange Bill. Report, 21 June 1882. 1882 (244) vii.

Select committee (HL) on the Copyright Bill and the Copyright (Amendment) Bill. Report, 29 July 1898. HL 1898 (189) ix.

Select committee (HL) on the Land Transfer Bill. Report, 16 May 1889. HL 1889 (67) vii.

Select committee (HL) on the Liability of Trustees Bill. Report, 14 May 1888. HL 1888 (110) x.

Select committee (HL) on private bills; standing order no.128. Report, 25 May 1886. HL 1886 (124) vii.

Select committee on the Registration (Occupation Voters) Bill. Report, 24 April 1885. 1884/5 (162) xi.

Select committee on salmon fisheries in Ireland. SEE: Walker, Samuel.

HERSCHEL, J.F.W.
Report on the reform of the Royal Mint. 2 Feb 1852. 1852 (76) xxviii; (MP Currency, 2). Treasury.

HERTFORD, E.   SEE:
Conway, F.S., *1st M. Hertford.*

HERTFORD, M.   [Peerage claim].   SEE:
Palmer, R.

HEWITT, James, *4th Vct. Lifford*
Select committee (HL) on the Contagious Diseases Act, 1866. SEE: Nelson, Horatio, *3rd E. Nelson.*

Select committee (HL) on the Drainage of Land (Ireland) Bill. Report, 6 March 1863. HL 1863 (32) xxxiii.

HIBBERT, John Tomlinson, *Sir*
Committee of inquiry into the wages of operatives, *etc* in the Royal Army Clothing Factory. Report, 10 July 1879. 1878/9 C.2433 xv. War Office.

Local Government Board inquiry committee
1st report, 3 Aug 1897. 1898 C.8731 xl.
2nd report, 16 June 1898. 1898 C.8999 xl. Treasury.

Select committee on Crown Lands Bill. Report, 1 Aug 1894. 1894 (252) xi.

Select committee on parliamentary debates. Report, 12 May 1893. 1893/4 (213) xiii.

Select committee on the Municipal Corporations (Borough Funds) Bill. Report, 1 May 1872. 1872 (177) xi.

Select committee on poor law guardians. Report, 18 July 1878. 1878 (297) xvii.

Select committee on the Shannon Navigation Bill. Report, 8 May 1885. 1884/5 (183) xii.

Select committee on Stationery Office printing contracts. Report, 2 July 1895. 1895 (362) xiii; (Industrial Relations, 22).

Select committee on the Summary Jurisdiction (Repeal, *etc*) Bill. Report, 19 June 1884. 1884 (224) xv.

HICK, John
Select committee on steam boiler explosions. Report, 21 July 1870. 1870 (370) x; (IR Factories, 27).

Select committee on steam boiler explosions. Report, 20 June 1871. 1871 (298) xii; (IR Factories, 27).

HICKLEY, Henry Dennis
Committee on Greenwich Hospital School. Report, 17 Oct 1882. 1882 C.3187 xvi. Admiralty.

HICKS-BEACH, Michael Edward, *1st E. St.Aldwyn*
Commission on Friendly and benefit building societies. SEE: Northcote, Stafford Henry, *1st E. Iddesleigh.*

HICKS-BEACH, Michael Edward, *1st E. St Aldwyn*
(continued)

Select committee on the Apothecaries Licenses Bill. Special report, 20 July 1874. 1874 (310) vi; (HE Food and Drugs, 3).

Select committee on the Earldom of Selborne. Report, 21 May 1895. 1895 (302) x.

Select committee on the jury system in Ireland. Report, 26 June 1874. 1874 (244) ix.

Select committee on Lloyds (Signal Stations) Bill. Report, 9 Aug 1888. 1888 (344) xii.

Select committee on local government and taxation of towns in Ireland. Report, 11 July 1876. 1876 (352) x.

Select committee on local government and taxation of towns in Ireland. Report, 20 July 1877. 1877 (357) xii. SEE ALSO: O'Brien, W.P.

Select committee on local government and taxation of towns in Ireland. Report, 2 July 1878. 1878 (262) xvi.

Select committee on members of Parliament personal interest. Report, 2 July 1896. 1896 (274) xi.

Select committee on Mr. Gladstone's funeral. Report, 23 May 1898. 1898 (218) x.

Select committee on the Municipal Privileges (Ireland) Bill. Special report, 19 May 1874. 1874 (178) x.

Select committee on poor rates assessment. SEE: Ayrton, Acton Smee.

Select committee on the Public Health (Ireland) Bill. Report, 2 Aug 1877. 1877 (384) xv.

Select committee on railway servants' hours of labour. Report, 16 July 1891. 1890/1 (342) xvi.

Select committee on railway servants' hours of labour. Special report, 24 March 1892. 1892 (125) xvi. Report, 3 June 1892. 1892 (246) xvi.

Select committee on the Sale of Intoxicating Liquors on Sunday (Ireland) Bill. Report, 9 May 1877. 1877 (198) xvi.

Select committee on the Sale of Intoxicating Liquors on Sunday (Ireland) (Re-committed) Bill. Report, 22 June 1877. 1877 (283) xvi.

HICKSON, W.E.
Report on the condition of hand-loom weavers. 11 Aug 1840. 1840 (639) xxiv; (IR Textiles, 9).

HIGGIN, W. Housman
Report on outrages alleged to have been committed by foreign fishermen on English fishing boats and fishermen. 8 Feb 1881. 1881 C.2878 lxxxii. Home Office.

HILL, Marcus, *Lord*   SEE:
Hill, Arthur Marcus Cecil, *Lord.*

HILL, Arthur Marcus Cecil, *Lord*
Standing committee on the kitchen and refreshment rooms, H.C.   Report, 26 Feb 1849. 1849 (66) xii.

Standing committee on the kitchen and refreshment rooms, H.C.   Report, 11 May 1852. 1852 (341) v.

HILL, Arthur Wills Blundell Sandys Trumbull Windsor, *4th M. Downshire*
Committee (HL) on the Dublin and Drogheda Railway Bill
> Min. of ev. 25 July 1836. HL 1836 (241) xxxiii.
> Report, 28 July 1836. HL 1836 (247) xii.

HILL, Edward Stock, *Sir*
Select committee on the Steam Engines (Persons in Charge) Bill. Special report and report, 22 May 1895. 1895 (274) xiii; (IR Factories, 31).

HILL, George Fitzgerald, *Sir*
Committee on the distilleries in Ireland. Report, 10 June 1813. 1812/3 (269) vi.

Select committee on illicit distillation in Ireland Report, 10 June 1816. 1816 (436) ix.
2nd report, 18 June 1816. 1816 (490) ix.

Select committee on the laws which regulate the linen trade of Ireland. Report, 17 July 1822. 1822 (560) vii.

Select committee on the linen trade of Ireland. Report, 6 and 22 June 1825. 1825 (411), (463) v.

HILL, Harry Charles
Report on the Forest of Dean. 19 July 1897. London, Stationery Office, 1897.

HILL, Lewin
Postage rates committee. Report on extension of newspaper post. 24 June 1896. 1897 (39) lxxii. Post Office.

HILL, Marcus, *Lord*   SEE:
Hill, Arthur Marcus Cecil, *Lord.*

HILL, Matthew Davenport
Select committee on the claim of the Baron de Bode. Report, 8 Aug 1834. 1834 (583) xviii.

HILL, Rowland
Report on the result of measures recently adopted for the reduction of Sunday labour in the Post Office. 28 Jan 1850. 1850 (185) liii. Post Office.

HILLSBOROUGH, E.   SEE:
Hill, Arthur, *2nd M. Downshire* (1753-1801)
Hill, Arthur Blundell Sandys Trumbull, *3rd M. Downshire* (1788-1845)
Hill, Arthur Wills Blundell Sandys Trumbull Windsor *4th M. Downshire* (1812-1868).

HIND, Henry Youle
Assinnibiore and Saskatchewan exploring expedition. Report of progress and a preliminary and general report. Aug 1860. 1860 [2743] xliv; (Canada, 23). Colonial Office.

HINDE, John Hodgson   SEE:
Hodgson-Hinde, John.

HINDLEY, Charles
Select committee on combination of workmen. SEE: Labouchere, Henry.

Select committee on Sunday trading in the Metropolis.   Report, 15 July 1847. 1847 (666) ix; (SP Sunday Observance, 1).

HINDMARCH, W.M.
Report of inquiry into the Patent Office accounts. 12 July 1864, 31 Jan 1865, 28 Feb 1865. 1865 (173) xliii; (GO Civil Service, 7). Commission of Patents. SEE ALSO: Leveson-Gower, Granville George, *2nd E. Granville.*

HINDS, Samuel, *Bp. of Norwich,* **1849-57**
Commission on Oxford University
> Report, 27 April 1852. 1852 [1482] xxii.
> Index. 1852/3 (1017-I) xxii.

HIPPISLEY, John Cox, *Sir*
Select committee on regulation of Catholics in foreign countries. Report, 25 June 1816. 1816 (501) vii; repr. 1851 (42) xx; (Religion, 1).

HOBART, *Lord* SEE:
Hobart, Vere Henry, *Lord.*

HOBART, Henry
Committee of the whole house on ways and means for raising the supply granted to H.M. Report, 17 May 1798. (Reps., 1731-1800, no.146, vol.22).

HOBART, Robert, *4th E. Buckinghamshire*
Committee (HL) on the charter of the East India Company. Min. of ev. 6 April 1813. HL 1812/3 (40) lxvii.

Select committee (HL) on the affairs of the East India Company. Report, 26 June 1811. HL 1811 (118) xliv.

HOBART, Vere Henry, *Lord Hobart*
Report on the financial condition of Turkey. 7 Dec 1861. 1862 [2972] lxiv. Foreign Office.

HOBHOUSE, Arthur, *1st Bn. Hobhouse*
Select committee (HL) on the Copyhold Enfranchisement Bill. Report, 20 June 1887. HL 1887 (128) ix.

HOBHOUSE, Benjamin
Commission to enquire into the state of Lancaster Prison. Report, 4 Dec 1812. 1812/3 (3) v; (CP Prisons, 7).

Committee on expired and expiring laws. 1st session, 3rd Parliament. Report, 22 Dec 1806. 1806 (3) ii.

Committee on expired and expiring laws. 1st session, 4th Parliament. Report, 29 June 1807. 1807 (5) ii.

Committee on the petition of the creditors of the Nabobs of Arcot. Report, 17 March 1806. 1806 (60) ii.

Committee on the resolution of the House of Commons of 11 Feb 1789 on controverted elections. Report, 16 July 1807. 1807 iii.

Committee on woollen clothiers petition. Report, 14 March 1803. 1802/3 (30) v; (IR Textiles, 1).

HOBHOUSE, Henry
Commission relative to Exchequer Bills. Report, 31 Jan 1842. 1842 (1) xviii; (National Finance, 2). Treasury.

Select committee on traction engines on roads. Report, 1 July 1896. 1896 (272) xiv.

HOBHOUSE, John, *Sir*
Committee appointed to prepare the militia estimates. Report, 19 June 1832. 1831/2 (541) v.

Select committee on plans for the Houses of Parliament. Report, 9 May 1936. 1836 (245) xxi.

HOBHOUSE, John Cam, *Bn. Broughton*
National Gallery site commission. Report, 15 June 1857. 1857, session 2 [2261] xxiv; (ED Fine Arts, 3).

Select committee on select and other vestries. Report, 10 Feb 1830. 1830 (215) iv.

HODGKINSON, Eaton
Experimental enquiries to determine the strength of wrought-iron tubes to supply data for the erection of tubular bridges across the Menai Straits and the River Conway. *In* 1849 [1123] xxix.

Report on experiments into the application of iron to railway structures. *In* 1849 [1123] xxix.

HODGSON, W.B.
Report on the state of popular education in the Metropolitan district. 30 July 1859. *In* 1861 [2794-III] xxi, pt.3; (Education, 5).

HODGSON-HINDE, John
Select committee on freeman of cities and boroughs. Report, 9 July 1840. 1840 (465) xi.

HOFMANN, A.W.
Report on the chemical quality of the supply of water to the Metropolis. 1856 [2137] lii. General Board of Health.

HOGG, James Wier, *Sir*
Select committee on Clitheroe Borough election. Proc., 19 March 1842. 1842 (548) v.

Select committee on the Nottingham Town election petition. Min. of proc. and ev. 24 March 1843. 1843 (130) vi.

Select committee on Reading Borough election. Proc. 2 May 1842. 1842 (548) v.

Select committee on Waterford city election. Proc. 9 June 1842. 1842 (548) v.

HOGG, T.J.
Reports on certain boroughs [for the commission on municipal boroughs]. 6 Aug 1838. 1837/8 (686) xxxv; (GO Municipal Corporations, 6).

HOLDSWORTH, Arthur Howe
Committee on South Devon fisheries. Report, 20 June 1817. 1817 (394) iii; (Fisheries, 1).

HOLFORD, George
Committee on penitentiary houses
    1st report, 31 May 1811. 1810/1 (199) iii.
    2nd report, 10 June 1811. 1810/1 (217) iii.
    3rd report, 27 June 1812. 1812 (306) ii; repr. 1813/4 (35) iv; (CP Transportation, 1).

HOLKER, John, *Sir*
Select committee on the Bankruptcy Law Amendment Bill and the Bankruptcy Act (1869) Amendment Bill. Special report, 15 March 1880. 1880 (123) viii.

Select committee on the law of libel. Report, 6 Aug 1879. 1878/9 (343) xi; (Newspapers, 2).

HOLL, William Haworth
Royal commission on corrupt practices in the Borough of Sandwich. Report, 9 Feb 1880. 1881 C.2796 xlv.

HOLLAND, Henry Thurston, *Sir*
Colonial conference, 1887. Proc. 1887 C.5091 lvi. Colonial Office.

Committee of public accounts
    Report, 10 March 1880. 1880 (113) viii.
    Report, 12 July 1880. 1880 (245) viii.

Committee on public accounts
    1st report, 2 March 1881. 1881 (111) vii.
    2nd report, 11 May 1881. 1881 (217) vii.
    3rd report, 27 July 1881. 1881 (350) vii.

Committee of public accounts. Report, 5 July 1882. 1882 (269) vii.

HOLLAND, Henry Thurston, *Sir* (continued)
Committee of public accounts
1st report, 7 March 1883. 1883 (77) xi.
2nd report, 30 May 1883. 1883 (187) xi.
3rd report, 29 June 1883. 1883 (233) xi.

HOLLAND, P.H.
Reports on certain Metropolitan cemeteries. 26 Nov 1856, 28 Jan and 3 March 1856. 1856 (146) lii. Home Department.

HOLMES, Hugh
Commission of inquiry into the collection of rates in the City of Dublin. Report, 17 May 1878. 1878 C.2062 xxiii. Irish Secretary's Office.

Commission on the matter at issue between the Irish benchers and the Incorporated Law Society of Ireland regarding the allocation of part of the stamp duty on indentures of solicitors' apprentices in Ireland. Report, Jan 1892. 1892 (217) lxv. Treasury.

HOLMES, Timothy
Report on the proposed changes in hours and ages of employment in textile factories. 7 April 1873. 1873 C.754 lv; (IR Factories, 28). Local Government Board.

HOLMS, John
Select committee on public departments' purchases, *etc.* Report, 18 July 1873. 1873 (311) xvii.

Select committee on public departments' purchases, *etc.* Report, 3 July 1874. 1874 (263) xi.

HOLROYD, John Baker, *1st E. Sheffield*
Commission for the issue of exchequer bills. Report, 12 June 1796; repr. 7 March 1811. 1810/1 (51) iv.

Select committee (HL) on the Gas, Light and Coke Company (Metropolis) Bill. Min. of ev. 22 May 1810. HL 1810 (86) xxxi.

HOME, Everard
Committee on petition respecting purchase of the Hunterian collection. SEE: Evelyn, G.A.W.S.

HOOKER, W.J.
Report on the Royal Botanic Gardens and the proposed new palm house at Kew. 30 Dec 1844. 1845 (280) xlv. H.M. Commission of Woods, *etc.*

HOPE, Alexander James Beresford Beresford SEE: Beresford-Hope, Alexander James Beresford.

HOPE, Beresford SEE:
Beresford-Hope, Alexander James Beresford.

HOPE, C.
Commission on forms of process and appeals, Scotland. Report, 18 March 1824. 1824 (241) x.

Commission on trial of civil causes by jury in Scotland. Report, 15 May 1827. 1826/7 (340) vii.

Report of the Lords of Session on the future Entail Bill and the Bill for the Relief of Heirs of Entail. 13 April 1835. 1835 (163) xlvi.

HOPE, James, *Sir*
Commission on harbours of refuge
Report, 3 March 1859. 1859, session 1 [2474] x, pt.1.
Report, supplementary report and min. of ev. 15 April 1859. 1859, session 1 [2506 I-II] x, pts. 1 and 2.

Committee on the 'Inflexible'. Report, 4 Dec 1877. 1878 C.1917 xix. Admiralty.

Committee on the outbreak of scurvey in the Arctic Expedition, 1875-76. Report, 3 March 1877. 1877 C.1722 lvi. Admiralty.

HOPWOOD, Charles Henry
Select committee on the Merchandise Marks (Files) Bill. Special report, 27 June 1895. 1895 (335) xii.

HOPWOOD, Francis John Stephens, *1st Bn.Southborough*
Memorandum upon the use of automatic couplings on railway stock, with special reference to American Experience. 20 Dec. 1898 1899 C.9183 lxxxv. Board of Trade.

HORNER, Francis
Select committee on the high price of gold bullion. Report, 8 June 1810. 1810 (349) iii; (Monetary Policy, 1).

HORNER, Leonard
Report on the educational provisions of the factories act. 28 Jan 1839. 1839 (42) xlii; (IR Factories, 27). Home Department.

Special report on guarding of machinery in factories. 2 April 1841. 1841 [311] x; (IR Factories, 27).

HORNSBY, Alan
Mackerel fishing off the coast of Ireland during the spring of 1893. Interim report, 11 Sept 1893. 1893/4 C.7169 xviii. Irish Secretary's Office. (no final report).

Report on the allegation that fishing for herring off the south-west coast of Ireland before 1st June each year is detrimental to the mackerel and hake fisheries. 20 April 1893. 1893/4 C.7283 xviii. Irish Secretary's Office.

HORSFALL, Thomas Berry
Select committee on Inland Revenue and Customs establishments. Report, 2 July 1862. 1862 (370) xii.

Select committee on Inland Revenue and Customs Establishments. Report, 8 July 1863. 1863 (424) vi.

Select committee on merchant shipping. SEE: Gibson, Thomas Milner.

HORSMAN, Edward
Select committee on the Bath City election petition. Min. of ev. 4 Aug 1857. 1857, session 2 (240) v.

Select committee on fictitious notes, Scotland
1st report, 18 April 1837. 1837 (215) xii.
Report, 13 and 14 July 1838. 1837/8 (590) xiv.

HORTON, R.J.W. SEE:
Wilmot-Horton, R.J.

HOSKING, Anthony Hiley, *Sir*
Committee on the sick-berth staff of the Navy. Report, 18 Dec 1883. 1884 C.3959 xvii. Admiralty.

Committee on Navy medical officers. Report, 31 Aug 1880. 1881 C.2928 xxii. Admiralty.

HOTHAM, Beaumont, *3rd Bn. Hotham*
Commission on the present system of recruiting in the Army. Report, 30 June 1861. 1861 [2762] xv.

Committee on the details for carrying out the amalgamation of the local Indian and line armies. Report, 30 Aug 1860. 1861 (77) xliii. India Office.

Committee of selection on the grouping of private bills, 1864. SEE: Wilson-Patten, John.

Committee of selection relative to the grouping of private bills, 1865. SEE: Wilson-Patten, John.

Committee of selection relative to the grouping of private bills. 1st to 4th reports, 6 March to 24 April 1868. 1867/8 (126, 126 I-III) viii.

General committee on railway and canal bills, 1857. Report, 3 March 1857. 1857, session 1 (75) ii.

General committee on railway and canal bills
1st report, 13 May 1857. 1857, session 2 (29) ix.
2nd report, 20 May 1857. 1857, session 2 (44) ix.
3rd report, 25 May 1857. 1857, session 2 (53) ix.
4th report, 11 June 1857. 1857, session 2 (95) ix.

General committee on railway and canal bills
1st report, 22 March 1858. 1857/8 (141) xii.
2nd report, 20 April 1858. 1857/8 (216) xii.

Select committee on military reserve funds. Report, 22 July 1867. 1867 (453) vii.

Select committee on military reserve funds. Report, 22 May 1868. 1867/8 (298) vi.

Select committee on the petition of William Henry Baker. Report, 7 July 1858. 1857/8 (397) xii; (CP Transportation, 14).

HOULDSWORTH, William Henry, *Sir*
Select committee on the Agricultural Produce (Marks) Bill. Report and special report, 29 July 1897. 1897 (365) viii.

Select committee on the Belfast Corporation Bill and the Londonderry Improvement Bill. Report, 12 and 25 June 1896. 1896 (233) viii.

Select committee on the Watermen's and Lightermen's Company Bill and the Barge Owners', *etc* Liability Bill. Report and special report, 31 May and 16 June 1892. 1892 (237) (280) xviii.

HOWARD, Charles Wentworth George
Select committee on the Maidstone election petition. Min. of ev. 23 April 1866. 1866 (201) xi.

HOWARD, Edward Stafford
Royal commission on the fisheries of the Solway Firth
Pt.1: Report, 1896. 1896 C.8182 xlvi.
Pt.2: Witnesses, min. of ev., index. 1896 C.8183 xlvi.

Royal commission on the Tweed fisheries
Pt.1: Report. 1896 C.8086 xlvi.
Pt.2: Witnesses, min. of ev., index. 1896 C.8087 xlvi.

HOWARD, George James, *9th E. Carlisle*
Royal commission on the condition of cathedral churches in England and Wales
1st report, 8 Feb 1882. 1882 C.3141 xx.
2nd report, 20 Aug 1883. 1883 C.3822 xxi.
Reports on cathedral churches
Llandaff. 23 Feb 1883. 1883 C.3513 xxi.
Truro. 26 Feb 1883. 1883 C.3514 xxi.
St. Paul in London. 9 March 1883. 1883 C.3544 xxi.
Chester. 14 July 1883. 1883 C.3712 xxi.
Bristol. 20 Aug 1883. 1883 C.3823 xxi.
Wells. 20 Aug 1883. 1883 C.3824 xxi.
St. David's. 20 Aug 1883. 1883 C.3825 xxi.
Rochester. 14 July 1883. 1883 C.3713 xxi.
Ely. 20 Aug 1883. 1884 C.3870 xxii.
Norwich. 11 Dec 1883. 1884 C.3871 xxii.
Carlisle. 14 Feb 1884. 1884 C.3937 xxii.
Christ in Oxford. 14 Feb 1884. 1884 C.3938 xxii.
Worcester. 14 Feb 1884. 1884 C.3939 xxii.

Hereford. 20 June 1884. 1884 C.4113 xxii.
Canterbury. 8 April 1884. 1884 C.4017 xxii.
Ripon. 8 April 1884. 1884 C.4018 xxii.
St. Asaph. 8 April 1884. 1884 C.4019 xxii.
Manchester. 8 Aug 1884. 1884/5 C.4215 xxi.
Winchester. 24 Oct 1884. 1884/5 C.4235 xxi.
Durham. 15 Nov 1884. 1884/5 C.4236 xxi.
Salisbury. 28 Oct 1884. 1884/5 C.4237 xxi.
Lichfield. 28 Oct 1884. 1884/5 C.4238 xxi.
Bangor. 16 Dec 1884. 1884/5 C.4306 xxi.
Gloucester. 16 Dec 1884. 1884/5 C.4307 xxi.
Peterborough. 16 Dec 1884. 1884/5 C.4308 xxi.
Manchester. 2nd report, 27 Feb 1885. 1884/5 C.4330 xxi.
Exeter. 27 Feb 1885. 1884/5 C.4331 xxi.
Chichester. 27 Feb 1885. 1884/5 C.4332 xxi.
Lincoln. 27 March 1885. 1884/5 C.4377 xxi.
York. 27 March 1885. 1884/5 C.4378 xxi.
Final report, 23 March 1885. 1884/5 C.4371 xxi.

HOWARD, George William Frederick, *7th E. Carlisle*
Commission for the improvement of the Metropolis
1st report, 27 Jan 1844. 1844 (15) xv.
2nd report, 7 May 1845. 1845 (348) xvii.
3rd report, 9 April 1845. 1845 [619] xvii.
4th report, 23 April 1845. 1845 [627] xvii.
5th report: Improvement of Battersea Fields. 23 July 1845. 1846 [682] xxiv.
6th report: Proposed new record office and approaches. 15 July 1847. 1847 [861] xvi.
7th report, 7 Aug 1850. 1850 [1356] xxix.

Report on a general scheme for extramural sepulture. 15 Feb 1850. 1850 [1158] xxi. General Board of Health.

Report on quarantine. SEE: Cooper, Anthony Ashley, *7th E. Shaftesbury.*

Select committee (HL) on the Episcopal and Capitular Estates Management Bill. Report, 22 July 1851. HL 1851 (123) xix; HC repr. 1851 (589) xiii.

Select committee (HL) on the Manchester Rectory Division Bill. Report, 9 July 1850. HL 1850 (247) xxiii.

Select committee on the state of the northern roads. Report, 23 March 1830. 1830 (172) x.

Select committee on works of art. Report, 1 Sept 1848. 1847/8 (720) xvi; (ED Fine Arts, 3).

Supply of water to the Metropolis
Report, 28 May 1850. 1850 [1218] xxii.
Appendix 1: Returns to the queries addressed to the Metropolitan water companies. 1850 [1281] xxii.
Appendix 2: Engineering reports and ev. 1850 [1282] xxii.
Appendix 3: Medical, chemical, geological and miscellaneous reports and ev. 1850 [1283] xxii.
Appendix 4: Cesspool system in Paris. 1850 [1284] xxii. (UA Water Supply, 4). General Board of Health.

HOWARD, Henry
Report on the proceedings and awards of the mixed commission on British and American claims. 7 Feb 1874. 1874 C.1046 lxxv. Foreign Office.

HOWARD, James Kenneth
Report on the Isle of Man disafforestation and on the acts of Tynwald. 11 Jan 1865. 1865 (6) xxx. Office of Woods, *etc.*

Report on the operation of the New Forest Deer

HOWARD, James Kenneth (continued)
Removal Act. 5 Dec 1867. 1875 (141) xxi. Treasury.

Report on the New Forest; description, relation to the crown and the principles of management. 8 June 1871. 1871 (293) lviii; repr. 5 May 1875. 1875 (191) xxi. Treasury.

Report on the subject of the report of the select committee on the Inclosure Law Amendment Bill. 29 June 1871. 1871 (328) lviii; (Agriculture, 14). Treasury.

Report upon the recommendations of the select committee on the New Forest, 1875. 16 Oct 1875. 1877 (214) xxvii. Commission of Woods.

HOWARD, John Morgan
Royal commission on corrupt practices at the last parliamentary election for the City of Norwich. Report, 15 March 1876. 1876 C.1442 xxvii.

HOWARD, William Forward, *4th E. Wicklow*
Select committee (HL) on intercourse between the U.K. and the colonies of North America. SEE: Petty-Fitzmaurice, Henry, *3rd M. Landsdowne.*

HOWE, H.
Report on the investigation into the loss of the ship 'Eagle Speed'. 27 Sept 1865. 1866 (196) lxv. Board of Trade.

HOWELL, Henry
Committee of whole HC on Howell's Divorce Bill. SEE: Tooke, William.

HOWELL, Francis
Reports on the operation of the laws of settlement and removal of the poor in the County of Nottingham. 30 June 1848. 1850 [1152] xxvii; (Poor Law, 21). Poor Law Board.

HOWELL, Thomas Jones
Report on the educational provisions of the Factories Act. 14 Jan 1839. 1839 (42) xlii; (IR Factories, 27). Home Department.

HOWES, Edward
Select committee on the Barnstaple election petition. Min. of ev. 19 April 1864. 1864 (219) x.

Select committee on the Bristol election petition. Min. of ev. 30 June 1868. 1867/8 (372) viii.

Select committee on education (Inspectors' reports). Report, 11 July 1864. 1864 (468) ix.

Select committee on the Lancaster Borough election petition. Min. of ev. 25 April 1866. 1866 (210) xi.

Select committee on Leeds Bankruptcy Court. Report, 22 June 1865. 1865 (397) ix.

HOWICK, Vct. SEE:
Grey, Henry George, *3rd E. Grey.*

HOWLEY, William, *Archbp. of Canterbury,* **1828-48**
Commission on the Church of England with reference to ecclesiastical duties and revenues
    1st report, 19 March 1835. 1835 (54) xxii.
    2nd report, 10 March 1836. 1836 (86) xxxvi.
    3rd report, 20 May 1836. 1836 (280) xxxvi.
    4th report, 30 June 1836. 1836 (387) xxxvi.
    Draft 5th report, 22 Dec 1837. 1837/8 (66) xxviii.

Commission of ecclesiastical revenues of England and Wales
    Report, 26 July 1834. 1834 (523) xxiii.
    Report. 1835 [67] xxii.

Commission on the public records. General report, 24 Feb 1837. 1837 [71] xxxiv, pts.1 and 2.

Commission on practice and jurisdiction of the ecclesiastical courts in England and Wales. Report, 27 Feb 1832. 1831/2 (199) xxiv.

Commission on the state of bishopricks in England and Wales
    1st report, 20 April 1847. 1847 (324) xxxiii. (no others identified).

Ecclesiastical commission. Special and general report, 27 Feb 1832. 1832 (199) xxiv; repr. 1843 (132) xix.

Select committee (HL) on the revenues of canonries in Canterbury and Westminster. Report, 25 May 1841. HL 1841 (111) xxi.

HOWSON, J.S.
Report on popular education in Liverpool. 28 March 1859. *In:* 1861 [2794-IV] xxi, pt.4; (Education, 6).

HOWELL, Thomas Jones
Special report on guarding of machinery in factories. 10 March 1841. 1841 [311] x; (IR Factories, 27).

HUBBARD, John Gellibrand
Select committee on income and property tax. Report, 1 Aug 1861. 1861 (503) vii.

HUGESSEN, E.H.K. SEE:
Knatchbull-Hugessen, E.H.

HUGES, Henry George
Select committee on victualling house licenses, Holborn Division. SEE: Evans, Richard.

HUGES, J.
Report and ev. on the wreck of the 'San Francisco'. 23 April 1867. 1867 (265) lxvi. Board of Trade.

HUME, Joseph
Select committee on artizans and machinery exportation. 1st to 6th reports, 23 Feb to 21 May 1824. 1824 (51) v; (Industrial Relations, 1).

Select committee on controverted election fees. Report, 19 Dec 1837. 1837/8 (50) x; (GO Elections, 2).

Select committee on election expenses. Report, 8 Aug 1834. 1834 (591) ix.

Select committee on H.C. buildings. Report, 13 May 1833. 1833 (269) xii.

Select committee on H.C. officers' compensation. Report, 10 May 1836. 1836 (249) xxi.

Select committee on import duties. Report, 6 Aug 1840. 1840 (601) v; (National Finance, 1).

Select committee on income and property tax, 1851. SEE: Henly, Joseph Warner.

Select committee on income and property tax
    1st report, 17 May 1852. 1852 (354) ix.
    2nd report, 22 June 1852. 1852 (510) ix; (NF Income Tax, 1).

Select committee on King's printers' patents. Report, 8 Aug 1832. 1831/2 (713) xviii.

Select committee on laws relating to the export of tools and machinery. Report, 30 June 1825. 1825 (504) v.

Select committee on lighthouses. Report, 8 Aug 1834. 1834 (590) xii; (Shipping, 1).

Select committee on lighthouses. Report, 1 Aug 1845. 1845 (607) ix.

Select committee on lighting the H.C. Report, 7 Aug 1839. 1839 (501) xiii.

Select committee on members in office. Report, 15 Aug 1833. 1833 (671) xii.

Select committee on the method of engrossing bills. Report, 11 July 1823. 1823 (541) iv.

Select committee on national monuments and works of art. Report, 16 June 1841. 1841 (416) vi; (ED Fine Arts, 2).

Select committee on Orange institutions in G.B. and the colonies. Report, 7 Sept 1835. 1835 (605) xvii; (CP Civil Disorder, 1).

Select committee on printed papers
    1st report, 20 March 1835. 1835 (61) xviii.
    2nd report, 16 July 1835. 1835 (392) xviii.
    3rd report, 7 Sept 1835. 1835 (606) xviii.

Select committee on private bills. Report, 3 Aug 1846. 1846 (556) xii.

Select committee on private bills
    1st report, 26 Feb 1847. 1847 (116) xii.
    2nd report, 29 March 1847. 1847 (235) xii.
    3rd report, 21 July 1847. 1847 (705) xii.

Select committee on private business of the H.C. Report, 18 June 1824. 1824 (432) vi.
    2nd report, 24 June 1824. 1824 (468) vi.

Select committee on the settlements of Sierra Leone and Fernando Po. Report, 13 July 1830. 1830 (661) x; (Slave Trade, 1).

Select committee on slave trade treaties. Report, 12 Aug 1853. 1852/3 (920) xxxix; (Slave Trade, 7).

Select committee on the state of the coal trade. Report, 2 Aug 1836. 1836 (522) xi; (FP Coal Trade, 2).

Select committee on tobacco trade. Report, 1 Aug 1844. 1844 (565) xii; (TI Tobacco, 1).

HUME, Joseph Burnley
Commission on the outbreak of cholera in Newcastle-upon-Tyne, Gateshead and Tynemouth. Report, 15 July 1854. 1854 [1818] xxxv; (HE Infectious Diseases, 2). General Board of Health.

Report on the New and Waltham Forests. 3 May 1850. *In*: 1850 (707), [1267] xxx.

HUNT, Charles
Report and evidence taken at the investigation into charges by the Rev. J. O'Dwyer against the police of Limerick. 15 Oct 1850. 1851 (434) l. Irish Secretary's Office.

HUNT, George Ward
Committee on expiring laws, 1st session, 19th Parliament. Report, 27 July 1866. 1866 (448) xi.

Committee of public accounts
    1st report, 22 June 1870. 1870 (301) x.
    2nd report, 18 July 1870. 1870 (358) x.

Committee of public accounts
    1st report, 17 March 1871. 1871 (102) xi.
    2nd report, 29 March 1871. 1871 (138) xi.
    3rd report, 4 April 1871. 1871 (162) xi.
    4th report, 11 May 1871. 1871 (321) xi.
    5th report, 28 June 1871. 1871 (321) xi.
    6th report, 13 June 1871. 1871 (350) xi.

Select committee on the Election Petitions Bill. Report, 29 June 1863. 1863 (397) vii.

Select committee on game laws. Report, 26 July 1872. 1872 (337) x.

Select committee on game laws. Report, 8 July 1873. 1873 (285) xiii.

Select committee on prosecution expenses. Report, 14 July 1862. 1862 (401) xi.

Select committee on the Valuation of Property Bill. Report, 31 May 1867. 1867 (322) xiii.

HUNT, Henry
Select committee on reform of Parliament petitions. Report, 16 March 1831. 1830/1 (263) iii.

HUNT, Henry A.
Report on the sites proposed for the courts and offices of law. 18 June 1869. 1868/9 (273) xlvii. Commission of Works and Public Buildings.

HUNT, Robert
Commission on coal in the U.K., committee E. Report: Statistics of production, comsumpton and export of coal. 1871 C.435-II xviii; (FP Coal Trade, 4).

HUNTER, John
Committee on petition respecting purchase of the Hunterian collection. SEE: Evelyn, G.A.W.S.

HUNTER, Robert
Sub-committee of the Commission of Northern Light-houses on lighting the mouth of the River Tay. Report, 1867 (172) lxiv. Board of Trade.

HUNTER-RODWELL, B.B. SEE:
Rodwell, Benjamin Bridges Hunter.

HUNTLEY, *Lord* [Peerage claim]. SEE:
Cooper, C.A.

HURST, Robert
Committee on expired and expiring laws, 2nd session, 2nd Parliament. Report, 29 Nov 1803. 1803/4 (3) v.

HUTCHINS, Edward John
Select committee on accidents in coal mines
    1st report, 30 June 1853. 1852/3 (691) xx.
    2nd report, 11 July 1853. 1852/3 (740) xx.
    3rd report, 26 July 1853. 1852/3 (820) xx; (FP Mining Accidents, 14).

Select committee on accidents in coal mines
    1st report, 7 April 1854. 1854 (169) ix.
    2nd report, 19 May 1854. 1854 (258) ix.
    3rd report, 1 June 1854. 1854 (277) ix.
    4th report, 26 June 1854. 1854 (325) ix; (FP Mining Accidents, 5).

HUTCHINSON, Vct. SEE:
Hely-Hutchinson, Richard John, *4th E. Donoughmore* (1823-66)
Hely-Hutchinson, John Luke George, *5th E. Donoughmore* (1848-1900)
Hely-Hutchinson, Richard Walter John, *6th E. Donoughmore* (1875-1948).

[Peerage claim]. SEE: Freeman-Mitford, J.T.

HUTCHINSON, Bury
Select committee on petition relating to a debt of the Rajah of Travancore. SEE: MacKinnon, W.A.

HUTCHINSON, C. Scrope
Report of an inquiry into the present state and condition of, and the high rate of charges on the Dublin and Kingstown section of the Dublin, Wicklow and Wexford Railway. 30 March 1878. 1878 (147) lxvi. Board of Trade.

HUTCHINSON, C. Scrope (continued)

Inquiry on the train service from Dundalk to Bundoran and Enniskillen on the Great Northern (Ireland) Railway. Report, 18 July 1891. 1892 (83) lxx. Board of Trade.

Special committee on the improvement of railway communication on the western coast of Scotland. Report, 28 Nov 1891. 1892 C.6611 lxx. Treasury.

HUTCHINSON, John Luke George Hely   SEE:

Hely-Hutchinson, John Luke George, *5th E. Donoughmore.*

HUTCHINSON, Thomas

Communication on the poor laws. 21 Jan 1834. 1834 (44) xxxvii; (Poor Law, 17).

HUTCHINSON, W.N.

Committee on the Enfield and Whitworth rifles. Report, 1 Jan 1859. 1861 (187) xxxvi. War Office.

HUTT, William, *Sir*

Commission on Greenwich hospital. Report, 4 May 1860. 1860 [2670] xxx.

Select committee on bonded corn. Report, 14 July 1840. 1840 (472) v.

Select committee on bonded corn (Grinding Act). Report, 16 June 1842. 1842 (333) xiv.

Select committee on the laws affecting aliens. Report, 2 June 1843. 1843 (307) v.

Select committee on the Maidstone election petition. Report, 22 April 1853. 1852/3 (381) xvi.

Select committee on slave trade
1st report, 18 April 1848. 1847/8 (272) xxii.
2nd report, 30 May 1848. 1847/8 (366) xxii.
3rd report, 25 July 1848. 1847/8 (536) xxii.
4th report, 10 Aug 1848. 1847/8 (623) xxii; (Slave Trade, 4).

Select committee on the slave trade
1st report, 24 May 1849. 1849 (308) xix.
2nd report, 21 June 1849. 1849 (410) xix; (Slave Trade, 5).

Select committee on the Taunton election petition (second case)
Report, 23 June 1853. 1852/3 (652) xix.
Min. of ev. 1852/3 (660) xix.

Select committee on Thames Conservancy, *etc.* Report, 16 July 1863. 1863 (454) xii.

Select committee on the Thames Conservancy Bill. Report, 8 June 1864. 1864 (373) viii.

HUXLEY, Thomas Henry

Report on the disturbances during the Winter of 1880-81 in Radnorshire in carrying out or in defiance of the Salmon Fishery Acts, 1861 and 1876. 6 April 1881. 1881 C.2918 xxiii. Home Office.

IBBETSON, Henry John Selwin, *1st Bn. Rockwood*

Select committee on cattle plague and the importation of livestock. Report, 25 July 1877. 1877 (362) ix; (AG Animal Health, 2).

Select committee on commons. Report, 2 April 1884. 1884 (114) ix.

Select committee on commons. Report, 30 May 1883. 1883 (186) xiii.

Select committee on commons. Report, 21 April 1887. 1887 (114) ix.

Select committee on the Metropolitan fire brigade. Report, 20 July 1876. 1876 (371) xi.

Select committee on the Metropolitan fire brigade. Report, 17 July 1877. 1877 (342) xiv.

Select committee on police superannuation funds. Report, 23 July 1875. 1875 (352) xiii; (CP Police, 9).

Select committee on police superannuation funds. Report, 13 April 1877. 1877 (158) xv; (CP Police, 10).

IDDESLEIGH, E.   SEE:

Northcote, Stafford Henry, *1st E. Iddesleigh* (1818-1887)

Northcote, Walter Stafford, *2nd E. Iddesleigh* (1845-1927).

INCHIQUIN, *Lord*   [Peerage claim].   SEE:

Freeman-Mitford, J.T.;   AND SEE: Rolfe, R.M.

INDERWICK, Frederick Andrew

Select committee on tithe rent charges. Report, 22 July 1881. 1881 (340) xii.

INGESTRE, *Vct.*   SEE:

Chetwynd-Talbot, Henry John Chetwynd, *3rd E. Talbot* (1803-1863).

INGHAM, Robert

General committee on railway and canal bills.   SEE: Smith-Stanley, Edward Henry, *15th E. Derby.*

General committee on railway and canal bills. Report, 23 Feb 1859. 1859, session 1 (82) iii.

General committee on railway and canal bills
Report, 17 June 1859. 1859, session 2 (35) v.
2nd report, 30 June 1859. 1859, session 2 (43) v.
3rd report, 8 July 1859. 1859, session 2 (74) v.

General committee on railway and canal bills
Report, 10 Feb 1860. 1860 (62) xxi.
2nd report, 16 Feb 1860. 1860 (90) xxi.
3rd report, 22 March 1860. 1860 (163) xxi.
4th report, 28 March 1860. 1860 (188) xxi.
5th report, 21 May 1860. 1860 (316) xxi.
6th report, 13 June 1860. 1860 (382) xxi.
7th report, 21 June 1860. 1860 (398) xxi.

General committee on railway and canal bills
1st report, 21 Feb 1861. 1861 (51) xiv.
2nd report, 28 Feb 1861. 1861 (65) xiv.
3rd report, 20 March 1861. 1861 (118) xiv.
4th report, 17 April 1861. 1861 (172) xiv.
5th report, 24 April 1861. 1861 (189) xiv.
6th report, 7 May 1861. 1861 (225) xiv.
7th report, 6 June 1861. 1861 (311) xiv.
8th report, 14 June 1861. 1861 (338) xiv.
9th report, 21 June 1861. 1861 (368) xiv.
10th report, 8 July 1861. 1861 (413) xiv.

General committee on railway and canal bills. 1st to 12th reports, 21 Feb to 22 June 1865. 1865 (66, 66 I-XI) vii.

Select committee on the Derby election petition. Min. of ev. 10 March 1853. 1852/3 (219) xii.

Select committee on the Edinburgh Annuity Tax Abolition Act, 1860, and the Cannongate Annuity Tax Act. Report, 29 June 1866. 1866 (379) viii.

Select committee on the Lambeth Borough election petition. Min. of ev. 21 Aug 1857. 1857, session 2 (287) vi.

Select committee on the Liverpool election petition
Report, 21 June 1853. 1852/3 (641) xv.
Min. of ev. 1852/3 (653) xv.

Select committee on merchant seamen's fund. Report, 10 Aug 1840. 1840 (617) xiii.

Select committee on stoppage of wages (hosiery). Report, 25 July 1855. 1854/5 (421) xiv; (Industrial Relations, 6).

INGLEBY, Rupert
Commission on intestacy, real property and testamentary clauses acts, of South Australia. Report, 30 June 1873. 1874 C.1108 xliv; (Australia, 27). Colonial Office.

INGLEFIELD, Edward Augustus
Committee on mortar and rocket life-saving apparatus. Report on trials of the apparatus of Rogers and Anderson and of the Board of Trade apparatus. 20 March 1878. 1878 (214) lxvii. Board of Trade.

INGLIS, John, Lord
Royal commission on the Universities of Scotland. Report, ev., returns, documents. Feb 1878. 1878 C.1935 xxxii, xxxiii, xxxiv, xxxv.

Scottish universities commission. General report, 14 May 1863. 1863 [3174] xvi.

INGLIS, Robert Harry, Sir
Classification committee on railway bills
1st report, 19 March 1845. 1845 (151) x.
2nd report, 2 April 1845. 1845 (181) x.
3rd report, 7 April 1845. 1845 (194) x.
4th report, 8 April 1845. 1845 (196) x.
5th report, 15 April 1845. 1845 (218) x.
6th report, 18 April 1845. 1845 (230) x.
7th report, 22 April 1845. 1845 (237) x.
8th report, 5 June 1845. 1845 (353) x.
9th report, 26 June 1845. 1845 (413) x.
10th report, 10 July 1845. 1845 (478) x.

Select committee on Carrickfergus forgeries election petition. Report, 4 Feb 1831. 1830/1 (112) iii.

Select committee on the Glasgow lottery
1st report, 8 May 1834. 1834 (279) xviii.
2nd report, 5 Aug 1834. 1834 (560) xviii; (SP Gambling, 2).

Select committee on Indian territories. SEE: Wood, Charles.

Select committee on the law of mortmain. SEE: Headlam, T.E.

Select committee on the library of the H.C. Report, 16 July 1832. 1831/2 (600) v.

Select committee on the library of the H.C. Report, 7 Aug 1838. 1837/8 (691) xxiii.

Select committee on the Office of the Speaker. Report, 12 May 1853. 1852/3 (478) xxxiv.

Select committee on Westminster bridge. Report, 11 July 1844. 1844 (477) vi.

Select committee on Westminster Bridge and New Palace
Report, 1 April 1846. 1846 (177) xv.
2nd report, 29 May 1846. 1846 (349) xv.
3rd report, 5 Aug 1846. 1846 (574) xv.

Select committee on Westminster Temporary Bridge Bill. Report, 25 July 1850. 1850 (609) xix.

Standing committee on the library of the H.C. Report, 7 July 1834. 1834 (436) xi.

Standing committee on the library of the H.C. Report, 29 Feb 1836. 1836 (63) xxi.

Standing committee on the library of the H.C. Report, 1 July 1837. 1837 (468) xiii.

Standing committee on the library of the H.C. Report, 16 July 1839. 1839 (406) xiii.

Standing committee on the library of the H.C. Report, 18 June 1841. 1841 (422) ix.

IRVINE, M. Bell
Report on the Red River expedition of 1870. 25 Oct 1870. 1871 C.391 xlviii; (Canada, 27). Colonial Office.

IRVING, John
Committee on Guadeloupe claims petition
Report, 14 July 1820. 1820 (276) iii.
Petition, min. of ev., memorial. 17 July 1820. 1820 (289) iii.

ISMAY, Thomas H.
Committee on live-saving appliances. Report, 11 April 1889. 1889 C.5762 lxix; (Shipping, 9). Board of Trade.

JACK, William
Commission on the Queen's colleges in Ireland. Report, 1884/5 C.4313 xxv. Irish Secretary's Office.

JACKSON, C.R.M.
Commission on the failure of the Bank of Bombay. Report, 10 Feb 1869. 1868/9 [4162 I-III] xv. India Office.

JACKSON, Henry Mather, Sir
Select committee on hallmarking of gold and silver. Report, 31 July 1878. 1878 (328) xiii; (TI Silver and Gold Wares, 2).

Select committee on hallmarking of silver. Report, 19 May 1879. 1878/9 (191) x; (TI Silver and Gold Wares, 2).

Select committee on the General Carriers Act. Report, 1 July 1875. 1875 (295) x.

Select committee on the General Carriers Act. Report, 4 June 1877. 1877 (234) vii.

JACKSON, John, Sir
Select committee on the doctrine of contagion in the plague. Report, 14 June 1819. 1819 (449) ii.

JACKSON, Pilkington
Reports on the Soldiers' Institutes at Aldershot and Portsmouth. 3 Sept and 2 Dec 1861. 1862 (126) xxxii. War Office.

JACKSON, William
Select committee on Metropolitan communications. Report, 23 July 1855. 1854/5 (415) x.

Select committee on slave trade. SEE: Hutt, William.

Select committee on British South Africa. Report, 14 Aug 1895. 1895 (380) ix; (Africa, 18).

Select committee on British South Africa
Special report, 5 Feb 1897. 1897 (64) ix.
2nd report, 13 July 1897. 1897 (311) ix; (Africa, 41).

JAMES, Henry
Cam experiments. 1849. *In:* 1849 [1123] xxix.

Experiments made in Portsmouth Dockyard for determining the effects produced by passing weights over bars at different velocities. *In:* 1849 [1123] xxix.

Experiments by statical pressure on the strength of rectangular bars cast of iron. *In:* 1849 [1123] xxix.

Experiments with slowly moving weights. *In:* 1849 [1123] xxix.

JAMES, Henry, Sir

Committee on the system of conducting the legal business of the government. Report, 8 June 1888. 1888 (239) lxxx. Treasury.

Report on the Ordnance Survey and Topographical Depot at the date of transfer of the Ordnance Survey from the War Office to the Office of Works on 1 April 1870. 9 May 1870. 1870 (268) xliii. War Office.

Select committee on the Bankruptcy Act Amendment Bill. Special report, 2 Aug 1880. 1880 (324) viii.

Select committee on the Bills of Sale Act (1878) Amendment Bill. Report, 22 July 1881. 1881 (341) viii.

Select committee on the Conveyancing and Law of Property Bill. Report, 1 Aug 1881. 1881 (96) viii.

Select committee on the Court of Criminal Appeal Bill. SEE: Finlay, Robert Bannatyne.

Select committee on East India; Hyderabad Deccan Mining Company
1st report, 17 May 1888. 1888 (177) xi.
2nd report, 6 Aug 1888. 1888 (327) xi.

Select committee on the Eastbourne Improvement Act (1885) Amendment Bill. Report, 4 May 1892. 1892 (169) xi.

Select committee on the law of libel. Report, 14 July 1880. 1880 (248) ix; (Newspapers, 2).

Select committee on the Married Women's Property Bill. Report, 10 March 1881. 1881 (124) ix; (Marriage and Divorce, 2).

Select committee on privilege. Report on the commitment of Mr. Gray. 21 Nov 1882. 1882 (406) xii.

Select committee on town holdings. SEE: Pleydell-Bouverie, Jacob, Vct. Folkstone.

Standing committee on law. Liability of Trustees Bill. Report, 3 Aug 1888. 1888 (323) xii.

Standing committee on trade. Railway Servants (Hours of Labour) Bill. Report, 20 March 1893. 1893/4 (124) xv.

JAMES, William Milbourne, Sir

Commission on memorials from officers in the Army in reference to the abolition of purchase. Report, 1 June 1874. 1874 C.1018 xii. War Office.

Committee on supersession of colonels of the British Army by colonels of the Indian Army. Report, 15 Dec 1869. 1870 C.45 xii. War Office.

JAMESON, Andrew

Commission on the telephone exchange service in Glasgow
Report, 29 Nov 1897. 1898 C.8768 xlix.
Proc. 1898 C.8769 xlix. Treasury.

JAMESON RAID

Select committee of Cape of Good Hope Assembly on the raid. SEE: Upington, Thomas.

JARDINE, William

Commission on salmon fisheries in England and Wales. Report, 7 Feb 1861. 1861 [2768] xxiii.

JEBB, Joshua

Report on Bolton Corporation. 3 April and 26 May 1838. 1841 (251) xx. Privy Council.

Report on the construction, ventilation and details of Pentonville prison, 8 Aug 1844. 1844 [594] xxviii; (CP Prisons, 11). Home Department.

Report on the discipline and management of the military prisons. 14 June 1849. 1849 [1110] xxvi. War Office.

JEBB, Richard Claverhouse, Sir

Select committee on burial grounds. Report, 13 July 1897. 1897 (312) x.

Select committee on burial grounds. Report, 27 July 1898. 1898 (322) viii.

JEFFREY, Francis

Committee on the Exchequer Court (Scotland) Bill. Report, 23 March 1832. 1831/2 (307) v.

JENKINS, H.

Report on the agriculture of Denmark and France for the Royal commission on agriculture. 30 Nov 1881. 1882 C.3375-IV xv; (Agriculture, 19). SEE ALSO: Gordon-Lennox, Charles Henry, 6th D. Richmond.

Report on the state of popular education in Welsh specimen districts in North and South Wales. 4 July 1859. In: 1861 [2794-II] xxi, pt.2; (Education, 4).

JENKINS, H.M.

Report on agricultural education in North Germany, France, Denmark, Belgium, Holland and U.K. for the Royal Commission on Technical Instruction. 1884 C.3981-I xxx.

JENKINS, Richard

Select committee on Ipswich Borough election petition. Min. of ev. 28 Feb 1838. 1837/8 (173) x.

JENKINSON, Charles

Commission on Cold Bath Fields Prison. Report, 19 May 1809. 1809 (216) iv; (CP Prisons, 7).

JENKINSON, Robert Banks, Lord Hawkesbury

Committee on the assize and making of bread and the deficiency of the crop of 1799.
Report, 10 Feb 1800. CJ Reports, vol.9, p.65; (Reps., 1731-1800, no.158, vol.25)
2nd report, 6 March 1800. CJ Reports, vol.9, p.81; (Reps., 1731-1800, no.159, vol.25)

Committee on the state of the copper mines and the copper trade. Report, 17 May 1799. CJ Reports, vol.10, p.651; (Reps., 1731-1800, no.149, vol.22).

Select committee on the improvement of the Port of London. SEE: Abbot, C.

JENKINSON, Robert Banks, 2nd E. Liverpool

Select committee (HL) on the precedents respecting the use of proxies. Report, 22 Dec 1810. HL 1810/1 (3) xliii.

JENNER, Edward

Committee on petition respecting discovery of vaccine innoculation. SEE: Bankes, Henry.

JENNER, William

Commission on the sanitary state of the War Office. Report, 31 Jan 1877. 1877 (55) xxvii. War Office.

JEPHSON, C.D.O. SEE:
Jephson-Norreys, C.D.O.

JEPHSON-NORREYS, Charles Denham Orlando

Select committee on post communication with Ireland. Report, 9 Aug 1832. 1831/2 (716) xvii.

Select committee on Registry of Deeds (Ireland) Bill. Report, 10 July 1832. 1831/2 (592) xviii.

Select committee on steam carriages. Report, 12 Oct 1831. 1831 (324) viii.

JERVOIS, William Francis Drummond
Report on the progress made in the construction of the fortifications for the defence of dockyards and naval arsenals, *etc* of the U.K. 19 Feb 1867. 1867 [3787] xlv. War Office.

Observations on the report of the special committee on the iron shields supplied for Malta and Gibraltar. 16 March 1868. 1867/8 [4003-I] xvi. War Office. SEE ALSO: Hay, J.C.D., *Sir*.

JERVIS, John, *Sir*
Royal commission on the superior courts of common law. SEE: Cockburn, James Edmund, *Sir*.

JERVIS, Henry Jervis White
Select committee on Harwich harbour. Report, 2 June 1862. 1862 (296) vi.

Select committee on Royal Artillery and engineer officers' arrears of pay. Report, 31 July 1877. 1877 (382) viii.

Select committee on Royal Artillery and engineer officers' arrears of pay. Report, 29 May 1878. 1878 (204) x.

JERVIS, John
Select committee on the Stewardship of Denbigh. Report, 1 March 1839. 1839 (83) xiii.

JERVIS-WHITE-JERVIS, Henry SEE:
JERVIS, Henry Jervis White.

JESSEL, George, *Sir*
Departmental committee on the legal business of the government. 1st to 3rd reports, 6 July to 3 Dec 1875. 1877 (199) xxvii. Treasury.

Judicature Acts (Legal Offices) committee. Report, 1878. 1878 C.2067 xxv; (Legal Administration, 16).

JEUNE, Francis Henry, *Sir*
Committee on the North Atlantic Winter Freeboard. Report, 25 Nov 1898. 1899 (126) lxxiii. Board of Trade.

Committee on rule of the road at sea. Report on the screening of ships' side lights. 13 Nov 1895. 1895 C.7908 xlii. Board of Trade.

JOCELYN, *Vct.* SEE:
Jocelyn, Robert, *3rd E. Roden* (1788-1870)
Jocelyn, Robert, *Vct. Roden* (1816-1854)

JOCELYN, Robert, *3rd E. Roden*
Select committee on steam communications with India
  1st report, 5 June 1851. 1851 (372) xxi.
  2nd report, 29 July 1851. 1851 (605) xxi.

JOEL, Lewis
Mixed commission on the claims of British subjects against the government of Venezuela. 15 Nov 1869. 1871 C.308 lxxii. Foreign Office.

JOHNSON, George
Special committee of the coal trade on the explosion at the Haswell Collieries and on the means of preventing similar accidents. Report, 7 Feb 1845. 1845 (232) xvi. Home Department. SEE ALSO: Lyell, Charles; AND SEE: Faraday, M.

JOHNSON, Henry Vaughan
Commission of inquiry into the state of education in Wales. SEE: Shuttleworth, James Phillip Kay.

JOHNSON, W.M.
Select committee on the Coroners (Ireland) Bill. Report, 14 June 1881. 1881 (281) viii.

JOHNSTON, Andrew
Select committee on the Wildfowl Protection Bill. SEE: Cowper-Temple, William Francis.

JOHNSTONE, John James Hope
Commission on religious instruction in Scotland. SEE: Bell, Robert.

JOLLIFFE, William George Hylton
Select committee on the London (City) Traffic Regulation Bill. Special report, 13 April 1866. 1866 (174) xii.

Select committee on the Middlesex Industrial Schools Bill. Min. of ev. 25 May 1865. 1865 (313) xii.

Select committee on preserved meats (Navy). Report, 3 May 1852. 1852 (303) xv.

JONES, Harry David, *Sir*
Commission appointed to consider the defences of the U.K. Report. 1860 [2682] xxiii.

Defence commission.
  Report on Spithead forts. 26 Feb 1861. 1861 (219) xxxvi.
  Report on the proposed forts at Spithead. 20 May 1862. 1862 [3005], (277) xxvii.
  Report on the proposed fort behind Plymouth breakwater. 27 May 1862. 1862 [3006] xxvii.

Report on Dover harbour. 12 July 1845. 1847/8 (476) lx. Admiralty.

JONES, Henry Bence
Report on the accommodation in St. Pancras workhouse. 31 Jan 1856. 1856 [2008] xlix. Poor Law Board.

JONES, Richard
Report on the proposed harbours at Holyhead. Feb 1845. 1846 (630-II) xlv. Admiralty.

JONES, Theobald
Select committee on Derry bridge. Report, 22 July 1833. 1833 (557) xvi.

JUDGE ADVOCATE
1865, SEE: Phillimore, J.R., *Sir*
1884, SEE: Morgan, G.O.

JULYAN, Penrose G.
Report on the civil establishments of Malta. 25 March 1879. 1880 C.2684 xlix. Colonial Office.

KANE, Robert
Report of an inquiry into the composition and cultivation of sugar beet in Ireland. 1852/3 [1578] xcix. Museum of Irish Industry.

Report on the nature and products of the distillation of peat. 8 April 1851. 1851 [1393] l. Museum of Irish Industry, *and* Commission of H.M. Woods.

Report on processes proposed by Mr. Claussen and others for improvement in the preparation and uses of flax fibre. 20 May 1852. 1852 (379) li. Office of Works.

KAY, James Phillips

Report on the distress prevalent among the Spittal-fields' weavers. 27 April 1837. 1837 (376) li; *also in:* 1837 (546) xxxi. Poor Law Commission.

Training of pauper children
1st report. *In:* 1837/8 [147] xxviii.
2nd report, 1 May 1839. *In:* 1839 (239) xx.
Report. HL 1841 xxxiii (Command number not given). Poor Law Commission.

KAY-SHUTTLEWORTH, James Phillip

Commission of inquiry into the state of education in Wales
Report, pt.1: Carmarthen, Glamorgan and Pembroke. 1 July 1847. 1847 [870] xxvii, pt.1.
Report, pt.2: Brecknock, Cardigan, Radnor and Monmouth. 3 March 1847. 1847 [871] xxvii, pt.2.
Report, pt.3: North Wales. Oct 1847. 1847 [872] xxvii, pt.2; (Education, 1-2). Home Department.

Letter on the report of the commission on popular education. 24 April 1861. 1861 (231) xlviii; (Education, 8). Privy Council on Education.

KAY-SHUTTLEWORTH, Ughtred James, *1st Bn. Shuttleworth*

Committee of public accounts
1st report, 13 March 1889. 1889 (73) ix.
2nd report, 10 April 1889. 1889 (107) ix.
3rd report, 29 May 1889. 1889 (175) ix.
4th report, 17 July 1889. 1889 (259) ix.

Committee of public accounts
1st report, 26 Feb 1890. 1890 (71) x.
2nd report, 30 April 1890. 1890 (157) x.
3rd report, 14 May 1890. 1890 (177) x.
4th report, 2 July 1890. 1890 (278) x.
5th report, 23 July 1890. 1890 (319) x.

Committee of public accounts
1st report, 18 Feb 1891. 1890/1 (107) xi.
2nd report, 6 May 1891. 1890/1 (227) xi.
3rd report, 23 July 1891. 1890/1 (361) xi.

Committee of public accounts
1st report, 9 March 1892. 1892 (106) xi.
2nd report, 11 May 1892. 1892 (180) xi.
3rd report, 24 May 1892. 1892 (222) xi.
4th report, 15 June 1892. 1892 (277) xi.

Select committee on the Fishguard and Rosslare Railways and Harbours Bill. Report, 1 July 1898. 1898 (270) x.

KAYE, W.S.B.

Committee on the list of 1801 for the promulgation of the statutes in Ireland. Report, 4 Sept 1883. 1884 C.4198 xxiii. Irish Secretary's Office.

KECK, George Anthony Leigh

Select committee on the Penryn election. Report, 15 March 1827. 1826/7 (176) iv.

KEENAN, Patrick Joseph

Report on the educational system of Malta. June 1879. 1880 C.2685 xlix. Colonial Office.

KEKEWICH, George William

Departmental committee on the superannuation of teachers in public elementary schools. Report, 28 Nov. 1894. 1895 C.7636 lxxvi. Education Department.

KELLIE, *Lord* [Peerage claim]. SEE: Cooper, C.A.

KELLY, FitzRoy, *Sir*

Select committee on malt duty. Report, 20 July 1863. 1863 (460) vii.

KELLY, John W.

Report on the practicability of rendering the town of Ennis in the county of Clare, a seaport. 6 May 1848. 1849 (59) xlix. Commission of Board of Works in Ireland.

KELLY, William

Removal of Irish paupers to Ireland and his case. SEE: Gulson, E.

KEMMIS, Henry

Commission on duties, salaries and emoluments in courts of justice in Ireland
1st report: Court of Chancery. 6 Feb 1817. 1817 (9) x.
2nd report: Court of Exchequer. 6 Feb 1817. 1817 (10) xi.
3rd report: Court of Error. 11 July 1817. 1817 (487) xi.
4th report: Offices in the courts of justice in Ireland. 17 March 1818. 1818 (140) x.
5th report: Court of Common Pleas. 25 Jan 1819. 1819 (5) xii.
6th report: Court of the King's Bench. 25 Jan 1819. 1819 (6) xii.
7th report: Clerks of Nisi Privis or Judges Registers. 20 Dec 1819. 1819/20 (33) iii.
8th report: Registry of Memorials. 30 May 1819. 1820 (94) viii.
9th report: Chancellor and Court of Exchequer. 16 April 1821. 1821 (411) xi.
10th report: Equity side of the Court of Exchequer. 21 Feb 1822. 1822 (31) xiv.
11th report: Court of Exchequer. 16 May 1822. 1822 (332) xiv.
12th report: Revenue side of the Court of Exchequer. 22 June 1824. 1824 (467) xii.
13th report: Sheriffs Office. 12 May 1825. 1825 (313) xv.
14th report: Judge or Commissary of the Courts of Perogative and Faculties. 21 Feb 1826. 1826 (68) xii.
15th report: Office of Sheriff. 26 April 1826. 1826 (310) xii.
16th report: Crown Office. 15 May 1827. 1826/7 (341) xi.
17th report: Courts of Quarter Sessions and assistant barristers. 14 March 1828. 1828 (144) xii.
18th report: High Court of Admiralty. 9 Feb 1829. 1829 (5) xiii.
19th report: Courts of perogative and faculties. 27 April 1830. 1830 (311) xv.
19th report, supplemental report. 10 June 1830. 1830 (518) xv.
20th report: Office for Registry of Deeds. 15 April 1831. 1830/1 (365) iv.
21st report: Metropolitan and Consistorial courts. 8 Aug 1831. 1831 (146) x.

KENDALL, Nicholas

Select committee on rating of mines. Report, 11 July 1856. 1856 (346) xvi.

Select committee on rating of mines. Report, 5 Aug 1857. 1857, session 2 (241) xi.

Select committee on the River Thames. Report, 19 July 1858. 1857/8 (442) xi.

Select committee on forestry. SEE: Lubbock, John, *Bn. Avebury.*

KENNAWAY, John Henry, *Sir*

Select committee on the Military Lands Consolidation Bill. Report, 13 June 1892. 1892 (259) xiv.

Select committee on nonconformist marriages; attendance of registrars. Report, 8 Aug 1893. 1893/4 (368) xiii; (Marriages and Divorce, 2).

Select committee on the Pluralities Bill. Report, 22 July 1885. 1884/5 (283) x.

KENNEDY, Evory

Report on the conditions and treatment of infant children in the workhouse of the North Dublin Union. SEE: Hall, Richard.

KENNEDY, J.P.

Memorandum on Indian railways. 14 Sept 1852. 1854 (131) xlviii. East India Office.

KENNEDY, Thomas Francis

Committee on the Exchequer Court (Scotland) Bill. Min. of proc. 2 April 1832. 1831/2 (354) xxv.

Committee of the whole HC on Hamerton's Divorce Bill. Min. of ev. 3 June 1830. 1830 (490) x.

Referees to inquire into charges of fraud. SEE: Matthews, J.

Select committee on Glasgow and Port Patrick roads. Report, 24 June 1823. 1823 (486) v.

Select committee on Glasgow and Port Patrick roads. Report, 17 June 1824. 1824 (428) vii.

Select committee on the salmon fisheries. Report, 17 June 1824. 1824 (427) vii; (Fisheries, 1).

Select committee on salmon fisheries
   Report, 30 March 1825. 1825 (173) v.
   2nd report, 3 June 1825. 1825 (393) v; (Fisheries, 1).

Select committee on the Salmon Fisheries Bill. Min. of ev. 31 May 1827. 1826/7 (417) vi; (Fisheries, 1).

Select committee on Scottish entails. Report, 23 March 1829. 1829 (102) iii.

Select committee on Scottish entails. Report, 25 March 1833. 1833 (109) xvi.

Select committee on Scottish Entails Bill
   1st report, 28 March 1828. 1828 (198) vii.
   2nd report, 9 June 1828. 1828 (404) vii.

KENRICK, William

Committee of whole HC on charge against. SEE: Gordon, Robert.

KENRY, *Lord* SEE:
Wyndham-Quin, Windham Henry, *2nd E. Dunraven and Mount-Earl* (1782-1850)
Wyndham-Quin, Edwin Richard, *3rd E. Dunraven and Mount-Earl* (1812-1871)
Wyndham-Quin, Windham Thomas, *4th E. Dunraven and Mount-Earl* (1841-1926)

KENSINGTON, *Lord* SEE:
Edwardes, William, *4th Bn. Kensington* (1835-96)

[Peerage claim]. SEE: Freeman-Mitford, J.T.

KENYON, *Lord* SEE:
Kenyon, Lloyd, *1st Bn. Kenyon* (1732-1802)
Kenyon, George, *2nd Bn. Kenyon* (1776-1855)
Kenyon, Lloyd, *3rd Bn. Kenyon* (1805-1869)
Kenyon, Lloyd, *4th Bn. Kenyon* (1864-1927)

KENYON, George, *2nd Bn. Kenyon*

Committee (HL) on the health and morals of apprentices and others in cotton factories. Min. of ev. 22 May 1818. HL 1818 (90) xcvi.

Committee (HL) on the Warrington and Newton Railway Bill. Min. of ev. 29 Aug 1831. HL 1831 (72) ccxciv.

Select committee on the London Grand Junction Railway Bill
   Report, 3 June 1836. HL 1836 (110) xii.
   Min. of ev. 10 May 1836. HL 1836 (94) xxxi.

Committee (HL) on the Manchester and Leeds Railway Bill. Report, 17 June 1836. HL 1836 (147) xii.

Select committee (HL) on children employed in cotton manufactories of the U.K. Min. of ev. 8 March 1819. HL 1819 (24) cx.

Select committee (HL) on the Liverpool and Manchester Railway Bill. Report, 18 April 1826. HL 1826 (68) ccix.

Select committee (HL) on the Pauper Lunatics Bill and the Lunatics Regulations Bill. Min. of ev. 1 May 1828. HL 1828 (85) ccxxxvii.

Committee (HL) on the Sunderland Dock Bill. SEE: Dundas, Lawrence, *1st E. Zetland.*

KEOGH, William

Select committee on Court of Chancery (Ireland) Bills. Report, 24 June 1856. 1856 (311) x.

Select committee on the Court of Perogative (Ireland) Bill. Report, 1 July 1850. 1850 (493) xvi.

Trial of the County of Tipperary election petition. Judgement and ev. 21 May 1875. 1875 (241) lx.

Trial of the Drogheda election petition, 1869. Min. of ev. Feb 1869. 1868/9 (27) xlix.

Trial of the Dublin City election petition, 1869. Min. of ev. Feb 1869. 1868/9 (29) xlix.

Trial of the Galway County election petition. Judgement and ev. 13 June 1872. 2 pts. 1872 (241) xlviii.

Trial of the Sligo Borough election petition, 1869. Min. of ev. March 1869. 1868/9 (85) xlix.

KEPPEL, William Coutts, *7th E. Albemarle*

Committee on the volunteer force in G.B. Reports, 8 July 1878, 31 Jan 1879. 1878/9 C.2235-I xv. War Office.

Select committee on the cadastral survey. Report, 26 July 1861. 1861 (475) xiv.

Select committee on the cadastral survey. Report, 10 April 1862. 1862 (161) vi.

KER, Henry Bellenden

Board for the revision of the statute law
   Report of proc. 12 Aug 1853. 1854 (438) xxiv.
   2nd report of proc. 27 Jan 1854. 1854 (302) xxiv.
   3rd report of proc. 31 May 1854. 1854 (302-I) xxiv. Lord Chancellor's Office.

Commission on criminal law
   1st report: Penalties and disabilities in regard to religious worship. 30 May 1845. 1845 [631] xiv.
   2nd report, 14 May 1846. 1846 [709] xxiv.
   3rd report, 10 June 1847. 1847 [830] xv.
   4th report, 30 March 1848. 1847/8 [940] xxvii.
   5th report, 13 July 1849. 1849 [1100] xxi; (LA Criminal Law, 5).

Report on the law of partnership. 14 July 1837. 1837 (530) xliv.

KERR, Hem Chunder
Report on the cultivation of, and trade in jute in Bengal, and on Indian fibres available for the manufacture of paper. 18 Dec 1873. 1874 C.982-II xlviii. Indian Office.

KERR, Schomberg Henry, *9th M. Lothian*
Royal commission on a scheme of colonisation in Canada by crofters and cottars from the western highlands and islands of Scotland. SEE: Bruce, Alexander Hugh, *6th Bn. Balfour of Burleigh.*

KERR, Walter Talbot, *Lord*
Joint committee on floating derelicts. Report, 23 Aug 1894. 1894 C.7568 lxxvi. Admiralty *and* Board of Trade.

KERRY, *E.* SEE:
Petty-Fitzmaurice, William Thomas, *4th E. Kerry.*

[Peerage claim]. SEE: Freeman-Mitford, J.T.

KESWICK, William
Commission on the working of the Hong Kong Contagious Diseases Ordnance, 1867. SEE: Hayllar, Thomas Child.

KETTLE, Rupert
Committee on the working of the Bankruptcy Act, 1869. 28 July 1875. 1877 (152) lxix. Lord Chancellor's Office.

KEY, Astley Cooper, *Sir*
Committee on engineers for HM Navy. Report, 29 Jan 1876. 1877 C.1647 xxi. Admiralty.

KEYSER, Solomon
Report on hand-loom weavers in Germany, 1839. 1840 (43-I) xxiii; (IR Textiles, 9).

Report on the linen weavers of Yorkshire and the silk weavers of Macclesfield. 1839. 1840 (43-I) xxiii; (IR Textiles, 9).

KILDARE, *M.* SEE:
Fitzgerald, Charles William, *5th D. Leinster.*

KIMBERLEY, *E.* SEE:
Wodehouse, John, *1st E. Kimberley.*

KINCHELA, John
Report on captured Negroes at Demerara. 12 June 1827. 1826/7 (464) xxii; (Slave Trade, 72).

KING, Gilbert
Report on the fever at Boa Vista, Cape Verd Islands. 10 Oct 1847. 1847/8 (163) li. Home Department.

KING-HARMAN, Edward Robert
Select committee on Municipal Regulation (Constabulary, *etc*) (Belfast) Bill. Report, 15 Aug 1887. 1887 (288) x.

KINGSCOTE, Robert Nigel Fitzhardinge
Select committee on Dean Forest. Report, 10 July 1874. 1874 (272) vii.

KINLOSS, *Lord* [Peerage claim]. SEE:
Freeman-Mitford, J.T.

KINNAIRD, George William Fox, *9th Bn. Kinnaird and 1st Bn. Rossie*
Commission on the condition of mines in G.B.
Report, 4 July 1864. 1864 [3389] xxiv, pt.1.
Min. of ev. 1864. 1864 [3389] xxiv, pt.2; (FP Mining Accidents, 6-8).

Select committee (HL) on the Coalwhippers Act. Report, 24 July 1857. HL 1857, session 2 (97) xx; HC repr. 1857, session 2 (286) xii.

Select committee (HL) on railways. Report, 31 March 1846. HL 1846 (76) xxvi; HC repr. 1846 (489) xiii.

KINNEAR, Alexander Smith, *1st Bn. Kinnear*
Scottish universities commission. Report on the subscription of tests by principals, professors and other officers in the Scottish universities. 20 June 1892. 1892 C.6790 xlvii.

KINROSS, *Lord* SEE:
Balfour, John Blair, *Bn. Kinross.*

KNATCHBULL, Edward, *Sir*
Committee on the Broadstairs pier petition. Report, 2 March 1808. 1808 (64) ii.

Committee on the Shoreham Roads Repeal Bill. Min. of ev. 30 July 1811. 1810/1 (196) ii.

Select committee on the Parish Constables Bill. SEE: Sutton, J.H.T.M.

Select committee on union workhouses in Ireland. Report, 3 July 1844. 1844 (441) xiv.

KNATCHBULL-HUGESSEN, Edward Hugessen
Commission on the constabulary in Ireland. 8 March 1866. 1886 [3658] xxxiv. Treasury.

Select committee on Metropolis Commons Act, 1866, Amendment Bill. SEE: Cowper, William Francis.

Select committee on registration of voters in counties in England and Wales. Report, 18 July 1870. 1870 (360) vi.

Select committee on Turnpike Trusts Bill. Special report, 18 June 1867. 1867 (352) xii.

KNIGHT, H. Gally SEE:
Gally- Knight, Henry.

KNIPE, Thomas
Royal Commission on the Land Acts, Ireland. SEE: Cowper, Francis Thomas De Grey, *7th E. Cowper.*

KNOLLYS, W.
Council of military education on Army schools. SEE: Napier, William, C.E.

KNOWLES, Lees, *Sir*
Select committee on the Plumbers' Registration Bill. Report, 8 April 1892. 1892 (140) xiv.

KNOX, Alexander A.
Commission on the treatment of the treason-felony convicts in the English convict prisons. Report, 8 June 1867. 1867 [3880] xxxv; (CP Prisons, 21).

KOOP, Matthias
Committee on Mr. Koop's petition for establishing a company for remanufacturing paper. SEE: Adams, William.

KYNMOUND, G.E.M. SEE:
Elliott-Murray-Kynmound, Gilbert, *2nd E. Minto.*

LABOUCHERE, Henry, *Bn. Taunton*
Commission on agreements made by the Fine Arts Commission with artists in respect to wall-paintings for the palace of Westminster. Report, 19 July 1864. 1864 [3410] xix.

Commission on the state of London Corporation. Report, 1854. 1854 [1772] xxvi.

Committee on the Liverpool Docks Bill, and the Birkenhead and Liverpool Docks (Trust Property of Birkenhead Dock Trustees, *etc*) Bill. Special report, 19 June 1855. 1854/5 (328) vii.

Schools inquiry commission
   Vol.1: Report, 2 Dec 1867. 1867/8 [3966] xxviii, pt.1.
   Vol.2: Miscellaneous papers. 1867/8 [3966-I] xxviii, pt.2.
   Vol.3: Answers to commission's questions. 1867/8 [3966-II] xxviii, pt.2.
   Vol.4-5: Min. of ev. 1867/8 [3966 III-IV] xxviii, pts. 3-4.
   Vol.6-20: General and special reports of assistant commissioners. 1867/8 [3966 V-XIX] xxviii, pts. 5-16.
   Vol.21: Tables. 1867/8 [3966-XX] xxviii, pt.17.
   Report on technical education. 2 July 1867. 1867 [3898] xxvi.
   Report on the common school system of the United States and Canada, by James Fraser. 1 March 1866. 1867 [3837] xxvi; (Education, 14, 17-33).

Select committee on admiralty courts. Report, 15 Aug 1833. 1833 (670) vii; repr. 1843 (133) v; (Legal Administration, 6).

Select committee on Channel Islands (corn trade). Report, 17 June 1835. 1835 (289) xiii.

Select committee on the Coal Trade (Port of London) Bill. Report, 13 June 1838. 1837/8 (475) xv; (FP Coal Trade, 2).

Select committee on Coalwhippers (Port of London) Bill. Report, 11 July 1851. 1851 (525) x.

Select committee on combinations of workmen
   1st report, 14 June 1838. 1837/8 (488) viii.
   2nd report, 30 July 1838. 1837/8 (646) viii; (Industrial Relations, 3).

Select committee on Edinburgh and Leith agreement. Report, 12 June 1838. 1837/8 (479) xxiii.

Select committee on the harbours of Leith and Newhaven. Report, 6 July 1835. 1835 (370) xx.

Select committee on the Hudson's Bay Company. Report, 31 July and 11 Aug 1857. 1857, session 2 (224), (260) xv; (Canada, 3).

Select committee on the Kafir tribes. Report, 2 Aug 1851. 1851 (635) xiv; (Africa, 4).

Select committee on the Kingston-upon-Hull election petition. Min. of ev. 8 March 1853. 1852/3 (209) xiv.

Select committee on Negro apprenticeship in the colonies. Report, 13 Aug 1836. 1836 (560) xvi; (Slave Trade, 3).

Select committee on Negro apprenticeship in the colonies. Report, 12 July 1837. 1837 (510) vii; (Slave Trade, 3).

Select committee on New Zealand. Report, 9 July 1857. 1857, session 2 (171) ix; (New Zealand, 10).

Select committee on the Port of London. Report, 21 Aug 1836. 1836 (557) xiv.

Select committee on private bills. Report, 14 Dec 1847. 1847/8 (32) xvi.

Select committee on railroad communication. Report, 28 March 1838. 1837/8 (257) xvi.

Select committee on the Royal Mint. Report, 30 June 1837. 1837 (465) xvi; (MP Currency, 1).

LACAM, Benjamin
Committee on petition on the New Harbour, Bengal. SEE: Preston, R.

LAING, Samuel
Committee on expiring laws. 2nd session, 17th Parliament. Report, 11 June 1860. 1860 (371) xxii.

Select committee on Chain Cables and Anchors Bill. Report, 15 March 1864. 1864 (139) viii.

LAMB, William, *2nd Vct. Melbourne*
Committee (HL) on the Cheltenham and Great Western Railway Bill. Report, 16 June 1836. HL 1836 (141) xii.

LAMBERT, John
Boundary commission for England and Wales
   Report, 10 Feb 1885. 1884/5 C.4287 xix.
   Supplementary report: Certain boroughs of the Metropolis. 22 April 1885. 1884/5 C.4382 xix. Local Government Board.

Boundary commission for Ireland
   Report, 16 Feb 1885. 1884/5 C.4291 xix.
   Reports (informal) on the local inquiries relative to the provisional scheme for the county of Down. 1884/5 C.4374 xix. Irish Secretary's Office.

Boundary commission for Scotland. Report, 10 Feb 1885. 1884/5 C.4288 xix. Scottish Office.

Report of inquiry into the state and management of the workhouse of Farnham Union. 21 Jan 1868. 1867/8 (134) lx. Poor Law Board.

Report on the system of medical relief to the outdoor poor in Ireland under the Dispensaries Act, 1851. 9 Nov 1866. 1867 (17) lx. Poor Law Board.

Royal commission on municipal boundaries in Ireland. SEE: Cotton, C.P.

LAMBTON, William Henry, *1st E. Durham*
Report on the affairs of British North America. Report, 11 Feb 1839. 1839 (3) xvii; (Canada, 2).

LANE, Richard James
Report on the Office for the Registry of Deeds, Ireland. 20 April 1861. 1861 [2867] li. Irish Secretary's Office.

LANESBOROUGH, *E.* [Peerage claim]. SEE:
Cooper, C.A.

LANGDALE, *Lord* SEE:
Bickersteth, Henry, *1st Bn. Langdale.*

LANGON, Charles
Commission appointed to ascertain the equitable amount to be repaid by the counties in Ireland transferred to other lunatic asylum districts. Report, 2 Feb 1857. 1857, session 2 (277) xvii. Lunatic Asylum Commission.

LANGTON, William Gore
Select committee on the Camelford election. Report, 16 June 1819. 1819 (458), (459) iv.

LANSDOWNE, *M.* SEE:
Petty-Fitzmaurice, John, *2nd M. Lansdowne* (1765-1841)
Petty-Fitzmaurice, Henry, *3rd M. Lansdowne* (1780-1863)
Petty-Fitzmaurice, Henry, *4th M. Lansdowne* (1816-1866)
Petty-Fitzmaurice, Henry Charles Keith, *5th M. Lansdowne* (1845-1927).

LARCOMBE, Thomas Aiskew
Commission for dividing the City of Dublin into wards. Report, 22 Nov 1849. 1850 (559) xxv. Irish Secretary's Office.

Poor law boundary commission, Ireland
  1st report. 1849. 1849 [1015] , [1015-II] xxiii.
  2nd report, 10 Sept 1849. 1850 [1145] xxvi.
  3rd report, 26 Sept 1849. 1850 [1146] xxvi.
  4th report, 29 Sept 1849. 1850 [1147] xxvi.
  5th report, 1 Nov 1849. 1850 [1148] xxvi.
  6th report, 1 Dec 1849. 1850 [1149] xxvi.
  7th report, 1 Jan 1850. 1850 [1155] xxvi.
  8th report, 1 Feb 1850. 1850 [1199] xxvi.
  9th report, 1 March 1850. 1850 [1191] xxvi.
  10th report, 1 April 1850. 1850 [1223] xxvi.
  11th report, 1 May 1850. 1850 [1257] xxvi.
  12th report, 1 June 1850. 1850 [1266] xxvi.
  13th report, 1 July 1850. 1850 [1277] xxvi.
  14th report, 1 Aug 1850. 1850 [1278] xxvi.

LASCELLES, Edward, *Vct. Lascelles*
Committee on the re-committed report on the petition of Sheffield and Hallamshire cutlers. Report, 17 April 1818. 1818 (204) iii.

LASCELLES, Edwin
Select committee on the Berwick-upon-Tweed election petition
  Report, 13 June 1853. 1852/3 (604) viii.
  Min. of ev. 24 June 1853. 1852/3 (661) viii.

Select committee on the Cirencester election petition. Report, 6 April 1853. 1852/3 (353) ix.

Select committee on the Newry election petition. Report, 6 April 1853. 1852/3 (346) xvi.

Select committee on the Sligo Borough election. SEE: Seymer, Henry Ker.

Select committee on the Totnes election petition. Report, 2 May 1853. 1852/3 (428) xix.

LASCELLES, Henry, *2nd E. Harewood*
Committee (HL) on the Bridlington Harbour Bill. Min. of ev. 28 June 1837. HL 1837 (145) xvi.

Committee on woollen manufacturers petition. Report, 24 April 1804. 1803/4 (66) v.

Select committee (HL) on the Sheffield and Rotherham Railway. Min. of ev. 8 July 1835. HL 1835 (102) xliii.

LATHAM, P.M.
Report of the physicians on the state of the General Penitentiary at Milbank. 16 April 1823. 1823 (256) v; (CP Prisons, 10).

LATHAM, William
Commission on the matter at issue between the Irish benchers and the Incorporated Law Society of Ireland regarding the allocation of part of the stamp duty on indentures of solicitors' apprentices in Ireland. Report, Jan 1892. 1892 (217) lxv. Treasury.

LA TOUCHE, John David
Commission on the House of Industry, Dublin. Report, 19 May 1820. 1820 (84) viii.

LATROBE, C.J.
Negro education in British Guiana and Trinidad. Report, 14 Aug 1838. 1839 (35) xxxiv. Colonial Office.

Negro education in Jamaica, with correspondence. Report, 7 Feb 1838. 1837/8 (113) xlviii. Colonial Office.

Negro education in the Windward and Leeward Islands. Report, 21 June 1838. 1837/8 (520) xlviii. Colonial Office.

LAUDERDALE, *Lord* SEE:
  Maitland, James, *8th E. Lauderdale* (1759-1839)
  Maitland, James, *9th E. Lauderdale* (1784-1860)
  Maitland, Anthony, *10th E. Lauderdale* (1785-1863)
  Maitland, Thomas, *11th E. Lauderdale* (1803-1878)
  Maitland, Charles, *12th E. Lauderdale* (1822-1884)
  Maitland, Frederick Henry, *13th E. Lauderdale* (1840-1924)

[Peerage claim]. SEE: Freeman-Mitford, J.T.

LAURENSON, J.
Committee on the organisation and establishment of the yeomanry force. Report, 7 May 1861. 1861 [2817] xxxvi. War Office.

LAW, Edward, *1st E. Ellenborough*
Commission on Fleet and Marshalsea prisons. Report, 16 March 1819. 1819 (109) xi; (CP Prisons, 8).

Commission on the Merchant Seamen's Fund. Report, 1847/8 [931] xxviii.

Committee (HL) on the London and Cambridge Railway Bill. Report, 21 June 1836. HL 1836 (161) xii.

Select committee (HL) on the petition of the East India Company for relief. Report. 1840 (43) xxii; HC repr. 1840 (353) vii.

Select committee (HL) on the Post Office revenue. Report, 21 June 1847. HL 1847 (225) xxv.

LAW, Ewan
Naval enquiry commissioners. SEE: Pole, C.M.

LAW, Hugh
Commission on corrupt practices amongst the freeman electors of the City of Dublin. Report, 3 May 1870. 1870 C.93 xxxiii.

LAW, William John
Supplementary paper on bankruptcy and insolvency. 1841 [289] xii.

LAWES, Edward
Report on the Westminster Improvement Acts Amending Bill. 29 May 1850. 1850 (396) xxxiii. Commission of H.M. Woods.

LAWES, John Bennett
Report of experiments undertaken to determine the relative values of unmalted and malted barley as food for stock. Aug 1865. 1866 [3597] lxvi. Board of Trade.

LAWLEY, Francis
Select committee on civil government charges. Report, 14 Oct 1831. 1831 (337) iv.

LAWRENCE, John Laird Mair, *1st Bn. Lawrence*
Commission on H.M.S. 'Megaera'. Report, 6 March 1872. 2 vols. 1872 C.507 xv. Admiralty.

LAWRENCE, S.
Commission on salable offices in the courts of law. Report, 15 June 1810. 1810 (358) ix.

LAWSON, John Grant
Departmental committee on the Universities and Colleges Estates Act
  Report, 6 Aug 1897. 1897 C.8646 xlv.
  Min. of ev. 1897 C.8647 xlv. Board of Agriculture.

LAWSON, William
Trial of the Borough of Galway election petition. Ev. and judgement. 5 June 1874. 1874 (201) liii.

LAYARD, Austen Henry
Select committee on the Paris exhibition. Report, 11 July 1867. 1867 (433) x; (ED Fine Arts, 6).

Select committee on plans for new dining rooms, *etc.* in the Houses of Parliament. Report, 4 Aug 1869. 1868/9 (392) vii.

LAYARD, Edgar Leopold
Report on the offer of the cession of the Fiji Islands to the British Crown. 13 April 1874. 1874 C.1011 xlv. Colonial Office.

LAYER, Christopher
Committee to examine him relating to conspiracy. SEE: Pulteney, W.

LEACH, George Alexander
Departmental committee on civil assistants employed on the ordnance survey. Report, 31 March 1892. 1892 C.6692 xliv. Board of Agriculture.

LEATHAM, Edward Aldam
Select committee on Hyde Park Corner (New Streets) Bill. Report, 14 April 1886. 1886, session 1 (114) x.

LECHMERE, Edmund Anthony Harley, Sir
Select committee on forestry. Report, 3 Aug 1887. 1887 (246) ix.

LECLERE, P.E.
Commission of indemnification for losses sustained during the rebellion in Lower Canada, 1837 and 1838
  1st report, 14 Dec 1838. 1840 (483) xxxii.
  Appendix. 1849 (353) xxxv; (Canada, 14). Colonial Department. (no further reports identified)

LEE, James
Committee on patent petition. SEE: Courtenay, T.P.

LEECH, Henry Brougham
Committee on the Registry of Deeds Office, Dublin. Report, 22 Dec 1885. 1887 (37) lxvii. Treasury.

LEESON, Edward Nugent, 6th E. Milltown
Select committee (HL) on the Pharmacy Act (Ireland) 1875 Amendment Bill. Report, 21 June 1888. HL 1888 (167) x; HC repr. 1888 (362) xiv.

Select committee (HL) on the Poor Law Guardians (Ireland) Bill. Report, 12 June 1885. 1884/5 (130) vii; HC repr. 1884/5 (297) x.

LEFEVRE, C. Shaw SEE:
Shaw-Lefevre, Charles (1758-1823)
Shaw-Lefevre, Charles, *1st Vct. Eversley* (1794-1888)

LEFEVRE, George John Shaw SEE:
Shaw-Lefevre, George John.

LEFROY, John Henry
Committee on the trials at Woolwich of Enfield rifles converted to breech loaders. Reports, 8 Feb and 14 March 1865. 1865 (355) xxxii. War Office.

Committee on the trials at Woolwich of Enfield rifles converted to breech loaders. Report, 21 June 1866. 1866 (435) xli. War Office.

Committee on the trials in firing shot from the 7-inch rifled guns. Report, 1 May 1865. 1865 (459) xxxii. War Office.

Ordnance select committee on coiled wrought-iron inner tubes for ordnance. Report, 29 Jan 1868. 1867/8 [3998] xvi. War Office.

LEGARD, Charles, Sir
Select committee on oyster fisheries. Report, 7 July 1876. 1876 (345) xii.

LEGGE, William, 4th E. Dartmouth
Select committee (HL) on the Metropolis water supply. Min. of ev. 29 June 1852. HL 1852 (253) xxi.

LEIGH, Lord [Peerage claim]. SEE:
Cooper, C.A.

LEIGHTON, Baldwin, Sir
Select committee on the Metropolitan Subways Bill. Report, 13 June 1864. 1864 (378) xi.

LEINSTER, D. SEE:
Fitzgerald, Charles William, *5th D. Leinster.*

[Peerage claim]. SEE: Giffard, H.S.

LEITRIM, E. SEE:
Clements, William Sydney, *3rd E. Leitrim.*

LEMON, Charles, Sir
Select committee on the Cambridge Borough election petition. Min. of ev. 29 April 1840. 1840 (258) ix.

Select committee on lighting the H.C. Report, 20 May 1842. 1842 (251) xiv.

LENNARD, Thomas Barrett
Select committee on the law relative to patents for inventions. Report, 12 June 1829. 1829 (332) iii; (Inventions, 1).

LENNOX, Charles SEE:
Gordon-Lennox, Charles, *5th D. Richmond.*

LENTAIGNE, John
Report on the escape of James Stephens from Richmond Bridewell. 7 Dec 1865. 1866 (147) lviii; (CP Prisons, 21). Irish Secretary's Office.

LE POER-TRENCH, William Thomas SEE:
Trench, William Thomas Le Poer.

LESSEPS, M. de
Inquiry into reasoning on the practicability of the Suez Canal. SEE: Spratt, T.

LETHBRIDGE, A.S.
Indian factory commission. Report, 1890/1 (86) lix. India Office.

LETHBRIDGE, Thomas Buckler, Sir
Committee on Mr. Palmer's petition on improvement of the Posts
  Report, 13 July 1807. 1807 (31) ii.
  Min. of ev. 18 May 1808. 1808 (241) vi.

Committee on the Western Ship-Canal Bill. Extract from min. of ev. 6 June 1825. 1825 (403) v.

LEVESON, Granville, Lord SEE:
Gower, Granville-Leveson, *Vct. Granville-Leveson.*

LEVESON-GOWER, Francis, *Lord* SEE:
Egerton, Francis, *1st E. Ellesmere.*

LEVESON-GOWER, George Granville
Select committee on kitchen and refreshment rooms, H.C. Report, 4 Jan 1894. 1893/4 (474) xii.

Select committee on kitchen and refreshment rooms, H.C.
    1st report, 27 Feb 1895. 1895 (76) x.
    2nd report, 5 July 1895. 1895 (385) x.
    Special report, 29 Aug 1895. 1895 (442) x.

LEVESON-GOWER, Granville George, *2nd E. Granville*
Commission for the exhibition of 1862. Report, 20 April 1863. HL 1863 xliv (Command number not given).

Commission on the proposal for an Irish packet station. Report. 1851 [1391] xxv. Treasury.

Committee on the management of Ramsgate harbour and its property. Report, 2 May 1876. 1876 (97) lxxiii. Board of Trade.

Joint committee on the despatch of business in Parliament. Report, 2 Aug 1869. HL 1868/9 (48) xxvii; HC repr. 1868/9 (386) vii.

Joint committee on railway schemes for the Metropolis. Report, 29 Feb 1864. HL 1864 (10) xxvii; HC repr. 1864 (87) xi.

Select committee (HL) on the Cattle Plague Bill. Report, 5 March 1866. HL 1866 (34) xxviii.

Select committee (HL) on the Designs Act Extension Bill. Min. of ev. 12-13 March 1851. HL 1851 (47) xviii; HC repr. 1851 (145) xviii.

Select committee (HL) on the government of Indian territories
    1st report, 12 May 1853. HL 1852/3 (20) xxviii; HC repr. 1852/3 (627) xxxi.
    2nd report, 4 Aug 1853. HL 1852/3 (20) xxix; HC repr. 1852/3 (627-I) xxxii.
    3rd report, 18 Aug 1853. HL 1852/3 (20) xxx; HC repr. 1852/3 (627-II) xxxiii.
    Index. HL 1852/3 (20-Ind) xxx; HC repr. 1852/3 (627-III) xxxiii; (East India, 15-16).

Select committee (HL) on Metropolitan railway communication
    1st report, 20 April 1863. HL 1863 (70-I) xxxiv; HC repr. 1863 (500) viii.
    2nd report, 24 April 1863. HL 1863 (70-II) xxxiv; HC repr. 1863 (500-I) viii.
    3rd report, 16 July 1863. HL 1863 (70-III) xxxiv; HC repr. 1863 (500-II) viii.

Select committee (HL) on national education in Ireland. Report, 20 July 1854. HL 1854 (47) xxii, xxiii; HC repr. 1854 (525) xv, pts. 1, 2.

Select committee (HL) on the Patent Law Amendment (No.2) Bill. Report, 1 July 1851. HL 1851 (77) xviii; HC repr. 1851 (486) xviii; (Inventions, 1).

Select committee (HL) on the printing of papers for the H.L. Report, 26 June 1854. HL 1854 (119) xxi.

Select committee (HL) on the printing of the proceedings and reports of the select committees of the H.L. Report, 21 June 1852. HL 1852 (185) xxi.

Select committee (HL) on the Public Revenue and Consolidated Fund Charges Bill. Min. of proc. 31 July 1854. HL 1854 (282) xxi.

Select committee (HL) on the resignation by Mr. Edmunds of certain offices. Report, 2 May 1865. HL 1865 (30) xxii; HC repr. 1865 (294) ix; (GO Civil Service, 7). SEE ALSO: Greenwood, John.

Select committee (HL) on the Sale of Poisons *etc* Bill. Report, 10 Aug 1857. HL 1857, session 2 (37) xx; HC repr. 1857, session 2 (294) xii; (HE Food and Drugs, 3).

Select committee (HL) on the Turner and Vernon pictures. Report, 30 July 1861. HL 1861 (201) xxiv.

LEVI, Leone
Report of the International Conference on Weights, Measures and Coins. Paris, June 1867. *In:* 1867/8 [4021] xxvii; (MP Currency, 3). Foreign Office.

Report on technical, industrial and professional instruction in Italy and other countries. 1867/8 (33) liv. Privy Council.

LEWIS, George Cornewall, *Sir*
Commission appointed to make inquiries relating to Smithfield Market. Report, 24 May 1850. 1850 [1217] xxxi.

Commission on the affairs of the Island of Malta
    Reports and correspondence, pts. I and II. 16 Feb 1838. 1837/8 (141) xxix.
    Report and correspondence, pt.III. 27 March 1839. 1839 (140) xvii.
    Further correspondence. 22 April 1839. 1839 (211) xvii.

Committee on expiring laws, 4th session, 15th Parliament. Report, 7 April 1851. 1851 (189) xiii.

Remarks on the third report of the Irish Poor Law Commission. 22 and 25 July 1836. 1837 [91] li. Home Department.

Select committee on Bank Acts. Report, 30 July 1857. 1857, session 2 (220) x, pts. 1 and 2; (Monetary Policy, 7-8). SEE ALSO: Cardwell, Edward.

Select committee on civil service superannuation. Report, 7 July 1856. 1856 (337) ix; (GO Civil Service, 3).

Select committee on the militia estimates, 1862/3. Report, 10 July 1862. 1862 (395) vi.

Select committee on the Parochial Assessments Bill. SEE: Villiers, Charles Pelham.

Select committee on public establishments; exemption from rates. Report, 19 July 1858. 1857/8 (444) xi.

LEWIS, Thomas Frankland
Commission for consolidating and adjusting the turnpike trusts in South Wales. Final report, 29 Sept 1845. 1849 (105) xlvi. Home Department. (no others identified).

Commission on education in Ireland
    1st report, 3 June 1825. 1825 (400) xii.
    2nd report: Schools of all denominations. 28 Nov 1826. 1826/7 (12) xii.
    3rd report: Education of the lower classes. 28 Nov 1826. 1826/7 (13) xiii.
    4th report: Belfast Academical Institution. 26 Feb 1827. 1826/7 (89) xiii.
    5th report: Diocesan schools. 8 June 1827. 1826/7 (441) xiii.
    6th report: Hibernian Society for the Care of Soldiers' Children. 8 June 1827. 1826/7 (442) xiii.
    7th report: Royal Cork Institution. 8 June 1827. 1826/7 (443) xiii.
    8th report: Roman Catholic College of Maynooth. 19th June 1827. 1826/7 (509) xiii.
    9th report: General view, conclusion. 18 June 1827. 1826/7 (510) xiii.

Commission of inquiry for South Wales. Report, 6 March 1844. 1844 [531] xvi.

Committee on Country Bakers Bill. Min. of ev. 3 June 1813. 1812/3 (259) iii.

Committee on laws relating to the assize of bread. Report, 6 June 1815. 1814/5 (186) v.

Committee on the petition of country bakers. Report, 12 March 1813. 1812/3 (82) iii.

Select committee on the civil government of Canada. Report, 22 July 1828. 1828 (569) vii; (Canada, 1).

Select committee on Durham election petitions (special inquiry). Report, 23 June 1853. 1852/3 (649) xii.

Select committee on malt drawbacks. SEE: Baring, F.

Select committee on petitions from Berkshire for shortening the duration of polls at elections. Report, 13 July 1820. 1820 (274) ii.

Select committee on Stamford Borough. Report, 22 July 1848. 1847/8 (532) xiv.

Select committee on the state of the coal trade. Report, 13 July 1830. 1830 (633) viii; (Corn Trade, 1).

Select committee on seeds and wool
    1st report, 29 April 1816. 1816 (272) vi.
    2nd report, 9 May 1816. 1816 (272) vi.
    3rd report, 9 May 1816. 1816 (272) vi.

LEWIS, Waller
Report on the laws and ordnances of France for the regulation of noxious trades and occupations. July 1855. 1854/5 [1979] xlv. Home Department.

LEYCESTER, Hugh
Committee of secrecy (disturbed northern counties). Report, 8 July 1812. 1812 (335) ii.

LICHFIELD, Bp. SEE:
Lonsdale, John, Bp. of Lichfield, 1843-67.

LIDDELL, Adolphus Frederick Octavius
Committee on the list of 1801 for the promulgation of the statutes. Report, 18 May 1883. 1883 [3648] xxii. Home Department.

LIDDELL, Henry George, 2nd E. Ravensworth
Committee on conditions under which contracts are invited for the building or repairing of ships. Report, 1884/5 C.4219 xiv. Admiralty.

Select committee on East India railways. Report, 13 July 1858. 1857/8 (416) xiv.

Select committee on the vicar's rate at Halifax. Report, 15 May 1876. 1876 (220) x.

LIDDELL, Henry Thomas, 1st E. Ravensworth
Select committee on dog stealing in the Metropolis. Report, 26 July 1844. 1844 (549) xiv.

Select committee (HL) on the Sewage Utilization Bill. Report, 30 May 1865. HL 1865 (139) xxi.

LIFFORD, Vct. SEE:
Hewitt, James, 4th Vct. Lifford.

[Peerage claim]. SEE: Freeman-Mitford, J.T.

LIMERICK, Vct. SEE:
Hamilton, James, 3rd E. Clanbrassil.

LIMERICK, Lord SEE:
Pery, Edward Henry, 1st E. Limerick (1758-1844)
Pery, William Henry Tennison, 2nd E. Limerick (1812-1866).

LINCOLN, E. SEE:
Fiennes-Pelham-Clinton, Henry Pelham, 5th D. Newcastle.

LINDLEY, John
Report on the present condition of the Botanical Garden at Kew. 28 Feb 1838. 1840 (292) xxix.

Report on the present state of the Irish potato crop and the prospect of approaching scarcity. 15 Nov 1845. 1846 (28) xxxvii; (Famine, 8). Home Department.

LINDSAY, Lord SEE:
Lindsay, James Ludovic, 26th E. Crawford and 9th E. Balcarres.

[Peerage claim]. SEE: Freeman-Mitford, J.T.

LINDSAY, James
Committee on claims of officers promoted to the rank of Colonel for distinguished service. Report of dissent. 25 July 1861. In: 1863 (73) xxxii. War Office.

Select committee on Army (general officers). Report, 7 Aug 1860. 1860 (528) viii.

LINDSAY, James Ludovic, 26th E. Crawford and 9th E. Balcarres
Committee on electrical communication between light vessels and the shore
    Report, 2 July 1887. 1887 C.5152 lxxiii.
    2nd and final report, 1 July 1889. 1889 C.5763 lxix. Board of Trade.

Edinburgh Royal Observatory commission. Report, 11 Nov 1876. 1877 (359) xxxiii. Home Department.

LINDSAY, William Schaw
The Navy and its sources of supply as regards officers and seamen. 1 Jan 1870. 1870 (247) xliv. Admiralty.

Select committee on transport service. Report, 24 July 1860. 1860 (480) xviii.

Select committee on transport service. Report, 26 June 1861. 1861 (380) xii.

LINGEN, Ralph Robert Wheeler, Bn. Lingen
Commission of inquiry into the state of education in Wales. SEE: Kay-Shuttleworth, James Phillip.

Royal commission on the aged poor. SEE: Bruce, Henry Austin, 1st Bn. Aberdare.

LISGAR, Lord SEE:
Young, John, Bn. Lisgar.

LISTER, Thomas, 4th Bn. Ribblesdale
Select committee (HL) on Metropolitan Water Companies Bill. Report, 9 May 1899. HL 1899 (82) x.

LISTOWEL, E. [Peerage claim]. SEE:
Freeman-Mitford, J.T.

LITTLE, William Cutlack
Royal commission on agriculture. Reports on Devon, Cornwall, Dorset and Somerset. Jan 1882. 1882 C.3375 xv; (Agriculture, 19). SEE ALSO: Gordon-Lennox, Charles Henry, 6th D. Richmond.

LITTLETON, Edward John, 1st Bn. Hatherton
Select committee on constitution of committees on private bills. Report, 21 June 1825. 1825 (457) v.

Select committee on the limits of Dungarvon, Youghall and Mallow Boroughs. Report, 23 and 24 July 1832. 1831/2 (613), (635) v.

LITTLETON, Edward John, *1st Bn. Hatherton* (continued)
Select committee (HL) on Sunday trading on canals, *etc.* Report, 4 May 1841. HL 1841 (92) xxi.

Select committee on turnpike trusts renewal bills. Report, 25 May 1827. 1826/7 (383) vi.

LITTON, Edward
Commission on the duties of the officers and clerks of the Court of Chancery, Ireland. Report, 21 Dec 1858. 1859, session 1 [2473] xii.

LIVERPOOL, E. SEE:
Jenkinson, Robert Banks, *2nd E. Liverpool* (1770-1828)
Jenkinson, Charles Cecil Cope, *3rd E. Liverpool* (1784-1851)

LLANDAFF, *Lord* SEE:
Matthews, H., *1st Vct. Llandaff.*

LLOYD, F.J.
Report on cheddar cheese-making. Jan 1899. 1899 C.9374 xxx. Board of Agriculture.

LOCK, Granville G.
Report on the fisheries of Newfoundland and Labrador. 2 Oct 1848. 1849 (327) xxxv; (Canada, 18). Admiralty.

LOCKE, John
Select committee on open spaces in the Metropolis
1st report, 3 April 1865. 1865 (178) viii.
2nd report, 30 June 1865. 1865 (390) viii; (UA Planning, 3).

LOCKHART, John
Select committee on Insolvent Debtors Acts, 53 and 54 Geo III. Report, 13 June 1816. 1816 (472) iv.

Select committee on poor laws. SEE: Bourne, Struges.

LOCKHART, John Ingram
Committee on American claimants petition. Report, 25 March 1812. 1812 (134) ii.

Committee on the report from the committee on the petition of American claimants. Report, 1 March 1813. 1812/3 (66) iii.

Committee on the petition of the High Bailiff of Westminster (Mr. Morris) [on Westminster elections]. Report, 30 June 1814. 1813/4 (271) iii.

Committee on public breweries. Report, 3 June 1818. 1818 (399) ii.

LOCKWOOD, Frank, *Sir*
Select committee on trusts administration. Report, 7 Aug 1894. 1894 (269) xv.

LOGAN, Charles B.
Committee on the list of 1801 for the promulgation of the statutes in Scotland. Report, 3 April 1884. 1884 C.4197 xxiii.

LONDON, *Bp.* SEE:
Porteous, Beilby, 1787-1809.
Randolph, John, 1809-13.
Howley, William, 1813-28.
Blomfield, Charles James, 1828-56.
Tait, Archibald Campbell, 1856-68.
Jackson, John, 1869-85.
Temple, Frederick, 1885-96.
Creighton, Mandell, 1897-1901.

LONDON, C.J.
Commission on the administration and operation of the poor laws
Report, 21 Feb 1834. 1834 (44) xxvii; HC repr. 1884/5 (347) xxxii.
Ev., appendix. 1834 (44) xxvii-xxix; (Poor Law, 8-18).

LONDONDERRY, M. [Peerage claim]. SEE:
Freeman-Mitford, J.T.

LONG, Charles, *1st Bn. Farnborough*
Commission of inquiry into Customs and Excise
1st-6th reports: Customs: Board of Customs; warehousing systems; reweighing goods for exportation; Long Room; London and West India Docks; East India Department. 8 May 1820. 1820 (46) vi.
7th-10th reports: Customs: Warehousing system; Solicitor's Department; Port of Liverpool; Customs in Ireland. 9 Feb 1821. 1821 (25) x.
11th report: Customs, Scotland. 15 March 1822. 1822 (87) xi.
12th report: Out-ports. 15 March 1822. 1822 (87) xi.
13th report: Customs: Out-ports. 5 June 1823. 1823 (425) vii.
14th report: Customs: General observations. 5 June 1823. 1823 (425) vii.
15th report: Excise: Import and Export Department. 15 April 1824. 1824 (141) ix.
16th report: Excise Department. 17 June 1824. 1824 (429) ix.

Committee on the British Museum's petition relative to the Lansdowne manuscripts. Report and proc. 10 July 1807. 1807 (22) ii.

Committee on the British Museum petition respecting medals and coins. Report, 24 June 1814. 1813/4 (255) iii.

Committee on the petition of the British Museum respecting Mr. Townley's collection of ancient sculptured marbles. Report, 19 June 1805. 1805 (172) iii.

Committee on the report and memorial of the commission for improvement of Westminster
Report, 9 June 1808. 1808 (293) iii.
2nd report, 29 June 1808. 1808 (328) iii.

Committee on the Royal Library. Report, 18 April 1823. 1823 (271) iv.

Select committee (HL) on the price of foreign grain. Report, 11 April 1827. HL 1826/7 (56) ccxix; HC repr. 1826/7 (333) vi.

LONG, John Charles
Select committee to examine the physicians who have attended His Majesty during his illness, touching on the state of His Majesty's health. Report, 13 Jan 1812. 1812 (7) ii.

LONG, Walter Hume
Select committee on police and sanitary regulations bills. Special report, 11 July 1893. 1893/4 (321) xiii.

Select committee on police and sanitary regulations bills. Special report, 10 July 1894. 1894 (213) xv.

Select committee on police and sanitary regulations bills. Special report, 5 July 1895. 1895 (386) xii.

Select committee on the Public Health Acts Amendment Bill. Report, 20 May 1890. 1890 (185) xvii; (Health, 11).

LONGFIELD, M.
Committee on an invention of Mr. Dillon for simplifying the Registry of Deeds, Ireland. Reports, 23 Sept 1874 and 13 April 1875. 1876 (425) lx. Treasury.

Select committee on the Berwick-upon-Tweed election petition. Min. of ev. 15 March 1864. 1864 (127) x.

LONGLEY, Charles Thomas, *Archbp. of Canterbury,* **1862-8**
Clerical subscription commission. Report, 9 Feb 1865. 1865 [3441] xv.

Durham University Commission
    Report, 4 June 1863. 1863 [3173] xvi.
    Min. of ev. 1863 (77) xlvi.

Royal commission on ritual of the Church of England. SEE: Tait, Charles Campbell, *Archbp. of Canterbury,* 1868-83.

Select committee (HL) on the Ecclesiastical Dilapidations Bill. Report, 27 June 1862. HL 1862 (130) xxix.

LONGMORE, G.
Report on the condition and treatment of children sent out by the Children's Friend Society to the Cape of Good Hope. 24 Dec 1839. 1840 (323) xxxiii; (Africa, 21).

LONGWORTH, John Augustus
Report on the primary causes of the insurrection in Crete. Extracts. 20 Aug 1858. 1867/8 [3965-I] lxxiii. Foreign Office.

LONSDALE, John, *Bp. of Lichfield,* **1843-67**
Commission on the state and operation of the law of marriage. SEE: Wortley, James Stuart.

LOPES, Massey, *Sir*
Select committee on co-operative stores. Report, 6 Aug 1879. 1878/9 (344) ix.

Select committee on co-operative stores. Report, 10 March 1880. 1880 (111) viii.

Select committee on the law of distress. SEE: Goschen, George Joachim.

Select committee on the North British Railway (Tay Bridge) Bill. Report, 4 Aug 1880. 1880 (311) xii.

LOPEZ, Baldomero M.
Commission on the claims of the British Auxiliary Legion against the Spanish Government. Reports, 26 Oct 1839 and 20 March 1840. HL 1840 xxxvi. Command number not given.

LORD ADVOCATE FOR SCOTLAND SEE:
Advocate for Scotland, Lord.

LORD CHANCELLOR SEE:
Chancellor, Lord.

LORD PRIVY SEAL SEE:
Privy Seal, Lord.

LOTHIAN, *M.* SEE:
Kerr, Schomberg Henry, *9th M. Lothian.*

LOUDOUN, *E.* [Peerage claim]. SEE:
Freeman-Mitford, J.T.

LOUGHBOROUGH, *Bn.* SEE:
Wedderburn, Alexander, *1st E. Rosslyn.*

LOVAT, *Lord*
[Peerage claim, 1827-55]. SEE: Cooper, C.A.
[Peerage claim, 1856-85]. SEE: Freeman-Mitford, J.T.

LOW, Alexander, *Lord Low*
Committee on the system of land registration in Scotland. Report, 18 Oct 1898. 1898 C.8727 xxxiv. Scottish Office.

LOWE, Robert, *1st Vct. Sherbrook*
Commission on cattle plague. SEE: Spencer, John Poyntz, *5th E. Spencer.*

Joint select committee on the Stationery Office controller's report. Report, 29 July 1881. HL 1881 (143) x; 1881 (356) xii.

Select committee on the Chartered Banks (Colonial) Bill. Report, 11 March 1880. 1880 (115) viii.

Select committee on the Companies Acts, 1862 and 1867. Report, 26 July 1877. 1877 (365) viii.

Select committee on the Corrupt Practices Prevention Act and the Election Petitions Act. Report, 28 May 1875. 1875 (225) viii; (GO Elections, 5).

Select committee on the Electric Telegraphs Bill. Special report, 16 July 1868. 1867/8 (435) xi; (Posts and Telegraphs, 3).

Select committee on employers' liability for injuries to their servants. Report, 21 July 1876. 1876 (372) ix; (Industrial Relations, 19).

Select committee on employers' liability for injuries to their servants. Report, 25 June 1877. 1877 (285) x; (Industrial Relations, 19).

Select committee on Mr. Goffin's [teaching] certificate. Report, 1 Aug 1879. 1879 (334) x.

Select committee on Homicide Law Amendment Bill. Special report, 21 July 1874. 1874 (315) ix; (LA Criminal Law, 6).

Select committee of the Legislative Council of New South Wales on Crown Lands. Report, 2 Oct 1849. 1850 [1220] xxvii; (Australia, 12). Colonial Office.

Select committee on loans to foreign states
    Special report, 19 April 1875. 1875 (152) xi.
    Report, 29 July 1875. 1875 (367) xi; (Monetary Policy, 10).

Select committee on local charges upon shipping. Report, 3 July 1856. 1856 (332) xii.

Select committee on the office of coroner. Report, 30 March 1860. 1860 (193) xxii.

Select committee on the South Kensington Museum. Report, 1 Aug 1860. 1860 (504) xvi.

LOWRY-CORRY, Somerset Richard, *4th E. Belmore*
Royal commission on manual and practical instruction in primary schools, Ireland. SEE: Walsh, William J.

Royal commission on Dublin University. Report, 1878 C.2045 xxix.

Select committee (HL) on railway borrowing powers. SEE: Hely-Hutchinson, John Luke George, *5th E. Donoughmore.*

Select committee (HL) on the Traffic Regulation (Metropolis) Bill. Report, 8 March 1867. HL 1867 (21) xxvii; HC repr. 1867 (186) xi.

LOWTHER, William, *2nd E. Lonsdale*
Commission on the laws and regulations relating to pilotage in the U.K. Report. 1836 [56] xxviii.

Select committee on Metropolis turnpike trusts. Report, 27 May 1825. 1825 (355) v.

LOWTHER, William, *2nd E. Lonsdale* (continued)
Select committee on the Midwives Registration Bill. Report, 18 July 1890. 1890 (311) xvii; (Health, 15).

Select committee on the Tottenham and Wood Green Sewerage Bill. Report, 13 July 1891. 1890/1 (308) xviii; (UA Sanitation, 7).

LOYD, Samuel Jones, *1st Bn. Overstone*
Commission on decimal coinage. SEE: Rice, Thomas Spring, *1st Bn. Monteagle.*

LOYD-LINDSAY, Robert James, *1st Bn. Wantage*
Committee on the terms and conditions of service in the Army. Report, 27 Jan 1892. 1892 C.6582 xix. War Office.

LUARD, William Garnham
Committee on the cause of the bursting of one of the 38 ton guns in the turret of 'HMS Thunderer'. 13 Feb 1879. 1878/9 C.2248 xv. Admiralty.

Committee on education of naval executive officers. Report, 28 June 1886. 1886 C.4885 xiii. Admiralty.

Committee on explosions of gas in coal bunkers, *etc* Report, 11 Nov 1882. 1883 C.3572 xvii.
Report on the explosive power of xerotine siccative. 14 Sept 1882. 1883 C.3766 xvii. Admiralty.

Committee on the filling up of certain vacancies in the Royal Marine Artillery. Report. 1884 (159) l. Admiralty.

LUBBOCK, John, *Bn. Avebury*
Committee on aid to university colleges. Report. 1889 (250) lix. Treasury.

Committee of public accounts. Report, 29 June 1887. 1887 (201) vii.

Committee of public accounts
1st report, 14 March 1888. 1888 (87) viii.
2nd report, 1 Aug 1888. 1888 (317) viii.
3rd report, 28 Nov 1888. 1888 (405) viii.
4th report, 12 Dec 1888. 1888 (417) viii.

Select committee on the Ancient Monuments Bill. Report, 9 July 1877. 1877 (317) vii; (ED Fine Arts, 6).

Select committee on the Bills of Exchange Bill. SEE: Herschell, Farrer.

Select committee on forestry. Report, 24 July 1885. 1884/5 (287) viii.

Select committee on forestry. Report, 18 June 1886. 1886, session 1 (202) ix.

Select committee on the Lochearnhead, St. Fillans and Comrie Railway Bill. Report, 1 July 1897. 1897 (275) xi.

Select committee on the Public Libraries Law Consolidation Bill. Report, 24 May 1892. 1892 (221) xiv.

Select committee on the Shops (Early Closing) Bill. Report, 21 May 1895. 1895 (273) xii; (IR Factories, 30).

Select committee on the Shop Hours Regulation Bill. Report, 18 May 1886. 1886, session 1 (155) xii; (IR Factories, 2).

LUCAS, Edward
Commission of inquiry into matters concerned with the failure of the potato crop. Extracts from report, 20 Jan 1846. 1846 (33) xxxvii; (Famine, 8). Home Department.

LUCAS, W.H.
Report on the management of Kilrush union. 14 April 1851. 1851 (234) xlix. Poor Law Board.

LUSH, Robert, *Sir*
Boston election petition trial. Ev. and judgement. 31 July 1880. 1880 (330) lvii.

Chester City election petition trial. Ev. and judgement. 17 July 1880. 1880 (301) lvii.

Harwick election petition trial. Judgement and proc. 8 June 1880. 1880 (227) lviii.

Knaresborough election petition trial. Ev. 23 July 1880. 1880 (410) lviii.

Lichfield election petition trial. Ev. and judgement. 5 July 1880. 1880 (278) lviii.

Norwich election petition trial. Judgement and min. of ev. 8 May 1875. 1875 (209) lx.

Oxford election petition trial. Ev. 4 Aug 1880. 1880 (349) lviii.

Sandwich election petition trial. Ev. 10 Aug 1880. 1880 (350) lviii.

LUSHINGTON, Godfrey
Departmental committee on Metropolitan police superannuation. Notes of ev. and papers. 1890 C.6075 lix; (CP Police, 10). Home Department.

Departmental committee on reformatory and industrial schools
Vol.1: Report, 30 Oct 1896. 1896 C.8204 xlv.
Vol.2: Ev., index. 1897 C.8290 xlii; (CP Juvenile Offenders, 5-6). Home Department

LUSHINGTON, Stephen Rumbold
Committee on the compensation to the American commissioners. Report, 22 July 1814. 1813/4 (335) iii.

Committee on expired and expiring laws, 5th session, 4th Parliament. Report, 17 Jan 1811. 1810/1 (7) ii.

Committee on expired and expiring laws, 6th session, 4th Parliament. Report, 9 Jan 1812. 1812 (3) ii.

Committee on expired and expiring laws, 1st session, 5th Parliament. Report, 2 Dec 1812. 1812/3 (2) iii.

Committee on expired and expiring laws, 2nd session, 5th Parliament. Report, 6 Nov 1813. 1813/4 (2) iii.

Committee on the Hides and Skins Bill. Min. of ev. 18 May 1824. 1824 (323) vii.

Committee on the nightly watch and police of the metropolis. Report, 24 March 1812. 1812 (127) ii; (CP Police, 1).

Committee on the office of High Bailiff of Westminster. Report, 11 June 1811. 1810/1 (220) ii.

Committee on the public income and expenditure of Ireland. Report, 25 June 1813. 1812/3 (309) vi.

Committee of the whole H.C. on the affairs of the East India Company. SEE: Sullivan, John.

Min. of ev. on the right of search [of ships in suppression of the slave trade]. 31 March to 4 April 1845. 1847 [851] lxviii; (Slave Trade, 89).

Select committee on the criminal law of England; forgery
Report, 2 April 1824. 1824 (205) iv.
Further report, 7 May 1824. 1824 (444) iv; (LA Criminal Law, 2).

Select committee on laws relating to leather
1st report, 30 May 1816. 1816 (386) vi.
2nd report, 6 June 1816. 1816 (386) vi.

LUSHINGTON, William
Committee on the Grenada and St. Vincent petition. Report, 23 Feb 1802. 1801/2 (25) ii.

Committee on the petition of the proprietors of estates in the Island of Grenada. Report, 1 June 1801. 1801 (98) iii.

LYALL, George
Committee on British shipping. Report, 25 July 1844. 1844 (545) viii.

LYALL, James Broadwood, Sir
Indian Famine Commission
    Report, 20 Oct 1898. 1899 C.9178 xxxi.
      Appendix, vol.1-7. 1899 C.9252, C.9253, C.9254, C.9255, C.9256, C.9257, C. 9258 xxxii, xxxiii. India Office.

LYELL, Charles
Report on the explosion at the Haswell Collieries and on the means of preventing similar accidents. 21 Oct 1844. 1845 (232) xvi. Home Department.

Report on the geological, topographical and hydrographical departments of the New York Industrial Exhibition. 1854 [1793] xxxvi. Foreign Office.

LYGON, Frederick, 6th E. Beauchamp
Select committee (HL) on the Burial Grounds Bill. Report, 3 July 1871. HL 1871 (230) viii.

Select committee (HL) on reporting
    Report, 11 March 1880. HL 1880 (28) vii.
    1st and 2nd reports (session 2), 18 June and 20 July 1880. HL 1880 (66) vii.

Committee (HL) on the Drainage of Fens Bill. Min. of ev. 22 April 1818. HL 1818 (41) xcv.

LYNAGH, Matthew
Commission on his death. SEE: Tufnell, Jolliffe.

LYNAM, James
Report on the rivers Shannon and Suck. 25 April 1867. 1867 (298) lix. Treasury.

LYNCH, Andrew Henry
Select committee on advances made by the Commission of Public Works in Ireland
    1st report, 26 June 1835. 1835 (329) xx.
    1st and 2nd report, 27 Aug 1835. 1835 (573) xx.

LYNCH, David
Commission for dividing the City of Dublin into wards. Report, 22 Nov 1849. 1850 (559) xxv. Irish Secretary's Office.

Commission on the riots in Belfast in July and Sept 1857. Report, 30 Nov 1857. 1857/8 [2309] xxvi; (CP Civil Disorder, 7).

LYNDHURST, L. SEE:
Copley, John Singleton, 1st Bn. Lyndhurst.

LYNN, William
Report of the trials at Wigan of the steam coals of South Lancashire and Cheshire. 16 July 1867. 1867 (563) xliv. Admiralty.

LYTTELTON, Lord SEE:
Lyttelton, George William, 3rd Bn. Lyttelton.

LYTTLETON, Charles George, 1st Vct. Cobham
Royal commission on agricultural depression
    1st report, 4 May 1894. 1894 C.7400 xvi, pt.1.
    Min. of ev. Vol.1-3. 1894 C.7400 I-III xvi, pts.1-3.

Reports of assistant commissioners
    Reports on districts of Hampshire and Kent. 1894 C.7365 xvi, pt.1.
    Reports on districts of Somerset and Warwickshire. 1894 C.7372 xvi, pt.1.
    Reports on districts of Lancashire and Northumberland. 1894 C.7334 xvi, pt.1.
    Reports on districts of Lincolnshire and Essex. 1894 C.7374 xvi, pt.1.
    Reports on districts of Scotland. 1894 C.7342 xvi, pt.1.
    North Devon. 1895 C.7728 xvi.
    Vale of Aylesbury and the County of Hertford. 1895 C.7691 xvi.
    Lincolnshire. 1895 C.7671 xvi.
    Suffolk. 1895 C.7755 xvi.
    Heatherfield district of Sussex. 1895 C.7623 xvi.
    Salisbury Plain district of Wiltshire. 1895 C.7624 xvi.
    South Durham and selected districts of the N. and E. Ridings of Yorkshire. 1895 C.7735 xvi.
    Counties of Bedford, Huntingdon and Northampton. 1895 C.7842 xvii.
    County of Cambridge. 1895 C.7871 xvii.
    County of Dorset. 1895 C.7764 xvii.
    County of Norfolk. 1895 C.7915 xvii.
    County of Cumberland. 1895 C.7915-I xvii.
    Counties of Ayr, Wigtown, Kirkcudbright and Dumfries. 1895 C.7625 xvii.
    Counties of Roxburgh, Berwick, Selkirk, Peebles, Linlithgow, Edinburgh, Haddington, Banff, Nairn and Elgin. 1895 C.7742 xvii.
2nd report, 8 Feb 1896. 1896 C.7981 xvi.
    Particulars of expenditure and outgoings on certain estates in G.B. and farm accounts. 1896 C.8125 xvi.
    Min. of ev., vol.4. 1896 C.7400-IV xvii.
    Alphabetical digest of the Min. of ev. 1896 C.8146 xvii.
    Final report, 25 June 1897. 1897 C.8540 xv.
    Appendix. 1897 C.8541 xv.
    Statements showing the rateable value of 'lands' in 1894 as compared with 1890 and the gross annual value of 'lands'. 1897 C.8300 xv; (Agriculture, 26, 28-32).

LYTTELTON, George William, 3rd Bn. Lyttelton
Endowed schools commission. Report, 21 Feb 1872. 1872 C.524 xxiv. Privy Council Committee on Education.

Endowed schools commission. Report, 31 Dec 1874. 1875 C.1142 xxviii. Privy Council Committee on Education.

Select committee (HL) on the Subdivision of Dioceses Bill. Report, 25 June 1861. HL 1861 (148) xxiv.

McADAM, John Loudon
Select committee on his petition. SEE: Baring, Thomas, Sir.

MACAULAY, Thomas Babington
Indian law commission. Penal code for India. Report, 14 Oct 1837. 1837/8 (673) xli. SEE ALSO: Amos, Andrew.

Report on the Indian civil service. In: 1854/5 (34) xl.

Select committee appointed to prepare the militia estimates. Report, 13 July 1840. 1840 (478) xv.

Select committee appointed to prepare the militia estimates. Report, 8 June 1841. 1841 (386) ix.

Select committee on medical registration. Report, 16 July 1847. 1847 (620) ix; (HE Medical Profession, 3).

MACBETH, John
Commission on the state of the fairs and markets in Ireland. Report, 21 May 1853. 1852/3 [1674] xli. Irish Secretary's Office.

MACCABE, Francis Xavier Frederick
Royal commission on the sewerage and drainage of the City of Dublin. Report, 19 June 1880. 1880 C.2605 xxx.

McCLINTOCK, John
Committee on petition. SEE: Barry, John Maxwell.

M'CLELLAN, John
Committee of the General Assembly of the Church of Scotland on the mode of striking the fiars. Report, 1 May 1834. 1834 (259) xlix.

M'CLELLAND, J.
Report on the coal fields of India. 11 July 1845. 1863 (372) xlv. India Office.

McCULLAGH-TORRENS, William Torrens
Select committee on extradition. SEE: Bouverie, Edward Pleydell.

Select committee on witnesses (HC). Report, 8 July 1869. 1868/9 (305) vii.

MACDONALD, E.M.
Report and evidence of inquiry at Halifax, Nova Scotia, into the loss of the steamship 'Atlantic'. 24 April 1873. *In:* 1873 (373) lx. Board of Trade.

MACDONALD, Hugh Guion
Remarks on the River Plate republics as a field for British emigration. 14 March 1872. 1872 C.659 lxx; (Emigration, 25). Foreign Office.

MacDONALD, J.H.A.
Glasgow boundary commission. Report, 24 April 1888. 1888 C.5382 xlvi, xlvii. Scottish Office.

MACDOUGALL, Patrick L.
Committee on the organisation of the various military land forces of the country.
Report. Feb 1872. 1872 C.493 xxxvii; repr. 1881 C.2792 xxi.
Supplementary report, 4 July 1872. 1872 C.588 xiv; repr. 1881 C.2792 xxi.
Final report, 21 Feb 1873. 1873 C.712 xviii; repr. 1881 C.2792 xxi. War Office.

MACEVOY, Edward
Select committee on Ecclesiastical Titles and Roman Catholic Relief Acts. Report, 2 Aug 1867. 1867 (503) viii.

MACGREGOR, John
Report on the commercial statistics of the two Sicilies. 30 June 1840. 1840 [269] xxi.

M'HARDY, A.B.
Departmental committee on inebriate reformatories, Scotland. Report, 1 Feb 1899. 1899 C.9175 xii. Scottish Office.

MCINTYRE, Aeneas John
Royal commission on corrupt practices at parliamentary elections in the Borough of Boston. Report, 1876 C.1441 xxviii.

MACKDONALD, James, *Sir*
Select committee on the affairs of the East India Company. SEE: Villiers, Hyde.

MACKENZIE, J.H.
Committee of the judges of the Court of Session on the fees of the sheriff clerks in Scotland. Report, 16 March 1837. 1837 (119) xliv.

MACKENZIE, William Forbes
Select committee on public houses, Scotland. Report, 3 July 1846. 1846 (457) xv; (SP Sunday Observance, 2).

Select committee on the South Western and Epsom, and Croydon and Epsom Railway Bills. Min. of ev. relating to the atmospheric principle of traction. 10 June 1844. 1844 (358) xiv.

M'KERLIE, John Graham
Inquiry into the survey and valuation of lands to be relieved from inundation by works proposed under the Shannon Navigation Act, 1874. Report, 19 March 1875. 1875 (206) xxi. Commission of Public Works Ireland.

Observations on the report of the committee on the Board of Works, Ireland. 2 July 1878. 1878 C.2080 xxiii. Treasury. SEE ALSO: Crichton, John Henry, *4th E. Erne.*

MACKINNON, William Alexander
Committee on the bill for prevention of cruelty to animals. Report, 1 Aug 1832. 1831/2 (667) v.

Select committee on Arctic expedition. Report, 20 July 1855. 1854/5 (409) vii.

Select committee on Fourdrinier's patent. Report, 1 June 1837. 1837 (351) xx. SEE ALSO: Mosley, Oswald, *Sir.*

Select committee on improvement of the health of towns. Report: effect of interment of bodies in towns. 14 June 1842. 1842 (327) x. SEE ALSO: Chadwick, Edwin.

Select committee on masters and operatives (equitable councils of conciliation). Report, 8 July 1856. 1856 (343) xiii; (Industrial Relations, 7).

Select committee on masters and operatives. Report, 15 May 1860. 1860 (307) xxii; (Industrial Relations, 7).

Select committee on the petition of Mr. Hutchinson relating to a debt of the Rajah of Trovancore. 7 Aug 1832. 1831/2 (PB 2) v.

Select committee on Ramsgate and Margate harbours. Report, 1 Aug 1850. 1850 (660) xiv.

Select committee on Smithfield Market. Report, 22 June 1849. 1849 (420) xix.

Select committee on smoke prevention. Report, 17 Aug 1843. 1843 (583) vii.

Select committee on smoke prevention
Report, 9 May 1845. 1845 (289) xiii.
2nd report, 11 July 1845. 1845 (489) xiii.

Select committee on the steam navy. Report, 22 May 1849. 1849 (305) xvii.

Select committee on turnpike trusts. Report, 6 June 1839. 1839 (295) ix.

Select committee on turnpike trusts and tolls. Report, 9 Aug 1836. 1836 (547) xix.

MACKINTOSH, James, *Sir*
Select committee on the affairs of the East India Company. SEE: Villiers, H.

Select committee on criminal laws. Report, 6 July 1819. 1819 (585) viii; (LA Criminal Law, 1).

M'LAGAN, Peter
Select committee on fire protection. Report, 25 July 1867. 1867 (471) x.

M'MAHON, Patrick
Select committee on the Fisheries (Ireland) Bill. Report, 27 June 1862. 1862 (360) ix.

McNEILL, Duncan
H.M. sole and only master printers in Scotland. SEE: Rutherford, Andrew.

McNEILL, Duncan, *Bn. Colonsay*
Commission on courts of law in Scotland
    1st report. Ev. to 12 Feb 1869. 1868/9 [4125] xxv.
    2nd report. Ev., 29 March to May 1869. 1868/9 [4188] xxv.
    3rd report. Ev., 25 Oct to 6 Dec 1869. 1870 C.36 xviii.
    4th report. 1870 C.175 xviii.
    5th report. 1871 C.260 xx; (Legal Administration, 11-12)

Select committee on prisons in Scotland. Report, 7 July 1845. 1845 (460) xiii.

McNEILL, John, *Sir*
Commission of inquiry into the supplies of the British Army in the Crimea
    Report, 10 June 1855. 1856 [2007] xx.
    Appendix. 1856 [2007-I] xx.
    Index. 29 July 1856. 1856 (422-I) xx.

Report on the western highlands and islands. 7 July 1851. 1851 [1397] xxvi. Board of Supervision.

McNEILL, Malcolm
Report on the condition of the cottar population of Lewes. 21 Jan 1888. 1888 C.5265 lxx; (Agriculture, 25). Scottish Office.

MACONOCHIE, A.
Report on the state of prison discipline in Van Diemen's Land, *etc.* 30 Sept 1837. 1837/8 [121] xl; (CP Transportation, 6). Home Office.

MACPHERSON, J.C.
Reports (informal) on the local inquiries relative to the provisional scheme of the Boundary Commission for the County of Down. 1884/5 C.4374 xix. SEE ALSO: Lambert, John.

MACQUEEN, Thomas Potter
Select committee on the law of parochial settlements. Report, 9 June 1828. 1828 (406) iv.

McWILLIAM, J.O.
Report on the fever at Boa Vista, Cape Verd Islands. 10 July 1846. 1847 [806] xlix. Admiralty.

MADDEN, Dogson Hamilton
Select committee on Sunday Closing Acts, Ireland. Report, 2 July 1888. 1888 (255) xix.

MAGEE, William Connor, *Bp. of Peterborough,* **1868-91**
Select committee (HL) on the Children's Life Insurance Bill. Report, 25 July 1890. HL 1890 (225) x; HC repr. 1890 (344) xi.

Select committee (HL) on church patronage. Report, 7 July 1874. HL 1874 (44) viii; HC repr. 1874 (289) vii.

Select committee (HL) on the Church Patronage Bill. Report, 30 April 1875. HL 1875 (78) x.

Select committee (HL) on the Parish Churches Bill. Report, 23 June 1886. HL 1886 (201) vii.

MAGUIRE, John Francis
Select committee on the Prisons and Prison Ministers Acts. Report, 30 May 1870. 1870 (259) viii; (CP Prisons, 17).

Select committee on the Tenure and Improvement of Land (Ireland) Act. Report, 23 June 1865. 1865 (402) xi.

MAHON, *Vct.* SEE:
Stanhope, C., *3rd E. Stanhope.*

MAINSTY, Henry, *Sir*
Harwich election petition trial. Judgement and proc. 8 June 1880. 1880 (227) lviii.

MAINWARING, William
Committee on petition for money to complete the repairs of St. Margaret's Church, Westminster. Report, 20 May 1802. 1801/2 (89) ii.

MAITLAND, Edward Francis
Select committee on the Offences Against the Person *etc* Bill. Report, 7 May 1861. 1861 (240) xiv.

MAITLAND, Frederick Henry, *13th E. Lauderdale*
Joint select committee on electric and cable railways in the Metropolis. Report, 23 May 1892. HL 1892 (126) x; HC repr. 1892 (215) xii.

MAITLAND, James, *8th E. Lauderdale*
Committee (HL) on the London Bridge Approaches Bill
    Min. of ev. 1 June 1829. HL 1829 (83) cclix.
    Appendix. HL 1829 (83) cclx.

MAITLAND, Thomas
H.M. sole and only master printers in Scotland. SEE: Rutherford, Andrew.

MAITLAND, Thomas, *11th E. Lauderdale*
Committee on turret ships. Report, 28 June 1865. 1866 (87) xlvii. Admiralty.

MAJENDIE, Vivian Dering
Inquiry into the suitability of the existing position of the gunpowder magazines on the River Mersey. Report, 24 June 1890. 1890 C.6169 xxvii; (TI Explosives, 2). Home Department.

Report on the necessity for the amendment of the law relating to gunpowder and other explosives. 16 May 1872. 1872 C.977 lii; (TI Explosives, 2). Home Department.

MAJOR, James
Commission of inquiry into the state of the municipal affairs of the Borough of Belfast
    Report. 1859, session 1 [2470] xii; repr. 1859, session 2 [2470] x.
    Min. of ev. and plans. 1859, session 2 [2526] x.

MALCOLM, E.D.
Templeton Mills disaster inquiry commission. Report, 23 Jan 1890. 1890 C.5921 xxvii. Scottish Office.

MALLISON, William Henry
Committee on his petition. SEE: Whitbread, Samuel.

MALMESBURY, E. SEE:
Harris, James Edward, *2nd E. Malmesbury* (1778-1841)

MALMESBURY, *E.* SEE: (continued)
Harris, James Howard, *3rd E. Malmesbury* (1807-1889)
Harris, Edward James, *4th E. Malmesbury* (1842-1899).

MANBY, George William
Committee on apparatus for saving lives of ship-wrecked seamen
1814. SEE: Rose, George.
1823. SEE: Curwen, J.C.

MANN, Andrew
Report of the special inspectors appointed to inquire into the circumstances attending the loss of the steam ship 'City of Philadelphia', 26 Dec 1854. 1854/5 (45) xlvi. Board of Trade.

MANNERS, *L.* SEE:
Manners-Sutton, John Thomas, *2nd Bn. Manners.*

MANNERS, John, *Lord*
Manners, John James Robert, *Lord.*

MANNERS, John
Commission on accommodation of public departments
Report, 18 May 1868. 1867/8 (281) lviii.
Sub-committee on the concentration of the public offices. Report, 9 April 1867. 1867/8 (281-I) lviii. Treasury.

Select committee on mortmain. Report, 24 July 1844. 1844 (536) x.

MANNERS, John Henry, *5th D. Rutland*
Sub-committee of the Wellington military memorial committee. Report, 14 July 1839. 1846 (553) xliii.

MANNERS, John James Robert, *Lord*
Royal commission on copyright
Report, 24 May 1878. 1878 C.2036 xxiv.
Analysis and index of ev. HL 1878/9 C.2245 xxxvi.

Select committee on the Court of Probate, *etc* (Acquisition of Site) Bill. Min. of ev. 14 April 1859. 1859, session 1 (220) iii.

Select committee on the Factory Acts Extension and the Hours of Labour Regulation Bills. Special report, 9 July 1867. 1867 (429) ix; (IR Factories, 2).

Select committee on H.C. arrangements. SEE: Headlam, Thomas Emerson.

MANNERS-SUTTON, Charles, *Archbp. of Canterbury, 1805-1828*
Select committee (HL) on laws relative to marriage. Report, 13 May 1823. HL 1823 (33) cliii.

MANNERS-SUTTON, John Henry Thomas
Commission on local charges upon shipping. SEE: Bethune, Charles Ramsay Drinkwater.

Select committee on game laws
Report (1845). 1845 (602) xiii; repr. 1846 (463-I) ix, pt.1.
Report (1846). 6 July 1846. 1846 (463-II) ix, pts. 1 and 2.

Select committee on the Parish Constables Bill. Proc. 20 July 1842. 1842 (470) xiv.

MANNERS-SUTTON, John Thomas, *2nd Bn. Manners*
Select committee on bleaching and dyeing works
1st report, 6 July 1857. 1857, session 2 (151) xi.
2nd report, 28 July 1857. 1857, session 2 (211) xi; (IR Children's Employment, 12).

MANNING, William
Committee on the coal trade
Report, 23 June 1800. CJ Reports, vol.10, p.538; (Reps., 1731-1800, no.161, vol.26).
Report, 31 Dec 1800. CJ Reports, vol.10, p.640; (Reps., 1731-1800, no.161A, vol.26).

Select committee on the Camelford election. SEE: Langton, W.G.

Select committee on marine insurance. Report, 18 April 1810. 1810 (226) iv; repr. 1824 (323) vii.

MANSFIELD, John
Select committee on framework knitters petition. Report, 1 April 1819. 1819 (193) v.

MANSFIELD, William, *1st Vct. Sandhurst*
Committee on the accidents at the Royal Gunpowder Factory, Waltham Abbey on 13 December 1893 and 7 May 1894
1st report, 25 April 1894. 1894 C.7370 xx.
Report, 12 July 1894. 1894 C.7486 xx; (TI Explosives, 2). War Office.

Committee on the entrance examinations (in non-military subjects) of candidates for commission in the Army. Report, 27 April 1894. 1894 C.7373 xix. War Office.

Select committee (HL) on Metropolitan hospitals, *etc*
Report, 31 July 1890. HL 1890 (238) xii; HC repr. 1890 (392) xvi.
2nd report, 18 July 1891. HL 1890/1 (252) xi; HC repr. 1890/1 (457) xiii.
3rd report, 13 June 1892. HL 1892 (93) ix; HC repr. 1892 (321) xiii; (Health, 12-14).

MANSFIELD, William Rose, *Sir*
Commission on the provision of a government paper currency. Report, 4 Oct 1866. 1867/8 (148) xlix. India Office.

MAPLETON, Henry
Report on the sanitary condition of the Army of the East. 5 Feb 1855. 1857/8 (425) xxxvii. War Office.

MAR, *Lord* [Peerage claim]. SEE:
Freeman-Mitford, J.T.

Select committee on restoration of Earldom. SEE: Palmer, R.

MARCH, *E.* SEE:
Gordon-Lennox, Charles Henry, *6th D. Richmond* (1818-1903)
Gordon-Lennox, Charles Henry, *7th D. Richmond* (1845-1928).

MARCHMONT, *Lord* [Peerage claim]. SEE:
Cooper, C.A.

MARINDIN, Francis Arthur, *Sir*
Committee on the system of ventilation of tunnels on the Metropolitan Railway. Report, 1898 C.8684 xlv. Board of Trade.

Report on inspection of Thornton Junction Station, North British Railway. 1 Aug 1899. 1899 (315) lxxxvi. Board of Trade.

MARJORIBANKS, Edward, *2nd Bn. Tweedsmouth*
Committee on the condition of the Scottish mussel and bait beds. Report, 5 March 1889. 1889 C.5660 xxii. Scottish Office.

Interdepartmental committee on Post Office establishments

Report, 15 Dec 1896. 1897 (121) xliv.
Ev. 1897 (163) xliv; (Posts and Telegraphs, 6-7). Treasury.

Select committee on harbour accommodation. Report, 13 July 1883. 1883 (255) xiv.

Select committee on harbour accommodation. Report, 23 July 1884. 1884 (290) xii.

Select committee on sea fisheries. Report, 17 Aug 1893. 1893/4 (377) xv; (Fisheries, 7).

MARKHAM, William Orlando
Report on the Metropolitan workhouses. 18 Jan 1867. 1867 (18) lx. Poor Law Board.

MARLBOROUGH, D. SEE:
Spencer-Churchill, John Winston, *7th D. Marlborough* (1822-1883).

MARMYON, *Lord* [Peerage claim]. SEE:
Cooper, C.A.

MARRIOTT, William Thackeray, *Sir*
Investigation on the inspection and reception of leather at the Ordnance Store Department at Woolwich. Report, 23 Nov 1887. 1888 C.5282 xxv. War Office.

Select committee on emigration and immigration of foreigners. Report, 27 July 1888. 1888 (305) xi; (Emigration, 8).

Select committee on emigration and immigration of foreigners. Report, 8 Aug 1889. 1889 (311) x; (Emigration, 8).

Select committee on the Irish Society's and City Companies' Irish estates. Report, 30 July 1889. 1889 (290) xi.

Select committee on Sunday postal labour. Report, 10 Aug 1887. 1887 (274) xii.

MARRYATT, Joseph
Committee on the petition of Messrs. Phelps, Troward and Bracebridge respecting the Strand Bridge Bill. Report, 19 May 1813. 1812/3 (211) iv.

MARSHAM, Charles, *Vct.*
Select committee on petitions complaining of an undue election and return for the County of Middlesex. Report, 9 and 11 July 1804. 1803/4 (171) ii.

MARSHAM, Charles, *3rd E. Romney*
Select committee (HL) on charging of entailed estates for railways. Report. HL 1863 (48) xxxiv; HC repr. 1863 (209) vii.

Select committee (HL) on the Great Southern and Western and Limerick and Castleconnell Railways, *etc* Bill. Min. of ev. 28 March 1862. HL 1862 (0. 8-30) xxxiv; HC repr. 1862 (483) ix.

MARSON, James F.
Report on the vaccination of sheep. 8 June 1864. 1864 [3362] l. Privy Council.

MARTEN, Alfred
Select committee on the Parliamentary and Municipal Registration Bill. Report, 3 June 1878. 1878 (212) xiii.

MARTEN, Philip Wykenham
Select committee on the Parliamentary and Municipal Registration Bill. Report, 31 July 1877. 1877 (381) xv.

MARTIN, Francis Offley
Report on Sir John Port's hospital in Etwall and school in Repton, County of Derby. 19 July 1865. 1867 (287) liv. Charity Commission.

Report on the Tancred charities. 5 Nov 1866. 1867 (139) liv. Charity Commission.

MARTIN, George
Committee on his petition. SEE: Tierney, George.

MARTIN, Henry
Select committee on sinecure offices. SEE: Bankes, Henry.

MARTIN, James Ranald
Report on the capabilities of the Metropolitan workhouses for the reception and treatment of cholera cases. 19 Jan 1848. 1847/8 [917] li; (HE Infectious Diseases, 1). Poor Law Board.

MARTIN, R. Montgomery
Minute on the British position and prospects in China. 19 April 1845. 1857, session 1 (148) xii. Colonial Office.

Report on the island of Chusan. 30 Aug 1849. 1857, session 1 (148) xii. Colonial Office.

Report on the island of Hong Kong. 22 July 1844. 1857, session 1 (148) xii. Colonial Office.

MARTIN, Samuel
Trial of the Beverley election petition. Min. of ev. 18 March 1869. 1868/9 (90) xlviii.

Trial of the Bradford election petition. Min. of ev. 19 Feb 1869. 1868/9 (28) xlviii.

Trial of the Norwich election petition. Min. of ev. 22 Jan 1869. 1868/9 (8) xlix.

MARTIN, Thomas Byam
Commission upon the subject of harbours of refuge. Report, 7 Aug 1844. 1845 [611] xvi. Treasury.

Committee of flag officers on the validity of claims to a Naval War Medal. Report, Nov 1850. 1851 (24) xxxiii. Admiralty.

Committee of inquiry into the expediency of diminishing the present quantity of spirits in the Royal Navy. Report, 30 Jan 1850. 1850 [1174] xxxv. Admiralty.

Report on the harbour of refuge to be constructed in Dover Bay. 28 Jan 1846. 1847 [821] xvi. Admiralty.

MASKELYNE, Mervin Herbert Nevil Story SEE:
Story-Maskelyne, M.H.N.

MASSEY, *Lord* [Peerage claim]. SEE:
Freeman-Mitford, J.T.

MASSEY, William Nathaniel
Royal commission on contagious diseases. Report. 2 pts. 1871 C.408 xix; (HE Infectious Diseases, 5).

Select committee on the Contagious Diseases Acts. Report, 30 July 1879. 1878/9 (323) viii; (HE Infectious Diseases, 6).

Select committee on the Contagious Diseases Acts. Report, 10 March 1880. 1880 (114) viii. Report, 26 July 1880. 1880 (308) viii; (HE Infectious Diseases, 6).

Select committee on the Contagious Diseases Acts. Report, 28 July 1881. 1881 (351) viii; (HE Infectious Diseases, 6).

MASSEY, William Nathaniel (continued)
Select committee on Burgh and Populous Places (Scotland) Gas Supply Bill
Report, 6 April 1876. 1876 (161) viii.
2nd report, 30 May 1876. 1876 (254) viii.

Select committee on seat of Under Secretary of State. 1st and 2nd reports, 22 and 27 April 1864. 1864 (226) x.

MASTER OF ROLLS
1836 Lord Langdale
1852 Lord John Romilly
1873 George Jessel, *Sir*
1883 William Brett, *Lord Esher*
1897 Nathaniel Lindley, *Sir*
1900 Lord Alverstone

MATHER, W.
Report on technical education in the U.S.A. for the Royal Commission on Technical Instruction. 1884 C.3081-I xxx.

Notes on technical instruction in Russia for the Royal Commission on Technical Instruction. 28 Aug 1884. 1884 C.3981-II xxxi.

MATTHEW, James Charles, *Sir*
Evicted tenants, Ireland, Commission. Report, 25 Feb 1893. 1893/4 C.6935 xxxi. Irish Secretary's Office.

MATTHEW, T.P.
Medical and surgical history of the British Army which served in Turkey and the Crimea in the war against Russia, 1854-56
Vol.1: Military medical history of individual corps
Vol.2: History of disease; history of wounds and injuries. 2 pts. 1857/8 [2434] xxxviii, pts. 1 & 2. War Office.

MATTHEWS, George
Report on protestant dissenting ministers in Ireland. 28 June 1847. 1847/8 (458) xlix. Irish Secretary's Office.

MATTHEWS, Henry, *1st Vct. Llandaff*
Select committee on privilege. Report on the service of a writ on Mr. Sheehy in the outer lobby. 8 Dec 1888. 1888 (411) xvi.

Royal commission on Metropolitan water companies
1st report, 20 Dec 1898. 1899 C.9122 xli.
Final report, 30 Dec 1899. 1900 Cd.25 xxxviii.
Ev.
Vol.1 1900 Cd.45 xxxviii, pt.1.
Vol.2 1900 Cd.198 xxxviii, pt.2.
Appendix. 1900 Cd.108 xxxix.
Index to report. 1900 Cd.25 xxxviii.
Index to min. of ev. 1900 Cd.198 xxxviii.
Maps, plans and diagrams. 1900 Cd.267 xxxix.

MATTHEWS, J.
Referees to inquire into the charges of fraud, etc. made against the deputy surveyors of Holt Forest by Mr. Kennedy and Mr. Brown. Report, 15 April 1854. 1854 (244) lxvii. Treasury.

MAULE, Fox SEE:
Maule-Ramsay, Fox, *11th E. Dalhousie*.

MAULE-RAMSAY, Arthur George, *14th E. Dalhousie*
Select committee (HL) on the Burgh Police and Health (Scotland) Bill. Report, 20 July 1885. HL 1884/5 (189) vii.

MAULE-RAMSAY, Fox, *11th E. Dalhousie*
Commission on recruiting for the Army. Report, 31 Oct 1866. 1867 [3752] xv.

Committee on Sunday labour in the Post Office. Report, Dec 1871. 1872 C.485 xviii. Treasury.

Select committee on Army and Ordnance expenditure. Report, 21 July 1851. 1851 (564) vii; (Military and Naval, 4).

Select committee on the Kafir tribes. SEE: Labouchere, Henry.

Select committee on the militia estimates. Report, 27 July 1846. 1846 (525) xv.

Select committee on the militia estimates, 1847/8. Report, 23 June 1847. 1847 (553) viii.

Select committee on militia estimates, 1848/9. Report, 28 July 1848. 1847/8 (552) xvi.

Select committee on militia estimates, 1849/50. Report, 22 June 1849. 1849 (415) xii.

Select committee on militia estimates, 1850/1. Report, 9 July 1850. 1850 (530) xiii.

Select committee on railway bills classification, 1846. SEE: Wilson-Patten, John.

Select committee on the Supreme Court of Judicature in Scotland. Report, 28 May 1840. 1840 (332) xiv; (Legal Administration, 6).

MAULE-RAMSAY, John William, *13th E. Dalhousie*
Royal commission on trawl net and beam trawl fishing. Report. 1884/5 C.4324 xvi.

MAXWELL, Charles Francis
Report on the state of education in the country districts of Scotland. 1 March 1866. 1867 [3845-III] xxv; (Education, 14). Education commission, Scotland. SEE ALSO: Campbell, George Douglas, *8th D. Argyll*.

Statistical report on the state of education in the lowland country districts of Scotland. 1867 [3845-I] xxv; (Education, 14). Education Commission, Scotland. SEE ALSO: Campbell, George Douglas, *8th D. Argyll*.

MAXWELL, Herbert Eustace, *Sir*
Committee on the Crown rights in salmon fisheries in Scotland. Report, May 1890. 1890 C.6036 xxi. Scottish Office.

Departmental committee on the plague of field voles in Scotland. Report, 1892. 1893/4 C.6943 lxxiii. Board of Agriculture.

Report on the international Congress on Tuberculosis, Berlin, 24-27 May 1899. 1899 C.9368 xlv. Privy Council.

Royal commission on tuberculosis
Report, 4 April 1898. 1898 C.8824 xlix.
Min. of ev., appendix. 1898 C.8831 xlix.

Select committee on commons. Report, 14 April 1893. 1893/4 (177) x.

Select committee on the Fisheries Acts (Norfolk and Suffolk) Amendment Bill. SEE: Fitzgerald, Robert Uniacke Penrose, *Sir*.

Select committee on friendly societies. Report, 13 Nov 1888. 1888 (389) xii; (Insurance, 10).

Select committee on the Friendly Societies Act, 1875. Report, 6 Aug 1889. 1889 (304) x; (Insurance, 10).

Select committee on the Industrial and Provident

Societies Bill. Report, 13 July 1893. 1893/4 (330) xii; (Insurance, 10).

Select committee on national provident insurance. Report, 16 July 1885. 1884/5 (270) x; (Insurance, 9).

Select committee on national provident insurance. Report, 21 June 1886. 1886, session 1 (208) xi; (Insurance, 9).

Select committee on national provident insurance. Report, 2 Aug 1887. 1887 (257) xi; (Insurance, 9).

Solway white fishery commission. Report, March 1892. 1892 C.6798 xlvii. Scottish Office.

MAXWELL, John
Select committee on hand-loom weavers' petitions. Report, 4 Aug 1834. 1834 (556) x.

Select committee on hand-loom weavers' petitions Report, 1 July 1835. 1835 (341) xii.
Analysis of the evidence, 1834-35. 10 Aug 1835. 1835 (492) xiii; (IR Textiles, 7).

MAXWELL, John Hall
Report of the Highland Agricultural Society of Scotland on the agricultural statistics of small holdings in Scotland, and agricultural statistics of Orkney, 1854. 20 June 1855. 1854/5 (343) xlvii. Board of Trade.

Report of the Highland Agricultural Society of Scotland on the agricultural statistics of Scotland, 1854. 23 Jan 1855. 1854/5 [1876] xlvii. Board of Trade.

Report of the Highland and Agricultural Society of Scotland on the agricultural statistics of Scotland, 1855. 11 Dec 1855 and 23 Jan 1856. 1856 (2) lix. Board of Trade.

MAXWELL, William Sterling
Committee on the annual grant in aid of meteorological observations. Report. 1877 C.1638 xxxiii. Treasury.

MAY, George Augustus Chichester
Royal commission on registration of deeds and assurances in Ireland
1st report, 12 Aug 1879. 1878/9 C.2443 xxxi.
2nd report, 30 Oct 1880. 1881 C.2818 xxx.

MAY, Samuel W.
Potteries committee of inquiry. Report, July 1893. 1893/4 C.7240 xvii. (IR Factories, 29). Home Department.

MAYERS, William S. Frederick
Report and papers on the famine in the northern provinces of China. 30 Oct 1877. 1878 C.1957, C.2052, C.2107 lxxv. Foreign Office.

MAYNE, Richard
Commission on the constabulary in Ireland. SEE: Knatchbull-Hugessen, E.H.

MAYO, E. SEE:
Bourke, Richard Southwell, *6th E. Mayo.*

[Peerage claim]. SEE: Cooper, C.A.

MAYO, John J.
Committee on the Royal Naval reserve regulations. Report, 6 Jan 1870. 1870 C.46 xii. Admiralty and Board of Trade.

MEADE, R.J., Sir
Commission on the administration of the Baroda state. Report, 1874. 1875 C.1203 lvi. India Office.

MEADE-KING, William Oliver
Departmental committee on conditions of work in wool-sorting and other kindred trades (dangerous trades (anthrax) committee). Report, 7 April 1897. 1897 C.8506 xvii; (IR Factories, 31). Home Department.

MEADOWS, C. SEE:
Medows, C.

MEADOWS, John G.
Report of the select committee on the Bahamas Assembly on Rev. Capern's petition on seizure of packages directed to him. 5 May 1853. 1854 (362) xliii. Colonial Office.

MEAGHER, Thomas
Select committee on postal arrangements (Waterford, *etc*). Report, 31 July 1855. 1854/5 (445) xi.

MEATH, *Lord* SEE:
Brabazon, John Chambre, *10th E. Meath* (1772-1851)
Brabazon, William, *11th E. Meath* (1803-1929).

[Peerage claim]. SEE: Giffard, H.S.

MEDOWS, Charles Pierrepoint. SEE:
Pierrepont, Charles, *1st E. Manvers.*

MEDWAY, *Lord* SEE:
Gathorne-Hardy, John Stewart, *2nd E. Cranbrook.*

MELBOURNE, *Lord* SEE:
Lamb, William, *2nd Vct. Melbourne* (1799-1848)
Lamb, Frederick James, *3rd Vct. Melbourne* (1782-1853).

MELDON, Charles Henry
Select committee on the Births and Deaths Registration (Ireland) Bill. Report, 23 June 1880. 1880 (243) viii.

MELLISH, William
Committee on acts relating to fanners, *etc.* Report, 15 July 1807. 1807 (40) ii.

MELLOR, John, *Sir*
Report of the Metropolitan Buildings Act. 14 Dec 1850. 1851 (114) xlviii. Commission of HM Woods.

MELLOR, John William, *Sir*
Select committee on the Clare election petition. Min. of ev. 18 June 1860. 1860 (392) xi.

Committee on the distribution of the grant in aid for university colleges, G.B. Report, 20 May 1897. *In:* 1897 (245) lxx. Treasury.

Select committee on the Tithe Rent Charge (Extraordinary) Amendment Bill. Report, 7 June 1886. 1886, session 1 (181) xii.

Trial of the Launceston election petition. Ev. and judgement. 30 June 1874. 1874 (250) lii.

MELROSE, *Lord* SEE:
Baillie, Thomas, *9th E. Haddington* (1780-1858)
Baillie-Hamilton, George, *10th E. Haddington* (1802-1870)
Baillie-Hamilton-Arden, George, *11th E. Haddington* (1827-1917)

MELVILLE, *Lord* SEE:
Dundas, Henry, *3rd Vct. Melville.*

MEREWETHER, Charles George
Royal commission on corrupt practices in the Borough of Macclesfield. Report, 22 March 1881. 1881 C.2853 xliii.

METHUEN, Frederick Henry Paul, *2nd Bn. Methuen*
Commission on regulations for a constant supply of water to the Metropolis. Min. of proc. 1872. 1873 C.679 xxxviii. Board of Trade.

MIDLETON, *Lord* SEE:
Broderick, William St. John Freemantle, *1st E. Midleton.*

[Peerage claim]. SEE: Freeman-Mitford, J.T.

MILES, Philip William Skyner
Select committee on Halifax and Boston mails. Report, 3 Aug 1846. 1846 (563) xv.

MILNES, Richard Monckton
Second special committee of the Council of the School of Design on the management of the School. 1847 [850] lxii; (IR Design, 3). Board of Trade. SEE ALSO: Shaw-Lefevre, G.J.

MILES, William
Select committee on the Clare election petition
 Report, 9 June 1853. 1852/3 (587) ix.
 Min. of ev. 10 June 1853. 1852/3 (595) ix.

Select committee on county rates in Ireland. Report, 13 July 1858. 1857/8 (420) xiii.

Select committee on the Dartmouth election. Report, 12 April 1853. 1852/3 (322) xii.

Select committee on the Wigton Burghs election petition. Report, 6 April 1853. 1852/3 (351) xix.

MILES, William Augustus
Report on hand-loom weavers in the West of England and in Wales. 16 March 1839. 1840 [220] xxiv; (IR Textiles, 9).

MILLER, Taverner John
Select committee on the London (City) Traffic Regulation Bill. SEE: Jolliffe, William, *Sir.*

MILLS, Arthur
Select committee on colonial military expenditure. Report, 11 July 1861. 1861 (423) xiii.

MILLTOWN, *E.* SEE:
Leeson, Joseph, *4th E. Milltown* (1799-1866)
Leeson, Joseph Henry, *5th E. Milltown* (1829-1871)
Leeson, Edward Nugent, *6th E. Milltown* (1835-1890)
Leeson, Henry, *7th E. Milltown* (1837-1891)

MILNE, Alexander, *Sir*
Committee on the rank, pay and position of medical officers of the Navy and Army. Report, 8 Feb 1866. 1866 (515) lx. Admiralty *and* War Office.

Special committee on the alterations requisite in the original plan for the defence of Spithead. Report, 15 July 1864. 1864 [3387], [3387-I] xxxv. War Office.

MILNE, Patrick
Select committee on corn laws. Report, 26 July 1814. 1813/4 (339) iii.

MILNER-GIBSON, Thomas SEE:
Gibson, Thomas Milner.

MILNES, Richard Monckton
Select committee on consular service appointments. Report, 27 July 1858. 1857/8 (482) viii; (GO Diplomatic Service, 1).

Select committee on diplomatic service. Report, 23 July 1861. 1861 (459) vi; (GO Diplomatic Service, 2).

MILNES-GASKELL, James SEE:
Gaskell, James Milnes.

MILROY, Gavin
Report on cholera epidemic in Jamaica, 1850/51. July 1852. 1854 (235) xliii. Colonial Office.

Report on leprosy and yaws in the West Indies. 30 Dec 1872. 1873 C.729 l. Colonial Office.

MILTON, *Lord* SEE:
Wentworth-FitzWilliam, Charles William, *5th E. Fitz-William.*

MINTO, *E.* SEE:
Elliot-Murray-Kynynmound, Gilbert, *2nd E. Minto* (1782-1859)
Elliot-Murray-Kynynmound, William Hugh, *3rd E. Minto* (1814-1891)
Elliot-Murray-Kynynmound, Gilbert John, *4th E. Minto* (1845-1914)

MITCHELL, James
Report on hand-loom weavers of the East of England. 24 April 1839. 1840 (43-I) xxiii; (IR Textiles, 9).

MITCHELL, Thomas
Report on the present state of trade between G.B. and Russia. 4 Dec 1865. 1866 [3603] lxxii. Foreign Office.

MITCHELL, Thomas Alexander
Select committee on customs
 1st report, 14 April 1851. 1851 (209) xi, pt.1.
 2nd report. Min. of ev. 1851 (604) xi, pts. 1 and 2
 Appendix. 1851 (604) xi, pts. 3 and 4.

Select committee on customs. Report, 21 June 1852. 1852 (498) viii, pts. 1 and 2.

MITFORD, Bertram
Commission on the duties, salaries and .emoluments in courts in Ireland. SEE: Kemmis, Henry.

MITFORD, Robert Sidney
Departmental committee on the education and moral instruction of prisoners
 Report, 5 May 1896. 1896 C.8154 xliv.
 Min. of ev. 1896 C.8155 xliv; (CP Prisons, 20). Home Department.

MOFFAT, George
Select committee on the Bankruptcy Act. Report, 22 July 1864. 1864 (512) v.

Select committee on the Bankruptcy Act. Report, 21 March 1865. 1865 (144) xii.

Select committee on charges on foreign trade (Customs Act, 1860). Report, 18 July 1862. 1862 (429) xii; (National Finance, 4).

MOLESWORTH, *Vct.* [Peerage claim]. SEE:
Cooper, C.A.

MOLESWORTH, Guilford Lindsey, *Sir*
Report on the Uganda Railway. 28 March 1899. (Africa, no.5, 1899). 1899 C.9331 lxiii. Colonial Office.

MOLESWORTH, William, Sir

Select committee on Downing Street Public Offices Extension Bill. Report, 10 July 1855. 1854/5 (382) vii.

Select committee on Mr. Goldsworthy Gurney's case. Report, 17 July 1834. 1834 (438) xi; (Transport, 1).

Select committee on the Metropolitan Buildings Bill. Proc. 29 June 1855. 1854/5 (349) vii.

Select committee on small arms. Report, 12 May 1854. 1854 (236) xviii.

Select committee on transportation. Report, 14 July 1837. 1837 (518) xix; (CP Transportation, 2).

Select committee on transportation. Report, 3 Aug 1838. 1837/8 (669) xxii; (CP Transportation, 3).

Select committee on the Westminster Bridge Bill. Min. of ev. 16 June 1853. 1852/3 (622) xxxix.

Standing committee on ventilation and lighting of the H.C. Report, 6 June 1853. 1852/3 (570) xxxiv.

MONACUTE, Lord [Peerage claim]. SEE: Freeman-Mitford, J.T.

MONAHAN, James Henry

Select committee on the Administration of Justice (Metropolitan Districts) Bill. Report, 27 June 1849. 1849 (432-II) viii.

Select committee on the Bankrupt Law Consolidation Bill. Report, 24 July 1849. 1849 (551) viii.

MONCK, Vct. [Peerage claim]. SEE: Cooper, C.A.

MONCK, Charles Stanley, 4th Vct. Monck

Commission on the condition of the civil service in Ireland

Report on the Local Government Board and the General Register Office. 14 Dec 1872. 1873 C.789 xxii.

Report on the Dublin Metropolitan Police. 29 Nov 1872. 1873 C.788 xxii.

Report on the Royal Irish Constabulary. 7 Dec 1872. 1873 C.831 xxii.

Report on resident magistrates. 7 Dec 1872. 1874 C.923 xvi. Treasury.

Commission of inquiry on the King's Inns, Dublin in respect of sums received on the admission of attorneys and solicitors as 'deposits for chambers', etc. Report, 5 Feb 1872. 1872 C.486 xx.

Committee on barrack accommodation for the Army. Report, 18 June 1855. 1854/5 (405) xxxii. War Department.

Royal commission on inland navigation in Ireland. Report, 8 Feb 1882. 1882 C.3173 xxi.

MONCKTON-MILNES, R. SEE: Milnes, Richard Monckton.

MONCRIEFF, Bn. SEE: Moncrieff, James, 1st Bn. Moncrieff.

MONCRIEFF, A.

Committee on letter with reference to his invention for mounting guns. SEE: Baring, Thomas George, 2nd Bn. Northbrook.

MONCRIEFF, J.

Report on the administration of the law in the Justice of the Peace Court held in the City of Glasgow. 25 May 1841. 1841, session 2 (9) ii. Scottish Office.

MONCRIEFF, James, 1st Bn. Moncrieff

Royal commission on endowed institutions in Scotland

1st report, 15 Sept 1879. 1880 C.2493 xxiv.

Report. 15 Nov 1880. 1881 C.2768 xxxvi.

2nd report, 30 Dec 1880. 1881 C.2790 xxxvi.

3rd report, 30 July 1881. 1881 C.3076 xxxvi. Education Department, Privy Council Office.

Select committee (HL) on claims of peerage, etc. Report, 12 June 1882. HL 1882 (128) vii.

Select committee on Leith Harbour and Docks Bill. Min. of ev. 27 June 1860. 1860 (412) xv.

MONK, Charles James

Select committee on the Partnerships Bill. Report, 23 May 1882. 1882 (204) xii.

MONK BRETTON, Bn. SEE:

Dodson, John George, 1st Bn. Monk Bretton (1825-1897)

Dodson, John William, 2nd Monk Bretton (1869-1933)

MONKSWELL, Bn. SEE:

Collier, Robert, 2nd Bn. Monkswell.

MONSELL, William

Select committee on contracts for public departments. Report, 15 July 1856. 1856 (362) vii.

Select committee on ordnance. Report, 25 July 1862. 1862 (448) vi.

Select committee on ordnance. Report, 23 July 1863. 1863 (487) xi.

Select committee on the Piccadilly and Park Land New Road Bill. Min. of ev. 8 May 1865. 1865 (260) viii.

Select committee on Tramways (Ireland) Acts Amendment Bill. Report, 17 July 1866. 1866 (418) xi.

Select committee on the Wakefield election petition. Min. of ev. 29 July 1859. 1859, session 2 (126) iv.

MONSON, William John, Vct. Oxenbridge

Royal commission on horse breeding. SEE: Cavendish-Bentinck, William John Arthur Charles James, 6th D. Portland.

Select committee (HL) on the Jubilee service in Westminster Abbey. Reports, 9 and 20 July 1887. HL 1887 (114) (130) ix.

MONTAGU, Robert, Lord

Select committee on art union laws. Report, 7 June 1866. 1866 (332) vii; (ED Fine Arts, 6).

Select committee on the Metropolitan Foreign Cattle Market Bill

1st report, 24 April 1868. 1867/8 (227) xii.

2nd report, 12 May 1868. 1867/8 (261) xii.

3rd report, 28 May 1868. 1867/8 (303) xii.

Select committee on sewage (Metropolis). Report, 14 July 1864. 1864 (487) xiv; (UA Sanitation, 2).

Select committee on Sir John Port's Charity Bill. Min. of proc. 2 July 1867. 1867 (413) xiii.

Select committee on Tancred's Charities Bill. Min. of proc. 25 June 1867. 1867 (396) xiii.

MONTAGU-DOUGLAS-SCOTT, Walter Francis, 5th D. Buccleugh and 7th D. Queensferry

Commission of inquiry into the state of large towns and populous districts

1st report, 27 June 1844. 1844 [572] xvii.

2nd report, 3 Feb 1845. 1845 [602], [610] xviii.

MONTAGU-DOUGLAS-SCOTT, Walter Francis, 5th D.
Buccleugh and 7th D. Queensferry (continued)
Committee of the council of the British Association for the Advancement of Science on the best means of promoting scientific education in schools. Sept 1867. 1867/8 (137) liv. Privy Council.

Committee (HL) on the Glasgow, Paisley, Kilmarnock and Ayr Railway Bill. Min. of ev. 28 June 1837. HL 1837 (146) xviii.

Select committee (HL) on the Burial Acts. Report, 4 July 1856. HL 1856 (219) xxiv; HC repr. 1856 (367) vii.

Select committee (HL) on the condition of parochial schoolmasters in Scotland. Report, 7 Aug 1845. HL 1845 (112) xix.

Select committee (HL) on the Scottish Episcopal Clergy Disabilities Removal Bill. Report, 10 June 1864. HL 1864 (124) xxvii.

MONTEAGLE OF BRANDON, Bn. SEE:
Rice, Thomas Spring, *1st Bn. Monteagle*.

MONTEATH, A.M.
Note on the state of education in India, 1865-66. March 1867. 1867/8 (244) l. India Office. SEE ALSO: Grant, Alexander.

MONTEITH, Alexander E.
Commission on lunatic asylums in Scotland. Report, 1857, session 1 [2148] v; (HE Mental, 7).

MONTGOMERIE, Archibald William, 13th E. Eglinton
Select committee (HL) on the elections of the representative peers of Scotland. Report, 4 June 1847. HL 1847 (132) xxv; HL repr. 1868/9 (103) xxvii.

MONTGOMERY, James
Commission on the duties, salaries and emoluments in courts in Scotland
1st report: Court of Session. 31 May 1816. 1816 (419) viii.
2nd report: Court of Session (cont.) 31 Jan 1817. 1817 (3) ix.
3rd report: Sheriff and Commissary Courts. 11 Feb 1818. 1818 (16) x.
4th report: Inferior commissariat courts and courts of Admiralty. 6 April 1818. 1818 (157) x.
5th report: Court of Justiciary. 25 Jan 1819. 1819 (4) xi.
6th report: Court of Exchequer. 5 July 1819. 1819 (546) xi.
7th report: Court of Exchequer (cont.) 1 May 1820. 1820 (6) vii.
8th report: Office of Chancery. 1 May 1820. 1820 (7) vii.
9th report: Justice of Peace Courts. 3 July 1821. 1821 (729) x.
10th report: Office and Court of the Lord Lyon. 10 June 1822. 1822 (412) viii.
11th report: Burgh Courts. 17 July 1822. 1822 (558) viii.
12th report: Charges of agents or law practitioners before the inferior courts. 23 July 1822. 1822 (595) viii.

MONTHERMER, Lord [Peerage claim]. SEE:
Freeman-Mitford, J.T.

MONTROSE, D. [Peerage claim]. SEE:
Freeman-Mitford, J.T.

MOODY, Thomas
Remarks on J. Dougan's report on the state of captured Negroes at Tortola. 12 June 1827. 1826/7 (462) xxii; (Slave Trade, 72).

Remarks on Mr. John Dougan's report on captured Negroes at Tortola. 12 July 1828. 1828 (535) xxvi; (Slave Trade, 75). SEE ALSO: Dougan, John.

MOORE, Arthur William
Committee on the Training of Naval Medical Officers. Report, 29 May 1899. 1899 C.9515 lv. Admiralty.

MOORE, George
Committee of inquiry into the money order system of the Post Office. Report, 22 July 1876. 1877 (289) xxvii; (Post and Telegraphs, 4). Treasury.

MOORE, Peter
Committee on Mr. Bradbury's petition relative to machinery for engraving and etching. Report, 19 May 1818. 1818 (328) iii.

Committee on Mrs. Whitfield's petition. Report, 11 July 1814. 1813/4 (309) iii.

Committee on petitions of watchmakers of Coventry. Report, 11 July 1817. 1817 (504) vi.

Committee on poor houses and poor rates. Report, 26 March 1813. 1812/3 (113) iii; repr. 1813/4 (27) iv.

Committee on silk ribbon weavers petition
Report, 3 June 1818. 1818 (398) ix.
Min. of ev. 18 March 1818. 1818 (134) ix.
2nd report, 20 and 28 April and 8 May 1818. 1818 (211) (278) ix; (IR Textiles, 4).

Committee of the whole H.C. on the Camelford election. Min. of ev. 5 July 1819. 1819 (544) iv.

Committee of the whole H.C. on the Grampound bribery indictments. Min. of ev. 3 June to 5 July 1819. 1819 (388) iv.

Select committee on sewers in the Metropolis. Report, 10 July 1823. 1823 (542) v; (UA Sanitation, 1).

Select committee on laws relating to watchmakers. Report, 18 March 1818. 1818 (135) ix.

MOORSOM, W.S.
Report on the Bay of Balcary in the Solway Firth. 30 April 1846. 1846 (278) xlv. Admiralty.

MORE, Robert Jasper
Select committee on corn averages
Report, 31 July 1888. 1888 (312) x.
2nd report, 11 Dec 1888. 1888 (413) x.

Select committee on corn sales. Report, 17 July 1891. 1890/1 (347) xii.

Select committee on corn sales. Report, 16 June 1892. 1892 (279) xi.

Select committee on corn sales. Report, 15 May 1893. 1893/4 (220) xi.

MORE-O'FERRALL, Richard
Committee of the Board of Treasury on the estate of the late Samuel Troutbeck. Report, 5 June 1838. 1839 (28) xxx. Treasury.

Select committee on turnpike roads in Ireland. Report, 26 July 1832. 1831/2 (645) xvii.

MOREHEAD, W.A.
Commission sent to Ceylon on documents presented to the Select Committee on Ceylon, 1849.
Reports, 10 and 20 June 1850. 1851 (99) xxii.
Ev. 8 May 1851. 1851 (634) xxii. Colonial Office.

Commission to prepare a scheme for the amalgamation of the Supreme and Sudder courts [in Madras]. 1860 (199) lii. India Office.

MORGAN, George Osborne, *Sir*
Select committee on land titles and transfer. Report, 16 July 1878. 1878 (291) xv.

Select committee on land titles and transfer. Report, 24 June 1879. 1878/9 (244) xi.

Select committee on the Yorkshire Land Registries Bill and the Yorkshire Registries Bill. Report, 27 June 1884. 1884 (243) xv.

Standing committee on law. Bail (Scotland) Bill. Report, 7 June 1888. 1888 (208) ix.

Standing committee on law. County Courts Consolidation Bill. Report, 14 May 1888. 1888 (172) x.

Standing committee on law. Elections (Scotland) Corrupt and Illegal Practices Bill. Report, 9 June 1890. 1890 (215) xiii.

Standing committee on law. Employer's Liability for Inquiries to Workmen Bill. Report, 12 July 1888. 1888 (275) xii.

Standing committee on law. Housing of the Working Classes Bill. Report, 10 July 1890. 1890 (294) xiii.

Standing committee on law. Mortmain and Charitable Uses Bill. Report, 7 June 1888. 1888 (207) xii.

Standing committee on law. Pistols Bill. Report, 19 March 1895. 1895 (165) xii.

Standing committee on law. Places of Worship Enfranchisement Bill. Report, 23 March 1893. 1893/4 (132) xiii.

Standing committee on law. Summary Jurisdiction (Married Women) Bill. Report, 17 June 1895. 1895 (307) xiii; (Marriage and Divorce, 3).

Standing committee on trade. Factories and Workshops Bill. Report, 4 May 1891. 1890/1 (221) xii.

Standing committee on trade. Merchant Shipping (Pilotage) Bill. Report, 8 July 1889. 1889 (239) xi.

Standing committee on trade. Merchant Shipping (Tonnage) Bill. Report, 27 June 1889. 1889 (218) xi.

Standing committee on trade. Weights and Measures Bill. Report, 16 May 1889. 1889 (149) xvi.

MORLEY, *E.* SEE:
Parker, Albert Edmund, *3rd E. Morley.*

MORLEY, Arnold
Select committee on the Post Office (Acquisition of Sites) Bill. Report, 8 March 1893. 1893/4 (106) xiii.

Select committee on the telephone service. Report, 1 July 1895. 1895 (350) xiii; (Posts and Telegraphs, 8).

MORLEY, John
Select committee on Irish Society's and London Companies' Irish estates. Report, 24 July 1890. 1890 (322) xiv.

Select committee on the Irish Society's and London Companies' Irish estates. Report, 4 May 1891. 1890/1 (222) xii.

Select committee on the Land Acts, Ireland. Report, 20 Aug 1894. 1894 (310) xiii.

MORLEY, S.
Committee of the Commission on the state of popular education. Report, 5 May 1859. 1861 (410) xlviii; (Education, 8).

MORRIS, Arthur
Committee on petition on Westminster elections. SEE: Lockhart, J.I.

MORRISON, James
Select committee on Railway Acts enactments
Report, 7 Aug 1846. 1846 (590) xiv.
2nd report, 25 Aug 1846. 1846 (687) xiv; (Transport, 7).

MORPETH, *Lord* SEE:
Howard, G.W.F., *7th E. Carlisle.*

MORSHEAD, W.H.
Report on the death by starvation of Commander A.F. Gardiner and the whole party sent out by the Patagonian Missionary Society in Sept 1850, to Picton Island. 22 Jan 1852. 1852 (332) xxx. Admiralty.

MORTON, Alpheus Cleophas
Select committee on the Commission of the City of London (Baths and Wash houses) Bill. Report, 12 March 1895. 1895 (112) vii; (Health, 17).

MORTON, Charles
Commission on the estate of the registers of land rights in the counties and burghs of Scotland. Reports, July 1862 and Feb 1863. 1863 [3110] xv.

Departmental committee on the Register House Departments, Edinburgh, relating to the system of registration and searching in the Register of the Sasines. 3 Feb 1881. 1882 C.3377 xxi. Treasury.

MORTON, John Chalmers
Commission on preventing the pollution of rivers, 1868. SEE: Frankland, Edward.

MORTON, Thomas
Select committee on his patent slip. SEE: Cockburn, George, *Sir.*

MOSELEY, Henry
Report on the Kneller Hall training school. March 1855. 1854/5 [1957] xlii.

MOSLEY, Oswald, *Sir*
Select committee on the Coventry City election petition. Report, 16 April 1833. 1833 (188) viii.

Select committee on the re-committed report from the select committee on Fourdrinier's patent. Report, 16 June 1837. 1837 (405) xx. SEE ALSO: Mackinnon, William Alexander.

MOTT, Charles
Report on distress in Bolton relative to cases of destitution and death. 24 Sept 1841. 1841, session 2 (58) ii. Poor Law Commission.

Report of an inquiry into the administration of the Board of Guardians of Hartismere Union. Suffolk, 4 July 1838. 1837/8 (550) xxxviii. Poor Law Commission.

Report of the proc. of the Board of Guardians of the Keighley Union and of the magistrates interference therewith. 23 April 1842. 1842 (359) xxxv. Poor Law Commission.

Report on the state of the Macclesfield and Bolton Unions. 30 April 1841. 1846 (661) xxxvi. Poor Law Commission.

MOUAT, Frederick John
Report on the home and cottage system of training

MOUAT, Frederick John (continued)
and educating the children of the poor. 4 Feb 1878.
1878 (285) lx; (ED Poorer Classes, 7). Local Government Board.

MOUAT, James
Report on the organisation of the Russian medical
department and the sanitary state of their Crimean
hospitals. 15 May 1856. 1857, session 1 (135) ix.
War Office.

MOUNT, William George
Select committee on police and sanitary regulations
bills. Report, 17 July 1896. 1896 (305) xiii.

Select committee on police and sanitary regulations
bills. Special report, 22 July 1897. 1897 (336) xiii.

MOUNT-EDGCUMBE, E. SEE:
Edgcumbe, William Henry, *4th E. Mount-Edgcumbe.*

MOUNTGARRETT, Vct. [Peerage claim]. SEE:
Freeman-Mitford, J.T.

MOWBRAY, Lord [Peerage claim]. SEE:
Freeman-Mitford, J.T.

MOWBRAY, John Robert
Select committee on gas for the Metropolis. SEE:
Byng, George Henry Charles, *3rd E. Stafford.*

Select committee on the Great Yarmouth election
petition. Min. of ev. 23 March 1866. 1866 (140) xi.

MUDGE, Richard Z.
British commission on the north-eastern boundary
of the United States. Report, 16 April 1840. 1840
[257] xxxii.

MUDGE, T.
Select committee on his petition. SEE: Windham, W.

MUGGERIDGE, Richard Michaux
Commission appointed to inquire into the condition
of the frame-work knitters. Report, 20 Feb 1845.
1845 [609] [618] [641] xv.

Report on hand-loom weavers of Lancaster, Westmorland, Cumberland and part of the West Riding
of Yorkshire. 30 March 1839. 1840 [220] xxiv;
(IR Textiles, 9).

Report on home migration. July 1837. *In:* 1837
(546) xxxi.

Report on the linen and cotton manufacturers of
Ireland. 1839. 1840 (43-II) xxiii; (IR Textiles, 9).

MULGRAVE, E. SEE:
Phipps, George Augustus Constatine, *2nd M. Normanby.*

MULOCK, W.B.
Bombay factory commission. Report, 6 Jan 1885.
1888 (321) lxxvii. India Office.

MULVANY, William T.
Preliminary examination of the country between
the rivers Shannon and Erne, with a view to the formation of a proposed junction canal. 11 March 1839.
1839 [193] xxviii. Commission for improvment of
the River Shannon.

MUNDELLA, Anthony John
Departmental committee on poor law schools
Report, 28 Feb 1896. 1896 C.8027 xliii
Min.of ev. 1896 C.8032 xliii

Appendix. 1896 C.8033 xliii; (ED Poorer Classes,
8). Local Government Board.

Select committee on perpetual pensions. Report,
29 July 1887. 1887 (248) xi; (GO Civil Service, 12).

Select committee on petroleum. Report, 27 July
1894. 1894 (244) xiv.

Select committee on petroleum. Report, 23 July
1896. 1896 (311) xii.

Select committee on petroleum. Report, 9 July 1897.
1897 (309) xiii.

Select committee on petroleum, 1898. SEE: Collings,
Jesse.

Select committee on school board elections; voting.
Report, 17 July 1885. 1884/5 (275) xi.

Trade and treaties committee
1st report, 24 Jan 1891. 1890/1 C.6286 lxxviii.
3rd report, 24 April 1891. 1890/1 C.6349 lxxviii.
7th report, 29 Jan 1892. 1892 C.6641 lxxii.
9th report, 11 March 1892. 1892 C.6648 lxxii.
Board of Trade.
(2nd, 4th-6th, 8th reports not printed).

MUNTZ, George Frederick
Select committee on postage label stamps. Report,
21 May 1852. 1852 (386) xv.

Select committee on the ship 'Novello'. Report,
13 July 1853. 1852/3 (748) xxxix.

Select committee on strangers and divisions. Report,
27 May 1853. 1852/3 (525) xxxiv.

MUNTZ, Philip Henry
Select committee on the Railway Rolling Stock (Dis-
traint) Bill. Report, 12 July 1872. 1872 (303) xii.

MURCHINSON, Roderick I., Sir
Commission on coal in the U.K. Committee E. Report:
Statistics of production, consumption and export of
coal. 1871 C.435-II xviii; (FP Coal Trade, 4).

MURCHISON, Charles
Commission on the condition and organisation of
Naval hospitals. Report, July 1869. 1868/9 (343)
xxxviii. Admiralty.

MURDOCH, T.W. CLINTON, Sir
Committee of inquiry on the Colonial Land and
Emigration Office. Report, 10 Aug 1853. 1854 [1715]
xxvii. Treasury.

Report of the colonial land and emigration commission
on the application that Bristol should be made a
government emigration port. 13 Jan 1855. 1854/5
(523) xvii; (Emigration, 23).

Report on the subject of emigration. 5 Aug 1870.
1871 C.296 xlvii; (Emigration, 24). Colonial Office.

MURE, William
Commission of inquiry into the state of the universities of Aberdeen. Report, 1858. 1857/8 [2368]
xx.

Select committee on the National Gallery. Report,
4 Aug 1853. 1852/3 (867) xxxv; (ED Fine Arts, 4).

MURPHY, James
Commission of inquiry into the riots and disturbances
in the City of Londonderry, 1869. Report, 30 Nov
1869. 1870 C.5* xxxii; (CP Civil Disorder, 7). Irish
Secretary's Office.

MURPHY, Shirley F.
Inquiry on the immediate sanitary requirements of the parish of St. Mary, Rotherhithe. Report, 19 March 1889. 1889 C.5688 lxv; (Health, 11). Home Department.

MURRAY, A. Graham
Royal commission on the colonisation of Canada of crofters from the western Highlands and Islands of Scotland. SEE: Bruce, Alexander Hugh, *6th Bn. Balfour of Burleigh.*

MURRAY, Augustus William
Commission on the outbreak of yellow fever in the garrison at Demerara in 1866. Report, 23 May 1867. 1867 (554) xli. War Office.

MURRAY, Charles Adolphus, *7th E. Dunmore*
Select committee (HL) on the Locomotives Bill. Report, 13 July 1871. HL 1871 (256) viii.

MURRAY, D.
International code of signals committee
    Interim report, 15 Jan 1889. 1889 C.5695 lxix.
    2nd interim report, July 1892. 1892 C.6836 lxxi.
    3rd and final report, Sept 1896. 1897 C.8354 lxxviii.
    Board of Trade. SEE ALSO: Collinson, R.

MURRAY, Herbert
Committee on an invention of Mr. Dillon for simplifying the Registry of Deeds, Ireland. SEE: Longfield, M.

MURRAY, John Archibald
Select committee on King's printers' patent, Scotland
    Report, 12 July 1837. 1837 (511) xiii.
    Report, 3 Aug 1838. 1837/8 (670) xxiii.

Select committee on the Roxburghshire election petition. Min. of ev. poll books, suppl. 21 and 27 Feb 1838. 1837/8 (152) xii.

MURRAY, Patrick, *Sir*
Select committee on East India Company. SEE: Wallace, Thomas.

Select committee on mail coach exemption. Report, 8 June 1811. 1801/1 (212) iii.

MURRAY-KYNYMOUND, G.E. SEE:
Elliott-Murray-Kynymound, Gilbert, *2nd E. Minto.*

MUSGRAVE, Thomas, *Archbp. of York,* **1847-69**
Commission of subdivision of parishes.
    1st report, 27 July 1849. 1849 (582) xxii.
    Min. of ev. 1849. 1854 (0.4) lxix.
    2nd report, 3 May 1850. 1850 [1224] xx.
    3rd report, 14 March 1855. 1854/5 [1922] xv.

NAAS, *Bn.* **SEE:**
Bourke, Richard Southwell, *6th E. Mayo.*

NAIRNE, *Lord* [Peerage claim]. **SEE:**
Freeman-Mitford, J.T.

NAPIER and ETTRICK, *Bn.* **SEE:**
Napier, Francis, *9th Bn. Napier.*

NAPIER, Charles, *Sir*
Select committee on district asylums, Metropolis. Report, 12 June 1846. 1846 (388) vii.

NAPIER, Francis, *9th Bn. Napier and Ettrick*
Royal commission on the crofters and cottars of the highlands of Scotland
    Report, 1884 C.3980 xxxii.
    Ev. 4 vols. 1884 C.3890 I-IV xxxiii, xxxiv, xxxv, xxxvi; (Agriculture, 21-25).

NAPIER, James M.
Report on European mints. 5 Aug 1870. *In:* 1870 (466) xli; (MP Currency, 3). Treasury.

NAPIER, Joseph, *Sir*
English and Irish law chancery commission. Separate report, June 1866. 1867 (285) xix; (Legal Administration, 10). SEE ALSO: Blackburne, Francis.

Select committee on the Dungarvon election petition
    Report, 6 April 1854. 1854 (162) viii.
    Decision, 20 July 1854. 1854 (162-I) viii.

Select committee on receivers, courts of chancery and exchequer in Ireland
    1st report, 29 June 1849. 1849 (438) viii.
    2nd report, 11 July 1849. 1849 (494) viii.

NAPIER, Mark
Report on the recent disturbances in Caithness-shire connected with the statute labour assessments upon the inhabitants of that county. 9 July 1844. 1844 (466) xlii.

NAPIER, William C.E.
Committee on the admission of university candidates to the scientific corps. Report, 23 May 1873. 1874 C.935 xii. War Office.

Committee on the advanced class of artillery officers. Report, 25 March 1872. 1872 C.589 xiv. War Office.

Council of military education
    Report. 1860 [2603] xxiv.
    2nd general report, 29 Dec 1864. 1865 [3502] xxxvi.
    3rd general report. 1868/9 [4153] xxii. War Office.

Council of military education on Army schools, libraries and recreation rooms
    1st report, 31 Dec 1861. 1862 [2957] xxxii.
    2nd report, 1 Oct 1864. 1865 [3422] xxxiv.
    3rd report, 25 Oct 1865. 1866 [3604] xliv.
    4th report. 1866 [3737] xlv.
    5th report. 1868/9 [4108] xxii.
    6th report, 31 March 1870. 1870 C.131 xxv. War Office. SEE ALSO: Pocklington, E.H.F.

Education of officers. Report by the Director-General of military education. SEE: Biddulph, Robert.

NASH, Charles Lacy
Select committee on conduct. SEE: Stonor, T.

NEILSON HANCOCK, W. SEE:
Hancock, W. Neilson.

NEATE, Charles
Select committee on mines. Report, 23 July 1866. 1866 (431) xiv; (FP Mining Accidents, 9).

Select committee on mines. Report, 31 July 1867. 1867 (496) xiii.

NELSON, Horatio, *3rd E. Nelson*
Select committee (HL) on the contagious Disease Act, 1866. Report, 2 July 1868. HL 1867/8 (113) xxx; HL repr. 1871 (46) viii.

NESBITT, Thomas
Commission of paving. Report to the Irish government on lighting the City of Dublin with gas. 10 March 1817. 1817 (102) viii.

NETTERVILLE, *Lord* [Peerage claim]. SEE: Freeman-Mitford, J.T.

NEWARK, *Vct.* SEE:
Pierrepont, Charles, *1st E. Manvers* (1737-1816)
Pierrepont, Charles Herbert, *2nd E. Manvers* (1778-1860)
Pierrepont, Charles Evelyn, *Vct. Newark* (1805-1850)

NEWBURGH, *E.* SEE:
Radcliffe, James Bartholomew, *4th E. Newburgh*.
[Peerage claim]. SEE: Freeman-Mitford, J.T.

NEWCASTLE, *D.* SEE:
Pelham-Clinton, Henry Pelham, *5th D. Newcastle*.

NEWLANDS, James
Report on the abattoirs of La Villitte in Paris and at Brussels. 1867. 1868/9 (404) l. Home Department.

NEWPORT, John, *Sir*
Committee on petition relating to the registry of freeholds in Ireland. Report, 12 June 1817. 1817 (357) viii.

Committee of ·privileges on complaint against W.W. Quin
Petition, 15 March 1819. 1819 (96) v.
Min. of ev. 11 to 15 March 1819. 1819 (96) v.
Reports, 12 and 15 March 1819. 1819 (97) v.

Committee respecting the poor of Ireland. Report, 1 June 1804. 1803/4 (109) v.

Select committee on the contagious fever in Ireland
Report, 8 May 1818. 1818 (285) vii.
2nd report, 26 May 1818. 1818 (359) vii.

Select committee on Grand Jury presentments, Ireland. SEE: Rice, T.S.

Select committee on Milford Haven Communication
Report, 11 April 1827. 1826/7 (258) iii.
2nd report, 14 June 1827. 1826/7 (472) iii.

Select committee on public records. Report, 29 March 1822. 1822 (134) iv.

Select committee on the state of disease and condition of the labouring poor in Ireland
1st report, 17 May 1819. 1819 (314) viii.
2nd report, 7 June 1819. 1819 (409) viii; repr. 1829 (347) iv.

NEWTON, Isaac
Report on the state of gold and silver coins. 21 Sept 1717. repr. 1830 (110) xvii, and 1847/8 (718) xxxix; (MP Currency, 2).

NICHOLL, John
Select committee on the ship 'Guiana' and the dismissal of the appeal by the Judicial committee of the Privy Council. Report, 11 July 1843. 1843 (421) xi.

Select committee on the Glasgow lottery. SEE: Inglis, Robert Harry, *Sir*.

Select committee on the management of the poor in Keighley Union. Report, 15 July 1842. 1842 (452) ix.

Select committee on tithes. Report, 18 June 1816. 1816 (486) iv.

NICHOLLS, George
Poor laws, Ireland commission
1st report, 15 Nov 1836. 1837 [69] li.
2nd report, 3 Nov 1837. 1837/8 [104] xxxviii.
3rd report: Condition of the labouring classes in Holland and Belgium. 5 May 1838. 1837/8 [126] xxxviii. Home Department.

Report on charitable institutions, Dublin. 1—Foundling Hospital, 2—House of Industry. 19 May 1842. 1842 (389) xxxviii. Irish Secretary's Office.

Report on the law concerning the maintenance of bastards. 31 Jan 1844. 1844 (31) xix. Poor Law Commission.

Report on local taxation. 1 June 1843. 1843 [486], [487], [488] xx. Poor Law Commission.

Report on medical charities in Ireland. 1841 [324] xi. Poor Law Commission, Ireland.

Report on the relief of the poor in the parishes of St. Marylebone and St. Pancras. 9 April 1847. 1847 [802] xxviii. Poor Law Commission.

Valuations for poor rates and registered elective franchise in Ireland. SEE: Haig, Charles.

NICHOLS, D. Cubitt
Inquiry on the immediate sanitary requirements of the parish of St. Mary Rotherhithe. Report, 19 March 1889. 1889 C.5688 lxv; (Health, 11). Home Department.

NICHOLSON, Charles
Select committee of the Legislative Council of New South Wales on immigration. Report, 30 Sept 1845. 1846 (418) xxix; (Australia, 9). Colonial Office.

NICOLL, Robert
Report of the trials at Wigan of the steam coals of south Lancashire and Cheshire. 16 July 1867. 1867 (563) xliv. Admiralty.

NICOLSON, Alexander
Report on the state of education in the Hebrides. May 1866. 1867 [3845-IV] xxv; (Education, 14). Education Commission, Scotland. SEE ALSO: Campbell, George Douglas, 8th D. Argyll.

NIMMO, Alexander
Report on Dunmore harbour. 10 May 1821. 1821 (492) xi.

NOEL, Charles Noel, *2nd Bn. Barham*
Commission on the civil affairs of the Navy
1st report: Dockyards. 13 June 1805. 1806 (8) v.
2nd report: Dockyards. 6 Feb 1806. 1806 (98) v.
3rd report: Dockyards. 24 June 1806. 1806 (312) v.
4th report: Navy Office. 9 July 1806. 1809 (120) vi.
5th report: Foreign yards. 2 Aug 1806. 1809 (121) vi.
6th report: Dockyards at the outposts. 4 Dec 1806. 1809 (122) vi.
7th report: Naval hospitals. 26 Feb 1807. 1809 (123) vi.
8th report (not printed)
9th report: Transport Office. 25 June 1807. 1809 (124) vi.
10th report: Victualling Office. 11 Aug 1807. 1809 (125) vi.
11th report: Victualling establishment at the outposts. 22 Dec 1807. 1809 (126) vi.
12th report: Victualling departments abroad. 22 Dec 1807. 1809 (127) vi.
13th report: Transport Board. 22 Dec 1807. 1809 (128) vi.

NOLAN, John
Commission on death in Clerkenwell prison. SEE: Bennett, James Risdon.

NOLAN, John Philip
Select committee on potato crop [failures]. Report, 9 July 1880. 1880 (274) xii.

NORBURY, E. [Peerage claim]. SEE:
Palmer, R., *1st E. Selborne.*

NORMAN, Henry Wylie, Sir
West India Royal Commission
Report, appendix A-B. 25 Aug 1897. 1898 C.8655 l.
Appendix C
Vol.1: Ev., appendices received in London. 1898 C.8656 l.
Vol.2: Ev., appendices relating to British Guiana, Barbados, Trinidad and Tobago. 1898 C.8657 l.
Vol.3: Ev., appendices relating to the Windward Islands, the Leeward Islands and Jamaica. 1898 C.8669 li.
Vol.4: Analysis of verbal ev. 1898 C.8799 li.

NORMAN, John Paxton
Commission on cases of claimants against the late state of Oude. Report, 10 Feb 1865. 1866 (301) lii. India Office.

NORMANBY, M. SEE:
Phipps, Constantine Henry, *1st M. Normanby* (1797-1863)
Phipps, George Augustus Constantine, *2nd M. Normanby* (1819-1890)

NORREYS, Charles Denham Orlando Jephson, Sir
Select committee on committees of supply. SEE: Russell, John, *1st E. Russell.*

Select committee on the map of Ireland. Report, 12 Aug 1853. 1852/3 (912) xxxix.

Select committee on Ordnance Survey Ireland. Report, 20 Aug 1846. 1846 (664) xv.

NORTH, Lord [Peerage claim]. SEE:
Cooper, C.A.

NORTH, Charles Napier
Select committee on mortality of troops in China. Report, 24 July 1866. 1866 (442) xv.

NORTHAMPTON, M. SEE:
Compton, Spencer Joshua Alwyne, *2nd M. Northampton* (1790-1851)
Compton, Spencer Joshua Alwyne, *3rd M. Northampton* (1816-1877)

NORTHBROOK, E. SEE:
Baring, Thomas George, *1st E. Northbrook.*

NORTHCOTE, Stafford Henry, 1st E. Iddesleigh
Commission on friendly and benefit building societies
1st report. 1871 C.451 xxv.
2nd report. 1872 C.514 xxvi.
Supplement by F.T. Bircham. 27 Jan 1873. 1873 C.678 xxii.
3rd report. 1873 C.842 xxii.
4th report. 1874 C.961 xxiii, pt.1.
Assistant commissioners reports. 1874 C.995, C.996, C.997, C.998 xxiii, pt.2; (Insurance, 4-8).

Committee on the employment of supplemental and temporary clerks in the civil service. Report, 1 July 1860. 1865 (251) xxx; (GO Civil Service, 6). Treasury.

Committee of inquiry on the Board of Ordnance. Report, 17 Dec 1853. 1854 [1715] xxvii. Treasury.

Committee of inquiry on the Copyhold, Enclosure and Tithe Commission. Report, 17 Aug 1853. 1854 [1715] xxvii. Treasury.

Committee of inquiry on the Department of Practical Sciences and Art. Report, 25 May 1853. 1854 [1715] xxvii. Treasury.

Committee of inquiry into public offices. Index to reports. 14 Aug 1855. 1854 [1715] xxvii; 1854/5 (530) xlix. Treasury.

Committee of inquiry on the Office of Works. Report, 14 Jan 1854. 1854 [1715] xxvii. Treasury.

Committee on soldiers dietary. Report, 15 May 1889. 1889 C.5742 xvii. War Office.

Organisation of the permanent civil service
Report, 23 Nov 1853. 1854 [1715] xxvii; repr. 1854/5 [1870] xx.
Index. 1854/5 (530-I) xx; (GO Civil Service, 2). Treasury.

Royal commission on depression of trade and industry
1st report, 7 Nov 1885. 1886 C.4621 xxi.
2nd report, 31 March 1886. 1886 C.4715 xxi; Appendix. 1886 C.4715-I xxii.
3rd report, 18 June 1886. 1886 C.4797 xxiii.
Final report, 21 Dec 1886. 1886 C.4893 xxiii; (TI Depression, 1-3)

Select committee on banks of issue. Report, 22 July 1875. 1875 (351) ix; (Monetary Policy, 9).

Select committee on the Corrupt Practices at Elections Bill. Min. of proc. 12 July 1867. 1867 (436) viii.

Select committee on the education of destitute children. 23 July 1861. 1861 (460) vii; (ED Poorer Classes, 7).

Select committee on Euphrates Valley railway. Report, 27 July 1871. 1871 (386) vii.

Select committee on Euphrates Valley railway. Report, 22 July 1872. 1872 (322) ix.

Select committee on police and sanitary regulations bills. Report, 11 July 1898. 1898 (291) xi.

Select committee on police and sanitary regulations bills. Report, 20 July 1899. 1899 (285) x.

Select committee on public business. Report, 8 July 1878. 1878 (268) xviii.

Select committee on schools of art. Report, 8 July 1864. 1864 (466) xii; (ED Fine Arts, 6).

Select committee on the taxation of Ireland. Report, 1 June 1865. 1865 (330) xii.

NORTHUMBERLAND, D. SEE:
Percy, Algernon George, *6th D. Northumberland.*

NORTON, Bn. SEE:
Adderley, Charles Bowyer, *Bn. Norton.*

NORWICH, Bp. SEE:
Hinds, Samuel, *Bp. of Norwich,* 1849-52.

NORWOOD, Charles Morgan
Committee on sea fishing trade. Report, 18 Dec 1882. 1882 C.3432 xvii. Board of Trade.

Royal commission on the measurement of tonnage
Report, 25 Aug 1881. 1881 C.3074 xlix
Digest of ev., index. 1882 C.3380 xxi.

NORWOOD, Charles Morgan (continued)

Select committee on Customs out-door officers at the outports. Report, 25 July 1881. 1881 (342) viii; (GO Civil Service, 10).

Select committee on trade partnerships. Report, 5 June 1872. 1872 (228) xii.

NUGENT OF RIVERSTON, *Lord* [Peerage claim]. SEE: Cooper, C.A.

OAKES, H.

Commission of military enquiry. SEE: Drinkwater, J.

O'BRIEN, Edward, *Sir*

Select committee on the expenses of sheriffs, *etc,* at elections in Ireland. Report, 30 June 1820. 1820 (226) iii.

O'BRIEN, Michael

Commission on corrupt practices at elections for the Borough of Beverley
 Report on witnesses. 19 Oct 1869. 1870 (310) lvi.
 Report, 29 Jan 1870. 1870 C.15 xxix.
 Min. of ev. 1870 C.16 xxix.

O'BRIEN, Terence

Committee on Netley hospital. Report on the site, etc, of the Royal Victoria Hospital near Netley Abbey. 1 July 1858. 1857/8 [2401] xix.

O'BRIEN, W.P.

Local government and taxation in Ireland inquiry. Special report, 10 Jan 1878. 1878 C.1965 xxiii. Irish Secretary's Office. SEE ALSO: Hicks-Beach, Michael Edward, *Sir.*

O'BRIEN, William Smith

Select committee on the Royal Dublin Society. Report, 14 July 1836. 1836 (445) xii.

O'CALLAGHAN, E.B.

Standing committee of grievances of the Assembly of Lower Canada. 4th report respecting the conduct of Lord Aylmer. 16 Aug 1836. 1836 (570) xxxix; (Canada, 7). No other reports printed in BPP.

O'CONNELL, Daniel

Select committee on the Belfast election compromise. Report, 11 July 1842. 1842 (431) v.

Select committee on Carrickfergus election petition. Report, 15 April 1833. 1833 (181) viii.

Select committee on the Dublin and Kingstown Ship Canal. Report, 30 July 1833. 1833 (591) xvi.

Select committee on the Inns of Court
 1st report, 21 July 1834. 1834 (503) xviii.
 2nd report, 4 Aug 1834. 1834 (555) xviii.

O'CONNELL, John

Select committee on emigrant ships
 1st report, 6 April 1854. 1854 (163) xiii.
 2nd report, 5 July 1854. 1854 (349) xiii; (Emigration, 7).

O'CONNELL, Morgan John

Select committee on the Cheltenham election petition. Min. of ev. 2 June 1848. 1847/8 (382) xi.

Select committee on combinations of workmen. SEE: Labouchere, Henry.

Select committee on the Lincoln election petition. Min. of ev. 4 May 1848. 1847/8 (296) xiii.

Select committee on manor courts, Ireland. Report, 10 July 1837. 1837 (494) xv.

Select committee on manor courts in Ireland. Report, 30 July 1838. 1837/8 (648) xvii.

O'CONNOR, Arthur

Committee of public accounts
 1st report, 10 June 1896. 1896 (227) viii.
 2nd report, 1 July 1896. 1896 (271) viii.
 3rd report, 15 July 1896. 1896 (297) viii.

Committee of public accounts
 1st report, 10 March 1897. 1897 (122) viii.
 2nd report, 5 May 1897. 1897 (196) viii.
 3rd report, 30 June 1897. 1897 (274) viii.
 4th report, 14 July 1897. 1897 (314) viii.

Committee of public accounts
 1st report, 9 March 1898. 1898 (105) viii.
 2nd report, 29 June 1898. 1898 (261) viii.

Committee of public accounts
 1st report, 8 March 1899. 1899 (97) viii.
 2nd report, 26 April 1899. 1899 (169) viii.
 3rd and 4th reports, 28 June 1899. 1899 (253) viii.

Committee on Stationery Office contracts. Report, 7 Sept 1896. 1897 (145) lxxii. Treasury.

Standing committee on law. Building Societies (No.2) and the Building Societies (No.3) Bills. Special report and report, 24 May 1894. 1894 (130) ix.

Standing committee on law. Fatal Accidents Inquiry (Scotland) Bill. Report, 13 July 1893. 1893/4 (329) xi.

Standing committee on law. Municipal Franchise (Ireland) Bill. Report, 8 April 1895. 1895 (208) xii.

Standing committee on law. Poor Law (Scotland) Bill. Report, 10 June 1898. 1898 (234) xi.

Standing committee on law. Poor Law Unions Associations Bill. Report, 3 May 1898. 1898 (191) xi.

Select committee on law. Prisons Bill. Report, 7 June 1898. 1898 (229) xi.

Standing committee on law. Solicitors (Ireland) Bill. Report, 26 April 1898. 1898 (176) xi.

Standing committee on trade. Bankruptcy Bill. Report, 30 June 1890. 1890 (266) x.

Standing committee on trade. Companies (Memorandum of Association) Bill and the Companies (Winding-up) Bill. Report, 17 April and 19 May 1890. 1890 (133) xiii.

Standing committee on trade. Directors' Liability Bill. Report, 22 May 1890. 1890 (188) xiii.

Standing committee on trade. Market Gardens Compensation Bill. Report, 3 July 1894. 1894 (197) xiv.

Standing committee on trade. Merchant Shipping (Life Saving Appliances) Bill. Report, 2 Aug 1888. 1888 (318) xii.

Standing committee on trade. Notice of Accidents Bill. Report, 5 June 1894. 1894 (149) xiv.

Standing committee on trade. Sea Fisheries Regulation Bill. Report, 27 July 1888. 1888 (303) xviii.

O'CONNOR, Charles Owen, *The O'Connor Don*

Royal commission on the financial relations between G.B. and Ireland
 1st report, 28 March 1895. 1895 C.7720 xxxvi. Final report. 1896 C.8262 xxxiii.
 Min. of ev. 1896 C.7720-II xxxiii; (National Finance, 6).

Select committee on the Grand Jury Presentments, Ireland. Report, 6 July 1868. 1867/8 (392) x.

O'CONNOR DON, The SEE:
O'Connor, Charles Owen, *The O'Connor Don.*

ODLING, William
Committee on photometric standards to be used for testing the illuminating power of coal gas. Report, March 1895. 1895 C.7743 lxxxviii; (FP Gas, 6). Board of Trade.

O'DONNELL, J.W.
Committee of inquiry into the Dublin Metropolitan Police. Report, 3 Jan 1883. 1883 C.3576 xxxii. Irish Secretary's Office.

O'DWYER, J.
Report and evidence on charges against the police of Limerick. SEE: Hunt, C.

O'FERRALL, R. More SEE:
More-O'Ferrall, Richard.

OGILVY, David Graham Drummond, *9th E. Airlie*
Select committee (HL) on the law of hypothec in Scotland. Report, HL 1868/9 (45) xxvii; HC repr. 1868/9 (367) ix.

O'GORMAN, Purcell
Charges against sub-inspector Flinter. Report, 1 Aug 1833. 1833 (605) xxxii.

O'HAGAN, Thomas, *1st Bn. O'Hagan*
Select committee (HL) on the Bankruptcy (Ireland) Amendment Bill and the Debtors (Ireland) Bill. Report, 27 June 1872. HL 1872 (177) ix.

OLIVEIRA, Benjamin
Select committee on Metropolitan bridges. Report, 14 July 1854. 1854 (370) xiv.

OLIVER, Thomas
Report on lead compounds in pottery. 21 Feb 1899. 1899 C.9207 xii. Home Office.

Report upon the pottery industry in France. 6 July 1899. 1899 C.9526 xii. Home Office.

Report on the use of phosphorus in the manufacture of lucifer matches. Jan 1899. 1899 C.9188 xii. Home Office.

O'LOGHLEN, Colman Michael, *Sir*
Select committee on Bank Holidays Bill. Report, 22 June 1868. 1868/9 (354) vii; (IR Factories, 2).

Select committee on the Libel Bill. Report, 8 April 1867. 1867 (208) ix.

O'LOGHLIN, Michael
Report respecting the court for relief of insolvent debtors in Ireland. 17 April 1834. 1834 (205) xlviii.

OMMANNEY, Francis Molyneux, *Sir*
Select committee on poor rate returns. Report, 10 July 1821. 1821 (748) iv.

ONSLOW, E. SEE:
Onslow, William Hillier, *4th E. Onslow.*

ONSLOW, Arthur
Select committee on admission of attorneys and solicitors. Report, 5 March 1821. 1821 (137) iv.

Select committee on standing orders relating to bills

regulating trades, *etc.* Report, 23 June 1820. 1820 (193) ii.

Select committee on usury laws. Report, 28 May 1818. 1818 (376) vi.

Select committee on usury laws. Report, 16 April 1821. 1821 (410) iv.

Select committee on writs of *Habeas Corpus ad Subjiciendum.* Report, 20 June 1815. 1814/5 (418) iii.

ONSLOW, William Hillier, *4th E. Onslow*
Departmental committee on the prevalence of venereal disease among the British troops in India. Report, 20 Feb 1897. 1897 C.8379 lxiii. India Office.

Select committee (HL) on the marking of foreign and colonial produce
Report, 19 July 1893. HL 1893/4 (121) ix; HC repr. 1893/4 (214) xii.
2nd report, 9 July 1894. HL 1894 (30) viii; HC repr. 1894 (293) xiv.

ORD, Henry St. George
Commission on the condition of the British settlements on the west coast of Africa. Report, 9 March 1865. 1865 (170) xxxvii; (Africa, 50). Colonial Office.

ORD, William Henry
General committee of elections
Report, 5 March 1840. 1840 (102) ix.
Report, 31 July 1840. 1840 (477) ix.

Select committee on bribery at elections. Report, 20 Aug 1835. 1835 (547) viii; (GO Elections, 1).

O'REILLY, Miles William
General committee on railway and canal bills, 1868/9. SEE: Goldsmid, Francis, *Sir.*

Select committee on the Sale of Liquors on Sunday (Ireland) Bill. Report, 26 May 1868. 1867/8 (280) xiv.

ORMONDE, *Lord* [Peerage claim]. SEE:
Cooper, C.A.

ORMSBY-GORE, William
Select committee on privileges. Report on Sligo election. 21 July 1848. 1847/8 (526) xiv.

Select committee on Smithfield Market. Report, 9 July 1847. 1847 (640) viii.

OSBORNE, Edward Haydon
Conditions of work, *etc* in flax mills and linen factories. Reports, 1894. 1893/4 C.7287 xvii; (IR Factories, 29). Home Department.

Report on the effects of heavy sizing in cotton weaving upon the health of the operatives employed. 1 Oct 1883. 1884 C.3861 lxxii; (IR Factories, 28). Home Department.

OSBORNE-MORGAN, G. SEE:
Morgan, George Osborne.

OSGOODE, W.
Commission to enquire into the condition and treatment of prisoners at Lincoln Castle prison. Report, 4 Dec 1812. 1812/3 (4) v; (CP Prisons, 7).

O'SHAUGHNESSY, Richard
Select committee on the Contagious Diseases Acts. Report, 7 Aug 1882. 1882 (340) ix; (HE Infectious Diseases, 7).

O'SHAUGHNESSY, W.B.
Report on the electric telegraph from Calcutta to Kedgeree, Bengal. 30 March 1852. 1852/3 (87) lxxvi.

OSLER, Edward
A practical essay on the administration and improvement of the poor laws. 16 Aug 1832. *In:* 1834 (44) xxxvii.

OSWALD, James
Select committee on the conduct of General Darling while governor of New South Wales. SEE: Tooke, William.

OTWAY, Arthur John
Select committee on civil service writers. Report, 30 July 1873. 1873 (370) xi; (GO Civil Service, 8).

OTWAY, C.G.
Report on hand-loom weavers in Ireland, 1839. 1840 (43-II) xxiii; (IR Textiles, 9).

OVEREND, William
Sheffield outrages inquiry. Report to the Trades unions commission. Vol.1—report; vol.2—ev. 2 Aug 1867. 1867 [3952-I] xxxii; (Industrial Relations, 8). SEE ALSO: Erle, William, *Sir.*

OVERSTONE, *Lord* SEE:
Loyd, Samuel Jones, *1st Bn. Overstone.*

OWEN, Aneurin
Report on vagrancy. 17 Feb 1848. 1847/8 [987] liii. Poor Law Board.

OWEN, Richard
Report on prepared and preserved alimentary substances at the Paris Universal Exhibition. 30 Nov 1855. 1856 [2049-I] xxxvi. Board of Trade.

OXENBRIDGE, *Vct.* SEE:
Monson, William John, *Vct. Oxenbridge.*

OXFORD, *Bp.* SEE:
Wilberforce, Samuel, *Bp. of Oxford*, 1845-69.

PACKE, Charles William
Select committee on stoppage of wages; hosiery. SEE: Ingham, Robert.

PACKINGTON, John Somerset
SEE: Pakington, John Somerset.

PAGE, Thomas
Report on Chelsea embankment and Chelsea Bridge works. 21 April 1856. 1856 (193) lii. Commission of Works.

Report on the comparative merits of Holyhead and Portdynllaen as a harbour of refuge. 16 June 1846. 1846 (630) xlv. Admiralty.

Report on the eligibility of Holyhead and Porth-Dyn-Llaen as harbours of refuge and packet stations for communicating with Kingston, Jamaica. 30 April 1844. 1844 (633) xlv.

Report of an inquiry on the prevalence of disease at Croydon and on the plan of sewerage. Engineering report. 21 April 1853. 1852/3 [1648] xcvi; (UA Sanitation, 3). Home Department. SEE ALSO: Arnott, Neil.

Report on the progress and present state of the new bridge at Westminster. 18 June 1855. 1854/5 (347) liii.

PAGET, Clarence Edward, *Lord*
Select committee on the Contagious Diseases Bill. Report, 20 April 1866. 1866 (200) xi; (HE Infectious Diseases, 4).

Select committee on dockyards
1st report, 5 May 1864. 1864 (270) viii.
2nd report, 15 July 1864. 1864 (496) viii.

Select committee on the Naval Medical Supplemental Fund Society Bill. Min. of ev. 8 July 1861. 1861 (414) xiii.

PAGET, James
Committee to inquire into *M.* Pasteur's treatment of hydrophobia. Report, June 1887. 1887 C.5087 lxvi; (HE Infectious Diseases, 8). Local Government Board.

PAGET, Richard Horner, *Sir*
Departmental commission on agricultural and dairy schools
Report, 9 Dec 1887. 1888 C.5285 xxxii.
Final report, 27 Feb 1888. 1888 C.5313 xxxii. Privy Council Office.

Select committee on the Butter Substitutes Bill. Special report, 4 July 1887. 1887 (208) ix.

PAKINGTON, John Slaney, *2nd Bn. Hampton*
Committee on Army examinations. Report, 26 April 1878. 1878 (254) xix. War Office.

PAKINGTON, John Somerset, *Sir*
Select committee on the Athlone election petition. Min. of proc., ev. 11 March 1844. 1844 (97) xiv.

Select committee on the business of the H.C. Report, 3 May 1854. 1854 (212) vii.

Select committee on classification of railway bills, 1847. SEE: Wilson-Patten, John.

Select committee on education. Report, 23 June 1865. 1865 (403) vi.

Select committee on education. Report, 5 July 1866. 1866 (392) vii.

Select committee on the Ipswich election petition. Min. of proc. and ev. 26 April 1842. 1842 (207) vii.

Select committee on railway bills classification, 1846. SEE: Wilson-Patten, John.

Select committee on the Rye election petition. Report, 6 April 1853. 1852/3 (350) xviii.

Select committee on the Rye election petition (further inquiry). Resolutions and report, 21 April 1853. 1852/3 (377), (377-I) xviii.

Select committee on Thetford Borough election. Proc. 4 May 1842. 1842 (548) v.

Select committee on West India colonies. Report, 25 July 1842. 1842 (479) xiii; (West Indies, 1).

PALLES, Christopher
Intermediate education (Ireland) commission
First report, 22 Dec 1898. 1899 C.9116, C.9117 xxii.
Final report, 11 Aug 1899. 1899 C.9511 xxii.
Appendix. 2 parts. 1899 C.9512, C.9513 xxiii, xxiv. Irish Secretary's Office.

PALMER, C.
Commission on the cattle plague, Calcutta, 1864. Report, 7 Oct 1865. 1866 (28) lii. India Office.

PALMER, Charles Fyshe
Select committee on the office of high sheriff. Report, 11 June 1830. 1830 (520) x.

PALMER, George
Select committee on shipwrecks
    1st report, 10 Aug 1843. 1843 (549) ix.
    2nd report, 15 Aug 1843. 1843 (581) ix; (Shipping, 3).

Select committee on shipwrecks of timber ships. Report, 18 June 1839. 1839 (333) ix; (Shipping, 2).

PALMER, John
Committee on his account of Post Office revenues due. SEE: Eden, George, *1st E. Auckland.*

Committee on agreement for reform of the Post Office. SEE: Byng, George.

Committee (HL) on agreement with the Post Office for its reform. SEE: Eliot, J., *1st E. St. Germans,* AND SEE: Ryder, Dudley, *1st E. Harrowby.*

PALMER, Robert
Select committee on the Aylesbury election petition. Min. of ev. 29 March 1848. 1847/8 (220) x.

Select committee on Irish vagrants. Report, 17 June 1833. 1833 (394) xvi.

Select committee on medical relief. SEE: Pigott, Francis.

PALMER, Roundell, *1st E. Selborne*
Commission on Oxford University. Ev., circulars. 1881 C.2868 lvi.

Committee for privileges (HL)
    Vct. Bangor's peerage claim. Report, 25 April 1882. HL 1882 (69) vii.

Committee for privileges (HL)
    Marquess of Donegal's peerage claim. Report, 28 March 1884. HL 1884 (48) vii.

Committee for privileges (HL)
    Vct. Galway's peerage claim. Report, 25 July 1884. HL 1884 (215) vii.

Committee for privileges (HL)
    Marquess of Hertford's peerage claim. Report, 28 Feb 1884. HL 1884 (21) vii.

Committee for privileges (HL)
    Earl of Norbury's peerage claim. Report, 12 Feb 1884. HL 1884 (12) vii.

Judicature commission. SEE: Cairns, Hugh Mac-Calmont, *Bn. Cairns.*

Royal commission on a university for London. Report, 29 April 1889. 1889 C.5079 xxxix.

Select committee (HL) on appellate jurisdiction. Report, 9 July 1872. HL 1872 (149) ix; HC repr. 1872 (325) vii; (Legal Administration, 14).

Select committee (HL) on the Earldom of Mar Restitution Bill. Report, 28 July 1885. HL 1884/5 (216) vii.

Select committee (HL) on the Stolen Goods Bill. Report, 18 Aug 1881. HL 1881 (146) viii; HC repr. 1881 (447) xii.

Select committee (HL) on the Stolen Goods Bill. Report, 22 June 1882. HL 1882 (155) vii; HC repr. 1882 (275) xiii.

Select committee (HL) on the Supreme Court of Judicature Bill. Report, 24 April 1873. HL 1873 (72) ix.

PALMER, William Waldegrave, *2nd E. Selborne*
Pacific cable committee. Report, 5 Jan 1897. 1899 C.9247 lix. Colonial Office.

PALMERSTON, *Vct.* SEE:
Temple, Henry John, *3rd Vct. Palmerston.*

PANMURE, *Bn.* [Peerage claim]. SEE:
Freeman-Mitford, J.T. Committee for privileges, Dalhousie and Panmuir claims of peerage.

PARIS, John Ayrton
Report of the Medical Council in relation to the cholera epidemic of 1854. 26 July 1855. 1854/5 [1989] xlv; (HE Infectious Diseases, 3). General Board of Health.

Report on the results of the different methods of treatment of epidemic cholera. 1854/5 [1990] xlv; (HE Infectious Diseases, 3). General Board of Health. SEE ALSO: Sutherland, John.

PARISH, Woodbine
Two reports on illicit distillation in Scotland. 7 June 1816. 1816 (432) viii.

PARKE, James
Commission on circuit regulation. Report, 3 June 1845. 1845 [638] xiv.

PARKER, Albert Edmund, *3rd E. Morley*
Army hospital services inquiry. Report, 25 April 1883. 1883 C.3607 xvi. War Office.

Committee on artillery localization. Report, 26 Jan 1882. 1882 C.3168 xvi. War Office.

Committee on the manufacturing departments of the Army. Report, 14 Aug 1887. 1887 C.5116 xiv. War Office.

Committee on officers of the Ordnance Corps. Report, 8 Jan 1881. 1881 C.2816 xx. War Office.

Committee for privileges (HL)
    Precedence of H.R.H. the Duke of Clarence and Avondale. Min. of ev. HL 1890 (124) x.

Committee for privileges (HL)
    Precedence of the Duke of York
      Min. of proc. 17 June 1890. HL 1890 (124) x.
      Min. of proc. 14 June 1892. HL 1892 (171) ix.

Committee on Royal hospitals at Chelsea and Kilmainham, Royal Military Asylum, Chelsea, and Royal Hibernian Military School, Dublin
    Report, 20 Nov 1882. 1883 C.3679 xv.
    Min. of ev. 1883 C.3720 xv. War Office.

Joint select committee on the Houses of Lords and Commons permanent staff. Report, 20 July 1899. HL 1899 (171) x; HC 1899 (286) ix.

Joint committee on the statute law revision bills. Report, 27 July 1893. HL 1893/4 (170) ix; HC 1893/4 (348) xv.

Select committee (HL) on the Parliament Office and the office of the Gentleman Usher of the Black Rod
    1st report, 13 May 1889. HL 1889 (61) vii; HC repr. 1889 (339) xi.
    2nd report, 8 Aug 1889. HL 1889 (218) vii; HC repr. 1889 (340) xi.

Select committee (HL) offices
    1st report, 23 Feb 1890. HL 1890 (30) x.
    2nd report, 29 July 1890. HL 1890 (233) x.

Select committee (HL) on the HL offices. Report, 24 July 1891. HL 1890/1 (266) xi.

Select committee (HL) on the HL offices
    1st report, 7 March 1892. HL 1892 (34) ix.
    2nd report, 24 June 1892. HL 1892 (218) ix.

PARKER, Albert Edmund, *3rd E. Morley* (continued)
Select committee (HL) on HL offices
    1st report, 16 March 1893. HL 1893/4 (38) ix.
    2nd report, 8 May 1893. HL 1893/4 (88) ix.
    3rd report, 21 July 1893. HL 1893/4 (214) ix.

Select committee (HL) on the HL offices. Report, 4 June 1894. HL 1894 (81) viii; HC repr. 1894 (201) xii.

Select committee (HL) on the HL offices
    1st report, 26 March 1895. HL 1895 (50) vi.
    2nd report, 5 July 1895. HL 1895 (199) vi.

Select committee (HL) on HL offices
    1st report, 10 March 1896. HL 1896 (29) ix.
    2nd report, 30 April 1896. HL 1896 (75) ix.
    3rd report, 12 May 1896. HL 1896 (90) ix.
    3rd report, amended, 18 May 1896. HL 1896 (101) ix.
    4th report, 13 Aug 1896. HL 1896 (254) ix.

Select committee (HL) on the HL offices
    1st report, 4 March 1897. HL 1897 (23) ix.
    2nd report, 30 July 1897. HL 1897 (196) ix.

Select committee (HL) on the HL offices
    1st report, 24 March 1898. HL 1898 (35) ix.
    2nd report, 9 Aug 1898. HL 1898 (209) ix.

Select committee (HL) on the HL offices
    1st report, 16 May 1899. HL 1899 (91) x.
    2nd report, 4 Aug 1899. HL 1899 (212) x.

Select committee (HL) on the Petroleum Bill. Report, 5 July 1872. HL 1872 (135) ix.

PARKER, Charles Stuart
Committee on education in Scotland
    1st and 2nd reports, 12 Feb 1887, 17 March 1888. 1888 C.5336 xli.
    3rd report, 20 June 1888. 1888 C.5425 xli. Committee of the Privy Council on Education in Scotland.

PARKER, H.W.
Report on the East Preston Gilbert's incorporation. 1 May 1843. 1843 (247) xlv. Poor Law Commission.

PARKER, John
Committee of the Board of Treasury on the estate of the late Samuel Troutbeck. Report, 5 June 1839. 1839 (28) xxx. Treasury.

Committee on expired and expiring laws. 3rd session, 13th Parliament. Report, 11 Feb 1840. 1840 (62) xv.

Committee on expiring laws. 7th session, 14th Parliament. Report, 12 March 1847. 1847 (178) viii.

Select committee on expiring laws. 1st session, 15th Parliament. Report, 16 March 1848. 1847/8 (173) xvi.

Committee on expiring laws. 2nd session, 15th Parliament. Report, 4 April 1849. 1849 (216) xii.

Select committee on the fresh fruit trade. Report, 12 July 1839. 1839 (398) viii.

Select committee on the Scottish Central Railway Bill. Report, 8 May 1845. 1845 (291) x.

PARKER, W.
Committee on manning of the Navy
    Report, 14 Feb 1853. 1852/3 [1628] lx.
    Appendix. 1859, session 2 (45) xvii. Admiralty.

PARKES, Josiah
Inquiry into steam-vessel accidents. Report, 29 May 1839. 1839 (273) xlvii. Board of Trade.

PARNELL, Henry, *Sir*
Commission of excise inquiry
    1st report: Tea permits and surveys. 26 July 1833. 1833 [1], (762) xxi.
    2nd report: Wine permits and surveys. 1834 [2] xxiv.
    3rd report: Summary jurisdiction. 1834 [3] xxiv.
    4th report: Survey of brewers. 1834 [4] xxiv.
    5th report: Stone bottles and sweets. 1834 [5] xxiv.
    6th report: Tobacco and foreign spirits. 1834 [6] xxiv; (TI Tobacco, 2).
    7th report: British spirits. pt.1. 1834 [7] xxv. pt.2. 1835 [8] xxx.
    8th report: Starch. 1834 [9] xxv.
    9th report: Vinegar. 1834 [10] xxv.
    10th report: Malt duty, Ireland. 1834 [11] xxv.
    Digest of the first 10 reports. 1835 [12] xxx.
    11th report: Excise accounts. 1835 [13] xxx.
    12th report: Auctions. 1835 [14] xxx; repr. 1845 (57) xxvii.
    13th report: Glass. 1835 [15] xxxi.
    14th report: Paper. 1835 [16] xxxi.
    15th report: Malt. 1835 [17] xxxi.
    16th report: Hops. 1835 [18] xxxi.
    Digest of reports 11-16. 1835 [19] xxxi.
    17th report: Soap. 1836 [19] xxvi.
    18th report: Bricks. 1836 [20] xxvi.
    19th report: Excise licences. 1837 [21] xxx.
    20th report: Excise establishment. 1836 [22] xxvi.
    Digest and index. 1837 [84] xxx.

Commission of public accounts. Report, 10 Oct 1831. 1831 (313) x.

Select committee on the affairs of the East India Company. Report, 30 June and 11 Oct 1831. 1831 (65), (320) v, vi.

Select committee appointed to prepare militia estimates. Report, 8 July 1831. 1831 (85) iv.

Select committee on combinations of workmen. SEE: Labouchere, Henry.

Select committee on the corn trade of the U.K. Report, 11 May 1813. 1812/3 (184) iii; repr. 1813/4 (57) iv.

Select committee on the growth and cultivation of tobacco. Report, 21 June 1830. 1830 (565) x; (TI Tobacco, 2).

Select committee on the Holyhead and Liverpool roads
    Report, 20 May 1830. 1830 (432) x.
    2nd report, 9 July 1830. 1830 (652) x.

Select committee on Holyhead roads, etc
    Report, 6 June 1815. 1814/5 (363) iii.
    2nd report, 27 June 1815. 1814/5 (395) iii.

Select committee on Holyhead roads
    1st report: North Wales. 25 Feb 1822. 1822 (41) vi.
    2nd report: Steam packets. 2 April 1822. 1822 (180) vi.
    3rd report: Chester road. 3 May 1822. 1822 (275) vi.
    4th report: Road through England from north Wales to London. 17 May 1822. 1822 (343) vi.
    5th report: Steamboats, *etc.* 12 June 1822. 1822 (417) vi.
    6th report: Irish roads. 4 July 1822. 1822 (513) vi.

Select committee on public income and expenditure
    1st report, 10 March 1828. 1828 (110) v.
    2nd report: Ordnance estimates. 12 June 1828. 1828 (420) v.

3rd report: Superannuations. 26 June 1828. 1828 (480) v.

4th report: Revenue, expenditure and debt. 10 July 1828. 1828 (519) v.

Select committee on the roads from Holyhead to London
  1st report, 3 June 1817. 1817 (313) iii.
  2nd report, 6 June 1817. 1817 (332) iii.
  3rd report, 23 June 1817. 1817 (411) iii.
  4th report, 3 July 1817. 1817 (459) iii.

Select committee on the roads from London to Holyhead
  1st report, 2 March 1819. 1819 (78) v.
  2nd report, 6 April 1819. 1819 (217) v.
  3rd report: Menai Bridge. 19 April 1819. 1819 (256) v.
  4th report: Post Office packets. 24 June 1819. 1819 (501) v.
  5th report: Holyhead mails and packets. 6 July 1819. 1819 (548) v.
  6th report: Turnpike trusts between London and Holyhead. 6 July 1819. 1819 (549) v.

Select committee on the state of Ireland. Report, 2 Aug 1832. 1831/2 (677) xvi.

Select committee on the Whetstone and St. Alban's turnpike trusts. Report, 18 July 1828. 1828 (546) iv.

PARRY, W.E., *Sir*
Report on the Caledonian Canal. 13 Jan 1842. 1842 (74) xxxvii. Treasury.

PARSONS, Henry Franklin
Report on the influenza epidemic of 1889-90. 1890/1 C.6387 xxxiv; (HE Infectious Diseases, 8). Local Government Board.

Further report on the influenza epidemics of 1889-90 to 1891-92. 1893/4 C.7051 xlii; (HE Infectious Diseases, 8). Local Government Board.

PARSONS, Laurence, *4th E. Rosse*
Commission on endowed schools in Ireland. Report, 30 Oct 1880. 1881 C.2831 xxxv. Irish Secretary's Office.

PARSONS, William, *3rd E. Rosse*
Commission on the College of Science, Dublin. Report, 9 July 1866. 1867 (219) lv. Privy Council Committee on Education.

Select committee (HL) on the drainage of lands in Ireland. Report, 29 June 1852. HL 1852 (178) xxi; HC repr. 1852/3 (10) xxvi.

PASLEY, C.W.
Report on Captain Powell's patent sectional transferable railway carriages for carrying goods either on the broad or narrow gauge. 8 May 1846. 1846 (415) xxxviii. Board of Trade, Railway Department.

Report on the state of the works of the North British Railway. 2 Nov 1846. 1847 (436) lxiii. Board of Trade.

PASTEUR, Louis
Committee to inquire into treatment of hydrophobia. SEE: Paget, James.

PATER, J.
Commission for the investigation of the circumstances connected with the mutiny at Vellore. Report, 9 Aug 1860. 1861 (284) xlii. India Office.

PATTEN, John Wilson SEE:
Wilson-Patten, John.

PATTERSON, Robert H.
Gas Referees
  Construction of gas burners with reference to the principles of gas illumination
    1st report, 22 June 1871. 1871 (394) lvii. Board of Trade (no others identified)

  Report, 3 May 1869. 1868/9 [4156] li. Board of Trade.

  Report on the ammonia impurity in gas. 1 June 1871. 1871 (393) lvii. Board of Trade.

  1st report on the sulphur question. 13 July 1870. 1870 C.200 liv. (no others identified). Board of Trade.

  Sulphur purification at the Beckton gas works
    Report, 31 Jan 1872. *In:* 1872 (199) xlix.
    Further reports, 3 and 17 June 1872. 1872 (281) xlix. Board of Trade.

PATTESON, J.H.
Report of inquiry into the loss of sailing ship 'Spindrift' on 21 Nov 1869. 7 Dec 1869. 1870 (82) lx. Board of Trade.

PATTESON, John
Committee on the account between the public and the East India Company. Report, 26 June 1805. 1805 (197) vi; (East India, 1).

Committee on the petition of the brewers of Dublin, Cork and Waterford. Report, 11 June 1811. 1810/11 (222) v.

Committee on the petition of owners of collieries in South Wales. 7 June 1810. 1810 (344) iv.

Committee on woollen manufacture of England. Report, 4 July 1806. 1806 (268) iii; (IR Textiles, 2).

PATTISON, Mark
Report on the state of elementary education in Germany. 30 Oct 1859. *In:* 1861 [2794-IV] xxi, pt.4; (Education, 6).

PAULET, John, *14th M. Winchester*
Select committee (HL) on the York, Newcastle and Berwick Railway (Newcastle-upon-Tyne and Carlisle Railway Lease and Amalgamation) Bill and the York, Newcastle and Berwick Railway and Maryport and Carlisle Railway Lease and Amalgamation Bill (on re-commitment). Report, 10 July 1849. HL 1849 (209) xxxii.

PAULL, Henry
Select committee on the Piers and Harbours Bill. Min. of ev. 12 July 1860. 1860 (448) xv.

PAXTON, Joseph, *Sir*
Select committee on Thames embankment. Report, 27 July 1860. 1860 (494) xx.

PEASE, Henry Fell
Select committee on midwives registration. Report, 17 June 1892. 1892 (289) xiv; (Health, 15).

Select committee on midwives registration. Report, 8 Aug 1893. 1893/4 (367) xiii; (Health, 15).

PEASE, Joseph
Select committee on accidents in mines. Report, 4 Sept 1835. 1835 (603) v; (FP Mining Accidents, 1).

PEASE, Joseph Albert, *Sir*
Select committee on the London Water Companies Bill. Special report, 7 July 1896. 1896 (282) xi.

PEEL, *Vct.* SEE:
Peel, Arthur Wellesley, *1st Vct Peel.*

PEEL, Arthur
Joint select committee on trade partnerships. Report, 5 June 1872. (HL not located); HC 1872 (252) xii.

Select committee on merchant ships laden in bulk. Report, 9 March 1880. 1880 (170) xi.

Select committee on tramways' use of mechanical power bills. Report, 7 June 1878. 1878 (224) xviii.

PEEL, Arthur Wellesley, *1st Vct. Peel*
Royal commission on liquor licensing laws
   1st report. 1897 C.8355 xxxiv.
      Min. of ev., appendix, vol.1. 1897 C.8356 xxxiv.
      2nd report, June 1897. 1897 C.8523 xxxv.
      Min. of ev., appendix, vol.2. 1897 C.8523-I xxxv.
      3rd report, Aug 1898. 1898 C.8693 xxxvi.
      Min. of ev., appendix, vol.3. 1898 C.8694 xxxvi.
      Return of clubs in G.B. and Ireland, appendix, vol.4 1898 C.8695 xxxvii.
      Statistics of licensed premises [and] a comparative statement of licensing laws in the three Kingdoms, appendix, vol.5. 1898 C.8696 xxxvii.
      4th report, April 1898. 1898 C.8821 xxxviii.
      5th report, June 1898. 1898 C.8979 xxxviii.
      Min. of ev: Scotland. Vol.6. 1898 C.8822 xxxviii.
      Min. of ev: Ireland. Vol.7. 1898 C.8980 xxxviii.
      Ev., appendix and index, vol.8. 1899 C.9075 xxxiv.
      Precis of min. of ev. with summary of reports of commissioners and committees since 1800, special cases, etc. 1899 C.9076 xxxv.
      Final report and index to ev. 1899 C.9379 xxxv.

PEEL, Frederick
Committee on the storekeeping arrangements of the Navy. Report, 28 April 1876. 1877 C.1646 xxii. Admiralty.
Select committee on the Berwick-upon-Tweed election petition. Min. of ev. 31 March 1860. 1860 (194) x.

Select committee to prepare the militia estimates, 1855/6. Report, 31 July 1855. 1854/5 (446) vii.

Select committee on the Red Sea and India Telegraph Bill. Min. of ev. 7 March 1861. 1861 (86) xiv.

PEEL, John
Committee on expiring laws. 3rd session, 18th Parliament. Report, 4 June 1861. 1861 (304) xiv.

Committee on expiring laws. 4th session, 18th Parliament. Report, 11 July 1862. 1862 (400) xvi.

Committee on expiring laws. 6th session, 18th Parliament. Report, 4 July 1864. 1864 (459) x.

Committee on expiring laws. 7th session, 18th Parliament. Report, 20 June 1865. 1865 (191) xii.

PEEL, Jonathan
Committee of inquiry into the organisation of the Indian Army.
   Report, 7 March 1859. 1859, session 1 [2515] v. (also bound in 1859, session 2, vol.viii) SEE ALSO Hancock, Henry.
   Supplement. Papers connected with the re-organisation of the Army in India. 1859, session 2 [2541] viii.

Royal commission on the claims of distinguished-service colonels, *etc.* Report, 15 June 1863. 1863 [3196] xiii.

Select committee on the militia estimates, 1858/9. Report, 14 July 1858. 1857/8 (428) x.

PEEL, Robert, *Sir*
Committee on Mr. Foden's petition on discovery of his crystalline size. Report, 23 May 1800. CJ, vol.55, p.564; (Reps., 1731-1800, no.162, vol.26).

Secret committee on the expediency of the Bank [of England] resuming cash payments
   1st report, 5 April 1819. 1819 (202) iii.
   2nd report, 6 May 1819. 1819 (202) iii; (Monetary Policy, 2).

Select committee on the British Museum. Report, 30 June 1838. 1837/8 (545) xxiii; (ED British Museum, 4).

Select committee on East India built shipping. Min. of ev. 19 April to 30 June 1814. 1813/4 (115) viii.

Select committee on election petition recognizances. Report, 1 June 1838. 1837/8 (441) x; (GO Elections, 2).

Select committee on Evesham election petition. Min. of ev. 8 June 1838. 1837/8 (460) x.

Select committee on police of the metropolis. Report, 17 June 1822. 1822 (440) iv; repr. 1852/3 (292) xxxviii; (CP Police, 3).

Select committee on promisory notes in Scotland and Ireland. Report, 26 May 1826. 1826 (402) iii.

Select committee on public petitions. Report, 25 July 1832. 1831/2 (639) v; repr. 1833 (2) xii.

Select committee on the state of children employed in the manufactures of the U.K. Min. of ev. 25 April to 18 June 1816. 18 May and 19 June 1816. 1816 (397) iii; (IR Children's Employment, 1).

PEELE, R. SEE:
Peel, R.

PELHAM, Charles Anderson Worsley Anderson SEE:
Anderson-Pelham, Charles Anderson Worsley.

PELHAM, Henry Thomas, *3rd E. Chichester*
Commission to inquire into the management of Milbank Prison
   Report, 9 Jan 1847. 1847 [760] xxx.
   Min. of ev. 20 Jan 1847. 1847 [768] xxx; (CP Prisons, 13).

Commission for inquiring into those cases which were investigated and reported upon by the Charity Commission, but not certified to the Attorney-General, 1849
   1st report, 25 June 1850. 1850 [1242] xx.
   2nd report, 29 May 1851. 1851 [1373] xxii.

Communication on the poor laws. 18 Jan 1834. *In*: 1834 (44) xxxvii; (Poor Law, 17).

Select committee (HL) on the petitions respecting the Birmingham and Oxford Junction Railway. Report, 8 June 1847. HL 1847 (190) xxv.

PELHAM, Thomas
Commitee of secrecy relative to the state of Ireland
   1st report, 13 April 1801. CJ Reports, vol.10, p.828; 1801 (39) iii.
   2nd report, 15 May 1801. CJ Reports, vol.10, p.829; 1801 (71) iii.

PELHAM-CLINTON, Henry Pelham, *5th D. Newcastle*
Commission on popular education in England
   Report (vol.1). 18 March 1861. 1861 [2794-I] xxi, pt.1.
   Reports of assistant commissioners (vols.2-4). 1861 [2794 II-IV] xxi, pts. 2-4.

Answers to circular of questions (vol.5). 1861 [2794-V] xxi, pt.5.

Min. of ev. (vol.6). 1861 [2794-VI] xxi, pt.6; (Education, 3-8)

Council of the Prince of Wales on the Duchy of Cornwall. Report, 8 Nov 1862. 1863 [3088] xxvi.

Select commitee (HL) on the Illegitimate Children (Ireland) Bill and the Poor Relief (Ireland) Act Amendment Bill. Report, 19 March 1863. HL 1863 (49) xxxiv.

PELL, Albert
Royal commision on agriculture. Reports of assistant commissioners. July 1880. 1880 C.2678 xviii; (Agriculture, 19). SEE ALSO: Gordon-Lennox, Charles Henry, *6th D. Richmond.*

Select committee on borough auditors and assessors. Report, 22 July 1874. 1874 (321) vii.

PEMBROKE, Lord   SEE:
Herbert, S., *14th E. Pembroke and Montgomery.*

PENDARVES, E.W.W.   SEE:
Wynne-Pendarves, E.W.

PENNETHORNE, James
Commision of inquiry into the execution of the contracts for certain union workhouses in Ireland. Report, 2 April 1844. 1844 [562], [568] xxx.

Metropolis improvements: New Street from Spitalfields Church to Shoreditch. 9 May 1856. 1856 (193-II) lii. Commission of Works.

Report and plan for opening a street between the Thames embankment and the Horse Guards through Whitehall Yard and the Garden of Fife House. 24 April 1868. 1867/8 (399) lviii. Commission of Woods, *etc.*

Report on the damage sustained by Crown property in the precincts of Whitehall by the operations of the Metropolitan Commission of Sewers. 10 May 1851. 1851 (663) xlviii; (UA Sanitation, 3). Commission of Woods, *etc.*

Report on New Street works from Lower Sloan Street to Chelsea Bridge and on Battersea Park. 15 and 25 April 1856. 1856 (193) lii. Commission of Works.

Report respecting Pimlico improvements. 12 March 1856. 1856 (193-I) lii. Commission of Works.

PENROSE-FITZGERALD   SEE:
Fitzgerald, Robert Uniacke Penrose, *Sir.*

PENZANCE, *Bn.*   SEE:
Wilde, James Plaisted, *Bn. Penzance.*

PEPYS, Charles Christopher, *1st E. Cottenham*
Select committee (HL) on the Administration of Justice Bill. Min. of ev. 2 July 1840. HL 1840 (160) xxii; HC repr. 1840 (500) xv; (Legal Administration, 6).

Select committee (HL) on the Bankruptcy Law Amendment Bill, the Bankruptcy and Insolvency Bill (No.2), and the Debtor and Creditor Bill. Report, 8 June 1847. HL 1847 (194) xxiii.

Select committee (HL) on the Ecclesiastical Courts (Consolidation) Bill. Report, 29 March 1836. HL 1836 (46) ix.

Select committee (HL) on the extension of the Dissenters Chapels Bill to Ireland. Report, 15 March 1844. HL 1844 (38) xix.

PEPYS, Lucas
Royal College of Physicians of London. Report on vaccination. Report, 8 July 1807. 1807 (14) ii.

PERCEVAL, Charles Spencer
Sepulchral monuments committee of the Society of Antiquaries of London. Report, 1869. 1872 C.558 xlvi. Office of Works.

PERCY, Algernon George, *6th D. Northumberland*
Royal commission on the condition and administration of the parochial charities in the City of London. Report, 12 March 1880. 4 vols. 1880 C.2522 xx.

Select committee (HL) on the Pollution of Rivers Bill. Report, 21 July 1873. HL 1873 (132) ix.

PERCY, Henry George, *E. Percy*
Select committee on the Ecclesiastical Buildings (Fire Insurance) Bill. Report, 28 June 1878. 1878 (253) xi.

PERRIN, Louis
Commission on municipal corporations in Ireland
  1st report, and supplementary report. 1835 [23], [24] xxvii.
  Report on the City of Dublin
    Pt.1 1835 [25] xxvii.
    Pt.2 1836 [26] xxiv.
  Appendix, pts. 1 and 2. 1835 [27], [28] xxvii, xxviii.
  Appendix, pt.3. 1836 [29] xxiv.

PERRY, Erskine, *Sir*
Select committee on Bills of Exchange Bill, and Bills of Exchange and Promissory Notes Bill. Report, 15 May 1855. 1854/5 (237) vii.

PERRY, Harold Arthur
Commission on the affairs of the Macclesfield Trustee Savings Bank. Interim report. 1889 C.5778 xxxix; (MP Savings Banks, 4). Treasury. (no others identified)

PERTH, *Lord*
[Peerage claim]. 1846-8, SEE: Cooper, C.A.
                1853, SEE: Freeman-Mitford, J.T.

PERY, Edmund Sexton
Committee on the petitions of freemen of Limerick. Report, 23 Dec 1761; repr. 1820 (270) iii.

PERY, Edward Henry, *1st E. Limerick*
Committee (HL) on the Gas Light and Coke Company Bill. Min. of ev. 27 June 1816. HL 1816 (117) lxxxi.

Committee of privileges (HL). Borthwick claim of peerage. SEE: Cooper, C.A., *6th E. Shaftesbury.*

PETERBOROUGH, *Bp.*   SEE:
Jeune, Francis, 1864-68
Magee, William Connor, 1868-91
Creighton, Mandell, 1891-96
Glyn, Edward Glyn, 1896-1916

PETERKIN, William Arthur
Report on the system of boarding pauper children in private dwellings. 15 April 1893. 1893/4 C.7140 xliv. Board of Supervision.

PETO, Samuel Morton, *Sir*
Select committee on the Burials Bill. Min. of proc. 3 June 1862. 1862 (306) xiv; repr. 1870 (0.61) vi.

PETTY, Henry, *Lord*   SEE:
Petty-Fitzmaurice, Henry, *3rd M. Lansdowne.*

PETTY-FITZMAURICE, Henry, *3rd M. Lansdowne*

Committee on the petition of the Sierra Leone Company. Report, 27 Feb 1804. 1803/4 (24) v; (Africa, 1).

Report of the judges appointed to examine the models submitted in competition for a monument to the late Duke of Wellington. 7 Aug 1857. 1857/8 (400) xxxiv. Commission of Works.

Secret committee (HL) on the commercial distress. Report. HL 1847/8 (31) xxiv; repr. HL 1857, session 1 (16) ix; HC repr. 1847/8 (565) viii, pt.3; repr. 1857, session 1 (0.50) ii; (MP Commercial Distress, 3).

Select committee (HL) on the affairs of the East India Company
    Report, 19 July 1830. HL 1830 (11) cclxxiv.
    Appendix, index. HL 1830 (11) cclxxv.

Select committee (HL) on the appointment of sheriff in Ireland. Report, 3 Aug 1838. HL 1837/8 (330) xxi.

Select committee (HL) on the burdens affecting real property
    Report, 17 Feb 1846. HL 1846 (29) xxii.
    Index. HL 1846 (29-II) xxii.
    Appendix. HL 1846 (29-III, IV) xxiii.

Select committee (HL) on certain prisoners confined in the penitentiary at Milbank. Report, 30 March 1838. HL 1837/8 (81) xxi.

Select committee (HL) on the coal trade of the U.K. Report, 19 July 1830. HL 1830 (12) cclxxv.

Select committee (HL) on the collection and payment of tithes in Ireland
    1st report. HL 1831/2 (44) cccv.
    2nd report, 28 June 1832. HL 1831/2 (178) cccv.
    Ev., appendix. HL 1831/2 (14) cccv.

Select committee (HL) on the Court of Chancery Regulation Bill. Min. of ev. 16 May to 15 June 1833. HL 1833 (66) cccxviii.

Select committee (HL) on foreign trade
    1st report: Timber trade. 3 July 1820. HL 1820 (59) cxvii; HC repr. 1820 (269) iii.
    2nd report: Silk and wine trade. 8 June 1821. HL 1821 (98) cxxii; HC repr. 1821 (703) vii; (IR Trade, 3).

Select committee (HL) on foreign trade with the East Indies and China. Report. HL 1821 (42) cxxii; repr. HL 1829 (110) ccxlix; HC repr. 1821 (476) viii; (IR Trade, 3).

Select committee (HL) on gaols and houses of correction. SEE: Gordon-Lennox, Charles, *5th D. Richmond.*

Select committee (HL) on intercourse between the U.K. and the colonies of North America. Report, 13 June 1836. HL 1836 (56) ix.

Select committee (HL) on the new plan of education in Ireland. Report, 14 July 1837. HL 1837 (27) xxi, xxii; HC repr. 1837 (543) viii, pts. 1 and 2.

Select committee (HL) on the operation of the criminal law
    Report, 26 April 1847. HL 1847 (49) xxiv.
    2nd report, 14 June 1847. HL 1847 (49-I) xxiv.
    Appendix. HL 1847 (49-APP) xxv.

Select committee (HL) on the operation of the Irish poor law
    1st report, 9 March 1849. HL 1849 (19-I) xxxi; HC repr. 1849 (192) xvi.
    2nd report, 22 March 1849. HL 1849 (19-II) xxxi; HC repr. 1849 (228) xvi.

    3rd report, 30 March 1849. HL 1849 (19-III) xxxii; HC repr. 1849 (209) xvi.
    4th report, 10 May 1849. HL 1849 (19-IV) xxxii; HC repr. 1849 (365) xvi.
    5th report, 25 May 1849. HL 1849 (19-V) xxxii; HC repr. 1849 (507) xvi.
    6th report, 2 July 1849. HL 1849 (19-VI) xxxii; HC repr. 1849 (507) xvi.
    Appendix. HL 1849 (19-APP) xxxii; HC repr. 1849 (507) xvi.

Select committee (HL) on precedents relating to the King's signature. Report, 26 May 1830. HL 1830 (150) cclxxv.

Select committee (HL) on the progress and operation of the new plan of education in Ireland. Report, 14 July 1837. HL 1837 (241) xx.

Select committee (HL) on railway bills
    Report, 5 Feb 1846. HL 1846 (12) xxvi.
    2nd report, 12 Feb 1846. HL 1846 (22) xxvi.
    3rd report, 27 Feb 1846. HL 1846 (45) xxvi.
    4th report, 6 March 1846. HL 1846 (50) xxvi.
    5th report, 10 March 1846 HL 1846 (52) xxvi.
    6th report, 13 March 1846. HL 1846 (56) xxvi.
    7th report, 17 March 1846. HL 1846 (60) xxvi.
    8th report, 11 May 1846. HL 1846 (135) xxvi.

Select committee (HL) on the rebuilding of the Houses of Parliament
    1st report, 17 March 1836. HL 1836 (30) ix.
    2nd report, 28 April 1836. HL 1836 (74) ix.

Select committee (HL) relative to the suspension of railway bills. 1st report, 8 June 1847. HL 1847 (191) xxv.

Select committee (HL) on standing orders respecting railway bills. Report, 16 Aug 1836. HL 1836 (310) ix.

Select committee (HL) on temporary accommodation of the H.L. Report, 2 July 1835. HL 1835 (96) xxviii.

Select committee (HL) on tithes in Ireland
    1st report, 19 Jan 1832. HL 1831/2 (44) cccv; HC repr. 1831/2 (271) xxii.
    2nd report. HL 1831/2 (178) cccv; HC repr. 1831/2 (663) xxii.
    Min. of ev. HL 1831/2 (14) cccv; HC repr. 1831/2 (663) xxii.

Stafford Borough Disfranchisement Bill. Min. of ev. upon the second reading. 16 June 1836. HL 1836 (137) xxx; HC repr. 1836 (541) xix.

PETTY-FITZMAURICE, Henry Charles Keith, *5th M. Lansdowne*

Committee on employment of officers of Royal Engineers in civil departments of the state. 24 Sept 1870. 1871 C.276 xiv; (GO Civil Service, 8). War Office.

Committee on the housing of the Wallace Collection. Report. 1897 C.8445 lxxii; (ED Fine Arts, 6).

Joint select committee on the channel tunnel. Report, 10 July 1883. HL 1883 (47) x; HC repr. 1883 (248) xii.

Select committee (HL) on Irish jury laws. Report, 12 Aug 1881. HL 1881 (117) viii; HC repr. 1881 (430) xi.

PETTY-FITZMAURICE, John, *2nd M. Lansdowne*

Committee on British Museum petition on the Lansdowne manuscripts. SEE: Long, Charles.

PETTY-FITZMAURICE, William Thomas, *4th E. Kerry*

Select committee on Shannon navigation. Report, 29 July 1834. 1834 (532) xvii.

Select committee on education in England and Wales. Report, 3 Aug 1835. 1835 (465) vii; (ED Poorer Classes, 6).

PHELAN, Denis
Report on the arrangements for carrying into effect the provisions of the Vaccination Extension Act, and their results. 25 March 1842. In: 1842 [399] xix.

Report on the mortality of infant children in the workhouse of the North Dublin Union. SEE: Hall, Richard.

PHILIPPS, John Henry
Select committee on the Great Yarmouth election petition. Min. of ev. 2 March 1860. 1860 (127) xi.

PHILIPS, Mark
Select committee on the exportation of machinery
1st report, 1 April 1841. 1841 (201) vii.
2nd report, 11 June 1841. 1841 (400) vii.

PHILLIMORE, John George
Select committee on public prosecutors. Report, 9 Aug 1855. 1854/5 (481) xii.

Select committee on public prosecutors. Report, 9 May 1856. 1856 (206) vii.

PHILLIMORE, Joseph
Commission on the claims of British subjects trading with Spain for losses sustained since 1804
Report, 20 Feb 1839. 1839 (167) xxx.
Report, 25 Feb 1841. 1841 (78) xiii.

Commission for investigating the Danish claims
Report, 3 April 1835. 1835 (121) xxxvii.
Report, 6 Feb 1839. 1839 (75) xxx.
Report, 12 May 1840. 1840 (440) xxix.

Commission on registers or records of births, baptisms, deaths or burials and marriages in England and Wales. 18 June 1838. 1837/8 [148] xxviii.

PHILLIMORE, Robert Joseph, Sir
Select committee on the Metropolis Sewage and Essex Reclamation Bill. SEE: Headlam, Thomas Emerson.

PHILLIPPO, George
Commission on smuggling from Hong Kong into China of opium and other goods. Report, 1 Sept 1883. 1884 C.3983 liv. Colonial Office.

PHILLIPS, George
Report on the use of Barley, malt, sugar and molasses in breweries and distilleries. 14 Nov 1846. 1847 (26) lix. Board of Excise.

PHILLIPS, John
Report on the ventilation of mines and collieries. 1850 [1222] xxiii; (FP Mining Accidents, 6). Home Department.

PHILLIPS, R.
Report on the specific gravity of soap. 20 Nov 1839. 1840 (253) xliv. Commission of Excise.

PHILLPOTTS, George
Select committee on conduct. SEE: Beardsley, B.C. SEE ALSO: Rolph, J.

PHIPPS, Edmund Constantine Henry
Emigration to Brazil. 23 March 1872. (Brazil, no.1, 1872). 1872 C.550 lxx; (Emigration, 25).

PHIPPS, George Augustus Constantine, 2nd M. Normanby
Select committee on the kitchen and refreshment rooms, H.C. Report, 17 Feb 1853. 1852/3 (138) xxxiv.

Select committee (HL) on Sunday trading on canals, etc. SEE: Littleton, Edward John, 1st Bn. Hatherton.

PICKERING, Percival Andree
Trades union commission: Manchester outrages inquiry. Report, 10 Feb 1868. 1867/8 [3980] xxxix; (Industrial Relations, 9). SEE ALSO: Erle, William.

PICKWOOD, R.W.
Commission on the state of the community in Anguilla. Report, 17 March 1826. 1826 (174) xxvi.

PIERREPONT, Charles, 1st E. Manvers
Select committee (HL) on the Poor (St. Pancras Parish) Act (Amendment) Bill. 21 June 1805. HL 1805 (59) xv.

PIGOTT, Arthur, Sir
Committee appointed to inspect the HL Journals in relation to the bills sent from the HL for declaring the law on witnesses being liable to answer and for interrogation of witnesses against Henry, Vct. Melville. Report, 29 March 1806. 1806 (69) ii.

PIGOTT, Francis
Select committee on medical relief. Report, 5 July 1854. 1854 (348) xii; (Health, 8).

PIGOTT, Gillery
Commission on the existence of corrupt practices for the Borough of Wakefield. Report, 28 Jan 1860. 1860 [2601] xxviii.

PIGOTT, Grenville
Report on returns relating to the operation of the laws of settlement and removal of the poor in the counties of Berkshire, Buckingham and Oxford. 1850 [1152] xxvii; (Poor Law, 21). Poor Law Board.

Report on vagrancy. 18 Dec 1847. 1847/8 [987] liii. Poor Law Board.

Committee on the expenditure and practice of different government departments in regard to stationery and printing. Report, 30 Dec 1884. 1884/5 C.4367 xxii. Treasury.

PIRBRIGHT, Bn. SEE:
De Worms, Henry, Bn. Pirbright.

PITT, J.
Report on the state of the enclosures in H.M. Forests. 1782. (Reps., 1731-1800, no.48, vol.5).

PITT, John, 2nd E. Chatham
Lords' committee of secrecy relating to the Bank of England. Report, 6 Feb 1810. 1810 (17) iii; (Monetary Policy, 1).

PITT, William
Committee appointed to examine His Majesty's physicians on the state of His Majesty's health
Report, 10 Dec 1788. CJ, vol.44, p.6.
Report, 13 Jan 1789. CJ, vol.44, p.47.

Committee of secrecy. Reports on seditious societies
1st report, 17 May 1794. (Reps., 1731-1800, no.112, vol.14)
2nd report, 6 June 1794. CJ, vol.49, p.656; (Reps., 1731-1800, no.113, vol.14)

PITT, William (continued)
Appendix. 7 June 1794. (Reps., 1731-1800, no.114, vol.14)
Supplement and appendix. 16 June 1794. (Reps., 1731-1800, no.115, vol.14)

PLAYFAIR, Lyon, *Sir*
Civil service inquiry commission
1st report, Jan 1875. 1875 C.1113 xxiii.
2nd report, 19 May 1875. 1875 C.1226 xxiii.
3rd report, 23 July 1875. 1875 C.1317 xxiii
Index. 1876 C.1444 xxii; (GO Civil Service, 9). Treasury.

Coals suited to the steam navy
1st report, 5 Jan 1848. 1847/8 [915] xxxviii.
2nd report, 24 May 1849. 1849 [1086] xxxii.
3rd report, 2 April 1851. 1851 [1345] xxxiii.
Museum of Practical Geology *and* Commission of HM Woods.

Committee on the retirement of professors. Report, 5 Aug 1895. 1895 C.7889 lxxx. Treasury.

Report on the gases and explosions in collieries
1 June 1846. 1846 (529) xliii; (FP Mining Accidents, 6)
1 June 1846. 1847 [815] xvi; (FP Mining Accidents, 6). Home Department.

Report on the present state of the Irish potato crop and the prospect of approaching scarcity. 15 Nov 1845. 1846 (28) xxxvii; (Famine, 8). Home Department.

Report on smoke prohibition. 30 March 1846. 1846 (194) xliii. Home Department.

Royal commission on trawling for herring on the coasts of Scotland. Report. 1863 [3106], [3106-I] xxviii.

Select committee on British and foreign spirits. Report, 22 July 1890. 1890 (316) x.

Select committee on British and foreign spirits. Report, 30 April 1891. 1890/1 (210) xi.

Select committee on the City of London (Fire Inquests) Bill. Report, 13 April 1888. 1888 (116) ix.

Select committee on Coal Duties (London) Abolition Bill. Report, 2 July 1889. 1889 (228) ix.

Select committee on Endowed Schools Acts. 11 June 1886. 1886, session 1 (191) ix.

Select committee on Endowed Schools Acts, 1869, and amending acts. Report, 21 April 1887. 1887 (120) ix.

Select committee on lighting by electricity. Report, 13 June 1879. 1878/9 (224) xi.

Select committee on the Manchester Corporation Water Bill. Report, 8 April 1878. 1878 (136) xvi.

Select committee on the Post Office Telegraph Department. Report, 13 July 1876. 1876 (357) xiii; (Post and Telegraphs, 5).

Standing committee on law. Criminal Lunatics Bill. Report, 17 July 1884. 1884 (277) ix.

Standing committee on trade. Patents for Inventions Bill. Report, 9 July 1883. 1883 (247) xiv.

PLEYDELL-BOUVERIE, William, *3rd E. Radnor*
Select committee (HL) on the Stafford Bribery Bill. Ev. 30 March 1836. HL 1836 (49) xxx.

Select committee on town holdings. Report, 5 Aug 1887. 1887 (260) xiii; (UA Planning, 5).

Committee (HL) on the Great Western Railway Bill. SEE: Stuart-Wortley-Mackenzie, James Archibald, *1st Bn. Wharncliffe.*

Select committee (HL) on the inquisition on the body of Thomas Culver in Marshalsea Prison. 5 June 1811. HL 1810/1 (84) xliv.

Select committee (HL) on the London to Southampton Railway Bill. Report, 9 June 1834. HL 1834 (106) xxiii, pt.2.

Select committee (HL) on the Stafford Bribery Bill. Min. of ev. 30 March 1836. HL 1836 (49) xxx.

PLOWDEN, George
Commission on salt in British India
Report, 30 Jan 1856. 1856 [2084-I] xxvi.
Conclusion to report, 24 May 1856. 1856 [2084-IV] xxvi.
Appendix. 1856 [2084-II, III, V] xxvi.

PLUMER, Thomas, *Sir*
Report on the petition of the Lord Mayor and Alderman of London respecting the office of a guager at West India and London docks. 26 July 1814. 1813/4 (344) iv.

PLUMER, William
Committee on franking by members of Parliament. Report, 16 April 1735. CJ, vol.22, p.462.

PLUNKET, David Robert, *1st Bn. Rathmore*
Committee on Celtic ornaments found in Ireland and the relations between the British Museum and the museums of Edinburgh and Dublin. Report, 5 April 1899. 1899 (179) lxxvii. Treasury.

Royal committee on Westminster Abbey
1st report, 30 July 1890. 1890/1 C.6228 xliv.
Final report, 24 June 1891. 1890/1 C.6398 xliv.

Select committee on the Admiralty and War Office sites. Report, 15 June 1887. 1887 (184) vii.

Select committee on the Bann Drainage Bill. Report, 22 July 1889. 1889 (272) ix.

Select committee on H.C.; re-arrangement of rooms. Report, 16 June 1892. 1892 (288) xii.

Select committee on the H.C. ventilation. Report, 24 July 1891. 1890/1 (371) xii.

Select committee on London Water (Transfer) Bills. Report, 4 July 1895. 1895 (384) xi; (UA Water Supply, 9).

Select committee on the Public Parks and Works (Metropolis) Bill. Report, 12 July 1887. 1887 (219) xi.

Select committee on registration of parliamentary voters in Ireland. Report, 3 July 1874. 1874 (261) xi.

Select committee on theatres and places of entertainment. Report, 2 June 1892. 1892 (240) viii; (Stage and Theatre, 3).

POCKLINGTON, Evelyn H.F.
Education of officers. Report by the Director-General of military education. SEE: Biddulph, Robert.

Report of Director-General of military education on Army schools and libraries
1st report, 15 July 1872. 1872 C.654 xiv.
2nd report, 1 July 1874. 1874 C.1085 xii.
3rd report, 1 July 1877. 1877 C.1885 xxx. War Office.

POLE, Charles Morice, *Sir*
Naval enquiry commission

1st report: Naval store-keepers at Jamaica. 12 May 1803. 1802/3 (78) iv.

2nd report: Chest at Chatham. 6 June 1803. 1802/3 (97) iv.

3rd report: Block contract; cooper's contract. 13 June 1803. 1802/3 (109) iv.

4th report: Prize Agency. 18 July 1803. 1802/3 (160) iv.

5th report: Sixpenny Office. 10 Aug 1803. 1802/3 (174) iv.

6th report: Plymouth Yard; Woolwich Yard. 2 May 1804. 1803/4 (83) iii.

7th report: Naval Hospital at East Stonehouse; Le Caton Hospital Ship. 11 July 1804. 1803/4 (172) iii.

8th report: H.M. victualling department at Plymouth; embezzlement of the King's Casks. 16 July 1804. 1803/4 (179) iii.

9th report: Receipt and issue of stores in Plymouth yard. 16 Jan 1805. 1805 (1) ii.

10th report: Offices of the Treasurer of HM Navy. 13 Feb 1805. 1805 (9) ii.

11th report: Issue of Navy bills. 11 March 1805. 1805 (47) ii.

12th report: Purchases of hemp, masts and fir timber; transfer of contracts. 22 Jan 1806. 1806 (1) iv.

13th report: Contracts for victualling sick prisoners of war. 15 May 1806. 1806 (161) iv.

14th report: Royal Hospital at Greenwich. 30 June 1806. 1806 (256) iv.

Select committee on the min. of ev. respecting calico printers, printed 4 July 1804. Report, 17 July 1806. 1806 (319) iii.

Select committee on the embankments in Catwater. Report, 12 July 1806. 1806 (298) iii.

Committee on public income and expenditure of Ireland
Report, 14 June 1811. 1810/11 (262) v.
2nd report, 22 July 1812. 1812 (370) v.

POLLARD-URQUHART, William SEE:
Urquhart, William Pollard.

POLLOCK, Charles Edward, *Bn. Pollock*
Gloucester City election petition trial. Min. of ev. and judgement. 9 June 1880. 1880 (229) lviii.

POLLOCK, George D.
Commission on the treatment of the treason-felony convicts in the English convict prisons. Report, 8 June 1867. 1867 [3880] xxxv; (CP Prisons, 21).

POLLOCK, Jonathan Frederick
Commission on courts of common law
1st report, 20 Feb 1829. 1829 (46) ix.
2nd report, 8 May 1830. 1830 (123) xi.
3rd report, 13 July 1831. 1831 (92) x.
4th report, 6 March 1832. 1831/2 (239) xxv, pts. 1 and 2
5th report, 3 May 1833. 1833 (247) xxii.
6th report. 1834 (263) xxvi; (Legal Administration, 1-5).

POLWARTH, *Lord* [Peerage claim]. SEE:
Cooper, C.A.

PONSONBY, *Lord* SEE:
Ponsonby, John William, *4th E. Bessborough* (1781-1847)
Ponsonby, John George Brabazon, *5th E. Bessborough* (1809-1880)

Ponsonby, Frederick George Brabazon, *6th E. Bessborough* (1815-1895)

PONSONBY, Frederick George Brabazon, *6th E. Bessborough*
Royal commission of inquiry into the working of the Landlord and Tenant (Ireland) Act, 1870. Report, 4 Jan 1881. 1881 C.2779 xviii, xix.

PONSONBY, George
Select committee on the administration of justice in Wales. Report, 4 July 1817. 1817 (461) v; repr. 1818 (109) vii.

PONSONBY, John George Brabazon, *5th E. Bessborough*
Select committee (HL) on petitions respecting the Irish Great Western Railway. Report, 17 July 1845. HL 1845 (275) xviii.

PONSONBY, John William, *4th E. Bessborough*
Commission of Holyhead roads. Report on origin of their commission and the present jurisdiction and duties of the present commissioners. Report, 4 Oct 1831. 1831 (298) xii.

Commission of inquiry into the Post Office Department
Reports: Mail-coach contract. 8 July 1835. 1835 (313) xlviii.
5th report: Mail-coach contracts. 19 Aug 1835. 1835 (542) xlviii.

Commission on the Post Office Department
(1st-3rd reports not printed)
4th report. 1836 [49] xxviii.
5th report: Prices current. 1836 [50] xxviii.
6th report: Packet establishments. 1836 [51] xxviii.
7th report, 8 Feb 1837. 1837 [70] xxxiv, pt.1.
8th report: Fees, pt.1. 15 April 1837. 1837 [85] xxxiv, pt.1.
9th report: Two-penny post. 7 July 1837. 1837 [99] xxxiv, pt.1.
10th report: Registration of letters. Jan 1838. 1837/8 [112] xxxv.

Destruction by fire of the two Houses of Parliament. Report, 25 Feb 1835. 1835 (1) xxxvii.

POPHAM, Home, *Sir*
Select committee on papers relating to repairs of ships under his command. SEE: Stewart, John, *Sir.*

PORCHESTER, *Lord* SEE:
Herbert, H.G., *2nd E. Carnarvon.*

PORT, John
Select committee on his charity bill. SEE: Montagu, Robert.

PORTLAND, D. SEE:
Scott-Bentinck, William Henry Cavendish, *4th D. Portland* (1786-1854)
Scott-Bentinck, William John, *5th D. Portland* (1800-1879)
Cavendish-Bentinck, William John Arthur Charles James, *6th D. Portland* (1857-1950)

PORTMAN, Edward Berkely, *1st Vct. Portman*
Royal New and Waltham forests commission. Report, 16 May 1850. 1850 (707), [1267] xxx.

Select committee (HL) on the East Gloucestershire Railway Bill. Report, 7 July 1862. HL 1862 (161) xxix.

PORTMAN, Edward Berkely, *1st Vct. Portman* (continued)
Select committee (HL) on the Glasgow Waterworks Bill. Min. of ev. 5 July 1838. HL 1837/8 (293) xx.

Select committee (HL) on the Infant Life Protection Bill. Report, 4 July 1872. HL 1872 (188) ix.

Select committee (HL) on laws relating to parochial assessments. Report, 18 July 1850. HL 1850 (150) xxiii; HC repr. 1850 (622) xvi; repr. 1867/8 (0.113) xiii.

POTTER, Richard
Select committee on Potter's Patent Bill. SEE: Temple-Nugent-Chandos-Grenville, Richard Plantagenet Campbell, *3rd D. Buckingham and Chandos.*

POULETT-SCROPE, G. SEE:
Scrope, George Poulett.

POULETT-THOMSON, Charles Edward
Select committee on manufactures, commerce and shipping. Report, 19 Aug 1833. 1833 (690) vi; (IR Trade, 2).

Select committee on the Port of London. SEE: Labouchere, Henry.

Select committee on private business (of the HC). Report, 4 Aug 1838. 1837/8 (679) xxiii.

Select committee on private business (of the HC).
1st report, 25 Feb 1839. 1839 (51) xiii.
2nd report, 9 Aug 1839. 1839 (520) xiii.

Select committee on the public and private business of the HC. Report, 13 July 1837. 1837 (517) xiii.

Select committee on railway bills. Report, 1 Aug 1836. 1836 (511) xxi.

Select committee on standing orders on private bills
1st report, 1 June 1837. 1837 (367) xiii.
2nd report, 7 July 1837. 1837 (489) xiii.

POULTER, John Sayer
Select committee on Poole Borough municipal election. Report, 25 March 1836. 1836 (128) xxi.

POWELL, Francis Sharp, *Sir*
Select committee on museums of the Science and Art Department
1st report, 21 May 1897. 1897 (223) xii.
2nd report, 23 July 1897. 1897 (341) xii.

Select committee on museums of the Science and Art Department
1st report, 26 April 1898. 1898 (175) xi.
2nd report, 19 July 1898. 1898 (327) xi.

Select committee on police and sanitary regulations bills. Proc. 22 June 1892. 1892 (328) xiv.

Select committee on police and sanitary regulations bills, 1893. SEE: Long, Walter Hume.

POWELL, Thomas S.
Report on patent sectional transferable railway carriages for carrying goods on the broad or narrow gauge. SEE: Pasley, C.W.

POWER, A.
Report on the Bedworth Incorporation under Gilbert's Act. 18 March 1843. 1843 (172) xlv. Poor Law Commission.

Report and ev. on the state of the population of Stockport. 9 Feb 1842. 1842 (158) xxxv. Poor Law Commission.

POWER, W.H.
Report on the cause of the late outbreak of diptheria in North London. 10 Dec 1878. 1878/9 (99) lviii. Local Government Board.

POWER, William James Tyrone, *Sir*
Committee on equalisation on stoppages from soldiers' rations at home, abroad, in hospital and on board ship. Report, 2 March 1866. 1871 (197) xxxix. War Office.

POWIS, E. SEE:
Herbert, Edward, *2nd E. Powis* (1785-1848)
Herbert, Edward James, *3rd E. Powis* (1818-1891)

POWLETT, Harry George, *4th D. Cleveland*
Commission on the property and income of the universities of Oxford and Cambridge
Vol.1: Report, 31 July 1873. 1873 C.856 xxxvii.
Vol.2: Returns from the University of Oxford. 1873 C.856-I xxxvii.
Vol.3: Returns from the University of Cambridge. 1873 C.856-II xxxvii.

Royal commission on the sale, exchange and resignation of ecclesiastical benefices
Report. 1878/9 C.2375 xx.
Min. of ev. 1880 C.2507 xviii.

Select committee on the Mayo election petition
Report, 20 April 1853. 1852/3 (372) xvi.
Min. of ev. 28 April 1853. 1852/3 (415) xvi.

Select committee on miscellaneous expenditure. Report, 25 July 1860. 1860 (483) ix; (National Finance, 4).

Select committee of privileges. Report on a petition complaining of the interference of E. Fitzhardinge at the election in the Western division of Gloucester county. 9 March 1848. 1847/8 (160) xi.

POWNALL, Thomas
Committee on laws relative to the assize of Bread. Report, 21 Dec 1772. CJ Reports, vol.3, p.55; (Reps., 1731-1800, no.11, vol.1).

POZER, C.H.
Select committee of the Parliament of Canada on immigration and colonisation. 1st report, 31 March 1875. 1875 (275) lii; (Canada, 28). Colonial Office. (No others identified).

PRAED, William Mackworth
Report on the auditors of public accounts on the deductions of the civil list. 16 Feb 1808. 1808 (38) ii; repr. 1830 (616) ix.

PRATT, Charles, *1st E. Camden*
Select committee (HL) on the dearth of provisions. Report, 22 Dec 1800. 1801 (3) ii. (HL not located).

PRATT, John Jeffreys, *1st M. Camden*
Select committee (HL) to examine the physicians attending His Majesty on the state of His Majesty's health. Report, 20 Dec 1810. HL 1810/1 (1) xliii.

Select committee (HL) on precedents on the proceedings in the case of the personal exercise of the Royal authority being prevented or interrupted. Report, 17 Dec 1788; LJ, vol.38, p.276; repr. HL 1810 (2) xliii.

PRENDERGAST, Michael
Commission on the existence of corrupt practices in the Borough of Barnstaple. Report, Dec 1853. 1854 [1704] xxi.

PRESIDENT OF COUNCIL, *Lord*
1796 *E. Chatham*
1801 *D. Portland*
1805 *Vct. Sidmouth*
1805 *E. Camden*
1806 *E. Fitzwilliam*
1806 *Vct. Sidmouth*
1807 *E. Camden*
1812 *Vct. Sidmouth*
1812 *E. Harrowby*
1827 *D. Portland*
1828 *E. Bathurst*
1830 *M. Lansdowne*
1834 *E. Rosslyn*
1835 *M. Lansdowne*
1841 *Lord Wharncliffe*
1846 *D. Buccleuch*
1846 *M. Lansdowne*
1852 *E. Lonsdale*
1852 *E. Granville*
1854 *Lord John Russell*
1855 *E. Granville*
1858 *M. Salisbury*
1859 *E. Granville*
1866 *D. Buckingham and Chandos*
1867 *D. Marlborough*
1868 *E. De Grey and Ripon*
1873 *H.A. Bruce*
1874 *D. Richmond*
1880 *E. Spencer*
1883 *Lord Carlingford*
1885 *Vct. Cranbrook*
1886 *E. Spencer*
1886 *Vct. Cranbrook*
1892 *E. Kimberley*
1894 *E. Rosebery*
1895 *D. Devonshire*

PRESTON, Robert, *Sir*
Committee on the petition of Benjamin Lacam on the New Harbour, Bengal. Report, 10 July 1806. 1806 (289) iii.

PRICE, Edward Plumer
Commission on corrupt practices at elections for the Borough of Bridgewater
1st report, 4 Nov 1869. 1870 C.10 xxx.
2nd report, 20 Dec 1869. 1870 C.11 xxx.
Min. of ev. 1870 C.12 xxx.
Index. 1870 C.78 xxx.

PRICE, Eliza
Commission on inquiry into allegations in her petition. SEE: Rogers, T.N.

PRICE, Rees
Report on death in Carmarthen Asylum. SEE: Campbell, William G.

PRICE, Robert, *Sir*
Select committee on the Pembroke County election petition. Report, 23 Sept 1831. 1831 (262) iv.

PRIMROSE, Archibald John, *4th E. Rosebery*
Committee on the amount of the joint charge on the U.K. and of G.B. and Ireland. Report, 11 July 1806. 1806 (296) iii.

Commission of inquiry on the universities and colleges of Scotland. Report, 7 Oct 1831. 1831 (310) xii.

Commission for visiting the universities of Scotland. Evidence, oral and documentary, indexes
Vol.1: University of Edinburgh. 28 Oct 1830. 1837 [92] xxxv.

Vol.2: University of Glasgow. 11 Oct 1827. 1837 [93] xxxvi.
Vol.3: University of St. Andrews. 4 Aug 1827. 1837 [94] xxxvii.
Vol.4: University of Aberdeen. 21 Sept 1827. 1837 [95] xxxviii.

Select committee (HL) on the Future Entails (Scotland) Bill and the Entails Relief (Scotland) Bill. Report, 25 June 1834. HL 1834 (126) xxi.

Select committee (HL) on the Future Entails Bill and the Entails Relief Bill. Report, 15 May 1835. HL 1835 (57) xxviii.

Select committee (HL) on the laws for election of peers for Scotland. Report, 7 May 1832. HL 1831/2 (123) cccvii.

Select committee (HL) on the report of the Lords of Session on the Future Entails Bill and the Bill for the Relief of Heirs of Entail. Report, 15 May 1835. HL 1835 (57) xxviii.

Select committee (HL) on the Salmon Fisheries (Scotland) (No.2) Bill. Report, 27 June 1842. HL 1842 (151) xvi; HC repr. 1842 (522) xiv; (Fisheries, 2).

PRIMROSE, Archibald Philip, *5th E. Rosebery*
Select committee (HL) on horses. Report, 14 July 1873. HL 1873 (32) viii; HC repr. 1873 (325) xiv.

Select committee (HL) on the representative peerage of Scotland and Ireland. Report, 23 July 1874. HL 1874 (140) viii.

PRINGLE, Alexander
Select committee on Custom House frauds. Report, 1 Aug 1844. 1844 (566) xiv.

PRINGLE, Hall
Report on certain atrocities of slave traders. 9 Aug 1839. 1839 (157) l; (Slave Trade, 87). Colonial Office.

PRINGLE, James W.
Inquiry into steam-vessel accidents. Report, 29 May 1839. 1839 (273) xlvii. Board of Trade.

Report on prisons in the West Indies
Pt.I: Jamaica. Report, 17 July 1838. 1837/8 (596) xl.
Pt.II: Barbados; Antigua, Montserrat, Tortola, St. Lucia. Report, 17 July 1838. 1837/8 (596-II) xl. Colonial Department.

PRINGLE, R.K.
Commission on the conduct of His Highness Meer Allee Moorad. Report, 8 May 1850. 1852/3 (73) lxxvii. East India Office.

PRINSEP, C.R.
Commission of inquiry into certain matters connected with the position of Sir James Brooke, consul-general in Borneo. Reports, 6 and 11 Jan 1855. 1854/5 [1976] xxix. East India Office.

PRIVY SEAL, *Lord*
1798 *E. Westmorland*
1801 *D. Portland*
1805 *Vct. Sidmouth* (–July)
1805 *E. Camden* (July–)
1806 *E. Fitzwilliam* (Feb–)
1806 *L. Holland* (Oct–)
1807 *E. Westmorland*
1827 *D. Portland*
1827 *E. Carlisle*
1828 *L. Ellenborough*
1829 *E. Rosslyn*

PRIVY SEAL, *Lord* (continued)
1830 *L. Durham*
1834 *E. Mulgrave*
1834 *L. Wharncliffe*
1835 *Vct. Duncannon*
1841 *D. Buckingham*
1842 *D. Buccleuch*
1842 *E. Haddington*
1846 *E. Minto*
1852 *M. Salisbury*
1853 *D. Argyll*
1855 *E. Harrowby*
1858 *E. Hardwicke*
1859 *D. Argyll*
1866 *E. Malmesbury*
1868 *E. Kimberley*
1870 *Vct. Halifax*
1874 *E. Malmesbury*
1876 *E. Beaconsfield*
1878 *D. Northumberland*
1880 *D. Argyll*
1881 *L. Carlingford*
1884 *E. Rosebery*
1885 *E. Harrowby*
1886 *W.E. Gladstone*
1886 *E. Cadogan*
1892 *W.E. Gladstone*
1894 *L. Tweedmouth*
1895 *Vct. Cross*

PROTHEROE, Edward
Select committee on highways. Report, 25 June 1819. 1819 (509) v; repr. 1820 (301) ii.

PROVIS, William A.
Report to the Commission of Woods and Forests on the Menai Bridge. 13 May 1840. 1840 (418) xxix.

Report on the Menai Bridge. 1 Oct 1843. 1844 (214) xlv. Commission of Woods, Forests, *etc.*

PULLER, Christopher William Giles
Select committee on the Kingston upon Hull election petition. Min. of ev. 13 Aug 1859. 1859, session 2 (219) iv.

PULTENEY, William, *Sir*
Committee to examine Christopher Layer and others relating to the conspiracy to establish the Pretender on the Throne. Report, 1 March 1722. CJ Reports, vol.1, p.99.

Select committee on a lighthouse on Bell Rock. Report, 1 July 1803. 1802/3 (137) v; (Shipping, 1).

PUSEY, Philip
Committee on the Middle Level Drainage and Navigation Bill. Proc. 4 July 1844. 1844 (446) xiv.

Select committee on agricultural customs. Report, 3 July 1848. 1847/8 (461) vii; repr.1866 (461) vi; (Agriculture, 8).

Select committee on York City election bribery petition. Report, 9 Sept 1835. 1835 (612) x.

PYE-SMITH, Philip Henry
Report on the International Congress on Tuberculosis, Berlin, 24-27 May 1899. 1899 C.9368 lxv. Privy Council.

PYM, William, *Sir*
Report on the fever at Boa Vista, Cape Verd Islands. 15 May 1848. 1847/8 (674) li. Home Department.

QUETELET, A.
Report on conference held at Brussels respecting meteorological observations. 8 Sept 1853. 1854 (4) xlii. Admiralty.

QUINN, W.W.
Committee of privileges on complaint against him. SEE: Newport, John.

RADCLIFFE, John Netten
Report on certain cases of erysipelas following upon vaccination. 16 Dec 1876. 1877 (50) lxxi. Local Government Board.

Report on the recent diffusion of cholera in Europe. 7 May 1872. 1872 (340) xlvii; (HE Infectious Diseases, 3). Local Government Board.

RADNOR, E. SEE:
Pleydell-Bouverie, Jacob, *2nd E. Radnor* (1750-1828)
Pleydell-Bouverie, William, *3rd E. Radnor* (1779-1869)
Pleydell-Bouverie, Jacob, *4th E. Radnor* (1815-1900)

RAE, John
Report of the proc. of the Arctic searching expedition, since 10 June. 27 Sept 1851. 1852 (248) l. Admiralty.

RAE, William
H.M. sole and only master printers in Scotland. SEE: Rutherford, Andrew.

Select committee on the state of prisons in Scotland. Report, 18 May 1826. 1826 (381) v.

RAFFLES, T.S.
Report on the loss of the 'Barbadian' with min. of ev. 21 Dec 1865. *In:* 1866 (56) lxv. Board of Trade.

RAIKES, Henry Cecil
Select committee on elections, intervention of peers, *etc.* Report, 18 Feb 1887. 1887 (80) ix; (GO Elections, 5).

Select committee on standing orders revision. Report, 8 Aug 1876. 1876 (404) xiv.

RAINALS, Harry
Report on the affairs of Schleswig and Holstein. 22 Feb 1861. 1864 [3292] lxv. Foreign Office.

RAMMELL, Thomas W.
The cess pool system in Paris. 1850 [1284] xxii. General Board of Health.

Report on the soft-water springs of the Surrey sands as a gathering ground for the supply of the Metropolis. 5 Nov 1850. 1851 (345) xxiii.

RAMSAY, Fox Maule SEE:
Maule-Ramsay, Fox, *11th E. Dalhousie* (1801-1874)
Maule-Ramsay, George, *12th E. Dalhousie* (1806-1880)
Maule-Ramsay, John William, *13th E. Dalhousie* (1847-1887)
Maule-Ramsay, Arthur George, *14th E. Dalhousie* (1878-1928)

RAMSAY, George Dalhousie
Committee on the system of clothing the militia and Army reserve. Report, 24 April 1872. 1873 C.717 xviii. War Office.

RAMSAY, William
Committee on marine engines. Amended report, 2 Oct 1858. 1859, session 2 [2583] xvii. Admiralty.

RAMSDEN, John, *Sir*
Select committee on the militia estimates, 1857/8. Report, 22 July 1857. 1857, session 2 (200) ix.

RANKIN, James, *Sir*
Select committee on Metropolitan Gas Companies. Report, 24 July 1899. 1899 (294) x.

RANKINE, W.J. MacQuorn
Remarks on the stability of mastless ships of low freeboard, as affected by the waves submitted to the scientific sub-committee on designs of ships of war. 23 Feb 1871. *In:* 1871 C.333 xiv. Admiralty.

RASSAM, Hormund
Report respecting mission to the late King of Abyssinia. 1 Sept 1868. 1868/9 [4088] lxiii. Foreign Office.

RATHDONNELL, *Lord* [Peerage claim]. SEE: Freeman-Mitford, J.T.

RATHMORE, *Lord* SEE:
Plunket, D.R., *1st Bn. Rathmore.*

RAVENSWORTH, *Lord* SEE:
Liddell, Henry Thomas, *1st E. Ravensworth* (1797-1878)
Liddell, Henry George, *2nd E. Ravensworth* (1821-1903)

RAWDON-HASTINGS, Francis, *1st M. Hastings*
Committee (HL) on imprisonment for civil debt Report, 27 April 1809. HL 1809 (61) xxvii. Appendix, min. of ev. HL 1809 (16) xxvii.

RAWLINS, W. Wharton
Commission on the state of the community in Anguilla. Report, 17 March 1826. 1826 (174) xxvi.

RAWLINSON, Robert
Commission on preventing the pollution of rivers
1st report: River Thames. 29 March 1866. 1866 [3634] xxxiii.
2nd report: River Lee. 6 May 1867. 1867 [3835] xxxiii.
3rd report: Rivers Aire and Calder. 15 Aug 1867. 1867 [3850] xxxiii. SEE ALSO: Frankland, Edward.

Committee on the modes of treating town sewage. Report, 21 July 1876. 1876 C.1410 xxxviii; (UA Sanitation, 5). Local Government Board.

Inquiry into the pollution of the River Thames at Barking. Report, Nov 1869. 1870 C.7 xl. Home Department.

Remarks on the Croton aqueduct, New York, and on ancient and modern works of water supply. *In:* 1850 [1282] xxii. General Board of Health.

Report on Dale Dyke and Agden reservoirs. 5 Dec 1864. 1866 (25) lx. Home Department.

Report on the failure and bursting of a reservoir embankment belonging to the Sheffield Waterworks Company, 11 March 1864. 20 May 1864. 1864 (290-I) l. Home Department.

Report on the pollution of the River Blackwater by sewage permitted to flow unclarified from the Camp Farm, Aldershot. 10 March 1870. 1870 (174) lvi. Home Department. Sent.

Report on the public works executed in cotton manufacturing districts and the employment of operatives. 16 Jan 1869. 1868/9 (6) liii. Poor Law Board.

Report on the Public Works (Manufacturing Districts) Acts, 1863-64. 25 Jan 1865. 1865 (5) xlviii. Home Office.

Reports on the Public Works (Manufacturing Districts) Acts, 1863-64. 12 Jan and 12 May 1866. 1866 (375) lxi. Poor Law Board.

Report on St. Giles Cemetery, St. Pancras. 13 June 1850. 1850 [1228] xxi. General Board of Health.

Report on the state of the several reservoirs belonging to the Corporation of Bradford. 7 May 1864. 1864 (290) l. Home Department.

Royal commission on the sewerage and drainage of the City of Dublin. Report, 19 June 1880. 1880 C.2605 xxx.

RAWSON, Rawson W.
Finance committee of Mauritius on overland communication with Europe. Report, 26 Oct 1847. 1851 (430) xxxv. Colonial Office.

Finance committee of Mauritius on steam communication with Europe via Ceylon. Report, 2 April 1846. 1851 (430) xxxv. Colonial Office.

RAYLEIGH, *Bn.* SEE:
Strutt, John William, *3rd Bn. Rayleigh.*

READ, Clare Sewell
Committee on the modes of treating town sewage. Report, 21 July 1876. 1876 C.1410 xxxviii; (UA Sanitation, 5). Local Government Board.

Royal commission on agriculture. Reports of assistant commissioner. July 1880. 1880 C.2678 xviii; (Agriculture, 19).

Select committee on the Adulteration of Food Act, 1872. Report, 3 July 1874. 1874 (262) vi; (HE Food and Drugs, 3).

REDESDALE, *Lord* SEE:
Freeman-Mitford, John, *1st Bn. Redesdale* (1748-1830)
Freeman-Mitford, John Thomas, *1st E. Redesdale* (1805-1886)

REDGRAVE, Alexander
Report on precautions for the protection of persons employed in whitelead works. 29 April 1882. 1882 C.3263 xviii; (Factories, 28).

REDINGTON, Christopher Talbot
Departmental committee on the National School Teachers' (Ireland) Pension Fund. Report, 31 Dec 1896. 1897 C.8471 lxxi. Treasury.

Poor relief, Ireland inquiry commission. Report, 2 April 1887. 1887 C.5043 xxxviii. Home Office.

REDINGTON, Thomas Nicholas, *Sir*
Commission on lunatic asylums in Ireland. Report. 1857/8 [2436] xxvii.

Select committee on the Southampton Town election petition. Min. of ev. 9 May 1842. 1842 (239) viii.

Select committee on the Sudbury election petition. Min. of proc. and ev. 15 April 1842. 1842 (176) vii.

REED, Edward James, *Sir*
Committee on the manning of merchant ships
Vol.1: Report, 4 June 1896. 1896 C.8127 xl.
Vol.2: Min. of ev. 1896 C.8128 xl.
Vol.3: Names of witnesses, digest and index of ev., list of ships. 1896 C.8129 xli. Board of Trade.

REED, Edward James, *Sir* (continued)
Load line committee. Report, 14 Aug 1885. 1884/5 C.4566 lxix. Board of Trade.

Report and ev. of the inquiry into explosion of the steamboat 'Druid'. 12 Feb 1873. 1873 (162) lx. Board of Trade.

REID, Robert Threshie, *Sir*
Select committee on rule of the road at sea. Report, 14 April 1896. 1896 (140) xiii.

RENDEL, James M.
Report and plans for a harbour of refuge at the Isle of Portland. 14 Aug 1846. 1847 (327) lxi. Admiralty.

Report on the Chester and Holyhead Railway and Holyhead harbour. 24 April 1844. 1844 (262) xlv. Admiralty.

Report on Dover harbour. 9 Sept 1845. 1847/8 (476) lx. Admiralty.

Report on the Harbours of Holyhead and Portdynllaen as harbours of refuge. 27 May 1845. 1846 (630) xlv. Admiralty.

Report on a proposed harbour of refuge at Holyhead. 5 Dec 1845. 1846 (380) xlv. Commission of H.M. Woods, *etc.*

Report on the proposed railway bridge over the River Mersey at Runcorn. 30 April 1845. 1846 (379) xxxviii. Admiralty.

Report on the restoration of Ardglass harbour. 17 May 1852. 1852/3 (1007) xciv. Admiralty.

Report on the state of New Westminster Bridge. 28 June 1856. 1856 (318) lii. Commission of Works.

RENDLESHAM, Lord SEE:
Thellusson, Frederick, *4th Bn. Rendlesham.*

RENNIE, George
Report on the construction of a harbour of refuge and breakwater in Dover Bay. 28 July 1845. 1847/8 (476) lx. Admiralty.

RENNIE, John, *Sir*
Report on Dover harbour. 11 Aug 1845. 1847/8 (476) lx. Admiralty.

Report on the harbours of Holyhead and Port Dyllaew. 30 March 1844. 1844 (633) xlv.

Report on the Harbours of Holyhead and Portdynllaen as a harbour of refuge for the channel trade. 14 June 1846. 1846 (630) xlv. Admiralty.

Report on Ramsgate harbour in reply to Capt. James Vetch's report. 4 April 1853. 1852/3 (337) xcviii. Board of Trade.

Report on Ramsgate harbour, in reply to Capt. James Vetch's report of 18 May 1853. 19 June 1853. 1852/3 (745) xcviii. Board of Trade.

RENNY, G.
Commission on charitable institutions in Dublin. Report, 8 Feb 1830. 1830 (7) xxvi.

RENSHAW, Charles Bine, *Sir*
Select committee on the Orkney and Zetland Small Piers and Harbours Bill. Report, 23 June 1896. 1896 (253) xi.

RESTELLI, Giuseppe
Secret committee (HL) on his mission to Milan. SEE: Ryder, D., *1st E. Harrowby.*

REVANS, John
Report on the operation of the law of settlement in Dorsetshire, Hampshire and Somersetshire. 1848. 1850 [1152] xxvii; (Poor Law, 21). Poor Law Board.

REVANS, Samuel
Report on emigration to Upper Canada. 22 Feb 1834. *In:* 1834 (44) xxxvii; (Poor Law, 17).

RHODE, J.
Commission sent to Ceylon on documents presented to the select committee on Ceylon, 1849
Reports, 10 and 20 June 1850. 1851 (99) xxii.
Ev. 8 May 1851. 1851 (634) xxii. Colonial Office.

RHODES, Thomas
Report on the port of Limerick for the purposes of making floating docks. 13 May 1834. 1834 (300) li.

Reports on River Shannon navigation. 10 June 1833. *In:* 1833 (371) xxxiv.

RIBBLESDALE, Lord SEE:
Lister, Thomas, *1st Bn. Ribblesdale* (1752-1826)
Lister, Thomas, *2nd Bn. Ribblesdale* (1790-1832)
Lister, Thomas, *3rd Bn. Ribblesdale* (1828-1876)
Lister, Thomas, *4th Bn. Ribblesdale* (1854-1925)

RICE, Edward B.
Committee on the systems of training naval cadets on board H.M.S. Britannia. Report, 6 Oct 1874. 1875 C.1154 xv. Admiralty.

RICE, Edward Royds
Select committee on police
1st report, 10 June 1853. 1852/3 (603) xxxvi.
2nd report, 5 July 1853. 1852/3 (715) xxxvi; (CP Police, 8).

RICE, Thomas Spring, *1st Bn. Monteagle*
Chairman's committee on the London and North-western Railway Bill. Report, 24 July 1856. HL 1856 (191) xxiv.

Decimal coinage commission
Preliminary report, 4 April 1857. 1857, session 2 [2212] xix.
Final report, 5 April 1859. 1859, session 2 [2529] xi.
Appendix. 1860 [2591] xxx.
Min. of proc. 30 March 1859. 1859, session 1 (176) viii.
Questions communicated to the Commission. April 1857. 1857, session 1 [2213] xix.
Questions communicated by Lord Overstone with answers. 1857/8 [2297] xxxiii; (MP Decimal Coinage, 1-2).

Report on burdens on land. 12 June 1846. 1846 (449) xl. Board of Trade.

Secret committee on joint stock banks. Report, 25 July 1838. 1837/8 (626) viii; (MP Joint Stock Banks, 1).

Select committee on the accounts of income and expenditure of the Civil list, 1831-1836. Report, 5 Dec 1837. 1837/8 (22) xxiii.

Select committee on the affairs of Lower Canada. Min. of ev., papers, 1834. 11 March 1837. 1837 (96) vii; (Canada, 1).

Select committee (HL) on the amending of the Railway Acts as to audit of accounts
1st report, 26 March 1849. HL 1849 (21-I) xxix; HC repr. 1849 (381) x.

2nd report, 8 May 1849. HL 1849 (21-II) xxxix; HC repr. 1849 (371) x.

3rd report, 18 June 1849. HL 1849 (21-III) xxix; HC repr. 1849 (421) x.

Appendix. HL 1849 (21-APP) xxix.

Select committee on church leases. Report, 17 July 1837. 1837 (538) vi.

Select committee (HL) on colonisation from Ireland. Report, 21 July 1847. HL 1847 (200) xxiii; HC repr. 1847 (737) vi; (Emigration, 4).

Select committee (HL) on colonisation from Ireland
1st report, 2 June 1848. HL 1847/8 (46) xxiii; HC repr. 1847/8 (415) xvii.
2nd report, 23 June 1848. HL 1847/8 (46) xxiii; HC repr. 1847/8 (593) xvii.
3rd report. HL 1847/8 (46) xxiii; HC repr. 1849 (86) xi; (Emigration, 5).

Select committee (HL) on consolidated annuities, Ireland. Report, 29 June 1852. HL 1852 (64) xx; HC repr. 1852 (585) vi.

Select committee (HL) on a consolidated annuity for Ireland. Report, 29 June 1852. HL 1852 (64) xx.

Select committee on committee rooms and printed papers
1st report: Committee rooms and library. 28 June 1825. 1825 (496) v.
2nd report, 30 June 1825. 1825 (515) v.
3rd report: Selection of printed reports, etc. 1 July 1825. 1825 (516) v.

Select committee (HL) on consolidated annuities, Ireland. Report, 29 June 1852. HL 1852 (64) xx.

Select committee on Dublin local taxation
Report, 16 May 1823. 1823 (356) vi.
Report, 9 July 1823. 1823 (549) vi.

Select committee on Dublin local taxation. Report, 25 June 1824. 1824 (475) viii; repr. 1825 (329) v.

Select committee on Dublin local taxation. Report, 18 May 1825. 1825 (403) v.

Select committee on education in Ireland reports. Report, 19 May 1828. 1828 (341) iv; repr. 1829 (80) iv.

Select committee on employment of the poor in Ireland. Report, 16 July 1823. 1823 (561) vi.

Select committee (HL) on extending the functions of the constabulary in Ireland to the suppression or prevention of illicit distillation. Report, 20 Aug 1853. HL 1852/3 (262) xxxi; HC repr. 1854 (53) x.

Select committee (HL) on the General Board of Health (No.3) Bill. Min. of ev. 5 Aug 1853. HL 1852/3 (374) xxxi.

Select committee on Grand Jury presentments in Ireland
1st report, 21 May 1822. 1822 (353) vii.
2nd report, 11 June 1822. 1822 (413) vii.
3rd report, 19 June 1822. 1822 (451) vii.

Select committee on Grand Jury presentments, Ireland. Report, 29 June 1827. 1826/7 (555) iii.

Select committee on joint stock banks. Report, 20 Aug 1836. 1836 (591) ix; (MP Joint Stock Banks, 1).

Select committee on joint stock banks. Report, 15 July 1837. 1837 (531) xiv; (MP Joint Stock Banks, 1).

Select committee on local taxation of Dublin, 1822. SEE: Ellis, Charles Rose.

Select committee (HL) on the Manchester and Southampton Railway Bill. Report, 24 Aug 1846. HL 1846 (317) xxvi.

Select committee on petitions relating to the local taxation of Limerick. Report, 31 July 1822. 1822 (617) vii.

Select committee (HL) on the state of the lunatic poor in Ireland. Report, HL 1843 (193) xx; HC repr. 1843 (625) x.

Select committee on the state of the poor in Ireland
Summary report, 16 July 1830. 1830 (667) vii.
1st report, 30 June 1830. 1830 (589) vii.
2nd report, 9 July 1830. 1830 (654) vii.
3rd report, 16 July 1830. 1830 (665) vii.

Select committee on the survey and valuation of Ireland. Report, 21 July 1824. 1824 (445) viii.

Select committee on the survey of Ireland. Report, 27 May 1824. 1824 (360) viii.

RICHARDS, John
Canada waste lands and emigration. Report, 30 March 1832. 1831/2 (334) xxxii. Colonial Department.

RICHARDSON, John, *Sir*
Report on the search for Sir John Franklin's expedition to the Arctic. 16 Sept 1848. 1849 (497) xxxii.

RICHEY, James Bellot
Commission on the causes of the riots, 1875, in the Poona and Ahmednagar districts of the Bombay Presidency. (Deccan Riots Commission). Report, 1878 C.2071 lviii. India Office.

RICHMOND and GORDON, D. SEE:
Lennox, Charles, *3rd D. Richmond* (1734-1806)
Lennox, Charles, *4th D. Richmond* (1764-1819)
Gordon-Lennox, Charles, *5th D. Richmond and Gordon* (1791-1860)
Gordon-Lennox, Charles Henry, *6th D. Richmond and Gordon* (1818-1907)
Gordon-Lennox, Charles Henry, *7th D. Richmond and Gordon* (1845-1928)

RICHMOND, H.S.
Report on the conditions of work in the fish-curing trade of the U.K. 1 Feb 1898. 1898 C.8753 xiv; (IR Factories, 31). Home Office.

Report on the prevention of accidents from machinery in the manufacture of cotton. Aug 1899. 1899 C.9456 xii. Home Office.

RIDLEY, Matthew White, *Sir*
Royal commission on civil establishments
1st report, 6 Sept 1887. 1887 C.5226 xix.
2nd report, 10 Sept 1888. 1888 C.5545 xxvii.
3rd report, 5 June 1889. 1889 C.5748 xxi.
4th report, 30 July 1890. 1890 C.6172 xxvii; (GO Civil Service, 10-12).

Select committee on the City of London Police Bill. Report, 17 July 1889. 1889 (264) ix; (CP Police, 10).

Select committee on the Coroners Bill. Special report, 10 July 1879. 1878/9 (279) ix.

Select committee on the election and return for the Borough of Great Grimsby, County of Lincoln. Report, 18 and 24 March 1803. 1802/3 (33) iii.

Select committee on Freshwater Fish Protection Bill. Report, 2 July 1878. 1878 (261) xiii.

Select committee on government contracts; fair wages resolution. Report, 3 July 1896. 1896 (277) x; (Industrial Relations, 22).

RIDLEY, Matthew White, Sir (continued)

Select committee on government contracts; fair wages resolution. Report, 22 July 1897. 1897 (334) x; (Industrial Relations, 22).

Select committee on the London Water Commission Bill. Special Report, 14 July 1891. 1890/1 (334) xii; (UA Water Supply, 6).

Select committee on parliamentary and municipal elections; hours of polling. Report, 30 July 1878. 1878 (325) xiii.

Select committee on precedents respecting the Church in Ireland Bill. Report, 19 March 1833. 1833 (86) xii.

Select committee on printing done for the H.C. Report, 10 July 1828. 1828 (520) iv.

Select committee on the Superannuation Acts Amendment (No.2) Bill. SEE: Gorst, John, Sir.

Select committee on tea duties. Report, 25 July 1834. 1834 (518) xvii.

Select committee on the victualling establishment at Cremill Point. Report, 13 March 1832. 1831/2 (272) v.

Standing committee on law. Church Patronage Bill. Report, 13 May 1895. 1895 (263) vii.

Standing committee on law. Corrupt and Illegal Practices Prevention Act (1883) Amendment Bill. Report, 28 May 1895. 1895 (282) vii.

Standing committee on law. Criminal Code (Indictable Offences Procedure) Bill and the Court of Criminal Appeal Bill. Report, 26 June 1883. 1883 (225) xi.

Standing committee on law. Employers' Liability Bill. Report, 22 June 1893. 1893/4 (284) xi.

Standing committee on law. Places of Worship (Sites) Bill. Report, 27 April 1893. 1893/4 (192) xiii.

Standing committee, Scotland. Local Government (Scotland) Bill. Report, 27 July 1894. 1894 (243) xiv.

Standing committee on trade. Railway and Canal Traffic Bill. Report, 16 July 1888. 1888 (286) xvii.

RIDLEY-COLBORNE, Nicholas William, *1st Bn. Colborne*

Secret committee of the HL on the Post Office. Report. HL 1844 (250) xviii; HC repr. 1844 (601) xiv.

Select committee on Carlow election petitions. Report, 11 March 1836. 1836 (89) xi.

RIGBY, John, *Sir*

Interdepartmental committee on the limits of the action of the Board of Trade as regards the liquidation of companies under the Companies (Winding Up) Act, 1890. Report, 25 July 1893. 1893/4 C.7221 lxxxi. Board of Trade.

Select committee on the Witnesses (Royal Commissions and Parliament) Protection Bill. Special report, 23 May 1892. 1892 (216) xviii.

RIPON, *M.* SEE:
Robinson, George Frederick Samuel, *1st M. Ripon.*

RITCHIE, Charles Thomson

Committee on the financial arrangements at the Admiralty. Reports, 23 Sept, 16 Nov 1885. 1886 C.4615 xiii. Admiralty.

Committee on re-arrangement of the Department of the Accountant-General of the Navy. Report, 5 Nov 1885. 1886 C.4615 xiii. Admiralty.

Select committee on colonisation. Report, 23 July 1889. 1889 (274) x; (Emigration, 9).

Select committee on sugar industries. Report, 29 July 1879. 1878/9 (321) xiii.

Select committee on sugar industries
Report, 9 March 1880. 1880 (106) xii.
Report, 4 Aug 1880. 1880 (332) xii.

RIVERS-WILSON, C.

Reports on the administration of the Mint. 6 and 17 Nov 1869. 1870 (7) xli; (MP Currency, 3). Treasury.

Report on the International Monetary Conference, Paris, June 1867. 2 Dec 1867. *In:* 1867/8 [4021] xxvii; (MP Currency, 3).

ROBERTS, William Chandler

Report on chemical and metallurgical processes practiced in European mints. 5 Aug 1870. *In:* 1870 (466) xli; (MP Currency, 3). Treasury.

ROBERTSON, C.

Royal commission on agriculture. Preliminary report of the assistant commissioner for Ireland. 1 Jan 1880. 1881 C.2951 xvi; (Agriculture, 16).

ROBERTSON, James Patrick Bannerman

Select committee on Burgh Police and Health (Scotland) Bill. Report, 23 July 1888. 1888 (294) ix.

Select committee on the Police (Scotland) Bill. Report, 25 July 1890. 1890 (324) xvii; (CP Police, 10).

ROBERTSON, Robert

Report on the collision between the 'Josephine Willis' and the 'Mangerton' steamer. 21 Feb 1856. 1856 (76) li. Board of Trade.

Report of an investigation into the loss of the 'Charlotte' of London. 15 Feb 1855. 1854/5 [1889] xlvi. Board of Trade.

Report of an investigation into the loss of the steam ship 'Erin's Queen' of Belfast. 16 Jan 1855. 1854/5 [1874] xlvi. Board of Trade.

Report of an investigation into the loss of the 'Morna' of Belfast. 20 March 1855. 1854/5 [1909] xlvi. Board of Trade.

ROBERTSON, Thomas

Committee on Irish day mails
Report, 17 May 1898. 1898 C.9023 xxxiv.
Min.of ev. 1898 C.9024 xxxiv. Treasury.

ROBERTSON, W.W.

Templeton Mills disaster inquiry commission. Report, 23 Jan 1890. 1890 C.5921 xxvii. Scottish Office.

ROBERTSON, William

Report on the proposed trunkline of railway from Nova Scotia, through New Brunswick to Quebec. 31 Aug 1848. 1849 [1031] xxxv; (Canada, 18). Colonial Office.

ROBINSON, Denham

Report on the probable cost of abolishing purchase in the Army. Feb 1871. 1871 (47) xxxix. War Office.

ROBINSON, Frederick John, *1st E. Ripon*

Committee on the charge upon H.M.'s civil list revenue. Report, 29 March 1804. 1803/4 (42) iv; repr. 6 July 1830. 1830 (615) ix.

ROBINSON, George Frederick Samuel, *1st M. Ripon*
Select committee (HL) on thanksgiving in the Metropolitan Cathedral. Report, 22 Feb 1872. HL 1872 (25) x.

Select committee (HL) on tramways. Report, 31 March 1879. HL 1878/9 (15) vii; HC repr. 1878/9 (148) xiv.

ROBINSON, George Richard
Select committee on East India maritime officers. Report, 27 May 1835. 1835 (242) xviii.

ROBINSON, Henry A.
Royal commission on municipal boundaries in Ireland. SEE: Cotton, Charles P.

ROBINSON, Hercules George Robert, *Sir*
Commission on the state of the fairs and markets in Ireland
    Report, 21 May 1853. 1852/3 [1674] xli.
    Min. of ev. 1854/5 [1910] xix. Irish Secretary's Office.

Royal commission on the settlement of the Transvaal Territory
    Report. 1882 C.3114 xxviii.
    Report of conferences and ev. 1882 C.3219 xxviii; (Africa, 36).

ROBINSON, Hugh G.
Report on training colleges. 7 Feb 1860. *In:* 1861 [2794-IV] xxi, pt.4; (Education, 6).

ROBINSON, John
Committee on West India free labour. Report, 12 June 1811. 1810/1 (225) ii; (Slave Trade, 1).

ROBINSON, Robert Spencer, *Sir*
Letter on the report of the committee on designs for ships of war. 25 Nov 1871. 1872 C.487 xxxix. Admiralty. SEE ALSO: Hamilton-Temple-Blackwood, Frederick Temple, *1st M. Dufferin and Ava.*

Report on the operation of the laws of settlement and removal of the poor in the counties of Surrey and Sussex. July 1848. 1850 [1152] xxvii; (Poor Law, 21). Poor Law Board.

Review of naval expenditure with reference to dockyard wages and contract ships. 14 Feb 1870. 1874 (109) xxxviii. Admiralty.

ROBINSON, T.R.
Report on the subject of the tremor produced by railway trains as affecting astronomical observations. 13 June 1846. 1846 (436) xxxviii. Admiralty.

ROCHFORT, J.S.
Commission to enquire into fees, gratuities, perquisites and emoluments of public offices in Ireland
    1st report: Customs. 24 Jan 1806. 1806 (6) viii.
    2nd report: Stamps. 1806 (270) viii.
    3rd report: Assessed tasks. 20 Dec 1806. 1806/7 (1) vi.
    4th report: Land revenue of the Crown. 20 Dec 1806. 1806/7 (2) vi.
    5th report: Excise—distillation of spirits. 18 March 1807. 1806/7 (124) vi.
    6th report: Excise—malt. 25 Jan 1808. 1808 (4) iii.
    7th report: Excise and inland duties, continued—auctions, etc. 31 Jan 1809. 1809 (15) vii.
    8th report: Mode of accounting for the excise duties. 21 Feb 1809. 1809 (52) vii.
    9th report: General Post Office. 2 and 6 Feb 1810. 1810 (5) x.
    Supplement. 1810 (366) x.
    10th report: Arrears and balances. 30 April 1810. 1810 (234) x.
    11th report, pt.1: Arrears and balances. 8 March 1811. 1810/1 (55) iv.
    11th report, pt.2: Arrears and balances—stamp office. 7 Feb 1812. 1812 (34) v.
    11th report, pt.3: Arrears and balances. 30 March 1813. 1812/3 (123) vi.
    12th report: Board of Works. 7 Feb 1812. 1812 (33) v.
    Supplement to 8th and 10th reports. 7 Feb 1812. 1812 (35) v.
    Memorial relating to the 8th report. 20 Feb 1812. 1812 (70) v.
    13th report: Director General of Inland Navigation. 14 Feb 1813. 1812/3 (61) vi.
    14th report: Treasury. 5 April 1814. 1813/4 (102) vii.

RODWELL, Benjamin Bridges Hunter
Select committee on the law of libel. SEE: Holker, J., *Sir.*

Select committee on railway passenger duty. Report, 23 June 1876. 1876 (312) xiii.

ROE, Frederick Adair, *Sir*
Wolverhampton Inquiry. Min. of ev. 1 July 1835. 1835 (343) xlvi. Home Office.

ROEBUCK, John Arthur
Select committee on the Army before Sebastopol
    1st report, 1 March 1855. 1854/5 (86) ix, pt.1.
    2nd report, 30 March 1855. 1854/5 (156) ix, pt.1.
    3rd report, 3 May 1855. 1854/5 (218) ix, pt.2.
    4th report, 17 May 1855. 1854/5 (247) ix, pt.3.
    5th report, 18 June 1855. 1854/5 (318) ix, pt.3.

Select committee on the Bankruptcy Act 1861. Report, 9 July 1862. 1862 (393) xvi.

Select committee on debts from foreign governments. Report, 31 July 1849. 1849 (603) xii.

Select committee on election proceedings. Report, 18 July 1842. 1842 (458) v.

Select committee on Sir Thomas Turton (late Registrar of the Supreme Court of Calcutta). Report, 11 June 1850. 1850 (440) xix. SEE ALSO: Colville, James William.

Select committee on the Trade Marks Bill and the Merchandise Marks Bill. Report, 6 May 1862. 1862 (212) xii.

Select committee on Waterworks Bill. Special report, 23 June 1865. 1865 (401) xii.

ROGERS, Frederick, *1st Bn. Blachford*
Report of the Colonial land and emigration commission on the application that Bristol should be made a government emigration port. 13 Jan 1855. 1854/5 (523) xvii; (Emigration, 23).

Royal commission on small-pox fever hospitals. Report, 21 July 1882. 1882 C.3314 xxix.

Select committee (HL) on the Colonial Church Bill. Report, 10 July 1873. HL 1873 (203) viii.

ROGERS, J.W.
Report on a draft bill for consolidation of the statute law relating to the relations between master and servant and master and workman. 1854 (302-I) xxiv. Lord Chancellor's Office.

ROGERS, Thomas Newman
Commission of inquiry into certain allegations, in a

ROGERS, Thomas Newman (continued)
petition from Eliza Prince of ill-treatment towards her on the part of two constables of the County of Stafford. Report, 1845. 1845 [658] xxvii. Home Department.

ROGET, Peter M.
Commission on supply of water in the Metropolis. Report, 21 April 1828. 1828 (267) ix.

Report of the physicians on the state of the General Penitentiary at Milbank. 16 April 1823. 1823 (256) v; (CP Prisons, 10).

ROKEBY, *Lord* [Peerage claim]. SEE:
Cooper, C.A.

ROLFE, Robert Monsey, *Bn. Cranworth*
Commission for consolidating the statute law. SEE: Stanley, Edward Henry, *15th E. Derby.*

Commission on the memorials of Indian officers. Report, 9 Nov 1863. 1864 [3254] xvi.

Committee for privileges (HL). Inchiquin claim to vote for representative peers for Ireland. Ev. 11 April 1862. HL 1862 (C) xxviii.

Digest of law commission
1st report, 13 May 1867. 1867 [3849] xvii.
2nd report. SEE: Bethell, Richard, *1st Bn. Westbury.*

Neutrality laws commission. Report. 1867/8 [4027] xxxii.

Select committee (HL) on the appellate jurisdiction of the HL. Report, 20 May 1856. HL 1856 (46) xxiv; HC repr. 1856 (264) viii.

Select committee (HL) on the Charitable Uses Bill and the Roman Catholic Charities Bill. Report, 28 July 1857. HL 1857, session 2 (125) xx; HC repr. 1857, session 2 (278) ix.

Select committee (HL) on the County Courts Equitable Jurisdiction Bill. Report, 4 May 1865. HL 1865 (81) xxi.

Select committee (HL) on the Criminal Law Bills, etc. Report, 11 Aug 1854. HL 1854 (339) xxi.

Select committee (HL) on the Mercantile Law Amendment Bill (on recommitment). Report, 22 May 1856. HL 1856 (112) xxiv; HC repr. 1856 (294) xiv.

Select committee (HL) on the Transfer of Estate Simplification Bill. Report, 4 June 1858. HL 1857/8 (128) xx.

Statute law commission
Report, 10 July 1855. 1854/5 [1983] xv.
2nd report, 5 March 1856. 1856 [2045] xviii.
3rd report, June 1857. 1857, session 2 [2219] xxi.

ROLLESTON, George
Report on Smyrna. 1 Nov 1856. 1857, session 1 (0.51) ix.

ROLPH, John
Select committee of the House of Assembly, Upper Canada on the conduct of Capt. Phillpotts. Report, 18 July 1833. *In:* 1833 (543) xxvi.

ROMILLY, John, *1st Bn. Romilly*
Commission on the Court of Chancery
1st report, 27 Jan 1852. 1852 [1437] xxi.
Supplement. 1852 [1454] xxi.
2nd report, 11 Jan 1854. 1854 [1731] xxiv.
3rd report, 14 April 1856. 1856 [2064] xxii; (Legal Administration, 8).

Commission to prepare a body of substantive law for India. Report, 23 June 1863. 1864 [3312] xiv.

Commission on the state and practice of county courts. Report, 31 March 1855. 1854/5 [1914] xviii; (Legal Administration, 9).

Commission on superior courts of common law and courts of chancery in England and Wales. SEE: Blackburne, Francis.

Royal commission on land transfer, and the condition of the registry of Deeds for Middlesex. Report, 24 Nov 1869. 1870 C.20 xviii.

Select committee on fees in courts of law and equity
1st report, 8 March 1848. 1847/8 (158) xv.
2nd report, 8 May 1848. 1847/8 (307) xv; (Legal Administration, 7).

Commission on the reform of the judicial establishments, judicial procedure and laws of India
1st report. 1856 [2035] xxv.
2nd report, 13 Dec 1856. 1856 [2036] xxv.
3rd report, 20 May 1856. 1856 [2097] xxv.
4th report, 20 May 1856. 1856 [2098] xxv.

ROMNEY, *E.* SEE:
Marsham, Charles, *3rd E. Romney.*

RONAYNE, P.
Report on the state of the Castlebar Union workhouse. 20 April 1850. 1850 (382) l. Poor Law Board.

ROOS, *Bn.* [Peerage claim] SEE:
De Grey, Thomas, *2nd Bn. Walsingham.*

ROOKWOOD, *Bn.* SEE:
Ibbetson, Henry John Selwyn, *1st Bn. Rookwood.*

ROSCOE, Henry Enfield, *Sir*
Committee on cotton cloth factories
Report, 17 Feb 1897. 1897 C.8348 xvii.
Min. of ev. 1897 C.8349 xvii; (IR Factories, 31).

Select committee on the Aire and Calder Navigation Bill. Report, 14 July 1888. 1888 (296) viii.

Select committee on ventilation of the H.C.
1st report, 13 April 1886. 1886, session 1 (107) x.
2nd report, 31 May 1886. 1886, session 1 (173) x.
Report, 20 Sept 1886. 1886, session 2 (37) x.

Select committee on weights and measures. Report, 1 July 1895. 1895 (346) xiii.

ROSCOMMON, *Lord* [Peerage claim]. SEE:
Cooper, C.A.

ROSE, George
Committee on Barrack-Masters Memorial. Report, 6 June 1815. 1814/5 (366) v.

Committee on Capt. Manby's experiments for saving the lives of shipwrecked mariners. Report, 10 June 1814. 1813/4 (227) iii.

Committee on madhouses in England. Report, 11 July 1815. 1814/5 (296) iv; (HE Mental, 1).

Committee on the petition from the Royal College of Surgeons. Report, 13 April 1810. 1810 (202) ii.

Committee on petitions respecting apprentice laws. Report, 31 May 1813. 1812/3 (243) iv.

Committee of privileges. Report on arrest of Lord Cochrane in the H.C. 23 March 1815. 1814/5 (176) iii.

Min. of ev. and supplement on the Liskeard return. 18 May and 5 June 1804. 1803/4 (102) ii.

Select committee on guaging in the Port of London. Report, 26 July 1814. 1813/4 (343) iv.

Select committee on guaging in the Port of London. Report, 11 July 1815. 1814/5 (472) v.

Select committee on laws relating to leather. SEE: Lushington, S.R.

Select committee on madhouses in England
    Min. of ev. 25 May to 12 June 1815. 1814/5 (296) iv.
    Report, 11 July 1815. 1814/5 (296) iv; (HE Mental, 1).

Select committee on madhouses in England
    1st report, 26 April 1816. 1816 (227) vi.
    2nd report, 28 May 1816. 1816 (398) vi.
    3rd report, 11 June 1816. 1816 (451) vi; (HE Mental, 1).

Select committee on the state of mendicity in the Metropolis. Report, 11 July 1815. 1814/5 (473) iii.

Select committee on the state of mendicity in the Metropolis. Report, 28 May 1816. 1816 (396) v.

ROSE, Hugh Henry, *1st Bn. Strathnairn*
Committee on the administration of the Transport and Supply Departments of the Army. Report, 5 March 1867. 1867 [3848] xv. War Office.

ROSEBERY, *E*. SEE:
Primrose, Archibald John, *4th E. Rosebery* (1783-1868)
Primrose, Archibald Philip, *5th E. Rosebery* (1847-1929)

ROSSE, *E*. SEE:
Parsons, William, *3rd E. Rosse* (1800-1867)
Parsons, Laurence, *4th E. Rosse* (1840-1929)

ROSSE, Alexander
Ev. taken at an inquiry held at Manchester, 4 June 1850, with the view of ascertaining the effect of the introduction of the warehousing system into that town. 8 July 1851. 1851 (510) liii. Board of Customs.

ROSSIE, *Bn*. SEE:
Kinnaird, George William Fox, *9th Bn. Kinnaird and 1st Bn. Rossie* (1807-1878)
Kinnaird, Arthur Fitzgerald, *10th Bn. Kinnaird* (1814-1887)
Kinnaird, Arthur Fitzgerald, *11th Bn. Kinnaird* (1847-1923)

ROSSLYN, *E*. SEE:
Wedderburn, Alexander, *1st E. Rosslyn* (1773-1805)
St. Clair-Erskine, James, *2nd E. Rosslyn* (1762-1837)
St. Clair-Erskine, James Alexander, *3rd E. Rosslyn* (1802-1866)

ROTHERY, Henry Cadogan
Report on the fall of a portion of the Tay Bridge, 28 Dec 1879. 30 June 1880. 1880 C.2616 xxxix. Board of Trade.

ROTHSCHILD, Nathan Mayer, *2nd Bn. Rothschild*
Committee on old age pensions. Report, 7 June 1898. 1898 C.8911 xlv; (Poor Law, 30). Treasury.

ROUS, John Edward Cornwallis, *2nd E. Stradbroke*
Committee (HL) on the Lough Swilly and Lough Foyle Drainage Bill. Min. of ev. 10 July 1837. HL 1837 (214) xvi.

ROWAN, James
Commission of inquiry into the state of Sierra Leone. Report, 7 May and 29 June 1827. 1826/7 (312), (552) vii; (Africa, 52).

ROWSELL, Francis W.
Report on the system of supply of provisions and stores for the workhouses of the Metropolis. 20 July 1871. 1872 (275) li. Local Government Board.

RUGGLES-BRISE, Evelyn John
Some observations on the treatment of crime in America. April 1899. 1899 (156) xliii.

RUMBOLD, Charles Edward
Select committee on Crown Leases. Report, 19 June 1829. 1829 (343) iii.

RUMLEY, Randal
Special committee on Armstrong and Whitworth guns. Report, 3 Aug 1865. 1866 [3605] xlii. War Office.

RUSSELL, David
Committee on breach-loaders for the Army. Report, 11 July 1864. 1864 (578) xxxv. War Office.

RUSSELL, *E*. SEE:
Russell, John, *1st E. Russell* (1792-1878)
Russell, John Francis Stanley, *2nd E. Russell* (1865-1931)

RUSSELL, *Bn*. SEE:
Russell, Charles, *Bn. Russell of Killowen*.

RUSSELL, Charles, *Bn. Russell of Killowen*
Select committee on the Metropolis Management (Plumstead and Hackney) Bill. Report, 1 Sept 1893. 1893/4 (403) xiii.

Select committee on the Sale of Goods Bill. SEE: Asher, Alexander.

RUSSELL, George William Erskine
Committee of inquiry on the cab service of the Metropolis. Report, 1895. 1895 C.7607 xxxv. Home Department.

Committee on the rules, regulation and practice in the Indian cantonments and elsewhere in India with regard to prostitution and the treatment of veneral disease. Report, 31 Aug 1893. 1893/4 C.7148 lxiv. India Office.

Select committee on telephone and telegraph wires. Report, 12 May 1885. 1884/5 (188) xii.

RUSSELL, John, *1st E. Russell*
Select committee on the Bribery, etc. Bill. SEE: Walpole, Spencer Horatio.

Select committee on committees of supply. Report, 11 Aug 1857. 1857, session 2 (261) ix.

Select committee on the conduct of Northampton Corporation in the late election. Report, 9 March 1827. 1826/7 (158) iv.

Select committee on county rates. Report, 31 July 1834. 1834 (542) xiv.

Select committee on criminal commitments and convictions. Report, 22 June 1827. 1826/7 (534) vi.

Select committee on criminal commitments and convictions. Report, 17 July 1828. 1828 (545) vi.

Select committee (HL) on the Ecclesiastical Commission Bill. Report, 8 June 1866. HL 1866 (148) xxviii.

RUSSELL, John, *1st E. Russell* (continued)
Select committee on the Ecclesiastical Corporations Bill and the Ecclesiastical Commission, etc. Bill. Report, 17 July 1857. 1857, session 2 (192) ix.

Select committee on education. Report, 7 Aug 1834. 1834 (572) ix.

Select committee on the Ecclesiastical Commission, etc.
> 1st report, 25 April 1856. 1856 (174) xi.
> 2nd report, 13 June 1856. 1856 (278) xi.
> 3rd report, 18 July 1856. 1856 (369) xi.

Select committee on election polls for cities and boroughs. Report, 28 May 1827. 1826/7 (394) iv.

Select committee (HL) on the national education in Ireland. SEE: Leveson-Gower, Granville George, *2nd E. Granville.*

Select committee on labourers wages. Report, 4 June 1824. 1824 (392) vi; (Agriculture, 1).

Select committee on laws relating to prisons. Report, 15 July 1836. 1836 (454) xxi; (CP Prisons, 11).

Select committee on oaths taken by members of the H.C. Report, 10 Aug 1857. 1857, session 2 (253) ix.

Select committee on the order of the HC proceeding to the HL. Report, 6 Aug 1851. 1851 (653) vii.

Select committee on public documents
> 1st report, 1 March 1833. 1833 (44) xii.
> 2nd report, 23 Aug 1833. 1833 (717) xii.

Select committee (HL) on public petitions, 1868. SEE: Herbert, Henry Howard Molyneux, *4th E. Carnarvon.*

Select committee on slavery. SEE: Graham, J.

Select committee on the suppression of the Calcutta Journal. SEE: Bains, Edward.

RUSSELL, Thomas Wallace
Select committee on the Cottage Homes Bill. Special report, second special report and report, 4 and 7 July 1899. 1899 (261), (271) ix.

Select committee on distress from want of employment. Report, 30 July 1896. 1896 (321) ix; (Industrial Relations, 24).

Select committee on food products adulteration. Report, 9 July 1896. 1896 (288) ix; (HE Food and Drugs, 4).

Select committee on the Industries (Ireland) Bill. Report, 7 May 1897. 1897 (202) x.

Select committee on money lending. Report, 29 July 1897. 1897 (364) xi; (Monetary Policy, 12).

Select committee on money lending. Report, 29 June 1898. 1898 (260) x; (Monetary Policy, 12).

Select committee on Public Health Acts Amendment Bill. Special report and report, 28 June 1899. 1899 (252) x.

RUSSELL, W.J.
Report on the action of light on water colours. 30 June 1888. 1888 C.5453 lxxviii. Art Department, Privy Council committee on education.

RUSSELL, Whitworth
Report of inquiry into the conduct of Mr. George, governor of the county gaol of Carnarvon. 22 April 1843. 1843 (422) xliii; (CP Prisons, 11). Home Department.

Report respecting the circumstances which occurred on the occasion of the condemned sermon in the Chapel of Newgate Gaol in the case of convict Hocker. 6 May 1845. 1845 (366) xxv. Home Department.

RUSSELL, William, *Lord*
Select committee on the petition relating to the return for the Borough of Knaresborough. Report, 4 March 1805. 1805 (43) iii.

RUTHERFORD, Andrew
Board of H.M. sole and only master printers in Scotland
> Report, 17 June 1840. 1840 [259] xxviii.
> 2nd report, June 1842. 1842 [411] xxxvii.
> Report, 5 June 1846. 1846 [720] xxiii.
> Report, March 1848. 1847/8 [922] xxxviii.
> Report, April 1850. 1850 (728) xx.

Select committee on the Supreme Court of Judicature in Scotland. SEE: Maule, Fox.

Select committee on marriage in Scotland. Report, 24 May 1849. 1849 (310) xii; (Marriage and Divorce, 3).

Select committee on medical registration and medical law amendment
> 1st and 2nd reports, 28 and 31 March 1848. 1847/8 (210) xv.
> 3rd report, 25 Aug 1848. 1847/8 (702) xv; (HE Medical Professions, 3).

RUTLAND, D. SEE:
Manners, John Henry, *5th D. Rutland.*

RYAN, Edward
Commission on criminal law. SEE: Starkie, Thomas.

RYAN, William
Lurgan riots inquiry commission. Report, 31 Oct 1879. 1880 (130) lx. Irish Secretary's Office.

RYDER, Alfred Phillipps
Committee on the designs upon which ships of war have recently been constructed. Dissenting report, 14 Oct 1871. 1872 C.489 xiv. Admiralty. SEE ALSO: Hamilton-Temple-Blackwood, Frederick Temple, *1st M. Dufferin and Ava.*

Memorandum report on the design of ships of war: 'Devastation' and 'Thunderer' class. 11 March 1871. *In:* 1871 C.333 xiv. Admiralty.

RYDER, Dudley, *1st E. Harrowby*
Committee (HL) on the agreement made with Mr. Palmer for the reform and improvement of the Post Office. Report, 5 July 1813. HL 1812/3 (123) lxiii.

Committee appointed to consider the manner of the H.C. going to St. Paul's Church. Report, 14 Dec 1797. (Reps., 1731-1800, no.142, vol.20).

Committee on the high price of provisions
> 1st report, 24 Nov 1800. 1801 (174) ii.
> 2nd report, 9 Dec 1800. 1801 (174) ii.
> 3rd report, 13 Dec 1800. 1801 (174) ii.
> 4th report, 17 Dec 1800. 1801 (174) ii.
> 5th report, 18 Dec 1800. 1801 (174) ii.
> 6th report, 31 Dec 1800. 1801 (174) ii; CJ Reports, vol.9; (Reps., 1731-1800, no.174, vol.28).

Committee on the high price of provisions, 1801. SEE: Yorke, C.

Committee on the trade of Newfoundland. SEE: Taylor, M.A.

Secret committee (HL) on the mission of Giuseppe

Restelli to Milan. Report, 23 Oct 1820. HL 1820 (112) cxviii.

Secret committee (HL) on papers delivered by command of H.R.H. the Prince Regent. Report, 12 June 1817. HL 1817 (65) lxxxiv; HL repr. 1818 (7) xci; HC repr. 1817 (399) iv.

Secret committee (HL) on the papers laid before the HL presented by H.M.'s command. Report, 4 July 1820. HL 1820 (57) cxix.

Secret cdmmittee on the Post Office. Report, 5 Aug 1844. 1844 (582) xiv.

Secret committee (HL) on the preservation of the public tranquility. Report, 18 Feb 1817. HL 1817 (5) lxxxiv; repr. HL 1818 (7) xci.

Secret committee (HL) on the state of the Bank of England with reference to the resumption of cash payments. Reports, 7 May 1819. HL 1819 (30) xcviii; repr. HL 1844 (5) xviii; HC repr. 1819 (291) iii; (Monetary Policy, 2).

Select committee (HL) on the circulation of promissory notes in Scotland and Ireland
    Report, 26 May 1826. HL 1826 (126) ccxvii.
    Min. of ev. HL 1826 (130) ccvii; HC repr. 1826/7 (245) vi; (Monetary Policy, 3).

Select committee (HL) on disturbances in Ireland
    Report, 21 June 1824. HL 1824 (150) clxv.
    Min. of ev. HL 1825 (35) cxc; HC repr. 1825 (200) vii.

Select committee (HL) on disturbances in Ireland
    Report. HL 1825 (36) clxxxviii.
    Min. of ev. HL 1825 (37) clxxxviii; HC repr. HL 1825 (181) ix.

Select committee on the expedition to the Arctic seas commanded by Capt. John Ross. Report, 28 April 1834. 1834 (250) xviii.

Committee (HL) on the Office of Clerk of the Parliaments and Black Rod
    Report, 4 June 1824. HL 1824 (101) clxviii.
    2nd report, 21 June 1824. HL 1824 (132) clxviii.

Select committee (HL) on the Parliament Offices. Report, 5 July 1825. HL 1825 (206) cxcii.

Select committee (HL) on the state of Ireland
    Report, 4 July 1825. HL 1825 (202) cxci.
    Min. of ev. HL 1825 (103) cxcii; HC repr. 1825 (521) ix.

Select committee (HL) on weights and measures. Report, 16 July 1823. HL 1823 (120) cliii; HC repr. 1824 (94) vii.

Select committee on votes of elections. Report, 29 June 1846. 1846 (451) viii.

Select committee on the west coast of Africa. Report, 5 Aug 1842. 1842 (551) xi, xii; (Africa, 2-3).

RYDER, Dudley, 2nd E. Harrowby
Commission of inquiry into the management and government of Maynooth College
    Report, 1 March 1855. 1854/5 [1896] xxii.
    Min. of ev. 1854/5 [1896-I] xxii.

Commission on the realisation and distribution of Army prize. Report, 3 May 1864. 1864 [3333] xvi.

Episcopal and capitular revenues commission
    1st report, 31 May 1850. 1850 [1135] xx.
    Min. of ev. 1850 [1175] xx.
    2nd report. 30 July 1850. 1850 [1263] xx.

Select committee (HL) on the operation of the acts for the sale of beer

Min. of ev. 23 July 1849. HL 1849 (160) xxxii; HC repr. 1850 (398) xviii.
    Report, 3 May 1850. HL 1850 (25) xviii; HC repr. 1850 (398) xviii; repr. 1852/3 (292) xxxviii.

Select committee (HL) on the Sale of Beer Regulation Bill. Min. of ev. 4 July 1848. HL 1847/8 (187) xxvi; HC repr. 1847/8 (501) xvi; (SP Sunday Observance, 1).

Select committee (HL) on the Sunday Trading Prevention Bill. Report, 13 May 1850. HL 1850 (75) xxiv; HC repr. 1850 (441) xix; (SP Sunday Observance, 1).

Select committee (HL) on the Weights and Measures Bill. Report, 8 June 1855. HL 1854/5 (133) xxii.

Select committee on commercial relations with China. Report, 12 July 1847. 1847 (654) v.

Select committee (HL) on transportation. Report, 10 July 1856. HL 1856 (124) xxiv; HC repr. 1856 (404) xvii; (CP Transportation, 4).

RYE, Maria S.
Emigration of pauper and other children to Canada. Dec 1876. 1877 (392) lxxi. Local Government Board.
SEE ALSO: Doyle, Andrew.

SADLER, Michael Thomas
Committee on the Bill to regulate the labour of children in factories. Report, 8 Aug 1832. 1831/2 (706) xv.

ST. ALDWYN, E. SEE:
Hicks-Beach, Michael Edward, 1st E. St. Aldwyn.

ST. CLAIR-ERSKINE, James, 2nd E. Rosslyn
Commission of Post Office inquiry
    Report: Postal arrangements between France and G.B. 20 July 1835. 1835 (416) xlviii.
    2nd report: Contract for mail coaches. 22 June 1835. 1835 (313) xlviii.

Commission of inquiry into the receipt and expenditure of colonial revenue
    1st-3rd reports: Malta, Gibraltar and Australian colonies. 8 Dec 1830. 1830/1 (64) iv.
    4th report: Mauritius. 26 Feb 1830. 1830/1 (194) iv; (Colonies, 2).

Select committee (HL) on the Helleston Election Bill. Report, 22 March 1815. HL 1814/5 (41) lxxiv.

Select committee (HL) on the library of the HL. Report, 11 March 1834. HL 1834 (20) xxi.

ST. GEORGE, John, Sir
Ordnance select committee on systems of rifling for small arms. Report, 26 Nov 1862. 1863 (139) xxxiii. War Office.

Special committee on muzzle-loading vs breech-loading field guns. Report, 28 Nov 1870. 1871 C.283 xiv. War Office.

ST. GERMANS, E. SEE:
Eliot, Edward Granville, 3rd E. St. Germans.

ST. LEONARDS, Lord SEE:
Sugden, Edward Burtenshaw, 1st Bn. St. Leonards.

ST. MAUR, Edward Adolphus, 11th D. Somerset
Select committee (HL) on Regulations of Linen and Hempen Manufacturers in Scotland Bill. Min. of ev. 12 June 1823. HL 1823 (59) clvi.

Select committee (HL) on the Weights and Measures Bill. SEE: Ryder, Dudley, 1st E. Harrowby.

ST. MAUR, Edward Adolphus, *12th D. Somerset*

Commission appointed to consider a site for a new National Gallery. Report, 15 July 1851. 1851 (642) xxii; (ED Fine Arts, 3). Treasury.

Commission on the cost and applicability of the exhibition building in Hyde Park. Report, 19 Feb 1852. 1852 [1453] xxvi. Office of Works.

Commission on the purchase and sale of commissions in the Army. Report, 1857. 1857, session 2 [2267] xviii; (Military and Naval, 3).

Commission on the site of the new Westminster Bridge. Report, 1851. 1852 [1457] xviii. Treasury.

Royal commission on fugitive slaves. Report, 30 May 1876. 1876 C.1516-I xxviii; (Slave Trade, 92).

Royal commission on unseaworthy ships
Preliminary report, 22 Sept 1873. 1873 C.853 xxxvi.
Final report, 1 July 1874. 1874 C.1027 xxxiv; (Shipping, 6-7).

Select committee on Army and ordnance expenditure
1st report, 11 May 1849. 1849 (277) ix.
2nd report, 12 July 1849. 1849 (499) ix.

Select committee on Army and ordnance expenditure. Report. 1 Aug 1850. 1850 (662) x.

Select committee on army and ordnance expenditure, 1851. SEE: Maule-Ramsay, Fox, *11th E. Dalhousie.*

Select committee (HL) on the Board of Admiralty. Report, 30 March 1871. HL 1871 (30) viii; HC repr. 1871 (180) vii.

Select committee on dockyard appointments. Report, 23 May 1853. 1852/3 (511) xxv.

Select committee on dockyard appointments. Report on the case of Lieutenant Engledine. 22 July 1853. 1852/3 (803) xxv.

Select committee on the Dublin City election petition. Min. of proc. and ev. 9 Aug 1838. 1837/8 (703) x.

Select committee on East India produce. Report, 21 July 1840. 1840 (527) viii.

Select committee on Ecclesiastical Commission. Report, 16 July 1847. 1847 (681) ix.

Select committee on the Great London Drainage Bill. Min. of ev. 17 June 1853. 1852/3 (629) xxvi; (UA Sanitation, 3).

Select committee on the Guildford election petition. Report, 6 April 1853. 1852/3 (349) xiii.

Select committee (HL) on the harbour and fortifications of Alderney. Report, 25 April 1872. HL 1872 (56) ix.

Select committee (HL) on Highway Acts. Report, 4 Aug 1881. HL 1881 (54) vii; HC repr. 1881 (371) x.

Select committee (HL) on the Petroleum Bill. Report, 9 Aug 1883. HL 1883 (180) ix.

Select committee (HL) on poor rates and highway rates in respect of small tenements and on the municipal franchise. Report, 14 April 1859. HL 1859, session 1 (46) xii; 1859, session 2 (56) vii; repr. 1867 (74) viii.

Select committee on railway communication. Report, 28 March 1838. 1837/8 (257) xvi; repr. 1844 (25) xi.

Select committee (HL) on the Regulation of Railways (Prevention of Accidents) Bill. Report, 27 March 1873. HL 1873 (23) ix; HC repr. 1873 (148) xiv.

Select committee (HL) on the state of Ireland in respect of crime. SEE: Stuart-Wortley-Mackenzie, John Archibald, *1st Bn. Wharncliffe.*

Select committee on madhouses in England. SEE: Rose, G.

Select committee on the National Gallery. Report, 25 July 1850. 1850 (612) xv; (ED Fine Arts, 3).

Select committee on Navy, Army and Ordnance estimates. Report on Navy estimates, 28 July 1848. 1847/8 (555) xxi, pts. 1 and 2.

Select committee on printing; Houses of Parliament. Report, 1 Aug 1854. 1854 (434) vii.

Select committee on printing; Houses of Parliament. Report, 1 Aug 1855. 1854/5 (447) xi.

Select committee on railways
1st report, 26 April 1839. 1839 (222) x.
2nd report, 9 Aug 1839. 1839 (517) x; (Transport, 3).

Select committee on railways
1st report, 6 Feb 1840. 1840 (50) xiii.
2nd report, 2 March 1840. 1840 (92) xiii.
3rd report, 14 May 1840. 1840 (299) xiii.
4th report, 2 July 1840. 1840 (437) xiii.
5th report, 10 July 1840. 1840 (474) xiii; (Transport, 4).

Select committee on railways. Report, 27 May 1841. 1841 (354) viii; (Transport, 5).

Select committee (HL) on the Telegraphs Bill. Report, 1 July 1878. HL 1878 (141) vii.

SALISBURY, M. SEE:
Gascoyne-Cecil, James Brownlow William, *2nd M. Salisbury* (1791-1868)
Gascoyne-Cecil, Robert Arthur Talbot, *3rd M. Salisbury* (1830-1903)

SALOMONS, David

Select committee on the Metropolitan Toll Bridges Bill and the Chelsea Bridge Toll Abolition Bill. Special report, 19 June 1865. 1865 (380) viii.

Select committee on the Sidney branch mint. Report, 17 July 1862. 1862 (421) vii; (Australia, 24).

SALT, Thomas, *Sir*

Committee of public accounts
1st report, 12 March 1884. 1884 (98) viii.
2nd report, 26 June 1884. 1884 (237) viii.

Committee of public accounts
1st report, 11 March 1885. 1884/5 (112) vii.
2nd report, 15 July 1885. 1884/5 (267) vii.

Committee of public accounts, 1890. SEE: Kay-Shuttleworth, Ughtred, *Sir.*

Select committee on the Canal Boats Bill. Report, 12 July 1877. 1877 (327) vii.

Select committee on canals. Report, 12 July 1883. 1883 (252) xiii.

Select committee on poor removal. Report, 10 July 1879. 1878/9 (282) xii; (Poor Law, 26).

Select committee on the Public Worship Facilities Bill. Report, 13 July 1875. 1875 (331) xiv.

Select committee on the Southampton Docks Bill. Report, 6 May 1892. 1892 (177) xvii.

Select committee on tramways use of mechanical power. Report, 16 April 1877. 1877 (161) xvi.

Standing committee on law. Penal Servitude Bill. Report, 11 June 1891. 1890/1 (274) xiii.

Standing committee on law. Public Health (London) Law Amendment Bill. Report, 4 June 1891. 1890/1 (268) xiii.

Standing committee on trade. Factors Bill. Report, 25 July 1889. 1889 (277) x.

Standing committee on trade. Light Railways (Ireland) Bill. Report, 15 Aug 1889. 1889 (324) xi.

SALTOUN, *Bn.* [Peerage claim]. SEE: Freeman-Mitford, J.T.

SAMUELSON, Bernhard
Committee on light railways. Report, 23 Jan 1895. 1895 (49) lxxvi. Board of Trade.

Industrial progress and the education of the industrial classes in France, Switzerland, Germany, *etc.* 16 Nov 1867. 1867/8 (13) liv. Privy Council.

Royal commission on technical instruction
 1st report, 17 Feb 1882. 1882 C.3171 xxvii.
 2nd report.
  Report, 4 April 1884. 1884 C.3981 xxix.
  Report on agricultural education in North Germany, France, Denmark, Belgium, Holland and U.K., by H.M. Jenkins. 1884 C.3981-I xxx.
  Report on technical education in the U.S.A., by W. Mather. 13 Nov 1883. 1884 C.3981-I xxx.
  Notes on technical instruction in the U.S.A. 1884 C.3981-I xxx.
  Notes on technical instruction in Russia, by W. Mather. 28 Aug 1884. 1884 C.3981-II xxxi.
  Report on the English silk industry, by T. Wardle. 1884 C.3981-II xxxi.
  Technical instruction in Ireland, by W.K.Sullivan. 1884 C.3981-II xxxi.
  Min. of ev. 1884 C.3981-II xxxi.
  Ev. relating to Ireland. 1884 C.3981 -III xxxii.
  Foreign reports, appendices. 1884 C.3981-IV lxix; (ED Scientific and Technical, 5-8).

Select committee on letters patent. Report, 20 July 1871. 1871 (368) x; (Inventions, 2).

Select committee on letters patent. Report, 8 May 1872. 1872 (193) xi; (Inventions, 2).

Select committee on Rating of Machinery Bill. Special report, 20 July 1887. 1887 (231) xi.

Select committee on scientific instruction. Report, 15 July 1868. 1867/8 (432) xv; (ED Scientific and Technical, 1).

SANDERSON, James SEE:
Saunderson, James.

SANDHURST, *Bn.* SEE:
Mansfield, William, *1st Vct. Sandhurst* (1855-1933)

SANDON, *Vct.* SEE:
Ryder, Dudley, *2nd E. Harrowby.*

SANDFORD, Edward Ayshford
Select committee on the Ludlow election petitions. Min. of ev. 13 April 1840. 1840 (229) ix.

Select committee on pensions
 1st report, 30 March 1838. 1837/8 (263) xxiii.
 Report, 24 July 1838. 1837/8 (621) xxiii.

Select committee on St. Albans election. Proc., min. of ev. 5 April 1841. 1841 (219) ix.

Select committee on the silk trade. SEE: Stuart, D.C.

SANFORD, Herbert B.
Reports to the Philadelphia International Exhibition. 30 April 1877. 1877 C.1774, C.1848, C.1890 xxxiv, xxxv, xxxvi. Privy Council, Education Committee.

SAUNDERS, Robert John
Report on the educational provisions of the Factories Act. 1 Jan 1839. 1839 (42) xlii; (IR Factories, 27). Home Department.

Report on the establishment of schools in factory districts. 16 Feb 1842. 1843 [500] xxvii; (IR Factories, 27). Home Department.

Special report on guarding of machinery in factories
 1st report, 27 March 1841. 1841 [311] x.
 2nd report, 14 April 1841. 1841 [311] x; (IR Factories, 27).

SAUNDERSON, James, *Sir*
Select committee on commercial credit. Report, 29 April 1793. CJ, vol.48, p.702; (Reps., 1731-1800, no.101, vol.10); repr. 1826 (23) iii.

SAXE-COBURG, Albert Edward, *Prince of Wales*
Commission on the Vienna Universal Exhibition. Reports, 12 June 1874. 1874 C.1072 lxxiii, pts.1-4.

Committee on the decoration of the new Palace at Hyde Park Corner. Report: Wellington statute. 8 March 1884. 1884 (130) lxviii.

Royal commission for the Colonial and Indian Exhibition, 1886. Report, 30 April 1887. 1887 C.5083 xx.

Royal commission for the Australian international exhibitions. Report, 19 Dec 1881. 1882 C.3099 xxviii; (Australia, 29).

Royal commission for the Melbourne Centennial International Exhibition of 1888. Report, 1889. 1889 C.5848 xxxiv; (Australia, 31).

Royal commission for the Paris Universal Exhibition of 1878. 1880 C.2588 xxxi, xxxii.

SAXE-COBURG, Alfred Ernest Albert, *D. Edinburgh*
Committee on pensions or gratuities to the widows and children of seamen. Report, 3 Feb 1886. 1886 C.4689 xiii. Admiralty.

Report of the conference on the proposal for a uniform system of buoyage for the U.K. 1 May 1883. 1883 C.3622 xvii. Board of Trade.

SAXE-COBURG, Francis Albert Augustus Charles Emanuel, *Prince Saxe-Coburg-Gothe*
Commission for the exhibition of 1851
 1st report, 24 April 1852. 1852 [1485] xxvi.
 2nd report, 11 Nov 1852. 1852/3 [1566] liv.
 3rd report, 12 April 1856. 1856 [2065] xxiv.
 4th report, 3 May 1861. 1861 [2819] xxxii.
 5th report, 15 Aug 1867. 1867 [3933] xxiii.
 6th report, 29 July 1878. 1878/9 C.2378 xxvii.

Commission on the fine arts [for the Parliament buildings]
 Report, 22 April 1842. 1842 [412] xxv.
 2nd report, 28 July 1843. 1843 [499] xxix.
 3rd report, 9 July 1844. 1844 [585] xxxi.
 4th report, 25 April 1845. 1845 [671] xxvii.
 5th report, 7 Aug 1845. 1846 [685] xxiv.
 6th report, 4 Aug 1846. 1846 [749] xxiv.
 7th report, 13 July 1847. 1847 [862] xxxiii.
 8th report, 5 Sept 1848. 1849 [1009] xxii.
 9th report, 11 March 1850. 1850 [1180] xxiii.
 10th report, 8 July 1854. 1854 [1829] xix; (ED Fine Arts, 2-3).

Royal commission on the patriotic fund
 1st report, 10 May 1855. 1857/8 (163) xix.
 2nd report, 9 Feb 1858. 1857/8 (163) xix.

SAXTON, Charles, *Sir*
Commission on duties, salaries and emoluments in courts of justice in Ireland. SEE: Webber, D.W.

SAYE and SELE, *Lord* [Peerage claim]. SEE: Cooper, C.A.

SCARLETT, James, *Sir*
Commission on the courts of the Count Palatine of Lancaster
    Report, 20 July 1832. 1831/2 (621) xxxv.
    2nd report and final report: County Court. 25 April 1836. 1836 (202) xxxvi.

SCHOLEFIELD, William
General committee on railway and canal bills. 1st to 7th reports, 21 Feb to 5 June 1867. 1867 (73, I-VI) viii.

General committee on railway and canal bills. 1st to 8th reports, 26 Feb to 5 July 1866. 1866 (69, I-VII) xi.

Select committee on adulteration of food
    1st report, 27 July 1855. 1854/5 (432) vii.
    2nd report, 8 Aug 1855. 1854/5 (480) vii; (HE Food and Drugs, 1).

Select committee on the adulteration of food. Report, 22 July 1856. 1856 (379) viii; (HE Food and Drugs, 2).

Select committee on the Mayo County election petition. Min. of ev. 15 July 1857. 1857, session 2 (182) vii.

SCHOMBERG, Charles F.
Report and ev. of inquiry at Liverpool, on the loss of the steamship 'Atlantic'. 11 June 1873. *In:* 1873 (373) lx. Board of Trade.

SCLATER-BOOTH, George, *1st Bn. Basing*
Committee on public accounts. Report, 4 Aug 1866. 1866 (475) vii.

Committee of public accounts
    1st report, 13 March 1872. 1872 (104) vii.
    2nd report, 13 May 1872. 1872 (198) vii.

Committee of public accounts
    1st report, 20 March 1873. 1873 (110) vii.
    2nd report, 9 July 1873. 1873 (290) vii.

Royal commission on redemption of the tithe rent charge in England and Wales. Report, 18 Feb 1892. 1892 C.6606 xlvii.

Select committee on the Butter Substitutes Bill. SEE: Paget, Richard, *Sir.*

Select committee on commons. Report, 22 June 1877. 1877 (282) x; (Agriculture, 14).

Select committee on diplomatic and consular services
    1st report, 18 May 1871. 1871 (238) vii.
    2nd report, 24 July 1871. 1871 (380) vii; (GO Diplomatic Service, 4).

Select committee on diplomatic and consular services. Report, 16 July 1872. 1872 (314) vii; (GO Diplomatic Service, 4). SEE ALSO: Bouverie, Edward Pleydell.

Select committee on Electric Lighting Provisional Orders Bills. Report, 31 July 1883. 1883 (288) xi.

Select committee on the Hampstead fever and small pox hospital. Report, 27 July 1875. 1875 (363) x.

Select committee on Liverpool Corporation Water Bill. Special report, 1 July 1880. 1880 (255) x.

Select committee on the New Mint Building Site Bill. Report, 4 July 1871. 1871 (334) xi.

Select committee on the Northallerton election petition. Min. of ev. 1 May 1866. 1866 (223) xi.

Select committee on police and sanitary regulations. Report, 9 June 1882. 1882 (226) xii.

Select committee on police and sanitary regulations. Special report, 2 June 1886. 1886, session 1 (178) xi.

Select committee on the Sale of Food and Drugs Act (1875) Amendment Bill. Report, 19 April 1879. 1878/9 (155) x; (HE Food and Drugs, 3).

Select committee on town holdings. Report, 24 June 1886. 1886, session 1 (213) xii; (UA Planning, 4).

Select committee on law. Criminal Code (Indictable Offences Procedure) Bill, and Court of Criminal Appeal Bill. SEE: Ridley, Matthew White.

Standing committee on law. Law of Evidence in Criminal Cases Bill. Report, 20 May 1884. 1884 (184) xiii.

Standing committee on law. Municipal Elections (Corrupt and Illegal Practices) Bill. Report, 17 June 1884. 1884 (220) xv.

SCOBELL, Edward
Committee on the general treatment, health and morality of children in the infant school of Marylebone workhouse. Report, Jan 1843. 1843 (483) xlv. Poor Law Commission.

SCOTT, George Robertson
Commission on duties salaries, fees and emoluments in courts in Scotland. SEE: Montgomery, James.

SCOTT, John, *1st E. Eldon*
Chancery commission. Report, 9 March 1826. 1826 (143) xv, xvi.

Commission to enquire into the administration of justice in Scotland. Report, 9 June 1809. 1809 (257) iv.

SCOTT, Walter Francis Montagu Douglas SEE: Montagu-Douglas-Scott, W.F., *5th D. Buccleuch and 7th D. Queensbury.*

SCOTT-BENTINCK, William Henry Cavendish, *4th D. Portland*
Committee of the Privy Council for coin. Min. of ev. 19 and 26 April 1828. 12 Feb 1830. 1830 (31) xvii; repr. 1847/8 (718) xxxix.

SCOURFIELD, John Henry
Select committee on the Private Bill Costs Bill. Min. of proc. 6 March 1865. 1865 (104) vii.

Select committee on standing orders (parliamentary deposits). Report, 22 June 1864. 1864 (423) x.

Select committee on standing orders. Sheffield, Chesterfield and Staffordshire Railway Bill
    Report, 18 May 1864. 1864 (140) x.
    Min. of ev. 25 April 1864. 1864 (233) x

SCROPE, George Poulett
Committee on the Dublin Wide Streets Bill. Min. of ev. 24 July 1846. 1846 (519) xii.

Select committee on Kilrush Union. Report, 25 July 1850. 1850 (613) xi.

SCUDAMORE, Frank Ives
Report and supplementary report on the proposal for transferring to the Post Office the control and management of electric telegraphs throughout the U.K. June 1866 and Feb 1868. 1867/8 (202) xli; (Posts and Telegraphs, 5).

Report on the financial results of the transfer of the telegraphs to the government. 3 June 1871. 1871 (378) xxxvii; (Posts and Telegraphs, 5). Treasury.

Report on the re-organisation of the telegraph system of the U.K. Jan 1871. 1871 C.304 xxxvii; (Posts and Telegraphs, 5).

SEALY, Edward
Committee on petition respecting his patent for tanning of leather. SEE: Dickinson, W.

SECCOMBE, Thomas Lawrence
Committee on the expense of the recruits for the regiments serving in India
 1st to 3rd reports, 11 March 1869 to 28 Feb 1870. 1871 (129) l.
 4th report, 12 April 1872. 1874 (129) xlvii.
 Report, 26 July 1872. 1874 (129) xlvii; India Office *and* War Office.

SEELY, Charles
Select committee on Admiralty monies and accounts. Report, 27 July 1868. 1867/8 (469) vi.

SEGRAVE, Lord [Peerage claim]. SEE:
Freeman-Mitford, J.T.

SELBORNE, Lord SEE:
Palmer, Roundell, *1st E. Selborne* (1812-1895)
Palmer, William Waldegrave, *2nd E. Selborne* (1859-1942)

Select committee on the Earldom of Selborne. SEE:
Hicks-Beach, M.E.

SELFE, Henry Selfe
Commission appointed to inquire into the state of the store and clothing depots at Weedon, Woolwich and the Tower, etc. SEE: Turner, James Aspinall.

SELKIRK, E. SEE:
Douglas, Dunbar James, *6th E. Selkirk.*

SELLAR, A.C.
Commission on the truck system. SEE: Guthrie, W.

Report on the state of education in the country districts of Scotland. 1 March 1866. 1867 [3845-III] xxv; (Education, 14). Education Commission, Scotland. SEE ALSO: Campbell, George Douglas, *8th D. Argyll.*

Statistical report on the state of education in the lowland country districts of Scotland. 1867 [3845-I] xxv; (Education, 14). Education Commission, Scotland). SEE ALSO: Campbell, George Douglas, *8th D. Argyll.*

SELWIN-IBBETSON, Henry SEE:
Ibbetson, Henry John Selwin, *1st Bn. Rookwood.*

SENIOR, Nassau W.
Letter on the third report of the Irish poor law commission. 14 April 1836. 1837 [90] li. Home Department.

Royal commission on hand-loom weavers. Report, 19 Feb 1841. 1841 [296] x; (IR Textiles, 10).

SETON-KER, W.S.
Indigo commission. Report, 27 Aug 1860. 1861 (72-I) xliv. India Office.

SEYMER, Henry Ker
Select committee on the Berwick-upon-Tweed election petition

Report, 25 April 1853. 1852/3 (401) viii.
Min. of ev. 20 May 1853. 1852/3 (509) viii.

Select committee on the Canterbury election petition. Mins. of ev. 22 Feb 1853. 1852/3 (151) ix.

Select committee on the Great Yarmouth election petition. Min. of ev. 15 Feb 1848. 1847/8 (95) xii.

Select committee on the Harwich election petition. Min. of ev. 13 June 1851. 1851 (396) xii.

Select committee on the Leicester election petition. Min. of ev. 2 June 1848. 1847/8 (381) xiii.

Select committee on the Marlborough Borough election petition. Min. of ev. 25 Aug 1857. 1857, session 2 (311) vii.

Select committee on the Peterborough election petition
 Report, 8 June 1853. 1852/3 (580) xvii.
 Min. of ev. 9 June 1853. 1852/3 (589) xvii.

Select committee on the Sligo Borough election. Report, 7 March 1854. 1854 (78) viii.

SEYMOUR, Lord SEE:
St. Maur, Edward Adolphus, *11th D. Somerset* (1775-1855)
St. Maur, Edward Adolphus, *12th D. Somerset* (1804-1885)

SEYMOUR, Henry Danby
Select committee on the Ecclesiastical commission. Report, 29 July 1862. 1862 (470) viii.

Select committee on the Ecclesiastical commission. Report, 17 July 1863. 1863 (457) vi.

SHADWELL, Charles Frederick Alexander
Committee on the higher education of naval officers. Report, 8 July 1870. 1870 C.203 xxv. Admiralty.

SHAFTESBURY, E. SEE:
Cooper, Cropley Ashley, *6th E. Shaftesbury* (1768-1851)
Cooper, Anthony Ashley, *7th E. Shaftesbury* (1801-1885)

SHARPE, T.W.
Departmental committee on defective and epileptic children
 Report, 7 Jan 1898. 1898 C.8746 xxvi.
 Min. of ev. 1898 C.8747 xxvi. Education Department.

Departmental committee on the pupil-teacher system
 Report, 12 Jan 1898. 1898 C.8761 xxvi.
 Min. of ev. 1898 C.8762 xxvi. Education Department.

SHAW, Benjamin
Committee on petitions relating to East India docks. Report, 5 June 1818. 1818 (430) vi.

SHAW, Frederick
Select committee on the Oxford, Worcester and Wolverhampton Railway Bill and the Oxford and Rugby Railway Bill. Min. of ev. 10 June 1845. 1845 (360) xi.

SHAW, Robert, Sir
Committee on Alnage Laws of Ireland. Report, 3 June 1817. 1817 (315) viii.

Select committee on local taxation of Dublin. SEE:
Ellis, Charles Rose.

SHAW, William Nap'er
Report on the ventilation and warming in certain Metropolitan poor law schools. 21 Sept 1897. 1898 C.9001 xlv. Local Government Board.

SHAW-LEFEVRE, Charles, 1st Vct. Eversley
Boundary commission for England and Wales. Report, 5 Feb 1868. 1867/8 [3892] xx.

Commission on the condition of the volunteer force in G.B. Report. 1862 [3053] xxvii.

Commission on the constabulary force in England and Wales. 1st report, 27 March 1839. 1839 [169] xix; (CP Police, 8). (No other reports identified).

Commission on municipal corporation boundaries, England and Wales. Report, 25 April 1837. 1837 (238) xxvi, xxvii, xxviii.

Committee on the North Metropolitan Cemetery Bill. Min. of ev. 12 June 1837. 1837 (394) li.

Committee on standing orders on private bills, 1837. SEE: Poulett-Thomson, Charles Edward.

Joint select committee on tramways in the Metropolis. Report, 17 June 1872. HL 1872 (55) xi; HC repr. 1872 (252) xii.

Petition of Messrs. Hansard in the case of Stockdale *vs* Hansard
    Min. of ev. 18 Jan 1840. 1840 (3) xlv.
    Petition and proceedings of the case of Stockdale *vs* Hansard. 16 Jan 1840. 1840 (1) xlv.

Select committee on agriculture
    1st report, 4 March 1836. 1836 (79) viii, pt.1.
    2nd report, 15 April 1836. 1836 (189) viii, pt.1.
    3rd report, 21 July 1836. 1836 (465) viii, pt.2; (Agriculture, 3-4).

Select committee (HL) on the despatch of public business in the H.L. Report, 7 May 1861. HL 1861 (95) xxiv.

Select committee (HL) on the Elementary Education Provisional Order Confirmation (No.1) Bill. Report, 20 June 1873. HL 1873 (119) viii.

Select committee on the Highway Rates Bill. Report, 30 June 1837. 1837 (457) xx.

Select committee (HL) on the Lands Improvement Company Bill. Report, 20 July 1859. HL 1859, session 2 (41) xvii.

Select committee (HL) on the New Forest Deer Removal Act, 1851. Report, 9 July 1868. HL 1867/8 (131) xxx; HC repr. 1867/8 (479) viii.

Select committee on printing. Report, 26 March 1841. 1841 (181) ix.

Select committee on printing. Report, 25 Aug 1846. 1846 (685) xv.

Select committee on printing. Report, 13 June 1850. 1850 (447) xvi.

Select committee on printing. Report, 17 March 1857. 1857, session 1 (122) ii.

Select committee (HL) on public business of the HL. Report, 7 May 1861. HL 1861 (95) xxiv; HC repr. 1861 (321) xi.

Select committee on standing orders revision. Report, 10 Aug 1838. 1837/8 (700) xxiii.

Select committee on survey of parishes; Tithe Commutation Act. Report, 8 May 1837. 1837 (285) vi.

Standing committee on the library of the H.C. Report, 10 June 1852. 1852 (453) v.

Standing committee on the library of the H.C. Report, 29 July 1856. 1856 (426) vii.

Standing committee on the library of the H.C. Report, 17 March 1857. 1857, session 1 (123) ii.

SHAW-LEFEVRE, Charles (ca. 1758-1823)
Committee on the petitions of General Martin [on Lord Fairfax's will]. Report, 30 July 1807. 1807 (82) iii.

SHAW-LEFEVRE, George John
Committee on the audit, *etc.* of Naval accounts. Report, 16 Aug 1872. 1873 (70) xviii. Admiralty.

Committee on the Central Post Office buildings and establishment. Report, 23 June 1884. 1884/5 C.4267 xxii. Treasury.

Letter respecting the annuity tax in Edinburgh. 29 April 1850. 1850 [1208] xlix. Home Department.

Report on the annuity tax in the City of Edinburgh and Cannongate. 27 April 1848. 1849 [1057] xlvi. Home Department.

Report on the expediency of an alteration of the law in respect to the rating of stock in trade. 14 May 1840. 1840 (325) xxix. Poor Law Commission.

Report of the Poor Law Commission on the further amendment of the Poor Laws. 31 Dec 1839. 1840 [226], [227] xvii.

Report respecting the erection of galleries of art at Edinburgh (National Gallery) and other papers in explanation of the estimate no.16, in class 4. 13 Dec 1847. 1850 (586) xxxiv. Treasury.

Royal commission on agricultural depression. SEE: Lyttleton, Charles George, *1st Vct. Cobham.*

Royal commission on loss of life at sea
    1st report: Ev. 31 July 1885. 1884/5 C.4577 xxxv.
    Final report, 27 Aug 1887. 1887 C.5227 xliii; (Shipping, 8-9).

Select committee on Agricultural Tennants (Compensation) Bill (nos. 1 and 2) Bills. Reports, 1 Aug 1882. 1882 (336) vii.

Select committee on the Belfast Corporation (Lunatic Asylums, *etc.*) Bill. Report, 25 May 1892. 1892 (228) xi.

Select committee on Charitable Trusts Acts. Report, 29 July 1884. 1884 (306) ix.

Select committee on the Charitable Trusts Acts. Report, 4 Dec 1884. 1884/5 (33) viii.

Select committee on H.C. accommodation. Report, 24 May 1881. 1881 (248) ix.

Select committee on the hop industry. Report, 8 Aug 1889. 1889 (307) xi.

Select committee on the hop industry. Report, 15 July 1890. 1890 (302) xiii.

Select committee on the Inclosure Law Amendment Bill. Report and special report, 23 June 1871. 1871 (314) vii; (Agriculture, 14).

Select committee on the Irish Land Act, 1870. Report, 12 July 1877. 1877 (328) xii.

Select committee on the Irish Land Act, 1870. Report, 27 June 1878. 1878 (249) xv.

Select committee on the London City Lands (Thames Embankment) Bill. Report, 30 June 1881. 1881 (304) ix.

Select committee on Married Women's Property Bill. Special report, 17 July 1868. 1867/8 (441) vii; (Marriage and Divorce, 2).

Select committee on the Parochial Charities (London) Bill and the London Parochial Charities Bill. Report, 23 May 1882. 1882 (205) xii.

Select committee on Parochial Charities (London) Bill. Report, 5 June 1883. 1883 (185) xiv.

Select committee on the Parochial Electors (Registration Acceleration) Bill. Report, 14 June 1894. 1894 (163) xiv.

Select committee on the Pilotage Bill. Report, 8 and 12 July 1870. 1870 (343) ix.

Select committee on Post Office Sites Bill. Report, 21 May 1885. 1884/5 (208) x.

Select committee on Public Offices Sites Bill. Report, 28 June 1882. 1882 (253) xii.

Select committee on railway rates and charges
    1st report, 22 Aug 1893. 1893/4 (385) xiv.
    2nd report, 14 Dec 1893. 1893/4 (462) xiv; (Transport, 22).

Select committee on Tramways Bill. Report, 2 May 1870. 1870 (205) x.

Select committee on the Tramways (Ireland) Acts Amendment Bill. Report, 4 April 1881. 1881 (156) xii.

Select committee on Trustee savings banks. Report, 28 Nov 1888. 1888 (406) xxiii; (MP Savings Banks, 3).

Select committee on Trustee savings banks. Report, 2 Aug 1889. 1889 (301) xvi; (MP Savings Banks, 3).

Select committee on Westminster Hall restoration. Report, 27 April 1885. 1884/5 (166) xiii.

Special committee of the Council of the School of Design on the management of the school. Report, 23 June 1847. 1847 [835] lxii; (IR Design, 3). Board of Trade. SEE ALSO: Milnes, R.M.

Statute law committee
    Min. and memorandum on consolidation of the statutes. 1875 (157) lxi.
    Papers relative to proceedings and reports preliminary to consolidation. 1878 (320) lxiii.
    Memorandum: Poor law acts. 8 Aug 1877. 1878 (45) lxiii. Lord Chancellor's Office.

SHEEHY, David
Select committee on privilege. Report on the service of a writ. SEE: Matthews, Henry, *1st Vct. Llandaff.*

SHEFFIELD, Lord SEE:
Holroyd, John Baker, *1st E. Sheffield* (1735-1821)
Holroyd, George Augustus Frederick Charles, *2nd E. Sheffield* (1802-1876).

SHEIL, Richard Lalor
Commission of inquiry into the Royal Mint. Report. 1849 [1026] xxviii; (MP Currency, 2).

Select committee on Ministers' money, Ireland. Report, 28 July 1848. 1847/8 (559) xvii.

SHELBURNE, E. SEE:
Petty-Fitzmaurice, Henry Charles Keith, *5th M. Lansdowne.*

[Peerage claim]. SEE: Freeman-Mitford, J.T. Kerry and Shelburne claims.

SHELLEY, John, *Sir*
Select committee on coal duties in the Metropolis. Report, 12 Aug 1853. 1852/3 (916) xxii.

SHERBROOK, *Vct.* SEE:
Lowe, Robert, *1st Vct. Sherbrook.*

SHERIDAN, John E.
Report on convent schools in Ireland. 1860. 1864 (179) xlvi. Office of National Education, Ireland.

SHERIDAN, Richard Brinsley
Select committee on the Railways (Guards' and Passengers' Communication) Bill. Special report, 2 Aug 1866. 1866 (465) xi.

SHIPPARD, Sidney Goldophin Alexander
Commission on land claims and a land settlement in British Bechuanaland. Report, 29 May 1886. 1886 C.4889 xlvii; (Africa, 44). Colonial Office.

SHORE, Charles John, *2nd Bn. Teignmouth*
Select committee on the office of coroner for Middlesex. Report, 27 July 1840. 1840 (549) xiv.

SHREWSBURY, *E.* [Peerage claim]. SEE:
Freeman-Mitford, J.T.

SHUTTLEWORTH, *Bn.* SEE:
Kay-Shuttleworth, Ughtred James, *1st Bn. Shuttleworth.*

SHUTTLEWORTH, J.P.K. SEE:
Kay-Shuttleworth, James Philip.

SIBTHORPE, Charles De Laet Waldo
Select committee on steam navigation. Report, 14 Oct 1831. 1831 (335) viii.

SIDMOUTH, *Vct.* SEE:
Addington, Henry, *1st Vct. Sidmouth* (1757-1844)
Addington, William Leonard, *2nd Vct. Sidmouth* (1794-1864)

SIFTON, T.E.
Interdepartmental committee on mail steamer services on the North and West Coasts of Scotland. Report, 15 Jan 1898. 1898 (130) xxxiv. Post Office.

SIMMONS, J.L.A.
Report on the fatal accident, 24 May 1847, by the falling of the bridge over the River Dee, on the Chester and Holyhead Railway. 15 June 1847. 1847 (584) lxiii. Board of Trade, Railway Commission.

SIMMS, F.W.
Commission on the practicability of establishing railway communication throughout India. Report, 13 March 1846. 1846 (571) xxxi. India Office.

Report upon the practicability of introducing railways into India and upon an eligible line to connect Calcutta with Mirzapore and the Northwest provinces. 13 March 1846. 1847 (68) xli. East India Office.

Report upon the proposed Madras and Wallajanuggur railroad. 30 Dec 1845. 1847 (151) xli. East India Office.

SIMON, John
Letter on the Russian epidemic. 19 April 1865. 1865 (246) xlvii. Privy Council.

Report on the last two cholera epidemics of London as affected by the consumption of impure water. 13 May 1856. 1856 [2137] lii.

SIMONDS, James B.
Report on the vaccination of sheep. 8 June 1864. 1864 [3362] l. Privy Council.

SIMPSON, James
Report on the state of New Westminster Bridge. 28 June 1856. 1856 (318) lii. Commission of Works.

Report on the Victoria Street sewer. 4 June 1853. 1852/3 (541-I) xcvi; (UA Sanitation, 3). Metropolitan Commission of Sewers.

SINCLAIR, Daniel
Select committee on Gilbert and Sinclair's Patent Bill. SEE: Temple-Nugent-Chandos-Grenville, R.P.C., *3rd D. Buckingham.*

SINCLAIR, George
Select committee on church patronage, Scotland. Report, 23 July 1834. 1834 (512) v.

Select committee on judges' salaries, Scotland. Report, 1 July 1834. 1834 (438) xi.

SINCLAIR, John, *Sir*
Committee on Broad-Wheel Acts
    1st report, 13 June 1806. 1806 (212) ii; repr. 1808 (76) ii.
    2nd report, 18 July 1806. 1806 (321) ii; repr. 1808 (77) ii.

Committee on Broad-Wheel Acts
    Report, 2 May 1809. 1809 (179) iii.
    2nd report, 30 May 1809. 1809 (138) iii.
    3rd report, 19 June 1809. 1809 (271) iii.

Committee on funds arising from the forfeited estates in Scotland. Report, 16 June 1806. 1806 (221) ii.

Committee on highways and turnpike roads in England and Wales. Report, 14 June 1811. 1810/1 (240) iii.

Committee on the highways of the Kingdom
    1st report, 11 May 1808. 1808 (125) ii.
    2nd report, 30 May 1808. 1808 (275) ii.
    3rd report, 17 June 1808. 1808 (315) ii.

Committee on the re-committed report on the rate of duty payable on Scotch barley and malt. Report, 15 June 1804. 1803/4 (129) v.

Royal commission on the colonisation of Canada of crofters and cottars from the western Highlands and Islands of Scotland. SEE: Bruce, Alexander Hugh, *6th Bn. Balfour of Burleigh.*

SKEY, Frederick C.
Committee on the pathology and treatment of venereal disease in the Army and Navy. Report, 27 May 1867. 1868/9 [4031] xxxvii; (HE Infectious Diseases, 4). Admiralty.

SKIRROW, Walter
Report of an inquiry into the state and management of the estates and property of the Charterhouse and into the general affairs of that Charity. 3 Dec 1854. 1857/8 (9) xlvi. Charity Commission.

SKRIVANOW, Gregory George
Select committee Skrivanow's Patent Bill. SEE: Temple-Nugent-Chandos-Grenville, R.P.C., *3rd D. Buckingham.*

SLADE, Frederick William
Commission on the existence of bribery in the Borough of St. Alban's. Report, 2 Feb 1852. 1852 [1431] xxvii.

Commission on corrupt practices in the City of Canterbury. Report, 23 July 1853. 1852/3 [1658] xlvii.

SLADE, Wyndham
Commission on corrupt practices at elections for the

Borough of Great Yarmouth. Report, 20 Dec 1866. 1867 [3775] xxx.

SLANE, *Lord* [Peerage claim]. SEE: Cooper, C.A.

SLANEY, Robert Aglionby
Select committee on education of the poorer classes in England and Wales. Report, 13 July 1838. 1837/8 (589) vii; (ED Poorer Classes, 6).

Select committee on the health of towns. Report, 17 June 1840. 1840 (384) xi; (Health, 2).

Select committee on investments for the savings of the middle and working classes. Report, 5 July 1850. 1850 (508) xix; (MP Savings Banks, 1).

Select committee on the law of partnership. Report, 8 July 1851. 1851 (509) xviii.

Select committee on manufacturers' employment. Report, 2 July 1830. 1830 (590) x.

Select committee on poor laws relating to employment or relief of able-bodied persons from the poor rate. Report, 3 July 1828. 1828 (494) iv; (Agriculture, 1).

Select committee on public walks. Report, 27 June 1833. 1833 (448) xv.

SLOGGETT, W.H.
Report on the moral effects of the Contagious Diseases Acts. 8 May 1873. 1873 (209) xl. War Office.

SMART, Robert
Committee on dockyard economy. Report, 14 June 1859. 1859, session 2 (139), (139-I) xviii. Admiralty.

SMITH, Andrew
Board of inquiry held at the Office of the Army Medical Departmental, 1849-50, on the nature of yellow fever. Report, 1850. *In:* 1852 [1473] xx. General Board of Health.

SMITH, Edward
Dietaries for the inmates of workhouses. 1866 [3660] xxxv. Poor Law Board.

Report of inquiry into the state and management of the workhouse of Farnham Union. 21 Jan 1868. 1867/8 (134) lx. Poor Law Board.

Report on the Metropolitan workhouse infirmaries and sick-wards. 19 June 1866. 1866 (372) lxi. Poor Law Board.

Report on the sufficiency of the existing arrangements for the care and treatment of the sick in provincial workhouses in England and Wales. 15 April 1867. 1867/8 (4) lx. Poor Law Board.

SMITH, Frederick, *Sir*
Committee on railway communications between London, Dublin, Edinburgh and Glasgow
    Report, 16 April 1840. 1840 (250) xlv.
    Report, 16 May 1840. 1840 (312) xlv.
    3rd report, 14 Nov 1840. 1841 (8) xxv.
    4th report, 15 March 1841. 1841 (132) xxv. Treasury.

Report on the atmospheric railway. 15 Feb 1842. 1842 [368] xli. Board of Trade.

Select committee on the Navy gun and mortar boats. Report, 13 Aug 1860. 1860 (545) viii.

SMITH, Frederick James
Commission on corrupt practices at the last election for the Borough of Reigate. Report, 2 Feb 1867. 1867 [3774] xxviii.

SMITH, James
Report by the Marine Board of Liverpool on the shipping of crews at Liverpool. 30 June 1863. 1863 (464) lxiii. Board of Trade.

SMITH, James Parker
Committee on the inland transit of cattle
    Report, 1 May 1898. 1898 C.8928 xxxiv.
    Min. of ev. 1898 C.8929 xxxiv; (AG Animal Health, 4). Board of Agriculture.

SMITH, John
Committee on Irish tontine annuities
    Report, 14 June 1811. 1810/1 (237) v.
    2nd report, 4 May 1812. 1812 (221) v.
    Report, 29 June 1813. 1812/3 (321) vi.

Select committee on bankrupt laws. Report, 11 July 1817. 1817 (486) v.

Select committee on the bankrupt laws
    Report, 8 May 1818. 1818 (276) vi.
    Min. of ev. 16 March 1818. 1818 (127) vi.
    Further report, 8 May 1818. 1818 (277) vi.

Select committee on law relating to merchants, agents, or factors. Report, 13 June 1823. 1823 (452) iv.

SMITH, John Abel
Select committee on the Beversley Borough election petition. Min. of ev. 7 Aug 1857. 1857, session 2 (243) v.

Select committee on savings banks. 1st report, 28 June 1849. 1849 (437) xiv; (MP Savings Banks, 1).

Select committee on savings banks. Report, 1 Aug 1850. 1850 (649) xix; (MP Savings Banks, 1).

Select committee on trade with China. Report, 5 June 1840. 1840 (359) vii.

SMITH, John Mark Frederick
Commission on harbours of refuge. SEE: Hope, James.

Commission of inquiry into the guage of railways. Report. 1846 [684], [699], [700] xvi; (Transport, 8).

SMITH, Joseph
Report on the state and condition of the Victoria St. sewer. 1 March 1851. 1851 (338) xlviii; (UA Sanitation, 3). Metropolitan Commission of Sewers. SEE ALSO: Forster, Frank.

SMITH, Montague
Commission on the affairs of the Borough of Queensborough. Report, 17 Aug 1843. 1844 (575) xxxi. Home Department.

SMITH, Montague Edward, Sir
Royal commission on municipal boundaries. SEE: Cave, Stephen.

SMITH, R. Baird
Report on the commercial condition of the north west provinces of India. 8 May 1861. 1862 (29) xl. India Office.

Reports on the famine of 1860-61 in the north west provinces of India. 25 May and 14 Aug 1861. 1862 (29) xl. India Office.

SMITH, Robert Angus
Reports on air and water of towns and supply problems. *In:* 1850 [1283] xxii. General Board of Health.

SMITH, Robert Vernon
Select committee on church leases. Report, 7 Aug 1838. 1837/8 (692) ix.

Select committee on church leases. Report, 6 May 1839. 1839 (247) viii.

Select committee on civil list charges. Report, 9 Aug 1833. 1833 (646) vii.

Select committee on the Highways Bill. Min. of proc. 17 July 1847. 1847 (683) viii.

Select committee on the militia estimates, 1852/3. Report, 11 June 1852. 1852 (444) v.

Select committee on miscellaneous expenditure. Report, 27 July 1848. 1847/8 (543) xviii, pts.1 and 2; (National Finance, 3).

Select committee on the plan of education in Ireland. Report, 6 July 1837. 1837 (485) ix.

Select committee on printing
    1st report, 16 Aug 1848. 1847/8 (657) xvi.
    2nd report, 29 Aug 1848. 1847/8 (710) xvi.

SMITH, Thomas Berry Cusack
Commission on the mercantile laws and the law of partnership
    1st report: Law of partnership. 1854 [1791] xxvii.
    2nd report. 1854/5 [1977] xviii.

SMITH, Thomas Southwood
Report on Mr. Ledoyen's disinfecting fluid. 20 March 1847. 1847 (599) lvii; (UA Sanitation, 3). Commission of H.M. Woods.

Report on Metropolitan drainage. 4 Aug 1854. 1854 (180) lxi; (UA Sanitation, 4). General Board of Health.

Report on the prevalence of fever in Metropolitan unions and parishes during 1827/8. 29 April 1839. *In:* 1839 (239) xx; (Health, 3). Poor Law Commission.

Statement of the preliminary inquiry on the epidemic at Croydon. Jan 1853. 1852/3 [1683] xcvi; (HE Infectious Diseases, 2). Board of Health.

SMITH, Vernon
Select committee on the Cambridge election petition. Min. of ev. 2 March 1853. 1852/3 (185) ix.

SMITH, William
Select committee on extents in aid. Report, 11 July 1817. 1817 (505) v.

Committee on Messrs. Chalmers and Cowie's petition on Swedish herrings. Report, 21 March 1806. 1806 (48) ii; (Fisheries, 1).

Committee on the Norwich and Lowestoft Navigation Bill. Min. of ev. 12 May 1826. 1826 (369) iv.

Committee on the Queensferry passage. Report, 3 May 1814. 1813/4 (139) iii.

SMITH, William Henry
Select committee on the jubilee thanksgiving service, Westminster Abbey. Report, 14 June 1887. 1887 (183) ix.

Select committee on the member of the Royal family. Report, 22 July 1889. 1889 (271) xi.

Select committee on the New Forest. Report, 16 July 1875. 1875 (341) xiii.

Select committee on the New Forest Bill. Report, 22 June 1877. 1877 (281) xiv.

Select committee on parliamentary reporting. Report, 31 July 1878. 1878 (327) xvii.

SMITH, William Henry (continued)

Select committee on parliamentary reporting. Report, 23 May 1879. 1878/9 (203) xii.

Select committee on the Public Works Loans Acts Amendment Bill, and the Public Works Loans Act Consolidation Bill, consolidated into the Public Works Loans Bill. Special report, 26 July 1875. 1875 (358) xiv; (National Finance, 5).

Select committee on the ventilation of the H.C. Report, 30 July 1884. 1884 (309) xiii.

SMITH-STANLEY, Edward, *13th E. Derby* SEE: Stanley, Edward Smith, *13th E. Derby*.

SMITH-STANLEY, Edward Geoffrey, *14th E. Derby* SEE: Stanley, Edward Geoffrey, *14th E. Derby*.

SMITH-STANLEY, Edward Henry, *15th E. Derby* SEE: Stanley, Edward Henry, *15th E. Derby*.

SMYTH, James Carmichael

Committee on petition respecting discovery of nitrous fumigation. SEE: Bankes, Henry.

SMYTH, John

Select committee on the election and return for the Borough of Ilchester Somerset. Report, 29 and 31 March 1803. 1802/3 (41) iii.

SMYTH, John Henry

Committee on African forts. Report, 25 June 1817. 1817 (431) vi; (Africa, 1).

SMYTH, Warrington Wilkinson

Report on the metallurgical products at the Paris Universal Exhibition. 1 March 1856. 1856 [2049-II) xxxvi, pt.2. Board of Trade.

Royal commission on accidents in mines
    Preliminary report. 1881 C.3036 xxvi.
    Final report, 15 March 1886. 1886 C.4699 xvi;
        (FP Mining Accidents, 10-11).

SMYTHE, Hamilton

Commission on the riots in Belfast in July and Sept 1857. Report, 30 Nov 1857. 1857/8 [2309] xxvi; (CP Civil Disorder, 7).

SOLICITOR-GENERAL

1799	*Sir* William Grant
1801	Spencer Perceval
1802	T.M. Sutton
1805	*Sir* Vicary Gibbs
1806	*Sir* Samuel Romilly
1807	*Sir* Thomas Plumer
1812	*Sir* William Garrow
1813	*Sir* Robert Dallas
1814	*Sir* Samuel Shepherd
1817	*Sir* Robert Gifford
1819	*Sir* S. Copley
1824	*Sir* C. Wetherell
1826	*Sir* N.C. Tindal
1829	*Sir* Edward B. Sugden
1830	*Sir* William Horne
1832	*Sir* J. Campbell
1834	R.M. Rolfe
1834	*Sir* William Follett
1835	*Sir* R.M. Rolfe
1839	*Sir* T. Wilde
1841	*Sir* William Follett
1844	*Sir* F . Thesiger
1845	*Sir* F. Kelly
1846	*Sir* David Dundas
1848	*Sir* J. Romilly
1850	*Sir* A.J.E. Cockburn
1851	*Sir* W.P. Wood
1852	*Sir* F. Kelly
1853	*Sir* R. Bethell
1856	J.S. Wortley
1857	*Sir* H.S. Keating
1858	*Sir* H.M. Cairns
1859	*Sir* H.S. Keating
1860	*Sir* Wm. Atherton
1861	*Sir* Roundell Palmer
1863	*Sir* Robert P. Collier
1866	*Sir* W. Bovill
1866	*Sir* J.B. Karslake
1867	*Sir* Charles J. Selwyn
1868	*Sir* W.B. Brett
1868	*Sir* Richard Baggallay
1868	*Sir* J.D. Coleridge
1871	*Sir* George Jessel
1873	*Sir* Henry James
1873	*Sir* W.G.V. Harcourt
1874	*Sir* Richard Baggallay
1874	*Sir* John Holker
1875	*Sir* Hardinge S. Giffard
1880	*Sir* Farrer Herschell
1885	*Sir* J.E. Gorst
1886	*Sir* Horace Davey
1886	*Sir* Edward Clarke
1892	*Sir* John Rigby
1894	*Sir* Robert T. Reid
1894	*Sir* Frank Lockwood
1895	*Sir* Robert B. Finlay
1900	*Sir* E. Carson

SOLICITOR-GENERAL FOR IRELAND

1884	Samuel Walker
1888	Dodgson H. Madden

SOLICITOR-GENERAL FOR SCOTLAND

1789	Robert Blair of Avonton
1806	John Clerk of Eldin
1807	David Boyle of Shewalton
1811	David Moneypenny of Pitmilly
1816	James Wedderburn
1822	John Hope
1830	Henry Cockburn
1834	Andrew Skene
1834	Duncan McNeill
1835	John Cunninghame
1837	Andrew Rutherfurd
1839	James Ivory
1840	Thomas Maitland of Dundrennan
1841	Duncan McNeill
1842	Adam Anderson
1846	Thomas Maitland of Dundrennan
1850	James Moncrieff
1851	John Cowan
1851	George Deas
1852	John Inglis
1852	Charles Neaves
1853	Robert Handyside
1853	James Craufurd
1854	Thomas Mackenzie
1855	Edward Francis Maitland
1858	Charles Baillie
1858	David Mure
1859	George Patton
1859	Edward Francis Maitland
1862	George Young
1866	Edward Strathearn Gordon
1867	John Millar
1868	George Young

1869 Andrew Rutherfurd Clark
1874 John Millar
1874 William Watson
1876 John Hay Athole Macdonald
1880 John Blair Balfour
1881 Alexander Asher
1885 James Patrick Bannerman Robertson
1886 Alexander Asher
1886 James Patrick Bannerman Robertson
1888 Moir Tod Stormonth Darling
1890 *Sir* Charles John Pearson
1891 Andrew Graham Murray
1892 Alexander Asher
1894 Thomas Shaw
1895 Andrew Graham Murray
1896 Charles Scott Dickson
1903 David Dundas

SOMERHILL, *Bn.* SEE:
De Burgh, Ulick John, *1st M. Clanricarde* (1802-1874)
De Burgh-Canning, Hubert George, *2nd M. Clanricarde* (1832-1916)

SOMERS, *E.* SEE:
Cocks, John Somers, *2nd E. Somers.*

SOMERS, John Patrick
Select committee on Sligo Borough election. SEE: Fitzgerald, J.D.

SOMERSET, *D.* SEE:
St. Maur, Edward Adolphus, *11th E. Somerset* (1775-1855)
St. Maur, Edward Adolphus, *12th D. Somerset* (1804-1885)

SOMERSET, Granville Charles Henry, *Lord*
Commission on the Department of Stamps. Report, 5 March 1821. 1821 (156) x.

Commission of revenue inquiry. Report, 19 April 1844. 1844 (508) xxxi. Treasury.

Commission of revenue inquiry
Report on Customs frauds. 22 May 1843. 1843 [480] xxix.
Special report relating to Mr. Rolls. 22 May 1843. 1844 (491) xxxviii.
Liverpool customs establishment. Report, 21 Feb 1847. 1847 [400] xxv; (National Finance, 1). Treasury.

Select committee on controverted elections. Report, 12 June 1844. 1844 (373) xiv; (GO Elections, 2).

Select committee on fictitious votes, Ireland
1st report, 12 May 1837. 1837 (308) xi, pt.1.
2nd report, 25 May 1837. 1837 (335) xi, pt.2.
3rd report, 5 July 1837. 1837 (480) xi, pt.2.

Select committee on fictitious votes, Ireland
1st report, 28 March 1838. 1837/8 (259) xiii, pt.1.
2nd report: Supplementary appendix of returns of voters for Cork City. 9 April 1838. 1837/8 (294) xiii, pt.1.
3rd report, 30 July 1838. 1837/8 (643) xiii, pt.2.

Select committee on railway bills
1st report, 28 Feb 1845. 1845 (82) x.
2nd report, 17 March 1845. 1845 (135) x.

Select committee on railway bills
Report, 20 June 1845. 1845 (395) x.
2nd report, 4 July 1845. 1845 (442) x.

Select committee on railway bills
1st report, 5 Feb 1846. 1846 (41-I) xiii.

2nd report, 10 Feb 1846. 1846 (41) xiii.
3rd report, 17 Feb 1846. 1846 (61) xiii.

Select committee on rebuilding the Houses of Parliament. Report, 3 June 1835. 1835 (262) xviii.

Select committee on standing orders revision, 1842.
Report, 1 Aug 1842. 1842 (513) xiv.
Report, 2 Aug 1842. 1842 (530) xiv.

Select committee on standing orders revision, 1843.
Report, 10 Aug 1843. 1843 (550) xi.

Select committee on standing orders revision, 1844.
Report, 2 Aug 1844. 1844 (572) xiv.

Select committee on standing orders revision, 1845.
Report, 25 July 1845. 1845 (570) xiii.

Select committee on the stationery contract
1st report: Appointment of storekeeper. 16 Aug 1833. 1833 (674) xvi
2nd report, 16 Aug 1833. 1833 (674) xvi.

SOMERVILLE, William, *Sir*
Select committee on railway bills classification, 1846. SEE: Wilson-Patten, John.

SOTHERN, Thomas Henry Sutton
Committee of selection on the grouping of private bills
1st report, 25 Feb 1853. 1852/3 (163) xxxiv.
2nd report, 3 March 1853. 1852/3 (186) xxxiv.
3rd report, 10 March 1853. 1852/3 (218) xxxiv.
4th report, 17 March 1853. 1852/3 (242) xxxiv.
5th report, 7 April 1853. 1852/3 (305) xxxiv.
6th report, 20 April 1853. 1852/3 (373) xxxiv.
7th report, 25 April 1853. 1852/3 (393) xxxiv.
8th report, 29 April 1853. 1852/3 (419) xxxiv.
9th report, 2 May 1853. 1852/3 (427) xxxiv.
10th report, 5 May 1953. 1852/3 (445) xxxiv.
11th report, 23 May 1853. 1852/3 (520) xxxiv.
12th report, 27 May 1853. 1852/3 (526) xxxiv.
13th report, 3 June 1853. 1852/3 (563) xxxiv.

Committee of selection on the grouping of private bills, 1856. SEE: Green, Thomas.

Committee of selection on the grouping of private bills, 1857. SEE: Wilson-Patten, John.

Select committee on the Friendly Societies Bill. Report, 3 July 1849. 1849 (458) xiv; (Insurance, 2).

Select committee on friendly societies. Report, 25 June 1852. 1852 (531) v; (Insurance, 2).

Select committee on Friendly Societies Bill. Report, 26 July 1854. 1854 (412) vii; (Insurance, 2).

Select committee on Henry Stonor. Report, 1 June 1854. 1854 (278) viii.

SOTHERON-ESTCOURT, Thomas Henry Sutton
Select committee on the Drogheda election petitions. Min. of ev. 11 Aug 1857. 1857, session 2 (255) vi.

Select committee on the Duchy of Lancaster (Bertolacci's petition). 29 July 1857. 1857, session 2 (218) xii; (GO Civil Service, 5).

Select committee on the Gas (Metropolis) Bill
Special report, 18 July 1860. 1860 (493) xxi.
Min. of ev. 29 June 1860. 1860 (417) xxi; (FP Gas, 1).

Select committee on irremovable poor
Report, 29 June 1858. 1857/8 (374) xiii.
Min. of ev. 5 Aug 1859. 1859, session 2 (146) vii; (Poor Law, 23).

Select committee on prosecution expenses. SEE: Hunt, George Ward.

Select committee on the Sale of Gas Act Amendment

SOTHERON-ESTCOURT, Thomas Henry Sutton
(continued)

(No.2) and (No.3) Bills. Min. of ev. 18 July 1860. 1860 (462) xxi; (FP Gas, 1).

Select committee on savings banks. Report, 19 July 1858. 1857/8 (441) xvi; (MP Savings Banks, 2).

SOUTH, James, Sir

Report on the probable danger of any railway passing within a given distance of the Royal Observatory, Greenwich. 22 June 1846. 1846 (470) xxxviii. Admiralty.

SOUTHBOROUGH, Lord SEE:
Hopwood, F.J.S., 1st Bn. Southborough.

SOUTHESK, Lord [Peerage claim]
1848, SEE: Cooper, C.A.
1854-55, SEE: Freeman-Mitford, J.T.

SPARK, John

Report on certain charges of proselytism in the workhouse of Dingle union. 7 May 1851. 1851 (427) xlix. Poor Law Board, Dublin.

SPEAKER, Mr.

1789 Henry Addington
1801 Sir J. Mitford
1802 Charles Abbot
1817 C. Manners-Sutton
1835 J. Abercromby
1839 C. Shaw-Lefevre
1857 J.E. Denison
1872 H.B.W. Brand
1884 A.W. Peel
1895 W.C. Gully

SPEARMAN, Alexander Young, Sir

Commission on railways in Ireland
Report, 30 April 1868. 1867/8 [4018], [4018-I] xxxii.
2nd report, 7 Dec 1868. 1868/9 [4086] xvii. Treasury.

SPENCER, E. SEE:
Spencer, George John, 2nd E. Spencer (1758-1834)
Spencer, John Charles, 3rd E. Spencer (1782-1845)
Spencer, Frederick, 4th E. Spencer (1798-1857)
Spencer, John Poyntz, 5th E. Spencer (1835-1910)

SPENCER, George John, 2nd E. Spencer

Select committee (HL) on the Revenue Laws Penalty Bill
1st report, 14 May 1810. HL 1810 (83) xxxv.
2nd report, 14 June 1810. HL 1810 (133) xxxv.

Select committee (HL) on the Revenue Laws Penalty Bill. Report, 1 March 1811. HL 1811 (31) xliv.

SPENCER, John Charles, 3rd E. Spencer

Committee of secrecy on the Bank of England charter. Report, 11 Aug 1832. 1831/2 (722) vi.

Select committee on acts respecting insolvent debtors. Report, 10 May 1819. 1819 (287) ii.

Select committee on the civil list. Report, 21 March 1831. 1830/1 (269) iii.

Select committee on the County Courts Bill. Min. of ev. 4 May 1825. 1825 (276) v.

Select committee on county election polls. Report, 16 May 1827. 1826/7 (349) iv.

Select committee on recovery of small debts. Report, 27 May 1823. 1823 (368) iv.

SPENCER, John Poyntz, 5th E. Spencer

Commission on cattle plague
1st report, 31 Oct 1865. 1866 [3591] xxii.
2nd report, 5 Feb 1866. 1866 [3600] xxii.
3rd report, 1 May 1866. 1866 [3656] xxii; (AG Animal Health, 1).

Select committee (HL) on the Rivers Conservancy and Floods Prevention Bill. Report, 25 Feb 1881. HL 1881 (38) viii.

Report respecting the action of water on lead. 9 May 1850. In: 1850 [1283] xxii. General Board of Health.

SPENCER-CHURCHILL, John Winston, 6th D. Marlborough

Select committee (HL) on the assessment and levy of church rates. Report, 5 Aug 1859. HL 1859, session 2 (24) xvii; HC repr. 1859, session 2 (179) v.

Select committee (HL) on the assessment and levy of church rates. Report, 28 Feb 1860. HL 1860 (19) xxiv; HC repr. 1860 (154) xxii.

Select committee (HL) on the Contagious Diseases (Animals) Bill. Report, 31 May 1867. HL 1867 (121) xxvii.

Select committee on the Formation, etc. of Parishes Bill. Report, 14 March 1856. 1856 (106) vii.

Select committee (HL) on Mr. France's pamphlet. Report, 26 Feb 1867. HL 1867 (25) xxvii.

Select committee on his pension. SEE: Harcourt, G.G.

Select committee (HL) on the Vaccination Bill. Report, 19 July 1867. HL 1867 (242) xxvii.

SPENCER-CHURCHILL, Randolph Henry, Lord

Select committee on Army and Navy estimates
1st report, 8 July 1887. 1887 (216) viii.
2nd report, 15 July 1887. 1887 (223) viii.
3rd report, 20 July 1887. 1887 (232) viii.
4th report, 26 July 1887. 1887 (239) viii.
5th report, 5 Aug 1887. 1887 (259) viii.

Select committee on Army estimates
1st report, 17 April 1888. 1888 (120) viii.
2nd report, 8 June 1888. 1888 (212) viii.
3rd report, 15 June 1888. 1888 (225) viii.
4th report, 10 July 1888. 1888 (269) ix.
5th report, 17 July 1888. 1888 (285) ix.

SPENCER-COMPTON, Cavendish, 7th D. Devonshire

Select committee on parliamentary procedure. Report, 10 June 1886. 1886, session 1 (186) xi.

SPOONER, R.

Committee of the Government of Bombay on the decline of the cotton trade. Report, 23 March 1847. 1847 (712) xli. East India Office.

SPRATT, T.

Inquiry into the soundness of M. de Lesseps' reasonings and arguments on the practicability of the Suez Canal. Extracts. 30 Jan 1858. In: 1860 (61) xlii. Admiralty.

SPRING-RICE, Thomas SEE:
Rice, Thomas Spring.

STAFFORD, Lord [Peerage claim]. SEE:
Cooper, C.A.

STAFFORD, Augustus Stafford O'Brien

Select committee on the Medical Department of the Army. Report, 3 July 1856. 1856 (331) xiii.

Select committee on the new Houses of Parliament
    1st report: Kitchen, *etc.* 10 May 1848. 1847/8
      (316) xvi.
    2nd report: Kitchen, *etc.* 9 June 1848. 1847/8
      (396) xvi.
    3rd report: Sergeant-at-Arms. 23 June 1848. 1847/8
      (430) xvi.

STANFORD, C.S., *Rev.*
Dismissal from North Dublin Union. SEE: Crawford,
William.

STANHOPE, E. SEE:
Stanhope, Charles, *3rd E. Stanhope* (1753-1816)
Stanhope, Philip Henry, *4th E. Stanhope* (1781-1855)
Stanhope, Philip Henry, *5th E. Stanhope* (1805-1875)
Stanhope, Arthur Philip, *6th E. Stanhope* (1838-
1905)

STANHOPE, Arthur Philip, *6th E. Stanhope*
Royal commission on copyright. SEE: Manners,
John James Robert.

STANHOPE, Edward
Committee on plans for the fortification and arma-
ment of our military and home mercantile ports.
Report, 17 Feb 1888. 1888 C.5305 xxv. War Office.

Select committee on Army estimates, 1888. SEE:
Spencer-Churchill, Randolph Henry, *Lord.*

Select committee on East India public works. Report,
24 July 1879. 1878/9 (312) ix.

Select committee on East India public works, 1878.
SEE: Hamilton, George Francis, *Lord.*

Select committee on the Electric Lighting Bill. Report,
12 June 1882. 1882 (227) x.

Select committee on the Merchant Seamen Bill. Report, 31 May 1878. 1878 (205) xvi.

Select committee on national provident insurance,
1885. SEE: Maxwell, Herbert Eustace, *Sir.*

Select committee on the Private Bill Procedure (Scotland) Bill. Special report and reports, 1 and 5 May
1891. 1890/1 (216), (226) xiii.

Select committee on the Trust Funds Investment Bill.
Report, 19 June 1889. 1889 (200) xv.

Select committee on the Weights and Measures Bill.
Report, 5 April 1878. 1878 (133) xviii.

STANHOPE, Philip Henry, *5th E. Stanhope*
Commission on the present position of the Royal
Academy in relation to the fine arts. Report, 10 July
1863. 1863 [3205], [3205-I] xxvii; (ED Fine Arts,
5).

Select committee (HL) on ecclesiastical titles in G.B.
and Ireland. Report, 16 June 1868. HL 1867/8 (66)
xxx; HC repr. 1867/8 (348) viii.

Select committee (HL) on the printing of the Minutes
and Journals of the H.L. Report, 27 Feb 1857. HL
1857, session 1 (30) ix.

Select committee (HL) on transportation. SEE: Ryder,
Dudley, *2nd E. Harrowby.*

STANLEY, Lord SEE:
Stanley, Edward Smith, *13th E. Derby* (1775-1851)
Stanley, Edward Geoffrey, *14th E. Derby* (1799-1869)
Stanley, Edward Henry, *15th E. Derby* (1826-1893)
Stanley, Frederick Arthur, *16th E. Derby* (1841-1893)
Stanley, Edward George Villiers, *17th E. Derby* (1865-
1948)

STANLEY, Lord SEE:
Stanley, John Thomas, *6th Bn. Stanley.*

STANLEY OF ALDERLEY, Bn. SEE:
Stanley, Edward John, *2nd Bn. Stanley of Alderley.*

STANLEY, E. Lyulph
Report on friendly societies in the midland counties
of England. 1874 C.996 xxiii, pt.2; (Insurance, 8).
SEE ALSO: Northcote, Stafford Henry, *Sir.*

Commission on the Trustee Savings Bank at Cardiff.
Interim report. 1888 C.5287 xliv; (Savings Bank, 3).
(No further reports printed).

STANLEY, E.S. SEE:
Smith-Stanley, E., *Lord Strange.*

STANLEY, Edward Geoffrey, *14th E. Derby*
Commission on the exhibition of 1851. SEE: Saxe-
Coburg, Francis Albert Augustus Charles Emanuel,
Prince of Saxe-Coburg-Gothe.

General committee on railway and canal bills
    1st report, 20 Feb 1862. 1862 (57) xvi.
    2nd report, 27 Feb 1862. 1862 (69) xvi.
    3rd report, 13 March 1862. 1862 (105) xvi.
    4th report, 21 March 1862. 1862 (114) xvi.
    5th report, 8 April 1862. 1862 (152) xvi.
    6th report, 6 May 1862. 1862 (211) xvi.
    7th report, 22 May 1862. 1862 (265) xvi.
    8th report, 29 May 1862. 1862 (283) xvi.
    9th report, 30 May 1862. 1862 (288) xvi.
    10th report, 5 June 1862. 1862 (308) xvi.
    11th report, 7 July 1862. 1862 (378) xvi.

Select committee on Chatham election. Report,
19 May 1835. 1835 (215) ix.

Select committee (HL) on injury from noxious vapours.
Report, 21 July 1862. HL 1862 (95) xxix; HC repr.
1862 (486) xiv; (Health, 8).

Select committee on the Religious Worship Bill
    Report, 2 July 1855. HL 1854/5 (191) xxii.
    Proc. 9 July 1855. HL 1854/5 (208) xxii.

Select committee on tithes in Ireland
    1st report, 18 Feb 1832. 1831/2 (177) xxi.
    2nd report, 4 June 1832. 1831/2 (508) xxi.

STANLEY, Edward George Villiers, *17th E. Derby*
Departmental committee on Glanders. Report, 2 June
1899. 1899 C.9397, C.9398 xxxiii.

Select committee on kitchen and refreshment rooms,
H.C. Report, 11 Aug 1896. 1896 (355) x.

Select committee on kitchen and refreshment rooms,
H.C. Report, 5 Aug 1897. 1897 (409) x.

Select committee on kitchen and refreshment rooms,
H.C. Report, 4 Aug 1898. 1898 (360) x.

Select committee on South Eastern, London, Chatham and Dover Railway Companies Bill. Report,
25 April 1899. 1899 (171) x.

STANLEY, Edward Henry, *15th E. Derby*
Commission for consolidating the statute law
    Report. 1854/5 [1963] xv.
    2nd report, 5 March 1856. 1856 [2045] xviii.
    3rd report, June 1857. 1857, session 2 [2219]
      xxi.
    4th report, Feb 1859. 1859, session 2 [78] xiii,
      pt.1.
    Proc. 8 Feb 1858. 1857/8 (46) xlvii.

Commission on the law relating to letters patent
for inventions. Report, 29 July 1864. 1864 [3419]
xxix; (Inventions, 2).

STANLEY, Edward Henry, *15th E. Derby* (continued)

Commission on the sanitary state of the Army in India. Report, 19 May 1863. 1863 [3184] xix.

General committee on railway and canal bills
1st to 7th reports, 19 Feb to 29 June 1863. 1863 (50, 50 I-VI) vii.

General committee on railway and canal bills
1st to 9th reports, 16 Feb to 7 July 1864. 1864 (55, 55 I–VIII) xi.

Local government act commission. Report, 15 Aug 1892. 1892 C.6839 xxxvii.

Royal commission on City of London livery companies
Report, 28 May 1884. 1884 C.4073 xxxix, pt.1.
Returns of great companies. 1884 C.4073-I xxxix, pt.2.
Returns of minor companies. 1884 C.4073-II xxxix, pt.3.
Reports on charities administered by the livery companies. 1884 C.4073 III, IV xxxix, pts.4 and 5.

Royal commission on market rights and tolls
1st report, 9 Aug 1888. 1888 C.5550 liii, liv, lv
Vol.2: Ev: Westminster. 1888 C.5550-I liii.
Vol.3-4: Ev: England. 1888 C.5550-II, -III liv, lv.
Vol.5: Ev: Ulster and portions of Leinster and Connaught. 1889 C.5888 xxxviii.
Vol.6: Ev: Munster, and portions of Leinster and Connaught. 1889 C.5888 xxxviii.
Vol.7: Min. of ev. July 1888-June 1890. 1890/1 C.6268-I xxxvii.
Vol.8: Min. of ev. taken before Mr. A.J. Ashton. 1890/1 C.6268-II xxxviii.
Vol.9: Min. of ev. taken before Mr. C.M. Chapman. 1890/1 C.6268-III xxxviii.
Vol.10: Min. of ev. taken in Ireland. 1890/1 C.6268-IV xxxix.
Vol.11: Final report, 15 Jan 1891. 1890/1 C.6268 xxxvii.
Vol.12: Precis of min. of ev. 1890/1 C.6268-V xxxix.
Vol.13: Statistics. 3 vols. 1890/1 C.6268-VI xxxix, xl, xli.
Vol.14: Reports as to foreign markets. 1890/1 C.6268-VII xli.

Select committee (HL) on the Children's Life Insurance Bill. Report, 16 July 1891. HL 1890/1 (236) xi; HC repr. 1890/1 (393) xi.

Select committee on civil service appointments. Report, 9 July 1860. 1860 (440) ix; (GO Civil Service, 6).

Select committee on the Clare election petition. Min. of ev. 27 March 1860. 1860 (178) xi.

Select committee on the new law courts. Report, 30 July 1869. 1868/9 (381) x.

Select committee on railway companies powers. Report, 18 March 1864. 1864 (141) xi.

Select committee (HL) on the sweating system. SEE: Wyndham-Quin, Windham Thomas, *4th E. Dunraven and Mount Earl.*

STANLEY, Edward John, *2nd Bn. Stanley of Alderley*

Select committee (HL) on agricultural statistics. Report, 26 July 1855. HL 1854/5 (162) xxii; HC repr. 1854/5 (501) viii; (Agriculture, 9).

Select committee (HL) on the Highways Act Amendment Bill. Report, 22 July 1864. HL 1864 (227) xxvii.

Select committee on Orange lodges in Ireland. SEE: Wilson-Patten, John.

Select committee (HL) on proceedings on private bills.

Report, 16 July 1858. HL 1857/8 (176) xx; HC repr. 1857/8 (450) xii.

Select committee (HL) on the Railways Construction Facilities Bill and the Railway Companies Powers Bill. Report, 22 July 1864. HL 1864 (229) xxvii.

Select committee (HL) on the Railways (Guards and Passengers Communication) Bill. SEE: Freeman-Mitford, John Thomas, *1st E. Redesdale.*

Select committee (HL) on the Salmon Fisheries (Scotland) Bill. Report, 24 April 1866. HL 1866 (85) xxviii.

Select committee (HL) on the Telegraphs Bill. Report, 23 June 1863. HL 1863 (155) xxxiv.

STANLEY, Edward Smith, *13th E. Derby*

Committee on Manchester and Salter's Brook Roads Bill relating to standing orders. Min. of ev. 2 March 1818. 1818 (77) iii.

Select committee on Irish and Scotch vagrants. Report, 7 July 1828. 1828 (513) iv.

STANLEY, Frederick Arthur, *16th E. Derby*

Committee on yeomanry cavalry. Report, 17 July 1875. 1875 C.1352 xv. War Office.

Committee on the militia and the present brigade depot systems. Report, 9 Nov 1876. 1877 C.1654 xviii; repr. 1881 C.2792 xxi. War Office.

Report on Army pay accountants. 8 May 1877. 1878 C.1922 xix. War Office.

Select committee on Commissariat and transport services in the Egyptian campaign. Report, 18 July 1884. 1884 (285) x.

Select committee on the Corporation of London Tower Bridge Bill. Report, 19 June 1885. 1884/5 (228) viii.

Select committee on the Metropolitan Railway (Park Railway and Parliament Street Improvement) Bill. Special report, 26 May 1884. 1884 (194) xv.

STANLEY, Thomas

Committee on cotton weavers petitions. Min. of ev. 16 June 1803. 1802/3 (114) vii.

Committee on petition of several weavers. Report, 13 June 1811. 1810/1 (232) ii; (IR Textiles, 3).

Committee on petitions of cotton manufacturers and journeymen weavers. Report, 12 April 1808. 1808 (177) ii; (IR Textiles, 3).

Committee on petitions relating to settling of disputes between masters and workmen in the cotton manufacture. Min. of ev., 16 June 1803. 1802/3 (114) viii; (IR Textiles, 3).

Committee on the petition of the cotton spinners of Lancaster. Report, 27 June 1780. (Reps., 1731-1800, no.38, vol.5).

Committee on petitions of masters and journeymen weavers. Report, 8 May 1800. (Reps., 1731-1800, no.170, vol.28).

Committee on petitions relating to the Isle of Man. Report, 23 May 1805. 1805 (139) iii.

Committee on the petition of Scottish callico printers. Min. of ev. 4 July 1804. 1803/4 (150) v.

STANLEY, William Owen

Select committee on the Barnstaple election petition
Report, 21 April 1853. 1852/3 (376) viii.
Min. of ev. 22 April 1853. 1852/3 (382) viii.

Select committee on the Waterford election petition
Report, 6 April 1853. 1852/3 (348) xix.
Min. of ev. 22 April 1853. 1852/3 (389) xix.

STANSFIELD, James, _Sir_
Joint select committee (HL) on electric and cable railways in the Metropolis. Report, 23 May 1892. HL 1892 (126) x; HC repr. 1892 (215) xii.

Select committee on boundaries of parishes, unions and counties. Report, 17 July 1873. 1873 (308) viii.

Select committee on the Government Departments (Transfer of Powers) Provisional Order Bill. Special report, 23 July 1889. 1889 (275) xi.

Select committee on the Metropolis Local Management Acts Amendment Bill. Report, 6 May 1875. 1875 (194) xii.

Select committee on the Metropolis Management and Building Acts Amendment Bill. Report, 22 March 1878. 1878 (98) xvi.

Select committee on the Metropolis Toll Bridges Bill. Report, 12 April 1877. 1877 (156) xiv.

Select committee on revenue departments estimates. Report, 11 July 1888. 1888 (272) xviii.

Select committee on toll bridges over the River Thames. Report, 26 May 1876. 1876 (244) xiv.

Select committee on the Toll Bridges (River Thames) Bill. Report, 30 June 1876. 1876 (328) xiv.

Select committee on the Ulster Canal and Tyrone Navigation Bill. Report, 20 June 1888. 1888 (233) xxiii.

Standing committee on law. Church Patronage Bill. Report, 11 June 1894. 1894 (158) xi.

Standing committee; Scotland. Fatal Accidents Inquiry (Scotland) Bill. Report, 24 June 1895. 1895 (320) x.

Standing committee on trade. Plumber Registration Bill. Special report, 27 July 1893. 1893/4 (347) xiii.

STAPLETON, Miles Thomas, _1st Bn. Beaumont_
Select committee (HL) on the accommodation of the H.L., 1849. SEE: Cooper, Cropley Ashley, _6th E. Shaftesbury._

Select committee (HL) on the burdens affecting real property. Report. HL 1846 (29) xxii; HC repr. 1846 (411) vi, pts. 1 and 2.

Select committee (HL) on the Liverpool Corporation Waterworks petition. Report, 2 Aug 1850. HL 1850 (274) xxiii.

Select committee (HL) on the petition of Donald Grant respecting his patent for ventilation. Report, 17 March 1848. HL 1847/8 (66) xxvi; repr. HL 1852/3 (18) xxxi. SEE ALSO: Courtenay, William, _11th E. Devon._

Select committee (HL) on the petition of the Board of Guardians of the Carrick-on-Shannon Union. Report, 6 Aug 1850. HL 1850 (170) xxii; HC repr. 1850 (725) xi.

Select committee (HL) on the Provident Associations Fraud Prevention Bill. Report, 24 July 1848. HL 1847/8 (126) xxvi; HC repr. 1847/8 (648) xvi; (Insurance, 1).

STARKIE, Thomas
Commission on the consolidation of the statute law. Report, 21 July 1835. 1835 (406) xxxv.

Commission on criminal law
1st report, 30 July 1834. 1834 (537) xxvi.

2nd report: Defence of prisoners by counsel and capital punishment. 20 June 1836. 1836 (343) xxxvi.
3rd report: Juvenile offenders. 10 March 1837. 1837 [79] xxxi.
4th report, March 1839. 1839 [168] xix.
5th report: Burglary, offences against administration of justice, forgery, offences against the public peace. 22 April 1840. 1840 [242] xx.
6th report, 3 May 1841. 1841 [316] x.
7th report, 11 March 1843. 1843 [448] xix.
8th report, 5 July 1845. 1845 [656] xiv; (Criminal Law, 3-4).

Commission on criminal law, 1846-1849. SEE: Ker, Harry Bellenden.

STENTON, _Lord_ [Peerage claim]. SEE:
Freeman-Mitford, J.T. Belhaven and Stenton claims.

STEPHEN, Henry John
Commission on county rates
Preliminary report, 12 Aug 1835. 1835 (508) xxxvi.
Report, 16 June 1836. 1836 [58] xxvii.
Appendix. 1837 [97] xxxiii.

STEPHEN, James Fitzstephen
Royal commission on the system under which patterns of war-like stores are adopted, the stores obtained and passed for H.M. service
Report, 16 May 1887. 1887 C.5062 xv.
2nd report, 30 April 1888. 1888 C.5413 xxv.

STEPHENS, Archibald John
Commission on endowed schools in Ireland. Letter of dissent. 26 Feb 1858. 1857/8 [2345] xlvi. Home Department. SEE ALSO: Fitzgerald, Charles William, _M. Kildare._

STEPHENS, James
Report on escape from Richmond Bridewell. SEE: Connellan, J.C.

STEPHENSON, Frederick Charles Arthur
Committee on the mode of appropriating for the benefit of the Army the money stopped from soldiers as fines for drunkenness. Report, 30 June 1870. 1870 C.199 xii. War Office.

STEPHENSON, William Henry
Reports of the Commission of Customs and Inland Revenue on the Revenue Officers Disabilities Bill. 9 and 13 April 1874. 1874 (116) liii; (GO Civil Service, 8).

Report of the Commission of Inland Revenue on the duties under their management, 1856-1869, with some retrospective history. 2 vols. Feb 1870. 1870 C.82 xx. Inland Revenue.

Report on the Poor Law Commission, Ireland. 4 March 1854. 1854/5 (0.28) xlvi. Treasury.

STEUART, Robert
Select committee on the Caledonian Canal. Report, 18 June 1840. 1840 (387) xv.

Select committee on the Caledonian and Crinan Canals. Report, 21 Aug 1839. 1839 (551) viii.

Select committee on Dover Harbour. Report, 1 July 1836. 1836 (398) xx.

Select committee on the state of education in Scotland. Report, 14 Aug 1838. 1837/8 (715) vii.

STEVENSON, David
Report on the Victoria (Redcar) Harbour and Docks Bill. 15 Feb 1851. 1851 (390) xxix. Admiralty.

STEWARD, *Lord*
    1799 *E.* Leicester
    1802 *E.* Dartmouth
    1804 *E.* Aylesford
    1812 *E.* Cholmondeley
    1821 *M.* Conyngham
    1830 *D.* Buckingham
    1830 *M.* Wellesley
    1833 *D.* Argyll
    1835 *E.* Wilton
    1835 *D.* Argyll
    1839 *E.* Erroll
    1841 *E.* Liverpool
    1846 *E.* Fortescue
    1850 *M.* Westminster
    1852 *D.* Montrose
    1853 *D.* Norfolk
    1854 *E.* Spencer
    1857 *E.* St. Germans
    1858 *M.* Exeter
    1859 *E.* St. Germans
    1866 *E.* Bessborough
    1866 *D.* Marlborough
    1867 *E.* Tankerville
    1868 *E.* Bessborough
    1874 *E.* Beauchamp
    1880 *E.* Sydney
    1885 *E.* Mount-Edgcumbe
    1886 *E.* Sydney
    1886 *E.* Mount-Edgcumbe
    1892 *M.* Bredalbane
    1895 *E.* Pembroke

STEWART, John, *Sir*
Select committee on papers relating to repairs of H.M. ships Romney and Sensible while under the command of Sir Home Popham. Reports, 5 and 24 June 1805. 1805 (156), (188) iv.

STEWART, Mark John, *Sir*
Select committee on commons. Report, 30 June 1896. 1896 (269) ix.

Select committee on commons
    1st report, 1 April 1898. 1898 (148) ix.
    2nd report, 18 May 1898. 1898 (208) ix.

STEWART, Patrick Maxwell
Select committee on Ipswich Borough election petition. Report, 11 June 1835. 1835 (286) ix.

Select committee on the Ipswich election petition. Min. of proc. and ev. 1 Aug 1842. 1842 (516) vii.

Select committee on the Salmon Fisheries (Scotland) Bill. Report, 4 Sept 1835. 1835 (601) xx; (Fisheries, 2).

Select committee on salmon fisheries, Scotland. Report, 30 June 1836. 1836 (393) xviii; (Fisheries, 2).

Select committee on Weymouth and Melcombe Regis Borough election. Proc. 2 April 1842. 1842 (548) v.

STEWART, Robert, *Vct. Castlereagh*
Committee on the petition of the Court of Directors of the Sierra Leone Company. Report, 25 May 1802. 1801/2 (100) ii; CJ Reports, vol.10, p.735; (Africa, 1).

STEWART, William, *Archbp. Armagh*, 1800-22
Commission on the Board of Education in Ireland
    1st report: Free schools of Royal foundation

2nd report: Schools of Navan and Ballyroan, of private foundation.
3rd report: Protestant charter schools. *All* 14 April 1809. 1809 (142) vii.

STEWART, William Houston
Committee on the systems of savings of provisions and victualling in the Royal Navy. Report, 29 Jan 1870. 1876 (204) xlvi. Admiralty.

STOKES, George Gabriel
Committee on solar physics
    Preliminary report. 1879. 1880 C.2547 xxv.
    Report, 22 Nov 1882. 1882 C.3411 xxvii.
    2nd report, 1889. 1889 C.5854 xxiv. Privy Council Committee on Education.

STOKES, William
Committee on dietaries of county and borough gaols in Ireland. Report, 18 Feb 1868. 1867/8 [3981] xxxv. Irish Secretary's Office.

STONOR, Henry
Select committee. SEE: Sothern, T.H.S.

STONOR, Thomas, *5th Bn. Camoys*
Select committee on the report of the select committee on the Waterford, Wexford, Wicklow and Dublin Railway Bill regarding the conduct of Charles Lacy Nash. Report, 1 Aug 1851. HL 1851 (242) xix.

STOPFORD, Montagu
Anchor committee. Report, 1 Feb 1853. 1860 (71) xlii. Admiralty.

STORKS, Henry Knight, *Sir*
Jamaica Royal Commission
    Report, 9 April 1866. 1866 [3683] xxx.
    Min. of ev. 1866 [3683-I] xxxi.
    Papers laid before the commission by governor Eyre. 1866 [3682] xxx; (West Indies, 4-5).

STORY-MASKELYNE, Mervin Herbert Nevil
Select committee on the Thames River (No.2) Bill. Report, 12 June 1885. 1884/5 (218) xii.

Select committee on the Thames River preservation. Report, 4 Aug 1884. 1884 (321) xv.

STRACHEY, John, *Sir*
Observations on some questions of Indian finance. 1874 (326) xlvii. India Office.

STRACHEY, Richard
Indian famine commission. Report.
    Famine relief. 7 July 1880. 1880 C.2591 lii.
    Measures of protection and prevention. 31 July 1880. 1880 C.2735 lii.
    Famine histories. 1881 C.3086 lxxi, pt.1.
    Appendices. 1881 C.3806 I-III lxxi, pt.2. India Office.

STRADBROKE, *E.* SEE:
Rous, John Edward Cornwallis, *2nd E. Stradbroke.*

STRAFFORD, *E.* SEE:
Byng, George Henry Charles, *3rd E. Strafford.*

STRANGE, *Lord* SEE:
Smith-Stanley, E.

STRATHEDEN AND CAMPBELL, *Bn.* SEE:
Campbell, William Frederick, *2nd Bn. Stratheden and Campbell.*

STRATHMORE, *Lord* [Peerage claim]. SEE:
Cooper, C.A.

STRICKLAND, George, *Sir*
Select committee on the Kingston-upon-Hull election petition. Min. of ev. 25 May 1838. 1837/8 (433) xi.

STRUTT, Edward, *1st Bn. Belper*
Commission on the operation of the Superannuation Act
> Report, 15 May 1857. 1857, session 2 [2216] xxiv.
> Supplemental report, 26 March 1858. 1857/8 [2375] xxv; (GO Civil Service, 5).

Select committee on railway bills, 1854. SEE: Wood, Charles.

General committee on railway and canal bills
> 1st report, 8 March 1855. 1854/5 (109) vii.
> 2nd report, 23 March 1855. 1854/5 (131) vii.
> 3rd report, 27 March 1855. 1854/5 (150) vii.
> 4th report, 7 May 1855. 1854/5 (224) vii.
> 5th report, 10 May 1855. 1854/5 (230) vii.

General committee on railway and canal bills.
> 1st report, 5 March 1856. 1856 (83) vii.
> 2nd report, 18 April 1856. 1856 (161) vii.
> 3rd report, 5 June 1856. 1856 (256) vii.

STRUTT, Henry, *2nd Bn. Belper*
Committee on Chelsea and Kilmainham hospitals. Report, 20 Aug 1894. 1894 C.7528 xix. War Office.

Departmental committee on water gas. Report, 17 Jan 1899. 1899 C.9164 xlv. Home Department.

STRUTT, John William, *3rd Bn. Rayleigh*
Committee on colour vision. Report. 1892 C.6688 lxiii. Royal Society.

Committee on establishing a national physical laboratory
> Report, 6 July 1898. 1898 C.8976 xlv.
> Min. of ev. 1898 C.8977 xlv. Treasury.

STRUTT, Joseph
Select committee on railway bills. Report, 7 June 1847. 1847 (473) xii.

Committee on standing orders relating to turnpike bills. Report, 17 July 1807. 1807 (41) iii.

STUART, *Bn.* SEE:
Stuart-Wortley, C.B., *1st Bn. Stuart.*

STUART, Dudley Coutts
Select committee on the silk trade. Report, 2 Aug 1832. 1831/2 (678) xix; (IR Textiles, 5).

STUART, James
Report on the educational provisions of the Factories Act. Jan 1839. 1839 (42) xliii; (IR Factories, 27). Home Department.

Special report on guarding of machinery in factories. 24 March 1841. 1841 [311] x; (IR Factories, 27).

STUART, Villiers
Select committee on agricultural labourers in Ireland. SEE: Walker, Samuel.

STUART DE DECIES, *Lord* [Peerage claim]. SEE:
Freeman-Mitford, J.T.

STUART-WORTLEY, Charles Beilby, *1st Bn. Stuart*
Select committee on the Infant Life Protection Bill. Report, 2 Aug 1890. 1890 (346) xiii.

Select committee on the London County Council (General Powers) Bill. Report, special report, 25 April 1893. 1893/4 (184) xii.

Select committee on the London Streets and Buildings Bill. Report, 9 July 1894. 1894 (208) xiv.

Select committee on Private Bill Procedure (Scotland) Bill. Special report, and report, 20 July 1898. 1898 (307) xi.

Select committee on the Shop Hours Bill. Report and special report, 16 June 1892. 1892 (287) xvii; (IR Factories, 2).

Standing committee on Law. Public Libraries (Scotland) Acts Amendment Bill. Report, 10 March 1899. 1899 (103) x.

Standing committee on law. Small Houses (Acquisition of Ownership) Bill. Report, 1 May 1899. 1899 (180) x.

Standing committee on trade. Chaff-cutting Machines (Accidents) Bill. Report, 5 July 1897. 1897 (282) x.

Standing committee on trade. Coal Mines Regulation Act (1887) Amendment (No.2) Bill. Report, 14 July 1896. 1896 (296) ix.

Standing committee on trade. Conciliation (Trade Disputes) Bill, and the Boards of Conciliation (No.2) Bill. Report, 7 July 1896. 1896 (281) ix.

Standing committee on trade. Factories and Workshops Bill. Report, 1 July 1895. 1895 (349) x.

Standing committee on trade. Locomotives on Highways Bill. Report, 5 July 1897. 1897 (283) xi.

Standing committee on trade. Railways (Ireland) Bill. Report, 24 July 1896. 1896 (315) xiii.

Standing committee on trade. Weights and Measures (Metric System) Bill. Report, 5 July 1897. 1897 (284) xiv.

STUART-WORTLEY-MACKENZIE, James Archibald, *1st Bn. Wharncliffe.*
Commission on the system of military punishments in the Army. Report. 1836 [59] xxii.

Committee (HL) on the Birmingham to London Railway Bill. Min. of ev. 29 June 1831. HL 1831/2 (181) cccxi.

Committee (HL) on the Cheltenham and Great Western Union Railway Bill. Ev. 29 April to 7 June 1836. HL 1836 (78) xxxi.

Committee (HL) on the Eau Brink Drainage Bill. Min. of ev. 24 Aug 1831. HL 1831 (67) ccxciv.

Select committee (HL) on the effect of the alterations made in the laws regulating the interest on money. Report, 24 May 1841. HL 1841 (113) xxi.

Select committee (HL) on the Great Western Railway Bill. Min. of ev. 18 June to 19 Aug 1835. HL 1835 (81) xxxix, xl, xli.

Committee (HL) on the Hull and Selby Railway Bill
> Report, 9 June 1836. HL 1836 (121) xii.
> Min. of ev. 3 May 1836. HL 1836 (83) xxxii.

Committee (HL) on the Manchester and Cheshire Junction Railway. Min. of ev. 14 July 1836. HL 1836 (216) xxxiii.

Committee (HL) on the Manchester and Leeds Railway Bill. SEE: Kenyon, George, *2nd Bn. Kenyon.*

Committee (HL) on the Midland Counties Railway Bill. Report, 16 June 1836. HL 1836 (142) xii.

Select committee (HL) on laws relating to game.

STUART-WORTLEY-MACKENZIE, James Archibald, *1st Bn. Wharncliffe.* (continued)

Report, 18 March 1828. HL 1828 (19) ccxxxvii; HC repr. 1828 (325) viii.

Select committee (HL) on the operation of the Poor Law Amendment Act. Report, 10 May 1838. HL 1837/8 (151) xxii, xxiii; HC repr. 1837/8 (719) xix, pts. 1 and 2; (Poor Law, 6-7).

Committee (HL) on the Oxford and Great Western Union Railway Bill. Min. of ev. 5 May 1837. HL 1837 (70) xix.

Select committee (HL) on the petitions touching on the Ecclesiastical Courts Consolidation Bill. Report. HL 1836 (46) ix; HC repr. 1843 (153) xi.

Select committee (HL) on the plan for ventilating and warming the Houses of Parliament. Report, 1 Oct 1841. HL 1841 (207) xxi.

Select committee (HL) on the progress of the building of the Houses of Parliament. Report, 13 March 1843. HL 1843 (40) xx; HC repr. 1844 (381) vi.

Select committee (HL) on the progress of the building of the Houses of Parliament
  1st report, 6 May 1844. HL 1844 (46) xix.
  2nd report, 8 Aug 1844. HL 1844 (46) xix.

Select committee (HL) on the rotation by which Irish Bishops sit in the H.L. Report, 7 Sept 1841. HL 1841 (198) xxi.

Select committee (HL) on the state of Ireland in respect of crime. Report, 22 April 1839. HL 1839 (72) xviii, xix, xx, xxi; HC repr. 1839 (486) xi, xii.

STUART-WORTLEY-MACKENZIE, John, *2nd Bn. Wharncliffe*

Select committee (HL) on the operation of the Irish Poor Law Acts relative to the rating of immediate lessors. Report, 20 July 1848. HL 1847/8 (189) xxvi; HC repr. 1847/8 (594) xvii.

Select committee (HL) on prevention of accidents in coal mines. Report, 26 July 1849. HL 1849 (164) xxvii; HC repr. 1849 (613) vii; (FP Mining Accidents, 2).

SUDELEY, Bn. SEE:
Hanbury-Tracy, Charles Douglas Richard, *4th Bn. Sudeley.*

SUGDEN, Edward Burtenshaw, *1st Bn. St. Leonards*
Select committee (HL) on the Bankruptcy Bill. Min. of ev. 12 May 1853. HL 1852/3 (196) xxxi; HC repr. 1852/3 (659) xxii.

Select committee (HL) on the Masters and Operatives Bill. Report, 13 July 1860. HL 1860 (241) xxv.

Select committee (HL) on the resolution for standing orders. Report, 9 Aug 1853. HL 1852/3 (390) xxxi.

SULIVAN, John
Committee of the whole HC on the affairs of the East India Company. Min. of ev. 30 March to 27 May 1813. 1812/3 (122) vii; (East India, 4).

SULIVAN, W.K.
Technical instruction in Ireland. Report for the Royal Commission on Technical Instruction. 1884 C.3981-III xxxii.

SUMNER, George Holme
Committee on petitions of country bakers. Report, 22 May 1818. 1818 (345) ix.

Committee on petition of ministers, church wardens and vestry of St. Margaret's, Westminster. Report, 25 June 1813. 1812/3 (308) iv.

Committee on South London Dock Bill. Special report, 3 June 1824. 1824 (391) vi.

Select committee on Darlington, *etc.* railway petitions, respecting standing orders. Report, 25 March 1819. 1819 (162) viii.

Select committee on the Orphans Fund. Report, 11 June 1812. 1812 (268) ii; repr. 1814/5 (292) v.

Select committee on petitions relating to agricultural distress. Report, 8 July 1820. 1820 (255) ii; (Agriculture, 1).

UMNER, John Bird, *Archbp. of Canterbury,* **1848-68**
Commission of inquiry into the state of the dioceses of Canterbury, London, Winchester, and Rochester. Report, 31 March 1858. 1857/8 [2365] xxiv.

Commission on the state of Cathedral and collegiate churches in England and Wales
  1st report, 6 April 1854. 1854 [1821], [1822] xxv.
  2nd report, 16 March 1855. 1854/5 [1935] xv.
  3rd and final report, 10 May 1855. 1854/5 [1936] xv.

SUNDRIDGE, Lord SEE:
Campbell, George Douglas, *8th D. Argyll.*

SURIDALE, Vct. SEE:
Hely-Hutchinson, John Luke George, *5th E. Donoughmore.*

SUSSEX, Lord [Peerage claim]. SEE:
Cooper, C.A.

SUTHERLAND, D. SEE:
Sutherland-Leveson-Gower, George Granville, *2nd D. Sutherland* (1786-1861)
Sutherland-Leveson-Gower, George Granville William, *3rd D. Sutherland* (1828-1892)
Sutherland-Leveson-Gower, Cromartie, *4th D. Sutherland* (1851-1913)

SUTHERLAND, John
Commission on improving the sanitary condition of barracks and hospitals
  General report, April 1861. 1861 [2839] xvi.
  Appendix: Interim reports. 1863 [3084] xiii.
  Report on the Mediterranean stations. 12 Jan 1863. 1863 [3207] xiii.

Committee on the causes of reduced mortality in the French army serving in Algeria. Report, July 1866. 1867 [3924] xv. War Office.

Medical report on soft water supplies. 22 May 1850. *In:* 1850 [1283] xxii. General Board of Health.

Report on epidemic cholera in the Metropolis in 1854. 30 Dec 1854. 1854/5 [1893] xlv; (HE Infectious Diseases, 3). SEE ALSO: Paris, John Ayrton.

Report on Metropolis burials. 23 Jan 1855. 1856 (146) lii. Home Department.

Report on the sanitary condition of Gibraltar with reference to the epidemic cholera of 1865. 20 Dec 1866. 1867 [3921-I] xxxvii. War Office.

Report on the sanitary condition of Malta and Gozo with reference to the epidemic cholera of 1865. 1 July 1867. 1867 [3921] xxxvii. War Office.

Statement of the preliminary inquiry on the epidemic at Croydon. Jan 1853. 1852/3 [1683] xcvi; (HE Infectious Diseases, 2). Board of Health.

Sanitary commission dispatched to the seat of war in the East, 1855-6. Report, 1 Dec 1856. 1857, session 1 [2196] ix. War Office.

SUTHERLAND-LEVESON-GOWER, George Granville, *2nd D. Sutherland*

Select committee (HL) on the Chimney Sweeps Bill under standing order no.198. Min. of ev. 9 June 1834. HL 1834 (107) xxiii, pt.1.

Select committee (HL) on the Chimney Sweeps Bill. Min. of ev. 16 June 1834. HL 1834 (118) xxiii, pt.1.

Select committee (HL) on the Warwick Borough Bill. Ev. 5 May to 5 Aug 1834. HL 1834 (60) xxiv.

SUTTON, C.M. SEE: Manners-Sutton, Charles.

SUTTON, J.H.T.M. SEE: Manners-Sutton, John Henry Thomas.

SWABEY, H. Committee for inquiry into misappropriation of monies. SEE: Greenwood, J.

SWANN, Henry Committee to inspect the Lords Journals, with relation to Hellestone Election Bill. Report, 25 May 1815. 1814/5 (325) iii.

SWANSTON, George J. Committee on drift net fishers. Report, 1 March 1887. 1887 C.5020 lxxv. Board of Trade.

SWANSTON, George J. International code of signals committee. SEE: Murray, D.

SYDNEY, E. SEE: Townshend, John, *4th M. Townshend* (1798-1855) Townshend, John Villiers Stuart, *5th M. Townshend* (1831-1899)

SYKES, William Henry Despatch relating to the system of police in the Bengal Presidency. 24 Sept 1856. 1857, session 1 (127) xi. East India Office.

Report on the land tenures of the Dekkan. Dec 1830. 1866 (226) lii. India Office.

SYMONS, Jellinger C. Commission of inquiry into the state of education in Wales. SEE: Shuttleworth, James Phillip Kay.

Report on hand-loom weavers, South of Scotland, Switzerland, Austria, France, Belgium. 27 March 1839. 1839 (159) xlii; (IR Textiles, 9). Home Department.

Report on hand-loom weavers in the south of Scotland. Note, 1839. 1840 [220] xxiv; (IR Textiles, 9).

TAAFFE, Lord [Peerage claim]. SEE: Freeman-Mitford, J.T.

TAIT, Charles Campbell, *Archbp. Canterbury,* **1868-83** Royal commission on the condition of cathedral churches in England and Wales. SEE: Howard, George James, *9th E. Carlisle.*

Royal commission on ritual of the church of England
1st report, 19 Aug 1867. 1867 [3951] xx.
2nd report, 1868. 1867/8 [4016] xxxviii.
3rd report, 12 Jan 1870. 1870 C.17 xix.
4th report, 31 Aug 1870. 1870 C.218 xix; (Religion, 2-3).

Select committee (HL) on the Ecclesiastical Courts Bill and the Clergy Discipline and Ecclesiastical Courts Bill. Report, 15 July 1869. HL 1868/9 (190) xxvii.

Select committee (HL) on the Ecclesiastical Offices and Fees Bill. Report, 26 May 1876. HL 1876 (93) vii; HC repr. 1876 (267) ix.

TALBOT, E. SEE: Chetwynd-Talbot, Henry John Chetwynd, *3rd E. Talbot.*

TALBOT, James, *4th Bn. Talbot de Malahide* Commission of inquiry into the hospitals of Dublin. 4 Dec 1855. 1856 [2063] xix.

TALBOT, John Gilbert Select committee on Colonial Clergy Bill. Report, 26 June 1874. 1874 (245) vii.

Select committee on police and sanitary regulations. Special report, 24 July 1884. 1884 (298) xv.

Select committee on police and sanitary regulations. Special report, 30 July 1885. 1885 (301) x.

TALBOT DE MALAHIDE, Bn. SEE: Talbot, James, *4th Bn. Talbot de Malahide.*

[Peerage claim]. SEE: Freeman-Mitford, J.T.

TANCRED, Henry William Select committee on privileges. Report on Sligo election. SEE: Ormsby-Gore, William.

TANCRED, Thomas Midland mining commission. 1st report: South Staffordshire. 30 May 1842. 1842 [508] xiii; (FP Mining Districts, 1). (No others identified).

TAUNTON, Lord SEE: Labouchere, Henry. *Bn. Taunton.*

TAYLOR, Alexander Commission of paving. Report to the Irish government on lighting the City of Dublin with gas. 10 March 1817. 1817 (102) viii.

TAYLOR, George Reports on the operation and administration of the poor laws
1st: State of the labouring classes, and on the operation and administration of the poor laws in the north of England. 27 March 1832
2nd: Investigation of parliamentary and other printed documents on allowance to children, payment of wages out of rates, and on unemployed labourers. 3 May 1832.
3rd: Remedial means for the evils consequent on the allowance system and on a redundant population. 30 May 1832.
4th: Jurisidiction of magistrates, and the constitution of vestries. 20 Oct 1832.
5th: Overseers. 29 Nov 1832.
6th: Rates. 2 Jan 1833.
7th: Extent of district. 29 Jan 1833.
8th: Settlement. 2 March 1833.
9th: Bastardy and improvident marriages. 15 March 1833.
In: 1834 (44) xxxvii.

Report on the proposed pier at Holyhead. 23 March 1808. 1808 (133) ii.

TAYLOR, Michael Angelo Committee on the High Court of Chancery
Report, 18 June 1811. 1810/1 (244) iii.
2nd report, 13 June 1812. 1812 (273) ii.

TAYLOR, Michael Angelo (continued)

Select committee on the administration of justice upon the northern circuit. Report, 28 April 1818. 1818 (240) vii.

Select committee on Newfoundland trade. Report, 26 June 1817. 1817 (436) vi; (Canada, 5).

Select committee on the pavement of the Metropolis. Report, 25 March 1816. 1816 (159) v.

Select committee on steam engines and furnaces. Report, 12 July 1819. 1819 (574) viii.

Select committee on steam engines and furnaces. Report, 5 July 1820. 1820 (244) ii.

TAYLOR, Richard C.H.

Committee on boy enlistment [into the Army]. Report, 1876. 1877 C.1677 xviii. War Office.

TEIGNMOUTH, Lord SEE:
Shore, Charles John, *2nd Bn. Teignmouth.*

TELFORD, Thomas

Report and estimate of a proposed Morpeth and Edinburgh road, 1 April 1822. 1822 (166) viii.

Report on Berwick and Morpeth road. 5 May 1825. 1825 (282) xv.

Report to Commission for improving the Holyhead road and on its general state. 28 May 1821. 1821 (575) x.

Report on Dunmore harbour. 10 May 1821. 1821 (492) xi.

Report on the means of supplying the Metropolis with pure water. 26 March 1834. 1834 (176) li.

Report respecting two lines of roads in the north of England. 14 July 1820. 1820 (279) vii.

Report on the road from Carlisle to Glasgow to the select committee. 10 June 1815. 1814/5 (436) iii.

Report on the road from Ketley Iron Works to Chirk in north Wales. 10 Feb 1830. 1830 (26) xxvii.

Report on Shrewsbury by Coventry to London road. 2 April 1822. 1822 (179) vi.

Report on the state of the mail road from London to Holyhead. 18 April 1823. 1823 (261) x.

Report on the state of the road from London to Liverpool. 17 May 1827. 1826/7 (362) vii.

Reports, estimates and plans for improving the road from London to Liverpool. (dated 17 June 1826, 3 Nov 1828 and 6 Feb 1829). 1829 (123) v.

Reports on the road between London and Shrewsbury, with maps and estimates dated 30 June 1819 and 5 June 1820. 1820 (126) vi.

Survey and report of the coasts and central highlands of Scotland. 5 April 1803. 1802/3 (45) iv.

TEMPEST, Vane, Lord SEE:
Vane-Tempest, Adolphus Frederick Charles William, *Lord.*

TEMPLE, E. SEE:
Temple-Brydges-Chandos-Grenville, Richard, *2nd M. Buckingham.*

TEMPLE, Frederick, Bp. of Exeter, 1869-85

Select committee (HL) on the Union of Benefices Bill. Report, 27 June 1876. HL 1876 (146) vii.

TEMPLE, Henry John, 3rd Vct. Palmerston

Committee appointed to prepare militia estimates.

Report, 26 June 1820. 1820(197) ii.

Committee appointed to prepare militia estimates. Report, 27 March 1821. 1821 (330) viii.

Committee appointed to prepare militia estimates. Report, 16 May 1823. 1823 (350) iv.

Committee appointed to prepare militia estimates. Report, 22 April 1825. 1825 (230) v.

Select committee on districts of Ireland under the Insurrection Act. Report, 31 May 1824. 1824 (372) viii.

Select committee on disturbances in Ireland
  Min. of ev. 11 Feb 1825. 1825 (20) vii.
  1st to 4th reports, 23 March to 30 June 1825. 1825 (129) viii; repr. 1826 (40) v.

Select committee on Gaming. Report, 20 May 1843. 1843 (297) vi; (SP Gambling, 1).

Select committee on the militia estimates, 1854/5. Report, 6 July 1854. 1854 (353) vii.

Select committee on the public accounts of the U.K. Report, 31 July 1822. 1822 (618) iv.

Select committee on the road from London, by Coventry to Holyhead
  Report: Bridge at Conway. 27 June 1820. 1820 (201) iii
  2nd report: Turnpike trusts. 28 June 1820. 1820 (224) iii.

TEMPLE, R.

Report on the income and expenditure of British Burma. 15 Dec 1860. 1865 (405) xxxix. India Office.

TEMPLE, Richard, Sir

Committee of public accounts
  1st report, 16 March 1894. 1894 (34) ix.
  2nd report, 11 July 1894. 1894 (215) ix.
  3rd report, 18 July 1894. 1894 (226) ix.
  4th report, 31 July 1894. 1894 (249) ix.

Committee of public accounts
  1st report, 6 March 1895. 1895 (103) vii.
  2nd report, 29 May 1895. 1895 (284) vii.
  3rd report, 27 June 1895. 1895 (339) vii.
  4th report, 27 June 1895. 1895 (340) vii.
  5th report, 1 July 1895. 1895 (348) vii.
  Report, 1 Aug 1895. 1895 (441) vii.

Select committee on elementary education; teachers' superannuation. Report, 27 May 1892. 1892 (231) xii.

Select committee on the School Board for London (Superannuation) Bill. Report, 20 July 1891. 1890/1 (350) xvii.

TEMPLE, William Francis Cowper SEE
Cowper-Temple, William Francis.

TEMPLE-BLACKWOOD, Frederick Temple H. SEE:
Hamilton-Temple-Blackwood, Frederick Temple, *1st M. Dufferin and Ava.*

TEMPLE-NUGENT-BRYDGES-CHANDOS-GRENVILLE, Richard, 2nd M. Buckingham

Committee on the petition of the Sierra Leone Company. Report, 3 Feb 1807. 1806/7 (55) ii; (Africa, 1).

Select committee on the sale of beer. Report, 21 June 1833. 1833 (416) xv; repr. 1852/3 (292) xxxviii.

Sugar distillery committee. Report, 17 Feb 1807. 1806/7 (83) ii.

TEMPLE-NUGENT-CHANDOS-GRENVILLE, Richard Plantagenet Campbell, *3rd D. Buckingham and Chandos*
Committee of inquiry on the Irish Office, etc. Report, 9 Dec 1852. 1854 [1715] xxvii. Treasury.

Select committee (HL) on the Metropolitan Tramways Provisional Orders Bill. Report, 21 July 1873. HL 1873 (228) ix.

Select committee (HL) on the Parliament Office and Office of the Black Rod
    1st report, 21 Feb 1887. HL 1887 (27) ix.
    2nd report, 11 Aug 1887. HL 1887 (225) ix.

Select committee (HL) on the Parliament Office and the Office of the Black Rod
    1st report, 11 June 1888. HL 1888 (144) x.
    2nd report, 5 July 1888. HL 1888 (198) x.
    3rd report, 7 Aug 1888. HL 1888 (259) x.

Select committee (HL) on the Potter's Patent Bill and the Skrivanow's Patent Bill and the Gilbert and Sinclair's Patent Bill. Report, 16 May 1887. HL 1887 (100) ix.

TEMPLEMAN, Giles
Commission of inquiry into the Office of Works. Report, 3 June 1813. 1812/3 (258) v.

TENNANT, Harold John
Departmental committee on dangerous trades
    Interim report. 1896 C.8149 xxxiii.
    2nd interim report: Electrical generating works. 1897 C.8522 xvii.
    3rd interim report. 1899 C.9073 xii.
    4th interim report. 1899 C.9420 xii.
    Final report, 1899 C.9509 xii; (IR Factories, 31). Home Department.

TENNENT, J. Emerson SEE:
Emerson-Tennent, James, *Sir.*

TENNANT, John T.
Report on the transit of animals from Ireland to ports in G.B. Feb 1878. 1878 C.2097 xxv. Veterinary Department, Privy Council.

TENNYSON, Charles
Committee of the whole H.C. on the Penryn Election Bill. Min. of ev. 18 May 1827. 1826/7 (365) iv.

Select committee on the Orphans Fund. Report, 3 June 1829. 1829 (307) iii.

THELLUSSON, Frederick, *5th Bn. Rendlesham*
Select committee on the Chester and Holyhead Railway (Extension of Holyhead) Bill. Min. of ev. 21 June 1847. 1847 (531) xii.

THESIGER, Frederick, *Bn. Chelmsford*
Royal commission on the laws of marriage. Report, July 1868. 1867/8 [4059] xxxii; (Marriage and Divorce, 1).

Select committee on the Administration of Justice (Metropolitan Districts) Bill. SEE: Monahan, James Henry.

Select committee (HL) on the Artizans and Labourers Dwellings Bill. Report, 7 July 1868. HL 1867/8 (227) xxx.

Select committee (HL) on the Landlord and Tennant (Ireland) Act, 1870. Report, 18 July 1872. HL 1872 (136) x; HC repr. 1872 (403) xi.

Select committee (HL) on the Policies of Insurance Bill. Report, 7 June 1867. HL 1867 (151) xxvii.

Select committee (HL) on the Union of Benefices Act Amendment Bill. Report, 11 June 1872. HL 1872 (139) x; HC repr. 1872 (332) xii.

THOM, Alexander
Medical report on the causes, character and treatment of spasmodic cholera in the H.M.'s 86th regiment at Kurrachee in June 1846. 18 March 1848. 1847/8 (190) xli. War Office.

THOM, John Nicholl
Select committee on his discharge from the lunatic asylum. SEE: Wynne-Pendarves, E.W.

THOMPSON, Ralph
Committee on candidates for the Army Medical Department
    Report, 22 July 1878. 1878/9 C.2200 xliv.
    Statement by the Board of Examiners for the Army Medical Department and rejoinder by the committee. 15 and 27 Nov 1878. 1878/9 C.2213 xliv. War Office.

THOMSON, Charles Edward Poulett SEE:
Poulett-Thomson, Charles Edward.

THOMSON, C.P.
Select committee on railways. SEE: St. Maur, Edward Adolphus, *12th D. Somerset.*

THOMSON, E. Deas
Select committee of the Legislative Council of New South Wales on steam communication with England. Report, 27 Oct 1846. 1851 (430) xxxv. Colonial Office.

Select committee of the Legislative Council of New South Wales on steam communication with England, India and China. Report, 13 June 1848. 1851 (430) xxxv. Colonial Office.

THOMSON, Robert
Committee on a report by the examining commission on the harbours of Scotland. Report to the commission of northern lighthouses. Report, 28 Dec 1847. 1847/8 (171) xxxvii.

Report on the plans of Mr. Cubitt for constructing a harbour of refuge at Dover. 9 Dec 1841. 1842 (444) xxxix. Admiralty.

THOMSON, Robert D.
Report on the relative value of barley and malt on the milk of cows when used as food. 20 Dec 1845. *In:* 1846 (190) xliv. Board of Excise.

Report on the relative value of grass, barley, malt, molasses, linseed and bean meal as food for cows. 20 Dec 1845. *In:* 1846 (190) xliv. Board of Excise.

THOMSON, Thomas
An account of a set of experiments on the specific gravity of soap. 1839. 1840 (253) xliv. Commission of Excise.

THOMSON, William
Scientific sub-committee of the Committee on designs of ships of war. Report on the stability of unmasted ships of low freeboard: 'Thunderer' and 'Devastation' class. 27 Feb 1871. *In:* 1871 C.333 xiv. Admiralty.

THORNTON, Henry
Committee on public expenditure of the U.K. SEE: Bankes, Henry.

THORNTON, John
Report on the composition for mileage duty. 9 July 1855. 1854/5 (389) xv. Inland Revenue.

THORPE, T. Edward
Report on lead compounds in pottery. 21 Feb 1899. 1899 C.9207 xii. Home Office.

Report on the use of phosphorus in the manufacture of lucifer matches. Jan 1899. 1899 C.9188 xii. Home Office.

THRING, Henry, *Bn. Thring*
Departmental committee on the importation into the U.K. of foreign prison-made goods. Report, 13 Sept 1895. 1895 C.7902 lxxxviii. Board of Trade.

Memorandum on the Merchant Shipping Law Consolidation Bill. 1854 (0.1) lxix. Board of Trade.

Select committee (HL) on the Floods Prevention Bill. Report, 13 June 1898. HL 1898 (95) ix.

TIERNEY, George
Committee on George Martin's petition. Report, 1 April 1803. 1802/3 (42) v.

TITE, William
Committee on the decay of the stone of the new palace at Westminster. Report, 7 Aug 1861. 1861 (504) xxxv. Commission of Public Works and Buildings.

Select committee on Metropolis Subways Bill. Min. of ev. 30 July 1867. 1867 (495) xi.

TODD, James H.
Commission for publication of the ancient laws and institutes of Ireland (Brehon Law Commission)
　Preliminary reports, 19 Feb 1852. 1859, session 2 (190) xiii, pt.2.
　1st and 2nd reports, Jan 1857. 1859, session 2 (190) xiii, pt.2.
　3rd and 4th reports, 16 Jan 1861 and 1 March 1863. 1864 (192) xlviii. Irish Secretary's Office.
　SEE ALSO: Blackburne, Francis *and* Gibson, Edward, *1st Bn. Ashbourne.*

TOOKE, Thomas
Commission on the employment of children
　1st report: Mines. 21 April 1842. 1842 [380], [381], [382] xv, xvi, xvii.
　2nd report: Trades and manufactures. 30 Jan 1843. 1843 [430] xiii.
　Appendix. 1843 [431], [432] xiv, xv.
　Index. 1845 [608] xlii; (IR Children's Employment, 3-11).

Commission on employment of children in factories (Factories Inquiry Commission)
　1st report, 12 Aug 1833. 1833 (450) xx.
　2nd report: Reports by medical commissioners. 12 Aug 1833. 1833 (519) xxi.
　Supplementary report, 25 March 1834. 1834 (167) xix, xx; (IR Children's Employment, 4-5).

TOOKE, William
Committee of the whole House on Howell's Divorce Bill. Min. of ev. 22 and 29 July 1834. 1834 (504) xviii; (Marriage and Divorce, 3).

Select committee on the conduct of General Darling while governor of New South Wales. Report, 1 Sept 1835. 1835 (580) vi; (Australia, 1).

TORRENS, William Torrens M'Cullagh SEE:
　M'Cullagh-Torrens, William Torrens.

TORRINGTON, *Vct.* SEE:
　Byng, George, *7th Vct. Torrington.*

TOWNSEND, J.S.
Commission on the Richmond Penitentiary, Dublin. Report, 14 May 1827. 1826/7 (335) xi.

TOWNSHEND, Charles
Committee on Milford Haven. Report, 9 June 1757. CJ, vol.27, p.921.

TOWNSHEND, John Villiers Stuart, *5th M. Townshend*
Select committee (HL) on the Highway Acts. Report, 23 July 1880. HL 1880 (126) vii.

Select committee (HL) on the Railways (Guards and Passengers Communications) Bill. SEE: Freeman-Mitford, John Thomas, *1st E. Redesdale.*

Select committee (HL) on reporting. SEE: Lygon, Frederick, *6th E. Beauchamp.*

TOWNSHEND, Thomas, *Jun.*
Committee on Mr. David Heartley's experiments respecting fire prevention. Report, 1774. CJ, vol.34, p.746.

TRACEY, *Lord* [Peerage claim].
　1839-49, SEE: Cooper, C.A.
　1854, SEE: Freeman-Mitford, J.T.

TRACEY, Richard E.
Committee on Haulbowline dockyard. Report. 1896 C.8069 liv. Admiralty.

TRACY, Charles Hanbury
Commission on plans for building the Houses of Parliament. Report, 1 March 1836. 1836 (66) xxxvi.

Select committee on Metropolis water. Report, 7 Aug 1834. 1834 (571) xv; (UA Water supply, 1).

TRELAWNY, John Salusbury, *Sir*
Select committee on church rates. Report, 15 July 1851. 1851 (541) ix.

Select committee on public institutions. Report, 27 March 1860. 1860 (181) xvi; repr. 1870 (0.54) vi.

TREMENHEERE, Hugh Seymour
Children's employment commission
　1st report, 15 June 1863. 1863 [3170] xviii.
　2nd report, Aug 1864. 1864 [3414] xxii.
　3rd report, Aug 1864. 1864 [3414-I] xxii.
　4th report, July 1865. 1865 [3548] xx.
　5th report, 11 June 1866. 1866 [3678] xxiv.
　6th report, 5 March 1867. 1867 [3796] xvi; (IR Children's Employment, 13-15).

Commission on the employment of children, young persons, and women in agriculture
　1st report, 2 pts. 31 Oct 1868. 1867/8 [4068] xvii.
　2nd report, 22 Oct 1869. 1868/9 [4202] xiii.
　3rd report, 28 March 1870. 1870 C.70 xiii.
　4th report, 13 Feb 1871. 1870 C.221 xiii; (Agriculture, 10-12).

Commission on employment of women and children in mines and on the state of the population in mining districts
　Report: Parts of Scotland and North and South Staffordshire. 25 July 1844. 1844 [592] xvi.
　Report: Parts of Scotland and the West Riding of Yorkshire. July 1845. 1845 [670] xxvii.
　Report: Northumberland, Durham and South Wales. July 1846. 1846 [737] xxiv.
　Report: June 1847. 1847 [844] xvi.

Report: Forest of Dean, Shropshire, Lanarkshire and Ayrshire. Aug 1848. 1847/8 [993] xxvi.

Report: Staffordshire, Northumberland, Durham and South Wales. June 1850. 1850 [1248] xxiii.

Report: Northumberland, Durham, Lanarkshire and other parts of Scotland, and Derbyshire. July 1849. 1849 [1109] xxii.

Report: Truck Acts. June 1852. 1852 [1525] xxi.

Report, July 1855. 1855 [1993] xv. Home Department.

Commission for inquiring into the expediency of extending the acts relative to factories and to bleaching works. Report, 7 June 1855. 1854/5 [1943] xviii; (IR Factories, 3).

Grievances complained of by journeymen bakers Report, 3 July 1862. 1862 [3027] xlvii.
2nd report, 12 Jan 1863. 1863 [3091] xxviii; (IR Factories, 3). Home Department.

Report on expediency of subjecting the lace manufacture to the regulations of the Factory Acts. 20 March 1861. 1861 [2797] xxii; (IR Factories, 3). Home Department.

Report on mining inspection in France and Belgium. Dec 1847. 1847/8 [995] xxvi.

Report on mining inspection in Germany. Nov 1848. 1849 [1021] xxii. Home Department.

Report on the operation of the Bakehouses Regulation Act, 1863. 6 July 1864. 1865 (175) xlvii; (IR Factories, 3). Home Department.

Report on the operation of the Bakehouses Regulation Act. Report, 6 July 1864. 1866 (394) lxvi. Home Department.

Report on popular education in England and Wales. 27 Jan 1860. 1861 (354) xlviii; (Education, 6). Education Commission.

Report on the Printworks Act and the Bleaching and Dyeing Works Acts. 24 May 1869. 1868/9 [4149] xiv; (IR Factories, 3). Home Department.

TRENCH, Frederick William
Select committee on the H.C. buildings. Report, 6 Oct 1831. 1831 (308) iv; repr. 1833 (17) xii.

TRENCH, William Thomas Le Poer, *3rd E. Clancarty*
Poor law union and lunacy inquiry commission, Ireland. Report, 7 Feb 1879. 1878/9 C.2239 xxxi. Irish Secretary's Office.

Select committee (HL) on the Chimney Sweepers Regulations Act Amendment Bill. Min. of ev. 7 June 1853. HL 1852/3 (227) xxxi.

Select committee (HL) on the laws relating to the relief of the destitute poor in Ireland
Report, 16 Feb 1846. HL 1846 (24) xxiv.
Appendix. HL 1846 (24-APP) xxv; HC repr. 1846 (694) xi, pts. 1 and 2.

TREVELYAN, Charles E., *Sir*
Committee of inquiry on the Board of Trade. Report, 20 March 1853. 1854 [1715] xxvii. Treasury.

Committee of inquiry on the Copyhold, Enclosure and Tithe Commission. Report, 17 Aug 1853. 1854 [1715] xxvii. Treasury.

Committee of inquiry on the Department of Practical Science and Art. Report, 25 May 1853. 1854 [1715] xxvii. Treasury.

Committee of inquiry on the Office of Works. Report, 14 Jan 1854. 1854 [1715] xxvii. Treasury.

Committees of inquiry into public offices. Index to reports. 14 Aug 1855. 1854/5 (530) xlix. Treasury.

Ev. before the commission on the purchase and sale of commissions in the Army. SEE: Hawes, Benjamin.

Explanation on supplies for the Army in Crimea. 2 Feb 1857. 1857, session 1 (117) ix. Treasury.

Report on the organisation of the permanent civil service
Report, 23 Nov 1853. 1854 [1713] xxvii; repr. 1854/5 [1870] xx.
Index. 1854/5 (530-I) xx; (GO Civil Service, 2). Treasury.

Report on proposed arrangements for the abolition of the purchase and sale of commissions in the Army. SEE: Tulloch, Alexander M.

TREVELYAN, George Otto, *Sir*
Committee on Greenwich Hospital School. Report, 15 June 1870. 1870 (334) xliv. Admiralty.

Royal commission on colonisation of Canada of crofters and cottars from the western highlands and islands of Scotland. SEE: Bruce, Alexander Hugh, *6th Bn. Balfour of Burleigh.*

Select committee on the Metropolis Management and Building Acts (Amendment) Bill and the Metropolis Management Amendment Act (1862) Amendment Bill. Reports, 24 June 1890. 1890 (245) xv.

TREVOR, C. Cecil
Report on the harbours of Holyhead. 29 July 1869. 1868/9 [4201] liv. Board of Trade.

TREVOR, Edward
Commission appointed to investigate abuses in the Convict Department at Cork. Report, 9 June 1817. 1817 (343) viii.

TROLLOPE, John, *Sir*
Select committee on the Aylesbury election petitions. Min. of ev. 3 Aug 1859. 1859, session 2 (141) iii.

Select committee on the London (City) Corporation Gas, etc. Bills. Report, 15 May 1866. 1866 (270) xii; (FP Gas, 2).

Select committee on Lunatic Asylums (Ireland)(Advances) Bill. Min. of ev. 24 May 1855. 1854/5 (262) viii.

Select committee on the Maldon Borough election petition. Report, 31 July 1857. 1857, session 2 (226) vii.

Select committee on medical relief. SEE: Pigott, Francis.

Select committee on Royal forests in Essex. Report, 9 June 1863. 1863 (339) vi.

TROUBRIDGE, Thomas, *Sir*
Select committee on Cinque Port pilots. Report, 8 Aug 1833. 1833 (636) vii.

Statistical report on the health of the Navy, 1830-36
Pt.1: South American, West Indian and North American, Mediterranean and Peninsular commands. 24 March 1840. 1840 (159) xxx.
Pt.2: Cape of Good Hope and west coast of Africa and East India commands, home and various forces. 5 Oct 1841. 1841, session 2 (53) vi. Admiralty.

TROUP, Charles Edward
Committee on the identification of habitual criminals. Report, 12 Feb 1894. 1893/4 C.7263 lxxii. Home Department.

TROUTBECK, Samuel
Committee on his estate. SEE: More-O'Ferrall, Richard.

TRYON, George, *Sir*
Committee on the Royal Naval Reserve. Report, 15 May 1891. 1892 C.6609 li.

TUCKER, William
Departmental committee on the condition of school attendance and child labour. Report, 4 July 1893. 1893/4 (311) lxviii. Education Department.

TUFNELL, Edward Carleton
Children's employment commission. SEE: Tremenheere, Hugh Seymour.

Commission on the employment of children, young persons, and women in agriculture
    1st report, 2 pts. 31 Oct 1868. 1867/8 [4068] xvii.
    2nd report, 22 Oct 1869. 1868/9 [4202] xiii.
    3rd report, 28 March 1870. 1870 C.70 xiii.
    4th report, 13 Feb 1871. 1870 C.221 xiii; (Agriculture, 10-12).

Report on the condition of the agricultural population in the West of England. 2 May 1846. *In:* 1846 [745] xix.

Report on distress in Rochdale. 2 Oct 1842. 1842 (89) xxxv. Poor Law Commission.

Report on emigration. 21 Dec 1840. *In:* 1841 [327] xi.

Report on the failure of potatoes and its effect on labourers. 26 Jan 1846. *In:* 1846 [745] xix. Poor Law Commission.

Report on pauper apprenticeship. *In:* 1837 (546) xxxi. Poor Law Commission.

Report on the training of pauper children. HL 1841 xxxiii. Poor Law Commission. (Command number not given).

TUFNELL, Henry
Select committee on annuity tax, Edinburgh. Report, 31 July 1851. 1851 (617) vii.

Select committee on buildings regulation and improvement of Boroughs. Report, 27 June 1842. 1842 (372) x.

Select committee on decimal coinage. SEE: Brown, William.

Select committee on parliamentary papers. Report, 7 July 1853. 1852/3 (720) xxxiv.

TUFNELL, Jolliffe
Commission on the circumstances concerning the death of a convict named Matthew Lynagh on 12 Feb 1867. Report, 4 March 1868. 1867/8 (155) lvii. Irish Secretary's Office.

TULLOCH, Alexander M.
Commission of inquiry into the supplies of the British Army in the Crimea
    Report, 10 June 1855. 1856 [2007] xx.
    Appendix. 1856 [2007-I] xx.
    Index. 1856 (422-I) xx.

Report on proposed arrangements of Sir Charles Trevelyan for the abolition of the purchase and sale of commissions in the Army. 1 June 1858. *In:* 1857/8 (498) xxxvii. War Office.

Statistical reports on the sickness, mortality and invaliding among H.M. troops in Ceylon, the Tenasserim provinces and the Burmese Empire. Aug 1841. 1842 [358] xxvii. War Office.

Statistical reports on the sickness, mortality and invaliding among the troops in the U.K., the Mediterranean and British America. March 1839. 1839 [166] xvi. War Office.

Statistical report on the sickness, mortality and invaliding among the troops in the West Indies. 28 May 1838. 1837/8 [138] xl. War Office.

Statistical reports on the sickness, mortality and invaliding among the troops in western Africa, St. Helena, the Cape of Good Hope and Mauritius. Feb 1840. 1840 [228] xxx; (Africa, 8).

TURNER, James Aspinall
Commission appointed to inquire into the state of the store and clothing depots at Weedon, Woolwich, and the Tower, etc. Report, 29 July 1859. 1859, session 2 [2577] ix.

TURTON, Thomas Edward Michell, *Sir*
Commission of inquiry into the defalcations of. SEE: Colville, James William.

Select committee on him. SEE: Roebuck, John Arthur.

TWEEDMOUTH, *Bn.* SEE:
Marjoribanks, Edward, *2nd Bn. Tweedmouth.*

TWISLETON, Edward
Report on the state of the population of Stockport. 9 Feb 1842. 1842 (158) xxxv. Poor Law Commission.

Report on local acts for the management of the poor. 10 Jan 1843. *In:* 1843 [491] xxi. Poor Law Commission.

TWISS, Edward Curtis
Report on the system of deep sea trawl fishing as conducted in the North Sea. 2 July 1883. 1883 C.3711 xviii. Board of Trade.

TYLER, Henry Whatley
Commission for the Channel tunnel and railway. Report, 31 May 1876. 1876 C.1576 xx. Treasury.

Report on the improvement of the means of communication between England and France. 29 June 1869. 1868/9 (353) lv. Board of Trade.

Report on inspection of the railways and ports of Italy with reference to the use of the Italian route for the conveyance of the Eastern mails. 19 July 1866. 1866 (466) xl. Treasury.

Report on the quantity and quality of water supplied by the East London Waterworks Company. 17 May 1867. 1867 (339) lvii. Home Department.

Report on the Royal harbour of Ramsgate. 5 June 1869. 1868/9 [4172] liv. Board of Trade.

Report on the water supplied by the Southwark and Vauxhall Water Company. 1 May 1871. 1871 (251) lvii. Board of Trade.

TYNDALL, John
Commission on the heating, lighting and ventilation of the South Kensington Museum. Report. 1868/9 [4206] xxiii. Privy Council.

TYRONE, *E.* SEE:
Beresford, Henry De La Poer, *6th M. Waterford.*

UNWIN, William Cawthorne
Committee on the manufacture of compressed gas cylinders. Report. 1896 C.7952 xix. Home Department.

UPINGTON, Thomas
Select committee of the House of Assembly of the Cape of Good Hope on the Jameson raid. Report, 17 July 1896. 1897 C.8380 lxii; (Africa, 42). Colonial Office.

URE, Andrew
Report of experiments on sugar refining. 30 July 1833. 1833 (590) xxxiii.

URQUHART, William Pollard
Committee of public accounts
　　1st report, 18 March 1869. 1868/9 (87) vi.
　　2nd report, 23 June 1869. 1868/9 (87) vi.
　　3rd report, 7 July 1869. 1868/9 (303) vi.
　　4th report, 27 July 1869. 1868/9 (356) vi.

Committee of public accounts, 1870. SEE: Hunt, George Ward.

Select committee on loan fund societies in Ireland. Report, 24 May 1855. 1854/5 (259) vii.

VALENTIA, Vct. SEE:
Annesley, Arthur, *11th Vct. Valentia.*

VALLANCEY, Charles
Commission on bogs in Ireland. SEE: Foster, John Leslie.

VANE, Harry, Lord SEE:
Powlett, Harry George, *4th D. Cleveland.*

VANE-TEMPEST, Adolphus Frederick Charles William, Lord
Select committee on land transport corps (Army). Report, 14 July 1858. 1857/8 (428) x.

VANSITTART, George
Committee on Bishopstone Inclosure Bill. Report, 3 May 1809. 1809 (180) iii.

Committee on the petitions of Mr. Du Bois [on Lord Fairfax's will]. Report, 29 July 1807. 1807 (76) iii; CJ, vol.62, p.954, app.72.

VANSITTART, Nicholas, 1st Bn. Bexley
Committee on British herring fisheries
　　Report, 12 May 1800. CJ Reports, vol.10, p.322; (Reps., 1731-1800, no.163, vol.26).
　　Report, 30 June 1800. CJ Reports, vol.10, p.323; (Reps., 1731-1800, no.164, vol.27).

Committee on the laws relating to salt duties
　　1st report, 16 June 1801. 1801 (35) iii; CJ Reports, vol.10, p.507; repr. 1818 (115) v.
　　2nd report, 30 June 1801. 1801 (142) iii; CJ Reports, vol.10, p.507; repr. 1805 (35) iii; repr. 1818 (115) v.

Committee on public income and expenditure of Ireland. SEE: Pole, Charles Morice.

Select committee on the improvement of the Port of London. Report, 3 June 1801. 1801 (102) iii; CJ Reports, vol.14, p.604.

Select committee (HL) on the London Bridge Approaches Bill. SEE: Maitland, James, *8th E. Lauderdale.*

Committee (HL) on Silk Manufacturers Bill. Min. of ev. 30 June 1823. HL 1823 (86) clvi.

VAUGHAN, Henry Halford
Report on the employment of women and children in agriculture; Kent, Surrey and Sussex. 15 March 1843. 1843 [510] xii; (Agriculture, 6). Poor Law Commission.

VAUGHAN, James
Commission on bribery at the last election (1859) for the town of Berwick-upon-Tweed. Report, 2 Feb 1861. 1861 [2766] xvii.

Committee on the existence of corrupt practices at the last Gloucester election (1859). Report. 1860 [2586] xxvii.

VAUX, Lord [Peerage claim]. SEE:
Cooper, C.A.

VERHEYEN, Pierre Joseph Seraphique
Belgian commission charged to test the value of the preservative process against pleuro-pneumonia proclaimed by Dr. Louis Willems. Report, 6 Feb 1853. *In:* 1852/3 [1661] cii. Foreign Office.

VERNON, George John SEE:
Warren, George John, *5th Bn. Vernon.*

VERNON, John
Commission on the state of Windsor Forest
　　1st report, 12 April 1809. 1809 (132) iv.
　　2nd report, 12 April and 9 May 1809. 1809 (133) iv.
　　3rd report, 12 April and 9 May 1809. 1809 (134) iv.

VERNON HARCOURT, W. SEE:
Harcourt, William George Granville Venables Vernon, *Sir.*

VETCH, James
Report on the improvement of the harbour of Wexford. 13 Jan 1855. 1856 (300) xi. Admiralty.

Report on Ramsgate harbour
　　6 Dec 1852. 1852/3 (250) xcviii. Admiralty.
　　18 May 1853. 1852/3 (550) xcviii. Board of Trade.
　　SEE ALSO: Rennie, John.

VICE-CHANCELLOR
1879, SEE: Chatterton, Hedges Eyre.

VIDAL, Alexander F.E.
Commission to inquire into the expediency of making a harbour of refuge at Holyhead. Report, 31 May and 16 June 1847. 1847 (446), (516) xvi.

VIGNOLES, Charles
Report on Dover harbour. 23 Aug 1845. 1847/8 (476) lx. Admiralty.

VILLIERS, Charles Pelham
Select committee on conventual and monastic institutions, *etc.* Report, 25 July 1870. 1870 (383) vii.

Select committee on conventual and monastic institutions. Report, 23 June 1871. 1871 (315) vii.

Select committee on the irremovable poor. Report, 6 Aug 1860. 1860 (520) xvii; (Poor Law, 24).

Select committee on the Parochial Assessments Bill. Report, 1 Aug 1861. 1861 (505) xiv.

Select committee on the Poor Law Boards (Payment of Debts) Bill. Min. of ev. 1 Aug 1859. 1859, session 2 (129) vii.

Select committee on poor relief
　　1st report, 19 April 1861. 1861 (180) ix.
　　2nd report, 10 June 1861. 1861 (323) ix.
　　3rd report, 26 July 1861. 1861 (474) ix.
　　4th report, 26 July 1861. 1861 (474-I) ix.
　　5th report, 26 July 1861. 1861 (474-II) ix.
　　6th report, 26 July 1861. 1861 (474-III)ix; (Poor Law, 25).

VILLIERS, Charles Pelham (continued)

Select committee on poor relief
    1st report, 11 April 1862. 1862 (171) x.
    2nd report, 13 June 1862. 1862 (321) x.
    3rd report, 29 July 1862. 1862 (468) xi; (Poor Law, 26).

Select committee on poor relief. Report, 23 June 1863. 1863 (383) vii; (Poor Law, 26).

Select committee on poor relief. Report, 31 May 1864. 1864 (349) ix; (Poor Law, 26).

Select committee on public houses, *etc.* Report, 2 Aug 1853. 1852/3 (855) xxxvii.

Select committee on public houses, *etc.* Report, 13 July 1854. 1854 (367) xiv.

Select committee on sound dues. Report, 22 July 1856. 1856 (380) xvi.

Select committee on the Valuation of Property Bill. SEE: Hunt, George Ward.

VILLIERS, Edward E.

Colonial land and emigration commission. Report on colonisation of the Falkland Islands and comments on a British port. 22 Aug 1840. 1841, session 2 (3) iii.

VILLIERS, George

Commercial relations between France and G.B. SEE: Bowring, John.

VILLIERS, George William Frederick, *4th E. Clarendon*

Public schools commission
    Report, 16 Feb 1864. 1864 [3288] xx.
    Appendix. 1864 [3288] xx.
    Ev., pt.1. Eton, Winchester and Westminster schools. 1864 [3288] xxi.
    Ev., pt.2. Charter House, St. Paul's Merchant Taylors, Harrow, Rugby and Shrewsbury schools. 1864 [3288] xxi; (Education, 9-12).

Royal commission on laws of naturalisation and allegiance. Report, 20 Feb 1869. 1868/9 [4109] xxv.

Select committee (HL) on the Public Schools Bill. Report, 5 May 1865. HL 1865 (90) xxv; HC repr. 1865 (481) x.

VILLIERS, Hyde

Select committee on the affairs of the East India Company
    Report, 16 Aug 1832. 1831/2 (734) viii.
    Min. of ev.
        Vol.1: Public. 1831/2 (735-I) ix.
        Vol.2: Finance and accounts, and trade. 1831/2 (735-II) x, 2 pts.
        Vol.3: Revenue. 1831/2 (735-III) xi.
        Vol.4: Judicial. 1831/2 (735-IV) xii.
        Vol.5: Military. 1831/2 (735-V) xiii.
        Vol.6: Political or Foreign. 1831/2 (735-V) xiv; (East India, 5-11).

VIVIAN, Henry Hussey, *Sir*

Committee on cutlass and cutlass sword bayonets supplied to the Royal Navy. Report, 17 March 1887. 1887 C.5014 xvi. War Office.

Select committee on the Galway Town election petitions. Min. of ev. 17 May 1866. 1866 (274) x.

Select committee on Metropolitan Board of Works (Thames Crossings) Bill. Reports, 4 July 1884. 1884 (255) xiv.

Select committee on the Reigate election petition. Min. of ev. 17 April 1866. 1866 (191) xi.

Standing committee on law. Criminal Lunatics Bill. Report. SEE: Playfair, Lyon, *Sir.*

VIVIAN, John Cranch Walker

Committee on promotion and retirement of officers of the Ordnance Corps. Report, 6 Aug 1870. 1870 C.206 xii. War Office.

Committee on the Royal hospitals at Chelsea and Kilmainham
    1st report, 5 July 1870. 1870 C.191 xii.
    2nd report, 24 Jan 1871. 1871 C.275 xiv. War Office.

Report on the Army Agency. 28 Jan 1871. 1871 (391) xxxix. War Office.

Select committee on Contagious Diseases Act, 1866. Report, 8 July 1869. 1868/9 (306) vii; (HE Infectious Diseases, 4).

WADDY, Samuel Danks

Select committee on nonconformist marriages; attendance of registrars. SEE: Kennaway, John, *Sir.*

WALES, *Prince* SEE:

Saxe-Coburg, Albert Edward, *Prince of Wales.*

WALKER, Beauchamp

Education of officers. Report by the Director-General of military education. SEE: Biddulph, Robert.

WALKER, Charles Arthur

Commission of inquiry into Irish fisheries
    1st report, 31 Oct 1836. 1837 [77] xxii.
    2nd report, 4 Nov 1836. 1837 [82] xxii.

WALKER, James

Navigation of the River Severn. Report, 1 Sept 1851. 1852 (225) xlix. Admiralty.

Report on the construction of a harbour of refuge and breakwater in Dover Bay. 19 June 1845. 1847/8 (476) lx. Admiralty.

Report on the effects of the new North River line of the Liverpool Docks upon the Cheshire shore. 18 Dec 1855. 1856 (306) xli. Admiralty.

Report on the fatal accident, 24 May 1847, by the falling of the bridge over the River Dee, on the Chester and Holyhead Railway. 15 June 1847. 1847 (584) lxiii. Board of Trade, Railway Commission.

Report on the Great Southern and Western (Irish) Railway. 13 May 1847. 1847 (459) lxiii. Commission for Loans to Public Works, Board of Trade.

Report on Holyhead and Port Dynllaen Harbour. 6 Oct 1843. 1844 (43) xlv. Admiralty.

Report on the proposed Plymouth Great Western Dock. 1 June 1846. 1846 (450) xlv. Admiralty.

Report on the proposed Sutton Harbour and docks, Plymouth. 1 June 1846. 1846 (450) xlv. Admiralty.

Reports on Ramsgate harbour. 15 and 21 May 1851. 1851 (678) lii; repr. 1852/3 (250-I) xcviii. Admiralty.

Report on the state of the North British Railway. March 1847. 1847 (248) lxiii. Railway Commission, Board of Trade.

WALKER, Samuel

Select committee on agricultural labourers in Ireland. Report, 1 Aug 1884. 1884 (317) viii.

Select committee on agricultural labourers in Ireland. Report, 4 Dec 1884. 1884/5 (32) vii.

Select committee on salmon fisheries in Ireland. Report, 16 July 1885. 1884/5 (271) xi.

WALLACE, Robert

Select committee on distress in Paisley. Report, 21 March 1843. 1843 (115) vii.

Select committee on postage
    1st report, 4 April 1838. 1837/8 (278) xx, pt.1.
    2nd report, 1 Aug 1838. 1837/8 (658) xx, pt.2.
    3rd report, 13 Aug 1838. 1837/8 (708) xx, pt.3;
    (Posts and Telegraphs, 1-2).

Select committee on turnpike roads, Ireland. Report,
6 July 1837. 1837 (484) xx.

WALLACE, Thomas, *1st Bn. Wallace*
Commission of inquiry into the collection and management of revenue
    Report, 27 Feb 1822. 1822 (53) xii.
    2nd report, 18 July 1822. 1822 (563) xii.
    3rd report, 26 July 1822. 1822 (606) xii.
    4th report, 5 Aug 1822. 1822 (634) xii.
        Supplement. 1823 (270) vii.
    5th report: Distilleries. 30 May 1823. 1823 (405) vii.
        Supplement: Intercourse in spirits. 25 June 1823. 1823 (498) vii.
    6th report: Out-ports of Scotland. 16 July 1823. 1823 (560) vii.
    7th report: Customs and Excise establishments in Dublin. 5 March 1824. 1824 (200) xi.
    8th report: Excise, Ireland. 19 May 1824. 1824 (331) xi.
    9th report: Revenue jurisdiction. 24 May 1824. 1824 (340) xi.
    10th report: Ports of Ireland, preventive coast guard, quarantine, *etc.* 21 June 1824. 1824 (446) xi.
    11th report: Customs, Scotland; Edinburgh establishments. 2 June 1825. 1825 (389) xiii.
    12th report: Excise, Scotland. 2 June 1825. 1825 (390) xiv.
    13th report: Board of Stamps, London. 26 May 1826. 1826 (435) x.
    14th report: Board of Stamps, London. 26 May 1826. 1826 (436) x.
    15th report: Revenue of stamps, Scotland. 5 Feb 1828. 1828 (6) xiii.
    16th report: Stamp revenue, Ireland. 5 Feb 1828. 1828 (7) xiv.
    17th report: Stamp revenue, Ireland. 5 Feb 1828. 1828 (8) xv.
    18th report: Post Office revenue, U.K. 15 April 1829. 1829 (161) xi.
    19th report: Post Office revenue, U.K., pt.2, Ireland. 22 June 1829. 1829 (353) xii.
    20th report: Post Office revenue, U.K., pt.3, Scotland. 19 Feb 1830. 1830 (63) xiii.
    21st report: Post Office revenue, U.K., pt.4, England. 3 March 1830. 1830 (94) xiii.
    22nd report: Post Office revenue, U.K., pt.5, Packet establishments, home stations. 9 July 1830. 1830 (647) xiv.

Committee on the East India Company's petition. Report, 16 June 1812. 1812 (280) vi.

Select committee on the affairs of the East India Company
    1st report: China trade. 8 July 1830. 1830 (644) v.
    2nd report, 8 July 1830. 1830 (655) v.

Select committee on combination laws. Report, 8 to 24 June 1825. 1825 (417) iv.

Select committee on the Dublin and Kingstown ship canal. SEE: O'Connell, Daniel.

Select committee on the East India Company
    1st report, 25 May 1808. 1808 (261) iii.
    2nd report, 11 May 1810. 1810 (363) v.
    3rd report, 21 June 1811. 1810/1 (250) vii.
    4th report, 10 April 1812. 1812 (148) vi.

        Supplement. 13 and 22 April 1812. 1812 (151), (182) vi.
    5th report, 28 July 1812. 1812 (377) vii.
        Glossary. 1812/3 (148) x; (East India, 1-3).

Select committee on East India-built shipping. SEE: Peel, Robert, *Sir.*

Select committee on the foreign trade of the country. Report, 18 July 1820. 1820 (300) ii; (IR Trade, 1).

Select committee on the foreign trade of the country
    1st report, 9 March 1821. 1821 (186) vi.
    2nd report, 18 May 1821. 1821 (535) vi.
    3rd report: East Indies and China. 10 July 1821. 1821 (746) vi; (IR Trade, 1).

Select committee on the foreign trade of the country. Report: Lights harbour dues and pilotage. 23 July 1822. 1822 (179) v.

Select committee on the foreign trade of the country. Report: West India Docks. 3 June 1823. 1823 (411) iv; (IR Trade, 4).

Select committee on the foreign trade of the country
    1st report: Pilotage. 14 June 1824. 1824 (416) vi.
    2nd report: Quarantine. 14 June 1824. 1824 (417) vi.
    3rd report: London port duty. 18 June 1824. 1824 (431) vi; (IR Trade, 5).

WALLIS, George
Report on manufactures of the New York Industrial Exhibition. 31 Dec 1853. 1854 [1717] xxxvi. Foreign Office.

WALPOLE, Spencer
Commission on the western highlands and islands
    Report, July 1890. 1890 C.6138 xxvii.
    2nd report, Dec 1890. 1890/1 C.6242 xliv; (Agriculture, 25).

Report on the disturbances during the Winter of 1880-81 in Radnorshire in carrying out or in defiance of the Salmon Fishery Acts, 1861 and 1876. 6 April 1881. 1881 C.2918 xxiii. Home Office.

Report of an inquiry into the Herne Bay oyster fishery. 8 Feb 1876. 1876 (65) lxviii. Board of Trade.

Report on the laws affecting the salmon fisheries of the Solway Firth. 30 Nov 1880. 1881 C.2769 xxiii. Home Office.

Report of inquiry on the use of dynamite for killing fish. 17 July 1877. 1877 C.1819 xxiv. Home Office.

Special commission on the operation of the Tweed Fisheries Acts. Report. 1875 C.1117 xvii. Home Office.

WALPOLE, Spencer Horatio
Christ's Hospital inquiry commission. Report, 10 Aug 1877. 1877 C.1849 xxvi. Home Office.

Commission on bankruptcy. Report, 10 April 1854. 1854 [1770] xxiii.

Commission on the registration of title with reference to the sale and transfer of land. Report, 15 May 1857. 1857, session 2 [2215] xxi.

Select committee on acts of Parliament. Report, 25 June 1875. 1875 (280) viii.

Select committee on boundaries of Boroughs
    Report, 29 May 1868. 1867/8 (311) viii.
    Petitions, letters, papers, memorials and reports of assistant commissioner. 8 June 1868. 1867/8 (318) lvi.

Select committee on the Bribery, *etc.* Bill. Proc. 30 June 1854. 1854 (340) vii.

WALPOLE, Spencer Horatio (continued)

Select committee on the Bury St. Edmund's election petition. Report, 6 June 1853. 1852/3 (569) viii.

Select committee on the Cheltenham election petition recognizances. Report, 22 Feb 1848. 1847/8 (114) xi.

Select committee on commons
1st report, 30 April 1878. 1878/9 (158) viii.
2nd report, 7 May 1879. 1878/9 (173) viii.
3rd report, 10 June 1879. 1878/9 (219) viii.
Special report, 20 May 1879. 1878/9 (198) viii.

Select committee on commons
1st report, 8 June 1880. 1880 (214) viii.
2nd report, 15 June 1880. 1880 (221) viii.

Select committee on commons
1st report, 3 March 1881. 1881 (115) viii.
2nd report, 8 March 1881. 1881 (120) viii.
3rd report, 15 March 1881. 1881 (133) viii.
4th report, 31 March 1881. 1881 (258) viii.

Select committee on commons
1st report, 21 March 1882. 1882 (126) viii.
2nd report, 29 March 1882. 1882 (139) viii.

Select committee on the Epping Forest Bill. Report, 15 July 1872. 1872 (306) ix.

Select committee on the Huddersfield election petition
Report, 6 April 1853. 1852/3 (352) xiii.
Min. of ev. 28 April 1853. 1852/3 (414) xiii.

Select committee on imprisonment for debt. Report, 24 July 1873. 1873 (348) xv.

Select committee on the Jews Act. Report, 11 April 1859. 1859, session 1 (205) iii.

Select committee on the Knaresborough election petition. Report, 25 April 1853. 1852/3 (394) xiv.

Select committee on the Local Courts of Record Bill. Report, 26 July 1872. 1872 (338) xi.

Select committee on London writ
1st report, 10 July 1855. 1854/5 (377) vii.
2nd report, 17 July 1855. 1854/5 (401) vii.

Select committee on the Lunatic Poor (Ireland) Bill. Min. of proc. 11 April 1859. 1859, session 1 (207) iii.

Select committee on lunatics. Report, 11 April 1859. 1859, session 1 (204) iii; (HE Mental, 3).

Select committee on lunatics. Report, 5 Aug 1859. 1859, session 2 (156) vii; (HE Mental, 4).

Select committee on lunatics. Report, 27 July 1860. 1860 (495) xxii; (HE Mental, 4).

Select committee on parliamentary oath. Report, 20 May 1980. 1880 (159) xii.

Select committee on parliamentary oath; Mr. Broadlaugh. Report, 16 June 1880. 1880 (226) xii.

Select committee on the Pontefract election (Childers' petition). Report, 12 Aug 1859. 1859, session 2 (214) iv.

Select committee on Navy promotion and retirement. Report, 24 July 1863. 1863 (501) x.

Select committee on the Office of Speaker. Report, 9 July 1855. 1854/5 (372) vii.

Select committee on the Parliamentary Elections (Returning Officers) Bill. Report, 13 July 1874. 1874 (280) xi.

Select committee on privileges. Report on the imprisonment of Mr. G.H. Whalley, a member of Parliament. 31 March 1874. 1874 (77) xi.

Select committee on privilege. Report on Tower High

Level Bridge (Metropolis) Bill Committee. 16 July 1879. 1878/9 (294) x.

Select committee on the protection of infant life. Report, 20 July 1871. 1871 (372) vii.

Select committee on the Public Schools Bill. Report, 22 May 1868. 1867/8 (292) xi.

Select committee on referees on private bills. Report, 17 March 1876. 1876 (108) xiv.

Select committee on the Rochdale Vicarage Bill. Min. of ev. 2 July 1866. 1866 (390) vii.

Select committee on tax bills. Report, 29 June 1860. 1860 (414) xxii.

Select committee on Union of Benefices Bill. Report, 20 March 1873. 1873 (130) xvii.

WALSH, William J.
Commission on manual and practical instruction in primary schools, Ireland
1st report, 26 Feb 1897. 1897 C.8383 xliii.
2nd report, 5 July 1897. 1897 C.8531 xliii.
3rd report, 31 July 1897. 1897 C.8518 xliii.
Min. of ev. Vol.1-3. 1897 C.8384, C.8532, C.8619 xliii.
Final report, 25 June 1898. 1898 C.8923 xliv.
Min. of ev. Vol.4, 29 Sept to 17 Dec 1898. 1898 C.8924 xliv.
Appendix. 1898 C.8925 xliv.

WALSHAM, John, Sir
Report on the agricultural statistics of Norfolk. 7 March 1854. 1854 [1761] lxv.
Supplementary report on the collection of agricultural statistics. 27 March 1854. 1854 (263) lxv. Poor Law Board.

Report on alleged abuses in the administration of the Poor law in Norfolk and Suffolk. 23 June 1844. 1846 (409) xxxvi. Poor Law Commission.

Report on Keighley Union. 9 June 1842. 1842 (347) xxxv. Poor Law Commission.

Report on workhouse and district schools in their relations to the education of pauper children and the powers of the Poor Law Board. 17 May 1862. 1862 (510) xlix; (ED Poorer Classes, 7).

Reports on vagrancy. 4 and 9 Jan 1848. 1847/8 [987] liii. Poor Law Board.

WALSINGHAM, Bn. SEE:
De Grey, Thomas, *2nd Bn. Walsingham* (1748-1818)
De Grey, George, *3rd Bn. Walsingham* (1776-1831)
De Grey, Thomas, *4th Bn. Walsingham* (1778-1839)
De Grey, Thomas, *5th Bn. Walsingham* (1804-1870)
De Grey, Thomas, *6th Bn. Walsingham* (1843-1919)

WANTAGE, Bn. SEE:
Loyd-Lindsay, Robert James, *1st Bn. Wantage.*

WARBURTON, George
Report on a petition from householders of the town of Brighton, praying for a municipal charter. 23 Sept 1853. 1854 (231) lxiii. Privy Council.

WARBURTON, Henry
Select committee on anatomy. Report, 22 July 1828. 1828 (568) vii; (HE Medical Profession, 1).

Select committee on the Londonderry City election petition. Report, 15 April 1833. 1833 (180) x.

Select committee on medical education. Report: Royal College of Physicians, London. 13 Aug 1834. 1834 (602) xiii; (HE Medical Profession, 1-2).

Select committee on Plymouth breakwater. Report, 10 Sept 1835. 1835 (631) xx.

Select committee on railway subscription lists
    1st report: Deptford and Dover Railway. 24 April 1837. 1837 (225) xviii, pt.1.
    2nd report: Westminster Bridge, Deptford and Greenwich Railway. 27 June 1837. 1837 (428) xviii, pt.1.
    3rd report: City of Southwark Bridge and Hammersmith Railway. 27 June 1837. 1837 (429) xviii, pt.1.
    4th report: South Midland Counties Railway. 10 June 1837. 1837 (495) xviii, pt.2.
    5th report: Direct London and Brighton Railway (Rennie's Line). 14 July 1837. 1837 (519) xviii, pt.2.
    6th report: South-Eastern Brighton, Lewes and Newhaven Railway. 14 July 1837. 1837 (520) xviii, pt.2.
    7th report: Brighton Railway (Stephenson's Line). 17 July 1837. 1837 (537) xviii, pt.2.

Select committee on the use of molasses in breweries and distilleries. Report, 21 July and 4 Oct 1831. 1831 (109), (297) vii.

Select committee on the Vaccine Board. Report, 28 Aug 1833. 1833 (753) xvi.

WARD, E.W.
Report on the mint at Sydney. 14 Jan 1860. 1860 (358) xlv; (Australia, 23). Colonial Office.

WARD, Henry George
Committee on the Thames Conservancy Bill. Min. of proc. 9 July 1847. 1847 (623) xii.

Letter on the subject of the culture of sugar (and the abolition of slavery). 19 June 1829. 1829 (345) xxiv.

Select committee on business of the H.C. SEE: Davies, T.H.H.

Select committee on the disposal of lands in the British Colonies. Report, 1 Aug 1836. 1836 (512) xi; (Colonies, 2).

Select committee on the divisions of the H.C. Report, 21 March 1834. 1834 (147) xi.

Select committee on Holyhead Harbour Bill. Report, 23 June 1847. 1847 (546) viii.

Select committee on Metropolis sewers. Report, 8 Aug 1834. 1834 (584) xv; (UA Sanitation, 1).

Select committee on publishing lists of divisions of the H.C. Report, 20 March 1835. 1835 (66) xviii.

Select committee on the Thames Conservancy (Recommitted) Bill. Report, 17 June 1847. 1847 (504) xii.

WARD, John
Report on the affairs of Schleswig and Holstein. 28 May 1857. 1864 [3292] lxv. Foreign Office.

WARD, Robert
Committee on Mr. Greathead's petition [on his lifeboat]. Report, 13 June 1811. 1810/1 (230) ii.

WARD, William
Select committee on the affairs of the East India Company. SEE: Wallace, Thomas.

WARD, William Humble, *2nd E. Dudley*
Committee on engagement and discharge of seamen abroad

Report, 8 July 1897. 1897 C.8577 lxxviii.
Min. of ev. 1897 C.8578 lxxviii. Board of Trade.

WARDE, Edward Charles, *Sir*
Committee on the education of artillery officers. Report, 30 Nov 1870. 1871 C.258 xiv. War Office.

WARDELL, Frank N.
Quarry committee of inquiry on working conditions in open quarries. Report, Nov 1893. 1893/4 C.7237 lxxxiii; (IR Factories, 30). Home Department.

WARDLAW, Robert
Cavalry organisation committee. Report, 19 Jan 1882. 1882 C.3167 xvi. War Office.

WARDLE, T.
Report on the English silk industry for the Royal Commission on Technical Instruction. 1884 C.3981-II xxxi.

WARRE, John Ashley
Select committee on the correspondence relating to an extra Post. Report, 26 June 1821. 1821 (688) iv.

Select committee on the land revenues of the Crown. Report, 16 Aug 1833. 1833 (677) xiv.

Select committee on land revenues of the Crown. Report, 7 Aug 1834. 1834 (579) xv.

WARREN, George John, *5th Bn. Vernon*
Select committee on the sale of corn. Report, 25 July 1834. 1834 (517) vii.

WARREN, Herbert Richard
Select committee on the Petit Juries (Ireland) Bill. Special report, 3 July 1868. 1867/8 (390) x.

WARREN, John Borlase, *Sir*
Committee on naval asylum petition. Report, 19 June 1805. 1805 (174) iii.

WASHINGTON, John
Report on the damage caused to fishing boats on the east coast of Scotland by the gale of 19 Aug 1848. 21 Dec 1848. 1849 (104) li. Admiralty.

Report on encroachments on the bed of the River Tivy between Cardigan and Llechryd. 10 Dec 1850. 1852/3 (306) xcviii. Admiralty.

Report on memorials relative to the harbours and coast lights of the county of Cork. 10 Nov 1848. 1849 (97) xlix. Admiralty.

WASON, Peter Rigby
Select committee on the improvements of Westminster. Report, 29 June and 18 July 1832. 1831/2 (567), (614) v.

WATERFORD, *M.* SEE:
Beresford, Henry De la Poer, *6th M. Waterford.*

WATERLOW, Sidney, *Sir*
Select committee on members holding contracts. SEE: Chambers, Thomas.

WATERS, George
Commission on corrupt practices at the last election for Cashel. Report, 18 Dec 1869. 1870 C.9 xxxii.

WATKIN, Edward William
Select committee on limited liability acts. Report, 28 May 1867. 1867 (329) x.

WATSON, J.
Account of the yellow fever on board H.M. ship
'Highflyer' in 1852. 10 Jan 1853. 1852/3 (547) lx.
Admiralty.

WATSON, Thomas
Committee on the cubic space of metropolitan work-
houses. Report, 7 Feb 1867. 1867 [3786] lx. Poor
Law Board.

WATSON, William Henry
Select committee on fees in courts of law and equity.
Report, 9 July 1847. 1847 (643) viii; (Legal Admini-
stration, 7).

WAUGH, A.S.
Report on the progress and expense of the Great
Trigonometrical Survey of India up to the year 1849-
50. 20 Oct 1850. 1851 (219) xli. East India Office.

WAUGH, Edward
Select committee on the Copyhold Enfranchisement
Bill. Report, 16 May 1884. 1884 (177) ix.

WEALE, Robert
Report on the Astonefield incorporation under Gil-
bert's Act. 27 Feb 1843. 1843 (172) xlv. Poor Law
Commission.

Reports on the Brassington incorporation. 23 May
to 5 June 1844. 1844 (614) xl. Poor Law Commission.

Report on the comparative state of pauperism in the
parishes of Aston and Birmingham
    21 July 1840. 1840 (543) xxxix.
    18 Jan 1856. 1856 (128) xlix. Poor Law Board.

Report on the comparative state of pauperism in
14 Agricultural unions, indifferently selected, and in
the 7 manufacturing unions in the district. 31 July
1840. 1840 (629) xxxix.

Reports on the education of pauper children. 28 Sept
to 11 Aug 1862. 1862 (510) xlix; (ED Poorer Classes,
7). Poor Law Board.

Report on the operatives employed in the ribbon
manufactories of Coventry, Foleshill and Nuneaton.
22 July 1864. 1864 (567) lii. Poor Law Board.

Report on the state of pauperism in the county of
Bedford, 1851 as compared with representations in
1829. 18 June 1851. 1851 (480) xlix. Poor Law
Board.

Report on the state of pauperism in the counties of
Bedford and Huntingdon. 9 Jan 1852. 1852 (61)
xlv. Poor Law Board.

Report on a table [giving statistics of parishes]. 2 Feb
1849. 1850 [1152] xxvii; (Poor Law, 21). Poor Law
Board.

Report on table [showing parish statistics] for the
county of Huntingdon. 8 Jan 1851. 1851 (244) xlix.
Poor Law Board.

WEBBER, Daniel Webb
Commission on duties, salaries and emoluments in
courts in Ireland. SEE: Kemmis, Henry.

WEBSTER, Richard Everard, *Vct. Alverstone*
Select committee on the Land Transfer Bill. Report,
2 July 1895. 1895 (364) xi.

Select committee on the rule of the road at sea. Report, 3 July 1895. 1895 (369) xii.

Select committee on trusts administration. Report,
6 May 1895. 1895 (248) xiii.

WEDDERBURN, Alexander, *1st E. Rosslyn*
Committee of secrecy (HL) on papers presented
by the Chancellor of the Exchequer, 1st and 2nd
April 1801.
    (1st report not identified)
    2nd report: London Corresponding Society. 27
        April 1801. (HL 1801 vol.1, p.477 — Oceana
        repr.)
    3rd report: Disturbances in Ireland. 15 June 1801.
        (HL 1801 vol.1, p.605 — Oceana repr.)

WELBY, Reginald Earle, *Bn. Welby*
Committee of inquiry to consider the memorial of
the civil service copyists. Report, 23 Dec 1886. 1887
(82) lxvi; (GO Civil Service, 10). Treasury.

Departmental committee on promotion and retirement in the Royasl Marines. Report, 10 Aug 1877.
1877 (422) xxi. Admiralty.

Royal commission on the administration of the expenditure of India
    Report, 10 Aug 1896. 1896 C.8258 xv.
    Appendix. 1896 C.8259 xvi.

Select committee on the Seeds Adulteration Bill.
Report, 19 July 1869. 1868/9 (335) ix.

WELENBERGH, P.M.J.
Dutch commission on Dr. Louis Willems' process
for preventing pleuro-pneumonia in cattle
    1st report, 21 Sept 1852. *In:* 1852/3 [1661] cii.
    2nd report, 28 Dec 1852. *In:* 1852/3 [1661] cii.
    Foreign Office.

WELLESLEY, Arthur, *1st D. Wellington*
Commission for inquiring into the naval and military
promotion and retirement. Report, 26 March 1840.
1840 [235] xxii.

Committee on expired and expiring laws. 2nd session,
4th Parliament. Report and lists, 25 Jan 1808. 1808
(2) ii.

Committee on Holyhead harbour. Report, 30 May
1808. 1808 (273) ii.

Committee on the Margate pier petition. Report,
23 Feb 1808. 1808 (46) ii.

Select committee on his funeral. SEE: Wood, Charles.

WELLESLEY, George Greville
Committee on life-boats. Report, 21 June 1872.
1872 C.627 xiv. Admiralty.

Committee on a site for a college for naval cadets.
Report, 30 Nov 1876. 1877 C.1673 xxi. Admiralty.

WELLESLEY, W.L.
Committee of privileges on his contempt of court.
SEE: Williams-Wynn, C.W.

WELLINGTON, *D.* SEE:
Wellesley, Arthur, *1st D. Wellington.*

WELLINGTON, Henry
Commission of inquiry into the state of Sierra Leone.
Reports, 7 May and 29 June 1827. 1826/7 (312),
(552) vii; (Africa, 52).

WELSBY, W.N.
Commission on the Birmingham Borough prison.
Report, 25 Jan 1854. 1854 [1809] xxxi; (CP Prisons,
15).

Commission on Leicester County gaol and house of
correction. Report, 25 Jan 1854. 1854 [1808] xxxiv;
(CP Prisons, 13).

WEMYSS, E. SEE:
Wemyss-Charteris-Douglas, Francis, *8th E. Wemyss* (1772-1853)
Wemyss-Charteris-Douglas, Francis, *9th E. Wemyss* (1796-1883)

WEMYSS-CHARTERIS-DOUGLAS, Francis, *8th E. Wemyss*
Select committee on the Eastern Counties Railway Company. Report, 11 June 1849. 1849 (366) x.

Select committee on Ordnance Survey, Scotland. Report, 10 July 1851. 1851 (519) x.

WEMYSS-CHARTERIS-DOUGLAS, Francis, *9th E. Wemyss*
Committee on volunteer capitation grant. Report, 16 March 1867. 1867 (184) xli. War Office.

Report on the Post Office. 20 May 1854. 1854 [1816] xxvii; (Posts and Telegraphs, 4). Treasury.

Select committee on the Hungerford Bridge and Wellington Street Viaduct
   1st report, 10 May 1869. 1868/9 (200) x.
   2nd report, 2 Aug 1869. 1868/9 (387) x.

Select committee on master and servant. Report, 30 July 1866. 1866 (449) xiii; (Industrial Relations, 18).

WENSLEYDALE, *Bn*. [Peerage claim]. SEE:
Freeman-Mitford, J.T.

WENTWORTH, *Lord* [Peerage claim]. SEE:
Freeman-Mitford, J.T.

WENTWORTH-FITZWILLIAM, Charles William, *5th E. Fitzwilliam*
Select committee (HL) on compensation for lands taken for or injured by railways. Report. HL 1845 (184) xviii; repr. HL 1847/8 (15) xxvi; HC repr. 1845 (420) x.

Select committee on life annuities. Report, 4 June 1829. 1829 (284) iii; (Insurance, 3).

WESTBURY, *Lord* SEE:
Bethell, Richard, *1st Bn. Westbury*.

WESTERN, Charles Callis
Select committee on East Retford election. Report, 2 May 1827. 1826/7 (288) iv.

WESTMEATH, *E*. [Peerage claim]. SEE:
Freeman-Mitford, J.T.

WESTMINSTER, *M. and D*. SEE:
Grosvenor, Robert, *2nd M. Westminster* (1767-1845)
Grosvenor, Richard, *3rd M. Westminster* (1795-1869)
Grosvenor, Hugh Lupus, *1st D. Westminster* (1825-1899)

WHALLEY, G.H.
Select committee on his imprisonment. SEE: Walpole, S.H.

WHARBURTON, Henry
Select committee on the Londonderry City election petition. Report, 15 April 1833. 1833 (180) x.

WHARNCLIFFE, *Lord* SEE:
Stuart-Wortley-Mackenzie, James Archibald, *1st Bn. Wharncliffe* (1776-1845)
Stuart-Wortley-Mackenzie, John, *2nd Bn. Wharncliffe* (1801-1855)
Montagu-Stuart-Wortley-Mackenzie, Edward Montagu, *1st E. Wharncliffe* (1827-1899)

WHARTON, *Lord* [Peerage claim]. SEE:
Cooper, C.A.

WHARTON, John
Committee on copyright Acts. Min. of ev. 20 July 1813. 1812/3 (292), (341) iv; repr. 1818 (177) ix.

Committee on expired and expiring laws, 3rd session, 4th Parliament. Report and lists, 24 Jan 1809. 1809 (5) iii.

Committee on the whole House on conduct of HRH, the Duke of York, the commander in chief. Min. of ev. 1 Feb 1809. 1809 (20) ii; (Military and Naval, 1).

Committee on the whole House on petitions respecting orders in Council. Min. of ev. 18 March to 26 May 1808. 1808 (119) x; repr. 1812 (231) iii.

Select committee on the civil list. Report, 2 July 1813. 1812/3 (342) iv; repr. 1830 (618) ix.

WHARTON, John Lloyd
Departmental committee on prison dietaries. Report, 27 Dec 1898. 1899 C.9166 xliii. Home Office.

Departmental committee on the treatment of inebriates. Report, 22 April 1893. 1893/4 C.7008 xvii. Home Department.

Select committee on the Cork (County and City) Court Houses Bill. Report, 18 June 1891. 1890/1 (283) xii.

WHATLEY, Richard, *Archbp. of Dublin*, 1831-64
Commission on the state of the poorer classes in Ireland
   1st report, 8 July 1835. 1835 (369) xxxii, xxxiii; 1836 [35]-[42] xxx to xxxiv.
   2nd report. 1837 [68] xxxi.
   3rd report. 1836 [43] xxx.

Commission on Dublin University
   Report. 13 April 1853. 1852/3 [1637] xlv.
   Index. 1852/3 (1017-II) xlv.

WHETTEN, J.
Report on Berthon's collapsing life boat. 19 May 1854. 1854 (336) xlii. Admiralty.

WHIFFIN, H.W.S.
Report on the Army agency. 28 Jan 1871. 1871 (391) xxxix. War Office.

WHITBREAD, Samuel
Committee to draw up articles of impeachment against Henry, Lord Viscount Melville
   Report, 4 July 1805. 1805 (206) ii.
   Report, 4 March 1806. 1806 (23) ii.
   Report on a further article of impeachment, 7 May 1806. 1806 (25) ii.

Committee on petition relating to Mr. Hargrave's books and manuscripts. Report, 29 June 1813. 1812/3 (316) iv.

Committee on the petition of William Henry Mallison [Preservation from drowning]. Report, 5 June 1811. 1810/1 (206) ii.

Select committee on Chatham dockyard extension. Report, 16 July 1861. 1861 (439) xiii.

Select committee on funding exchequer bills. Report, 14 May 1810. 1810 (271) iii.

Select committee on the Gloucester election petition; judges' report. Report, 15 July 1880. 1880 (287) ix.

WHITE, John Edward
Printworks Act and Bleaching and Dyeing Works Acts inquiry. Report, 6 May 1869. 1868/9 [4149] xiv; (IR Factories, 3). Home Department.

WHITE, Piers F.
Commission on disturbances in Londonderry on 1st Nov 1883. Report, 11 Feb 1884. 1884 C.3954 xxxviii; (CP Civil Disorder, 8). Irish Secretary's Office.

WHITESIDE, James
Select committee on Colonel Keogh's petition. Report, 4 July 1861. 1861 (401) xiii.

Select committee on the Debentures on Land (Ireland) Bill. Special report, 11 July 1862. 1862 (399) xvi.

WHITFIELD, Elizabeth
Committee on petition. SEE: Moore, Peter.

WHITLEY, George
Report of the results of an inquiry into the nature of the fever or fevers prevailing epidemically at St. Petersburg during the Winter of 1864/5. 10 May 1865. 1865 (435) xlvii. Privy Council.

WHITMORE, Charles Algernon
Departmental committee on laws relating to dogs Report, 28 Jan 1897. 1897 C.8320 xxxiv.
Min. of ev. 1897 C.8378 xxxiv. Board of Agriculture.

WHITMORE, Charles S.
Commission on corrupt practices in the Borough of Maldon. Report. 1852/3 [1673] xlviii.

WHITMORE, William Wolryche
Select committee on the duties of the Receivers General of Land and assessed taxes
Report, 8 June 1821. 1821 (630) viii.
Min. of ev. 15 June 1821. 1821 (667) viii.

WHITWELL, John
Select committee on elementary schools certified teachers' annuities. Report, 29 July 1872. 1872 (344) ix.

Select committee on pawnbrokers. Report, 21 July 1870. 1870 (377) viii. SEE ALSO: Ayrton, Acton Smee.

Select committee on the Pawnbrokers Bill. Report, 8 July 1872. 1872 (288) xii.

WHITWORTH, E. SEE:
Whitworth, Charles, 1st E. Whitworth.

WHITWORTH, Charles, 1st E. Whitworth
Select committee (HL) on the state of gaols in the U.K. Report, 12 July 1819. HL 1819 (31) xcix.

WHITWORTH, Joseph
Report on manufactures at the New York Industrial Exhibition. 1854 [1718] xxxvi. Foreign Office.

WICKLOW, E. SEE:
Howard, William Forward, 4th E. Wicklow (1788-1869)
Howard, Charles Francis Arnold, 5th E. Wicklow (1839-1881)
Howard, Cecil Ralph, 6th E. Wicklow (1842-1891)
Howard, Ralph Francis, 7th E. Wicklow (1877-1946)

[Peerage claim]. SEE: Freeman-Mitford, J.T.

WICKSTEED, Thomas
Report on the state of the works of drainage and sewerage in the town of Croydon. 5 Oct 1853. 1854 (450) lxi; (UA Sanitation, 4). General Board of Health.

WILBRAHAM, George
Select committee on salt (British India). Report, 2 Aug 1836. 1836 (518) xvii.

WILBERFORCE, Samuel, Bp. of Oxford 1845-69
Select committee (HL) on the African slave trade. Report, 23 July 1849. HL 1849 (32) xxviii; HC repr. 1850 (53) ix; (Slave Trade, 6).

Select committee (HL) on the African slave trade. Report, 15 July 1850. HL 1850 (35) xxiv; HC repr. 1850 (590) ix; (Slave Trade, 6).

Select committee (HL) on capital punishments. 7 July 1856. HL 1856 (127) xxiv; HC repr. 1856 (366) vii.

Select committee on the Sequestration Bill. Report, 27 May 1870. HL 1870 (115) viii.

WILBERFORCE, William
Commission for management of the Crown estates in the colony of Berbice. Report, 1 July 1816. 1816 (528) viii.

Committee on clothworkers petitions. Report, 3 May 1805. 1805 (105) iii.

Committee on General Boyd's petition. Report, 5 June 1818. 1818 (408) iii; repr. 1819 (329) viii.

Committee on Yorkshire woollen petitions. Report, 9 May 1803. 1802/3 (71) v; (IR Textiles, 1).

WILBRAHAM, Edward Bootle
Committee on parish apprentices. Report, 19 May 1814. 1814/5 (304) v.

WILD, A.E.
Report on the forests in the South and West of the Island of Cyprus. 8 Jan 1879. 1878/9 C.2348 lv. India Office.

WILDE, James Plaisted, Bn. Penzance
Commission on the London Stock Exchange. Report, 31 July 1878. 1878 C.2157 xix; (Monetary Policy, 11).

Royal commission on Army promotion and retirement. Report, 5 Aug 1876. 1876 C.1569 xv.

Royal commission on Wellington College. Report, 14 July 1880. 1880 C.2650 xiii. War Office.

Select committee (HL) on the Greek Marriages Bill. Report, 15 May 1884. HL 1884 (139) vii.

WILDE, Thomas, Sir
Select committee on courts of law and equity. Report, 2 July 1842. 1842 (476) x.

WILKIN, George
Report relative to the Mersey Conservancy. 28 April 1840. 1840 (589) xlv. Board of Trade.

WILKINSON, George
General report of the erection of the workhouse buildings in Ireland. 24 April 1847. In: 1847 [873] xxviii.

Report and plans for temporary fever hospitals. March 1847. In: 1847 [873] xxviii.

Report on matters requiring attention in the management of the workhouse buildings in Ireland. 10 March 1847. In: 1847 [873] xxviii.

WILKS, John
Select committee on parochial registration. Report, 15 Aug 1833. 1833 (669) xiv.

WILKINSON, Josiah
Report on the state of popular education in the Metropolitan district. 1 Oct 1859. In: 1861 [2794-III] xxi, pt.3; (Education, 5).

WILLEMS, Louis
Dutch commission on his process for preventing

pleuro-pneumonia in cattle. SEE: Wellenbergh, P.M.J.

Memorial [to the Belgian minister of the Interior] on the epizootic pleuro-pneumonia of cattle. 22 March 1852. 1852/3 [1616] cii. Foreign Office.

WILLES, George Ommanney
Committee on the Royal Naval reserve regulations. Report, 6 Jan 1870. 1870 C.46 xii. Admiralty *and* Board of Trade.

WILLES, James Shaw, *Sir*
Trial of the Coventry election petition, 1869. Min. of ev. 1 March 1869. 1868/9 (275) xlix.

WILLIAMS, Alexander
Report on the cattle plague in G.B., 1865 to 1867. 18 July 1868. 1867/8 [4060] xviii. Privy Council.

Report on the origin, etc. of the cattle plague. 20 March 1866. 1866 [3653] lix. Privy Council.

WILLIAMS, John
Report on the treatment and condition of the convicts in the hulks at Woolwich. 28 May 1847. 1847 [831] xviii; (CP Prisons, 12). Home Department.

WILLIAMS, S.
Report and estimate regarding Ramsgate Harbour. 9 Jan 1854. 1856 (28) xi. Board of Trade.

WILLIAMS, William
Select committee on the Sunday Trading Prevention Bill. Proc. 15 April 1851. 1851 (221) x; (SP Sunday Observance, 1).

WILLIAMS, William John
Commission on the Birmingham Borough Prison. SEE: Welsby, W.N.

Report of inquiry into the treatment of prisoners in the house of correction at Knutsford. 16 March 1843. 1843 (126) xliii; (CP Prisons, 11). Home Department.

WILLIAMS-WYNN, Charles Watkin
Committee on election recognizances. Reports, 9 March 1819. 1819 (88) iv.

Committee on elections and duration of polls. Report, 20 June 1817. 1817 (393) iii.

Committee on expediting the introduction of public bills. Report, 7 March 1821. 1821 (178) iv.

Committee on fees to examiners of election recognizances and bills of costs. Report, 2 July 1813. 1812/3 (330) iv.

Committee of precedents. Report on Naval and military officers accepting offices of profit from the Crown and continuing to sit as members of the H.C. 11 April 1816. 1816 (239) iii.

Committee of privileges. Report on complaint of a letter to influence a vote in election of a member, in breach of the privileges of the H.C. 5 May 1818. 1818 (258) iii.

Committee of privileges. Report: Contempt of court, by W.L. Wellesley. 26 July 1831. 1831 (117) iv.

Committee of privileges. Report on letters from the Lord Chancellor and Mr. Charlton concerning the latter's contempt of court. 16 Feb 1837. 1837 (45) xiii.

Committee of privileges. Report on members being summoned as jurymen. 21 Feb 1826. 1826 (71) iii.

Committee of privileges. Report on the petition of the freeholders of Wexford on the lunacy of a member (Mr. Alcock), with appendix. 24 April 1811. 1810/1 (122) v.

Select committee on accommodations for members of the H.C. at the solemnity of their majesties' coronation. Report, 1 Sept 1831. 1831 (220) iv.

Select committee on the Admiralty Court in Ireland. Report, 1 June 1829. 1829 (293) iv.

Select committee on the 9th report of the commission on courts of justice in Ireland, and the Chief Baron of the Court of Exchequer's letter. Report, 3 July 1821. 1821 (736) viii.

Select committee on the 11th report of the commission of inquiry into courts of justice in Ireland. Report, 16 May 1823. 1823 (352) vi.

Select committee on Copyright Acts
    Min. of ev. 13 April 1818. 1818 (177) ix.
    Min. of ev. 8 May 1818. 1818 (280) ix.
    Report, 5 June 1818. 1818 (402) ix.

Select committee on Ipswich Borough election petition. Report, 22 July 1835. 1835 (411) ix.

Select committee on orders respecting election recognizances. Report, 11 July 1828. 1828 (529) iv.

Select committee on printed papers. Report on proceedings in the action of Howard *vs.* Gosset
    1st report, 29 May 1845. 1845 (338) xiii.
    2nd report, 20 June 1845. 1845 (397) xiii.

Select committee on the privileges of the H.C. Report respecting the imposition of pecuniary penalties for offences. 23 March 1831. 1830/1 (277) iii.

Select committee on Quakers' affirmation. Report, 11 Feb 1833. 1833 (6) xii.

Select committee on Schoolmasters' Widows' Fund (Scotland) Bill. Report, 7 July 1843. 1843 (413) xi.

Select committee on the state of lunatics. Report, 15 July 1807. 1807 (39) ii; (HE Mental, 1).

Select committee on the stewardship of Denbigh. SEE: Jervis, John.

Select committee on the Sudbury Disfranchisement Bill. Report, 19 July 1843. 1843 (448) vi.

WILLIAMSON, Victor Alexander
Royal commission on the treatment of immigrants in Mauritius. Report, 5 Nov 1874. 1874 C.1115 xxiv, xxxv.

WILLIS, Robert
On the effects produced by causing weights to travel over elastic bars. *In:* 1849 [1123] xxix.

WILLMORE, Graham
Commission on corrupt practices in the Borough of Cambridge. Report, 17 Aug 1852. 1852/3 [1685] xlvi.

WILLOUGHBY, Henry Pollard, *Sir*
Commission on the control and management of H.M. naval yards. Report, 11 March 1861. 1861 [2790] xxvi.

Committee of public accounts, 1864. SEE: Bouverie, Edward Pleydell.

WILLOUGHBY, J.D.
Political and military committee of the Council of India. Report on the organisation of H.M. European forces serving in India. 4 July 1859. 1860 (330) l. India Office.

WILLOUGHBY DE ERESBY, *Lord* [Peerage claim] . SEE: Freeman-Mitford, J.T.

WILLS, Alfred
Committee on accommodation in court houses and other places for prisoners awaiting trial at Assizes and Sessions. Report, 21 Dec 1886. 1887 C.4971 xli; (CP Prisons, 18).

Committee on accommodation provided for prisoners in police courts and courts of summary jurisdiction. Report, 26 April 1888. 1888 C.5439 lviii; (CP Prisons, 18). Home Department.

WILMOT, Eardley SEE: Eardley-Wilmot, John Eardley, *2nd Bn.*

WILMOT-HORTON, Robert John
Select committee on emigration
　　1st report, 26 Feb 1827. 1826/7 (88) v.
　　2nd report, 5 April 1827. 1826/7 (237) v.
　　3rd report, 29 June 1827. 1826/7 (550) v; (Emigration, 2).

WILSON, C. Rivers SEE: Rivers-Wilson, C.

WILSON, Henry William, *2nd Bn. Berners*
Select committee (HL) on the Game Law Amendment (No.2) Bill. Report, 4 July 1862. HL 1862 (157) xxix; H.C. repr. 1862 (439) xvi.

WILSON, Jacob
Departmental committee on pleuro-pneumonia and tuberculosis in the U.K. Report, 10 July 1888. 1888 C.5461 xxxii; (AG Animal Health, 3). Privy Council Office.

WILSON, James
Committee on expiring laws. 1st session, 16th Parliament. Report, 1 March 1853. 1852/3 (184) xxxiv.

Committee on expiring laws. 1st session, 17th Parliament. Report, 2 July 1857. 1857, session 2 (153) ix.

Select committee on assurance associations. Report, 16 Aug 1853. 1852/3 (965) xxi; (Insurance, 3).

Select committee on harbours of refuge. Report, 11 Aug 1857. 1857, session 2 (262) xiv.

Select committee on harbours of refuge. Report, 17 June 1858. 1857/8 (344) xvii.

Select committee on silver and gold wares. Report, 1 May 1856. 1856 (190) xvi; (TI Silver and Gold Wares, 1).

WILSON, John
Report on the raw materials department and agriculture at the New York Industrial Exhibition. 1854 [1830] xxxvi. Foreign Office.

Reports on the agricultural exhibitions at Vienna and Aarhuus, Denmark. Dec 1866. 1867 [3828] lxx. Foreign Office.

Statistical reports on the health of the Navy, 1830-1836; South American, West Indian and North American, Mediterranean and Peninsular Commands. 24 March 1840. 1840 (159) xxx.

WILSON, Thomas
Select committee on the intended new Post Office, London. SEE: Curtis, W.

Select committee on the Orphans' Fund of the City of London. Report, 26 June 1822. 1822 (481) iv.

WILSON-PATTEN, John, *Bn. Winmarleigh*
Committee of selection on the grouping of private bills
　　1st report, 2 March 1849. 1849 (91) xii.
　　2nd report, 30 March 1849. 1849 (187) xii.
　　3rd report, 27 April 1849. 1849 (238) xii.
　　4th report, 7 May 1849. 1849 (264) xii.
　　5th report, 11 May 1849. 1849 (278) xii.

Committee of selection on the grouping of private bills, 1850. SEE: Greene, Thomas.

Committee of selection relative to the grouping of private bills
　　1st report, 3 March 1851. 1851 (88) x.
　　2nd report, 10 March 1851. 1851 (108) x.
　　3rd report, 14 March 1851. 1851 (120) x.
　　4th report, 20 March 1851. 1851 (129) x.
　　5th report, 4 April 1851. 1851 (181) x.
　　6th report, 14 April 1851. 1851 (210) x.
　　7th report, 8 May 1851. 1851 (277) x.
　　8th report, 16 May 1851. 1851 (299) x.
　　9th report, 27 June 1851. 1851 (445) x.

Committee of selection on the grouping of private bills
　　1st report, 23 Feb 1852. 1852 (108) v.
　　2nd report, 12 March 1852. 1852 (131) v.
　　3rd report, 18 March 1852. 1852 (161) v.
　　4th report, 23 March 1852. 1852 (183) v.
　　5th report, 26 March 1852. 1852 (199) v.
　　6th report, 30 March 1852. 1852 (224) v.
　　7th report, 20 April 1852. 1852 (258) v.
　　8th report, 29 April 1852. 1852 (293) v.

Committee of selection on the grouping of private bills
　　1st report, 21 Feb 1854. 1854 (58) vii.
　　2nd report, 24 Feb 1854. 1854 (65) vii.
　　3rd report, 28 Feb 1854. 1854 (73) vii.
　　4th report, 7 March 1854. 1854 (88) vii.
　　5th report, 10 March 1854. 1854 (97) vii.
　　6th report, 14 March 1854. 1854 (103) vii.
　　7th report, 21 March 1854. 1854 (114) vii.
　　8th report, 4 April 1854. 1854 (157) vii.
　　9th report, 7 April 1854. 1854 (170) vii.
　　10th report, 5 May 1854. 1854 (215) vii.
　　11th report, 9 May 1854. 1854 (226) vii.
　　12th report, 19 May 1854. 1854 (259) vii.
　　13th report, 1 June 1854. 1854 (279) vii.
　　14th report, 14 June 1854. 1854 (307) vii.

Committee of selection on the grouping of private bills
　　1st report, 22 Feb 1856. 1856 (57) vii.
　　2nd report, 29 Feb 1856. 1856 (73) vii.
　　3rd report, 12 March 1856. 1856 (98) vii.
　　4th report, 4 April 1856. 1856 (136) vii.
　　5th report, 15 April 1856. 1856 (152) vii.
　　6th report, 2 May 1856. 1856 (192) vii.

Committee of selection on the grouping of private bills, 1857
　　1st report, 24 Feb 1857. 1857, session 1 (64) ii.
　　2nd report, 27 Feb 1857. 1857, session 1 (68) ii.
　　3rd report, 3 March 1857. 1857, session 1 (74) ii.
　　4th report, 10 March 1857. 1857, session 1 (97) ii.
　　Special report, 6 March 1857. 1857, session 1 (83) ii.

Committee of selection relative to the grouping of private bills
　　1st report, 11 May 1857. 1857, session 2 (6) ix.
　　2nd report, 12 May 1857. 1857, session 2 (14) ix.
　　3rd report, 15 May 1857. 1857, session 2 (32) ix.
　　4th report, 19 May 1857. 1857, session 2 (42) ix.
　　5th report, 25 May 1857. 1857, session 2 (54) ix.

Committee of selection relative to the grouping of private bills
　　1st report, 19 Feb 1858. 1857/8 (87) xii.
　　2nd report, 26 Feb 1858. 1857/8 (97) xii.

3rd report, 12 March 1858. 1857/8 (114) xii.
4th report, 18 March 1858. 1857/8 (138) xii.
5th report, 23 March 1858. 1857/8 (146) xii.
6th report, 16 April 1858. 1857/8 (200) xii.

Committee of selection on the grouping of private bills
1st report, 23 Feb 1859. 1859, session 1 (81) iii.
2nd report, 28 Feb 1859. 1859, session 1 (89) iii.
3rd report, 25 March 1859. 1859, session 1 (163)iii.

Committee of selection relative to the grouping of private bills
1st report, 17 June 1859. 1859, session 2 (34) v.
2nd report, 30 June 1859. 1859, session 2 (44) v.
3rd report, 5 July 1859. 1859, session 2 (65) v.

Committee of selection on the grouping of private bills
1st report, 13 Feb 1860. 1860 (75) xxi.
2nd report, 17 Feb 1860. 1860 (91) xxi.
3rd report, 24 Feb 1860. 1860 (102) xxi.
4th report, 4 March 1860. 1860 (176) xxi.
5th report, 1 May 1860. 1860 (265) xxi.
6th report, 22 May 1860. 1860 (319) xxi.

Committee of selection relative to the grouping of private bills
1st report, 18 Feb 1861. 1861 (37) xiv.
2nd report, 22 Feb 1861. 1861 (54) xiv.
3rd report, 1 March 1861. 1861 (66) xiv.
4th report, 15 March 1861. 1861 (107) xiv.
5th report, 12 April 1861. 1861 (156) xiv.
6th report, 23 April 1861. 1861 (188) xiv.
7th report, 31 May 1861. 1861 (293) xiv.

Committee of selection on the grouping of private bills
1st report, 18 Feb 1862. 1862 (51) xvi.
2nd report, 21 Feb 1862. 1862 (59) xvi.
3rd report, 28 Feb 1862. 1862 (70) xvi.
4th report, 12 March 1862. 1862 (103) xvi.
5th report, 11 April 1862. 1862 (166) xvi.
6th report, 17 June 1862. 1862 (331) xvi.
7th report, 10 July 1862. 1862 (394) xvi.

Committee of selection relative to the grouping of private bills. 1st to 4th reports, 18 Feb to 5 June 1863. 1863 (47 I-III) viii.

Committee of selection on the grouping of private bills. 1st to 7th reports, 17 Feb to 24 June 1864. 1864 (62 I-VI) xi.

Committee of selection relative to the grouping of private bills. 1st to 9th reports, 21 Feb to 16 May 1865. 1865 (65 I-VIII) vii.

Committee of selection on the grouping of private bills. 1st to 9th reports, 23 Feb to 5 July 1866. 1866 (63 I-VIII) xi.

Committee of selection relative to the grouping of private bills. 1st to 7th reports, 21 Feb to 5 June 1867. 1867 (73 I-VI) viii.

Committee of selection on the grouping of private bills. 1st to 7th reports, 4 March to 4 June 1869. 1868/9 (64 I-VI) vii.

Committee of selection relative to the grouping of private bills. 1st to 5th reports, 25 Feb to 27 May 1870. 1870 (81 I-IV) vi.

Committee of selection relative to the grouping of private bills. 1st to 6th reports, 3 March to 6 June 1871. 1871 (71 I-V) ix.

Royal commission on courts-martial in the Army
1st report, 24 July 1868. 1867/8 [4114] xii.
2nd report, 14 May 1869. 1868/9 [4114] xii.

Select committee on classification of railway bills
1st report, 11 Feb 1847. 1847 (57) xii.
2nd report, 22 Feb 1847. 1847 (87) xii.

3rd report, 1 March 1847. 1847 (123) xii.
4th report, 4 March 1847. 1847 (138) xii.
5th report, 30 April 1847. 1847 (330) xii.
6th report, 4 May 1847. 1847 (350) xii.
7th report, 10 May 1847. 1847 (366) xii.
8th report, 13 May 1847. 1847 (393) xii.
9th report, 10 June 1847. 1847 (483) xii.

Select committee on conveyance of mails by railways. Report, 25 July 1854. 1854 (411) xi.

Select committee on county financial arrangements. Report, 13 July 1868. 1867/8 (421) ix.

Select committee (HL) on the Epping Forest Bill. Report, 19 July 1878. HL 1878 (162) vii.

Select committee on inland warehousing. Report, 9 July 1840. 1840 (464) v.

Select committee on local acts; preliminary inquiries
1st report, 19 July 1850. 1850 (582) xiii.
2nd report, 22 July 1850. 1850 (591) xiii.

Select committee on official salaries. Report, 25 July 1850. 1850 (611) xv; (GO Civil Service, 1).

Select committee on Orange lodges in Ireland
1st report, 20 July 1835. 1835 (377) xv.
2nd report, 6 Aug 1835. 1835 (475) xv.
3rd report, 6 Aug 1835. 1835 (476) xvi; (CP Civil Disorder, 5-6).

Select committee on private business. Report, 13 Feb 1851. 1851 (35) x.

Select committee on privileges. Report on Sligo election. SEE: Ormsby-Gore, William.

Select committee on railways and canals amalgamation
1st report, 8 April 1846. 1846 (200) xiii.
2nd report, 6 May 1846. 1846 (275) xiii; (Transport, 7).

Select committee on railway and canal legislation. Report, 12 July 1858. 1857/8 (411) xiv; (Transport, 9).

Select committee on Railways committee, 1846. Report, 29 March 1847. 1847 (236) xii; (Transport, 7).

Select committee on railway bills classification
1st report, 16 Feb 1846. 1846 (42) xiii.
2nd report, 20 Feb 1846. 1846 (69) xiii.
3rd report, 23 Feb 1846. 1846 (73) xiii.
4th report, 26 Feb 1846. 1846 (84) xiii.
5th report, 10 March 1846. 1846 (113) xiii.
6th report, 16 March 1846. 1846 (129) xiii.
7th report, 19 March 1846. 1846 (137) xiii.
8th report, 24 March 1846. 1846 (142) xiii.
9th report, 26 March 1846. 1846 (161) xiii.
10th report, 1 April 1846. 1846 (176) xiii.
11th report, 23 April 1846. 1846 (225) xiii.
12th report, 1 May 1846. 1846 (253) xiii.
13th report, 11 May 1846. 1846 (298) xiii.
14th report, 15 May 1846. 1846 (317) xiii.
15th report, 22 May 1846. 1846 (340) xiii.
16th report, 29 May 1846. 1846 (348) xiii.
17th report, 8 June 1846. 1846 (370) xiii.
18th report, 10 June 1846. 1846 (378) xiii.
19th report, 15 June 1846. 1846 (389) xiii.
20th report, 17 June 1846. 1846 (403) xiii.
21st report, 23 June 1846. 1846 (431) xiii.
22nd report, 6 July 1846. 1846 (462) xiii.
23rd report, 13 July 1846. 1846 (475) xiii.
24th report, 17 July 1846. 1846 (494) xiii.
25th report, 4 Aug 1846. 1846 (557) xiii.

Select committee on references on private bills. Report, 21 June 1865. 1865 (393) vii.

WILSON-PATTEN, John, *Bn. Winmarleigh* (continued)
Select committee on the Salmon and Trout Fisheries Bill. Min. of proc. 9 July 1861. 1861 (433) xiv.

Select committee on standing orders revision, 1849, Report, 19 July 1849. 1849 (525) xii.

Select committee on standing orders revision, 1850. Report, 1 Aug 1850. 1850 (659) xix.

Select committee on standing orders revision, 1852. Report, 23 June 1852. 1852 (512) v.

Select committee on standing orders revision, 1852-3. Report, 2 Aug 1853. 1852/3 (856) xxxiv.

Select committee on standing orders revision, 1854. Report, 14 July 1854. 1854 (371) vii.

Select committee on standing orders revision, 1855. SEE: Heathcote, William, *Sir.*

Select committee on standing orders revision, 1857-8. Report, 23 July 1858. 1857/8 (460) xii.

Select committee on standing orders revision, 1862. Report, 24 July 1862. 1862 (444) xvi.

Select committee on standing orders revision, 1864.
    Report, 21 July 1864. 1864 (510) x.
    Min. of ev. 1864 (510-I) x.

Wye River byelaws commission. Report, 8 June 1876. 1876 C.1537 xvi. Home Office.

WILTES, *Lord* [Peerage claim]. SEE:
Freeman-Mitford, J.T.

WINCHESTER, *M.* SEE:
Paulet, John, *14th M. Winchester.*

WINCHESTER, *Bp. of*
North, Brownlow, 1781-1820
Tomline, George, *Sir,* 1820-27
Sumner, Charles Richard, 1827-69
Wilberforce, Samuel, 1869-73
Browne, Harold, 1873-90
Thorold, Anthony Wilson, 1890-95
Davidson, Randall Thomas, 1895-1903

WINDER, J.S.
Report on the state of popular education in the specimen manufacturing districts of Rochdale and Bradford. July 1859. In: 1861 [2794-II] xxi, pt.2; (Education, 4).

WINDEYER, Richard
Select committee of the legislative council of New South Wales relative to the monetary depression. Report, 28 Oct 1843. 1844 (505) xxxv; (Australia, 7). Colonial Department.

WINMARLEIGH, *Lord* SEE:
Wilson-Patten, John, *Bn. Winmarleigh.*

WINERTON, *E.* [Peerage claim]. SEE:
Freeman-Mitford, J.T.

WODEHOUSE, Edmund
Select committee on the Limerick election. Report, 3 July 1820. 1820 (229) iii.

Select committee on petitions complaining of the distressed state of the agriculture of the U.K.
    Report, 1 April 1822. 1822 (165) v.
    2nd report, 20 May 1822. 1822 (346) v; (Agriculture, 1).

WODEHOUSE, Edmund Robert
Committee of public accounts
    1st report, 13 March 1893. 1893/4 (110) ix.

2nd report, 12 July 1893. 1893/4 (255) ix.
3rd report, 12 July 1893. 1893/4 (325) ix.

WODEHOUSE, John, *1st E. Kimberley*
Penal Servitude Acts commission. Report, 14 July 1879. 1878/9 C.2368 xxxvii, xxxviii; (CP Penal Servitude, 1-2).

Select committee (HL) on poor law relief. Report, 30 July 1888. HL 1888 (239) xi; HC repr. 1888 (363) xv; (Poor Law, 27).

Select committee (HL) on public petitions, 1868. SEE: Herbert, Henry Howard Molyneux, *4th E. Carnarvon.*

Select committee (HL) on the Tramways Bill. Report, 18 July 1870. HL 1870 (193) viii.

WOLFF, Henry Drummond, *Sir*
Select committee on consular chaplains. Report, 2 July 1874. 1874 (257) vii.

WOLSELEY, Garnet Joseph, *1st Vct. Wolseley*
Colour committee. Report, 25 July 1882. 1883 C.3536 xv. War Office.

Report on the manoeuvres held near Salisbury, 1898. 27 Oct 1898. 1899 C.9139 liii. War Office.

WOLVERHAMPTON, *Vct.* SEE:
Fowler, Henry Hartley, *1st Vct. Wolverhampton.*

WOOD, Charles, *1st Vct. Halifax*
Epping Forest Commission
    Preliminary report, 27 Feb 1875. 1875 (110) xxi.
    Final report, 1 March 1877. 1877 (187) xxvi.

Royal commission on international coinage. Report, 25 July 1868. 1867/8 [4073] xxvii; (MP Currency, 3).

Select committee on banks of issue. Report, 7 Aug 1840. 1840 (602) iv; (Monetary Policy, 5).

Select committee on banks of issue
    1st report, 4 June 1841. 1841 (366) v.
    2nd report, 15 June 1841. 1841 (410) v; (Monetary Policy, 6).

Select committee on the Bridport election. Min. of ev. 1 May 1846. 1846 (255) viii.

Select committee on commercial distress. SEE: Baring, Francis Thornhill.

Select committee on the funeral of the Duke of Wellington. 1st and 2nd reports, 17 Nov 1852. 1852/3 (8) xxxix.

Select committee on Indian territories
    1st report, 2 May 1853. 1852/3 (426) xxvii.
    2nd report, 12 May 1853. 1852/3 (479) xxviii.
    3rd report, 2 June 1853. 1852/3 (556) xxviii.
    4th report, 30 June 1853. 1852/3 (692) xxviii.
    5th report, 14 July 1853. 1852/3 (768) xxviii.
    6th report, 8 Aug 1853. 1852/3 (897) xxix.
    Supplement, appendix, index. 1852/3 (897 I-II) xxix; (East India, 14).

Select committee on Lewes Borough election. Proc. 19 March 1842. 1842 (548) v.

Select committee on the Nottingham Town election petition. Min. of proc. and ev. 12 June 1843. 1843 (328) vi.

Select committee on the Penryn and Falmouth election petition. Min of proc. and ev. 9 May 1842. 1842 (240) viii.

Select committee on railway bills

1st report, 16 Dec 1847. 1847/8 (35) xvi.
2nd report, 13 March 1848. 1847/8 (165) xvi.
3rd report, 19 April 1848. 1847/8 (287) xvi.

Select committee on savings banks in Ireland
Report, 24 Aug 1848. 1847/8 (693) xvii.
Min. of ev. 12 Feb 1849. 1849 (21) xiv.

WOOD, J. Stewart
Commission on the constabulary in Ireland. SEE:
Knatchbull-Hugessen, E.H.

WOOD, John
Report on the probable effect on the stamp revenue
by the Stamp Revenue Bill. 18 April 1850. 1850
(249) xxxiii. Inland Revenue.

WOOD, Matthew, *1st Bn. Wood*
Committee on the Canine Madness Bill. Report, 9 July
1830. 1830 (651) x.

Select committee on London Bridge
Report, 24 July 1820. 1820 (304) iii.
Min. of ev. 6 June 1821. 1821 (609) v.

Committee on London Bridge. Report, 25 May 1821.
1821 (569) v.

Select committee on Metropolis improvements. Report, 2 Aug 1836. 1836 (517) xx.

Select committee on Metropolis improvements
1st report, 23 May 1838. 1837/8 (418) xvi.
2nd report, 2 Aug 1838. 1837/8 (661) xvi; (UA
Planning, 1).

Select committee on Metropolis improvements. Report, 27 March 1839. 1839 (136) xiii; (UA Planning,
2).

Select committee on Metropolis improvements
1st report, 25 June 1840. 1840 (410) xii.
2nd report, 14 July 1840. 1840 (485) xii; (UA
Planning, 2).

Select committee on Metropolis improvements. Report, 11 June 1841. 1841 (398) ix; (UA Planning, 2).

Committee on prisons in London
Report, 8 May 1818. 1818 (275) viii.
2nd report, 1 June 1818. 1818 (392) viii; (CP
Prisons, 8).

Select committee on Thames embankment. Report,
29 July 1840. 1840 (554) xii.

Select committee on Mr. Young's petition relating
to police. Report, 6 April 1833. 1833 (627) xiii.

Committee on game laws. Report, 26 June 1816.
1816 (504) iv.

WOOD, William Page, *Bn. Hatherley*
Commission on the new courts of justice buildings.
Report, 3 Aug 1870. 1871 C.290 xx.

Commission of inquiry into the Inns of Court. Report, 10 Aug 1855. 1854/5 [1998] xviii.

Judicature commission. SEE: Cairns, Hugh Mac-
Calmont, *1st E. Cairns*.

Royal commission on the Royal Hospital of St. Katherine. Report. 1871 C.321 xvi.

Select committee (HL) on the Bankruptcy Bill. Report, 22 July 1869. HL 1868/9 (207) xxvii.

Select committee on business of the H.C. Report,
28 March 1871. 1871 (137) ix.

Select committee on oaths of members. Report,
25 April 1850. 1850 (268) xv.

Select committee on Thames embankment. Report,
3 Aug 1871. 1871 (411) xii.

WOODALL, William
Select committee on the Manchester, Sheffield and
Lincolnshire Railway (Extension to London) Bill.
Special report, 24 June 1891. 1890/1 (292) xii.

Select committee on the Post Office Sites Bill. Report, 14 Aug 1889. 1889 (323) xi.

Select committee on the Royal Patriotic Fund. Report, 1 July 1895. 1895 (347) xii.

Select committee on the Royal Patriotic Fund. Report, 12 Aug 1896. 1896 (368) xiii.

Select committee on the Volunteer Acts. Report,
17 July 1894. 1894 (224) xv.

Select committee on the Waltham Abbey Gunpowder
Factory Bill. Report, 23 Nov 1888. 1888 (403) xxiii.

Select committee on Waltham Abbey Gunpowder
Factory Bill. Report, 9 May 1889. 1889 (135) xvi.

WOODD, Charles, *Sir*
Committee on the Park Lane Improvement Bill.
Special report, 22 May 1868. 1867/8 (293) viii.

General committee on railway and canal bills, 1864.
SEE: Smith-Stanley, Edward Henry, *15th E. Derby.*

General committee on railway and canal bills. 1st
to 6th reports, 10 March to 2 July 1868. 1867/8
(130 I-V) viii.

WOODFORD, Alexander
Board of general officers on the report of the com-
mission of inquiry into the supplies of the British
Army in the Crimea
Report, 4 July 1856. 1856 [2119] xxi.
Index. 1856 (422) xxi.

WORSLEY, Lord SEE:
Anderson-Pelham, Charles Anderson Worsley, *1st E.
Yarborough.*

WORTHINGTON, T.
Commercial mission to South America
1st and 2nd reports: Chile. 14 April and 24 May
1898. 1899 C.9100 xcvi.
3rd report: Argentine Republic. 18 Aug 1898.
1899 C.9101 xcvi.
4th and 5th reports: Brazil. 4 Nov and 20 Dec
1898. 1899 C.9160, C.9161 xcvi.
6th report: Uruguay. 7 Feb 1899. 1899 C.9298
xcvi. Board of Trade.

WORTLEY, James Archibald Stuart
Commission on the alleged disturbances in Hyde
Park. 10 Nov 1855. 1856 [2016] xxiii; (CP Civil
Disorder, 3).

Select committee on the Harwich election petition.
Min. of ev. 16 March 1848. 1847/8 (172) xii.

Select committee on laws relating to the stamping
of woollen cloth. Report, 19 April 1821. 1821 (437)
vi.

Select committee on Mr. Thomas Croggon's imprisonment in Newgate. Report, 28 June 1813. 1812/3
(312) iii.

Select committee on shop windows duty. Report,
30 June 1819. 1819 (528) ii.

Select committee on the Southampton Town election petition inquiry. Report, 18 July 1842. 1842
(457) viii.

WORTLEY, James Stuart
Commission on the state and operation of the law
of marriage

WORTLEY, James Stuart (continued)
1st report. 1847/8 [973] xxviii.
2nd report: East India marriages. 18 April 1850.
1850 [1203] xx; (Marriage and Divorce, 1).

Select committee on Peterborough election petitions.
Report, 8 Aug 1853. 1852/3 (898) xvii.

WRIGHT, James
Committee on boilers. Report, 25 March 1880. 1880
C.2642 xiii. Admiralty.

WRIGHT, John Atkyns
Select committee on Penryn election. Report, 4 and
5 Feb 1807. 1806/7 (56) iii; repr. 1819 (85) iv; repr.
1826/7 (318) iv.

Select committee on the Penryn election. Report,
26 Feb 1819. 1819 (72) iv; repr. 1826/7 (318) iv.

WRIGHT, Thomas Guthrie
Report on the Jury Court, Scotland. 12 Jan 1827.
1844 (636) xlii; (Legal Administration, 6).

WRIGHTSON, William Battie
Committee on group no. 19 of private bills. Report,
16 July 1849. 1849 (508) xii.

Select committee on the Bewdley election petition.
Min. of ev. 22 March 1848. 1847/8 (194) x.

WROTTESLEY, John, *2nd Bn. Wrottesley*
Ordnance Survey Commission. Report, 20 May 1858.
1857/8 [2396] xix.

Select committee on Coventry election
Special report, 9 March 1827. 1826/7 (147) iv.
Report, 9 March 1827. 1826/7 (148) iv.

Select committee on the Hackney Coach Office.
Report, 10 June 1830. 1830 (515) x.

Select committee on losses by fire of the Houses of
Parliament. Report, 10 July 1837. 1837 (493) xiii;
repr. 1837/8 (8) xxiii.

WROTTESLEY, John, *2nd Bn. Wrottesley*
Commission of inquiry into the application of iron
to railway structures. Report, 26 July 1849. 1849
[1123] xxix.

WYATT, John
Report on the organisation of the Russian medical
department and the sanitary state of their Crimean
hospitals. 15 May 1856. 1857, session 1 (135) ix.
War Office.

WYATT, M. Digby
Report on furniture and decoration at the Paris Universal Exhibition. 1856 [2049-I] xxxvi.

WYNDHAM, George O'Brien, *3rd E. Egremont*
Committee (HL) on standing orders relating to bills
for harbours, *etc.* Report, 20 July 1812. HL 1812
(175) liii.

Committee (HL) on standing orders of the H.L. relating to bills for making harbours, canals, roads, *etc.*
Report, 25 June 1813. HL 1812/3 (110) lxiii.

WYNDHAM, Percy Scawmen
Select committee on Mines etc Assessment Bill. Special
report, 27 May 1867. 1867 (321) xiii.

WYNDHAM-QUIN, Windham Thomas, *4th E. Dunraven*
Commission on horse breeding in Ireland
Report, 19 July 1898. 1898 C.8651 xxxiii.

Min. of ev. 1898 C.8652 xxxiii. Irish Secretary's
Office.

Select committee (HL) on the sweating system
1st report, 30 July 1888. HL 1888 (240) xiii; HC
repr. 1888 (361) xx.
2nd report, 18 Dec 1888. HL 1888 (303) xiii;
HC repr. 1888 (448) xxi.
3rd report, 2 May 1889. HL 1889 (40) vii; HC
repr. 1889 (165) xiii.
4th report, 5 Aug 1889. HL 1889 (207) viii; HC
repr. 1889 (331) xiv, pt.1.
5th report, 28 April 1890. HL 1890 (62) x; HC
repr. 1890 (169) xvii.
Analysis of ev. HL 1889 (207-III) ix; HC repr.
1889 (331-III) xiv, pt.1.
Indexes. HL 1889 (207 I-II) ix; HL 1890 (207-
III) xi; HC repr. 1889 (331 I-II) xiv, pt.2; (Industrial Relations, 13-17).

WYNFORD, Bn. SEE:
Best, William Draper, *1st Bn. Wynford.*

WYNN, C.W.W. SEE:
Williams-Wynn, Charles Watkin.

WYNNE, George
Report on Prof. Gluckman's invention of a means
of communication between guards and drivers of
trains on railways. 3 April 1854. 1854 [1769] lxii.
Board of Trade.

WYNN-CARRINGTON, Charles Robert, *1st E. Carrington*
Royal commission on land in Wales and Monmouth-
shire
1st report, 29 June 1894. 1894 C.7439 xxxvi.
Report, 26 Aug 1896. 1896 C.8221 xxxiv.
Min. of ev., vols. 1 and 2. 1894 C.7439 I-II xxxvi,
xxxvii.
Min. of ev., vols. 3 and 4. 1895 C.7661, C.7757
xl, xli.
Min. of ev., vol.5. 1896 C.8222 xxxv.
Appendix. 1896 C.8242 xxxiii.

WYNNE, Edmund
Select committee on his letters. SEE: Aglionby,
Henry Aglionby.

WYNNE, James
Report on the epidemic cholera in the United States
in 1849 and 1850. 1852 [1523] xx. General Board
of Health.

WYNNE-PENDARVES, Edward William
Select committee on the discharge of John Nicholl
Thom from the lunatic asylums. Report, 31 July
1838. 1837/8 (651) xxiii; (HE Mental, 6).

Select committee on the suppression of the *Calcutta
Journal.* SEE: Bains, Edward.

WYNYARD, Edward Buckley
Commission on purchase and sale of commissions in
the Army. Note of dissent. 3 Aug 1857. 1857/8
[2293] xix; (Military and Naval, 3). SEE ALSO:
St. Maur, Edward Adolophus, *12th D. Somerset.*

WYSE, Thomas
Select committee on art unions. Report, 5 Aug 1845.
1845 (612) vii.

Select committee on education in Ireland. Report,
10 Sept 1835. 1836 (630) xiii; repr. 1836 (586) xiii.

Select committee on foundation schools in Ireland.
Report, 9 Aug 1838. 1837/8 (701) vii.

Select committee on legal education. Report, 25 Aug 1846. 1846 (686) x.

YARBOROUGH, E. SEE:
Anderson-Pelham, Charles, *1st Bn. Yarborough* (1749-1823)
Anderson-Pelham, Charles, *1st E. Yarborough* (1781-1846)
Anderson-Pelham, Charles Anderson Worsley, *2nd E. Yarborough* (1809-1862)

YARDE-BULLER, John, *3rd Bn. Churston*
Commission on militia surgeons. Report, 2 July 1862. 1863 (126) xxxiii. War Office.

Commission of selection on the grouping of private bills. SEE: Wilson-Patten, John.

Select committee on Cork City election petition
Report, 26 May 1853. 1852/3 (521) xi.
Min. of ev. 27 May 1853. 1852/3 (528) xi.

Select committee on the Great Marlow election. Min. of proc. and ev. 14 April 1842. 1842 (174) vii.

Select committee on the Lords' amendments to the Great Northern Railway (Isle of Axholme Extension) Bill. Report, 4 Aug 1848. 1847/8 (598) xvi.

Select committee (HL) on the Mersey, Weaver, Irewell, *etc*. Protection Bill. Min. of ev. 2 June 1862. HL 1862 (92) xxix.

Select committee on the Newcastle-under-Lyme election petition. Min. of proc. and ev. 20 May 1842. 1842 (250) viii.

Select committee on petitions for private bills. Report on the Midland Railway Branches Bill. 16 April 1845. 1845 (222) x.

Select committee on the Rochdale Borough election petition. Min. of ev. 17 July 1857. 1857, session 2 (185) viii.

Select committee on the Sligo Borough election petition. Min. of ev. 3 Aug 1857. 1857, session 2 (227) viii.

YOLLAND, William
Commission on the education and training of officers for the scientific corps of the military. Report, 12 Jan 1857. 1857, session 1 (0.52), (0.53) vi.

Commission on the system of training officers for the scientific corps. Report, together with an account of foreign and other military education. 25 July 1856. 1856 (406) xl. War Office.

Court of inquiry upon the fall of a portion of the Tay Bridge, 28 Dec 1879. Report, 30 June 1880. 1880 C.2616 xxxix. Board of Trade.

Report on experiments made on different systems of electrical communication between passengers and servants of railway companies in charge of those trains. 21 Feb 1868. 1867/8 [3992] lxii. Board of Trade.

Report on the Metropolitan railway schemes proposed by bills in the session of 1864. 9 Feb 1864. 1864 [3259] liii. Board of Trade.

YONGE, William
Lords commission on the High Court of Chancery. Report, 8 Nov 1740. 1814/5 (98) xi.

YORK, *Archbp. of*
Markham, William, 1777-1807
Vernon, Edward Venables Vernon, 1808-47
Musgrave, Thomas, 1848-60

Longley, Thomas, 1860-62
Thomson, William, 1863-91
Magee, William Connor, 1891
MacLagan, William Dalrymple, 1891-1909

YORK, *D.*
Precedence. SEE: Parker, A.E.

YORKE, Charles
Committee on the high price of provisions
1st report. CJ Reports, vol.9, p.129.
2nd report, 23 Feb 1801. 1801 (11) ii; CJ, vol. 9, p.132.
3rd report. CJ Reports, vol.9, p.137.
4th report, 20 March 1801. 1801 (23) ii; CJ, vol. 9, p.138.
5th report, 2 April 1801. 1801 (37) ii; CJ, vol.9, p.139.
6th report, 22 May 1801. 1801 (82), (84) ii; CJ Reports, vol.9, p.140.
7th report, 24 June 1801. 1801 (137) ii; CJ Reports, vol.9, p.144.

YORKE, Charles, *Sir*
Committee on the claims of officers promoted to the rank of Colonel for distinguished service. Report, 25 July 1861. *In:* 1863 (73) xxxii. War Office.

YORKE, Charles Philip, *4th E. Hardwicke*
Commission of inquiry into the best means of manning the Navy. Report, 19 Feb 1859. 1859, session 1 [2469] vi.

Select committee (HL) on the Direct London and Portsmouth Railway Bill, the Brighton and Chichester Railway Bill, and the Guildford, Chichester and Portsmouth Railway Bill. Reports, 28 July 1845. HL 1845 (328) xix.

Select committee (HL) on the Ecclesiastical Commission Bill and the Ecclesiastical Corporations Aggregate (Estates) Bill. Report, 21 June 1858. HL 1857/8 (155) xx.

Select committee (HL) on the Liverpool Corporation Waterworks Bill. Report, 9 July 1850. HL 1859 (246) xxiii.

Select committee (HL) on the Locomotives on Roads Bill. Report, 15 June 1865. HL 1865 (161) xxi.

Select committee (HL) on the navigation laws
1st report, 9 May 1848. HL 1847/8 (51) xxv; HC repr. 1847/8 (340) xx, pt.2.
2nd report, 9 June 1848. HL 1847/8 (51) xxv; HC repr. 1847/8 (431) xx, pt.2.
3rd report, 4 Aug 1848. HL 1847/8 (51) xxv; HC repr. 1847/8 (754) xx, pt.2; (TI Navigation Laws, 2).

YORKE, Philip, *3rd E. Hardwicke*
Committee (HL) on the Equitable Loan Bank Company's Bill. Min. of ev., 1824. 28 March 1825. HL 1825 (38) cxcvii. SEE ALSO: Brand, Thomas, *20th Bn. Dacre*.

Select committee (HL) on the corn laws. 1st and 2nd reports, 25 July 1814. HL 1813/4 (118) lxx.

Committee (HL) on grain and the corn laws. 1st and 2nd reports, 23 Nov 1814. HL 1814/5 (29) v.

Committee (HL) on the poor laws
Report, 10 July 1817. HL 1817 (101) lxxxiv.
Min. of ev. 19 May 1817. HL 1817 (43) lxxxvii.

Committee on the poor laws. Report, 1 June 1818. HL 1818 (62) xci; HC repr. 1818 (400) v.

YORKE, Phillip, *3rd E. Hardwicke* (continued)

Select committee (HL) on the use of corn in distillation. SEE: Gordon, George Hamilton, *4th E. Aberdeen.*

YOUNG, Archibald

Report on the laws affecting the salmon fisheries of the Solway Firth. 30 Nov 1880. 1881 C.2769 xxiii. Home Office.

Special commission on the operation of the Tweed Fisheries Acts. Report. 1875 C.1117 xvii. Home Office.

Special commission on salmon fisheries in Scotland. Report, July 1871. 1871 C.419 xxv. Home Department.

YOUNG, Frederick

Select committee on petition relating to police. SEE: Wood, Matthew.

YOUNG, George, *Sir*

Report on friendly societies in the southern and eastern counties of England. 1874 C.997 xxiii, pt.2; (Insurance, 8). SEE ALSO: Northcote, Stafford Henry, *Sir.*

Select committee on the Valuation of Lands and Assessments (Scotland) Bill. Report, 24 June 1870. 1870 (294) xi.

YOUNG, George Frederick

Select committee on East India maritime officers. Report, 26 May 1837. 1837 (336) vi.

YOUNG, John, *Bn. Lisgar*

Commission on administrative departments of the courts of justice
  1st report, 8 Dec 1873. 1874 C.949 xxiv.
  2nd report, 30 July 1874. 1874 C.1107 xxiv.
  Min. of ev. 1875 C.1245 xxx; (Legal Administration, 14-15).

Commission of inquiry into the Ordnance memo of Ireland. Report, Nov 1843. 1844 [527] xxx. Treasury.

Select committee on the Lagan Navigation Bill. Report, 8 Aug 1842. 1842 (537) xiv.

Select committee on poor laws, Ireland
  1st report, 23 Feb 1849. 1849 (58) xv, pt.1.
  2nd report, 2 March 1849. 1849 (93) xv, pt.1.
  3rd report, 20 March 1849. 1849 (137) xv, pt.1.
  4th report, 27 March 1849. 1849 (170) xv, pt.1.
  5th report, 29 March 1849. 1849 (148) xv, pt.1.
  6th report, 2 April 1849. 1849 (194) xv, pt.1.
  7th report, 27 April 1849. 1849 (237) xv, pt.1.
  8th report, 4 May 1849. 1849 (259) xv, pt.1.
  9th report, 21 May 1849. 1849 (301) xv, pt.1.
  10th report, 6 June 1849. 1849 (356) xv, pt.2.
  11th report, 8 June 1849. 1849 (357) xv, pt.2.
  12th report, 19 June 1849. 1849 (403) xv, pt.2.
  13th report, 22 June 1849. 1849 (416) xv, pt.2.
  14th report, 27 July 1849. 1849 (572) xv, pt.2.

Select committee on townland valuation of Ireland. Report, 18 July 1844. 1844 (513) vii.

Select committee on the trade of spirits in Ireland. Report, 17 June 1842. 1842 (338) xiv.

YOUNG, William, *Sir*

Committee on the booksellers and printers petition. Report, 22 March 1802. 1801/2 (34) ii; CJ Reports, vol.14, p.164.

YOUNGHUSBAND, C.W.

Special committee on gun-cotton and lithofracteur. Report on lithofracteur. 4 May 1872. 1872 (371) xxxvii. War Office.

ZLATAROFF,

Commission of inquiry into the occurences in the Kirdjali district of Turkey. Report, 23 May 1880. 1880 C.2610 lxxxi. Foreign Office.

Revise for GCSE
Citizenship Studies
for AQA

Joan Campbell • Sue Patrick

Heinemann
Inspiring generations

Heinemann Educational Publishers
Halley Court, Jordan Hill, Oxford OX2 8EJ
Part of Harcourt Education
Heinemann is the registered trademark of Harcourt Education Limited

First published 2003

ISBN 0 435 80826 5

08 07 06 05 04 03
10 9 8 7 6 5 4 3 2 1

British Library Cataloguing in Publication Data is available
from the British Library on request.

Edited by Janice Baiton
Typeset and illustrated by Tek-Art, Croydon
Original illustrations © Harcourt Education Limited, 2003

Printed and bound by Scotprint in the UK

Cover photo: © Getty/Stone/Colin Hawkins

Acknowledgements

Extracts
p.39 @ *Daily Mirror*, Voice of the Mirror; 13 March 2002;
James Hardy, 16 March 2002; *The Guardian*
Ian Black, 16 March 2002.

Photos
p.9 Impact/Tony Page.
Every effort has been made to contact copyright holders of material reproduced in
this book. Any omissions will be rectified in subsequent printings if notice is given to
the publishers.

Websites
On pages where you are asked to go to www.heinemann.co.uk/hotlinks to complete a
task or down load information, please insert the code **8265P** at the website.

Tel: 01865 888058   www.heinemann.co.uk